SOCIAL INEQUALITY IN CANADA
Patterns, Problems, Policies

Edited by

James Curtis
UNIVERSITY OF WATERLOO

Edward Grabb
UNIVERSITY OF WESTERN ONTARIO

Neil Guppy
UNIVERSITY OF BRITISH COLUMBIA

Sid Gilbert
UNIVERSITY OF GUELPH

Prentice-Hall Canada Inc., Scarborough, Ontario

Canadian Cataloguing in Publication Data

Main entry under title:
Social inequality in Canada

Bibliography: p.
Includes index.
ISBN 0-13-815606-9

1. Equality — Canada   2. Social classes — Canada
3. Canada — Social policy. I. Curtis, James E., 1943 —

HN110.Z9S66 1988   305'.0971   C87-095294-3

Prentice-Hall Inc., Englewood Cliffs, *New Jersey*
Prentice-Hall International, Inc., *London*
Prentice-Hall of Australia, Pty., Ltd., *Sydney*
Prentice-Hall of India Pvt., Ltd., *New Delhi*
Prentice-Hall of Japan, Inc., *Tokyo*
Prentice-Hall of Southeast Asia (PTE.) Ltd., *Singapore*
Editora Prentice-Hall do Brasil Ltda., *Rio de Janeiro*
Prentice-Hall Hispanoamerica, S.A., *Mexico*

ISBN 0-13-815606-9

Coordinating editor: Edward O'Connor
Production editor: John Metford
Cover and text design: Elaine Cohen
Manufacturing buyer: Matt Lumsdon
Composition: Convertype

Printed and bound in Canada by Imprimerie Gagné Lteé

  2 3 4 5 IG 92 91 90 89

Contents

Section IV   The State and Social Inequality / 371

Section V   Consequences of Social Inequality / 431

Preface

This volume is intended for students of contemporary Canadian society, particularly as a text or a supplement for courses in Social Inequality, Social Class, Social Stratification, Social Issues, and Canadian Society. It contains articles chosen to reflect the range of research approaches, theoretical perspectives, and major patterns of evidence in the current literature on social inequality in Canada.

In selecting the 42 articles for this book, we have placed a premium on imaginative and clear presentations of results and theories in the area of Canadian social inequality, and on pieces that suggest avenues for studying the topic further. Also, emphasis has been placed on studies that address social inequality in a historical perspective, so several trend studies are included among our selections. Finally, we have given considerable attention to *ideologies* and *social policies* pertaining to social inequality. We began from the premise that social inequality entails two broad components: objective or structural conditions of social inequality (power, income and wealth, occupations, and educational attainment, in particular) and ideologies that help support these differences. The ideologies—expressed in formal laws, public policies, dominant values, and so forth—provide justification for the objective patterns of inequality. There are also, of course, other, less influential, ideologies in the society—"counter-ideologies"—that often reflect the interests of the disadvantaged. These counter-ideologies frequently call for changes to existing conditions of inequality so as to better the lot of the disadvantaged. The proper study of social inequality can only involve the scrutiny of both these *structural* and *ideological* components.

The task of selecting the papers for this volume has at the same time been easy and difficult, because of the growing body of new research and theory on social inequality in Canada. Since the appearance of the first two summaries of research in this area, in two edited collections (Curtis and Scott, 1973, 1979; Harp and Hofley, 1980), a wealth of additional evidence has been gathered. This has lent significant breadth and depth to what we know, and made it easy for us to develop a volume based on top-quality materials.

Our difficulties resulted from the limited space available to us in one book. The space constraints have meant that we have had to include some choices to the exclusion of many other fine works on the same topic. Our Further Readings sections, and the references in the selections themselves, only begin to suggest the amount of important research now available and the difficulty we have had in making choices.

Our difficulties demonstrate that the study of social inequality in Canada is moving forward rapidly toward a much better understanding of the phenomenon. Those of us who would prefer to see our society changed to provide greater equality of opportunity and condition can take heart at this improved understanding. It is another matter, though, to turn our understanding into action and achieve social change. The following pages will show that many patterns of inequality are terribly resistant to change because they are maintained by formidable forces, especially by the *economic, political, and ideological control* of highly privileged groups. Much of this control operates through the apparatuses of the state, as some of the selections will emphasize. This volume will show that there are inequalities that are becoming more marked over time—as is the case with the increased concentration of wealth and corporate control. There are also other forms of inequality that have considerably diminished—as with differences in the attainment of university degrees by women relative to men. And finally, there are other patterns, such as the distribution of income, that show little change in recent decades. Thus, those readers who prefer a more egalitarian society than currently exists in Canada will find reasons for both optimism and pessimism in the research presented here.

We would like to thank several individuals for their help with this project. First, of course, are the contributors to the volume. The strengths of this book are largely their doing. Second, we would like to acknowledge our debts to several people for their very helpful suggestions on our materials. They include William Johnston and James Rinehart, University of Western Ontario; Gillian Creese, Melody Hessing, and Martin Meissner at the University of British Columbia; John Goyder and Ronald Lambert, the University of Waterloo; Lorne Tepperman, University of Toronto; Pat Ferrier, David Jolliffe, and Edward O'Connor, Prentice-Hall Canada; and Bernard R. Blishen, York University; J. Stolzman, Dalhousie University; and G. Teeple, Simon Fraser University, all of whom reviewed this text in the manuscript stage. Third, Lorraine Thompson, University of Waterloo, deserves a special note of thanks for her very capable work in helping organize the project across four universities and for her assistance in typing some of the manuscript. Also, at the University of Western Ontario, Veronica D'Souza and Denise Statham typed sections of the book and Lisa Jakubowski and Lynn Dalrymple provided research and library assistance. Jean Marchart at the University of British Columbia contributed to the typing as well.

J.C.
E.G.
N.G.
S.G.
1988

REFERENCES

Curtis, James E., and William G. Scott (eds.).
    1979   *Social Stratification: Canada* (2nd ed.). Scarborough: Prentice-Hall Canada.
    (1973)

Harp, John, and John R. Hofley (eds.).
    1980   *Structured Inequality in Canada.* Scarborough: Prentice-Hall Canada.

CONCEPTUAL ISSUES IN THE STUDY OF SOCIAL INEQUALITY

Edward G. Grabb

That human beings are often very different from each other is one of those basic truths about life of which we are all aware. We need only observe the various sizes, shapes, and colours of other people, the different group affiliations they adopt, and the distinct goals or interests they pursue, to be reminded of the numerous differences that can be drawn among us. It is also true that many of these differences probably have little or no lasting influence on our existence. And yet, it is clear that certain human differences regularly have significant consequences for the lives that we are able to lead in society.

The study of social inequality is really the study of these consequential human differences. In particular, inequality refers to differences that become socially *structured*, in the sense that they become a regular and recurring part of how people interact with one another on a daily basis. Structured inequality involves a process in which groups or individuals with particular attributes are better able than those who lack or are denied these attributes to control or shape rights and opportunities for their own ends. One major factor in this process is that the advantaged groups or individuals tend to obtain greater access to the various rewards and privileges that are available in society. These benefits, in turn, serve to reinforce the control over rights and opportunities enjoyed by the advantaged factions, in a cyclical process that structures and *reproduces* the pattern of inequality across time and place.

In general terms at least, such a view of what social inequality entails is held by most theorists and researchers in the social sciences, including many of those who study Canadian society. In this book we have brought together recent exemplary works by some noted Canadian writers, all of whom share an interest in understanding the consequential differences among people and the inequalities that they engender.

1

In this opening chapter our main goal is to provide an integrative background for the papers that have been selected, to provide a context within which the substance of our selections can be more easily located and comprehended. This is not an entirely straightforward task, since in the study of inequality, as in most vibrant and continuing areas of inquiry in sociology, there are clear divergences in theoretical orientations and research traditions.

Given these divergences, there is little possibility at present of establishing a single, universally accepted approach to analysing the problem; a complete synthesis of existing thought and knowledge is currently not feasible. Nonetheless, we can arrive at a general understanding of the major theoretical issues and empirical questions that have held the attention of contemporary students of social inequality. This understanding should also help us to appreciate important areas of agreement and dispute among scholars in the field.

The central questions we shall address in this opening chapter are theoretical in nature. In particular, we will assess the two most important ideas in theories of social inequality: the concept of *class* and the concept of *power*, or *domination*. In doing so, we will also demonstrate that class and power are closely tied to questions of *economic control* in society and to questions of *ideological and political control*. The combined effects of these factors are what gives rise to the key bases for social inequality that operate in Canada and most modern societies. Our discussion here will provide the conceptual background for the selection and classification of papers in this volume.

SOCIAL INEQUALITY AND THE CONCEPT OF CLASS

If we were to ask most people what inequality is all about, we would probably find that their responses put considerable stress on economic or material distinctions, on differences in economic rights, opportunities, rewards, and privileges between themselves and others. Although such differences might not be their sole focus, people do show a notable interest, for example, in whether or not they earn as much money as others in different occupations; they might wonder if their own share of society's wealth is growing or shrinking over time; they might even raise such questions as whether or not it is true that a small number of businesses increasingly controls more and more of their country's economic resources.

In fact, these same kinds of questions—about economic control and material privilege—have also been the predominant concern among most of the social scientists interested in the topic of inequality. Such a focus is understandable, of course, since economic differences involve the most immediate or fundamental inequality in social settings: people's relative access to the material necessities of life itself. Undoubtedly, this emphasis is at least partly responsible for the central role that the concept of economic *class* has always played in social analysis, particularly since the early writings of Karl Marx and Max Weber (cf. Marx, 1867; Weber, 1922).

Unfortunately, the concept of class has provoked long-standing and still unresolved questions about its precise meaning and significance. Of these questions, five in particular should be raised in this opening section. First, there is the question of whether classes are just categories of individuals who share similar economic circumstances, or whether the term class should refer only to an economic category which is also a real *social group*, a set of people with a shared sense of common membership or purpose. Second, analysts have debated whether classes are best thought of as simply the same as *strata*—ranked layers of people separated according to income or occupation level, for instance—or whether the dividing lines between classes are less arbitrary, less variable, and more fundamental than these stratum distinctions suggest. Third, some writers contend that classes are best understood as sets of *people*, while others say they are really sets of *places* or *positions*, like boxes or containers in which the people are located. Fourth, there is the question of whether classes should be defined principally by differences in the amount of material rewards *distributed* to them for consumption purposes, or whether such differences are secondary to, and largely derivative from, structured economic *relationships*, especially relationships which give sustained control over material life to some and not others. For some theorists, such control provides the real means by which classes are defined and delineated. Finally, many writers disagree on how many classes there are in modern societies. Are there just two, a small dominant one and a large subordinate one? Are there instead some intermediate classes between top and bottom and, if so, how many? Or is it in fact the case that there are no easily identifiable classes, but a continuous hierarchy without clear class distinctions?

The difficulties inherent in any attempt to answer all of these questions are obvious from the volume of work that has been generated on the concept of class (for a review of the work, see Grabb, 1984). The disparate viewpoints cannot be fully incorporated within a single conception or definition of class. Nevertheless, there is sufficient common ground for class to be viewed in a manner which, at least in general terms, is consistent with most major works in the field, including those of the key classical writers, Marx and Weber, and of subsequent writers broadly sympathetic to either or both of these theorists (for example, Poulantzas, 1975; Carchedi, 1977; Wright, 1979; 1985; Parkin, 1979; Giddens, 1981a; 1981b; 1984).

Our approach to defining the concept of class involves the following answers to the five questions listed above:

1. Classes exist primarily as *categories* of people, and need not be defined as real *groups*. In other words, classes typically will not be sets of people having a common sense of group membership and the capability to act in unison toward some collective goal. This is not to say that such united action is never possible; classes sometimes become groups, but only sometimes. As Giddens notes, for example, class systems exist on a national or even international scale in modern times, making such co-ordination and common purpose exceedingly difficult to generate, at least in the mass of the population (cf. Giddens, 1973:84). In those rare instances where simple economic classes also develop these group-like characteristics, some writers find it useful, following Weber, to refer to such groups as *social classes* (Weber, 1922:302-5; cf. Giddens, 1973:78-79; Grabb, 1986:146).

2. While classes normally are not real groups, neither are they merely equivalent to strata, as certain writers seem to suggest (for example, Johnson, 1960:469;

cf. Barber, 1957:73; Parsons, 1951:172). That is, strata are usually ranked statistical aggregates, for which the criteria used in ranking are quite variable (including such characteristics as income, education, occupation, and general prestige level) and where the choice of boundaries is an arbitrary decision made by the researcher. In contrast, class divisions are traceable to more fundamental, deep-seated, and uniform cleavages than the ones implied by these stratum distinctions.

3. Classes are most completely comprehended if we recognize that they are neither just sets of people nor just structural categories, the containers that separate or encapsulate sets of people; they really are both these things in combination. This double meaning of class is one aspect of a more general process that Giddens has called the "duality" of social structures (cf. Giddens, 1979; 1981b). Hence, classes exist as structural entities because certain enforceable rights or opportunities—such as the right to own and to exclude others from owning productive property—define them and distinguish them from each other. However, classes have almost no meaning if they are not also seen as real people, for it is people who create the rights or opportunities that define classes in the first place, it is people who enjoy or suffer the consequences of class inequalities, and it is people alone who are capable of changing or consolidating class structures through social action.

4. Classes are most readily defined as *economically based* entities. However, as will be discussed later, they also have an important part to play in the *political and ideological* spheres of society and can be said to exist, in a sense, within and across all social structures, not just the economic (cf. Wright, 1978; 1980). In delineating classes, we can conform with Marx, Weber, and most leading contemporary theorists by treating one distinction—between those who own or control society's productive property or resources and those who lack this attribute—as the initial and most fundamental division in modern class systems (for example, Marx and Engels, 1848a:58, 92; Weber, 1922:927; Giddens, 1973:100; Poulantzas, 1975:14; Wright, 1978:73; Parkin, 1979:53).

While this basic division is the crux of most class structures, there are other forms of social inequality that can occur. The relations of domination and exploitation established by this division are the primary factors in class formation, but the distribution of material benefits such as income can also be significant for delineating classes, if only in an indirect way. Such benefits can enhance or blur the division between the dominant and the subordinate classes, depending on whether or not these benefits are distributed so that the two classes have markedly distinct consumption habits and qualities of life.

In addition, despite what some writers seem to suggest, the distribution of material benefits need not be an insignificant factor in the formation of classes. For example, some Marxist theorists tend to consider all wage and salary employees as simply members of the working class, or *proletariat*, because they depend for their livelihood on the sale of labour power to the propertied owning class, or *bourgeoisie*. However, wage and salary employees sometimes are paid sufficiently high incomes for them to be able to accumulate some surplus funds, over and above what they need for basic survival. These funds can be, and occasionally are, used to gain some control over productive resources, in the acquisition of such holdings as stocks, rental properties, interest-bearing bonds, annuities, pension plans, and so forth. To be sure, these are relatively minor forms of economic control or ownership, in most cases, somewhat like that of the *petty bourgeoisie*, who own small-scale businesses or farms but employ no workers themselves. Nonetheless, such resources provide a means by which distributive inequalities can give rise to economic categories that are distinct to some degree from both the bourgeoisie and the proletariat.

A related point of note is the opportunity those with a distributive surplus have to expend these funds in another manner: to help finance special educational qualifications or technical training for themselves or their children. Here again, distributive inequalities need not merely signify consumption differences. Some writers suggest that educational credentials themselves are another form of productive "property." This may be true to the extent that educational certificates are tangible possessions that can generate material dividends all their own and that, as a result, can provide a basis for economic control otherwise unattainable by those who lack similar credentials (Giddens, 1973; cf. Collins, 1979; Parkin, 1979). Hence, educational advantage or opportunity may be yet another basis on which divisions can arise in the class structure and be passed on or reproduced over generations. The important role of educational certification or "credential assets" in class formation has increasingly been acknowledged by recent Marxist scholars (for example, Wright, 1985), in contrast to some earlier Marxists who ignored or downplayed the importance of this factor.

5. The final, and probably most controversial, question to address about class is how many classes actually exist in current capitalist societies. Again, complete agreement on this question is at present unattainable. Nevertheless, most writers now concur that modern class systems are more complex or plural in nature than the traditional Marxist division between bourgeoisie and proletariat is alone capable of representing. On the surface, this may seem to contradict standard Marxist accounts on the subject of class, especially those offered by Marx's early disciples. However, we should note that, on closer inspection, some allowance for a more complex portrayal of modern class systems is really quite consistent with Marx's own analysis and with more recent treatments by Marxist scholars.

At several points in his original writings, it is clear that Marx himself speaks of additional economic groupings that exist in real societies and that complicate the pure two-class model he believes will ultimately emerge in advanced capitalism. Marx refers to these complicating elements in various ways, calling them *Mittelstande* ("middle estates or strata"), *Mittelstufen* ("middle stages or ranks"), and *Mittelklassen* ("middle classes") (cf. Marx and Engels, 1848b:472; Marx, 1862:368; 1867:673, 688, 784, 791; 1894:892). Most current Marxists describe similar complications in contemporary class structures, although they usually avoid referring to these additional elements as genuine classes (but see Carchedi, 1977; Wright and Martin, 1987). Such elements may include the traditional petty bourgeoisie of small-scale owners but also involve a diverse range of salaried personnel that, because of attributes such as educational training, technical knowledge, or administrative authority, persist as "fractions" or "contradictory class locations," straddling the two basic classes of capitalism (cf. Poulantzas, 1975:23, 196-99, 297; Wright, 1978:90-91; 1979:46-47; 1985:88-89).

Among most non-Marxists, the existence of intermediate categories in the class structure is readily acknowledged. In fact, some non-Marxists argue that there are so many complexities and fine distinctions in today's economic structure that what we really have is a *continuous hierarchy* with no distinct classes at all (for example, Nisbet, 1959; Faris, 1972). Other non-Marxists have tried to adhere to this notion of a continuum while simultaneously retaining the concept of class in their analyses. One approach is to conceive of a general social hierarchy that is continuous and yet can also be divided into identifiable class clusters. In contrast to Marxist writers, some non-Marxist analysts, especially the so-called "structural functionalist school," see classes as sets of *occupations* that share a similar level of *prestige* because they are similar in their supposed value to society as a whole (for example, Parsons, 1940; 1953; Barber, 1957).

Among many recent non-Marxist scholars, however, it is common to reject this conception, primarily because it tends only to confuse classes with statistical categories or strata. Instead, leading contemporary writers outside the Marxist circle now conclude that it is essential to retain key aspects of Marx's original conception of class, provided these are revamped or supplemented to take account of subsequent developments in advanced class systems.

The latter approach is reminiscent of that adopted by Max Weber, the best known non-Marxist among major classical theorists in the field of inequality. Weber's work entails a constructive critique of Marx's writings. Weber envisions a class structure broadly akin to Marx's, involving a dominant bourgeoisie, or owning class, at the top, a propertyless working class at the bottom, and a mix of "various middle classes" (*Mittelstandklassen*) in between (cf. Weber, 1922:303-5). There are several differences between the views of Marx and Weber, of course. Perhaps the most crucial difference concerns their expectations for the eventual fate of the middle categories in the class system. In contrast to Marx, Weber believes that the growing need for intermediate bureaucratic and technical personnel in modern societies means that the middle class will not fall into the proletariat with time but will continue to endure as a significant force in the future; hence, Weber is far less convinced than Marx that a growing split will emerge between the top and the bottom classes or that an ultimate revolt by the working class against capitalism is likely to occur.

Weber's approach to the study of class has had a notable influence on virtually all current non-Marxist theorists. For example, some recent writers see classes arising because some people are able to gain greater access to certain important "capacities" and "mobility chances" (for example, Giddens, 1973:101-3) or to special "resources and opportunities" (for example, Parkin, 1979:44-46) that serve to exclude other people from advantaged positions. Certainly, these current approaches are not identical to one another, nor do they correspond precisely to the views of either Marx or Weber in their subtler details. Still, the class structures they portray are generally akin to one another and to the classical conceptions, for they also arrive at three key groupings: a *dominant class* composed mainly of those who own or control large-scale production; a *working class* made up of people who lack resources or capacities apart from their own labour power; and, in between, a *mixed intermediate range* that primarily comprises professional, technical, or white-collar personnel who have some degree of special training or education (cf. Giddens, 1973:101-10; Parkin, 1979:47-58, 102-10).

Thus, even a brief review of classical and contemporary conceptions of class indicates that what is mainly at issue among most theorists is not whether complications exist in the class system, but whether the complexities that do occur, especially those found in the centre of the structure, in fact constitute classes in their own right. Marxists usually say no, perhaps because they consider any middle segments as both transitional and heterogeneous, prone to plummet eventually into the proletariat and to blur only temporarily the real two-class system that underlies capitalism. In contrast, non-Marxists routinely treat such central segments as a middle class (or a set of middle classes), either because such writers use the term *class* differently or because they genuinely believe these intermediate categories are fundamental and persistent realities within modern class systems.

While no complete resolution of this debate is possible, the view put forth here is that, at least for the current stage of capitalist development, it is not unreasonable to use the term *middle class* to label these central categories. There are three reasons for taking this position.

First, there seems to be nothing inherent to the word *class* that suggests that it must be reserved solely to refer to permanent and lasting social categories. Thus, while all Marxists treat the bourgeoisie as a real class within capitalism, Marxists also contend that this class is destined for eventual dissolution in future socialist societies. Similarly then, whether or not the middle categories in the class system are destined to be transitional entities should not be a crucial concern for deciding whether or not they form a class at present. Marx clearly saw this himself since, as noted already, he sometimes spoke of the existence of a middle class even though he had no doubt that its days were numbered.

Second, it can be argued similarly that although the middle segments of the class structure are indeed heterogeneous, their diversity is insufficient grounds for denying that they form a distinct class. For, as leading Marxists and others acknowledge, the contemporary bourgeoisie and proletariat are also marked by considerable heterogeneity but are deemed to be classes all the same (for example, Poulantzas, 1975:23, 139, 198).

Finally, between the proletarian or bourgeois classes on the one hand and the set of intermediate categories on the other, there is some conceptual parity that suggests the latter also may be seen as a class. By *conceptual parity* we mean that the middle class is definable by means of the very same criteria used to delineate the bourgeoisie and the proletariat. These criteria are the measure of people's relative control over society's productive resources and the extent to which such control separates sets of individuals (and the positions they occupy) from one another. What is most distinct about the members of the middle class is their mixed, or hybrid, situation in the productive system relative to people from other classes. As suggested previously in point 4, middle-class incumbents are unlike those in the proletariat, and similar to people in the bourgeoisie, because they retain some control over productive resources or assets—the acquisition of property and investments or of educational credentials and skills, in particular. However, at the same time, middle-class members are unlike those in the bourgeoisie, and closer to people in the proletariat, because the resources they control are typically minor in scale and are often derived from a relatively small surplus fund accumulated from salaried or wage-based earnings. That these middle locations tend to commingle characteristics of the other two classes, and yet still remain marginal to both of them, is what most clearly identifies the middle class as a separate entity.

Given these considerations, we can deal with point 5 by provisionally suggesting that Canada, as well as most advanced capitalist countries, retains a class structure that, although highly complex and internally diverse, tends at its core to comprise three basic elements. The first is a predominant class of large-scale owners of productive property, the so-called *capitalist class*, or *bourgeoisie* in classical Marxian terminology. The second element is a subordinate class of workers who live primarily through the sale of their labour power to the owning class and who are usually termed the *working class* or *proletariat*. The third major element is a mixed and more heterogeneous middle category of small-scale business people, educated professional-technical or administrative personnel, and various salaried employees or wage earners possessing some certifiable credentials, training, or skills. The latter grouping, while it is for some writers just a set of complicating fractions or fragments within a basic two-class model, can be considered a third or *middle class* for the reasons already outlined.

Still, as has been pointed out from the beginning of this chapter, this provisional characterization cannot be presented as a universally acceptable conception of modern class structures. Rather, it can best be seen as an approximation, a compromise view with which the differing perspectives that are considered in this book can be compared and contrasted. Such an approximation allows us to recognize some level of agreement on how to think about the concept of class. Even so, other theoretical issues still remain to be addressed. In particular, we should be aware that many analysts believe a focus on class is too narrow to provide by itself a complete conceptualization of social inequality in all its forms. Such contentions move us beyond the problems of economic class and control over material or productive resources. They lead into a broader range of concerns that require us to consider the second key idea in most theories of social inequality—the concept of power or domination.

SOCIAL INEQUALITY AS POLITICAL AND IDEOLOGICAL CONTROL

In our opening remarks it was suggested that social inequality is primarily a question of consequential human differences, especially those that become structured, recurring features of our everyday lives. To this point, we have considered what many feel are the most familiar and fundamental illustrations of such differences: the inequalities that derive from differential *economic* control, people's command over material or productive resources in society. In addition, however, many writers suggest at least two other major mechanisms that are typically crucial to the creation and continuation of social inequality. The first of these involves control over people and their conduct, over what some might call "human resources." This command over human resources is the essence of *political* control, as broadly defined by various analysts. The third major mechanism can be referred to as *ideological* control. It entails the control of ideas, knowledge, information, and similar resources in the establishment of structured inequality between groups or individuals.

It can be taken as a basic premise of the current discussion that these two additional forms of control, though they typically occur in conjunction with economic control (and with each other), are not simply reducible to or a consequence of economic control, since both political and ideological control actually have their own distinct origins. In other words, it is possible to gain positions of dominance in society and to establish inequalities between factions without relying purely on control over material resources.

For example, inequality can result from political control when enforceable policies, statutes, or laws are invoked to ensure the compliance of subordinates with the will of others. The government or *state* is most commonly identified with the idea of political control, since it takes primary responsibility for creating the laws that govern the behaviour of people and can ensure compliance, if necessary, through the use of police or military force. However, political control in the broadest sense occurs whenever individuals' actions are constrained by rules of conduct established by others in authority over them in various organizations—when employees obey the work regulations of their jobs or when students comply with the academic regulations of their university, for example. The most extreme or blatant form that political control can take is one which is typically exercised by the state. This is the use of physical force by one faction on another, what Poulantzas quite literally calls the "coercion of bodies and the threat of violence or death" (Poulantzas, 1978:28-29).

In addition to economic and political control, inequalities can also be created through or reinforced by ideological forces. *Ideology* refers to the set of ideas, values, and beliefs that describe, explain, or justify various aspects of the social world, including the existence of inequality (cf. Porter, 1965, chs. 15, 16; Marchak, 1981). Thus, for example, a belief in racial superiority or inferiority is central to the ideological system that helped create and justify the unequal treatment of Blacks by Whites in the nineteenth-century southern United States and in present-day South Africa. Similarly, the belief in the divine right of kings was important in establishing and maintaining the rule of monarchs and nobles over other people in much of medieval Europe. Of course, it is also possible for ideologies to support *reductions* in inequalities among groups. For example, the Canadian Charter of Rights and Freedoms is one recent attempt in Canada to implement the belief in equal rights and opportunities for all people, regardless of race, national or ethnic origin, colour, religion, sex, age, or mental or physical disability. In each of these examples, ideas and beliefs about inequality were also converted by governments into official policy or formal laws. There often is a close connection between politics and ideology in society.

We should also recognize, though, that ideology can be fundamental to the third major type of control we have been discussing, economic control. For example, the belief that it is acceptable for people to own private property is clearly an essential ideological prerequisite for the existence of economic inequalities based on such ownership. Similarly, the belief that people with unequal talents or motivation should also be unequal in the material rewards they receive can be used as both an explanation and justification for the economic differences that arise among individuals. In both these examples, the extent to which people believe or reject ideas about themselves and their society will have an important bearing on how much inequality exists, and how likely it will change with time.

POLITICAL AND IDEOLOGICAL FACTORS IN CLASS DIFFERENCES

The recognition of multiple mechanisms of control and of the distinct resources they entail suggests that there is some degree of pluralism in the processes that generate social inequality. This, in turn, implies that any investigation based solely on economic class, especially if classes are conceived only in conventional terms as groupings within the structure of material production, is not sufficient by itself to capture and express this pluralism.

Perhaps for this reason, some recent Marxists have sought to include in their conceptions of class the sense that not only economic control but also political and ideological control are crucial to the formation of class structures (for example Poulantzas, 1975; Wright, 1979). Wright is especially noteworthy for his view that the standard Marxist emphasis on control of economic or material production as the criterion for defining classes should be broadened to include political and ideological "production" as well. In other words, those who control the production of the policies and laws that govern people and those who control the creation and communication of ideas, beliefs, information, or knowledge are clearly aligned with, if not part of, the economic upper class or bourgeoisie. He has suggested that people at the top of the political structure or state and those at the top of such ideologically oriented structures as the mass media, religion, education, and science share a similar general class location or class affinity with large-scale capitalists. Similarly, people who are employed within the political and ideological apparatuses of society, but who have no control over the products or resources of these structures, are basically equivalent to the industrial proletariat in their class position (cf. Wright, 1978:94-97; 1979:54; 1980:190).[1]

The incorporation of these additional elements into conventional conceptions of the class system is a significant innovation. Their inclusion permits us to recognize that classes, although they are primarily economic groupings, can also be important for other reasons and, in a way, may be fundamentally embedded within and across all social structures, both economic and non-economic. Here we should also note that, in addition to a revised notion of the class system, other complicating elements have come to be recognized in the multifaceted structure of inequality that characterizes most societies. As both Marxists and non-Marxists now generally acknowledge, various patterns of inequality exist that are at least partially independent of, and not reducible to, class inequality alone. The more prominent examples of these other bases for inequality include race, ethnicity, age, gender, and region, among others. Non-Marxists sometimes refer to these factors as different bases for "social closure" (Parkin, 1979), while Marxists sometimes call them "multiple oppressions" (Wright, 1985:57). However they are labelled, they represent additional areas of inquiry for students of inequality and require a conceptual approach which is somewhat broader than what the class concept by itself can provide.

SOCIAL INEQUALITY AS THREE FORMS OF POWER

It is primarily for this reason that some writers have recommended that the concept of power be used to supplement class theory, in an effort to move us toward a more general framework for analysing and thinking about inequality in all its forms. Some Marxist scholars have been reluctant to take this approach, especially if it relegates class analysis to a secondary concern (for example, Wright, 1985:57; cf. Clement, 1982:481). Other writers, however, have suggested that power can be employed as the more generalizable, if not the more fundamental, idea in theories of inequality, without belittling the importance of class at the same time (for example, Giddens, 1981a; cf. Grabb, 1984). Those who adopt the latter perspective contend that it is possible to treat class as the pivotal element in any complete understanding of social inequality. But, at the same time, they also argue that class differences represent one manifestation of the more general structure of power that is responsible for generating the overall system of inequality in most societies.

However, even if power can serve this more general conceptual purpose, the question still remains: What precisely does the concept of power signify? This is not a simple question to answer since power, like class, is an idea that has stimulated numerous debates over its definition and meaning (see, for example, Blau, 1964; 1977; Lukes, 1974; Wrong, 1979; Sennett, 1980; Galbraith, 1983; Mann, 1986). For our purposes, however, *power* can be defined briefly as the differential capacity to command resources and thereby to control social situations. We have already suggested that there are three major types of resources operating in social settings (material, human, and ideological) and three mechanisms of control corresponding to them (economic, political, and ideological). These three mechanisms can be seen as the key forms of power in society.

Whenever differences in economic, political, or ideological power are sufficiently stable and enduring that they promote regular, routinized relations of ascendance and subordination among people, the resulting pattern of interaction is a case of *structured power*, or what might be termed a *structure of domination* (cf. Grabb, 1984). Using abstract imagery, we can think of the overall system of inequality in a society as a kind of framework, involving all three forms of power and the three corresponding structures of domination. In more concrete terms, the structures of domination exist mainly as bureaucratic or corporate organizations: business enterprises in the economic sphere, departments of government in the political sphere, church hierarchies and institutions of higher learning in the ideological sphere, and so forth. It is within all these concrete settings that power differences among people (and among the positions they occupy) become manifested, thereby producing organized patterns of inequality.

Another point to note in this abstract imagery is that there is no perfect one-to-one linkage between each of the three forms of power and each set of concrete structures. These are just the *primary* linkages, since each of the means or forms of power can operate in at least a secondary fashion in any of the three structures. Thus, as noted earlier, political power (control over people or human resources) may indeed be the principal jurisdiction of the political structure of state organizations, but it is also exercised in the control imposed by owners on their workers in the economic structure. At the same time, the various political organizations composing the modern state do not derive all their power from the capacity to legislate or coerce human behaviour, for they also control material resources through their command over tax revenues, government ownership of some business enterprises, and so on. As for control of ideas or knowledge, this is most obviously identified with ideologically oriented structures such as the mass media, the education system, and the church. However, as mentioned in a previous section, such ideological control is clearly a means for wielding power elsewhere too. This is illustrated by the policy-making, information-gathering, and surveillance capacities within the state and by the control over technical ideas and knowledge that occurs in the economic sphere (cf. Giddens, 1981b; 1985).

It is the combined operation of all the structures of domination, or rather the concrete organizations to which they correspond, that establishes the major contours of the overall structure of inequality. The organizations themselves are patterned according to formal rules, laws, and rights of office, and their personnel exercise power in accordance with these formal guidelines. In addition, however, the inequalities that may develop within organizations, as well as the inequalities that organizations may engender for people outside them, are at least partly determined by informal practices or traditions, customs or habits, beliefs or prejudices. Not only formal rights or powers but informal privileges or advantages as well tend to determine the nature and extent of inequality in society. Both act together to designate what the key bases of social inequality will be and how much each of them will matter.

THE BASES OF SOCIAL INEQUALITY IN CANADA

There is a final conceptual issue to consider. This involves the identification of the central bases of social inequality that arise from the exercise of power in Canada. As we have already suggested, the notion that there are several distinct bases for inequality in society is one that has achieved increasing acceptance by theorists and researchers in the field, not only among non-Marxist writers but also among Marxist scholars. What has increasingly been argued is that there exists a multiple set of human characteristics or socially defined attributes that are consequential for determining the quality of life of most people. It will be recalled that this is the idea with which we began our introduction to the topic of social inequality in this chapter.

But what are these major bases for inequality, and why do these particular characteristics matter more than others? While it is difficult to provide answers to these questions that will satisfy all theoretical camps, we can see at least some common ground in the responses that most observers would give to both queries.

Perhaps the more difficult question to deal with is the second: why are some attributes of people more likely than others to lead to important inequalities? Why, for example, has colour of skin had such a sustained impact on the rights and rewards of people historically, but not colour of eyes or hair? In general terms, it is possible to conceive of this problem by looking once again at the idea of power, or domination, and by considering which factions within the population have histor-ically been the most or the least successful in turning to their advantage the various economic, political, and ideological mechanisms of power that operate within social structures. That is, to the extent that those in positions of ascendancy are able to use the three forms of power to establish and routinize structures of domination, they will be relatively more successful in reproducing across time and place impor-tant advantages for themselves and others with similar backgrounds or charac-teristics. For example, within any capitalist society, those individuals who retain private ownership or control over productive property will clearly enjoy special advantages and may well attempt to use their strategic position to encourage the further institutionalization of property rights in law, to foster belief systems favour-able to such rights, and to employ other comparable means to help ensure that the privileges of property are maintained for themselves and succeeding generations of capitalists. In a similar fashion, those who have recognized training and skills, notably those who possess formal credentials or degrees in such areas as medicine and law, will themselves benefit from the advantages such exclusive accreditation brings and will also tend to favour the continuation of the system of special certification (and attendant privileges) for themselves and the cohorts who follow.

In both of these illustrations, we have noted important bases for inequality—property and educational credentials—which also happen to correspond to two of the key types of economic or productive resources that are in demand in most societies. In the present context, however, these are not just resources but socially defined human attributes, or capacities of real people. In this form, they become recognized by others as crucial characteristics for differentiating some individuals or factions from others and for determining the rights, opportunities, rewards, and privileges of those who do or do not have them. We should note that this distinction, between resources on the one hand and human attributes on the other hand, illustrates once again what has elsewhere been referred to as the duality of social structures. In addition to these attributes, though, there is a whole range of other consequential human differences that should be identified. Each of these can likewise be conceived of as the product of long-standing factional antagonisms, struggles, or contests in which economic, political, and ideological mechanisms of power have played significant roles in establishing and structuring advantages for one grouping of people relative to others. The following set of attributes and capacities comprises the major bases of social inequality that can be identified in this way, especially in the context of the contemporary Canadian experience. The list includes property ownership, education, occupation, possession of wealth or income, ethnicity, race, language affiliation, regional or spatial location, gender, and age. As the papers in this volume will show, there is evidence to indicate that social groupings that are distinguishable from others on these dimensions (men relative to women or Anglophones relative to Francophones, for example) have often been able to maintain significant advantages within the system of social inequality in Canada, and have done so in part because of superior access to economic, political, and ideological power.

In considering such a list, of course, we should also be aware that not all of these factors must be equally influential in shaping the general patterns of inequality in Canadian society. It is also important to acknowledge that other factors may matter, in different historical periods or different places, and that there may be considerable variability over time in the importance or prevalence of some bases of inequality relative to others. An example is provided by religious affiliation. This is one social characteristic that we have not listed here, but which in the past was probably a significant basis for inequality in Canada. Nevertheless, most analysts would agree that now religion is of relatively little consequence in influencing the power or rank of Canadians, especially compared to a century ago. At the same time, though, it is true that religious differences still play a major part in shaping the structure of inequality in other countries, in contemporary Northern Ireland or Iran, for example.

PLAN OF THE BOOK

The selections that have been incorporated into this book reflect rather clearly the central role that the study of class and power has played in theory and research on inequality in Canada (see, in particular, Sections I and II). The various chapters also reveal the increasing attention that has been paid to the array of social characteristics that have arisen as important bases for inequality in this country (in particular, Sections II and III). As the title of the book suggests, we have also attempted within each section to attend not only to the patterns of social inequality and some of the problems these patterns pose for our society, but also to the policies and the ideology involved in inequality. The latter issue is especially prominent in Section IV, which focusses on the role of the state as an instrument of social control. Section V traces out some of the varied consequences of inequality for individuals.

Our choice of "Ownership and Class" as the topic for our first section is meant to underscore that control over productive property provides the fundamental context within which all the other bases for inequality operate in Canada and other capitalist societies. This section, therefore, provides necessary groundwork for understanding the patterns of inequality that are dealt with in the other sections.

We have said that certain key inherited or attained socio-economic characteristics are very important in defining the contours of inequality in our society. This issue is the principal focus of the second section of the book, which deals with the distribution of personal wealth or income, educational attainment, and occupational status. These are three bases for inequality that are distinct from each other and from the ownership factor itself, but which are also involved in shaping the system of economic classes. Ownership of productive property is the essential basis for class inequality, particularly that which exists between the owning class and the working class. At the same time, however, surplus wealth or income and educational credentials are, as we have seen, potentially important for distinguishing the "middle class," or comparable intermediate categories, from the two major classes. The reason for including occupation in the same section is perhaps less obvious, but follows from two considerations. First, occupation has long been employed in social research as an approximate indicator of class location, although the methodological problems associated with its use have been of some concern to many writers, especially Marxists. Second, the analysis of occupational inequality is useful in a supplementary or residual sense, because occupation subsumes such phenomena as skill level, manual versus non-manual labour power, and so on, which are not fully captured in research that is restricted to the study of ownership, wealth or income, and education.

In Section III the central concern is with factors of social ascription. In Canada, these include ethnicity, race, language, age, gender, and region of residence. This third set of attributes is discussed separately from class and the socio-economic status characteristics for two reasons. First, in contrast to the others, these bases for inequality are not fundamental to the definition of class or the delineation of class distinctions, although, as we shall see, they may be correlated with class location and may give rise to important divisions *within* classes. Second, these attributes are ascriptive in nature, involving statuses that are not achieved or attained by people, but rather given to them. The ascriptive process is most clear in such characteristics as ethnicity, race, and gender, which are all essentially assigned to people at birth. Age is another social characteristic that, though constantly changing, is assigned and beyond the control of people. Language and region of residence are also assigned characteristics. For adults, there is some reason to dispute the ascriptive label for these last two attributes, because adults can elect to alter the language they speak or move to another place to live. However, even in adulthood, these attributes are more ascriptive than they appear because of the pressures upon many Canadians to retain the language and place of residence they are born into. Language barriers and regional divisions reproduce themselves and their associated inequality over time, in spite of policy efforts to change them.

The selections in the fourth section of the book centre on the part played by the state in structuring social inequality in Canada. The importance of understanding the activities of governments and their influence on social inequality in modern societies has increasingly been recognized by sociologists in recent years. Governments are now seen to play a much more central part in society than they once did, not only in the political realm but also within the economic system, the education system, and elsewhere. Such issues as enlarged state ownership of business enterprises, wider state responsibility for providing social services, and increased calls for government policies to redistribute wealth or equalize opportunities are topics that are of considerable significance for understanding the patterns of social inequality. Perhaps the key way in which governments can have crucial influence is by establishing the bases of inequality themselves, through their formal capacity to legislate the official elimination or entrenchment of inequalities between groups. Once again, the Canadian Charter of Rights and Freedoms provides an example. The state is a central agent in deciding which social characteristics should *not* determine inequality in Canada. Other laws, however, such as those legitimating private property, may help reinforce inequality.

The first four sections of the volume, then, concentrate on structural questions: the character of class divisions and the other key bases of social inequality, and the ways in which such inequality has been developed and maintained. The final section serves a different purpose, by providing a broad sampling of evidence that class and the other bases of inequality have implications for the quality of life enjoyed or endured by all Canadians. Of course, the earlier parts of the book also deal with the consequences of inequality, to the extent that these sections examine the effects of class background on educational and occupational attainments, for example. In Section V, however, we have gone beyond this material to show the wide-ranging impact that social inequality can have on aspects of life as diverse as life expectancy, voting behaviour, criminal activity, political beliefs, and patterns of social interaction.

Our general purpose in this volume is to give the reader a sense of the rich array of important issues that research and theory on social inequality in Canada have addressed.

NOTES

1. In his most recent work, Wright has revised his first typology of classes so as to focus more narrowly once again on the control of economic or material production and away from other forms of control. This reversion to a more orthodox Marxist conception illustrates the continued controversy over how best to characterize class structures. Even here, however, it should be noted that Wright relies on three additional concepts in his new scheme that still parallel, at least roughly, the notions of economic, political, and ideological control that both he and Poulantzas used previously. These three corresponding concepts are respectively "assets in the means of production," "organization assets," and "skill/credential assets" (cf. Wright, 1985:64-104).

REFERENCES

Barber, Bernard
1957 *Social Stratification*. New York: Harcourt, Brace and World.

Blau, Peter
1964 *Exchange and Power in Social Life*. New York: Wiley.
1977 *Inequality and Heterogeneity: A Primitive Theory of Social Structure*. New York: The Free Press

Carchedi, Guglielmo
1977 *On the Economic Identification of Social Classes*. London: Routledge.

Clement, Wallace
1982 "Corporations, power, and class," in *Social Issues: Sociological Views of Canada*, ed. D. Forcese and S. Richer, pp. 469-85.Scarborough: Prentice-Hall Canada.

Collins, Randall
1979 *The Credential Society*. New York: Academic Press.

Curtis, James E., and William G. Scott, eds.
1979 *Social Stratification: Canada* (2nd ed.) Scarborough: Prentice-Hall Canada.

Faris, Robert E. L.
1972 "The middle class from a sociological viewpoint," in *Issues in Social Inequality*, ed. G. Thielbar and S. Feldman, pp. 26-32. Boston: Little, Brown and Company.

Galbraith, John Kenneth
1983 *The Anatomy of Power.* Boston: H. Mifflin.

Giddens, Anthony
1973 *The Class Structure of the Advanced Societies*. London: Hutchinson and Company.
1981a "Postscript (1979)", in *The Class Structure of the Advanced Societies* (2nd ed.). London: Hutchinson and Company.
1981b *A Contemporary Critique of Historical Materialism, Vol. I: Power, Property, and the State*. London: Macmillan.
1984 *The Constitution of Society*. Berkeley and Los Angeles: University of California Press.
1985 *A Contemporary Critique of Historical Materialism*, Vol. II: *The Nation State and Violence*. Berkeley and Los Angeles: University of California Press.

Grabb, Edward G
1984 *Social Inequality: Classical and Contemporary Theorists*. Toronto: Holt, Rinehart and Winston of Canada.
1986 "Social Stratification," in *Introduction to Sociology: A Canadian Focus* (2nd ed.), ed. James J. Teevan, pp. 143-81. Scarborough: Prentice-Hall Canada.

Johnson, Harry M.
1960 *Sociology: A Systematic Introduction*. New York: Harcourt, Brace and World.

Lukes, Steven
    1974   *Power: A Radical View*. London: Macmillan.

Mann, Michael
    1986   *The Sources of Social Power*. Cambridge: Cambridge University Press.

Marchak, M. Patricia
    1981   *Ideological Perspectives on Canada* (2nd ed.). Toronto: McGraw-Hill Ryerson.

Marx, Karl
    1862   *Theorien über den Mehrwert (Theories of Surplus Value)*, Vol. II, part 2. Stuttgart:
    (1910)   Verlag von J.H. Dietz Nachs.
    1867   *Capital*, Vol. I (German version). In *Marx Engels Werke*, Vol. I. Institut für
    (1967)   Marxismus-Leninismus Beim Zk Der Sed. Berlin: Dietz Verlag.
    1894   *Capital*, Vol. III (German version). In *Marx Engels Werke*, Vol. XXIII. Institut
    (1967)   für Marxismus-Leninismus Beim Zk Der Sed. Berlin: Dietz Verlag.

Marx, Karl, and Friedrich Engels
    1848a   *The Communist Manifesto*. New York: Washington Square Press.
    (1970)
    1848b   *The Communist Manifesto* (German version). In *Marx Engels Werke*, Vol. IV.
    (1967)   Institut für Marxismus-Leninismus Beim Zk Der Sed. Berlin: Dietz Verlag.

Nisbet, Robert A.
    1959   "The decline and fall of social class," *Pacific Sociological Review*, 2 (Spring):
            11-17.

Parkin, Frank
    1979   *Marxism and Class Theory: A Bourgeois Critique*. London: Tavistock.

Parsons, Talcott
    1940   "An analytical approach to the theory of social stratification," *Essays in Socio-*
    (1964)   *logical Theory*, pp. 69-88. New York: The Free Press.
    1951   *The Social System*. New York: The Free Press.
    1953   "A revised analytical approach to the theory of social stratification," *Essays in*
    (1964)   *Sociological Theory*, pp. 386-439. New York: The Free Press.

Porter, John
    1965   *The Vertical Mosaic*. Toronto: University of Toronto Press.

Poulantzas, Nicos
    1975   *Classes in Contemporary Capitalism*. London: New Left Books.
    1978   *State, Power, Socialism*. London: New Left Books.

Sennett, Richard
    1980   *Authority*. New York: Knopf.

Weber, Max
    1922   *Economy and Society*, Volumes I-III. New York: Bedminister Press.
    (1968)

Wright, Erik Olin
    1978   *Class, Crisis, and the State*. London: New Left Books.
    1979   *Class Structure and Income Determination*. New York: Academic Press.
    1980   "Class and occupation," *Theory and Society*, 9 (January):177-214.
    1985   *Classes*. London: Verso Editions.
Wright, Erik Olin, and Bill Martin
    1987   "The transformation of the American class structure, 1960-1980," *American Journal of Sociology*, 93, 1 (July):1-29.
Wrong, Dennis
    1979   *Power: Its Forms, Bases, and Uses*. Oxford: Blackwell.

FOR FURTHER READING

Clement, Wallace. 1983. *Class, Power, and Property*. Agincourt: Methuen. This is a collection of essays, some derived from Clement's earlier writings, others previously unpublished. The topics considered include the changing structure of the Canadian economy, access to the corporate elite, and the pattern of Canadian class cleavages.

Forcese, Dennis. 1986. *The Canadian Class Structure* (3rd ed.). Toronto: McGraw-Hill Ryerson. This book provides a range of materials on the Canadian class system, including sections on class and opportunity, class and lifestyle, class conflict, and the prospects of social change.

Grabb, Edward G. 1984. *Social Inequality: Classical and Contemporary Theorists*. Toronto: Holt, Rinehart and Winston. This book reviews and evaluates the major perspectives on social inequality that have emerged from classical and contemporary social theory.

Hunter, Alfred A. 1986. *Class Tells: On Social Inequality in Canada* (2nd ed.). Toronto: McGraw-Hill Ryerson. A general examination of social inequality in Canada, with a special focus on the importance of class, this book also investigates other key bases for social inequality, including gender and ethnic origin.

Porter, John. 1965. *The Vertical Mosaic: An Analysis of Class and Power in Canada*. Toronto: University of Toronto Press. This book is now dated, but remains one of the best works on social inequality in Canada. Porter employs the concepts of class, power, ethnicity, region, and institutional elites to describe and explain the complex structure of stratification in Canada in the 1950s and 1960s.

Porter, John. 1979. *The Measure of Canadian Society: Education, Equality and Opportunity*. Toronto: Gage. In this collection of essays Porter addresses a wide array of issues of importance to research and theory in the area of social inequality. Among the topics considered are the future of upward mobility, ethnic pluralism, education and equality, and the problem of power and freedom in Canadian democracy.

Section I

OWNERSHIP AND CLASS

Introduction

Most sociologists would agree that the best way to begin an investigation of social inequality is to examine its essentials, which in large part means understanding the underlying material foundations for its existence. This task requires that special attention be paid first to the key economic factors that operate in the formation of the Canadian class structure. The most important of these is ownership and control of productive property or resources.

There are three reasons for beginning our analysis in this way. First of all, differential access to material resources seems clearly to be the most elemental form of inequality to consider because such resources are a prerequisite for the very survival of all people. Second, concern over how material resources are distributed and who controls the productive apparatus that generates them has long been the central focus in much research in the field. Hence, a consideration of these and other economic questions is a crucial preliminary step for any general understanding of inequality in society. Third, it is apparent that the pattern of material inequalities can also be employed effectively to help us gauge the extent of inequality within other social hierarchies. For example, we can use information on who controls the means of material production not only to delineate economic classes but also to determine if people of different genders, ethnic groups, age groups, regions, and so on experience unequal access to economic resources. In other words, it is crucial that we understand differences in material or economic resources both as forms of inequality in their own right and as indicators of still other types of inequality.

With these considerations in mind, we will proceed initially by examining those features of society that most directly shape the system of economic inequality in Canada: *economic ownership* and the patterns of inequality that differential ownership tends to engender.

We have already noted that in capitalist societies like Canada's, and perhaps in all societies, the ownership of property is the most important topic of concern for those who wish to understand the problem of material inequality and the growth of economic classes. But what is really meant by the notion of *property ownership* in this context? Most theorists concur that property does not refer to the simple possession of material resources that are used only for personal consumption (such things as food, clothing, shelter, and the like). This is not to say that the distribution of these and other consumer items is unimportant to the study of inequality, nor is it to deny the tremendous significance of such goods for those who experience a shortage or abundance of them in their daily lives. Rather, it is to recognize that the possession of material benefits or products is not only, or even primarily, what in fact constitutes property ownership. As outlined by Wallace Clement in the first paper of this section, ownership of property, in its most complete and crucial sense, entails the right of disposition over the economic process in general.

The essence of property ownership is having the capacity to command the various activities and substructures that are inherent to producing, accumulating, investing, or expending society's material resources. Ultimately, it is from this capacity that decisions about the distribution of economic benefits to people stem, and it is through this capacity that some groups and individuals can exclude others from economic control or influence. Perhaps the most important outcome of this process is that the class of people who own society's productive property is in a position to establish relations of domination and exploitation over the class of non-owners, who in turn must sell their labour in order to survive. The non-owners, or working class, may resist this pattern of relationships through political organization, unionization, or other forms of collective action. However, as Clement's chapter argues, the owning class is typically able to override such opposition, given their rights of private property and the protection of these rights by the state or government.

In societies where private ownership of property is officially sanctioned, individuals or groups of individuals may purchase or otherwise acquire title to elements of the economy or of the productive apparatus. In earlier times, such acquisitions typically took the form of small farms, shops, and other businesses. People who owned these small-scale operations are often referred to as the *petite* (or petty) *bourgeoisie* and, as Clement's discussion reveals, they still play a role in the modern class system. Still, in more recent years, these simpler establishments have been superseded for the most part by large-scale corporate businesses, units of economic activity that are much more complex in their patterns of ownership, control, and operation.

In the second article, in this section, Robert Brym considers this group of large-scale owners—the so-called *bourgeoisie*, or *capitalist class*. His paper reviews and evaluates the research that has been done on Canada's capitalist class over the past two decades. Brym's overview takes note of such central concerns as the important role of foreign ownership in the Canadian economy, the historical development of internal cleavages in the Canadian capitalist class, and the effects of government policies on the power of private business to control the economy.

The third paper in this section is also concerned with the nature of the Canadian capitalist class and the system of large-scale business ownership in this country. William Carroll's chapter looks at recent evidence suggesting that ownership in Canada is more concentrated than ever before. His findings indicate that a relatively small *inner circle of capitalists* controls large segments of Canada's economy through densely interlocked corporate conglomerates.

For many observers, this high concentration of economic control in relatively few hands is a potentially serious problem. The main concern is that far too much economic power has been wielded historically by the owners of productive property. Any further centralization of ownership only increases the chances that such power will be abused by the owning class, and that inequalities will be significantly increased for the rest of the population.

In the final selection Deborah Coyne reviews some of the dangers of corporate concentration and offers some suggestions about what might be done to alleviate the problem. In particular, she considers some of the policy options that the state and various branches of government might consider to address and redress this issue.

The overall message conveyed by this section of the book is that ownership of productive resources, especially through the mechanism of giant business enterprises, is still the most fundamental and significant basis for inequality in Canada. Moreover, the evidence suggests that for the foreseeable future this will be as true in Canada as it is in capitalist societies generally.

1. Property, Labour, and Class Relations

Wallace Clement

Property is one of the most basic, yet least developed, concepts for the understanding of class. It incorporates a series of relationships characterizing different relations of production. The various *forms* of property (such as personal, communal, co-operative, and corporate property or common, state and private property) each designate specific relations between people and objects. They also designate, more importantly, relations between people and understandings about the rights of individuals to the use or benefit of things. To appreciate the concept of property, it is necessary to subdivide it into its various rights and specify the relations involved.

Property is a set of rights that determine *relationships* among and between people and things. The specification of relationships to the means of production as they affect relations between people is the essence of class analysis. The core relationship in a society dominated by the capitalist mode of production is that between capital and labour such that capital appropriates the right to the products of the labour power of workers. This relationship is not, however, the sole one. Other relationships, which, it is argued, are specified by the various rights of property, condition this core relationship. The most obvious example is the traditional petite bourgeoisie, which combines many of the rights of capital and obligations of labour in itself through independent commodity production whereby this class owns its own property and uses its own labour power. Aside from this core relationship, however, there are other property relations into which the petite bourgeoisie enters, such as market and capital relations with the capitalist class, or, intermittently, wage relations with capital, or employer relations with labour. Each must be disaggregated from the total bundle of relationships associated with various forms of property.

Crucial to understanding how the rights of property are reproduced and transformed is the existence of a state to mediate each process. Property rights always have some limitations on their exercise. As the embodiment of social relations, there must be limits, since various rights invariably interact and, therefore, require means to establish bounds. The state is often regarded as the "umpire" of these various claims. In some senses it is primarily arbitrating competing claims among capitalists (hence the Supreme Court's primary activity) and conditioning capital's right to exploit other classes. This is, however, too narrow a view of the state. The state in capitalist society has as its principal task the legitimation and enforcement of the rights of property, including the supply and containment of labour (the economic *and* social reproduction of the working class), ensuring that labour meets its obligation to provide capital with labour power. This task imposes severe limits on the state's infringement on the rights of capital. While it appears that the state creates property rights for capital, it is actually capital that created the capitalist state to enforce the rights capital had appropriated. The state, moreover, exercises the rights of state property, and an increasing part of labour enters its employ.

THE MEANING OF PROPERTY

Property is a social creation (*jure humano*) that orders and maintains specific relations between people. It is not, as it is used in an everyday sense, *what* is owned (or an object) but the rights attached to ownership; specifically, it is the right to control the use or benefit to which ownership is put. In the words of Morris Cohen, an American jurist, "'Property' denotes not material things but certain rights." He elaborated the specifically social content of the concept by saying, "A property right is a relation not between an owner and a thing, but between the owner and other individuals in reference to things" (1978:158–59). It is also a social relationship in another respect. Not only is it a right but "an enforceable claim to some use or benefit of something," in the words of C. B. Macpherson. As he goes on to say, "What distinguishes property from mere momentary possession is that property is a claim that will be enforced by society or the state, by custom or convention or law" (1978:3). We are obviously referring to property as much more than personal possessions (or chattels); it is the right to the use or benefit of things, tangible or not, enforceable by law.

Historically, *property* has been expressed in various forms of ownership. Out of feudalism grew capitalist ownership, which itself underwent changes in its property relations corresponding to an increasing division of labour. It is change in the content of capitalist property relations and its destruction of other forms that concerns us here.

Capitalism requires the subsumption of earlier property forms by "the complete separation of the labourers from all property in the means by which they can realize their own labour," as Marx argued, for two reasons. One is the requirement to transform "the social means of subsistence and of production into capital" and the other, to transform "the immediate producers into wage-labourers" (1967, I:714). This destruction turns individual property into social property by concentrating, in Marx's words, "the pigmy property of the many into the huge property of the few" (762). By divorcing labour from ownership of its means of production, it is transformed into wage labour capable of reproducing itself only by selling its labour power to capitalists, who own the means of production. Corresponding changes occur for both landed and manufacturing property. Both begin to correspond to the capitalist mode of production.

All forms of property under the capitalist mode of production are not capitalist, although all are shaped by capitalism as the dominant mode of production. As a first approximation of basic types of property relations under capitalism, we can begin with the three distinctions offered by C. B. Macpherson. *Private property* is "the right of an individual (or a corporate entity) to exclude others from some use or benefit of something." *State property* is "a right of a corporate entity—the state or the government or one of its agencies—to exclude others, not [as *common property* is . . .] an individual right not to be excluded" (1973:123). In analysing private property, it is important to recall, as Marx argued, that there are "two very different kinds of private property, of which one rests on the producers' own labour [and] the other on the employment of the . . . labour of others . . . [;] the latter not only is the direct antithesis of the former, but absolutely grows on its tomb only" (1967, I:765). This distinction within private property is, as will be argued later, the essential criterion separating the traditional petite bourgeoisie and the capitalist class (at the economic level).

State property arises, according to Macpherson, because the capitalist market fails to meet the necessary conditions of allocation. He points, for example, to transportation and communications "facilities necessary for, but not profitable to, private enterprise" (1973:134), and we could readily add a range of social welfare activities such as hospitals and schools. The state as an employer has adopted the *form* of capitalist relations and, as controller of state property, sets up similar relationships with labour to those used by capital.

It is crucial to locate correctly the state in our understanding of property, particularly, to distinguish state from common property and to specify the relationship between the state and private property. Macpherson convincingly argues that "the state indeed creates and enforces the right which each individual has in the things the state declares to be for common use [i.e., common property]. But so does the state create and enforce the exclusive rights which are private property. . . . The state *creates* the rights, individuals *have* the rights." And he quickly adds, corporate property (which is the recognized rights of a group) is an extension of individual property. The key, as far as state property is concerned, is that it "consists of rights which the state has not only created but has kept for itself" (178:4-5). There is no essential contradiction between state and private property. Both are hierarchically organized such that those claiming the property rights have what will later be referred to as economic ownership and possession, while those excluded have the obligation to labour. While the state appears to be the source of private property and is justifiably seen as its guardian, it would be more accurate to see the state in capitalism as arising to sanction private property and protect it from the antagonisms of civil society. Nonetheless, the state does have a crucial role in adjudicating and regulating the claims of property. The state can and often does regulate the profitability of particular activities; that is, it makes more or less valuable various property rights. For example, the striking of tariff duties determines whether certain industries will likely survive or be destroyed by imported goods. In fishing, it determines the jurisdictions; that is, makes into private property certain territories for the exclusive benefit of those it deems should use it. It also has the power of taxation, which is the right to take part of property (or revenue derived thereof) as its own. For the most part, however, it ensures what R. H. Tawney has referred to as "private taxation which the law allows certain persons to levy on the industry of others" (1978:143).

In order to understand property relations within, for instance, the farming and fishing industries, including the positions of independent commodity producers and capitalists, it is valuable to examine the relations between the state and property. It can be asked: Is the sea private property? As far as rights of access to fish, the sea has been transformed from common to private property for the most part. The state excludes some from the use or benefit of the products of the sea, not simply regulating its use (as can be the case with common property). The licences themselves, which are "tickets" to the amount of fish which may be gathered, the species, time, and location, take on a value of their own. They become private property—the state grants the rights, individuals (or corporations) have the rights, and, in the case of some fishing rights, these can be sold as private property. An important illustration of the state creating private property out of common property occurred in the initial stages of colonization in North America when the bulk of the land was alienated from the native people and turned into private property, often given over to corporations, such as the Hudson's Bay Company or the Canadian Pacific Railway (having passed through the various stages of common and state property).

The state is constantly engaged in creating or adjudicating private property rights for capitalists. Two cases illustrate this role. The first was a ruling concerning the lands of the Inuit of the Baker Lake area:

A Federal Court judge ruled yesterday that the Inuit have aboriginal title to about 130 000 square kilometres of the Northwest Territories. In his 65-page judgment, [Judge Patrick Mahoney] said the Inuit have no surface rights. He added that on Dec. 17 he will lift the order which has restricted exploration in the Baker Lake area since 1977. . . . [Federal Government lawyer Luther Chambers is quoted as saying,] "All they got was that they have the right to hunt and fish. The way I see it, the Government is free to deal with the land as it sees fit . . . to issue mining permits after Dec. 17." (*Globe and Mail*, November 16, 1979:4)

A second case concerns the lack of rights of farmers not only to the resources under their lands but to control access to these resources:

Contrary to popular belief, a farmer or rancher cannot prevent an industry operator from entering his property to drill, build storage and processing facilities or to drive pipelines through his fields and meadows. He has to yield the right of entry to a company that bought provincial mineral leases to explore and, if successful, develop crude oil, natural gas, or coal reserves beneath the surface.

That is, unless the farmer owns the mineral rights himself. Only descendants of a few early homesteaders in what was then part of the Northwest Territories, before Alberta became a province in 1905, and beneficiaries of land grants, such as the Canadian Pacific Railway, control both surface and mineral rights. . . .

On average, a well site would earn the farmer $3000 to $5000 in a once-only lump sum payment. If found productive, the completed well—fenced off and with a service road—would be worth up to $2500 in annual rental payments (*Globe and Mail*, November 19, 1979:B6)

In both illustrations, capitalist mining and energy companies are ensured access to "their" property rights (as created by the state) in the form of mineral claims. In both cases, these are claims created by the state and turned into private property, overriding the claims to the lands by those outside the capitalist class. Thus, in an analysis of class and property it is crucial to understand how the rights of property are subdivided, reproduced, and transformed. The state is often the mediary and acts to enforce the claims of capital.

The dominant ideology concerning the state and property is that the state is simply acting to ensure that those who own things are able to enjoy the benefits; that is, protecting the "natural" rights of the owners. Morris Cohen's observation that "the essence of private property is always the right to exclude others" and hence that "domination over things is also *imperium* over our fellow human beings" places this dominant ideology in a different light. As Cohen illustrates, the state's protection of property does not simply protect that property from others but "determines what men shall acquire. Thus, protecting the property rights of a landlord means giving him the right to collect rent, protecting the property of a railroad or a public service corporation means giving it the right to make certain charges," all of which ensures that the distribution of the benefits of these activities accrue to the property owner and exclude others (1978:159-60).

Property relations under feudalism involved mutual sets of rights and obligations and were limited to specific uses of land. The most important limitation was that the land was not disposable, particularly because different groups had various claims to the same land. Under capitalism these rights tended to become consolidated (that is, absolute). Contrasting modern private property with feudal rights, Macpherson says it "may be called an absolute right in two senses: it is a right to dispose of, or alienate, as well as to use, and it is a right which is not conditional on the owner's performance of any social function" (1978:7-10).

Hence, the restrictions on property under capitalism are less than under feudalism, with many of the obligations characteristic of property ownership under feudalism now falling to the state to perform. The rights of property under capitalism are, nonetheless, qualified in several respects, principally that the exercise of one person's rights does not impede another's use or benefit of his property. These qualifications are mainly to protect property holders from their fellows and not to ensure that the benefits of property enhance all. Property itself, however, has undergone some significant transformations with the development of capitalism.

FORMS OF OWNERSHIP

An important distinction that Marxists have come to accept for advanced capitalist societies is that between legal (or judicial) and real (or active) ownership. With the advent of the joint-stock company, a disjuncture became possible between what has often been called the ownership and the control of corporations. It is clear that not all stockholders control corporations in which they have holdings. Indeed, for most, the only claim their ownership ensures is that of revenue derived from dividends. Nonetheless, for a smaller number of concentrated owners, their claims do extend to control. This distinction is necessary to avoid the position that all legal owners are capitalists, when in fact only a fraction of owners are able to realize the *actual* property rights of corporations. The rest are *rentiers*, who retain only the right to income from their property, not the right to direct labour or the products of labour. These rights are transferred to capitalists in return for investment income. Most stock and bond holders are in a *rentier* position. Not all loan capital embodies this passive relationship. Banks, for instance, typically set conditions on their temporary "investments" and retain the rights of possession upon default or even a voice in the direction of the company (economic ownership). When sufficient capital is invested to command a say in management, then at least some additional rights of property are retained. The distinction, then, is basically between active and passive ownership, with capitalists as active and *rentiers* as passive.

Within active ownership, it is possible to make a distinction between economic ownership and possession. The need for this distinction arises with the increased division of labour that occurs with the development of corporate capitalism and its expanded hierarchy of control. Since the rights of capital are no longer activated by a single capitalist or even a handful of top managers, they become collectively performed by what Guglielmo Carchedi refers to as "a complex hierarchically organized ensemble of people" (1977:70). Nicos Poulantzas has defined the two forms of active ownership as follows: *economic ownership* is "real economic control of the means of production, i.e., the power to assign the means of production to given uses and so to dispose of the products obtained," while *possession* is "the capacity to put the means of production into operation" (1975:18-19). The two forms of control are directed at different levels within the firm: economic ownership refers to the activities of accumulation and investment, while possession refers to direction of the labour process. The capitalist class has both forms of ownership, while the working class is excluded from both, that is, the products of its labour and the control of the labour process. What is critical in this distinction is the recognition that possession is subject to a division of labour such that possession can be distinguished from economic ownership and thus assigned to a large number of positions within the labour process. For Poulantzas, economic ownership "is determinant in defining the places of social classes, that is to say, the place of the dominant and exploiting class" (1975:19). Possession is nevertheless crucial for determining the place of the intermediate class. The development of capitalism has meant the alienation of control over the labour process (possession) from the working class and subjected it to scientific control. The right to control one's own labouring practices, as has been the case for independent commodity producers and the early stages of capitalist relations characterized by the formal subordination of labour, has passed to the capitalist with the real subordination of labour. The real subordination of labour has been accomplished by a detailed division of labour (see Braverman, 1974). To the extent that control over the labour process has been retained by labour, it is only for that fraction of the working class still able to enforce the claims of tradesmen and craftsmen. This, of course, is a rapidly dwindling portion of the working class. The rest of the working class performs only the obligations of labour and not the rights of capital. The significance of the distinction between economic ownership and possession as two active aspects of property will become evident as we begin to apply them to class relations.

CLASS RELATIONS

Class may be defined at the economic level in terms of relationships to property and control over labour. What, then, is the capitalist class? Those who control property rights and command the labour power of others. And the working class? Those who are excluded from control over property rights and are obliged to sell their labour power. Estrangement from their *means* of labour and the rights of property are the key criteria for determining the working class. This distinguishes the working class from the traditional petite bourgeoisie, who control their own property (that is, their ability to labour). The modern petite bourgeoisie (or new middle class) performs both the tasks of capital (including surveillance and control, co-ordination and unity) and the tasks of labour, thus exercising both the rights of property and the obligations of labour, even though, like the working class, it has only its labour power to sell. The working class thus includes those excluded from the rights and benefits of property who also perform the obligations of labour. Its labour power is a living commodity sold to capitalists. In so doing, labour gives over to capital control of its labour power and is subject during specified periods to the command of capital. Labour is thus obliged to obey the rule of capital or face penalties. By virtue of their control over property and over employment of the labour power of others, capitalists control the means by which capital is accumulated, the products of labour, the use of labour, and the direction of the labour process. As a first approximation, this defines the basic classes of capitalism.

With the formal subordination of labour, capital strips labour of its rights to the products of its labour, but with the real subordination of labour, capital also strips labour of control over the labour process (that is, the right to conceive, design, and direct its own labour). In both cases capital appropriates the rights as its own. In the first case this right is retained as *economic ownership*, and in the second it subjects workers to a detailed division of labour as *possession*, thus leaving workers with only their obligation to labour under the direction of capital and without claims on the products of their labour.

The purpose of the remainder of this paper is not to explore property relations through an examination of capitalist and working classes but to examine the class which combines elements of each, namely, the petite bourgeoisie. It will be argued that what Carchedi calls the "functions of capital" and the "functions of labour" can be identified as the rights of capital and the obligations of labour within property relationships, and that these can be exposed through an examination of the petite bourgeoisie, which contains elements of both sets of rights and obligations.

THE PETITE BOURGEOISIE

The first distinction that must be offered is one which identifies fractions of this class found inside and outside capitalist relations. The classic petite bourgeoisie are those who own their own property and are thus "independent" of the capitalist class in the sense that they "work for themselves." This can be designated the *old middle class* to distinguish it from the *new middle class*, which is located within bureaucratic settings and performs both the "functions of capital and labour" (Carchedi, 1977:43-91). The key element of this analysis for the relationship between capital and labour will be to provide insight into the process known as proletarianization, whereby both the old and new middle classes are increasingly being drawn into a relationship with capital that destroys their rights of property—either their independent ownership in the case of the old middle class or their performance of the rights of capital in the case of the new middle class— and requires them to perform increasingly the obligations of labour. The analysis will proceed primarily on the economic level, but the political and ideological implications will partially be addressed. In terms of my immediate empirical interests, I intend to document the economic processes of proletarianization identified and correlate them with their political and ideological implications.

The existence of the middle classes has modified and to some extent cushioned the political and ideological struggle between capital and labour. The degree of proletarianization will, it is argued, facilitate the development of direct confrontation between capital and labour. Although Marx had little to say about the classes outside capital and labour under capitalism, he did observe "the continual increase in numbers of the middle classes . . . situated midway between the workers on the one side and capitalists and landowners on the other. These middle classes rest with all their weight upon the working class and at the same time increase the social security and power of the upper classes" (1956:190-91). This suggests that the proletarianization of the middle class would serve to polarize the two great classes of capitalism, thus laying bare the contradiction between them. This prospect runs counter, of course, to most analyses, which identify the expansion of the middle class with the development of capitalism. The present formulation recognizes that the old middle class shrinks with the development of capitalism but that the new middle class expands. The point in question is whether the new middle class will continue to expand or eventually begin to experience proletarianization as the labour process becomes further socialized. It is here suggested that the latter may be occurring, although it has not been demonstrated.

The traditional petite bourgeoisie, which was particularly characteristic of the early stages of capitalism, prior to its absorption into or destruction by the concentration and accumulation of capital on a large scale, includes two fractions. Those engaged in production are independent commodity producers, most notably artisans, farmers, and fishermen; those engaged in service, who may be called the urban petite bourgeoisie for lack of a better term, are small entrepreneurs such as restaurateurs, shopkeepers, and independent professionals (like accountants, doctors, and lawyers). The traditional petite bourgeoisie own their own property and use their own labour power with limited additional labour (usually family members or marginal workers). The ideal-type traditional petit bourgeois (who seldom existed) was one who owned his own means of production, controlled his supplies and directly sold his commodities or services to consumers. In practice, there has been a constant erosion of control over these dimensions, in addition to the overall displacement of the traditional petite bourgeoisie as a class. At the level of property, the petite bourgeoisie represent an identity between legal ownership, economic ownership, and possession, as well as a non-exploitive relationship with labour; that is, property controlled by the labourer is the means for realizing labour. Even though it no longer accurately reflects property relations (if it ever did), this continues to be a dominant *image* of property even in advanced capitalism. It is proposed here that an appropriate understanding of the process of proletarianization for the traditional petite bourgeoisie requires a specific analysis of the *various* property rights they have held.

Questions of economic ownership and possession of property relations are critical for the traditional petite bourgeoisie, but so too are those relations concerned with markets for the commodities of independent producers (particularly since they are engaged in exchange). Also of importance is the relationship to sources of finance, since petty commodity producers in Canada have traditionally been restricted in their effectiveness as primitive accumulators of capital and hence have relied on external financial sources; also included are sources of essential supplies, which are elements of the means of production. The traditional petite bourgeoisie are subordinate to capital insofar as they relate to capitalists in the capital, supply, and sales markets. Concentrated financial capital in the money markets (e.g., mortgages), industrial capital as the suppliers of instruments of production (e.g., equipment) or as buyers of their products (e.g., fish or food processors) are all illustrations of areas of possible subordination to capital. To the extent they are subordinated, they are no longer independent; that is, they lose some of the rights of property and experience proletarianization. Whether they actually become proletarian is determined by whether they lose all the rights of capital.

The key ideological characteristic of the traditional petite bourgeoisie is independence. This is the independence of working for oneself, of "being your own boss," and thus distinct from both big labour and big capital. The crucial economic relationship of the petite bourgeoisie in Canada, however, has been its dependence, its failure to remain autonomous from capital.

As for the new middle class, it experiences proletarianization differently but (one suspects) with similar ideological reactions. Its independence, or, more accurately, autonomy, within the labour process comes from its intermediary position between capital and labour such that it simultaneously has some of the rights of property and obligations of labour. Carchedi has argued that the process of proletarianization for the new middle class involves the "progressive decreasing of the time dedicated to the global function of capital and thus [. . .] a progressive increase of the time during which the function of collective work is performed" (1977:9). Stated in the terms used here, this means the new middle class progressively loses its rights of property, and its obligations as labourers increase. To determine precisely how this occurs is beyond the scope of this paper, but it is clearly an important political question for determining the relations of class with the further socialization of the means of production under capitalism.

CONCLUSION

Property relations, including both state and private property, are the axis upon which classes are drawn in capitalism. It is not a simple dichotomous structure but a complex dichotomy whereby the major criterion is the relationship of control over property. There are, however, other property relations to be considered. The principal task, therefore, is to locate the rights of ownership and hence the relationships involved in property. Only then is it possible to locate agents within these relationships. Some relationships may be "pure" in the sense of absolute rights or total absence of rights, while others may be mixed. In the latter it will be crucial to establish the determinant rights as they affect the economic, political, and ideological location of agents. Agents may "feel" independent and act politically on this belief while at the same time be economically dependent. In such cases it will be valuable to determine how this inconsistency is handled by agents; that is, by acceptance of a dominant ideology inconsistent with their subordinate location.

Individuals, particularly those within the middle classes, can stand in different relationships to various rights of property and can be expected to experience simultaneously a number of relationships through their position. For example, franchise dealers running corner stores, gasoline service stations, and so forth, may own their own "property" but enter into contracts with capital to market specific products under specific conditions, thus restricting their control over their property. These types of restrictions are particularly evident in agriculture, where outlets for products, generally under the control of monopoly capital, determine for the farmer both what is to be produced and how it is to be produced; that is, both the economic ownership and possession dimensions of their property relations are restricted.

The study of property, because it focusses the study of classes on their relationships and, hence, struggles between them, must incorporate the political and ideological confrontations over the rights of property that result. Since control over the rights and forms of property is at the core of class struggle, it brings to the fore the question of class alliances. Speaking of the traditional petite bourgeoisie, Marx commented:

> Against the coalesced bourgeoisie, a coalition between petty bourgeois and workers had been formed, the so-called *social-democratic party*. . . . The peculiar character of the Social-Democracy is epitomized in the fact that democratic-republican institutions are demanded as a means, not of doing away with the two extremes, capital and wage labour, but of weakening their antagonism and transforming it into harmony. However different the means proposed for the attainment of this end may be, however much it may be trimmed with more or less revolution-

ary notions, the content remains the same. This content is the transformation within the bounds of the petty bourgeoisie. (1963:49-50)

One may suspect, at first glance, that a focus on property might be in danger of economism. However, it is not property as a thing but its relationships that are being investigated, and these relationships inherently contain political and ideological dimensions. The struggles over the benefits or uses of property rights constitute the political dimensions; the justification of interests by those controlling or excluded from property rights constitutes the ideological dimension. There need not be a direct mechanical correspondence between the economic, political and ideological. To begin to determine the specific nature of the relationship is an empirical problem.

It is argued that the justifying theory of property, as used to unmask the political and ideological content of property in advanced capitalism, is one developed to correspond to petty commodity producers, or at best small capitalists, in terms of competition, free markets, the ingenuity of the owners, the hard work, the risk of innovators, etc. Modern capitalism continues to rely on this justifying theory (which is particularly useful for alliances with the petite bourgeoisie), but the economic structure it describes has been transcended. Nonetheless, the power of the ideology persists. It remains an important task to determine the resilience of this ideology under pressure from the proletarianization of the middle classes.

REFERENCES

Braverman, Harry
    1974   *Labor and Monopoly Capital: The Degradation of Work in the Twentieth Century.* New York: Monthly Review Press.

Carchedi, Guglielmo
    1975   "Reproduction of Social Classes at the Level of Production Relations," *Economy and Society,* vol. 4.
    1977   *On the Economic Identification of Social Classes.* London: Routledge and Kegan Paul.

Cohen, Morris
    1978   "Property and Sovereignty," in *Property: Mainstream and Critical Positions*, ed. C. B. Macpherson. Toronto: University of Toronto Press.

Macpherson, C. B.
    1973   *Democratic Theory: Essays in Retrieval.* London: Clarendon Press.
    1978   *Property: Mainstream and Critical Positions.* Toronto: University of Toronto Press.

Marx, Karl
    1956   *Selected Writings in Sociology and Social Philosophy*, ed. T. B. Bottomore and M. Rebel. Harmondsworth: C. A. Watts and Co.
    1963   *The Eighteenth Brumaire of Louis Bonaparte.* New York: International Publishers (original 1852).
    1967   *Capital*, Vols. I and III. New York: International Publishers (original 1867).

Poulantzas, Nicos
    1975   *Classes in Contemporary Capitalism.* London: New Left Books.

Tawney, R. H.
    1978   "Property and Creative Work," in *Property: Mainstream and Critical Positions*, ed. C. B. Macpherson. Toronto: University of Toronto Press (original 1920).

2. The Canadian Capitalist Class

Robert J. Brym

FROM THE DENIAL OF CLASS TO THE RISE OF LEFT-NATIONALISM

It is one of the more remarkable facts of Canadian intellectual life that, until some 20 years ago, few university professors or literary figures seem to have noticed that there are social classes in this country. Or at least, if many intellectuals did notice, they were not inclined to publicize the discovery. Thus, in 1963 a literary critic remarked that the theme of social class scarcely appears in Canadian literature (McDougall, 1963). In 1965 an historian made an identical observation in a review of Canadian historical writing (Mealing, 1965). And in that same year John Porter, who was soon to be acknowledged as the outstanding sociologist in the country, wrote:

> Even at times in what purports to be serious social analysis, middle-class intellectuals project the image of their own class onto the social classes above and below them. There is scarcely any critical analysis of Canadian social life upon which a conflicting image could be based. The idea of class differences has scarcely entered into the stream of Canadian academic writing ... (Porter, 1965:6).

Since the mid-1960s the situation has, of course, changed a great deal, and the study of social class has even become something of a "growth industry." This development is a result of a number of factors, among the most important of which are the influence of Porter's work; the recruitment of Canadian professors from more diverse class and ethnic backgrounds than was once the case; the immigration, during the days of rapid university expansion, of scholars from the U.S.A. and England, where the study of social class was better developed; and something which is perhaps best (if vaguely) labelled the changing "temper of the times."

This shift in the Canadian intellectual climate is worth reflecting upon. It is usually

Revised from Robert Brym (ed.), *The Structure of the Canadian Capitalist Class* (Toronto: Garamond Press, 1985), pp. 1-16. Reprinted with permission of Garamond Press Ltd. and the author.

and, I think, justifiably ascribed mainly to the weakening role of the U.S.A. in international affairs from the mid-1960s on (Resnick, 1977:145-99). The United States suffered defeat in Vietnam. The post-Second World War recovery of the Japanese and West German economies threatened the competitiveness of American manufacturers. Increasingly, wealth flowed from the U.S.A. and other highly industrialized countries to the petroleum- and mineral-exporting nations as OPEC and other cartels secured enormous increases in the price of natural resources.

How did Canadians respond? Many became aware of some of the negative consequences of being so tightly bound, economically and politically, to the fortunes of the U.S.A. Also, the realization grew that new possibilities for economic growth were afforded by changing international circumstances, especially rising world market prices for Canada's abundant natural resources.

Academics and university students tended to respond more radically to the American decline and Canada's expanded opportunities than did other segments of Canadian society. The most prominent manifestation of this trend was the formation, within the New Democratic Party, of a left-nationalist wing known as the "Waffle" (Hackett, 1980). Supported by roughly one third of NDP activists at its height, the Waffle was dominated by intellectuals, and central to its platform was the view that Canadian "dependency" upon the United States was chiefly responsible for a whole range of economic and other ills.

The term dependency was intended to signify an unequal relationship in which the United States uses its superior power to secure a wide range of economic advantages over Canada. As the left-nationalist argument has been developed in academic circles (see especially Britton and Gilmour,

1978; also Levitt, 1970; Lumsden, 1970; Rotstein and Lax, 1974), it is held that one of the chief features of the Canada/U.S.A. relationship is the control of substantial portions of the Canadian economy by American-based multinationals. This control facilitates the outflow of a great deal of capital— in the form of profits, dividends, interest payments, royalties, and management fees —from the country. In the absence of foreign control, that capital would presumably be available for investment and job creation in Canada. The magnitude of the problem is indicated by the fact that Canada has had growing deficits on the "non-merchandise account" of its international balance of payments throughout the post-Second World War period. By 1977 the annual deficit amounted to over $7 billion. Nearly 75 percent of that deficit is a result of capital transfers such as those listed above.

Not only does American direct investment cause a net capital drain but in addition (so the left-nationalist argument continues) the foreign capital which remains invested here creates fewer jobs than would an equal amount of domestic capital investment. This is the case because foreign capital is invested in Canada for two main purposes: to provide a secure source of raw materials for manufacturing plants in the U.S.A., and to produce manufactured goods for the Canadian market. Plants set up to produce only for the Canadian market are by definition prevented from trying to compete for international sales, from engaging in research and development, and in many cases from doing any more than assembling parts made outside the country. Thus, foreign direct investment seriously constrains growth in the manufacturing sector—which is one important reason why Canada imports substantially more manufactured goods than it exports ($11 billion more in 1977). Moreover, massive American direct investment in the resource sector is an inefficient creator of jobs: generally speaking, a unit of investment in resource extraction creates fewer employment opportunities than a unit of investment in manufacturing since resource extraction is generally more capital-intensive.

LEFT-NATIONALISM AND THE CAPITALIST CLASS

It has been argued that Canada's dependency is a function not of geography and technology but of the nature of Canada's capitalist class (Laxer, 1973). This corollary of the dependency thesis is particularly germane in the present context. It was first elaborated in a highly influential article by Tom Naylor (1972; see also Naylor, 1975). According to Naylor, the whole sweep of Canadian economic history is characterized by Canada's role as a supplier of raw materials to, and a purchaser of manufactured goods from, a progression of imperial centres: first France, then Great Britain, and finally the U.S.A. Naylor allowed that out of this trade there emerged a Canadian capitalist class which specialized in the construction and operation of transportation facilities, as well as the provision of insurance, banking, and short-term credit services. But he further insisted that this class has historically had a vested interest in blocking the development of a vigorous and independent manufacturing sector in this country. After all, he reasoned, using raw materials here rather than shipping them abroad, and producing manufactured goods here rather than bringing them in from elsewhere, would undermine the trading and related activities upon which the prosperity of the Canadian capitalist class was founded. The high import tariffs on manufactured goods

instituted by the Macdonald government in the National Policy of 1879, and eagerly backed by members of Canada's mercantile bourgeoisie, serve Naylor as an outstanding example of how the capitalist class stunted independent industrial growth in this country. The net effect of the tariff wall was to encourage the hothouse growth of foreign (mainly American) branch plants in Canada—plants designed to service only the local market and engage mainly in assembly and warehousing.

This argument, which came to be known as the "merchants against industry thesis," was widely accepted until the mid-1970s. Consider, for instance, the important studies undertaken by Wallace Clement (1975; 1977). One of the tasks Clement set himself was to analyse the density and pattern of ties among dominant corporations in Canada—ties formed by individuals sitting simultaneously on more than one corporate board of directors. According to Clement, the senior executives and members of the boards of directors of the country's dominant corporations, members of the "corporate elite," actually comprise two main groups. First, the "indigenous elite" consists of people, for the most part Canadian-born, who head corporations engaged mainly in commercial and transportation-related activities. Their business is conducted chiefly inside, but also to a degree outside, Canada. (An example of the latter is the case of Canadian banks setting up branches throughout the Caribbean region.) Second, the "comprador elite" consists of people, only some of whom are Canadian-born, who merely operate or manage the Canadian branch plants of multinational corporations. The economic activities of these branch plants are also largely restricted to Canada itself, although in some cases they serve as intermediaries for American direct investment in third countries. (For example, the Ford Motor Co. in the U.S.A. holds 85 percent of the stock in the Ford Motor Co. of Canada, which in turn holds 100 percent of stock in the Ford Motor Co. of Australia, New Zealand, South Africa, and Singapore.) Most of the multinationals with branch plants in Canada have head offices in the U.S.A., and most of them are engaged in manufacturing and resource extraction.

Clement does not suggest that the cleavage between indigenous and comprador "fractions" of the Canadian corporate elite implies conflict or rivalry between the two groups. Quite the contrary. The two groups play complementary roles in Canadian economic life, one basically financial, the other basically industrial and resource-related. Moreover, their boards of directors are highly interlocked, important financiers frequently serving on the boards of foreign-controlled companies engaged in manufacturing and resource extraction, and vice versa. They also share a "continentalist" outlook on the nature of Canada/U.S. relations, as evidenced by their opposition to the growth of an indigenous Canadian manufacturing sector that could disrupt the existing pattern of economic relations between the two countries.

The left-nationalists maintain that members of the Canadian corporate elite have successfully transformed this continentalist vision into what is widely perceived as "the national interest." This is significantly evident in the behaviour of the two establishment political parties, the Liberal and the Progressive Conservative. These parties have, by and large, acted to stultify the growth of a vigorous manufacturing sector and have reinforced the liaison between indigenous commercial and foreign-controlled comprador elites. Two of the most frequently cited examples of the manner in which gov-

ernments have acted in the interests of Canadian corporate leaders are the failure to enact a tough Foreign Investment Review Act limiting American takeovers of Canadian manufacturing and resource companies, and a readiness to introduce laws protecting Canadian banks, insurance companies, and transportation companies from foreign competition.

The theoretically important question is: How is it that the class interests of the corporate elite get translated into major government policies? Members of the left-nationalist school have differed in their answers to this question. Many of them have modified their opinions since the mid-1970s. With these qualifications in mind, I shall not distort matters greatly if I assert that the left-nationalists' original answer to the question posed above went something like this: The corporate elite controls governments largely in a direct manner, by forging a wide variety of strong social ties to the state and to state personnel. These ties ensure that the people who occupy the command posts of economic institutions form a ruling class.

The implications of this viewpoint may be more fully appreciated if we contrast it with the earlier formulation of John Porter. Porter had discovered that members of various Canadian elites—the chief power holders in our economic, political, media, bureaucratic, and intellectual institutions—tend to be recruited from well-to-do families of British and Protestant origin in far greater proportions than their representation in the general population. Moreover, Porter sought to establish that members of the different elites come to share certain values and attitudes as they interact with one another. This cohesion enables them to achieve "the overall co-ordination that is necessary for the continuity of the society" (Porter, 1965:523). Cohesion is attained informally by elite members' attending private schools together, intermarrying, and forming strong friendship ties. In addition, a number of formal mechanisms reinforce this cohesion. For example, various commissions and advisory boards are set up by governments, and members of the economic elite are usually the favoured appointees. Similarly, funding for the establishment political parties comes almost exclusively from wealthy corporate patrons. A "confraternity of power" is thereby established among the various elite groups.

In Porter's opinion this does not, however, amount to saying that Canada's elites form a ruling class: "The elite groups remain separated and never become merged into one effective power group" (Porter, 1965:215). He emphasized that harmony among elites has limits, as is indicated by the fact that various elite groups come into conflict over a wide range of issues.

A decade later, Clement, a student of Porter, acknowledged the existence of such conflict. But he underscored the limits of this conflict, not the limits of elite harmony. Clement concluded that Canada's major institutional elites do indeed form a cohesive group which represents the country's capitalist class and makes it a ruling class. The members of this class are presumably united around the goals of protecting private property, preventing the spread of public sovereignty over economic resources, and preserving continentalism as the dominant Canadian way of life. Yet Clement based his conclusion largely on the same types of data that Porter used to come to the opposite conclusion: data showing the relatively similar class, ethnic, religious, and even family origins of members of different elites, and the effective operation of formal and informal mechanisms which bind together corporate and political elites in particular.

Even among those scholars inclined to accord the state greater independence of, or autonomy from, the corporate elite, it was common in the mid-1970s to remark upon "a particularly striking characteristic of the Canadian state—its very close personal ties to the bourgeoisie. Whatever the merits of Poulantzas' contention that the most efficient state is that with the least direct ties to the dominant class, it is a rather academic point as applied to Canada" (Panitch, 1977:11).

The crux of the discussion thus far may be summarized as follows. In the decade or so following the publication of Porter's pathbreaking *The Vertical Mosaic*, students of the Canadian capitalist class tried to establish the validity of several ideas, three of which I have emphasized here. The first idea concerns the relationship between different segments of the Canadian capitalist class. That class was said to consist of two main groups: an indigenous commercial elite with deep historical roots in Canadian trade, transportation, banking, and insurance, and a more recently formed comprador elite whose role it is to manage manufacturing and resource-extracting branch plants to the principal advantage of head offices in the United States. These elites have allegedly conspired to block the growth of large Canadian-controlled manufacturing concerns.

The second idea concerns the boundaries of the Canadian capitalist class. According to the left-nationalists, that class is not a wholly independent and indigenous entity. One of its two major subgroups is wholly controlled by American multinationals, and the orientation of both subgroups is not national but continental. To be sure, the business activities of the Canadian capitalist class are supposedly restricted for the most part to Canadian soil, but that restricted base of operations, insofar as it provides American manufacturers with a secure supply of raw materials and a secure market for their products, favours American more than Canadian interests.

The third idea concerns the mechanisms that allow the capitalist class to rule, and especially the means by which it is able to shape at least the broad outlines of government policy. Direct ties between corporate leaders and powerful political figures were widely thought to transform wealthy capitalists into effective rulers; both formal and informal channels are supposedly used by members of the corporate elite to ensure their predominance.

These ideas, which together constitute the left-nationalist interpretation of Canadian capitalist class structure, are compelling in many respects. They were even more attractive 10 years ago or so, when the Canadian political and intellectual climate was more congruent with their policy implications. But the left-nationalist interpretation has nonetheless been criticized on a number of grounds.

CAPITALIST CLASS CLEAVAGES

The merchants against industry thesis was the first aspect of the left-nationalist view to come under critical scrutiny. Adherents of this school were charged with an error of emphasis, another of definition, and yet another of fact. The thesis stands or falls partly on the degree to which indigenous manufacturers in Canada formed a relatively small, poor, and uninfluential segment of the capitalist class, constrained in its development during the latter part of the nineteenth and the first part of the twentieth centuries by presumably more numerous, wealthy, and powerful commercial entrepreneurs. If, however, native industrialists

were in fact not so insignificant, then a central element of the merchants against industry thesis is called into question.

Several historians of Canadian industrial growth have made precisely that point, and they have done so with a wealth of material attesting to the industrialization that began in the British North America colonies as early as the 1850s. There is no denying the predominance of "staple" production (especially lumber and wheat) in the pre-Confederation years, but this does not prevent Stanley Ryerson from making the following remark:

> Together with a rise in the number engaged in "industrial employment" in the Province of Canada in the years 1851 to 1861 from 71 000 to 145 000, there was taking place at the top a consolidation of the new elite of railroad and factory owners; the shaping of that ruling class of industrial capitalists who were to be the real (not merely the titular) "fathers" of Confederation (Ryerson, 1973 [1968]:269; see also Ryerson, 1976).

By the 1880s and 1890s industrialization was certainly well under way, and by the early decades of the twentieth century, Canadian manufacturing industry was well developed by international standards. Thus, according to data presented by Gordon Laxer (1983:25 and *passim*), in 1913 Canada was the world's seventh largest manufacturing nation, outranked only by the U.S.A., Germany, the United Kingdom, France, Russia, and Italy. The great bulk of products manufactured in Canada were not semiprocessed, but fully finished goods such as farm implements, footwear, furniture, and so forth. With only 0.4 percent of the world's population, Canada produced 2.3 percent of all manufactured goods in the world that year (compared to Japan's 1.2 percent and Sweden's 1.0 percent).

Moreover, Canada's commercial sector

was not particularly "overdeveloped" in the first decades of this century, at least in comparison with that of the United States. Jack Richardson has computed ratios, for both Canada and the U.S.A., in which the numerator is the amount of national income generated by commercial businesses and the denominator is the amount of national income generated by industrial activity. He discovered that the Canadian ratio is about the same as, or lower than, the American ratio, depending on the precise definitions of "commercial" and "industrial" activity used. Yet this is exactly the opposite of what one would expect to find if the merchants against industry thesis were valid. (The ratios are for the years 1920-26; see Richardson, 1982:291).

In light of these facts it seems unjustified to speak of a tiny and uninfluential manufacturing elite in late nineteenth- and early twentieth-century Canada. The current weakness of Canada's manufacturing sector is undeniable, but the twentieth century was well advanced before its frailty became obvious. Why Naylor and Clement nonetheless held otherwise is partly a result of a definitional quirk. They alluded to Marx's distinction between industrial, or productive, capitalists who engage in "the sphere of production" (i.e., manufacturing) and mercantile, or non-productive, capitalists who engage in the "sphere of capital circulation" (i.e., banking, insurance, and the like). According to Marx, only the economic activity organized by productive capital directly adds value to raw materials. Moreover, industrial capital is characterized by a comparatively high ratio of fixed to circulating capital—which is to say that manufacturers tend to invest relatively more in plant and equipment than do mercantile capitalists, who prefer short-term liquid investments. That is why, in Marx's view, sustained and

substantial economic development depends upon the robustness of industry; only manufacturers organize the actual addition of value to raw materials by promoting the accumulation of long-term fixed investments.

The view that industry is generally the chief engine of economic development is unobjectionable. What is problematic is that Naylor and Clement classified entrepreneurs active in the railroad industry—one of the most important branches of the economy in late nineteenth-century Canada—not as industrialists, but as financial or commercial capitalists engaged in trade. Yet, according to L. R. Macdonald (1975: 267, 268), "railways had much the highest proportion of fixed to circulating capital of any nineteenth-century enterprise" in Canada; and Marx himself "went out of his way in *Capital* to insist that the transportation industry was productive because it added value to commodities; for him, a railway was an industry, not a trade." If Naylor and Clement had characterized the railroad barons as productive, rather than financial, capitalists they might not so readily have jumped to the conclusion that productive capitalists were a minor force in Canadian economic life. Neither do they seem to have been justified in positing a conflict of interest between financial and industrial capitalists. Not only was it the case that, by and large, financial capitalists in late nineteenth-century Canada had nothing against the formation of domestic manufacturing concerns. In point of fact, as Macdonald (1975) has noted, many financial capitalists promoted the growth of manufacturing, and even became manufacturers themselves. Richardson (1982:287-88) shows that this early tendency for merchants actually to become industrialists was clearly visible in the Brantford, Ontario, economic elite of the 1890s and in the Toronto economic elite of the 1920s. In Brantford, 55 percent of the 22 members of the economic elite were active in mercantile and industrial firms at the same time. In Toronto, 53 percent of the 164 most powerful men in the economic elite simultaneously held directorships in both types of corporations. If the economic interests of financial and industrial capitalists were opposed, one would not find such clear evidence of an identity of interest and personnel between these two groups.

Some analysts of the late twentieth-century Canadian capitalist class have taken this last point a step further. They question whether it makes any sense at all to talk about two main groups in the Canadian capitalist class, and hold that it may be altogether more accurate to posit a merger of commercial and industrial interests, at least in contemporary times. The most important pieces of research which develop this theme are by William Carroll (1982) and by Carroll, John Fox, and Michael Ornstein (1982).

Carroll, Fox, and Ornstein examined interlocking directorates among 100 of the largest financial, merchandising, and industrial firms in Canada in 1973. They discovered, first, that these firms are remarkably highly integrated by top corporate officials and managers serving simultaneously on more than one board of directors. Ninety-seven of the 100 firms were connected by single-director interlocks and 70 of the 100 by multiple-directorship ties. Their second important finding was actually a non-discovery: no evidence could be found in their interlock data to support the view that the largest Canadian firms are clustered in disconnected subgroups or cliques based on nationality of ownership or on sphere of economic activity. Such cliques would presumably have been discovered if the cleavages within the capitalist class posited by the

left-nationalists did in fact exist. Finally, Carroll, Fox, and Ornstein inferred from their data that non-financial corporations controlled by Canadians tend not to share directors with non-financial corporations controlled by non-Canadians; but both types of firms typically had multiple ties to Canadian-controlled financial firms. In other words, banks lie at the centre of the network of interlocking directorates, serving as the principal points of articulation and integration for the corporate elite.

Some of these interpretations were confirmed and elaborated on in Carroll's (1982) study. He examined the boards of directors of the 100 largest Canadian industrial, financial, and merchandising firms at five-year intervals over the period 1946-76, and discovered the existence of dense ties between Canadian-controlled financial firms and Canadian-controlled industrial firms, and markedly less dense ties between Canadian-controlled financials and U.S.-controlled industrials operating in Canada. Moreover, the directorship ties among indigenous Canadian financial and non-financial firms have become more dense over time, while the ties between Canadian financials and American-controlled industrials have become less dense. This is the opposite of what the left-nationalist theory predicts.

CAPITALIST CLASS BOUNDARIES

The evidence just reviewed leads one to conclude that the cleavages in the Canadian capitalist class which the left-nationalists purported to detect were greatly overdrawn. Does the left-nationalist theory fare any better with regard to the second question it raised, concerning the boundaries of the capitalist class? Carroll (1982), for one, thinks not. He suggests that the Canadian capitalist class is now indigenous and independent, not continental and dependent. Steve Moore and Debi Wells (1975) come to much the same conclusion, and Jorge Niosi (1981 [1980]; 1982; 1983) offers a more qualified assessment. Let us consider the evidence upon which they base their conclusions.

Carroll (1982:98) stresses the fact that the assets of top Canadian firms were overwhelmingly Canadian-controlled at the end of the Second World War and they exhibit the same characteristic today; in 1946 and in 1976 about 86 percent of such assets were Canadian-controlled (about 56 percent Canadian-controlled in the manufacturing sector alone) while roughly 11 percent were American-controlled (approximately 33 percent in the manufacturing sector). There was a period in the 1950s and 1960s when overall American control of assets in the largest Canadian firms nearly doubled, but that era began to fade into history after 1970. Similarly, Niosi (1981 [1980]:32; 1983: 132) cites government statistics showing that, among all non-financial companies in Canada, the value of assets under foreign control as a percentage of all assets has decreased from 36 percent in 1970 to 29 percent in 1978 to 26 percent in 1981. In manufacturing alone the decline was from 58 percent in 1970 to 52 percent in 1978. At the very least, these figures support the view that Canadian capitalism has become more indigenous and less controlled by non-Canadians over the past 15 years.

It is also worth noting that this independence has been reflected in the propensity of Canadian companies to increase their foreign investments: the boundaries of the capitalist class's activities are, in other words, less and less circumscribed by the country's political borders. The ratio of foreign direct investment in Canada to Canadian direct investment abroad was 4.6 in 1970, 3.6 in 1975, and 2.7 in 1979, the latest year for which figures are available. Significantly, in 1969 nearly 62 percent of Canadian direct investment abroad was investment by Canadian-controlled companies; that figure increased to 83 percent by 1978. In absolute terms, Canada was the seventh largest overseas investor in the world by 1976 (after the U.S.A., the U.K., West Germany, Japan, Switzerland, and France). In relative terms, too, Canada's overseas investment record was impressive: in 1978 Canadian direct investment abroad amounted to $700 per capita—not much less than the American figure of $750; and by 1980 the annual rate of growth of Canadian investment abroad was 13.7 percent, compared to 9.0 percent for the U.S.A. (Moore and Wells, 1975:72; Niosi, 1982:24, 25; 1983:132-3).

Some analysts are inclined, on the basis of these figures, to urge outright rejection of the view that the Canadian capitalist class is basically dependent and continentalist and largely constrained to Canadian territory in its business dealings. Carroll, Moore, Wells and others tend to think of Canadian capitalists as having "come of age," engaging in their own economic ventures overseas and no longer subordinate to American interests.

However, these interpretations probably go rather farther than facts warrant. For, as Niosi (1982; 1983:133-34) points out, Canadian-controlled multinationals are still technologically dependent upon research and development in the U.S.A., and they are restricted to supplying only a narrow range of products and services abroad (utilities, engineering, mining, banking, real estate services). Furthermore, the decline in foreign control of the Canadian economy which we have witnessed over the past 15 years has largely been confined to extractive and mineral processing industries (especially oil and gas, potash, coal, asbestos, and metals). The Canadian manufacturing sector is, as the left-nationalists stressed, still very weak. Most of it is still foreign-controlled, and because of the strict limits this places on its growth it still employs a smaller percentage of the labour force than is the case in any other industrialized country. It does not even come close to supplying Canadians with all the manufactured goods they need, and a large part of the manufacturing that takes place actually involves the mere assembly of parts made elsewhere (Williams, 1983).

From all this, Niosi concludes—quite sensibly I think—that the Canadian capitalist class cannot at present be characterized either as purely continentalist and dependent or as purely independent of foreign interests; either as tightly constrained to engage in business almost exclusively in Canada or as freely able to engage in wide-ranging business ventures abroad. The Canadian capitalist class possesses aspects of all these features simultaneously because of the local and international economic and political conditions within which it has evolved.

CAPITALIST CLASS RULE

There remains the vexing question of how the capitalist class rules, and especially of the relationship between the capitalist class and the state. The first post-Porter generation of class analysts has been faulted for taking too "instrumentalist" an approach to this problem. Instrumentalism refers to a school of Western neo-Marxism most closely associated with the early work of Ralph Miliband. Miliband (1973 [1969]) portrayed the various institutions which the state comprises—the government, legislature, judicial system, military, police, and public bureaucracy—as operating more to the advantage of the capitalist class than of other classes. He emphasized that this bias exists because the capitalist class directly controls state institutions. For example, top officials in all state institutions throughout the Western world are recruited substantially from the upper reaches of the class system. Therefore, he continued, they reflect the interests of the capitalist class. Similarly, state officials tend to rely upon members of the capitalist class for advice in policy formulation and, in the case of political parties, for material support in election campaigns. Thanks to the operation of these and other mechanisms, the state allegedly serves as an *instrument* of the capitalist class's will (hence the school's name).

One of the main criticisms of this viewpoint is that, frequently, dominant segments of the capitalist class do not in fact rule in any direct sense. For example, in Canada the Liberal Party has been in power for most of the post-Second World War era, yet it has rarely been supported by the overwhelmingly Tory corporate elite. In addition, critics point out that even the capitalist class as a whole cannot be said to rule directly through its control of the state since to do so it would have to display much more cohesion and unity of purpose than is frequently the case. This is especially evident in Canada. Some critics of instrumentalism hold that major political conflicts in Canada reflect cleavages within the capitalist class—between, say, its different ethnic or national segments (notably Québécois versus English Canadian) or between its different regional components (such as Western versus Ontarian). These conflicts supposedly testify to the disunity of the capitalist class and its inability to rule the state directly and with the stability necessary to promote its overall best interests.

In light of these perceived shortcomings, many Canadian scholars have come to accept the ideas of the late Nicos Poulantzas (1975 [1968]) as an alternative to instrumentalism. His theory of the relationship between the capitalist class and the state is usually referred to as "structuralism." This name is derived from his insistence that it is the environing system of socio-economic relations that is responsible for the state serving the long-run interests of the capitalist class as a whole. This system (or structure) allegedly places certain restrictions upon the state's freedom of operation. For example, state officials are unlikely to take actions which offend capitalist interests too profoundly for fear of provoking an "investment strike." It is restrictions like these, not direct ties between the state and the capitalist class, that, according to Poulantzas, makes the state act with its characteristic bias. At times state officials may even find it necessary, in order to ensure the persistence of capitalist economic relations, to take actions opposed by one or more powerful segments of the capitalist class. In this sense the state must not be closely tied to, but rather "relatively autonomous" of, the capitalist class. Only then can it perform its functions effectively.

The work of Tom Traves (1979) serves as a good illustration of how this theory has been applied to the Canadian case (see also Craven, 1980; van den Berg and Smith, 1981). Traves sought to explain how the Canadian state came to play a more interventionist and regulatory role in the country's economic life during the period 1917-31. He argued that a variety of competing claims were placed on the state—for and against tariff protection, for and against direct financial assistance, and so forth—by different segments of the capitalist class and by industrial workers and farmers as well. The governments of the day did not heed only the demands of the most powerful subgroups in the capitalist class, nor only the demands of the capitalist class as a whole. Rather, they tried to mediate conflicts by working out compromises and maintaining "a delicate balance of power between contending classes and interest groups" (Traves, 1979:156).

One might well ask how this analysis differs from the "pluralist" interpretations favoured by political analysts in the 1950s and 1960s, and now widely held in disrepute. Pluralists, too, thought of the state as performing certain "brokerage functions" and acting as a mediator of conflict between competing classes and other interest groups. But there is one critical difference between structuralism and pluralism. According to Traves (1979:158), the compromises worked out by governments are

not the equivalent of brokerage functions in pluralist theories of the state. For while the capitalist state does not directly represent the instrument for domination by a single class, it does assume the burden of perpetuating capitalism itself. In this sense it is not a value-free broker, but rather the protector and promoter of a specific set of rules and social relationships founded upon capitalist property relationships. . . .

This may seem like functionalist reasoning, and indeed it is. This introduces a number of serious conceptual and empirical problems. In the first place, imputing needs to socio-economic systems makes it seem as if these systems have human attributes, including the ability to engage in goal-directed behaviour. Of course, people have needs and goals, and powerful people are often able to convince, pay, or coerce others to act in ways which serve their needs and goals. Socio-economic systems do not, however, have needs and goals other than those which people, including entire classes of people, impose upon them. A capitalist system's "need" to perpetuate capitalist class relations is no more than a desire on the part of people who benefit from those relations to see things continue pretty much as they are.

Second, the argument made by Traves and other structuralists is circular. Why, they ask, is a particular government policy adopted? Because, they answer, it is functional for the capitalist system, i.e., it has certain salutary consequences for existing class relations. But how does one know that a given policy is functional? By virtue of the fact that it was adopted: in the structuralist view all existing state policies are functional. In other words, policies are enacted because they are functional, and they are functional because they are enacted.

Third, structuralists interpret the introduction of unemployment insurance, public health care, laws recognizing the right of workers to form unions, strike, and engage in collective bargaining, and all other reforms associated with the growth of the welfare state as "fundamentally" irrelevant to the long-term well-being of employees. What this wholly ignores, however, is that reformist changes may have a cumulative effect on the distribution of income in society. Thus, there is considerably less economic inequality in Sweden than in Canada, largely because Sweden has a better developed welfare system that provides universal public daycare and other benefits unknown in this country. This may indeed increase the longevity of capitalism, but one must remember that this more mature capitalism is not the same capitalism that existed in Dickensian England; and that, as Marx and Engels argued, it is at least possible that in the most advanced capitalist societies socialism may evolve through electoral politics. Electoral politics can matter, and hard-won reforms, including unemployment insurance, may indeed add up to "fundamental" change (cf. Hibbs, 1978; Shalev, 1983a; Stephens, 1979).

The fact that these reforms are hard-won suggests a fourth and final criticism of the structuralist viewpoint. By claiming that state policies are automatic responses to the "needs" of the capitalist system, structuralism plays down the fact that farmers and workers often endure bitter struggles in order to have these policies implemented. Structuralists also imply that workers and farmers are gullible or irrational to do so since they are "fundamentally" just contributing to a legitimizing myth which enables the process of capital accumulation to continue. It is especially ironic that some Marxists should minimize the significance of class (and other group) conflict and assume such an attitude toward working people. These people may, after all, frequently elect to engage in "mere" reformist action because that strategy assures them of more certain benefits and fewer likely costs than other possible strategies.

Despite these untenable functionalist assumptions, the idea that the state is relatively autonomous of the capitalist class nevertheless amounts to a useful insight. It seems to me to overcome the major weaknesses of instrumentalism and enables us to portray more accurately the relationship between capitalist classes and states.

The state's relative autonomy derives partly from the mundane fact that state officials want to keep their jobs. Thus, the occupational (if not class) interests of state officials demand that they not offend any class or group to such a degree that their reelection or reappointment is jeopardized. It is thus a matter of survival for the political elite to remain somewhat removed from the will of the capitalist class.

Normally, members of this elite will be able to remain in office if they succeed in sustaining conditions which promote economic growth, i.e., if they are able to facilitate both capital accumulation and increases in the real incomes of workers and others. Satisfaction with government will be widespread in such a situation. However, a variety of conditions—such as a sharp and prolonged downturn in the business cycle or sustained pressure on government by well-organized and effectively mobilized lower classes—may make it difficult to achieve both or either of these goals. This may heighten class and other forms of group conflict, as different classes and other groups make incommensurable claims on the state.

The outcome of such conflict depends on the distribution of power in society and the strategies adopted by the various political actors. It may result in sufficient pressure being placed on the state to effect reforms that benefit disadvantaged classes and groups. But even so, the more highly advantaged classes and groups are in a position to limit the gains of the disadvantaged and minimize their own losses: the outcome is analogous to the resultant of two or more vectors, with one vector having a greater magnitude than any of the others. For example, state medical care has historically been supported by labour unions and workers' political parties and opposed by business leaders and physicians. Pressured by the former, governments in Canada and all other Western countries have enacted legislation which has increased the minimum level of health care available to all citizens. But pressured by the latter, many governments have not sought to achieve equity in health care: the quality of medical services available seems still to be highly structured

along class, regional, ethnic, and racial lines in Canada, the United Kingdom, and the U.S.A. (Manga and Weller, 1980).

The fact that progressive laws and institutions may result from such episodes of class and other forms of group conflict suggests a second, and more profound, source of the state's relative autonomy. This derives from the frequently overlooked fact that state policies and institutions are no more than long-lasting legal resolutions of historically specific conflicts among classes and other groups. Put differently, states are social structures which reflect the distribution of resources, organization, and support—in short, of power—among classes and other groups at given points in time. These structures, once created, usually pattern political life for many years—specifically, until power is significantly redistributed, at which time new conflicts arise to cause change.

Laws regulating election procedures illustrate the point. These laws have a profound effect on who gets represented in parliaments, and how well they are represented. Thus, constituency-based electoral systems such as those in Canada ensure that parliamentary representation often reflects actual party support in a highly attenuated manner. This comes about because people who vote for unsuccessful candidates have no representative in the legislature. In the 1980 federal election this included, among others, the roughly 20 percent of Atlantic Canadians who voted for the New Democratic Party, the nearly 20 percent of Westerners who voted for the Liberal Party, and the 15 percent or so of Quebeckers who voted Progressive Conservative: these voters, perhaps a million or more, were represented by a total of only three or four parliamentarians. Is it any wonder that groups which suffer most from underrepresentation in the Canadian parliament are most in favour of adopting a system of proportional representation, such as exists, with variations, throughout continental Europe? In that part of the world, class and religious conflicts, often bitter, produced electoral systems which now represent major collectivities more equitably than does the Canadian system. Underrepresented groups in this country may be able to win similar changes, but only if they become sufficiently numerous, organized, and have enough material and other resources to force the hand of over-represented groups. Meanwhile, the electoral system, a resolution of past conflict, continues to affect the party composition of our parliaments. Canadian political life is thus no simple reflection of the current will of the capitalist class or of the country's present class structure as a whole. Electoral laws —and other state institutions and policies which remain relatively autonomous of the class system—also have a major impact on political life.

I suspect that when enough research has been done on the relationship between the state and the capitalist class in Canada, it will be possible to conclude, as did Robert R. Alford and Roger Friedland (1975:472) in a comprehensive review of relevant American studies, that the Canadian state structure has

(a) bureaucratically insulated dominant interests from political challenge; (b) politically fragmented and neutralized non-dominant interests; (c) supported fiscal and policy dependence on private economic power; and (d) therefore resulted in a lack of legislative or electoral control over the structure of expenditure and revenues.

But it is to be hoped that, if such conclusions indeed hold for the Canadian case, no functional imperatives will be invoked to explain them. The second generation of class analysts in Canada has forced us to discard the merchants against industry thesis and substantially qualify our interpretation of the boundaries of the Canadian capitalist class. So iconoclastic a group can surely perform an equally enlightening job on structuralism.

REFERENCES

Alford, Robert R., and Roger Friedland
    1975   "Political participation and public policy," *Annual Review of Sociology*, 1:429- 79.

Britton, J., and J. Gilmour
    1978   *The Weakest Link: A Technological Perspective on Canadian Industrial Development*. Ottawa: The Science Council of Canada.

Carroll, William
    1982   "The Canadian corporate elite: financiers or finance capitalists?" *Studies in Political Economy*, 8:89-114

Carroll, William K., John Fox, and Michael D. Ornstein
    1982   "The network of directorate interlocks among the largest Canadian firms," *The Canadian Review of Sociology and Anthropology*, 19:44-69.

Clement, Wallace
    1975   *The Canadian Corporate Elite: An Analysis of Economic Power*. Toronto: McClelland and Stewart.

    1977   *Continental Corporate Power: Economic Linkages Between Canada and the United States*. Toronto: McClelland and Stewart.

Craven, Paul
    1980   *'An Impartial Umpire': Industrial Relations and the Canadian State, 1900-1911*. Toronto: University of Toronto Press.

Hackett, Robert
    1980   "Pie in the sky: a history of the Ontario Waffle," *Canadian Dimension*, 15, no. 1-2:2-72.

Hibbs Jr., Douglas A.
    1978   "On the political economy of long-run trends in strike activity," *British Journal of Political Science*, 8:153-75.

Laxer, Gordon
    1983   "Foreign ownership and myths about Canadian development," Working Paper No. 50, Structural Analysis Programme (Toronto: Department of Sociology, University of Toronto).

Laxer, Jim
    1973   "Introduction to the political economy of Canada," in *(Canada) Ltd.: The Political Economy of Dependency*, ed. Robert M. Laxer, pp. 26-41. Toronto: McClelland and Stewart.

Levitt, Kari
    1970   *Silent Surrender: The Multinational Corporation in Canada*. Toronto: MacMillan of Canada.

Lumsden, Ian, ed.
    1970   *Close the 49th Parallel: The Americanization of Canada*. Toronto: University of Toronto Press.

Macdonald, L. R.
    1975   "Merchants against industry: an idea and its origins," *The Canadian Historical Review*, 56:263-81.

Manga, Pranial, and Geoffery R. Weller
    1980   "The failure of the equity objective in health: a comparative analysis of Canada, Britain, and the United States," *Comparative Social Research*, 3:229- 67.

McDougall, Robert L.
    1963   "The dodo and the cruising auk: class in Canadian literature," *Canadian Literature*, 18:6-20.

Mealing, S. R.
    1965   "The concept of class and the interpretation of Canadian history," *The Canadian Historical Review*, 46:201-18.

Miliband, Ralph
    1973   *The State in Capitalist Society*, London: Quartet.
    (1969)

Moore, Steve, and Debi Wells
    1975   *Imperialism and The National Question in Canada*. Toronto: privately published.

Naylor, Tom
    1972   "The rise and fall of the third commercial empire of the St. Lawrence," in *Capitalism and the National Question in Canada*, ed. Gary Teeple, pp. 1-41. Toronto: University of Toronto Press.
    1975   *The History of Canadian Business, 1867-1914*, 2 vols. Toronto: James Lorimer.

Niosi, Jorge
    1981   *Canadian Capitalism: A Study of Power in The Canadian Business Establishment*,
    (1980)   trans. Robert Chodos. Toronto: James Lorimer and Co.
    1982   "The Canadian multinationals," *Multinational Business*, 2:24-33.
    1983   "The Canadian bourgeoisie: towards a synthetical approach," *Canadian Journal of Political and Social Theory*, 7:128-49.

Panitch, Leo
    1977   "The role and nature of the Canadian state," in *The Canadian State: Political Economy and Political Power*, ed. Leo Panitch, pp. 3-27. Toronto: University of Toronto Press.

Porter, John
    1965   *The Vertical Mosaic: An Analysis of Social Class and Power in Canada*. Toronto: University of Toronto Press.

Poulantzas, Nicos
    1975   *Political Power and Social Classes*, trans. Timothy O'Hagan. London: New Left
    (1968)   Books.

Resnick, Philip
    1977   *The Land of Cain: Class and Nationalism in English Canada, 1945-1975*. Vancouver: New Star Books.

Richardson, R. J.
    1982   "'Merchants against industry': an empirical study of the Canadian debate," *The Canadian Journal of Sociology*, 7:279-95.

Rotstein, Abraham, and Gary Lax, eds.
    1974   *Getting It Back: A Program for Canadian Independence*. Toronto: Clarke Irwin & Co.

Ryerson, Stanley
    1973   *Unequal Union: Roots of Crisis in the Canadas, 1815-1873*. Toronto: Progress
    (1968)   Books.
    1976   "Who's looking after business?" *This Magazine*, 10, no. 5:41-46.

Shalev, Michael
    1983a   "Class politics and the Western welfare state," in *Evaluating the Welfare State: Social and Political Perspectives*, ed. S. Spiro and E. Yuchtman-Yaar, pp. 27-50. New York: Academic Press.
    1983b   "The social democratic model and beyond: two generations of comparative research on the welfare state," *Comparative Social Research*, 6:315-51.

Stephens, John D.
    1979   *The Transition from Capitalism to Socialism.* London: Macmillan.

Taves, Tom
    1979   *The State and Enterprise: Canadian Manufacturers and the Federal Government, 1917-1931.* Toronto: University of Toronto Press.

van den Berg, Axel, and Michael Smith
    1981   "The Marxist theory of the state in practice," *Canadian Journal of Sociology,* 6:505-19.

Williams, Glen
    1983   *Not for Export: Towards A Political Economy of Canada's Arrested Industrialization.* Toronto: McClelland and Stewart.

3. Class and Corporate Power

William Carroll

THE PROBLEMATIC OF CAPITALISTS AND CORPORATIONS

Studies of large corporations, of corporate directors and officers, and of corporate interlocking have contributed substantially to our understanding of the nature of economic power in advanced capitalist societies. Much of the research in this area has been divided between two analytic strategies: (1) the examination of individuals comprising a corporate elite, with attention to their biographical characteristics and social relationships (e.g., Mills, 1958; Porter, 1965; Clement, 1975; 1977a), and (2) the examination of networks of interlocked corporations, with attention to the positions of different firms and the relations between them (e.g., Levine, 1972; Sonquist and Koenig, 1975;

Allen, 1978b; Carroll, Fox, and Ornstein, 1982). Both these approaches have definite strengths as means of concretely describing the structure of corporate power, but they also share a problem in reconciling their descriptions with the general concept of "capitalist class" to which many authors ultimately appeal.

The rise of the corporation, culminating in the development of monopoly capital, introduced complexities into both the accumulation process and the structure of class domination. With the division of share ownership among multiple investors, the ownership and management of capital no longer necessarily entailed each other, providing the basis for "rentier" and "managerial" fractions of the bourgeoisie—an eventuality recognized by Marx himself (1967, III:436). But the large corporation also brought other transformations, including (1) elaboration of a hierarchy of management, a complex division of labour in the capitalist control of the production process (Marglin, 1974; Edwards, 1979); (2) development of a stratum of professional

Revised from William Carroll, "The Individual, Class, and Corporate Power in Canada," *The Canadian Journal of Sociology*, vol. 9, no. 3 (Spring 1984), pp. 245-68. Reprinted with permission.

advisors to the bourgeoisie—lawyers, financial consultants, and the like—who often occupy positions as "outsiders" on corporate directorates (Niosi, 1978); and (3) emergence of complex institutional relations between firms—of cartels, interlocking directorates, intercorporate ownership, and credit relations—which have to some extent supplanted atomized market relations at the higher levels of advanced capitalist economies (Mandel, 1968:398-403).

The long-range results of these transformations are evident in the composition of corporate directorates as well as in the broader structure of contemporary corporate power. Viewed from the perspective of capital, the accumulation process produces: (1) a complex intercorporate structure embracing industrial corporations, financial institutions, investment companies, etc.; as well as (2) a set of interdependent strata that together exercise the function of capital, including major shareholders, managers, and corporate advisors (cf. Carchedi, 1977:84; Niosi, 1981:15-16). A shortcoming of many empirical analyses of corporate power consists in overemphasizing one or another of these intertwined constituents of capitalist domination in the present era. Without undue oversimplification we can divide much of the empirical literature into network analyses of corporations and studies of corporate elites.

Networks of corporations

The network approach identifies the corporation as the locus of economic power and decision-making, and focusses on the structure of interlocking corporate directorates (cf. Levine, 1972; Sonquist and Koenig, 1975; Fennama and Schijf, 1979; Burt et al., 1980; Pennings, 1980). Within these intercorporate networks the motive for interlocking is often attributed to corporate needs for

exchange of information and expertise (Allen, 1974:395) or co-optation of external organizations with which a given firm is interdependent (Pfeffer, 1972; Burt et al., 1980; Pennings, 1980; Carrington, 1981). Studies of interlocked corporations, however, have generally not probed beneath the level of corporate actors to examine the "class composition" of intercorporate networks. Instead, corporate power structure is depicted as a network of interorganizational relations of communication, exchange, and co-optation.

The deficiencies of such a purely "organizational" approach have been pointed out by Robert Fitch, who holds that:

> The corporate firm has become the great fetish of modern economics. In the world of modern economics . . . the giant corporation controls men and bends their work to fit its purpose. . . . The economists . . . forget that the corporation is not a person, it is simply a legal device for structuring the flow of surplus value to various classes of investors under conditions that limit individual liability. . . . Like capital, it is a relationship between people. (Fitch, 1971:97-98)

Despite the distortions entailed in collapsing the concept of "capitalist" into that of the corporation, there is an important grain of truth in the analyses of interlocked corporations. As the social organizations in which capital accumulation occurs, corporations have a tangible existence that often extends beyond the career-spans of the particular capitalists who own or manage them. Further, relations *between* corporations sometimes show the same longevity, as is evident in Piedalue's (1976) and Sweeny's (1980) historical studies of corporate interlocking in Canada.

Corporate elites

In contrast to the first approach, numerous sociologists have focussed their analyses of corporate power on the individuals who occupy top positions in large corporations, the corporate elite (Mills, 1958; Porter, 1965; Domhoff, 1970; Clement, 1975; 1977a; Useem, 1978). The analysis centres on characteristics of these powerful individuals—their social background, club memberships, and so on. This research tradition presents a picture of a tightly knit group whose members have enormous latitude in exercising their personal prerogatives. The corporation is generally relegated to a merely nominal existence as the instrument of elite domination. It is the task of corporate elite analysis

> to penetrate the "corporate mirage" of competing, struggling corporations which obscures the reality of elite power and masks overriding factors which bring those at the top together to govern these legal fictions. (Clement, 1975:125)

This perspective raises a set of problems that may be viewed as complementary to those of intercorporate network analysis. First, corporations, in practice, are *not* mere legal fictions: they are the units for accumulation of capital in which labour power and means of production are combined to produce surplus value. Likewise, the power of corporate executives is rooted not in the capacity to "do as one pleases" but in a social relation of class domination (Sweezy, 1972:106-7).

A second problem concerns the degree to which the "corporate elite" may be so internally heterogeneous as to call into question its analytic integrity. Ashley (1957) and McKie (1976) suggest that the designation of all directors and executives of major corporations as elite members may be overinclusive, since most of them hold only one dominant directorship each (cf. Porter, 1965:589; Clement, 1975:166-67). The individuals who actually *constitute* corporate interlocks—what Useem has termed the "inner group" of the capitalist class—may be a

more appropriate population to analyse.

Jorge Niosi (1978; 1981) has also questioned the homogeneity of the corporate elite in his examination of the class locations of Canadian corporate directors. He concludes that the "economic elite" lacks internal coherence since it consists of three distinct groups: the large shareowners, the salaried managers, and a variety of advisors, each group occupying a very different position of stock ownership and of financial remuneration (1978:169).

Finally, corporate elite studies, by and large, have ignored important *relational* aspects of corporate power structure. Only the most rudimentary kinds of network analyses have been employed in studies of individual members of the corporate elite, and as a result, the *pattern* of relations between leading corporate directors remains largely unexplored.

Toward Synthesis

There is a need to move beyond both these perspectives. To do so requires an awareness that the structure of corporate power is not reducible to an elite of all-powerful corporate directors, nor is it merely a network of faceless corporations engaged in a variety of interorganizational relations. There is a need, in short, for an analysis that takes into account the *duality* of corporations and capitalists as interdependent units in a structure of accumulation and class domination, while retaining the methodological virtues of systematic network analysis.

There is, at this preliminary stage, no single method for analysing individuals and firms within corporate power blocs. In this paper the network of interlocks on the level of individual executives and directors, what we might call the "inner group" of Canadian corporate capitalism, is examined. In light of Niosi's findings, these interlocked individuals are depicted not as members of a homogeneous elite, but as capitalists associated with definite centres of accumulation or as advisors to the bourgeoisie.

RESEARCH QUESTIONS

Class and corporate power structure

It is essential to distinguish between capitalists who own or manage large corporations and their advisors who often serve as outside corporate directors. A corporate advisor may create a "weak tie" between firms by serving as an outside director of several companies; a capitalist may create an intercorporate relation of more substantive significance, corresponding to ownership or credit relations (cf. Knowles, 1973; Berkowitz et al., 1977; Kotz, 1978). In this regard we may ask whether the network of interlocked individuals is composed mainly of capitalists or of corporate advisors, and how central each of these groups might be in the larger structure.

Class fractions within the corporate power structure

Within the group of interlocked capitalists we may further distinguish between fractions of the bourgeoisie, following Clement (1977a: 24-25). Capitalists affiliated with a dominant firm can be usefully differentiated from those controlling smaller enterprises, giving us a very rough "monopoly-competitive" distinction. Analytic divisions between indigenous and comprador capitalists and between industrial and commercial capitalists are also worth drawing.

Clement has argued that ". . . a high de-gree of interconnection exists in Canada between indigenous and comprador fractions of the elite," with the indigenous elite being tightly linked to managers of American branch plants (1977a:287). Carroll's (1982) research, conducted on the level of corporations, shows no evidence of the high degree of interconnection that Clement has posited; indeed, in the post-war period the density of interlocking between Canadian- and American-controlled firms has actually declined. Niosi (1981:136-37) supplies a clue to possible reconciliation of these viewpoints. From an analysis of lawyers and brokers who advise indigenous and comprador sections of the bourgeoisie in Canada, he concludes that both class fractions employ the same consultants, giving rise to an illusion of close interconnection of *capitalists*. On these grounds we might expect the inner circle of corporate interlockers to be composed *primarily* of indigenous capitalists and corporate advisors, with relatively few compradors directly represented.

Finally, capitalists can be categorized as industrialists, bankers, and merchants on the basis of whether their home firm produces surplus value, circulates money capital, or circulates commodities (Kay, 1975). In addition, an important development in post-war Canada has been the emergence of diversified investment companies, which also deal in financial capital, through their ownership of blocs of corporate shares.

On the issue of the positions of industrialists, bankers, merchants, and financiers in the inner group, Carroll's research and that of Clement again lead in different directions. Clement (1977a) holds that ties between indigenous bankers and industrialists are only tenuous, particularly in light of the decline of indigenous industry in post-war Canada. Carroll's research, again on the level of the firm, indicates the reverse: indigenous industrial and financial companies are densely interlocked, and by 1976 investment companies show strong ties to both (Carroll, 1982; cf. Richardson, 1982). An analysis of individuals in the inner group, their primary corporate affiliations and their links to other individuals, can provide clarification on this issue.

Interest groups and corporate power structure

A third area for exploration is the matter of whether there exist "interest groups" of closely associated capitalists in control of several large firms. Many network analyses of interlocking in the United States and other advanced capitalist countries have documented the existence of groups of firms which are said to represent supra-corporate blocs of monopoly capital under the control of one or several allied capitalist interests and often focussed around large financial institutions (cf. Levine, 1972; Knowles, 1973; Sonquist and Koenig, 1975; Allen, 1978b; Overbeek, 1980).

In Canada, similar arguments have been advanced by Park and Park (1973) as well as by Piedalue (1976) and Sweeny (1980), who have analysed the network of strong intercorporate ties for the periods 1900-30 and 1948-77 respectively.

Carroll, Fox, and Ornstein have assessed the clusterability of the intercorporate network in the post-war period and find no evidence of discrete interest groups (1981; 1982). Instead, the network in 1972 is highly *centralized*, with chartered banks and other large financial institutions positioned near the core. Far from constituting the foci of *separate* financial groups, the banks tend to interlock with *common* firms, suggesting a widespread interpenetration of banks' spheres of influence (1982:61-62).

The absence of bank-centred interest groups, however, does not exclude the possibility that groups of associated *capitalists* might exist on the level of the individual, simultaneously with the broader integration of corporations by means of both bank interlocks and weak ties created by advisors. Hence, as a third research question, we may ask whether, within the inner group of corporate interlockers, distinct clusters of closely associated individuals exist, and if so, whether these groups of people tend to correspond to particular groupings of firms.

METHODS

Data for this analysis come from a sample of 114 large Canadian companies, including the 70 largest industrial corporations, 21 largest financial institutions, 10 largest merchandisers, five largest property developers, and eight prominent investment companies of 1976. In all cases, assets was employed as the criterion of firm size. For investment companies, where assets does not necessarily reflect a firm's economic importance, the operative criterion was control of a range of companies in more than one industry, including at least one economically dominant corporation. This procedure ensured representation in the sample of the major diversified investment companies in the Canadian economy.

For each of these corporations, data on directors and executives were gathered, as was information on the country in which controlling interest was held in 1976. All directors and executives holding positions in *two* or more of the 114 dominant corporations were selected for further analysis, yielding an "inner group" of 298 individuals. These interlockers were then assigned to five class categories: (1) *dominant owners* (major shareholders of one or more dominant companies, according to findings presented in Niosi, 1978:90-98); (2) *dominant executives* (those holding a position of chairman, president, vice-chairman, vice-president, secretary, treasurer, or general manager in a dominant corporation, without being major shareholders); (3) *non-dominant executives* in companies not included in the sample of dominant firms: (4) *lawyers* in active law practice; and (5) *other advisors* in such pursuits as financial consulting, accountancy, geology, engineering, academe, and the state. Adequate data were available to categorize 288 of the interlockers according to this scheme.

FIRST RESULTS

Three simple indicators of network position, summarized in Table 3-1, are (1) the number of other interlockers to whom an individual is *weakly* tied through common affiliation with a single dominant firm, (2) the number of other interlockers to whom an individual is *strongly* tied through common affiliation with two or more dominant firms; and (3) the extent to which interlockers are *very strongly* tied to other members of the inner group by means of three or more boards. On average, an interlocker is directly tied to 33 other interlockers by virtue of his own positions in dominant corporations. (Use of the masculine pronoun is intentional. The 298 interlockers studied here include only one woman.) The mean number of strong ties is much lower; that is, the preponderance of interlocks connect inner-group members by way of "weak", single-board ties.

Against this background we may interpret the tabulations in Table 3-1 of the degree of interlocking for individuals in different class positions. Overwhelmingly, members of the inner group tend to be capitalists, not advisors. Fully 58 percent are major share-

holders or executives of dominant corporations; another 28 percent are executives of non-dominant companies; while only 8 percent are lawyers and 6 percent other advisors. Moreover, most of these interlocked capitalists are affiliated with dominant corporations controlled in Canada: 16 are major shareholders in indigenous firms while 115 are executives.

The last three columns of Table 3-1 describe the degree of interlocking for members of each class category. With regard to single-board, or "weak", ties, dominant indigenous executives and non-dominant insiders show the highest incidence of interlocking, while corporate advisors and compradors are least interlocked.

The pattern for strong ties is somewhat different. Here, dominant indigenous capitalists—whether owners or managers—emerge unambiguously as the most interlocked individuals, averaging about five strong ties to other members of the inner group. Overall, only 14 percent of all interlockers participate in one or more of these relations, yet 38 percent of dominant indigenous owners and 30 percent of dominant indigenous executives are very strongly linked to other interlockers. In contrast, very few compradors, non-dominant capitalists, and advisors are involved in such practices.

To assess the extent to which financial or industrial capital predominates in the inner group, the 131 dominant indigenous capitalists depicted in Table 3-1 were divided into subgroups according to the *form* of capital with which each individual is principally affiliated. The resulting distribution indicated a strong presence in the inner group of indigenous industrial and financial capital.

To summarize, then, the network appears to be composed mainly of functioning

TABLE 3-1   Class positions of corporate interlockers, 1976.

Position	n	Percent	Single ties[1]	Multiple ties[2]	Percent[3]
Dominant indigenous owner	16	5.6	27.4	4.56	37.5
Dominant indigenous executive	115	39.9	31.8	4.98	30.4
Dominant American comprador	25	8.7	22.5	1.88	0.0
Dominant other comprador	10	3.5	21.8	1.00	10.0
Non-dominant executive	82	28.5	33.1	2.37	7.3
Lawyer	23	8.0	25.3	2.26	8.7
Other corporate advisor	17	5.9	26.5	1.41	5.9
Total	288	100.0	30.0	3.38	14.2

1. Mean n of single ties to other interlockers.
2. Mean n of multiple ties to other interlockers.
3. Percentage having ties to other interlockers via three or more boards

capitalists and only secondarily of corporate advisors. Within the capitalist section it is dominant *indigenous* interests that predominate, particularly in the network of strong ties. The indigenous capitalists who predominate in the inner group represent all major sectors of large-scale capital. The network, finally, includes a clear majority of top executives from large corporations controlled in Canada, but only a minority of top executives from dominant companies under foreign control, and this difference is especially notable when multi-board interlocks are considered.

EXPLORING THE NETWORK OF STRONG TIES

Consider now the third general issue raised earlier, namely the question of "interest groups" in the inner circle of corporate interlockers. This question can be addressed most directly by analysing connected subgraphs within the inner group, and the cliques of strongly tied individuals that make up these subgraphs. The 225 participants in strong ties divide into 12 networks, each isolated from all the others. The largest connected subgraph—the dominant component—includes 195 strongly tied individuals. Eleven small groupings of from two to six individuals account for the 30 isolates from the dominant component. The largest of these is made up of three executives with George Weston Limited (including owner Galen Weston), two executives with Loblaws (a subsidiary of Weston), and one executive with ITT Canada Limited.

To explore the structure of the dominant component, a clique analysis of its 195 members and their strong ties was performed. The result was a set of 14 candidate cliques, each having internal density statistically distinguishable from the overall density of interlocking in the dominant component. In addition to this statistical requirement, only cliques comprised of five or more strongly interlocked directors were retained for further analysis, eliminating five groups of four interlockers.

A clique could also be substantively trivial in terms of the number of corporate interests represented in it. A particularly obvious example is the parent-subsidiary relation between George Weston and Loblaws, involving several interlocked executives. Here the intertwining of capital between two firms creates a grouping of individuals that merely reflects a bilateral relation of intercorporate ownership. The rule of thumb adopted in this connection was to retain cliques in which *three* or more dominant corporations were directly represented in the person of interlocked executives. This restriction resulted in the deletion of three more candidate cliques. The remaining six cliques can be entertained as possible "interest groups" of associated capitalists, each comprised of five or more individuals and three or more dominant corporate interests.

These groupings are described in Table 3-2 in terms of both their global structure and their individual and corporate constituents. In all cases the density of strong ties within each clique is significantly above the overall network density indicating a good degree of internal coherence. However, the two largest cliques of 25 and 16 members are somewhat diffuse, with respective diameters of six and five. Moreover, only three cliques display a statistically significant degree of *isolation* from the rest of the network. The two largest cliques as well as clique 5 have such large peripheries that the degree of interlocking between members and non-members of these groups is not statistically distinguishable from the overall level of interlocking in the network. That is, while these cliques are internally integrated, they are also extensively connected with the rest of the network.

Particularly worthy of note are cliques 1 and 2, the largest groupings in the dominant component, with peripheries that include nearly 50 interlockers each. These subnetworks are not only large and well-ensconced in the broader structure, they also overlap with each other. This suggests that these subnetworks may not be proper "cliques" in the sense of being relatively isolated from the rest of the network. Rather, their extent of overlap and extraversion indicates that they may form the "dense centre of the network" (Alba, 1973:124).

Turning to the issue of class position, a majority of the members of each clique are indigenous capitalists associated with dominant corporations. Lawyers and other advisors are rarely clique members, though they do occupy positions on the peripheries. Finally, compradors are excluded from all cliques, with the exception of Jack Barrow, chairman of Simpson-Sears, a joint Canadian-American venture classified here as American controlled. By and large, then, the six cliques designate groups of functioning capitalists who own or control the largest indigenous firms.

It is also worthwhile to consider each clique with regard to its specific corporate representation. Clique 1 is clearly recognizable as the "Canadian Pacific" group, the interests that have been at the centre of Canadian monopoly capital from its inception (Chodos, 1973).

The second clique is a more diverse group of seven industrials, two banks, and one investment company. The largest industrial in the clique, Bell Canada, is also linked to another member, Northern Telecom, through intercorporate ownership. Clique 3 is obviously the Argus group of associated capitalists. Clique 4 is just as clearly the Power Corporation group. Interestingly, neither the Argus nor the Power groups show many ties to non-members. Instead they each present an introverted pattern of corporate affiliations that seems consistent with a highly centralized structure of intercorporate ownership and control.

TABLE 3-2 Memberships in 6 intercorporate cliques.

Dominant corporations represented by core members	Clique 1		Clique 2		Clique 3		Clique 4		Clique 5		Clique 6	
	Canadian Pacific Enterprises, Canadian Pacific Limited, Steel Co. of Canada, Cominco, C.I.B.C., Pan Canadian Petroleum, Bank of Montreal, Sun Life, Royal Bank, Marathon Realty		Bell Canada, Steel Co. of Canada, Inco, Northern Tel, TransCanada Pipelines, Consumers Gas, Brascan, Hiram Walker, T-D Bank, Bank of Montreal		Argus Corporation, Domtar Incorporated, Massey-Ferguson, Canadian General Investments, DOFASCO, Canadian Tire		Power Corporation, Investors Group, Consolidated Bathurst, Montreal Trust, Great West Life		Brascan, Hudson's Bay Company, Canadian Imperial Bank of Commerce		Simpsons Limited, Abitibi Paper, Simpsons Sears	
Clique #	1		2		3		4		5		6	
Clique density	0.267		0.392		0.694		0.750		0.733		1.000	
Density of ties to non-members	0.016		0.021		0.012		0.006		0.026		0.012	
Clique diameter	6		5		2		2		2		1	
Class position of clique members	Core	Peri-pheral	Core	Peri-pheral	Core	Peri-pheral	Core	Peri-pheral	Core	Peri-pheral	Core	Peri-pheral
Dominant indigenous owner	0	3	1	1	4	0	1	0	1	0	0	0
Dominant indigenous executive	14	22	9	25	4	7	7	2	2	17	4	6
Dominant American comprador	0	3	0	3	0	6	0	0	0	1	1	0
Dominant other comprador	0	3	0	0	0	0	0	2	0	0	0	0
Non-dominant executive	8	14	4	11	1	0	0	3	2	4	1	4
Lawyer	1	2	1	2	0	0	0	1	0	2	0	1
Other advisor	1	1	1	3	0	2	0	0	1	0	0	1
Not classified	1	0	0	2	0	0	0	0	0	0	0	0
Total	25	48	16	47	9	13	8	8	6	26	6	12

The fifth clique can be identified as the Brascan-Bank of Commerce group, one whose origins reach back to the formative period of monopoly capital in Toronto (Drummond, 1962; Nelles, 1974:234). Brascan's affiliate, Hudson's Bay Company, is directly represented within the clique, while its subsidiary, John Labatt Limited, is represented by N. E. Hardy.

Lastly, clique 6 is made up of five dominant executives representing Abitibi Paper, Simpsons Limited, and Simpsons' affiliate, Simpson-Sears, as well as one executive with a non-dominant company. Each of the three dominant firms has long-standing ties to the investment bank Wood Gundy (Niosi, 1978:58).

From these descriptions we can make the following generalizations. First, when we examine the network on the level of strongly tied individual interlockers, it is possible to discern definite groupings. These cliques consist mainly of Canadian capitalists: neither compradors nor advisors play major roles in any clique. Second, within the cliques we find capitalists associated with industrial corporations intermingling with bankers and executives or owners of investment companies, suggesting close, functional relations between large-scale industrial and financial capital.

As this paper has emphasized, there is an inherent *duality* to the structure of corporate power, which unites both individuals in varying class locations and corporations occupying different locations in the system of commodity production and circulation. Table 3-3 applies cumulative criteria of structural prominence to the *corporations* with which dominant capitalists are primarily affiliated. The table thus depicts the positions of different types of companies on the basis of the positions of their executives.

This aggregated analysis reveals that all major indigenous investment companies and a substantial proportion of other dominant indigenous firms are directly represented in the six cliques. Foreign-controlled firms, with the exception of Simpson-Sears, are entirely absent from the capitalist cliques, although a quarter of American-controlled industrials and 36 percent of industrials controlled outside of North America have peripheral ties to the cliques.

TABLE 3-3 Cumulative percentage distributions of corporations' positions in the interlock network.

Position in network	Canada				Foreign			
	Indus.	Finan.	Invest.	Other	Amer. Indus.	Other Indus.	Other	Total
Member and peripheral clique involvement	32.3	20.0	83.3	16.7	0.0	0.0	0.0	18.4
Clique member	48.4	35.0	100.0	33.3	0.0	0.0	16.7	28.9
Peripheral clique involvement	77.4	60.0	100.0	33.3	25.0	36.4	16.7	50.9
Member of dominant component	83.9	75.0	100.0	66.7	35.7	36.4	16.7	61.4
Participant in strong ties	93.5	85.0	100.0	75.0	42.9	45.5	16.7	69.3
Participant in weak ties	96.8	95.0	100.0	91.7	60.7	54.5	16.7	78.9
No involvement in interlocks	100.0	100.0	100.0	100.0	100.0	100.0	100.0	100.0
Number of firms	31	20	6	12	28	11	6	114

Considering membership in the dominant component, three quarters or more of dominant indigenous industrial and financial corporations are represented in the largest connected network, while slightly more than one third of foreign-controlled industrials meet this criterion. Over 95 percent of indigenous firms have at least one executive who sits on the board of another dominant company, constituting a weak tie, yet a large minority of foreign-controlled firms have no involvement in any interlocking.

Finally, Figure 3-1 presents a visual representation of the core network of 66 clique members, in the form of a two-dimensional plot derived from a non-metric multidimensional scaling. The clique members are represented by points, and the relative proximities of pairs of individuals in the interlock network are represented by the distances between points in the space.

There is no discernible "attraction" of these core interlockers to the centre of the space, but a rather diffuse cloud of points. The boundaries of the six cliques identified earlier are represented as solid lines along with broken lines which aggregate the individuals into intercorporate ownership groups, according to Niosi's findings (1978:101-5). The fact that clique boundaries can be drawn around the interesting points attests to the meaningfulness of these distinctions: the cliques do appear to occupy different regions of the network. Concomitantly, the memberships of several cliques overlap, and these overlaps do not include the contributions of overlapping clique peripheries nor of the many weak ties in the network. Generally, however, each individual—*and each corporation*—belongs to only one clique. The four corporate exceptions to this rule include two banks (the Commerce and the Bank of Montreal), one investment company (Brascan), and one industrial firm (Stelco).

The multidimensional plot also underlines an earlier finding concerning differences between cliques. The "Canadian Pacific-Royal Bank" and "Bell Canada-Bank of Montreal" groups are the most spatially diffuse, reflecting a lower density of interlocking among their members. These groups also show the most overlap with each other, sharing three capitalists.

Cliques organized around the major investment companies—Argus, Power and Brascan—are somewhat more compact. Moreover, the Argus and Power groups are generally detached from other cliques. In all other cliques a large majority of members are tied to members of other cliques, and some are members of two cliques. Hence, while cliques can be observed in the network, with the exception of the Argus and Power groups, they interpenetrate extensively.

The same cannot be said of intercorporate ownership relations in the network, depicted with broken lines in Figure 3-1. With the exception of Brascan, each of these is contained entirely *within* a single clique. It appears that much of the pattern of strong interlocks between individuals in the innermost circle reflects an intertwining of capital in the form of intercorporate ownership relations. To a considerable extent, the cliques we have identified on the basis of directorship interlocking seem built around relations directly indicative of the control of capital across different firms and among different individuals.

DISCUSSION

Let us return briefly to the three questions of class, class fractions, and interest groups, posed earlier in this paper. The network analysis has revealed an inner circle of Canadian corporate capital that is composed

FIGURE 3-1 Two-dimensional plot of 66 clique members showing clique boundaries (solid lines) and intercorporate ownership groupings (broken lines)

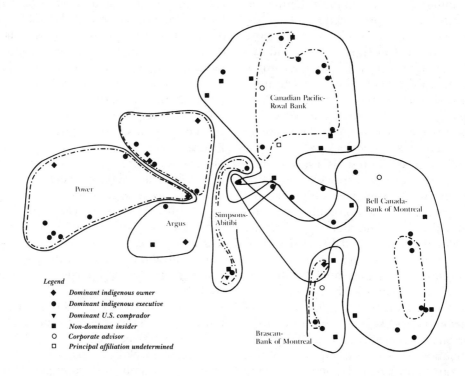

mainly of capitalists and only secondarily of their advisors. Both the industrial and the financial fractions of the indigenous bourgeoisie predominate in this network over the comprador industrial fraction, and their predominance increases as more stringent criteria of network membership are imposed. Lastly, the inner group divides into cliques of closely associated capitalists. Although these subgroups interpenetrate, they also exhibit a degree of internal coherence, especially given that the firms represented by individual members of a clique tend to belong to the same intercorporate ownership group.

This is not to suggest, however, that intercorporate ownership provides a *sufficient* explanation for the pattern of interlocking.

As we have seen, the preponderance of relations in the inner group are single-board, weak ties. Such links rarely correspond to lines of capitalist control, but exist for a variety of other reasons (Berkowitz et al., 1977:43) or as unintended consequences of other strong ties (Ornstein, 1982). Moreover, the financial institutions represented in the inner group are generally *not* major shareholders in dominant non-financial corporations. It is likely that their participation in the network and its cliques reflects institutionalized credit relations which fall short of control but are nevertheless crucial to the accumulation process.

The network analysis of interlocks points to the existence of close, functional relations between large financial and non-financial capital in Canada. In like measure, our findings call into question Clement's (1977:167, 179) notion of a "continental financial-industrial axis" in which Canadian financial capital maintains only tenuous connections with indigenous industry, coalescing instead with foreign-based multinationals. Alternatively, Aglietta's (1979) concept of "financial group" seems to suit these results rather well. As in other advanced capitalist societies, at the centre of the Canadian corporate power structure—and at the apex of the Canadian bourgeoisie—we find groups of interlocked capitalists who own or manage supra-corporate blocs of indigenous finance capital.

REFERENCES

Aglietta, Michel
   1979   *A Theory of Capitalist Regulation.* London: New Left Books.

Alba, R. D.
   1973   "A graph-theoretic definition of a sociometric clique," *Journal of Mathematical Sociology,* 3:113-26.

Allen, M. P.
   1974   "The structure of interorganizational elite cooptation: interlocking corporate directorships," *American Sociological Review,* 39:393-406.
   1978a   "Continuity and change within the core corporate elite," *Sociological Quarterly,* 19:510-21.
   1978b   "Economic interest groups and the corporate elite structure," *Social Science Quarterly,* 58:597-615.

Ashley, C. A.
   1957   "Concentration of economic power," *Canadian Journal of Economics and Political Science,* 23:105-8.

Baran, P., and P. M. Sweezy
   1966   *Monopoly Capital.* New York: Monthly Review Press.

Berkowitz, Stephen D., Yehude Kotowitz, Leonard Waverman, et al.
   1977   *Enterprise Structure and Corporate Concentration.* Royal Commission on Corporate Concentration Study No. 17. Ottawa: Minister of Supply and Services.

Burt, Ronald S., K. P. Christman, and H. C. Kilburn, Jr.
   1980   "Testing a structural theory of corporate cooptation," *American Sociological Review,* 45:821-41.

Carchedi, Guglielmo
   1977   *On the Economic Determination of Social Classes.* Boston: Routledge.

Carrington, Peter J.
   1981   "Anticompetitive effects of directorship interlocks," Working Paper No. 27, Structural Analysis Program. Department of Sociology, University of Toronto.

Carroll, William K.
   1981   *Capital Accumulation and Corporate Interlocking in Post-War Canada.* Doctoral Dissertation, York University, Downsview, Ontario.

1982 "The Canadian corporate elite: financiers or finance capitalists?" *Studies in Political Economy,* 8:89-114.

Carroll, William K., John Fox, and Michael D. Ornstein
1981 "Longitudinal analysis of directorate interlocks." Paper presented at the Annual Meeting of the Canadian Sociology and Anthropology Association, Halifax, May.
1982 "The network of directorate links among the largest Canadian firms," *Canadian Review of Sociology and Anthropology,* 19:44-69.

Chodos, Robert
1973 *The CPR: A Century of Corporate Welfare.* Toronto: James Lewis and Samuel, Publishers.

Clement, Wallace
1975 *The Canadian Corporate Elite.* Toronto: McClelland and Stewart.
1977a *Continental Corporate Power.* Toronto: McClelland and Stewart.
1977b "The corporate elite, the capitalist class, and the Canadian state," in *The Canadian State: Political Economy and Political Power,* ed. Leo Panitch. Toronto: University of Toronto Press.

Domhoff, G. W.
1970 *The Higher Circles.* New York: Vintage Books.

Drummond, Ian
1962 "Canadian life insurance companies and the capital market, 1890-1914," *Canadian Journal of Economics and Political Science,* 27:204-24.

Edwards, Richard
1979 *Contested Terrain.* New York: Basic Books.

Fennema, M., and H. Schijf
1979 "Analysing interlocking directorates: theory and methods," *Social Networks,* 1:297-332.

Fitch, R.
1971 "Sweezy and corporate fetishism," *Socialist Revolution,* 2(5):93-127.

Kay, Geoffrey
1975 *Development and Underdevelopment: A Marxist Analysis.* New York: St. Martin's Press.

Knowles, James C.
1973 "The Rockefeller financial group," in *Superconcentration/Supercorporation,* ed. R. L. Andreano, Andover, Mass.: Warner Modular Publications.

Kotz, David M.
1978 *Bank Control of Large Corporations in the United States.* Berkeley: University of California Press.

Levine, Joel
1972 "The sphere of influence," *American Sociological Review,* 37:14-27.

Mandel, Ernest
1968 *Marxist Economic Theory.* London: Merlin.

Marglin, Stephen
    1974   "What do bosses do? The origins and functions of hierarchy in capitalist production," *Review of Radical Political Economics,* 6(2):60-112.

Marx, Karl
    1967   *Capital,* 3 Vols. New York: International Publishers.

McKie, Craig
    1976   "Review of Wallace Clement's *The Canadian Corporate Elite,*" *Canadian Journal of Sociology,* 1(4):547-49.

Mills, C. Wright
    1958   *The Power Elite.* New York: Oxford University Press.

Nelles, H. V.
    1974   *The Politics of Development.* Toronto: Macmillan.

Niosi, Jorge
    1978   *The Economy of Canada.* Montreal: Black Rose Books.
    1981   *Canadian Capitalism.* Toronto: James Lorimer and Co.

Ornstein, Michael
    1982   "Post-war director interlocks in Canada: industrial, regional, or inter-firm alliances?" Paper presented at the Annual Meetings of the American Sociological Association, San Francisco.

Overbeek, Henk
    1980   "Finance capital and the crisis in Britain," *Capital and Class,* 2:99-120.

Park, Libbie, and Frank Park
    1973   *Anatomy of Big Business.* Toronto: James Lewis and Samuel.

Pennings, Johannes M.
    1980   *Interlocking Directorates.* San Francisco: Jossey-Bass.

Perlo, Victor
    1957   *The Empire of High Finance.* New York: International Publishers.

Pfeffer, Jeffrey
    1972   "Size and composition of corporate boards of directors: the organization and its environment," *Administrative Science Quarterly,* 17:218-28.

Piedalue, Gilles
    1976   "Les groupes financiers au Canada 1900-1930," *Revue d'Histoire de l'Amérique Française,* 30:3-34.

Porter, John
    1965   *The Vertical Mosaic.* Toronto: University of Toronto Press.

Richardson, R. J.
    1982   "Merchants against industry: an empirical study of the Canadian debate," *Canadian Journal of Sociology,* 7(2):279-95.

Sonquist, J. A., and T. Koenig
    1975   "Interlocking directorates in the top U.S. corporations: a graph theory approach," *Insurgent Sociologist,* 5(3):196-229.

Sweezy, Paul M.
1972   "Power elite or ruling class?" in *Modern Capitalism and Other Essays*, ed. Paul Sweezy. New York: Monthly Review Press.

Sweeny, Robert
1980   *The Evolution of Financial Groups in Canada and the Capital Market Since the Second World War.* Masters Thesis, Université du Québec à Montréal.

Useem, Michael
1978   "The inner group of the American capitalist class," *Social Problems*, 25:225-40.

4. Corporate Concentration and Policy

Deborah Coyne

Is corporate power in Canada now beyond political control? Is Canada becoming an economic oligarchy, whose economy will eventually be controlled by six or seven family dynasties? What are the consequences of such concentrated pools of wealth for our industrial structure, the level of innovation, the competitive business environment, the range of employment and investment opportunities available to Canadians, and, most importantly, our democratic political system?

These concerns cannot be dismissed as socialist rhetoric. Rather they reflect the views of keen observers of the Canadian business and political scene from both within and outside Canada, ranging from the current chairman of the Ontario Securities Commission, in a contribution to the Mac-

Reprinted with permission from Deborah Coyne, "Corporate Over-Concentration," *Policy Options* (published by the Institute for Research on Public Policy) vol. 7, no. 3 (April 1986).

donald Royal Commission, to a well-known commentator, Bill Javetski, in the American publication *Business Week*.

The level of corporate concentration in Canada has been under scrutiny for many years, but particularly since the late 1970s when a Royal Commission was established to study the issue. In its report the Bryce Commission concluded rather lamely that, while concentration in many key industries was high, it was not dangerously so and did not merit any particular policy action. It also decided that while there had been an increase in conglomerate corporations, the diversification had not been harmful.

Needless to say, the Bryce Report did not eliminate the widespread concern over corporate concentration. Most recently, the Macdonald Royal Commission commented on the continuing rising levels of aggregate concentration in Canada especially since 1975, as measured by the share of corporate assets controlled by the largest 25, 50, or 100 enterprises. It also noted that concentration, as measured by the percentage of shipments accounted for by the four largest enterprises (including government enterprises), increased in most of the major sectors between 1975 and 1980, notably, retail trade (5.1 percent increase), transportation, communications, and utilities (7.8 percent), finance (4.4 percent), and services (7.6 percent). With specific reference to the manufacturing sector, 82 percent of all manufactured products, taking each product separately (4080 products out of 167 industries) were manufactured by four or less firms.

According to the Commission, individual Canadian industries tend to be more highly concentrated than their counterparts in the United States, and nearly four fifths of economic activity in the U.S. (expressed in terms of GNP) is essentially competitive compared to only two fifths of the economic activity in Canada.

But while the Macdonald Commission documented the rising levels of concentration reasonably well and indeed acknowledged that the degree of corporate concentration may be harmful, its prescriptions for reform fall far short of what is required. On the whole, the Commission restricted itself to repeating the rather anodyne Bryce Report conclusions, and to the further observation that increases in producer concentration may be justified by the need for firms to rationalize in the face of stiff international competition.

Trade liberalization and reduced regulation of price, output, and entry into certain industries were then put forward as the two most important means of promoting competition and, presumably, minimizing any potential dangers of concentration. Brief reference was also made to the possibility of the occasional political decision to prohibit mergers involving major conglomerates, as a safeguard of the last resort.

Unfortunately, the superficial analysis in the Macdonald Report has once again inhibited proper consideration of the more fundamental issues relating to the increasing concentration of economic activity in Canada. For example, is there really any persuasive evidence to support the traditional argument that greater producer concentration is needed to achieve sufficient economies of scale, which in turn are necessary to enhance efficiency and competitiveness? Did the wave of mergers and rationalizations that occurred during the 1981-82 downturn do much to improve our economic competitiveness or increase employment? Or is a "merger mania" simply a manifestation of what Robert Reich has called "paper entrepreneurialism," and are not mergers prompted more by the lure of short-term financial rewards (for example, the target company's cash flow or tax losses) than by a desire to improve the long-term returns from actually making products or supplying services?

The time is long overdue for an adequate analysis of these issues. But more importantly, the time is long overdue for action, and the longer we shrink from taking effective remedial steps, the more difficult it will be to reverse the trend to increased concentration and to contain its deleterious effects.

In the meantime, the evidence continues to pile up. In late 1984, for example, the following startling statistics were reported: Close to 80 percent of the companies listed in the Toronto Stock Exchange 300 index were controlled by a single family and/or group. And almost 50 percent of the value of these companies was controlled by only nine families, notably the Thomsons of Hudson's Bay Company and *Globe & Mail* fame, the two branches of the Bronfman family, Paul Desmarais of Power Corporation, the Reichmann brothers, Conrad Black, and George Weston.

More recently, in 1985 it has been estimated that just 15 conglomerates control some $120 billion in financial assets. This is double the level of four years ago and represents one fifth of the country's total asset base.

With specific reference to the banking and financial services industry, the stability of which was rocked in 1985 by the collapse of the Canadian Commercial and Northland banks, some 60 percent of all of our financial assets are held by five financial service conglomerates and the six large banks. More importantly, several of the financial service conglomerates are each owned by one of the major family dynasties, and the largest is now controlled by Genstar Corporation (a Vancouver-based building materials and real estate group) following the mega merger of Canada Permanent Ltd. and Canada Trustco in December 1985.

This situation of closely held ownership is dangerously open to self-dealing and conflicts of interest. How can the shareholders of a trust company or the general public be certain that the financial institution will impartially examine all requests for financing when the same people control both the institution and the customer? Is there not a very real danger that such self-dealing will mean that the country's resources are going to the wrong places?

Similar concerns arise in respect of even the widely held big banks. They too are inevitably influenced by their major conglomerate customers by reason of extensive interlocking directorships. Some 231 bank directors held 306 other directorships in dominant firms—25 percent of all such directorships. Jack Gallagher's Dome Petroleum encountered apparently few problems in 1982 in obtaining $1.2 billion from the Canadian Imperial Bank of Commerce, on whose board Gallagher sat as a director, to help finance an ill-timed $4-billion takeover that soured and ultimately required a government—that is, taxpayer—bail out.

Perhaps the most troublesome aspect of the indisputable trend toward greater concentrations of wealth and economic activity, however, is the gradual but inexorable expansion of huge conglomerates: that is, the accumulation of unrelated corporate holdings in a variety of markets, both domestic and overseas, in the hands of a few individuals or family empires.

Illustrations of the extent of these empires are easy to find. The Thomson family holdings, for example, include a very large number of newspapers and the recently enlarged retailer, the Hudson's Bay Company. The value of all Thomson-controlled companies in 1984 was some $3.8 billion, with a market value of $2.3 billion. Edward and Peter Bronfman's holdings include controlling interests in the mining sector (Noranda), a brewery (Labatts), and a financial holding company (Trilon Financial Corporation). And the Reichmann brothers recently added Gulf Canada Ltd. to their extensive real estate, liquor, and lumber holdings.

Whether or not we realize it, these huge conglomerates dominate our daily lives—from our newspaper in the morning, to the office where we work, to the department stores where we shop, and to the liquor and beer we drink. Although the Hudson's Bay Company-Simpsons mega merger in 1979 may have passed unnoticed by most of us who frequent one or both stores, the elimination of a major source of competition in the retail market and the expansion of wealth in the hands of Lord Thomson have extremely significant implications for our present and future economic and social welfare.

But what exactly is the problem, and wherein lies the danger?

First, there is the impact on employment opportunities. Of course these conglomerates employ thousands of Canadians, but they also lay off thousands of workers as they consolidate and "down-size" in the face of a poor economic climate. As more and more of their competitors are eliminated, there are fewer and fewer job opportunities for Canadians outside the gigantic corporate web.

This has led some to conclude that the labour market is gradually splitting into two classes: one group of employees reasonably comfortably protected under the big corporate umbrella, while another group remains vulnerable, weak, employed or unemployed, struggling to survive in the smaller business sector.

Second, there is the impact of the conglomerates on the investment opportunities for both Canadians and non-Canadians. Few investors want to put money into an innovative business with the expectation that they will be gobbled up by an insatiable corporate giant. Furthermore, the pressure of such concentrated corporate power frequently stifles competitive forces and restricts the market available for aggressive investment strategies.

Finally, there is the element of enormous political power that is linked to such concentrations of wealth. Few governments have proved resistant to the suggestions, advice, requests, and so forth of companies that control such great proportions of our nation's wealth, labour force, and investment, whether on matters of tax reform, energy policy, foreign investment, or deficit-reduction.

Yet despite all the foregoing implications of conglomerate expansion, the Canadian public seems strangely quiescent. In part this may be due to our unseemly reverence of corporate power embodied in the likes of Conrad Black and Paul Reichmann. In part, it is also due to our exposure to the media's sympathetic business-oriented approach to issues: something which is itself an ines-

capable consequence of the extremely high concentration of corporate control of our newspapers and electronic media, concentration levels that are almost unparalleled in other western democracies.

Some informed observers, John Kenneth Galbraith among them, believe that little can be done to halt the runaway growth of conglomerates. As profits are accumulated, they must be reinvested, and the rational chief executive officer will more often than not choose to expand into unrelated, new, and challenging areas.

Take for example the Reichmanns' $2.8-billion takeover of Gulf Canada Ltd., which extended their empire well beyond its core real-estate base. This was the largest private transaction in Canadian history, assisted with a special tax exemption, kindness of the Canadian taxpayer, that has been estimated at anywhere between $400 million and $1 billion.

What has this done for the Canadian employee, the Canadian investor, the Canadian consumer? Admittedly it does have the effect of Canadianizing a large chunk of the energy sector. But at what price? As part of the deal, Gulf sold off its service outlets to PetroCanada, with a resultant loss of some 2000 jobs following the consolidation with PetroCanada stations. Further, the Gulf Canada deal concentrated the oil business even more, reducing the number of major refiners and marketers from five to four. And the close co-operation of the government in facilitating the deal unacceptably blurred the line between business and politics.

In a recent *Financial Post* interview, after being selected as business newsmaker of the year, Paul Reichmann firmly denied that he is anxious to become any bigger or wants more control. But in answering why the Reichmanns undertook yet another mega investment, he replied, "There is a sense of challenge, the challenge of doing something meaningful. In the end, though, it is an addiction."

It is this addiction that is leading inexorably to sprawling conglomerates that must now be seriously addressed as a pressing public policy issue. Unless we are willing to abdicate the public interest in the pursuit of a constructive industrial strategy—one that will ensure that, as we rapidly shift from a predominantly resource-based economy, we are able to generate a new economic dynamism, especially in the new high-technology growth sectors—our political leaders must take urgent steps to check this rise in concentration.

In doing so, they must also firmly break out of the traditional tripartite focus on big business, big labour, and government, and recognize that it is no longer, if it ever was, justifiable to believe that the country's biggest corporate players will necessarily do better than our small businesses and entrepreneurs at sparking economic growth and reducing unemployment.

A strategic approach involving firm initiatives on a number of fronts is now required in order to meet effectively the threat of ever-increasing concentration of economic activity and wealth in Canada. The primary role of the government is, of course, the establishment of a framework within which the economy should operate, while reserving direct intervention for critical areas of support or breakdown. But at this moment we clearly lack sensible framework policies in key areas such as competition policy, industrial policy, science and technology, and foreign investment.

First, we must take firm steps to revamp our competition laws and to facilitate reviews of mergers that may adversely impact on the public interest. The recent proposal by the federal government to establish a competition tribunal for such merger reviews is a small step in the right direction.

However, the tribunal ought to be much more private-sector-oriented (perhaps along the lines of the British Monopolies and Mergers Commission that involves no judicial element and merely advises the relevant Minister) rather than chaired by a Federal Court judge and potentially dominated by judges, as proposed in the draft legislation.

In addition, the jurisdiction of the tribunal should be extended to all mergers involving, for example, combined assets of at least $100 million. And the onus must be firmly placed on the merging parties to justify why the transaction is in the public interest, whether in terms of expanded output and employment or of the need for a larger domestic base to facilitate competitiveness in international markets.

In this connection, it is noteworthy that many of the larger Canadian companies, with the notable exceptions of Alcan Aluminum Ltd. and Bell Canada Enterprises, have had a less-than-stellar international competitive performance notwithstanding the putative advantages of economies of scale. The jury is clearly still out on this issue.

The jurisdiction of the competition tribunal should also include reviews of proposed takeovers of foreign companies by Canadian companies above the minimum threshold level, in much the same way that the British Mergers and Monopolies Commission has authority to review the British Telecom purchase of Mitel Corporation.

In this way, we may gain a greater insight into and perhaps influence over the billions of Canadian dollars that are invested outside our borders every year. Indeed it is estimated that the flow into the United States jumped from $11.4 billion in 1983 to $14 billion in 1984 and continues to rise steadily.

Other initiatives relating to competition policy include the establishment of ceilings for ownership measured in terms of market shares or on a sector-by-sector basis. In the United States, for example, there is an automatic investigation of any four companies having 60 percent of any market.

In addition, these competition policy initiatives should be linked to reforms to our foreign investment rules. Parallel ceilings could be placed on foreign ownership in the key sectors, and strong consideration should be given to the Science Council suggestion that foreign takeovers of any company that has received more than $100 000 in federal assistance over the previous five years, by way of grants, loans, subsidies, and so forth for research and development, should be subject to review notwithstanding the new threshold level established under the Investment Canada Act.

Most importantly perhaps, the foreign investment review mechanism should be integrated with the operations of the competition bureau and tribunal to ensure co-ordination and more streamlined reporting requirements.

A second area for specific government action relates to the financial services sector and the reduction of levels of concentrated ownership and the associated opportunities for abuse of corporate power. This should involve the imposition of strict ownership rules for trust companies similar to the limit for any single shareholder now imposed on the banks. Such a step will of course necessitate the appropriate divestiture of the existing controlling interests over a certain period of time.

There should also be a ban on self-dealing on the part of all financial institutions and all non-arm's length transactions should be prohibited in any instance where the true market value cannot be objectively ascertained by independent means.

With specific reference to banks, although they are widely held, stricter rules are required in respect of their corporate governance in order to ensure that the largest customers do not represent a dominant influence on the boards of directors, and that there is equal access to credit for all businesses and entrepreneurs regardless of size. In Britain, for example, the banks' biggest customers cannot sit on bank boards. This stands in stark contrast to the extensive interlocks between the five major Canadian banks and other dominant firms.

A third area for particular initiatives relates to the concentration of ownership in our media, especially the newspaper industry. Already two government-initiated studies—one prepared by the Special Senate Committee on Mass Media (1970), the other by the Kent Royal Commission on Newspapers—have warned Canadians of the dangers of the increasing concentration of the press, and have advised remedial measures.

Most Canadian communities have only one newspaper. Two huge newspaper chains, Thomson and Southam, control some 58 percent of the total English-language circulation. In New Brunswick, Irving Limited controls 90.6 percent of the daily circulation. Finally, Power Corporation controls at least 25 percent of the French-language circulation in Quebec, and its takeover in September 1985 of Télémetropole Inc., which includes most of Quebec's TVA private network, has raised additional concerns about cross-media ownership. In this connection, it is disturbing that in May 1985 the federal government annulled a 1982 directive to the CRTC designed to limit such cross-media ownership in the same region.

This overwhelming presence of powerful corporate interests does not necessarily entail overt or even covert censorship by the owners or publishers. But insofar as media coverage is frequently sympathetic to, or reflective of, the concerns of business, this inevitably strengthens the influence of business in the public policy process, and weakens the fully informed debate so essential to the effective functioning of a liberal democracy.

It is clearly time to review the proposals of both the Davey Report and the Kent Report, and to take action. Otherwise we risk a situation in which the revolution in information technology that is now taking place will come to be dominated by, and ever more entrenched in, the same groups, to the detriment of the social and political fabric of our society.

Corporation law reform is yet another means of addressing the problems of corporate concentration. To begin with, enhanced protections for minority shareholders, whose interests are too often forgotten or ignored in the course of mergers involving major corporate players, are clearly required. And measures must be taken to contain the deleterious effects of so-called "paper entrepreneurialism" that does so little to contribute to either economic growth or employment. In this connection, the New York legislature has recently passed a law that requires corporate raiders who buy more than 20 percent of a company's stock to wait five years before merging with the target company or selling off its assets.

Other possible approaches include amendments to our tax laws to eliminate built-in incentives to merger activity. Provisions for the deduction of interest on loans to finance takeovers should be removed, and consolidated tax filings for corporate conglomerates should be required in order to prevent interrelated companies from avoiding taxes by passing tax credits from one corporation to another.

Our company laws must also be amended in respect of the rules governing the composition of boards of directors in order to gradually dissolve the network of interlocking directorships and to ensure that a broader perspective is brought to bear on corporate decisions.

Furthermore, the need to expand the range of experience on boards of directors applies equally to the public sector. More specifically, governments must improve the range of government appointments to boards of crown corporations, regulatory agencies, research councils, universities, hospitals, granting bodies, and cultural, community, and charitable organizations.

Finally, consideration should be given to initiatives that are consciously aimed at broadening the ownership base of existing conglomerates and encouraging entrepreneurship. We could, for example, spur greater employee ownership of enterprises through tax-sheltered buy-back schemes such as those tried out in Sweden. This might be particularly useful as part of the divestiture recommended for the financial services and media sectors. We could also take steps to nurture the venture capital market and expand investment opportunities in Canada. This might help to stem the flow of the some $14 billion in Canadian investment south of the border, including 40 percent of Canadian venture capital.

Clearly, firm, positive government action is urgently required if we are to succeed in checking the inexorable expansion of concentrated pools of wealth in our economy, especially the conglomerate variety. Both the government and the general public have yet to fully appreciate the nature of this power and its implications for political influence as well as for the opportunities open to Canadians whether in terms of employment or investment. It is time to establish a strategic domestic agenda and to act decisively. Failure to do so could have irreparable long-term consequences for the social and economic fabric of this country.

FOR FURTHER READING

Brym, Robert J., ed. 1985. *The Structure of the Canadian Capitalist Class*. Toronto: Garamond Press. This collection of papers presents contemporary discussion of various class issues by leading writers in the field of social inequality. The main focal point is the capitalist class and its relevance to an understanding of class boundaries, class cleavages, and class rule in Canada.

Carroll, William K. 1986 *Corporate Power and Canadian Capitalism*. Vancouver: University of British Columbia Press. This book provides a thorough compilation and analysis of evidence about Canadian capitalism and the class of people that controls the economy. Carroll's approach departs from and extends earlier influential studies by Clement and others.

Clement, Wallace. 1977. *Continental Corporate Power: Economic Linkages Between Canada and the United States*. Toronto: McClelland and Stewart. Clement extends his earlier analysis of elites in Canada, *The Canadian Corporate Elite* (1975), by examining the linkages between the Canadian and the American economies, the relationship between Canadian and American elites, and Canada's position in a world system dominated by multinational corporations.

Marchak, Patricia. 1979. *In Whose Interests?* Toronto: McClelland and Stewart. In this essay Marchak's major concern is with the role of multinational corporations in shaping the structure of ownership in the Canadian economy. The first part of the book argues that major corporations tend to monopolize key sectors of our economy, to the general detriment of the population as a whole. The second part analyses the internal organization of corporations and the linkages between class and corporate structure.

Niosi, Jorge. 1985. *Canadian Multinationals*. Toronto: Garamond Press. This book looks at a topic that has received little attention elsewhere: the extent to which Canadian corporations have become involved in the economies of other nations. Niosi determines that in certain economic sectors Canadian businesses have made significant inroads into the international or world economy.

Palmer, Bryan D. 1983. *Working-Class Experience: The Rise and Reconstitution of Canadian Labour, 1800-1980*. Toronto: Butterworths. This historical analysis considers questions of ownership and class relations from the point of view of the workers, those individuals who must labour for the owning class. A major theme of this book is that Canadian workers, despite reversals in recent decades, have maintained a sense of collective identity and collective action in opposition to the injustices that arise in the capitalist economy.

Section II

SOCIO-ECONOMIC BASES OF SOCIAL INEQUALITY

A. WEALTH, INCOME, AND POVERTY

B. OCCUPATION

C. EDUCATION

Introduction

As we saw in the last section, the private ownership of productive economic property is fundamental to the social divisions characterizing Canadian society. There are other dimensions of social inequality though, and we explore three of them in this section. We turn to the issues of *wealth, income, and poverty; occupation; and education*.

These three dimensions of inequality are closely interrelated. For any individual, education is most often the key determinant of the range of occupational alternatives available, and the job one finds influences income. There is, thus, a causal connection between these three variables. Furthermore, the impact of income has important consequences for a person's family and in fact extends beyond an individual's lifetime, influencing, for example, the educational advantage of one's children. Several issues involved in this complex interrelationship must be emphasized.

First, it is important to clarify whether the focus is upon *individuals* or upon *families*. On some occasions sociologists study individuals, for example, when they seek to explain the occupations or incomes of people. At other times the emphasis is upon families, when, for instance, sociologists explore issues of intergenerational mobility or the inheritance of wealth. Being clear about the *unit of analysis* (individuals or families) is important.

Second, discussions of equality invariably confront the issue of transmission across the generations. To what degree is social inequality reproduced over time? Research in this vein investigates the influence of family origin or family background on the attainment or inheritance of education, occupation, and income levels. Questions concerning the openness or rigidity of society are paramount here. Inequalities in Canada have a history, and a historical perspective on patterns of inequality is useful (as the previous articles by Clement and Brym demonstrated).

Third, the relations between the three dimensions are not completely fixed, and, although they are intertwined, the correlation between any two dimensions is not perfect. So even though education, occupation, and income are closely aligned in contemporary Canada, it is true that some people with little education do earn large incomes and amass rather than inherit great fortunes (although the number of such people is remarkably low). These individuals are exceptions, though, as are people who live in poverty despite having attained high levels of education. In short, the connections between these factors are not deterministic, rather the relations are *probabilistic*.

Fourth, while social inequality is a feature of all societies, the degree of inequality is variable. Most simply, at different times and in different societies the amount of inequality varies. Sociologists studying inequality in Canada have, therefore, been concerned to investigate how inequality in this country compares to that in other countries and to account for how levels of inequality are changing over time in Canada.

Explanations for the levels of social inequality in contemporary Canada vary. While this section stresses facts about inequality in Canada, issues of interpretation are important too. Contrary to the popular wisdom, facts do not speak for themselves. For instance, how are we to understand the consistent finding that on average women earn much less than men (see Table 5-1 in the selection by Alfred Hunter)? This is a well-established fact, but it does not speak for itself. When you read Hunter's paper in this section, and then both the Saunders and the Calzavara selections in Section III, you will begin to appreciate the controversy of interpretations that swirls around this as well as around other facts of inequality.

To anticipate briefly some debates, you will encounter throughout this book ideas that provide consistent touchstones for interpretations of social inequality. The two basic approaches are raised here so that you will recognize them as you ponder the meaning and interpretation of patterns of structured inequality.

One way that some people have sought to explain inequality is by pointing to its positive benefits for the well-being of society. This line of reasoning holds that people will only be motivated to invest in the acquisition of skills, and will only undertake jobs competently and diligently, if they are likely to receive higher rewards by doing so. People with talent, ability, and drive will be encouraged to use these attributes for the benefit of all if they are rewarded for doing this. Great rewards, including income and influence, must go to the people filling those positions most crucial to the whole of society. The principle of *achievement* is central to this explanation for differences in income or prestige. Inequality functions to motivate people to work hard (see Davis and Moore, 1945, for a more elaborate statement of this theory).

A very different line of argument is taken by those who emphasize that certain groups in society benefit more than others from the labour that is undertaken in the economic workplace. Tensions and disputes over aspects of inequality are said to stem from opposing interests of different groups, as one group attempts to control profit at another group's expense. For some researchers, these interest groups are class-based, while for others, the major interest groups are defined by non-class factors such as sex or ethnicity. However the groups are defined, it is the centrality of conflict over scarce resources that holds the key to understanding social inequality in this interpretation. The struggle for control over economic resources, power, and wealth is understood as the motor of social change. The principle of *social control* is central to this explanation for differences in wealth and power. Inequality and conflict result from the struggle between groups for the control of scarce resources (see Wright, 1985, for a recent account of this perspective).

The tension between these two perspectives underlies much of the writing on inequality, although there are several variants of each theme. In the first paper on education, by Robert Pike, you will find a key distinction made between *equality of opportunity* (the freedom for individuals to pursue or to strive to attain goals or initiatives) and *equality of condition* (the availability to all of equal resources and the elimination of a monopoly on benefits and privileges). In the context of a foot race, equality of opportunity means that everyone is allowed to participate, whereas equality of condition ensures that everyone is at the same starting line, with no one suffering undue handicaps. Hugh McRoberts, in his paper on social mobility, also uses the contrast between equality of opportunity and of condition to interpret his results.

In terms of the two perspectives outlined previously, those who stress achievement tend to focus on equality of opportunity, emphasizing the freedom for individuals to pursue their own destiny. An emphasis on equality of condition comes from those who argue that the control and accumulation of power and profit by one group gives them, and especially their offspring, undue advantage and benefit.

Controversy surrounding debates between proponents of equality of opportunity and those of equality of condition is one important way in which the general tension around achievement versus social control is played out. Another way is portrayed in Morley Gunderson's paper on the advantages and disadvantages of income redistribution.

The general point which it is important to remember, and which is nicely illustrated in both Pike's and Gunderson's papers, is that the controversy continues about how best to interpret patterns of structured inequality.

WEALTH, INCOME, AND POVERTY

In the first part of this section we explore the distribution of money. At the two extremes of the income distribution are affluence and poverty, the rich and the poor. The readings examine how material rewards are distributed in Canadian society, how that distribution has changed over time, what the government has and has not done in attempting to make the distribution more equitable, and what arguments are made for and against income redistribution.

The first reading, by Alfred Hunter, demonstrates that while the economic pie has been expanding in the post-World War II era, the sizes of the slices apportioned to various income groups have remained remarkably stable. That is, the share of economic benefits is unequal and there has been very little discernible change in the amount of economic benefits going to different groups. What makes this surprising is that these decades since World War II have often been described in terms of the growth of the welfare state. Whatever else the state may have done during this period, it is not the case that the government played Robin Hood, taking from the rich and giving to the poor. It would appear that the state looked after everyone's welfare with the end result that very little, if any, redistribution of income occurred.

Many believe that the government uses the tax system to collect revenue which is then used to fund ameliorative programs. As Hunter describes, the poor do receive some transfer payments, but so too do the rich. The result is that little redistribution of income is in fact accomplished. One of the keys to understanding this process is to realize that of the various taxes we pay—sales tax, income tax, gasoline tax, excise tax and so forth—some are progressive forms of taxation which increase proportionally as the ability to pay increases, while others are regressive (that is, they increase proportionally as income decreases). In addition, people with larger incomes are able to take advantage of tax shelters (and to hire tax accountants who must be well paid to find these shelters). The net result is that the overall *rate* of tax paid by all Canadians varies surprisingly little over the entire income scale.

Income, however, is only one part of the material resources Canadians possess. For some, the super-rich, income is far less important than are assets. Wealth is accumulated and stored in the form of land, buildings, stocks, precious metals, art, and so forth. As Lars Osberg demonstrates in his paper on the distribution of wealth in Canada, there are some extremely rich families in this country. In fact, comparisons with the U.S. show that there are more rich families per capita in Canada. Furthermore, the distribution of wealth is much more unequally distributed than is the distribution of income. Finally, recent evidence would suggest that, if anything, wealth is becoming more unequally distributed as time passes.

At the other extreme of the distribution of material resources is poverty. Currently in Canada approximately 15 percent of the population lives in poverty, and this percentage increased in the early 1980s. The National Council of Welfare monitors the extent of poverty in Canada and publishes numerous informative papers on issues faced by the poor in this country. In the paper we reproduce here, the method employed by Statistics Canada to define poverty is described. Details are provided on how poverty lines compare to the expectations Canadians have of how much money is absolutely necessary to support a family, emphasizing especially the large discrepancy between the minimum wage lines and the amount of money a family of four needs to survive. The paper also analyses the *depth of poverty* by showing exactly how far below the poverty line some Canadian families are.

Juxtaposing poverty and wealth raises the issue of the actual distribution of economic benefits. We conclude this section with a paper which we hope will stimulate your thinking about issues of income redistribution. Morley Gunderson, an economist, discusses some of the pros and cons of income redistribution, examining the advantages and disadvantages of equalizing the distribution of income. As you read his paper it is important to keep in mind the results of Hunter's paper—that there is currently very little redistribution of income in Canada. As a policy concern, the question is whether or not redistribution should occur, and if it should, how it should be implemented.

OCCUPATION

In general, the occupations that people perform are of fundamental importance, since working is what many of us do with most of our waking lives. Our jobs or careers are often the crux of our personal identities, defining who we are in our own minds and in those of others. And, of course, the occupations we are engaged in generate the incomes with which most of us meet the material requirements of our daily existence. Occupation provides at least an approximate measure of where people stand on a wide variety of other inequality dimensions, not just income but education, skill level, degree of responsibility, amount of authority over others, and prestige ranking, among others.

Perhaps for these reasons, occupation has been said by some researchers to be the best indicator of a person's general social class location or socio-economic position. The relevance of occupation to the field is also revealed in the range of problems involving work or occupation that researchers in social inequality have addressed. These include, for example, the changing composition of the work force, the extent to which occupational status depends on the attainment of educational credentials, the degree to which the occupational backgrounds of parents influence the occupational attainments of their children, the question of who should decide or control the nature of the work process, and so on.

These issues form the focus of the three papers chosen for the section on occupational inequality. In the first article, Graham Lowe analyses recent changes in the Canadian occupational structure. He reviews and evaluates several developments, including the continued growth of professional, technical, and clerical occupations in the work force, the segmentation of the labour market by gender and ethnicity, and the possible implications of technological change for the organization of work.

The second paper, by Hugh McRoberts, assesses the question of occupational mobility in Canada, with specific concern for the extent to which the occupational advantages or disadvantages of parents are inherited by their offspring when the latter eventually enter the labour force as adults. He finds sufficient inheritance to suggest that Canada's occupational structure cannot be characterized as having full equality of opportunity; at the same time, however, McRoberts shows that there is clear evidence of mobility from one generation to the next, enough to conclude that there is a significant level of openness in the process by which occupations are attained.

The final paper on occupation concentrates more specifically on the organization and process of work. James Rinehart assesses the projections of some observers that future generations could experience a more liberated, less alienated work environment because of greater implementation of automation and a movement to advanced technology in production. Rinehart's analysis, however, suggests that any such transformation of work by automation will not provide these projected improvements, and that, despite expectations, there is little evidence that a significant need for highly trained technical personnel will arise in the near future. In contrast to other strategies, especially greater control over jobs by workers, automation is apparently not the answer to alienation in the workplace.

EDUCATION

The amount of education that a person acquires is arguably the most important of the three scarce rewards under discussion in this section—income, occupational status, and educational status. The argument would be that education is the most important because educational credentials are among the best predictors of attainment of the other two rewards. McRoberts' study of predictors of occupational mobility suggests that this is the case. Education is very often the sole avenue to the best jobs and the highest salaries.

No wonder then that academic researchers, educational practitioners, and politicians have devoted substantial attention to the question of providing equality in the opportunity to acquire education. The selection by Robert Pike describes the three policies that have been followed in several liberal democracies, Canada included, to try to assure such equality of opportunity. These are (1) "free access" to elementary and secondary schooling and sometimes to post-secondary schooling; (2) "compensating measures" to help the student from a disadvantaged background to catch up; and (3) opportunities for "lifelong learning." Pike makes it clear that the first two policies have been put to the test and have failed to achieve fully their objective; that is to say, people from economically disadvantaged backgrounds still do more poorly in school. The third policy is not long-standing enough in Canada for us to be able to assess its results properly, but Pike suggests that it, too, will not be very successful.

Pike goes on to describe the two sociological theories addressing the reasons why the policies have not worked well. The first theory emphasizes that the problem lies in the lack of equality of conditions outside the schools, in the family. Not all families are supportive of the pursuit of education for their children, either in the value they attach to education or in the time and resources they devote to encouraging education. The second theory argues that the problem lies in how the education system sorts people into different educational levels and occupational status levels and thus helps perpetuate class and status differences. Pike believes that each of these problems exists and argues that high levels of equality of educational opportunity cannot therefore come from educational reform alone. The structure of inequality pre-existing outside the school, and the school's effects upon it, would have to be addressed too.

The selection by Neil Guppy and his colleagues turns to the facts of educational inequality. Using a large national survey of adult Canadians, these researchers ask how much inequality there has been in the attainment of high-school education and college education, and whether the inequality has changed over time. Educational inequality is measured by asking if there are differences in participation in high school and university according to the socio-economic status backgrounds of students. The study shows that the socio-economic background of the family exerts a strong influence on educational attainment, although this influence appears to have weakened somewhat with time, especially in terms of the chances of graduating from high school. The more recent age groups in the study showed a lesser effect of socio-economic background upon education attained, especially at the high-school level.

The selection by Sid Gilbert and Neil Guppy shifts the focus to recent change in the overall educational participation rates for men and women. They show that there is currently little difference in the rates for women and for men for either university enrolment or the attainment of university degrees. This situation did not obtain in previous decades, when males were more advantaged. The educational participation rates have increased for both genders in recent decades, but the increase has been more rapid for females. The temporal data also show that women are progressively entering what used to be "male-dominated" professional fields of study, although there remains considerable difference between male and female participation rates in both traditionally "male" domains (for example, engineering) and traditional "female" specialties (for example, nursing).

The education subsection also contains two papers focussed on policy proposals. First, Stephen Schecter's paper begins from a point raised earlier by Pike—that the educational system reinforces the existing inequalities of the wider society's class structure. Schecter emphasizes that the educational system as we know it is, therefore, part of the problem of inequality. Schecter describes how the educational system teaches that inequalities are just: it slots people into different levels in the world of jobs and income, telling them all the while that their jobs and income are what they deserve, given their educational accomplishments or lack of accomplishments. These messages are taught via what Schecter calls "the hidden curriculum" of the schools. He goes on to conclude that a radical reform of this "curriculum" is needed.

In the final selection Robert Pike presents a critical review of the policy recommendations of three major government commissions of recent years: the 1984 Commission on the Future Development of the Universities of Ontario; the 1985 Royal Commission of Post-secondary Education in Nova Scotia; and the federal government's 1985 Royal Commission on the Economic Union and Development Prospects of Canada. First, the policies proposed by these commissions are all very "modest." There is no call for a radical restructuring of what is taught and how it is taught, as there is with Schecter. Each of the policies falls under the broad "free access" and "compensatory" approaches described earlier by Pike as the popular types of panaceas for education in liberal democracies. However, Pike detects an important change in the ideology reflected in the recommendations of the three reports, a change to different ideas than those supporting the policy initiatives of the 1960s and 1970s. A common goal, now, is retrieving more of the costs of higher education through tuition fees. These fees are being justified by arguments that education greatly benefits the individual, and that the individual should therefore pay more. Earlier it was argued that there was a need for very low tuition costs because a highly educated population greatly benefited the society as a whole and the society should, therefore, invest in an effort to have a large proportion of the population become highly educated. Pike is not optimistic about the likelihood of the new policy measures producing major changes in the patterns of educational inequality, and he emphasizes the reasons why.

REFERENCES

Davis, Kingsley, and Wilbert Moore
    1945   "Some principles of stratification," *American Sociological Review*, 10:242-49.
Wright, Erik Olin
    1985   *Classes*. London: New Left Books.

A. Wealth, Income, and Poverty

---

5. *The Changing Distribution of Income*

Alfred A. Hunter

CHANGING DISTRIBUTIONS

Relative to other countries, Canada is wealthy, and has been throughout the period since World War II. In 1984 Canada's gross domestic product per capita was $14 600, versus $15 300 for the United States, which put Canada substantially ahead of such countries as West Germany, France, Japan, Belgium, the Netherlands, Britain, and Italy. Moreover, Canada's per capita productivity relative to that of the U.S. has increased considerably in the past 35 years or so. In 1950 it stood at about 80 percent of that of the U.S.; in 1976, at 102 percent; and in 1984, at 96 percent. Canada's position in this respect has improved not only in relative terms, it has improved in absolute terms as well. That is, real productivity per capita in Canada, as in the other countries mentioned above, is much higher today than it was 35 years ago.

Revised from Alfred A. Hunter, *Class Tells: Social Inequality in Canada*, 2nd. ed. (Toronto: Butterworths, 1986), pp. 60-67. Reprinted with permission.

Accompanying the increases in productivity over time in Canada have been increases in the earnings of Canadians, as Table 5-1 shows. In current dollars (columns 2 and 3), Canadians' incomes have shown about an eightfold increase since 1951, although much of this has been due to inflation. Even allowing for inflation, however (columns 4 and 5), they more than doubled in this period, although most of the increase occurred prior to 1975, and men's real incomes actually dropped in the late 1970s—the first time this had happened in the postwar period.

Both Canada as a country and individual Canadians on the average, then, have continued to fare better and better economically in all but very recent times. Changes in per capita productivity, however, do not translate themselves in any simple or direct way into changes in individuals' incomes, and changes in individuals' incomes tell us only part of the story of the purchasing power of individuals. One reason for this is that most people belong to family units, and a majority of families currently have more than one income earner. While single individuals who live alone may typically have only their own economic resources to draw upon, people who are members of families can often draw upon the income of more than one person. At the same time, it is normally individuals, and not families, who receive income, although it was once fairly common for employees to be paid according to their marital status and number of children. For some purposes, then, it is appropriate to analyse family incomes (e.g., to study economic resources), while for other purposes it is appropriate to analyse individual incomes (e.g., to study wage and salary determination). Table 5-2 shows the changing distribution of families by the number of income recipients, 1951-81. As these data show, the modal pattern of an earlier time, whereby the economic fortunes of the family were tied to the income of one person, has been replaced by a pattern in which the Canadian family is likely to have two or more income recipients.

While an analysis of increases and decreases in real income is informative in its own right, it, too, tells us only part of what we might wish to know about the changing economic resources of Canadians. In particular, it does not tell us anything in itself about income inequalities, since some families and unattached individuals make much less

TABLE 5-1   Earnings of men and women in Canada in current and constant (1981) dollars, selected years, 1951-85.

Year	Current dollars		Constant (1981) dollars	
	Men	Women	Men	Women
1951	$ 2 575	$ 1 061	$ 9 229	$ 3 803
1954	2 922	1 161	10 253	4 074
1957	3 381	1 441	11 308	4 819
1959	3 556	1 599	11 467	5 158
1961	3 869	1 692	12 244	5 354
1965	4 612	1 870	13 565	5 500
1967	5 322	2 454	14 581	6 723
1971	7 056	3 307	16 720	7 836
1973	8 402	3 887	17 651	8 166
1975	10 815	5 200	18 487	8 889
1977	12 690	6 442	18 689	9 487
1979	14 981	7 673	18 564	9 508
1981	18 159	9 653	18 159	9 653
1985	22 298	12 454	18 232	10 183

Sources: Calculated from *Incomes of Non-Farm Families and Individuals in Canada, Selected Years 1951-65* (Ottawa: Dominion Bureau of Statistics, 1969); *Earnings of Men and Women, Selected Years 1967 to 1979* (Ottawa: Statistics Canada, 1981); *Earnings of Men and Women, 1981 and 1982* (Ottawa: Statistics Canada, 1984); F. H. Leacy, ed., Historical Statistics of Canada (Ottawa: Statistics Canada, 1983); *Consumer Prices and Prices Indexes, January-March 1985* (Ottawa: Statistics Canada, 1985).

TABLE 5-2   Percentage of families by number of income recipients, 1951-81.

Number of income recipients in family	1951*	1961*	1971	1981	Change 1951-81
None	0.4	0.5	0.3	0.1	− 0.3
One	57.0	53.2	34.7	20.9	− 36.1
Two	29.7	34.7	47.6	57.2	+ 27.5
Three or more	12.8	11.6	17.3	21.8	+ 9.0

*Excludes families with one or more farmers.
Sources: Dominion Bureau of Statistics, *Income Distribution*, Cat. 13-529, Table 14. Statistics Canada, *Income Distributions by Size in Canada* (1971), Cat. 13-207, Table 25. Statistics Canada, *Income Distributions by Size in Canada* (1981), Cat. 13-207, Table 20.

than the average, while others make much more. Table 5-3 contains information on the changing distribution of the incomes of families and unattached individuals in Canada, 1951-85. These data show that, although real incomes more than doubled in the period surveyed, there are large and persistent inequalities in the distribution of incomes. The bottom quintile (i.e., 20 percent) of families and unattached individuals never received more than 4.7 percent of the total income going to these units in the years represented in the table, while the top quintile never received less than 41.4 percent of the total family income (also see Henderson and Rowley, 1978). As well, there has been a slight tendency for the top two quintiles to increase their hold upon the available income at the expense of the bottom three quintiles (also see Hamilton and Pinard, 1977 and Johnson, 1977). In 1951 the top two quintiles received 66.1 percent of individuals. This decreased in 1961 to 65.9 percent, rose in 1971 to 68.2 percent, then dropped to 67 percent in 1981, and rose again to 68 percent in 1985.

The levels of family income inequality in Canada over the past 30 years appear to be broadly similar to those in the United Kingdom (Atkinson, 1975) and the United States (Thurow, 1975) in the same period—slightly higher than in the former, perhaps, and slightly lower than in the latter. They are, however, clearly higher than those in at least certain of the Eastern bloc countries, such as the Soviet Union, Poland, Czechoslovakia, and Hungary (Lane, 1971), although the available data are inadequate to provide any very precise comparisons between nations East and West.

TAXES AND TRANSFERS

The data on income distributions presented to this point have concerned before-tax income only. Many of us take at least some comfort, however, in the notion that Canada has a system of progressive taxation, whereby those with high incomes pay proportionally more in taxes than do those with low incomes, with the result that the tax structure has an equalizing effect on the overall income distribution. In fact, the system of taxation in Canada seems not to be progressive at all, and actually appears to be regressive at the low end of the income range. That is, when direct and indirect taxes from all sources—federal, provincial, and municipal—are taken into account,

TABLE 5-3 Percentage of total before-tax income going to families and unattached individuals by quintile, 1951-85.

Income quintile	1951*	1961*	1971	1981	1985
Lowest	4.4	4.2	3.6	4.6	4.7
Second	11.2	11.9	10.6	10.9	10.4
Middle	18.3	18.3	17.6	17.6	17.0
Fourth	23.3	24.5	24.9	25.2	25.0
Highest	42.8	41.4	43.3	41.8	43.0

*Excludes families with one or more farmers.
Sources: Canada (1974a: Table 7.4). Statistics Canada, *Income Distributions by Size in Canada* (1981), Cat. 13-207, Table 74.

there is a general tendency for the well-to-do to pay proportionally *less* of their incomes in taxes than the less well-to-do. As Maslove puts it in his detailed analysis of taxation in Canada, "by far the most striking conclusion to be drawn from an examination of total tax payments is the extreme regressivity of the system at the lower end of the income scale and the lack of any significant progressivity over the remainder of the income range." "Indeed," he continues, "over the lower portion of the income scale, the system tends to contradict the ability-to-pay principle by taxing the poor at a higher rate than those who are better off" (1972:64).

Since transfer payments represent a significant proportion of the incomes only of persons who receive no wage or salary, they have little effect on the overall distribution of incomes of individuals, of income earners, or of families (Love and Wolfson, 1976)—despite the expansion in the postwar years of social security programs whose apparent purpose has been to redistribute income. The inclusion of transfer payments in income does eliminate the phenomenon of people paying out more in taxes than they receive in income, but the basic pattern of regressive taxation for the lowest income categories remains, if in somewhat weak-ened form (Maslove, 1972:72). The pattern of taxation for the remainder of the income scale is unaltered through the inclusion of transfer payments, as one might expect (see also Table 5-4).

The systems of taxation and social security in Canada, then, seem to effect no significant redistribution of incomes, despite their stated purpose of doing so. In fact, the taxation system is actually regressive at the lower end of the income scale, and neither particularly regressive nor progressive through the remainder of it. With regard to the taxation system, the poorest 22–39 percent of all families, depending upon the province, fall into the regressive range when broad income (i.e., income before taxes, including the imputed value of non-monetary components, and minus transfer payments) is used. When full income (i.e., income before taxes—including, again, non-monetary components—plus transfer payments) is used, the poorest 17–28 percent of families, depending upon the province, fall into the regressive range. Moreover, the more local the unit of government, the more regressive the taxes it levies tend to be. In fact, the personal income tax—the one we tend to think first about when we think of taxes—is the only one which is progressive for all

TABLE 5-4   Taxes and transfers: the family allowance in Canada, 1984.

Family income	Family allowance	Child tax credit, exemption	Child care deduction	Tax on family allowance	Benefit per child
$ 6 250	$ 359	$ 367	$ –	$ –	$ 726
12 500	359	487	–	60	786
25 000	359	567	100	100	926
50 000	359	265	400	125	899
100 000	359	310	800	150	1 319

Source: Based partly on *The Globe and Mail,* January 4, 1985.

income levels. Most other federal taxes are regressive for at least certain income levels, including the federal general sales tax, which is regressive for all income levels. This is of course a feature of all taxes based on consumption. At the provincial level, the progressivity of the personal income tax (a proportion of which is either returned to the provinces or, as in the case of Quebec, collected by the province itself) is offset by the regressivity of sales and excise taxes. Municipal taxes, finally, are the most regressive of all including, most importantly, municipal property taxes, which are regressive at almost all income levels.

Perhaps most surprising is the apparent failure of the massive and increasingly expensive social security system in Canada to redistribute incomes in any real way. A major reason for this would seem to be that, despite the seemingly large amounts of money involved, they have been small and relatively constant as a proportion of total income earned over the years, and they benefit, by and large, only those who do not work for a wage or a salary. And another major reason could be that increases in transfer payments over the past 30 years have come in a period when the poorer income earners have been losing in *relative* purchasing power and, most recently, in *absolute* purchasing power as well. If this is true, "then it should not be surprising that

'redistributive' programs are failing to 're-distribute.' Like Alice, in *Through the Looking Glass*, they are running as hard as they can to stay in the same place" (Johnson, 1977:342).

In general, then, taxes and transfer payments in Canada seem at most to have only a small redistributive effect with regard to incomes. Just how Canada fares in this regard relative to other nations cannot be determined very precisely, although Hewitt (1977) presents some data for a number of Western countries which suggest that direct and indirect taxes, coupled with government social service expenditures, in Canada have only a modest redistributive effect relative to elsewhere (also see Atkinson, 1975:71). At the top of the list of 17 countries (in order) were Sweden, Austria, the Netherlands, Germany, Norway, and New Zealand. In the middle were Belgium, Denmark, the United Kingdom, Finland, and Switzerland. And at the bottom were the United States, Australia, France, Canada, Ireland, and Japan. The relative positions of the U.S. and Canada on this list are consistent with Pipes and Walker's (1979) analysis, which suggests that the overall tax rate is higher for all income categories in Canada than in the U.S., with the largest differences occurring in the lowest income categories and the smallest differences in the highest categories.

REFERENCES

Atkinson, A. B.
   1975   *The Economics of Inequality*. London: Oxford University Press.

Hamilton, R., and M. Pinard
   1977   "Poverty in Canada: Illusion and Reality," *Canadian Review of Sociology and Anthropology*, 14:247-52.

Henderson, D. W., and J. C. R. Rowley
   1978   "Structural Changes and the Distribution of Canadian Family Incomes, 1965-1975." Discussion Paper No. 118. Ottawa: Economic Council of Canada.

Hewitt, C.
   1977   "The Effect of Political Democracy on Equality in Industrial Societies: A Cross-National Comparison," *American Sociological Review*, 42:450-64.

Johnson, L.
   1977   "Illusions or Realities: Hamilton and Pinard's Approach to Poverty," *Canadian Review of Sociology and Anthropology*, 14:341-46.

Lane, D.
   1971   *The End of Inequality? Stratification Under State Socialism*. Middlesex: Penguin.

Love, R., and M. C. Wolfson
   1976   *Income Inequality: Statistical Methodology and Canadian Illustrations*. Ottawa: Statistics Canada.

Maslove, A.
   1972   *The Pattern of Taxation in Canada*. Ottawa: Information Canada.

Pipes, S., and M. Walker
   1979   *Tax Facts: The Canadian Tax Index and You*. Vancouver: Fraser Institute.

Thurow, L.
   1975   *Generating Inequality*. New York: Basic Books.

6. *The Distribution of Wealth and Riches*

Lars Osberg

THE DISTRIBUTION OF WEALTH

How unequal is the distribution of wealth? In Canada, our data come primarily from the Survey of Consumer Finances. Table 6-1 presents SCF estimates of the distribution of wealth in Canada in 1970 and 1977.

Of course, there is a vast difference between the relatively wealthy (top 10 percent) and the very rich (top 1 percent). Davies (1979) has made very careful adjustments to the 1970 Statistics Canada figures to correct for errors and omissions in the initial survey, and estimates that the top 10 percent of Canadian families owned 58 percent of all net assets, but of that, roughly a third (19.6 percent) was owned by the top 1 percent of families and over two thirds (43.4 percent) owned

by the top 5 percent. He estimates the inequality of total wealth distribution to be considerably greater than the inequality of income distribution. If we look at the distribution of wealth *per adult* and update Davies' figures for the growth of GNP between 1970 and 1980 we get Table 6-2.

Neither Table 6-1 nor Table 6-2 reveals, however, that some forms of assets are very narrowly held in Canada. The Survey of Consumer Finances states that in 1970, 87.7 percent of Canadian family units reported owning no publicly traded stock at all, while only 3.2 percent reported owning $5000 or more (Statistics Canada, 13-547:105). This evidence may be flawed (see Davies, 1979) but it clearly shows that direct stock ownership is restricted to a very small fragment of Canadian society.

Davies (1979:242) has estimated that stock ownership constitutes only approximately 9 percent of the total assets of Canadian families. Other financial assets include equity in business interests, life insurance and funded pension plans, bonds, and deposits in banks

---

Revised from Lars Osberg, *Economic Inequality in Canada* (Toronto: Butterworths, 1981), pp. 1-2, 7-12, 35-40. Reprinted with permission.

and other financial institutions. For most Canadians, tangible assets such as houses, other real estate, automobiles, and consumer durables are the main form of wealth holdings. Davies is considering, of course, wealth as comprehensively defined, i.e., the value of *all* assets (minus debts) owned by the household. Were the definition narrower, the share of the top 10 percent or top 1 percent would be higher.

THE DISTRIBUTION OF RICHES

Most students consider discussion of definitions to be a bore and accept them uncritically, impatient to get on to the "real thing." This is a great mistake, as apparently quite subtle differences in initial wordings can be magnified by their subsequent logical development into very different perceptions of

TABLE 6-1   The wealth distribution of Canada (as measured by the Survey of Consumer Finance) 1970 and 1977.

| | Family units ranked by wealth | | | | | | Family units ranked by income −Share of net worth− | | |
| | Financial assets | | Total assets | | Net worth | | | | |
Decile	1970	1977	1970	1977	1970	1977	1970	1977	Decile
(Share of) poorest 10%	0.0	0.0	0.0	0.0	− 1.0	− 0.6	4.4	4.0	lowest income 10%
2	0.1	0.1	0.2	0.3	− 0.0	0.1	6.0	5.0	2
3	0.3	0.4	0.6	0.9	0.3	0.6	7.0	6.4	3
4	0.7	0.9	1.4	2.3	1.3	1.7	6.8	6.4	4
5	1.2	1.5	3.2	5.0	3.0	3.6	6.7	7.1	5
6	2.2	2.6	6.3	7.4	5.4	6.0	7.3	7.9	6
7	4.0	4.5	9.6	9.6	8.3	8.6	8.4	9.0	7
8	7.3	8.0	12.7	12.2	11.8	12.0	10.6	10.0	8
9	15.1	15.0	17.5	16.8	17.6	17.5	11.5	12.7	9
(Share of) richest 10%	69.1	67.0	48.5	45.6	53.3	50.6	31.3	31.6	highest income 10%

Financial assets   = deposits, cash, bonds, stocks, mortgages, etc.
Total assets   = financial assets, business equity, real estate, automobiles
Net worth   = total assets − debts.
Source: Oja, 1980:352
NB: The left column refers to decile rankings of family wealth from the poorest (in the top row) to the richest (in the bottom row). The three columns on the right array family units by income deciles, showing the percent of net worth controlled by each decile grouping.

the world around us. In 1977 the median wealth of Canadian family units was estimated by the Survey of Consumer Finances to be $22 298 (Oja, 1980:351), a sum which could easily be accounted for by a car, a small bank balance, and a modest amount of equity in a home. It is likely that many of those Canadians who are in fact in the *top* half of the wealth distribution do not consider themselves to be rich. When most people talk of "the rich" they usually appear to mean other people who have a large amount of money (or assets which can be converted to money) which they can spend as they wish. Suppose, therefore, that we had defined "riches" as an individual's stock of discretionary purchasing power, which might seem an unobjectionable, commonsense idea underlying wealth. We would then have had to define the difference between "discretionary" and "non-discretion-

ary," and might well have adopted the idea that "non-discretionary" expenditures on assets are those expenditures which are socially required by one's occupation or work role.

It is a commonplace observation that some occupations require the ownership of tools (e.g., mechanics) or expensive clothing, and that some positions require entertaining, which mandates a certain size of house and quality of home furnishings. More importantly, some occupations, such as fishing or farming, require the possession of assets for which rental markets in Canada are poorly developed. These assets may be worth a great deal if sold, yet the owners cannot sell without fundamentally changing their occupation and lifestyle. Hence, the owners have a relatively small stock of purchasing power which can be used for personal consumption. The extent to which other owner-

TABLE 6-2 Estimated wealth per Canadian adult*—1980.

	Number (1)	Total net worth (assets–debts) (2)	Share (3)	Per adult (2) ÷ (1)
Top 1%	165 000	$146 361M	18.8%	$887 040
Next 4%	661 000	187 623M	24.1	283 847
Next 5%	826 000	110 549M	14.2	133 837
(Total top 10%)	(1 653 000)	(444 534M)	(57.1)	(268 925)
Next 10%	1 653 000	126 120M	16.2	76 297
(Total top 20%)	(3 306 000)	(570 654M)	(73.3)	(172 611)
Next 40%	6 612 000	200 857M	25.8	30 377
Bottom 40%	6 612 000	6 228M	0.8	1 002
Totals	16 530 000	$778 519M	100.0	47 097

*i.e., wealth per household ÷ number of adults in household; M = million
Sources: Davies (1979); Statistics Canada, 91-202; Bank of Canada 5/80.

ship patterns are socially required would be a grey area of such a definition, but grey areas also exist in the computation of income in kind or of "wealth" in the standard definition. If we adopted the stock of discretionary purchasing power held by an individual as our idea of riches, we would probably have to exclude from its measurement most consumer durables (e.g., automobiles) and a good fraction of farm real estate and housing stock. We would also have to exclude the "transactions balances" which Canadians hold to finance current purchases.

Since most of the assets of the poorest 80 percent of Canadian families are of exactly these types the resulting riches would be distributed more unequally than "financial assets" (column 1 of Table 6-1), which are considerably more unequally distributed than the total wealth of Canadians as conventionally defined. One would then make statements such as: "According to the SCF, over 70 percent of the riches of Canada were owned by the richest 10 percent of family units in 1977," rather than saying: "According to the SCF, 50.6 percent of the wealth

TABLE 6-3   Illustrative list of Canadian companies controlled by five Canadian families (July 1979).

Weston	*Black*	*Thomson*
B. C. Packers	Massey-Ferguson	Thomson Newspapers
Loblaws	Perkins Engines	Hudson's Bay Co.
Weston Bakeries	Argus Corp.	Simpson's
Bowes	Standard Broadcasting	Zellers
Neilson	Dominion Stores	Scottish & York Insurance
Super Valu	General Bakeries	McCallum Transport
Nabob	Hollinger Argus	Fields Stores
Eddy Paper	Labrador Mining	International Thomson
Donlands Dairy	CFRB, CJAD	Woodbridge
& 166* others	& 70* others	& 119* others

Desmarais	*Irving*	
Power Corp.	Irving Oil	
Laurentide Financial	Saint John Shipbuilding	
Canada Steamship	Saint John Pulp and Paper	
Davie Shipbuilding	Consolidated Fisheries	
Consolidated Bathurst	Kent Homes	
Kingsway Transport	Chipman Timber	
Montreal Trust	Atlantic Truck & Trailer	
Great West Life	N.B. Publishing	
Voyageur Colonial	First Maritime Mining	
& 208* others	& 156* others	

*approximate number
Source: Statistics Canada, 61:517 and Calura, special tabulation.

(net worth) of Canada was owned by the richest 10 percent of family units of 1977." Clearly, our idea of the extent of inequality would be considerably altered.

THE GREAT FAMILY FORTUNES OF CANADA

Great family fortunes are clearly an important part of the Canadian picture, as the largest of them are very large by any standards. Table 6-3 provides a partial list of the major companies controlled by the Weston, Black, Thomson, Desmarais, and Irving families. Other families whose companies make the top 100 industries are the Schneider, Webster, Mara, Gordon, Bentley, Prentice, Sobey, McLean, and Child families. Among the top 50 merchandisers of 1979 one can count 20 foreign-controlled enterprises and 26 family firms. In addition to those families already mentioned, they include the Eaton, Steinberg, Wolfe (Oshawa Group), Billes (Canadian Tire), Woodward, Scrymgeour (Westburne), Kay, Posluns

(Dylex), Cohen (General Distributing), Richardson, Reitmans, and Birks families (and a dozen others). Other sectors show the same picture. As many have noted (e.g., Porter, 1965:241), it is a very different picture from the U.S., where dispersal of stock ownership has produced, much more frequently, a separation between ownership and control. After examining the 146 private Canadian-owned companies which had assets of more than $100 million in 1975, Niosi (1978: 167) concludes, "Of the 136 companies for which we possess information, 68 percent are controlled by individuals, groups of associates, or families."

Although these families control, in some cases, billions of dollars in assets and hundreds of millions in annual investment, the probability of any of them being selected in the random sample of 15 000 families from the Canadian population on which wealth distribution statistics are based is nearly zero, and the probability of their co-operating in such a survey is almost certainly even less. Their holdings do not, therefore, appear in the statistics cited in Tables 6-1 and 6-2. They do, however, exist.

REFERENCES

Davies, J. B.
        1979   "On the Size Distribution of Wealth in Canada," *Review of Income and Wealth* (September): 237-60.

Niosi, J.
        1978   *The Economy of Canada*. Montreal: Black Rose.

Porter, J.
        1965   *The Vertical Mosaic*. Toronto: University of Toronto Press.

Oja, G.
        1980   "Inequality of the Wealth Distribution in Canada, 1970 and 1977," *Reflections on Canadian Incomes*. Ottawa: Economic Council of Canada.

Statistics Canada
        Occasional   "Incomes, Assets and Indebtedness of Families in Canada," Cat. No. 13-547.

7. *Poverty in Canada*

National Council of Welfare

DEFINING POVERTY

The most widely used Canadian poverty lines are the "low-income cut-offs" which Statistics Canada employs to produce data on the low-income population. Though Statistics Canada does not regard its low-income cut-offs as poverty lines, the National Council of Welfare follows common practice in using them as poverty lines. We use the terms "poverty line" and "low-income line" interchangeably.

The 1978 Survey of Family Expenditure found that Canadian families spend on average 38.5 percent of their income on food, clothing, and shelter. Since poor families devote an above-average proportion of their limited income to basic necessities, the low-income cut-offs are set at levels where, on average, 58.5 percent of income (20 percentage points above the average) go to the

essentials of life. Any family or single person with an income at or below the relevant poverty line is defined as low-income. (Since the 1982 Survey of Family Expenditure found little significant change in these proportions, Statistics Canada has continued to base its low-income cut-offs on the 58.5 percent criterion.)

Income is defined as money income received by all family members 15 years old and older from the following sources: wages and salaries (before deductions for taxes, pensions, etc.), net income from self-employment, investment income (interest, dividends, rental income, etc.), government transfer payments (e.g., Family Allowances, the Child Tax Credit, Old Age Security, provincial tax credits), pensions (e.g., retirement pensions, annuities and superannuation), and miscellaneous income (e.g., scholarships, alimony). Thus the poverty lines are based on gross rather than net (after-tax) income.

The definition of income excludes the following: gambling wins and losses, capital gains or losses, lump-sum inheritances, receipts from the sale of property or personal

Revised from National Council of Welfare, *1986 Poverty Lines* (Ottawa: Supply and Services, 1986), pp. 1-11. Reprinted with permission.

belongings, income tax refunds, loans received or repaid, lump-sum settlements of insurance policies, and income in kind (e.g., food and fuel produced on one's own farm).

Figure 7-1 is a symbolic representation of how the poverty lines are determined. The slanted line links expenditure on necessities with level of income: the higher the income, the lower the proportion devoted to necessities, for the simple reason that there is more money available to cover the cost of food, clothing, and shelter. In fact higher-income Canadians spend more in absolute terms on necessities, even though that expenditure is low in relative (percentage) terms.

The average family spends 38.5 percent of its income on necessities. To establish the low-income cut-offs, Statistics Canada in effect finds the point on the slanted line where 58.5 percent (38.5 plus 20) of income goes to food, clothing, and shelter and then drops a vertical line down to the income axis (the straight line at the bottom of the graph) to find the level of income that corresponds to the 58.5 percent expenditure. That level of income is termed the "low-income cut-off" (or "poverty line," in everyday speech).

A SET OF POVERTY LINES

There is no single poverty line for all of Canada. To take into account two factors which affect living costs, Statistics Canada varies its low-income cut-offs according to the size of the family and of the place of residence.

There are seven categories of family size ranging from one person to seven or more persons. Communities are divided into five groups according to population: metropolitan areas with half a million or more residents (Vancouver, Edmonton, Calgary, Winnipeg, Hamilton, Toronto, Ottawa, Montreal, and Quebec City), large cities (100 000 to 499 999), medium-sized cities (30 000 to 99 999), smaller centres (cities of 15 000 to 30 000 and small urban areas under 15 000), and rural areas (both farm and non-farm). The result is a set of 35 poverty lines as shown in Table 7-1.

The low-income lines shown in the first three columns of Table 7-1 apply to more than half of the population: six in 10 Canadians live in cities of 30 000 or more. Of these, 41.2 percent are in metropolitan cen-

FIGURE 7-1 Relationship between expenditure on necessities (food, clothing, and shelter) and income

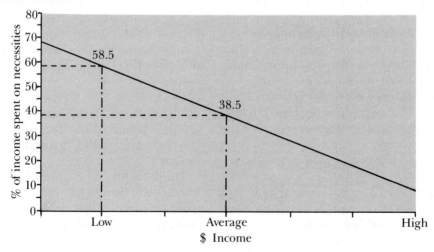

TABLE 7-1 National Council of Welfare estimates of low-income lines for 1987.

	Population of area of residence				
	500 000 and over	*100 000 – 499 999*	*30 000 – 99 999*	*Less than 30 000*	*Rural*
Family size					
1	$11 079	$10 522	$ 9 870	$ 9 126	$ 8 193
2	14 617	13 874	12 944	12 010	10 708
3	19 554	18 529	17 318	16 110	14 338
4	22 532	21 414	20 018	18 621	16 575
5	26 256	24 861	23 185	21 601	19 274
6	28 677	27 094	25 326	23 556	21 042
7 or more	31 564	29 887	27 933	25 977	23 185

tres (half a million or more), 10.5 percent in large cities (100 000 to 499 999) and 8.2 percent in medium-sized cities (30 000 to 99 999). Of the remainder, 15.8 percent are in cities and towns with less than 30 000 residents and 24.3 percent live in rural areas.

THE POVERTY LINES IN CONTEXT

In response to those who believe Statistics Canada's low-income lines are too high, it is worth pointing out that alternate measures produce higher poverty lines. The Canadian Council on Social Development, which sets its poverty line at one half of average family income, published a set of poverty line estimates for 1984 that for the most part exceed Statistics Canada's low-income cut-offs (the latter are higher only for single persons living in cities with 100 000 or more residents). Our estimates indicate that the situation is the same in 1987.

A national survey by Health and Welfare Canada found that aged Canadians reported an average after-tax income of $10 600 as necessary "to cover essential needs" in 1981 —substantially higher than the Statistics Canada low-income lines for one person, which in 1981 ranged from $5949 for rural areas to $8045 for the largest cities. This finding is significant in two ways. First, it shows what a sizeable segment of the population itself regards as a minimally adequate income, as opposed to a poverty line determined according to a formula. Second, the survey indicates that, at least in the eyes of elderly Canadians, the Statistics Canada low-income lines are anything but generous.

Even more telling are results from a Gallup poll taken in March 1986 which asked respondents what they consider "the least amount of money a family of four—husband, wife, and two children—needs each week to get along." The average amount was $400 a week. The average weekly poverty level for a family of four is an estimated $367 in 1986—less than the Gallup result.

In any event, the debate over what is the "right" poverty line and the "real" number of poor people contributes little if anything to an understanding of the economic situation of low-income Canadians. Poverty lines only establish the upper limit of the low-income population. Most poor Canadians live on incomes that are hundreds and more often thousands of dollars under the poverty line.

Few people would regard these incomes as adequate by any standard.

Take, as an illustration, a single mother on welfare who supports one child aged four and lives in the largest city in her province. Her family's total income from provincial social assistance, refundable tax credits, federal family allowances, and the child tax credit ranged from 63 percent to 85 percent of the poverty line in 1986, depending on her province of residence. If she lives in Toronto, her income in 1986 was about $10 230, which represents just 62 percent of the amount the Social Planning Council of Metropolitan Toronto considers necessary for her family to maintain "an adequate but modest" standard of living.

The 1986 adult minimum wage ranged from $3.65 an hour in British Columbia to $5.00 an hour in the Northwest Territories. (A typical rate was $4.00 an hour, payable in Newfoundland, Prince Edward Island, Nova Scotia, and New Brunswick, and in industries within federal jurisdiction.) A worker in Nova Scotia paid the provincial minimum wage ($4.00 an hour) earned $8320 in 1987 from a full-time year-round job. For all but rural parts of the province, this wage was below the poverty line, which ranges from $10 522 for Halifax to $8193 for rural communities. After paying federal and provincial income taxes, Canada Pension Plan contributions, and unemployment insurance premiums, the minimum wage worker took home only $7426.

An estimated 3 951 000 Canadians—one in six—lived on low incomes in 1985, the most recent year for which data are available. This figure represents a substantial increase of 476 000 men, women, and children over 1980. There are 908 000 families and 1 009 000 unattached individuals with incomes below the poverty line. Over a million children under 16—1 126 000 or one in five—are in low-income families.

Unattached elderly Canadians (i.e., the aged who live alone or in a household where they are not related to other members) run a very high risk of poverty. Almost half (46.8 percent or 356 000 women and men) were poor at last count. Six in every 10 women under age 65 who are single parents raise their children on an income below the poverty line.

Poor Canadians have incomes substantially below average. The poverty line for a family of four is less than half of the average income for a family of four. The low-income line for one person living in a metropolitan area is 47 percent of the average wage. Keep in mind that most poor people have incomes that are significantly less than the poverty line, so that the income gap between them and the average Canadian is even wider.

Figures 7-2 and 7-3 illustrate the "depth of poverty." They divide low-income Canadians into three groups—those with incomes below half the poverty line, those between one-half and three-quarters the poverty line and those with incomes between three-quarters the poverty line and the full poverty line. (The data are for 1982, the most recent available as we went to press.)

Figure 7-2 shows that the majority of low-income families and unattached individuals are below three quarters of the poverty line. Twenty-four percent of poor unattached individuals have incomes under half the poverty line and 33 percent are from one-half to three-quarters the low-income line. More than half of low-income childless couples (54.4 percent) fall between three-quarters the poverty line and the full poverty line. Single mothers, by contrast, are concentrated at the bottom of the income ladder—25 percent live below one-half the poverty level and another 46 percent are from half to three quarters of the line.

Figure 7-3 examines the depth of poverty for men and women. Two poor unattached men in three have incomes under 75 percent of the poverty line, in contrast to only

FIGURE 7-2   Depth of poverty, by family characteristics, 1982

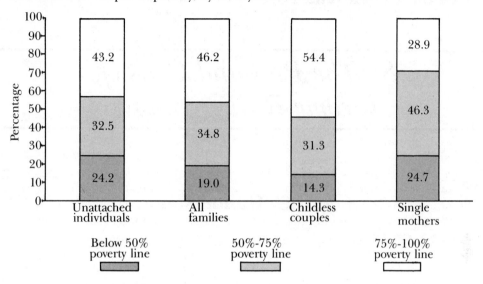

FIGURE 7-3   Depth of poverty, by sex, 1982

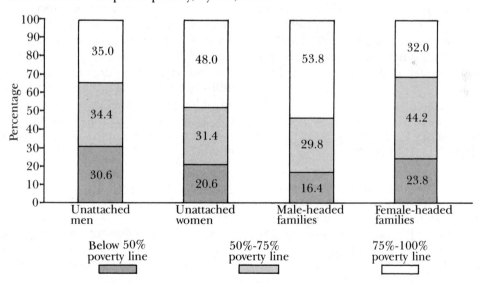

one poor unattached woman in two. As expected, low-income families led by women are worse off than those headed by men. More than half of male-headed poor families (54 percent) have incomes above three-quarters the low-income line. However most (68 percent) female-led families are below three-quarters the poverty line; 24 percent are very poor (under half the line).

---

8. The Pros and Cons of Income Redistribution

Morley Gunderson

Arguments about income redistribution often evoke emotional responses, because the well-being of individuals is involved and because the position of the debaters is often dependent upon where they themselves are on the income distribution scale. Whatever the motives, numerous arguments for and against income redistribution have been advanced.

ARGUMENTS FOR REDISTRIBUTION

In dealing with the arguments in favour of more equitable income distribution it is useful to distinguish between two interrelated issues. One is the normative issue of why income redistribution *should* occur; the other is the positive issue of why it *does* occur. Income redistribution may well occur

Revised from Morley Gunderson, *Economics of Poverty and Income Distribution* (Toronto: Butterworths, 1983), pp. 13-21. Reprinted with permission.

for reasons other than to satisfy a set of principles upon which society deems it should occur. The following arguments in favour of redistribution are advanced sometimes to explain why redistribution should occur, sometimes to explain why it does occur, and at other times to explain both. The first two arguments—diminishing marginal utility of income and underconsumption—are seldom advanced today; they are discussed because historically they have been advanced as arguments in favour of redistribution.

Diminishing Marginal Utility of Income

Early welfare economists advocated a move toward a more equal distribution of income on the grounds that the marginal utility of income of the rich was less than the marginal utility of income to the poor. Therefore, total utility or welfare could be increased by redistributing from the rich (who valued the income less) to the poor (who valued it more). This intuitively reasonable principle followed from the economic principle of diminishing marginal utility; that is, for a given individual the additional utility generated by an additional unit of consumption decreases as more of the commodity is consumed.

While it may be reasonable to assume that this principle eventually applies to the consumption activities of a given individual, there is no scientific basis upon which to make the comparison across individuals: interpersonal comparisons of utility are not valid.

It may well be reasonable to assume that an extra dollar to a rich person means less than an extra dollar to a poor person, even though one could never formally prove that statement. Decisions often have to be made on the basis of beliefs that cannot be proven; for this reason, the concept of diminishing marginal utility of income may not be a bad rule of thumb.

Underconsumptionist View

To the extent that the poor consume a greater portion of their incomes than do the rich, redistribution from the rich to the poor could increase consumption—and hence aggregate demand—in the economy. This view has taken on particular appeal in periods of depression: redistributing from the rich who save to the poor who consume would help the economy spend its way out of the depression. The argument is in contrast to the one often advanced today that tax cuts to the rich would encourage them to invest (thereby improving the ability of the economy to produce without inflationary pressures), and this spending would eventually trickle down to the poor in the form of job opportunities and lower product prices.

While the underconsumptionist view has some intuitive appeal, there are a number of problems with the argument. First, it is not always clear that aggregate demand should be increased; in inflationary times the opposite forces may be needed. Constantly changing the income distribution so as to achieve macroeconomic objectives of having just the right amount of aggregate demand could clearly be dangerous. Second, if the objective is to change aggregate demand, then there are other well-known policy instruments, such as monetary and fiscal policies, to achieve the objective; there is no need to tinker with the income distribution. Third and most important, it is not clear what redistribution would do to aggregate consumption in the economy. Redistribution involves *changes* in income and, while the poor may well consume a larger portion of their *level* of income, it is not clear that they would consume a larger portion of small changes in that income.

It is hazardous to support redistribution on the ground that it will have a desirable effect on aggregate demand in the economy; numerous hidden assumptions are involved for it to have such an impact. In recent years this rationale has also lost much of its effect because higher aggregate demand has not always been desirable owing to its inflationary impact. For these reasons the underconsumption view or the diminishing marginal utility of income idea tend not to be advanced today as rationales for redistribution.

Interdependent Utility

An economic efficiency rationale for redistribution can occur if potential donors (e.g., rich persons) care about the welfare of potential recipients (e.g., poor persons); that is, if the utility of the rich is a function not only of their own welfare but also of the welfare of others. Such benevolence or interdependent utility means that the donors can be made better off when the recipients are better off.

Unfortunately, such redistribution will not occur automatically through the marketplace because of the public-goods nature of redistribution. There would be insufficient incentive for an individual who cares about the poor to give to the poor, because the benefits of that redistribution would also go to other individuals who care about the poor but who do not give to the poor. In such circumstances it would make sense for the potential donors to vote for a certain amount of redistribution and to pay for that by taxes upon themselves. In that way they can share the costs of the redistribution they desire. The public-goods nature of redistribution implies that it may have to occur through the public sector under its tax system rather than through the private sector and its marketplace.

Donors may not only care about the welfare of the recipients; they may also care about the things that make up the welfare of the recipients. For example, donors may not value an increase in the leisure of the poor, but they may attach considerable weight to the poor spending on education, shelter, or food for their children. In such circumstances efficient redistribution may involve transfers-in-kind of these items rather than unconditional lump-sum transfers that the poor can use as they want.

Buy Behaviour and Avoid Conflict

Redistribution may also be seen as a device to influence the behaviour of the recipients, usually in the hope of reducing conflict between the rich and the poor. It can be used, for example, to avoid rioting, or in the extreme, revolution. Although the "War on Poverty" in the United States was conceived prior to the rioting in the 1960s, some would regard the substantial social expenditures at

that time as attempts to bribe the poor to end the rioting. Marxists often regard redistribution (e.g., from land reform or from social expenditures) as a way of buying off the working classes in an attempt to thwart ultimate revolution. Such is especially the case if the redistribution is to those who pose the main threat, for example, potential leaders.

Buy Insurance

Redistribution to influence the behaviour of the poor can be thought of as insurance against consequences such as rioting or revolution, with taxes on the donors being the insurance premium. Donors may also want redistribution so as to guarantee a certain income floor in case *they themselves* should become poor. In this case they are insuring not against the behaviour of others but rather against a possible calamity that may happen to them. For this reason, donors may support, for example, certain programs like welfare, health care, or unemployment insurance.

Voting and the Political Process

The importance of voting and the political process has already been alluded to in the discussion of the rationales for income redistribution. Basically the political process was seen as a device to set up taxes and transfers through the public sector, since the private marketplace would not guarantee the income distribution desired by society—the socially optimal distribution. Individuals were seen as willing to tax themselves so as to provide redistribution transfers because donors simply cared about the recipients, wanted to buy the good behaviour of the recipients, or wanted to buy the insurance in case they themselves became poor.

The political process, however, may also be used in a more narrow self-interested fashion for voters to redistribute income in their favour. Downs (1957), for example, argued that individuals form political coalitions so that the state will redistribute income in their favour. Since the average income is inflated by the very high income of a few very rich people, more people will have an income that is below, rather than above, average. In seeking to maximize the probability of being reelected, politicians will try to obtain the support of the mass of voters with below-average incomes by redistributing in their favour.

This process may be offset, in part at least, by other factors. The rich, having the most to lose, will try to control the political process through mechanisms other than the "one-person one-vote" procedure which gives them little influence. They may use their wealth and influence to support a candidate; they may support policies to restrict the voting franchise to those with property; and they may support amending formulas requiring more than a majority vote. The rich may also try to "bribe" some of the lower-income groups out of a coalition that would involve mass redistribution. The poor themselves may not always support such coalitions because they feel they themselves will be upwardly mobile.

Marxists tend to emphasize that the rich will use the instruments of the state to maintain their position and prevent redistribution through the voting mechanism. Hence, transfers to the poor will be used selectively to co-opt revolution, and public expenditures on such items as the police and military will be used by the rich to protect their privileged position. In such circumstances the political process may be used to redistribute from the rich to the poor; however, in general it will be used to redistribute from the poor to the rich.

Raise Income of Providers of Redistribution

Redistribution may also be supported to raise the income of those whose jobs and livelihood depend upon the redistribution *process* (as opposed to recipients who receive the transfers and donors who pay). In some cases this may be an obvious motive, for example, in the case of rich countries providing conditional aid to poor countries (on the condition that they use it to make purchases in the donor country), or providing transfers-in-kind such as farm produce or military equipment. In such circumstances the objective of the donor is probably a mixed one: to provide aid but to provide it in a form that benefits the donor country.

The motivation may be more subtle, for example, in the case of government employees whose jobs depend upon the redistribution process. (It is probably no accident that voters in Washington, D.C., tended not to support Reagan in the 1980 United States election.) Other groups, such as social workers (and even economists who do research in the area of income redistribution!), may also depend for their livelihood on the redistribution process. That is not to say that they would support income redistribution programs mainly to increase their own incomes; however, it certainly is easier to support redistribution when it is consistent with one's self-interest.

Social Contract Perspective

While theories of social justice (e.g., Rawls, 1971) are mainly concerned with the issue of developing a set of first principles for determining how income ought to be distributed in society, and often with critically assessing the market as one instrument of income distribution, they can provide a rationale for redistribution within a market perspective.

That is, income redistribution may be supported on the grounds that it is part of a social contract. We may simply prefer a society that provides a reasonable degree of equality to one that does not provide any. As Rawls (1971) suggested, if we were risk averse and had no information on where we could be in the income redistribution, we might well agree to a social contract that guaranteed a degree of equality. The fact that some individuals would not currently support such a notion simply reflects that they know where they are in the income distribution, and hence would not support redistribution from themselves to others. If they did not know whether they were going to be rich or poor, however, they might well support a social contract involving redistribution.

In this context the social contract can be thought of as a form of insurance. It is a set of principles that we agree to be bound by, presumably because the existence of the contract makes society better off than it would be without the contract—even though the contract may turn out to make some individuals worse off than they would be without the contract, once their position in society is determined or changes.

ARGUMENTS AGAINST REDISTRIBUTION

Incentive Problem

The main concern with income redistribution probably stems from its possible effect on incentives, and hence on economic growth and the size of the pie to be distributed. The concern is that if public policy taxes the rich to make transfers to the poor, then the work incentives of the rich and poor may be reduced.

The rich may have less incentive to work or invest because their earnings from these activities are being taxed. The poor may also have less incentive to work because they can afford not to, and because they often have to give up some of their transfer payments when they work.

While there may be counterarguments as to why these effects are theoretically or quantitatively not important, or at least overemphasized, the fact remains that they can be important. In the extreme, if redistribution were to guarantee complete equality of income, what would be the incentive to work or invest? While existing redistribution schemes are not designed to achieve complete equality, the fact remains that their redistribution toward equality can have effects on the incentive to work or invest; these effects may reduce economic growth and hence the size of the economic pie available.

For this reason, those who are concerned with the adverse incentive problem tend to emphasize that it is easier to share a growing economic pie than to share one that is dwindling because redistribution reduces incentives. Their belief is that the best way to raise the income of the poor is not through redistribution but rather through attaining growth through economic efficiency. This belief that the benefits of growth will "trickle down" to the poor is exemplified by the statement of goals in the *First Annual Review* of the Economic Council of Canada (1964:200): "The most effective 'war on poverty' will be effective achievement of potential output. . . . Steady economic growth would also make possible significant improvements in standards for low-income groups, and provide rising margins of income and resources over time for further advances toward more comprehensive and adequate services and facilities in the social welfare field."

Encroachment of the State

Concerns are also expressed over the fact that redistribution involves an encroachment of the state in areas where some feel that individuals or the family should be the principal decision-making unit. This can give rise to "state sovereignty" over "consumer sovereignty" and it can lead to the redistribution process being demeaning to the self-respect of recipients. It can give rise to large administrative costs that support public employees administering the redistribution. These costs may be irreversible and not necessarily responsive to the needs of the poor once a bureaucracy becomes entrenched.

Perverse Redistribution

Redistribution may end up benefiting the well-to-do more than the needy; in that sense it becomes perverse. This may occur not only because those who administer the redistribution may depend upon it for their livelihood (and they may be well-to-do professionals), but also because those who need the redistribution least may be better able than those who need it most to appropriate the benefits of redistribution. In addition, some universal programs designed to benefit everyone may in fact go disproportionately to high-income families, if, for example, they live longer to receive pensions or if they have larger families to receive family allowances.

Some people may be poor because they lack the skills to make themselves eligible for income transfers. On the other hand, those who are skilled at making themselves eligible for transfer payments may be the least in need because they can utilize their skills elsewhere to earn a reasonable income. They are also the ones most likely to be able to obtain information on the availability of transfers and how best to become eligible, and they are probably more skilled at hiding their long-term position of wealth as opposed to their short-term low income.

As a result, there is some concern that income distribution programs beginning with the best intentions may evolve into perverse redistribution as those least in need are best able to take advantage of the programs. This argument is not so much against the principle of redistribution but rather against what redistribution may evolve into. It becomes an argument against redistribution if such an evolution is inevitable.

REFERENCES

Downs, A.
    1957   *An Economic Theory of Democracy.* New York: Harper and Row.
Economic Council of Canada
    1964   *First Annual Review: Economic Goals for Canada to 1970.* Ottawa: Queen's Printer.
Rawls, J.
    1971   *A Theory of Justice.* Cambridge, Mass.: Belknap Press.

FOR FURTHER READING

Anisef, Paul, and Etta Baichman. 1984. *What Jobs Pay: The Complete Guide to Careers and Salaries in Canada*. Edmonton: Hurtig. A compendium of facts and figures on the wages for various jobs, showing changes over time and comparisons between different occupations. More useful as a source of ideas and data than as a sociological analysis.

Blackley, Alan, and Anne Usher. 1984. *Not Enough: The Meaning and Measurement of Poverty in Canada*. Ottawa: Canadian Council for Social Development. A readable, sobering account of poverty in Canada, focussed on the debates over how poverty should best be measured and how extensive poverty is in this country. The report is based on a national task force which held public meetings in various Canadian locales.

Francis, Diane. 1986. *Controlling Interest: Who Owns Canada?* Toronto: Macmillan. Assessing the degree of concentration in the ownership of Canadian businesses, Diane Francis reveals the extent of wealth controlled by 32 families: their combined assets exceeded $122 billion in 1985. The book is a journalistic account of wealth in this country, rich in detail and description.

Statistics Canada. *Income Distributions by Size in Canada*. Ottawa: Ministry of Supply and Services. This annual report presents the most recent data on income distributions in Canada. The statistics are derived from the annual Survey of Consumer Finances conducted by Statistics Canada.

Vaillancourt, François. 1985. *Income Distribution and Economic Security in Canada*. Toronto: University of Toronto Press. One of the research reports for the Macdonald Commission. This collection of essays provides a mixed review of economic security indicators (e.g., pensions, tax burdens, health care). The opening essay by Vaillancourt is an excellent overview of a range of issues relevant to the distribution of income.

9. Jobs and the Labour Market

Graham S. Lowe

Basic to a capitalist economy is a market in which commodities are bought and sold. Labour, too, becomes a commodity and is subjected to market forces. A labour market in which workers are recruited by employers to fill vacant jobs is a prerequisite for the emergence and growth of capitalism. Following Edwards (1975:5), we will define a labour market as encompassing "those specific mechanisms and institutions through which the purchase and sale of labour power is arranged." In short, it is the vehicle for allocating workers to jobs. Ideally, this process matches a worker's experience, skills, and education with the requirements of a vacant job. In reality, however, the labour market operates to perpetuate existing social inequalities. A person's job is crucial to

his or her present socio-economic status and, indeed, future "life chances." The purpose of this chapter, then, is to illuminate how the labour market contributes to stratification in Canadian society.

INTERNAL AND EXTERNAL LABOUR MARKETS

It is useful to distinguish between two kinds of labour markets: external markets, which exist outside organizations, and internal markets, which operate within the confines of large bureaucratic organizations (see Osterman, 1984). External markets operate through the classified job advertisements in newspapers and through employment agencies. Internal markets, on the other hand, are found in large corporations or state bureaucracies, where vacancies above a certain level are filled from within by existing employees. Those organizations have specified "ports of entry," usually at the bottom of the job hierarchy. Once inside, an

Revised by the author from his "The Nature of Work and the Productive Process," in J. Paul Grayson (ed.), *Introduction to Sociology: An Alternate Approach* (Toronto, Gage Publishing Co., 1983). Reprinted with permission.

individual is "sheltered" from outside competition (see Ashton, 1986, ch.3). Thus, a principal characteristic of internal markets is the job ladder. This refers to: orderly and predictable career progression; job postings and a bidding system for filling vacancies internally; an emphasis on individual merit in hiring and promotion; and training and development programs designed to tap the "human potential" of employees, in the hope they will make a long-term commitment to the organization.

Katherine Stone (1974) has examined the origins of internal labour markets in major U.S. steel companies. Contemporary job structures emerged during the 1890-1920 period. A new system of employee administration was implemented, based on three facets: wage incentive schemes, such as bonus payments; promotion hierarchies, so that workers could have some degree of upward mobility within the firm; and welfare programs to look after the non-monetary needs of workers. These changes brought some improvements in working conditions. But, according to Stone, their more fundamental aims were to increase worker productivity and prevent collective opposition to managerial authority. Stone (1974:128) explains that "to solve the labour problem, employers developed strategies to break down the basis for a unity of interests among workers, and to convince them that, as individuals, their interests were identical with those of their company." The new payment and promotion systems, for instance, rewarded individual effort. This encouraged workers to be "out for themselves," seeking individual solutions to work problems.

In examining the creation of internal labour markets, or job shelters, it is necessary to begin with the transitional period leading up to capitalism. Looking at pre-Confederation Canada, Pentland (1959; 1981) examines how workers were induced to flow into a formal labour market and, once there, how they were prevented from leaving. A precapitalist economy is typified by a shortage of both wage labourers and industrial jobs. This situation fosters paternalistic arrangements between emergent industrial employers and employees. In Canadian industry, this personal employment relationship prevailed prior to the 1850s.

On one hand, the scarcity of wage labour inhibited industrialization. But, on the other hand, it can be noted with some irony that conditions were ripe for the creation of a capitalist labour market in colonial Canada by the 1840s (Teeple, 1972). A lack of cheap, arable land swelled the ranks of the propertyless unemployed. But because wage work was scarce, many migrated to the U.S., where either peasant farming or factory employment were viable alternatives.

Railway construction during the 1850s, coupled with massive inflows of Irish peasants who were too poor to acquire farm land, helped form the first permanent labour pool. The railways also attracted skilled artisans (a group already committed to wage work) from England. Increased agricultural productivity, land shortages, and immigration—all of which swelled the ranks of the urban working class—aided the creation of a labour market and an "industrial reserve army." This army, which included the underemployed as well as the unemployed, assured expanding enterprises of a steady labour supply.

LABOUR MARKET SEGMENTATION

According to labour economists, the labour market is essentially one massive pool of individuals who are shunted in and out of jobs by the forces of supply and demand. The only things differentiating workers are varying skill, educational and experience levels (human capital), and geographic location. Workers supposedly make "rational" choices, attempting to maximize their economic gains given their bargaining power. In sum, this "human capital" theory of the market emphasizes how supply and demand for labour tend toward an equilibrium, in which workers are matched with jobs on the basis of their human capital endowments (see Ostry and Zaidi, 1971).

An alternative to this perspective has been developed since the early 1970s. Known as segmentation theory, or dual labour market theory, this approach is more sociological (see Clairmont et al., 1983). The image of a homogeneous labour market is rejected as being, among other things, too simplistic. The market is reconceptualized as composed of a number of unequal and relatively impermeable segments. These segments reflect inequalities among workers and are linked directly to the labour process within firms.

Segmentation theory assumes that the advance of corporate capitalism since 1900 has fragmented a once fairly uniform working class. By rationalizing the labour process within firms, breaking down tasks into simplified parts, capitalists have divided the labour market according to distinct occupational characteristics, employee behaviours, and working conditions. Workers in one segment tend to compete among themselves, not with those in other segments, for jobs. Mobility between segments is made difficult by institutional barriers. Occupations at the bottom of the job ladder, or in small firms in highly competitive industries, demand fewer skills and less commitment from the employee than do upper-level technical or professional jobs. Discrete markets

thus are created for each type of worker. A worker's position in the labour market reflects his or her position within the firm's labour process. Workers in each segment tend to have similar characteristics. Hence, one finds different submarkets containing, for example, educated white males, ethnic minorities, or women. Employers use these worker traits to determine suitability for a given job. (See Edwards et al., 1975; Edwards, 1979; Gordon, Edwards and Reich, 1982; Kalleberg, 1983; Baron and Bielby, 1984; Garnsey et al., 1985; Hirsch, 1981.)

The different experiences of men and women in the workplace attest to the existence of unequal labour market segments. Women historically have been concentrated in a handful of unrewarding occupations mainly in the sales, service, and clerical areas. These are often referred to as "job ghettos." Strong barriers to employment of women in male-dominated managerial and professional jobs have only recently begun to weaken. Even so, the structure of the labour market militates against equality of earnings and opportunities for men and women. Sex-based inequalities are not the product of a "free market" in labour. On the contrary, they are a direct result of how employers have built into the organization of the labour process sex-linked characteristics which specify whether a male or a female is more appropriate for a given job. These issues will be examined in greater detail below.

Segmentation theory makes a further distinction between core and periphery firms. Core firms are the large corporations which dominate key resource, manufacturing, and service industries. Examples would include multinational corporations, such as General Motors and Imperial Oil, and major Canadian banks and insurance firms. The sheer size, market dominance, and profitability of these corporations allow them to create employment conditions which foster employment stability. Through internal labour markets, attractive job conditions are provided to create a stable work force. Firms in the competitive and labour-intensive industries at the periphery of the economy cannot afford to pay the price, in terms of high wages and generous benefits, for a stable work force. Moreover, they often do not require this type of employee behaviour, because much of the work is unskilled and routine.

MARGINAL AND CENTRAL WORK WORLDS

Researchers at Dalhousie University in Halifax use a segmentation model to explain how poverty is linked to the operations of a labour market in the Maritimes (Clairmont et al., 1980). A large portion of poor families in the Maritimes are headed by individuals who are employed for at least part of the year. Their poverty stems from lack of access to well-paying jobs. Social inequality, then, can be seen as a direct result of the prevalence of low-wage work in a region.

The researchers extend the core and periphery concepts outlined above to include occupations, in addition to establishments. This broader approach is captured in their use of the terms *marginal work world* and *central work world*. Workers in the marginal work world find it very difficult, if not impossible, to enter the central work world. The marginal work world includes occupations and places of employment which provide "for a majority of their work force or membership, employment packages characterized by low wages, limited fringe benefits, little job security, and restricted internal advancement opportunities . . ."

(Clairmont et al., 1980:290). Small, labour-intensive firms, and unorganized self-employed groups which serve a limited market fall into this category. Examples include textile plants, taxi drivers, motels, sawmills, and food processing plants. Even though some of these firms may be owned by giant corporations, their poor employment conditions confirm their marginal status.

In contrast, central work world establishments offer "high wages, extensive fringe benefits, internal career ladders, and job security provisions" (Clairmont et al., 1980:290). Both employers and employees in this category are powerful. Firms are able to meet demands for improved wages and working conditions because of their dominant market position. Employees have sufficient bargaining power to extract these conditions through their trade unions or professional associations. Included in this sector would be governments and large private corporations such as coal mines, petroleum refineries, auto assembly plants, and pulp and paper operations, as well as self-employed professionals and unionized skilled craftsworkers.

Clairmont and his colleagues argue that the inequalities identified by their model are "normal" under capitalism. They originate because of differences in economic power between workers and their employers. The key distinction between working conditions in the marginal and the central work worlds concerns employment stability. Central work world firms, because of their control of the product market, can offer attractive employment conditions which foster stability. In contrast, marginal firms are unable to do this because of the largely seasonal or fluctuating nature of their activity, low training costs and the resulting ease of replacing workers, or low capital investment.

OCCUPATIONAL CHANGES IN CANADA

An overview of historical changes in the composition of the labour force provides a solid empirical foundation for studying transformations in the labour process. Using data from the decennial censuses and the monthly *Labour Force* survey, we can trace the spread of wage labour, the growth or decline of major occupational groups, and shifts in the labour force among industries.

To begin, let us examine what changes have occurred in the distribution of workers across industries. As capitalism develops, labour moves out of agriculture, into manufacturing, and, especially since World War II, toward services. Precapitalist societies have predominantly agricultural labour forces. Advanced capitalist nations, including Canada, are called *service societies*, because the majority of workers are employed in the white-collar service sector. The proportion of the working population engaged in agriculture has steadily declined in Canada, from 50 percent in 1871 to 4.2 percent in 1986. However, only part of the shift away from agricultural employment was absorbed by manufacturing industries. Only 13.1 percent of the labour force was engaged in manufacturing in 1871 (Smucker, 1980:78). This figure had almost doubled by 1951. But Table 9-1 shows a steady shift in employment away from manufacturing between 1951 and 1986 (a decline of 9.2 percentage points).

This more recent decline in manufacturing can be attributed to technological advances which have permitted fewer workers to produce greater quantities of goods. At

TABLE 9-1   Changes in the industrial distribution of the total labour force, Canada, 1951 and 1986.

Industry	1951	1986	Net shift 1951-1986
	%	%	(percentage points)
Agriculture	18.4	4.2	− 16.2
Forestry, fishing, and trapping	2.9	0.9	− 2.0
Mines, quarries, and oil wells	1.5	1.6	− 0.1
Manufacturing	26.5	17.3	− 9.2
Construction	6.8	5.4	− 1.4
Transportation, communication, and other utilities	8.8	7.7	− 1.1
Trade	14.1	17.9	+ 3.8
Finance, insurance, and real estate	3.0	5.6	+ 2.6
Community, business, and personal service	18.0	32.5	+ 14.5
Public administration	—	6.9	+ 6.9
	(100.0)	(100.0)	
Total number in the labour force (000)	5 097	11 634	

Source: Statistics Canada, *Perspectives Canada III* (Ottawa: Supply and Services, 1980), Table 5.12, p.92 (for 1951); Statistics Canada, *The Labour Force*, December 1986 (Ottawa: catalogue 71-001 monthly), Table 71, p.105 (for 1986).

the same time, increased affluence and more leisure time have spawned a vast array of service industries. As Table 9-1 demonstrates, the greatest employment increases in the post-World War II period have occurred in services, public administration, trade, and finance. This signifies the development of a service society.

The changing industrial distribution of the labour force is clearly revealed through its occupational composition. The growth in service industries just noted indicates that more and more people have been entering white-collar employment. Figure 9-1 suggests that a dramatic shift has occurred since

1901. The decline in manual, or blue-collar, work has been more than offset by a growth in white-collar, or "mental," labour. At the turn of the century roughly 15 percent of the labour force performed white-collar jobs. Yet by 1986 these jobs accounted for about half of the labour force. Manual jobs, mostly in manufacturing, have declined somewhat in relative numbers since 1901. In contrast, employment in primary occupations—mainly farming—has plunged from about 45 percent in 1901 to around 5 percent in 1986. This largely is the result of the transformation of agriculture through technology, more scientific techniques, and the

FIGURE 9-1 Changes in the occupational composition of the total labour force, Canada, 1901–81

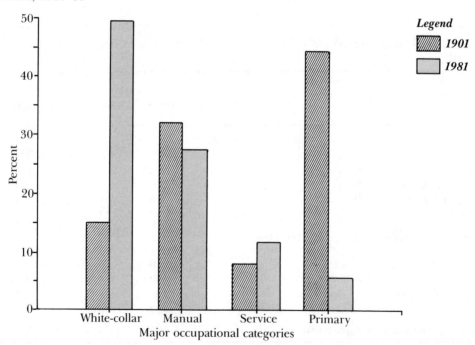

Source: Calculated from N. M. Meltz, *Manpower in Canada: Historical Statistics of the Canadian Labour Force* (Ottawa: Queen's Printer, 1969), Table A.1, p.58 (for 1901); *1981 Census of Canada* (Catalogue no. 92-920), Vol. 1, Table 1 (for 1981).

rise of corporate farming. Finally, service occupations have undergone a slight increase since the turn of the century. Service occupations include jobs such as firefighter, police officer, hairdresser and barber, cleaner, janitor, and security guard, which fall between the manual and the white-collar categories.

The growth of white-collar employment is associated with many important social changes. Generally it denotes the emergence of a large urban middle class. For some observers, white-collar work may also signal an upgrading of job conditions. Certainly the number of professional, technical, scientific, and managerial jobs has mushroomed. And many of these jobs are challenging and rewarding. But just because white-collar work is, as we noted above, mental rather than manual does not mean that office workers, for instance, are any less alienated or dissatisfied with their working conditions than are factory workers (see Rinehart, 1987, ch.4). In fact, for the average white-collar worker the rewards are meagre and the work monotonous. Clerical work is now the largest occupational group, employing 17 percent of all workers in 1986 (Statistics Canada, December 1986:105). Some clerical jobs are highly automated and regimented, resembling a paper-processing assembly-line.

Finally, we should make note of the extension of wage labour since 1900. Independent farmers, small entrepreneurs, and housewives have been increasingly drawn into wage employment. If we examine the agricultural sector, we discover that the proportion of owner-operators has declined from 72.6 percent in 1911 to 50.4 percent by 1971 (Johnson, 1980:94). In terms of the total labour force, self-employed workers comprised 13.5 percent in 1984 (Macredie, 1985:89). The vast majority of Canadians, then, are employees in business or government bureaucracies and, as such, must take orders from people above them in the hierarchy.

WOMEN'S EMPLOYMENT

Perhaps the most dramatic change in the character of the labour force since 1900 has been the rising participation rate of women. In 1901 the female labour force participation rate stood at 16.1 percent.[1] This participation rate shot steadily upward, spurred by labour shortages which women helped alleviate during both world wars, to 40.9 percent by 1975 (Canada, 1977:112). This upward trend still continues. By 1986, 55.1 percent of all adult women were gainfully employed outside the home (Statistics Canada, December 1986:84). Many social and economic factors underlie this rising female participation rate. Most notable are a tendency for greater numbers of wives to return to paid work after raising a family; an historically low birth rate; liberalized social norms regarding gender roles; expanding employment opportunities for women, especially in the service sector; rising female educational attainment; and higher female career aspirations (see Lowe and Krahn, 1985).

Historically, women have performed a critical, albeit unrecognized, role in the economy.[2] For example, Indian women directly contributed to the success of the fur trade by providing traders with a link between western and Indian cultures. Native women acted as interpreters, prepared food, and cleaned pelts for shipment to markets (Van Kirk, 1977). Little wonder that fur traders took Indian women as wives. Similarly, pioneer women performed essential chores in the toiler society of pre-Confederation Canada. While the males worked the fields, the women of a family performed all domestic tasks, from child-rearing, to tending the livestock and the garden, to spinning yarn for clothes. The death of a wife was a great economic blow to the subsistence farmer, making quick remarriage an act of survival (Johnson, 1974:16-17).

Beginning in the late nineteenth century women and children were recruited into the industrial work force as cheap, unskilled labour. The 1891 census, the first to break down occupational data by sex, reports only 11.4 percent of the female population over the age of 10 as gainfully employed. This percentage comprised 12.6 percent of the entire labour force (Lowe, 1980:363). The concentration of women into a handful of

unrewarding, dead-end occupations has been characteristic of female employment since the 1890s. These are referred to as female job ghettos.

Table 9-2 documents that in 1901 most women worked as domestic servants, teachers, seamstresses, or office clerks. (That "farmers and stockraisers" were listed among the leading female occupations probably reflects the direct role of many farm wives in the largely agricultural 1901 economy.) The current picture of female employment is strikingly different. By 1981 domestic work had been replaced by clerical work as the largest female occupation. Women are less concentrated within manufacturing and increasingly employed in the service sector. While the latter trend reflects

TABLE 9-2   The five leading female occupations, Canada, 1901 and 1981.

Occupation	Number of women employed	% of total female labour force in occupation	Females as % of total labour force in occupation
		1901	
1. Domestic servants	84 984	35.7	87.4
2. Seamstresses	32 145	13.5	100.0
3. School teachers	30 870	13.0	78.2
4. Office clerks	12 569	5.3	21.4
5. Farmers and stockraisers	8 495	3.6	1.9
	TOTAL	71.1	
		1981	
1. Secretaries and stenographers	368 025	7.4	98.9
2. Bookkeepers and accounting clerks	332 325	6.6	81.9
3. Tellers and cashiers	229 320	4.6	92.7
4. Waitresses, hostesses and stewards, food and beverage	200 710	4.0	85.7
5. Graduate nurses	167 710	3.4	95.4
	TOTAL	26.0	

Source: Canada, Dominion Bureau of Statistics, *Occupational Trends in Canada, 1901-1931* (Ottawa, 1939), Table 8; Statistics Canada, 1981 Census, Labour Force—Occupation Trends (catalogue number 92-920).

changes in the total labour force, it is more pronounced for women: 78 percent of female employees compared with 49 percent of male employees worked in service industries in 1984 (Labour Canada, 1986:16). However, within services women are still typically employed in the least desirable jobs. Over one third of all working women, including many female university graduates, occupy clerical positions.[3]

The current occupational distribution of males and females is presented in Table 9-3. The data show the effects of sex-based oc-cupational segregation. Barriers are constructed using sex-specific job definitions and requirements which channel women into certain jobs while restricting their entry into others. For example, there are few women in mining, trapping, forestry, fishing, construction, engineering, scientific, agricultural, managerial, or professional jobs, all of which are widely accepted as "men's work." In contrast, women predominate in clerical, service, teaching, social science, and medicine and health fields—areas traditionally considered appropriate female

TABLE 9-3 Employment concentration of women, Canada, 1984.

Occupation	Women as a percentage of the total labour force in each occupational category	Percentage distribution	
		Women	Men
Managerial and administrative	31.9	7.5	11.7
Natural sciences, engineering, and mathematics	16.9	1.3	4.8
Social sciences	55.1	2.1	1.2
Religion	20.6	0.1	0.4
Teaching	59.3	5.7	2.8
Medicine and health	78.1	8.5	1.7
Artistic and recreational occupations	39.2	1.5	1.7
Clerical	79.1	31.4	6.1
Sales	43.4	9.5	9.1
Service	55.8	18.6	10.8
Agriculture	24.8	2.6	5.7
Fishing, hunting, and trapping	—	—	0.5
Forestry and logging	5.5	0.1	1.2
Mining and quarrying	—	—	1.0
Processing	22.0	1.8	4.6
Machining	7.2	0.4	3.4
Product fabricating, assembling	23.6	4.8	11.4
Construction trades	1.8	0.2	10.1
Transport-equipment operation	7.0	0.6	5.9
Materials handling	20.4	1.2	3.5
Other crafts and equipment operating	21.7	0.6	1.7
Unclassified	63.3	1.3	0.6
All occupational categories	42.2	100.0	100.0

Source: Labour Canada, *Women in the Labour Force,* 1985-6 Edition (Ottawa: Supply & Services Canada, 1986), p. 19.

pursuits.[4] Moreover, the female employment is highly concentrated. Four occupations (clerical, service, sales, and health and medicine) employ fully 68 percent of the women in the labour force. Men are more widely distributed across a broader range of occupations.

One major effect of occupational sex segregation is that the social stereotypes condoning the female job ghettos noted above also justify paying women lower wages than males, even when the same work is performed. Table 9-4 documents the sex-based wage differentials for major occupational groups in 1983. The average earned income of full-year women workers was 60.2 percent of that of males. This is only a slight improvement over the 54.6 percent wage gap between the sexes in 1972. Clearly, wage discrimination is not abating (see Boulet and Lavallée, 1984). Turning to specific occupations, we find that the wage gap in 1983

ranged from over 60 percent in managerial, professional, and clerical jobs to under 50 percent in sales, service, and farming jobs. This wage spread has been fairly stable since the turn of the century. In clerical work, for example, women earned 53 percent of the average male wage in 1901 (Lowe, 1980:366).

Only a small part of the wage gap is due to employers directly discriminating against female employees by paying them less than males performing the same jobs. Rather, it is the result of the unequal structures of the labour market. Because women are channelled into a handful of female job ghettos, their occupational rewards are lower. As the 1984 federal Royal Commission on Equality in Employment recommended, legislation is needed to break down labour market divisions that prevent equal employment opportunities for women and, further, to provide "equal pay for work of equal value" (Canada, 1984).[5]

TABLE 9-4   Average earned income of full-year workers by occupation and sex, Canada, 1983.

	Average earned income		Difference between women's and men's earnings	Women's earnings as a percentage of men's earnings
	Women	*Men*		
Managerial	$21 883	$35 250	$13 367	62.1
Professional	21 695	34 038	12 343	63.7
Clerical	14 775	21 730	6 955	68.0
Sales	11 718	24 074	12 356	48.7
Service	9 319	19 806	10 487	47.1
Farming	7 643	15 477	7 834	49.4
Processing and machining	15 134	25 140	10 006	60.2
Product fabrication	12 443	23 038	10 595	54.0
Construction	*	25 159	*	*
Transportation	13 660	23 350	9 690	58.5
All occupations	15 751	26 171	10 420	60.2

*Sample inadequate for reliable estimate.
Source: Labour Canada, *Women in the Labour Force*, 1985-6 Edition (Ottawa: Supply & Services Canada, 1986), p. 46.

EXPLAINING GENDER INEQUALITIES IN EMPLOYMENT

Labour market segmentation theory is an insightful way of viewing sexual inequalities in the workplace. Over time, gender-specific characteristics became part of job requirements through the process of sex-labelling. Entry into a particular occupation could, as a consequence, be limited to either men or women. Many of the jobs created in the wake of twentieth century industrial expansion were quickly labelled women's work. Teaching, nursing, and social work traditionally had been sex-labelled because women's maternal instincts were thought appropriate for jobs devoted to caring for the sick, the young, and the needy. When typing emerged as a new occupation in the late nineteenth century, male office workers had little interest in acquiring the necessary skills. Within a short time female stereotypes—a delicate touch, attention to detail, manual dexterity—were attached to typing jobs, thus opening the way for women to enter. Likewise, by requiring unbroken career paths, geographic mobility, or physical exertion, employers could effectively limit applicants for managerial jobs to men.

It is mainly through this process of affixing sex-specific labels to jobs by manipulating job requirements that discrimination operates in the labour market. The notion of a free market efficiently allocating workers to jobs solely on the basis of qualifications becomes little more than a myth. Once a job is defined as female-only, the label tends to stick. The channelling of women into unchallenging, low-paying, dead-end jobs thus creates rigid institutional barriers for sexual equality in the world of work (see Armstrong and Armstrong, 1984; Kanter, 1977; Lowe, 1980; Kahn-Hunt et al., 1982).

The 1970s witnessed a liberalization of sex-role attitudes as the ideas of the women's liberation movement gained acceptance. At the same time great numbers of married women were streaming into the labour force. Despite these trends, the labour market remains stratified along sex-lines. Nowhere is this more apparent than in the office. The male office manager with the female secretary is the prototype of the male-female work relationship. In short, males dominate.

Since the turn of the century women have flooded into office jobs, only to end up performing the most tedious and routinized administrative tasks. Men, on the other hand, are usually recruited at the higher level of management trainee. The working conditions of a secretarial position compare very favourably to those of most other clerical jobs. Yet, despite its higher status and rewards, the job is infused with elements of the wife-mother role. Kanter (1977:89) describes the secretary as the "office wife" who performs personal favours for the boss, such as dropping off laundry, making coffee, and buying his family's birthday gifts. This patriarchal type of relationship is also found between male clients and female sales persons, female clerks, or waitresses.

The ideology of patriarchy assumes that men have a preordained right to dominate women. This view is still deeply entrenched in western culture. It makes it difficult for many women to stand up and challenge the authority of a male boss—either individually or collectively through unionization (White, 1980; Lowe, 1981). It is indeed paradoxical that society espouses the principle of equality between the sexes while at the same time women are limited by unequal opportunities in the economic sphere. Wilensky (1968:243) refers to this paradox as "the odd combination of emancipation and bondage."

Unfortunately, academic sociology has been of little help in critically analysing sexual inequities, for sociology has been mainly concerned with the study of male society (Acker, 1978:134). Male work behaviour is seen as resulting from the organization of industry and the worker's experiences on the job. But, in the case of women, this sociological approach lapses into a discussion of motivation based on distinctive female traits. Feldberg and Glenn (1979) call for a new perspective which examines both men and women workers using the same conceptual framework (also see Crompton and Mann, 1986). Contrary to conventional wisdom, the subordinate position of women in the job market does not result from their low job commitment, lack of ambition, unreliability, or maternal attachment to the home. Rather, these alleged personal traits are in fact a product of and a response to the poor working conditions most women face.

SEGMENTED LABOUR MARKETS AND ETHNIC WORKERS

Women are not the only group in society discriminated against in the labour market. The segmentation model also accurately portrays the labour market experiences of many immigrant groups. Negative stereotypes have been applied to restrict the access of certain racial and ethnic minorities to good jobs. A ready pool of labour to perform society's "dirty work"—undesirable jobs such as dishwasher, building cleaner, or chambermaid—is thus assured. Like gender, race and ethnicity are ascribed traits over which we have no control. The more visible an ascribed characteristic, as in the case of sex or race, the easier it is for an employer to discriminate when hiring or making promotions.

John Porter's (1965) image of Canadian society as a vertical mosaic indicates how class position and ethnicity are intertwined. Porter uses the concept of "entrance status" to show how immigrants enter the job market at the bottom in order to secure a niche in their new homeland. Certainly, not all immigrant groups begin in such low positions, and many individual immigrants have experienced upward mobility (Darroch, 1979). British engineers and technicians and American academics are obvious examples of successful immigrants. Most often it is the immigrant from the underdeveloped countries of Southeast Asia, the Caribbean, or even southern Europe who, attempting to escape poverty at home, becomes trapped in a low "entrance status" in Canada.

One measure of whether the labour market discriminates against ethnic minorities is the representation of individuals from ethnic backgrounds in the country's top jobs. Clement's (1975) study of the economic elite—individuals holding directorships in one of the major corporations—discovered that these powerful decision-makers were predominantly of British stock. Francophone Canadians, who comprised 28.6 percent of the population, held only 8.4 percent of the elite posts in 1972. Other ethnic groups, making up 26.7 percent of the population, were represented in only 5.6 percent of the directorships studied (Clement, 1975:231). The Anglo-British were disproportionately represented in the elite. They constituted only 44.7 percent of the population yet occupied 86 percent of the elite places. For true equality of opportunity to exist, each ethnic minority (or women) would have to be represented in the elite in the same proportion as their numbers in the total population. But, as Clement (1975:231) concludes: "In Canada, as in many modern societies built on conquest and immigration, ethnicity is interwoven into the class system so that it provides advantages to the conquerors while keeping the conquered and newly arrived at the bottom of the so-called 'opportunity structure'." A WASP (white, Anglo-Saxon, Protestant) elite thus retains a tight grasp on the reins of economic power by admitting to its echelons only those with similar class and ethnic backgrounds.

Government immigration policy has been instrumental in creating an unequal ethnic division of labour. Immigration policy has historically responded to the labour requirements of an expanding economy. For example, in the late nineteenth century the government explicitly encouraged the settlement of "stalwart peasants in sheepskin coats" on the prairies in order to build an agricultural economy. Avery's (1979) research documents that after 1896 immigration policy was reformulated to serve the requirements of a growing capitalist labour market. Railways, mining, and forestry companies joined industrialists to lobby actively for an "open door" immigration policy that would provide a steady flow of cheap labour. Today's immigration policy is based on a points system which assesses the eligibility of an immigrant mainly on the basis of skills and education. The stated motive behind the policy is to match the qualifications of immigrants with job openings. Critics claim, however, that the effects are racist, with the points system heavily weighted in favour of white, educated Western Europeans.

There can be little question that racial discrimination accounts for some of the existing inequalities in Canadian society. As a recent study in Toronto discovered, this stems partly from discriminatory hiring practices of employers (Henry and Ginzberg, 1985). Researchers tested hiring-dis-

crimination in two ways. First, teams of job applicants matched by the researchers on the basis of age, sex, education, and employment history applied for 201 jobs advertised in newspaper classifieds. The only difference among applicants was race. Second, members of the research team responded to 237 newspaper job ads over the phone. In this test, applicants gave ethnic-sounding names to prospective employers. Overall, the study found that white applicants in the first test had three job prospects for every one that blacks had. The second test revealed that over half of the employers contacted practised some form of discrimination against one or more of the ethnic callers.

Any discussion of Canada's ethnic division of labour must include the relative economic positions of French and English in Quebec. Politically dominant since the conquest in 1759, Anglophones have had the best opportunities and therefore have occupied the most rewarding jobs in Quebec. Everett Hughes' classic study, *French Canada in Transition* (1943), describes how the process of industrialization was controlled by British and American corporations. Based on field work in a Quebec textile town during the 1930s, the study focusses on the movement of Québécois from rural, agricultural backgrounds into the new urban, industrial society. However, work in the textile factories was sharply segmented along ethnic lines. English workers held supervisory, technical, and managerial positions, while French Canadians never rose above the rank of foreman.[6]

Ensuing decades have witnessed a reduction of the disparities portrayed by Hughes. Quebec's "Quiet Revolution" of the 1960s, the federal government's bilingualism and biculturalism policies, the rise of Quebec nationalism, and a more interventionist economic role for the provincial government have helped break down the barriers to equal Francophone participation in the work world. A strong Québécois business class and a large, upwardly mobile, professional middle class now exist. Indicative of these changes is the Quebec legislation making French the official language of work in the province.

CONCLUSION

This chapter has provided an overview of the changing occupational roles of Canadians since the turn of the century. Viewed historically, the labour force trends we have documented highlight how the rise of a modern, capitalist economy has reshaped the economic roles of men and women in society. If there is one outstanding theme running through all of these labour force changes, surely it is that many inequalities found in Canadian society are deeply rooted in labour market structures and processes. In short, access to a comfortable income through reasonably challenging and interesting work still eludes significant numbers of women, young people, members of racial and ethnic minorities, and residents of disadvantaged regions of the country. If we uphold equality of opportunity as a societal goal, then top priority must be given to eradicating labour market barriers and job ghettos.

NOTES

1. The participation rate is calculated as follows: the number of persons in the labour force divided by the population or group aged at 15 (14 prior to 1975) years of age or older.

2. There is a male bias in the concept of labour force, for the assumption is that only individuals working for wages are employed. This neglects the economic contribution of wives performing unpaid labour inside the home.

3. Devereaux and Rechnitzer (1980) report that, next to teaching, clerical work is the most likely job for women with B.A. degrees. Moreover, 40 percent of women with business diplomas end up as clerks.

4. The high percentage of women in the medicine and health category is accounted for by nurses, nurse's aides, and physical and occupational therapists—not by medical doctors.

5. This concept, also known as *comparable worth*, uses a job-evaluation system that assigns points on the basis of skill, responsibility, effort, and working conditions. In this way all employees in an organization are paid on the basis of their contribution, not according to arbitrary criteria such as sex.

6. The French middle class in the town predominated in commercial services, the professions, and small businesses. But, as Hughes points out, these traditional occupations were not central to the emerging industrial structure of the province.

REFERENCES

Acker, Joan
    1978   "Issues in the sociological study of women's work," in *Women Working*, ed. Ann H. Stromberg and Shirley Harkness, pp. 134-61. Palo Alto: Mayfield.

Armstrong, Pat, and Hugh Armstrong
    1984   *The Double Ghetto; Canadian Women and Their Segregated Work* (2nd ed.). Toronto: McClelland and Stewart.

Ashton, David
    1986   *Unemployment Under Capitalism: The Sociology of British and American Labour Markets.* Brighton: Harvester Press.

Avery, Donald
    1979   *"Dangerous Foreigners": European Immigrant Workers and Labor Radicalism in Canada, 1896-1932.* Toronto: McClelland and Stewart.

Baron, James N., and William T. Bielby
    1984   "The organization of work in a segmentated economy," *American Sociological Review,* 49:454-73.

Boulet, Jac-André, and Laval Lavallée
    1984   *The Changing Economic Status of Women.* Ottawa: Supply and Services Canada.

Canada
    1977   *Perspectives Canada II.* Ottawa: Statistics Canada.

Canada
    1984   *Report of the Commission on Equality in Employment [The Abella Report].* Ottawa: Supply and Services Canada.

Clairmont, Donald H., Martha Macdonald, and Fred C. Wein
    1980   "A segmentation approach to poverty and low-wage work in the Maritimes," in *Structured Inequality in Canada,* ed. John Harp and John R. Hofley, pp. 285-315. Toronto: Prentice-Hall.

Clairmont, Donald H., R. Apostle, and R. Kreckel
    1983   "The segmentation perspective as a middle-range conceptualization in sociology," *Canadian Journal of Sociology,* 8:245-71.

Clement, Wallace
    1975   *The Canadian Corporate Elite: An Analysis of Economic Power.* Toronto: McClelland and Stewart.

Crompton, Rosemary, and Michael Mann, eds.
    1986   *Gender and Stratification.* Cambridge: Polity Press.

Darroch, Gordon
    1979   "Another look at ethnicity, stratification, and social mobility in Canada," *Canadian Journal of Sociology,* 4:1-25.

Devereaux, M. S., and Edith Rechnitzer
    1980   *Higher Education - Hired? Sex Differences in Employment Characteristics of 1976 Postsecondary Graduates.* Ottawa: Statistics Canada and Labour Canada, Women's Bureau.

Edwards, Richard C.
  1975   "The social relations of production in the firm and labor market structure," in *Labor Market Segmentation*, ed. Richard C. Edwards, Michael Reich, and David M. Gordon, pp. 3-26. Lexington, Mass.: D. C. Heath.
  1979   *Contested Terrain: The Transformation of the Workplace in the Twentieth Century.* New York: Basic Books.

Feldberg, Roslyn L., and Evelyn Nakano Glen
  1979   "Male and female: job versus gender models in the sociology of work," *Social Problems*, 26:524-38.

Garnsey, E., J. Rubery, and F. Wilkinson
  1985   "Labour market structure and work-force divisions," in *Work, Culture and Society*, ed. R. Deem and G. Salaman, pp. 40-76. Milton Keynes and Philadelphia: Open University Press.

Gordon, D. M., R. Edwards, and M. Reich
  1982   *Segmented Work, Divided Workers: The Historical Transformation of Labor in the United States.* New York: Cambridge University Press.

Henry, Frances, and Effie Ginzberg
  1985   *Who Gets the Work: A Test of Racial Discrimination in Employment.* Toronto: Urban Alliance on Race Relations and Social Planning Council of Metropolitan Toronto.

Hirsch, Eric
  1980   "Dual labour market theory: a sociological critique," *Sociological Inquiry*, 50:133-45.

Hughes, Everett C.
  1943   *French Canada in Transition.* Chicago: University of Chicago Press.

Johnson, Leo
  1974   "The political economy of Ontario women in the nineteenth century," in *Women at Work: Ontario, 1850-1930*, ed. Janice Acton, Penny Goldsmith, and Bonnie Shepard, pp. 13-31. Toronto: Canadian Women's Educational Press.
  1980   "The development of class in Canada in the twentieth century," in *Structured Inequality in Canada*, ed. John Harp and John R. Hofley, pp. 99-136. Toronto: Prentice-Hall.

Kahn-Hunt, Rachel, Arlene Kaplan Daniels, and Richard Clovard, eds.
  1982   *Women and Work: Problems and Perspectives.* New York: Oxford University Press.

Kalleberg, Arne
  1983   "Work and stratification: structural perspectives," *Work and Occupations*, 10:251-69.

Kanter, Rosabeth Moss
  1977   *Men and Women of the Corporation.* New York: Basic Books.

Labour Canada
  1986   *Women in the Labour Force, 1985-86 Edition.* Ottawa: Women's Bureau.

Lowe, Graham S.
  1980   "Women, work, and the office: the feminization of clerical occupations in Canada, 1901-1931," *Canadian Journal of Sociology*, 5:361-81.

1981   "Causes of unionization in Canadian Banks," *Relations industrielles/Industrial Relations*, 36:865-92.

Macredie, Ian
1985   "Self-employment in Canada: an overview," *The Labour Force* (December, pp. 83-89) Statistics Canada. Catalogue no. 71-001, monthly.

Osterman, Paul, ed.
1984   *Internal Labor Markets.* Cambridge, MA: MIT Press.

Ostry, Sylvia, and Mahmood A. Zaidi
1972   *Labour Economics in Canada* (2nd ed.). Toronto: Macmillan of Canada.

Pentland, H. Claire
1959   "The development of a capitalistic labour market in Canada," *Canadian Journal of Economics and Political Science*, 24:450-61.
1981   *Labour and Capital in Canada, 1650-1860.* Toronto: James Lorimer.

Porter, John
1965   *The Vertical Mosaic: An Analysis of Social Class and Power in Canada.* Toronto: University of Toronto Press.

Rinehart, James W.
1987   *The Tyranny of Work: Alienation and the Labour Process* (2nd ed.). Don Mills: Longman Canada.

Smucker, Joseph
1980   *Industrialization in Canada.* Scarborough: Prentice-Hall Canada.

Statistics Canada
Monthly   *The Labour Force* (Catalogue no. 71-001).

Stone, Katherine
1974   "The origins of job structures in the steel industry," *Review of Radical Political Economics*, 6:113-73.

Teeple, G.
1972   "Land, labor, and capital in pre-confederation Canada," in *Capitalism and the National Question in Canada,* ed. G. Teeple, pp. 43-66. Toronto: University of Toronto Press.

Van Kirk, Sylvia
1977   "The impact of the white woman on fur trade society," in *The Neglected Majority,* ed. Susan Mann Trofimenkoff and Alison Prentice, pp. 27-48. Toronto: McClelland and Stewart.

White, Julie
1980   *Women and Unions.* Report for the Canadian Advisory Council on the Status of Women. Ottawa: Supply and Services Canada.

Wilensky, Harold
1968   "Women's work: economic growth, ideology, structure," *Industrial Relations*, 7:235-48

B. Occupation

10. Patterns of Occupational Mobility

Hugh A. McRoberts

In developing an analysis of inequality in any society there are two fundamental issues which must be addressed. First, there is the issue of how the differential allocation of the social product is tied to the structure of roles within the society. Second, given that this differential allocation is associated with certain types of roles, there remains the issue of how access to the different roles is managed. In most societies—certainly all industrial societies—the primary basis for the differential allocation of the social product is located in those roles which are associated with the social division of labour. Or, to put it more prosaically, the differential allocation of the scarce and desirable goods in our society is rooted very firmly in the differential rewards associated with occupational

Revised from the author's Social Mobility in Canada," in Dennis Forcese and Stephen Richer (ed.), *Social Issues: Sociological Views of Canada* (Scarborough: Prentice-Hall Canada Inc., 1982) pp. 375-94. Reprinted with permission.

positions. Beyond agreement on this basic fact, however, there is little consensus in the literature as to why this is so. In this paper I shall be focussing on the second issue, which is the study of how people do or do not gain access to these roles. In particular, I shall be concerned with the way in which the allocative process is managed in the context of the generational renewal of the occupational structure; that is, I shall be concerned with the degree of intergenerational occupational mobility and immobility. Or, to put it in a different way, I shall be concerned with the way in which the socio-economic status of a person's family of origin affects his own socio-economic position.

The concern with this aspect of stratification systems is a relatively recent one. Research has tended to focus on two key questions:

1. To what extent are industrial societies characterized by equality of opportunity? Or, in operational terms, to what extent is a son's occupational level associated with the father's occupational level?

2. Given that the amount of mobility observed is, or may be, less than perfect, is the trend in mobility toward greater amounts of mobility?

The primary studies were carried out in the late 1940s by David Glass and his associates in Great Britain (Glass, 1954) and Goldhamer and Rogoff in the United States (Rogoff, 1953). Since then, studies of occupational mobility have been carried out in almost every industrial society. Indeed some, like the United States and Great Britain, have carried out a second generation of studies as well. While there are many differences among these studies with respect to sampling, instrument design, and method of analysis, what remains striking about the results is their remarkable similarity. What they all show is that sons will tend to occupy occupations similar to their fathers' to a degree which substantially exceeds that which could be expected by chance alone. At the same time these studies show that those who do not stay at the same occupational level as their fathers are far more likely to move up in the occupational hierarchy than to move down. Studies done in Canada have also tended to conform to this pattern. I will now turn to the most recent of these, the Canadian Mobility Study, to examine in detail the patterns of occupational mobility in Canada.

PATTERNS OF OCCUPATIONAL MOBILITY IN CANADA

The Canadian Mobility Study was the first national study of mobility completed in Canada. It was carried out in 1973 by a team of sociologists from three Canadian universities in conjunction with Statistics Canada. The questionnaire was answered by more than 45 000 Canadian residents over 18 years of age and not in an institution. The analysis presented here is restricted to native-born males between the ages of 25 and 64 who were in the labour force at the time of the study (July 1973). This group represents a core labour force in a sense, and its experiences can best be used to typify opportunity in Canada.[1]

In analysing occupational mobility, at least two measurements must be taken for each person in the sample. First, we need a measure of the person's origin status or occupation. This is usually indicated by the occupation or occupational status of the head of the respondent's family of origin, and by convention this is usually measured at the minimum school-leaving age—in Canada where the respondent is 16 years of age. As the father is the head of household for the vast majority of our respondents, this measure is usually referred to as either father's occupation or father's occupational status. The second item which we need to know about is the respondent's current occupation or occupational status.

Table 10-1 presents the percentage distribution of these two measures for native-born males aged 25 to 64, from the Canadian Mobility Study. From these data we can observe a number of things. First, nearly half of both the fathers and the sons are engaged in blue-collar work (48.4 percent and 48.8 percent), although skilled work is slightly more prevalent in the sons' generation than in the fathers'. Second, sons are substantially more likely than their fathers to be engaged in some form of white-collar work with the difference being most marked with respect to the prevalence of sons in the highly qualified manpower occupations (the top two occupational categories in the table). Third, sons, on the other hand, are very much less likely to be engaged in farming than was the case with their fathers.

These changes are the results in turn of changes in the structure of the Canadian labour force over the last half-century. On the one hand, there has been a major rural-urban migration in Canada, which began in the 1930s as the sons of farmers, and indeed farmers themselves who could no longer make a living from their farms, began to drift into the towns and cities in search of work. This drift was accelerated during the war and post-war period by the demand for workers in the urban industries in combination with the growing capital intensivity of farm production. On the other hand, especially since the Second World War, there has been a very rapid growth in the tertiary, or service-producing, sector of our economy with a concomitant growth in the demand for professional and managerial workers.

With changes such as these, in which the prevalence of one type of occupation decreases from one generation to the next while another occupation grows in prevalence, it is clear that some intergenerational occupational mobility must occur. This occurs because even if all of the sons with fathers in the first occupation wished to remain in the occupation, there would be no room for them, and even if all of the sons with fathers in the second occupation wished to stay, there would not be enough of them to fill all of the jobs. As a result, some of those with fathers in the first occupation will be forced out of their origin occupation and "must," in a sense, be mobile. While we cannot identify whether or not specific individuals have been mobile in this way, as such mobility is a system or societal characteristic rather than an individual one, we can estimate the minimum extent of the phenomenon using a statistic called the Index of Dissimilarity. In the case of these data the index has a value of 21.65 percent, which means that at least 21.65 percent of the sample must have been mobile due solely to the changes in the relative prevalence of different occupational groups from the fathers' generation to the sons'.

TABLE 10-1   Father's occupation when respondent was 16 and respondent's occupation: native-born males aged 25–64 in civilian labour force, July 1973.

Occupation Group	Father's occupation	Son's (respondent's) occupation	S - F
Professional and executive	4.1	12.2	+ 8.1
Managerial and semi-professional	9.6	18.6	+ 9.0
White-collar lower-grade	10.4	13.1	+ 2.7
Blue-collar higher-grade	23.5	25.3	+ 1.8
Blue-collar lower-grade	24.9	23.5	− 1.4
Farm	27.5	7.2	− 20.3
	100.0 (8812)	99.9 (8812)	

In mobility analysis, mobility of this type is conventionally labelled *structural mobility*, and is conceived of as the mobility which is caused by changes in the external economic structure of society and in particular by changes in the labour force demand for different occupations. This term is used to distinguish this type of mobility from what is called *exchange mobility*, or *circulation mobility*, which is usually conceived of as the mobility which occurs independently of structural mobility and which involves a situation in which for every upward movement there must be a corresponding downward movement. Hence, the use of the image of "exchange" or "circulation." Although it is no doubt irrelevant to the individual whether or not his or her mobility, or lack thereof, is due to structural or circulation factors (again it is worth noting that one could not tell an individual this anyhow as both elements are properties of the society not of the individual), the difference is of considerable sociological importance.

To see why, let us consider an analogy with the distribution of income. The relative distribution of income in a society is often employed as a measure of the degree of inequality of condition, but it is not usable as a measure of well-being; for that we must know the amount of income to be divided as well. In many societies it has been possible through economic growth to increase the general level of well-being quite substantially, without altering in any significant way the distribution of income or, in other words, without changing the relative size of the shares. Structural mobility can be thought of as a process which is analogous to economic growth (indeed, empirically the two processes are often linked) in which the average level of occupations increases, and circulation mobility can be viewed as an analogue to the relative share of income, as a measure of, in this case, the actual degree of

inequality of opportunity in the society. To put it another way, circulation mobility is a measure of the amount of mobility which would occur in a society under the condition of no structural change in the labour force over the span of a generation.

Thus, when we examine social or occupational mobility there are in fact three things which we must consider. First, there is the total or observed mobility. This is the total amount of mobility which has occurred from one generation to the next regardless of cause. Second, there is the amount of structural mobility. Finally, there is the amount of circulation mobility. The division of the total amount of mobility into its component parts is not a simple issue. Indeed, it has been the principal focus of much of the literature on occupational mobility over the last three decades, and has not yet been resolved in a way which has been universally agreed upon. In the following pages I will examine the patterns of total mobility, and then move on to look at some of the simpler solutions to the decomposition problem.

To analyse the amount of occupational mobility in a society we need to know, in addition to the distributions of fathers' and sons' occupations, how these two elements are related to each other. More specifically, we would like to know what the probability of a son's ending up in a particular occupation is, given the occupation of his father. To find this out we cross-tabulate fathers' occupation by sons' occupation and calculate percentages for the table by row. Such a table is sometimes called an outflow table or an outflow matrix.

Table 10-2 presents an outflow table for males in the Canadian Mobility Study. Overall, the table conforms very much to the expectation which we would have, given the results of other national mobility studies. With two exceptions, occupational inheritance is the most likely single outcome, and upward mobility is clearly more prevalent than downward mobility. One of the exceptions, farm occupations, is not at all surprising in the light of the rural-urban migration discussed earlier. As can be seen in the table, only 22.9 percent of the sons of farmers stay in farming with over half going into blue-collar work. At the same time, we can note that the entrance of sons whose fathers were not in farming into this occupation is a rare event.

The other exception is in the category of lower-grade white-collar workers, where the degree of inheritance (18.1 percent) is the lowest in the entire table. Further, it will be noted that while upward mobility is more likely for sons with lower-grade white-collar origins than is downward mobility, the margin is not all that large (44.9 percent up

versus 37 percent down). This is probably a reflection of the group's relative powerlessness. Typically, the occupations in this group are ones for which the degree of external certification is low (that is, there are few qualifications for such occupations beyond literacy) and the degree of on-the-job training is high. As a consequence, such workers are highly dependent on their employers for the "recognition" of their "qualifications" and hence have less bargaining power than those in the professions or for that matter in the trades. Moreover, the lack of external qualifications makes such occupations unlikely *a priori* career choices for those who are selecting their career paths. Put bluntly, one may aspire to be a doctor, a farmer, or a machinist, but who ever heard of someone who yearns to be a clerk.

TABLE 10-2 Outflow percentages for father's occupation by son's occupation: native-born males aged 25–64 in the civilian labour force, July 1973.

	Son's occupation						
Father's occupation	Professional and executive	Managerial and semi-professional	White-collar lower-grade	Blue-collar higher-grade	Blue-collar lower-grade	Farm	Total
Professional and executive	42.5	28.8	13.2	9.2	5.4	0.9	100.0 (363)
Managerial and semi-professional	23.2	30.6	16.9	16.7	11.2	1.4	100.0 (842)
White-collar lower-grade	18.1	26.8	18.1	19.3	16.7	1.0	100.0 (920)
Blue-collar higher-grade	11.5	19.3	15.2	31.4	21.5	1.1	100.0 (2072)
Blue-collar lower-grade	7.5	16.9	12.9	28.1	32.9	1.7	100.0 (2197)
Farm	6.5	10.8	8.3	25.1	26.4	22.9	100.0 (2149)

By contrast, the degree of inheritance in the highly qualified manpower occupations and in the blue-collar occupations is quite high. Over 40 percent of those with professional or executive origins are in similar occupations and nearly 30 percent are in managerial or semi-professional occupations. Similarly, 30 percent of those whose fathers were in managerial or semi-professional jobs were themselves in like occupations, and just under a quarter (23.3 percent) were in professional or executive occupations. The picture is very much the same when we consider the two levels of blue-collar work for each case—just over 30 percent of the sons will remain in blue-collar occupations at the same level as their fathers, and over half of the blue-collar sons at each level will remain in blue-collar work.

Viewed in this way, the mobility table suggests that occupations can be divided into four broad occupational levels. First, there is farming which is, in a sense, separated from the rest of the table. Farm origins are a major source of supply for the remaining occupational groups (especially blue-collar occupations), but very few who were not born to it go into farming. Then there are two groupings which are typified by a fair amount of within-grouping mobility but at the same time by a tendency to low rates of mobility beyond the grouping: the highly qualified manpower occupations, and the blue-collar occupations. Finally, there is the lower-grade white-collar group of occupations, which may be seen as a transition zone located between the blue-collar and highly qualified manpower occupations.

These then are the patterns of occupational inheritance and mobility for Canadians. There is substantial inheritance but substantial mobility as well. The problem is, how can we tell if the amount of inheritance observed is a great deal, or simply trivial?

The answer requires going back to the theory which gave rise to the investigation. You will recall that the type of society envisaged by the functionalists would be typified by universalistic and achievement-based norms, and that in such a society the occupations of sons would be independent of those of their fathers. This notion can be expressed in statistical form in a model called the perfect mobility model, which was developed simultaneously by Rogoff in the United States (1953) and by Glass and his associates in England (1954). The perfect mobility model allows us to predict what the mobility table would have been for a society had that society enjoyed a mobility pattern wherein fathers' and sons' occupations were independent. We can then see the extent to which the society in question deviates from the perfect mobility pattern by comparing the observed mobility table with the perfect mobility model table. One way in which this can be done is to use Rogoff ratios, which are calculated by dividing the number of cases observed in each cell of the mobility table by the number of cases predicted for that cell by the model. A value for the ratio which is greater than the numeral one would indicate that the event occurred more often than expected, and a value of less than one would indicate that the event occurred less often than expected. A value of one would indicate that things happened at the same rate as would be expected in a society with perfect mobility. Overall, if there was perfect mobility in a society, a table of Rogoff ratios for that society would be all ones.

Table 10-3 gives the array of Rogoff ratios calculated for Canadian males. As can be seen, all of the ratios in the main diagonal are greater than one, which tells us that in Canada there is more inheritance in all occupational groups than we would expect under perfect mobility. With the exception of the cell for sons of professionals or executives who end up as managers or semi-professionals, and the cell for the sons of managers or semi-professionals who end up as lower-grade white-collar workers, all of the remaining cells above (to the right of) the main diagonal are less than or equal to one. This in turn tells us that in Canada one of the consequences of our failure to achieve perfect mobility has been that there is less downward mobility than would have been the case if we had. At the same time, while many of the cells below (to the left of) the main diagonal are less than or equal to zero, those immediately adjacent to the main diagonal are all greater than one. This indicates that while there is less long-distance upward mobility than would be expected under perfect mobility, there is more short-distance upward mobility than could be expected, especially mobility up a single occupational level.

Finally, if we divide the table into four quadrants along the blue-collar–white-collar line it can be seen that all of the ratios associated with white-collar downward mobility are less than one (upper right-hand quadrant), and, with one exception, that all of the

ratios associated with blue-collar upward mobility are less than or equal to one (lower left-hand quadrant). On the other hand, most of the ratios in the white-collar (upper left) and the blue-collar (lower right) quadrants are greater than zero. This suggests that in Canada, while there is a fair amount of mobility within these two very broad occupational groupings, there is relatively less mobility across the boundary which divides them. This would lead to the conclusion that the division between blue- and white-collar remains a salient (perhaps *the* salient) denomination for strata within the Canadian stratification system. Further, these findings, of course, lead inescapably to the conclusion that while there is much mobility, there is also much inheritance of occupational status and that, on that ground alone, Canada must be viewed as a society which has some way to go before it can call itself a meritocracy.

Thus, the answer to our first question has, in the case of Canada, been the same as in the case of every other society for which such studies have been done. There is a moderate association between fathers' and sons' status.

This brings us to the second question

TABLE 10-3 Rogoff ratios for father's occupation by son's occupation: native-born males aged 25–64 in the civilian labour force, July 1973.

	Son's occupation					
Father's occupation	Professional and executive	Managerial and semi-professional	White-collar lower-grade	Blue-collar higher-grade	Blue-collar lower-grade	Farm
Professional and executive	3.5	1.6	1.0	.4	.2	.1
Managerial and semi-professional	1.9	1.6	1.3	.7	.5	.2
White-collar lower-grade	1.5	1.4	1.4	.8	.7	.1
Blue-collar higher-grade	.9	1.0	1.2	1.2	.9	.2
Blue-collar lower-grade	.6	.9	1.0	1.1	1.4	.2
Farm	.6	.6	.6	1.0	1.1	3.2

raised by such research: Given that there is less than perfect mobility in Canada, is the direction of the trend towards greater mobility? The answer is both yes and no. Yes, there is greater mobility if one focusses attention on the total amount of mobility. Indeed, if we look at mobility from father's occupation to respondent's first occupation, and divide our sample up into five-year age groups, we find that of those who were 16 in the period 1925-29, 59.6 percent were mobile compared to 70.7 percent of those who were 16 in the period 1960-64. However, as McRoberts and Selbee have shown in their paper (1978), when we remove from consideration the effects of structural mobility (the mobility which is due to the differential demand for occupations from the father's time to the son's), we find that the rate of circulation mobility has remained virtually invariant from 1925 through to 1964. It is worth noting that other national mobility studies have pointed to similar conclusions in the United States (Hauser et al., 1975) and Great Britain (Hope, 1974).

From these results there has evolved a second and very much related stream of stratification research which must be considered as well—status attainment research. This line of research takes the existence of an association between fathers' occupational status and sons' occupational status as its starting point and asks, how does such an association come about? This question arises because while there is clearly some ascription present in industrial societies and, in the case of farming and small business, direct inheritance of status is possible, by and large fathers are simply not able to pass on their occupational positions to their sons. In industrial societies most people (85 percent of Canadians for example) work for others in relationships which are usually impersonal and often involve large bureaucratic organizations with personnel procedures which are, at least on paper, clearly achievement-oriented and universalistic. Indeed, it is in general not in the interest of managers to use obviously ascriptive or personalistic procedures in personnel decisions because in doing so they are required to accept a higher degree of responsibility for those decisions than would be the case had they simply allowed the decision to be made according to the rules of the system in which they work. As a result, when an employment decision turns sour the manager who has followed the established procedures in his firm can lay some, and at times all, of the blame on the personnel department and on its procedures. Whereas the manager who did his brother a favor must take the full brunt of blame for his nephew's non-performance, and unless his brother is chairman or chief executive officer, may well follow his nephew to the Unemployment Insurance Commission. This is not to argue that family of origin is irrelevant to the process of occupational attainment; rather it is to suggest that given the structures surrounding the process of job acquisition, it is unlikely that direct family intervention could begin to account for the degree of association which can be seen in the data which I have presented here, and which others have found for other societies.

To answer the question of how the father-to-son transmission of status occurs, Blau and Duncan in their landmark monograph *The American Occupational Structure* (1967) propose what has come to be known as the status attainment model. This model, displayed in schematic form in Figure 10-1, breaks the process which allows the transmission of status across generations into three distinct stages: educational attainment, labour force entry, career attainment. Before discussing the model further, I would note that while the model presented in Figure 10-1 was originally derived from American data, it has been found to be the optimal model for the Canadian labour force as well (McRoberts, 1975; McRoberts et al., 1976). Hence, the remarks which follow may be read as applying with equal force to either society.

The first stage of the status attainment model examines the way in which the socio-economic status of the family of origin as measured by father's occupational status and father's educational attainment affect the respondent's educational attainment. Both background factors are found to have independent effects on educational attainment that are of moderate strength, which means that family background has an important but by no means decisive impact on educational outcomes. In the second stage of the model the effects of family background and educational attainment on the status of the respondent at the time of labour force entry (first job) are examined. Here the strongest relationship (indeed the strongest in the model) is between educational attainment and entry status. That is, of course, not surprising in a society in which so much emphasis is placed on the use of educational credentials as a screening device in the personnel selection process. Of the two measures of socio-economic background, only one (father's occupation) has any direct effect on entry status, and that effect is a weak one. The existence of this effect is due to a combination of factors including: direct inheritance of small businesses and farms, the effects of influence and nepotism, and, probably most important, the effect which parental knowledge of the labour market has on the respondent's ability to search these sectors of the market where he can maximize the returns on his educational attainments. The weakness of the effect, on the other hand, is testament to the validity of the argument set out earlier with respect to the need for an explanation of the father-son association. The final stage of the model looks at the effects of background, educational attainment, and entry status on current occupational status. Education and entry status both have effects of moderate strength on current status. The effect of education underlines the long-term career value of education as an asset, the value of which extends well beyond the initial labour force entry stage. The effect of entry status on current status is a consequence of the obvious fact that in careers, as in races, the better one's position at the start the better, *ceteris paribus*, one's position at the end. As in the previous stage of the model, fathers' occupation is the only background factor to have an effect, and that is a very weak one.

Overall, the model shows that the single most important factor in the determination of current occupational status is educational attainment. This is especially so if we consider not only its direct influence on current status but the very strong effect which this factor has on entry status as well. At the same time, the effects of background factors seem to vary from weak to non-existent. However, to leave matters at that would be misleading inasmuch as it would ignore the potential indirect role which family background plays due to the effect of family background on educational attainment. Indeed, it is here that we find the link between the generations in the status transmission chain. While parents have relatively little ability to intervene directly in the careers of their offspring, this model and a voluminous body of other research have shown that the socio-economic status of parents does have a substantial capacity to determine the quantity and quality of education which the children will receive, and hence to advantage or disadvantage their offspring in the world of work (see e.g., Jencks et al., 1972; Gilbert and McRoberts, 1977).

CONCLUSIONS

I have examined the way in which the research on occupational mobility and occupational attainment addresses stratification in industrial societies. When we examined Canada we found (in concord with those who have done similar work in other societies) that there is substantial inequality of opportunity as represented by levels of father-son occupational inheritance which are much higher than would be found in a meritocratic society. Canada, in other words, remains very much a stratified society. Further, we drew on other research to ask whether, if Canada was not wholly a meritocracy, it was on a trajectory toward becoming one. It was pointed out that, while there has been an increase over time in the total amount of mobility, the amount of circulation mobility had remained invariant throughout the same period. This meant that the apparent increase in openness was due solely to structural changes in the labour force, but that the fundamental nature of the inequality of opportunity in Canada had remained unaltered. Finally, research on status attainment was briefly looked at in order to see how the father-son association could be explained. There it was found that the key link in the chain of status transmission was education. That is to say, it was found that the way in which parents transmit the advantages or disadvantages of their socio-economic status to their child is through the educational system. As a consequence, the structures surrounding the

FIGURE 10-1   Basic status attainment model

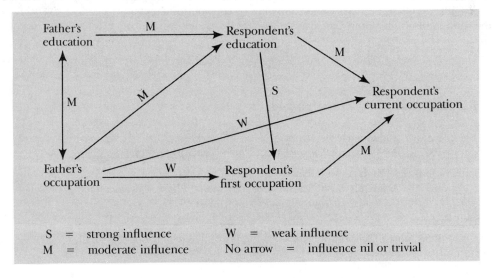

S = strong influence   W = weak influence
M = moderate influence   No arrow = influence nil or trivial

educational system in Canada were pointed to as the central set of institutions in the intergenerational reproduction of the stratification system.

All of these findings lead to the conclusion that Canada is a stratified society. At the same time, however, it should be pointed out that there are degrees of stratification. While there is significant status inheritance in Canada, there is also a good deal of mobility, most of it upward. In the table examined earlier, 55 percent of the sample were upwardly mobile compared with only 16 percent who were downwardly mobile. While Canada's educational institutions are rightly identified as the central institutions in the reproduction of the stratification structure, they are also the chief means by which many are able to transcend their origins. As I pointed out earlier, the effect of background on educational attainment is significant, but it is a long way from being decisive. Hence, although linkage between the generations via education is real, it is not all that strong. As Goyder and Curtis have shown, when one extends the chain of status transmission beyond two generations the linkages become rapidly weaker (1977). Thus, while like most other industrial societies Canada is a stratified society, like most it is also a society in which this stratification is not terribly rigid.

NOTES

1. Some will no doubt object to the exclusion of immigrants and women, but there are good reasons for both decisions. First, the exclusion of immigrants is done because for many immigrants their education and sometimes much of their career was in their country of origin, not in Canada, and hence reflects opportunity in the country of origin, not in Canada. The exclusion of women is done because research has shown that they have in important respects different patterns than men and as a consequence their inclusion would distort the results. At the same time, a male-female comparison would be an undertaking well beyond the scope of this chapter.

REFERENCES

Blau, Peter M., and Otis Dudley Duncan
  1967   *The American Occupational Structure*. New York: Wiley.

Gilbert, Sid, and Hugh A. McRoberts
  1977   "Academic Stratification and Educational Plans: a Reassessment," *Canadian Review of Sociology and Anthropology*, 14, no. 1:47.

Glass, D.V.
  1954   *Social Mobility in Britain*. London: Routledge and Kegan Paul.

Goyder, J. C., and J. E. Curtis
 1977 "Occupational Mobility in Canada over Four Generations," *Canadian Review of Sociology and Anthropology,* 14, no. 3:303-319.

Hauser, Robert M., John N. Koffel, Harry P. Travis, and Peter J. Dickinson
 1975 "Temporal Change in Occupational Mobility: Evidence for Men in the United States," *American Sociological Review,* 40 (June):279-97.

Hope, Keith
 1974 "Trends in the Openness of British Society in the Present Century." Paper presented at the Mathematical Social Sciences Board Conference on Measurement and Models in Comparative Social Stratification, Toronto, Canada, August.

Jencks, Christopher, et al.
 1972 *Inequality: a Reassessment of the Effect of Family and Schooling in America.* New York: Harper Colophon Books.

McRoberts, Hugh A.
 1975 *Social Stratification in Canada: A Preliminary Analysis.* Doctoral Dissertation, Carleton University, Ottawa.

McRoberts, Hugh A., Monica Boyd, John Porter, John Goyder, Frank E. Jones, and Peter C. Pineo
 1976 "Différences dans la mobilité professionnelle des Francophones et des Anglophones," *Sociologie et Sociétés,* 8:61-79.

McRoberts, Hugh A., and Kevin Selbee
 1981 "Trends in Occupational Mobility in Canada and the United States: a Comparison," *American Sociological Review,* 46 (August):406-21.

Myles, John F., and Aage B. Sorensen
 1975 "Elite and Status Attainment Models of Inequality of Opportunity," *Canadian Journal of Sociology,* 1 (Spring):75-88.

Rogoff, Natalie
 1953 *Recent Trends in Occupational Mobility.* Chicago: Free Press.

B: Occupation

11. Solving Alienation Through Automation?

James W. Rinehart

When we speak of alienation at work, we are referring to a condition in which individuals have little or no control over (1) the purposes and products of the labour process, (2) the overall organization of the workplace, and (3) the immediate work process itself. Defined this way, alienation is objective, or structural, in the sense that it is built into human relationships at the workplace and exists independent of how individuals perceive and evaluate their jobs. Alienation, then, can be viewed broadly as a condition of objective powerlessness.

Alienated labour extends throughout the world of work, affecting the traditional manual labour of heavy industry as well as reaching up through the ranks of white-collar

jobs—including the professional, scientific, and technical positions prototypical of post-industrial society. Even managers at the upper levels of the hierarchical authority structures of public and private organizations are not immune from the effects of alienation. But the burning issue is this: Can alienated labour be transcended?

Some writers contend that improved technology and various forms of automation could help to liberate us from alienating work, because the tremendous productive potential of automation could drastically reduce the amount of time people spend at paid labour. Robert Heilbronner believes we can look forward to "a time when as small a proportion of the labour force as now suffices to over-provide us with food will serve to turn out manufactured staples, the houses, the transportation, the retail services, even the government supervision that will be required" (Heilbronner, 1965:124). It is likely, however, that such a society would

Revised from James W. Rinehart, *The Tyranny of Work*, 2nd ed., © 1987 by Harcourt Brace Jovanovich Canada Inc. Reprinted by permission of the publisher.

be more of a nightmare than an Eden. Under capitalism, technological developments are utilized not to improve the lot of people in general but to enhance corporate profitability and augment the power and privileges of a tiny minority of the population. Consequently, instead of universally high living standards and extensive leisure time, the scenario envisioned by Heilbronner would likely feature the widening of present inequalities: a large *lumpenproletariat* of unemployed and underemployed citizens existing alongside an incredibly privileged and powerful minority benefiting from the new technology.

Automation, it is suggested, eliminates the more menial and physically exhausting tasks and allows for the creation of more challenging jobs than those available under earlier forms of technology. This is the position of the post-industrial theorists. Their forecasts emphasizing benign shifts in investment and employment between sectors of industry are complemented by visions of a high technology that will provide challenging jobs in manufacturing industries (Blauner, 1967). Recent trends, however, indicate that projections of growing job complexity both in manufacturing proper and the overall economy are exaggerated.

Advanced technology has indeed created jobs requiring special training and professional-type knowledge, but its major effect has been to drive employment out of those industries where new technology has been introduced into industries relatively immune from technological innovations. In recent decades the movement of employment from goods-producing to service-producing industries has brought with it in the United States a net increase of lower-skilled, poorly paid jobs (Roberts, 1984). Declines in manufacturing employment and a rapid increase in Canada of part-time jobs suggest

this tendency is not unique to the United States. Part-time jobs are for the most part held by women, are poorly paid, offer few or no benefits, and provide little job security. From 1979 to 1983 Canada lost 170 000 jobs in manufacturing, many of which were in unionized companies and were relatively well paid. Between 1975 and 1981 part-time jobs were created at a more rapid rate than full-time jobs, and part-time workers as a percentage of all workers in Canada increased from 10.6 to 13.5 percent. If part-time work continues to grow at this rate, one half of all jobs will be part-time in the year 2000. This surge of part-time employment has occurred alongside the rapid growth of the tertiary sector, large sections of which have been unaffected by recent advances in technology. Two thirds of all part-time workers are in service, clerical, and sales occupations (White, 1983; Harvey and Blakely, 1985).

It is often argued that the growth of high-technology industries will not only relieve unemployment but will provide complex, challenging jobs as well. However, the progressive use of sophisticated technology in high-tech industry and the small size of this sector limit its capacity to generate employment opportunities. For example, between 1971 and 1981, employment in Canada expanded annually by 3.1 percent, for a total of three million new jobs. In high-tech industries, employment growth averaged 3.9 percent per year, but this translated into only 900 000 new jobs over the 10-year period (Newton, 1985). Future developments can only be dimly perceived, but as micro-technology finds more and more realms of application in the 1980s and 1990s, the most rapidly growing jobs probably will require minimum skill and offer little remuneration. Forecasts by the Canadian government indicate there is no end in sight to the rapid growth of routine jobs. Table 11-1 shows projections to the year 1992 of the 30 fastest-growing Canadian occupations (in order of growth potential). Of the 30 occupations on the list, only one can be considered a high-tech occupation—systems analysts—and this is number 28 on the list. It is evident that the majority of jobs on the list are routine, require only modest educational training, and are not well paid. After examining these 30 occupations, an Economic Council of Canada analyst concluded: "The great majority of jobs in the foreseeable future will not require major shifts in educational preparation. For a relatively small number of very specialized jobs in high-tech occupations, qualifications in mathematics, computer science, and related disciplines will be in great demand. But for many jobs, even the recent emphasis on 'computer literacy for all' is increasingly questioned" (Newton, 1985:21).

It is also instructive to examine the kinds of jobs being created in high-technology manufacturing industries, that is, in businesses that (1) manufacture equipment in communications, semiconductors, information processing, robots, and biotechnology, or (2) use advanced technology (such as drugs, plastics, chemicals, and electronic components) in production. Most of the jobs being created in this sector are hardly challenging. After examining the relevant research in the United States, one economist concluded: "It's not news that most jobs in high-tech manufacturing industries are not high-tech jobs, but it is surprising to learn that many are not even very good jobs" (Appelbaum, 1984:21). In the semiconductor industry, for instance, 60 percent of the employees (mostly women) are semiskilled or unskilled production workers who occupy highly repetitive, poorly paid, and often unhealthy jobs. Even these unattractive

jobs are insecure; high-tech companies like Atari, Apple, and Wang have moved assembly operations to low-wage countries like Mexico, Taiwan, and the Phillipines.

Continuous-process industries, like chemical and petroleum industries, allegedly provide responsible, high-discretion production jobs aside from the necessary complement of highly skilled maintenance and repair personnel. The job of operators in such plants requires responsiblity (for monitoring the expensive equipment) but not high skill. Moreover, the separation of the conception of the work from its performance prevails here every bit as much as it does under mechanized production. Continuous-process operators are relegated to the role of passive spectators of the production process; their main responsibility is to ensure that dials and gauges are correctly set so that the quantity and quality of the throughput as programmed in the front office is maintained. Nor is much discretion involved in reading dials. Operator discretion comes into play when the equipment malfunctions or when there is some other operational problem. At these critical times, workers are required to detect quickly the sources of the problem and to take the appropriate corrective actions. Unpredictable malfunctions and other special production conditions in automated plants cannot be effectively and cheaply handled with a highly specialized division of labour and tight supervisory controls. Because a degree of worker flexibility and autonomy is the most profitable mode of operating continuous-process technology, workers ordinarily learn to perform multiple tasks and are accorded some control over such matters as job assignments and labour allocation. But this measure of discretion may be transitory. In the most advanced continuous-process plants, worker discretion is being severely restricted. Decisions once made by oper-ators are being made by computers capable of activating whatever work needs to be done. Instead of a number of operators pe-riodically walking through the plant to check dials, a single employee sits before a television console monitoring the meters (Sussman, 1972:43; Hill, 1981).

The most comprehensive study of the ef-fect of automation on the overall skill level of the manufacturing work force was con-ducted by James Bright (1958). From his survey of 13 automated plants, Bright was unable to draw any firm conclusions as to the general impact of automation on skill levels. In some cases, a reduction in the skill

TABLE 11-1   Projections of fastest-growing occupations, Canada, 1983-92.

| Rank | Occupation | Projected employment | | Total requirements |
		1983	1992	1983-92
1	Secretaries and stenographers	351 300	438 800	87 500
2	Bookkeepers	368 200	448 500	80 300
3	Truck drivers	238 000	310 000	72 000
4	Financial officers	140 000	180 000	39 100
5	Janitors	223 600	261 400	37 800
6	Cashiers and tellers	229 600	263 800	34 200
7	Carpenters	107 300	138 100	30 800
8	General office clerks	136 400	165 300	28 900
9	Waiters and waitresses	252 400	281 000	28 700
10	Guards and security personnel	76 900	101 500	24 600
11	Typists and clerk typists	95 700	118 400	22 700
12	Receptionists	90 400	112 000	21 600
13	Sales management occupations	169 900	191 100	21 200
14	Non-construction labourers	54 200	74 900	20 700
15	Graduate nurses, non-supervisory	185 500	206 100	20 600
16	Welders	79 800	99 800	20 000
17	Industrial farm mechanics	88 200	108 000	19 800
18	Auto mechanics	140 700	160 000	19 300
19	Sewing machine occupations	88 100	106 600	18 500
20	Bus drivers	49 000	67 400	18 400
21	Chefs and cooks	162 500	180 800	18 300
22	Non-construction supervisors	66 500	84 300	17 900
23	General managers	79 200	96 800	17 600
24	Nursery workers	58 800	75 900	17 100
25	E.D.P. equipment operators	71 300	88 100	16 800
26	Police officers	53 800	69 300	15 500
27	Stock clerks	91 500	106 600	15 100
28	Systems analysts	56 800	71 900	15 100
29	Shipping clerks	84 200	98 500	14 300
30	Commercial travellers	95 900	109 600	13 700

Source: Adapted from Government of Canada Consultation Paper on Training (Ottawa: Supply and Services, 1984).

of production workers was offset by a concomitant or proportionately greater increase in the skill levels of job setters and maintenance and repair personnel. In other cases, the net effect of the introduction of automated equipment was to reduce the overall skill level of plant workers. Had Bright undertaken his study more recently, he may have discovered a more pronounced tendency toward overall reduction of skill levels. In new continuous-process facilities, for example, management customarily minimizes its dependence on skilled workers by assigning maintenance and repair duties to semiskilled operators.

Automation has displaced skilled labour in other areas besides the continuous-process facilities and high-tech industries named above. Machine shops, which until recently were repositories of production skill, have been invaded by numerically controlled (NC) machines. Mass production plants are turning more and more to robotics. According to Shaiken (1984:8), "computer systems not only control the operations of machine tools, but track raw materials coming into the shop, inventory completed parts, monitor robots on the assembly line, and schedule production." While the productive capacity of this technology is of no little interest to management, profits and power are the major considerations. Numerically controlled machines enable management to transfer the control and operation of the machine from skilled workers to a preprogrammed set of instructions recorded on a tape. From management's point of view, all that should be left for the worker to do is to load and unload the machine. But the stakes involved here are workers' skills and control. There is no technical or other reason why skilled workers could not assume programming tasks, but management customarily prefers to hire university-trained (non-union) personnel for this job. This preference attests to management's intent to destroy the shop-floor and union power of skilled machinists (Noble, 1984; Howard, 1985). The magazine *Iron Age* quite candidly stresses this managerial advantage: "Numerical control is more than a means of controlling a machine. It embodies much of what the father of scientific management, Frederick Winslow Taylor, sought . . . [namely] taking the control of the machine shop out of the hands of many workmen and placing it completely in the hands of management" (cited in Shaiken, 1984:44). Not only are the skills and power of skilled machinists threatened, even the high-tech jobs of programmers and other software personnel are insecure due to the introduction of what is known as computer aided design (CAD). Engineers can now use electronic pencils, press buttons, or give keyboard instructions to design objects on an electronic drawing board; these designs can then be relayed directly to the numerically controlled machines. "With conventional methods, an engineer would design the part, a draftsman would draw it, and a machinist would build it. Now CAD is capable of translating a design directly into a part program that guides the cutting tool on an NC machine, eliminating all intervening steps between design and production" (Shaiken, 1984:219-20).

Robot usage is also growing at an exponential rate as this equipment is being refined and costs are dropping. Robots were initially employed to perform some of the most undesirable factory jobs like spot welding and spray painting, but as robots become more flexible they are beginning to take over more attractive jobs such as inspection. Finally, microtechnology has become the basis of new systems capable of monitoring workers' activities. These systems report, among other things, the rate at which parts are being produced on a machine and the length of time the operator is away from the machine (Shaiken, 1984).

Fortunately, we can qualify the bleakness of the scenario portrayed above if only because management's expectations for technology are not always realized. New machinery is often much less automatic and reliable and more "temperamental" than management anticipates or than advertising brochures lead them to expect. As a result, the skill and judgement of workers may still be required to get out production (Salzman and Mirvis, 1985). In addition, workers and unions have resisted encroachments on shopfloor skill and power, and in some cases they have succeeded in tempering the technology's degrading effects (Noble, 1984). But these are holding actions. In North America, the introduction, deployment, and uses

of technology are determined by owners and managers of the means of production. Unions have adopted, for the most part, a reactive approach to technological advances. Ideally, unions would challenge or veto management decisions about the character and purposes of new technology, but, as it is, they have largely restricted their concern to minimizing its adverse impact on employees. These tendencies are likely to persist as long as present configurations of political and economic power prevail.

It is not unreasonable to close the discussion on a pessimistic note. In the short run, there appears to be little likelihood that new, sophisticated forms of technology will have a liberating impact on the labour process and workers. This is not due to any intrinsically alienating properties of technology; it is a result of the manner in which technology is designed and selected, and the purposes for which it is employed.

REFERENCES

Appelbaum, E.
  1984   "High Tech and the Structural Employment Problems of the 1980s," in *American Jobs and the Changing Industrial Base,* ed. E. Collins and L. Dewey Tanner. Cambridge: Ballinger.

Blauner, R.
  1967   *Alienation and Freedom.* Chicago: University of Chicago Press.

Bright, J.
  1958   *Automation and Management.* Boston: Harvard University School of Business Administration.

Harvey, E., and J. Blakely
  1985   "Education, Social Mobility, and the Challenge of Technological Change," in *Transitions to Work,* ed. E. B. Harvey and J. Blakely, pp. 46-65. University of Manitoba: Institute for Social and Economic Research.

Heilbronner, R.
  1965   *The Limits of American Capitalism.* New York: Harper and Row.

Hill, S.
>
> 1981   *Competition and Control at Work.* London: Heinemann.

Howard, R.
>
> 1985   *Brave New Workplace.* New York: Viking.

Newton, K.
>
> 1985   "Employment Effects of Technological Change." Ottawa: Economic Council of Canada.

Noble, D. F.
>
> 1984   *Forces of Production: A Social History of Industrial Automation.* New York: Alfred A. Knopf.

Roberts, M.
>
> 1984   "A Labor Perspective on Technological Change," in *American Jobs and the Changing Industrial Base,* ed. E. Collins and L. Dewey Tanner, pp. 183-205. Cambridge: Ballinger.

Salzman, H., and P. Mirvis
>
> 1985   "The Work Force Transition to New Computer Technologies: Changes in Skills and Quality of Work Life," in *Transitions to Work,* ed. E. B. Harvey and J. Blakely, pp. 66-87. University of Manitoba: Institute for Social and Economic Research.

Shaiken, H.
>
> 1984   *Work Transformed: Automation and Labor in the Computer Age.* New York: Holt, Rinehart and Winston.

Sussman, G. I.
>
> 1972   "Process Design, Automation, and Worker Alienation," *Industrial Relations,* 11:34-45.

White, J.
>
> 1983   *Women and Part-Time Work.* Ottawa: The Canadian Advisory Council on the Status of Women.

FOR FURTHER READING

Boyd, Monica, John Goyder, Frank Jones, Hugh McRoberts, Peter Pineo, and John Porter. 1985. *Ascription and Achievement*. Ottawa: Carleton University Press. This is the most comprehensive work that has been conducted on occupational mobility and status attainment in Canada. Using national survey data and sophisticated techniques of analysis, the authors investigate the impact on mobility and attainment of a wide range of social background characteristics, including socio-economic origin, family size, gender, language, nativity, and immigration status.

Lowe, Graham S., and Harvey J. Krahn, eds. 1984. *Working Canadians: The Sociology of Work and Industry*. Toronto: Methuen. The essays in this collection assess a range of issues in the study of work and occupations that are of relevance to problems of inequality. These include questions of the relationship between management and labour, the organization of the workplace, the situation of working women, and the role of unions.

Lundy, Katherina, and Barbara Warme, eds. 1986. *Work in the Canadian Context* (2nd ed.). Toronto: Butterworths. The editors of this collection have compiled numerous articles dealing with various aspects of work in Canada. Many of these papers have relevance to the study of social inequality, including those dealing with the changing occupational structure, the earnings of occupations, working class ideology, and the impact of technological change on the organization of work.

Riddell, W. Craig, ed. 1985. *Work and Pay: The Canadian Labour Market*. Toronto: University of Toronto Press. This is one of several books produced in co-operation with the Royal Commission on the Economic Union and Development Prospects for Canada. This work assesses such topics as labour force trends, the labour market activities of Canadian women, the question of employment sharing to reduce unemployment, and the problems of discrimination, equal pay, and equal opportunity in the Canadian labour market.

Rinehart, James W. 1987. *The Tyranny of Work* (2nd ed.). Toronto: Harcourt Brace Jovanovich. This is a monograph on the nature of work in Canada, with particular concern for the labour process and the problem of alienation. Some of the key issues considered include the development of industrial capitalism in Canada, the sources of alienation at work, and the similarities and differences between the white-collar and the blue-collar worlds of work.

C: Education

---

12. Problems around Educational Opportunity

Robert M. Pike

As the late American scholar and administrator Frank Bowles (1965) noted, the notion that every person should have an opportunity for an education commensurate with his or her abilities has, under the general rubric of "Freedom of Education," been as influential in its policy outcomes in this century as freedom of speech and freedom of worship were in the eighteenth century. Essentially, at the roots of this notion lies the belief that all young people should be provided with the opportunity for an education commensurate with their abilities, irrespective of their origins, locality, race, or sex. In other words, equality of educational opportunity, and hence of policy designed to achieve it, is founded on the belief that ascriptive factors of environment over which the child has little control—for example, the

Revised from Robert M. Pike, "Equality of Educational Opportunity: Dilemmas and Policy Options," *Interchange,* vol. 9, no. 2 (1978/79), pp. 30-35. Reprinted with permission.

economic level of the family into which he or she is born, or social attitudes toward the race of which he or she is a member— should not be allowed to create barriers to the full realization of the child's intellectual potential.

On the one hand, I think we can recognize that the ideals which lie behind this concept are truly noble ones insofar as they are associated with a concern for the achievement of a more socially just society than presently exists in Canada or elsewhere. On the other hand, we would do little to further the attainment of this goal if we were to ignore the existence of a measure of disillusionment in some educational circles —a disillusionment which has been generated as a result of the apparent ineffectiveness of many of the policies which were formulated during the 1960s to provide a greater degree of educational equality for children from disadvantaged social and racial groups. In turn, this disillusionment has tended to extend beyond a critical appraisal of specific policies to encompass a thoroughgoing reappraisal of the general efficacy of the educational system as an agent for social equalization. In the light of this reappraisal, it is my purpose here to weave together the following major themes. First, I would like to explore the changing nature of educational policies which have been designed to achieve the ultimate goal of equality of educational opportunity in Western industrial countries. Second, I intend to look at two sets of intellectual and ideological responses which have emerged in response to the ongoing reappraisal of the social role of the educational system as an agent for social equalization. Finally, at various points in the paper, I hope to explore some of the relevant policy options that are now open to educators and educational administrators. I should stress that I make no claims to being an expert on the administration or planning of specific educational policies or practices. Rather, as a sociologist, my task is limited to a general review of the role of the educational system as an agent of social reform within the context of Canadian and American society.

EDUCATIONAL POLICIES LEADING TO EDUCATIONAL EQUALITY

Turning now to the first theme, it is interesting to note that there does appear to be a substantial measure of consensus in Western countries that such policies have tended to be introduced in a series of successive phases—the number of such phases is often taken to be three up to the present time (see notably OECD, 1976:38-40)—and that the reasons for the movement from the first to the second phase and from the second to the third phase are, where such movements have occurred, related to a recognition that

the policies of the preceding phase have failed to deliver the goods—that is, they have failed to facilitate the achievement of greater equality of educational opportunity to the satisfaction of many educationalists and educational administrators. Of course, since we are talking in general terms here, it will be recognized that not all Western countries have reached the same phase in this evolutionary movement. Some still restrict themselves mainly to policies at the first phase; others have moved well into the second phase; and a few of the wealthier ones, including Canada and the United States, are now into the third phase (OECD, 1976:39). Furthermore, it should be stressed that the policies introduced in the earlier phases are generally not discontinued but are maintained as essential features of a comprehensive program of educational equality into which the policies of the later phases can be incorporated.

At this point, I should obviously provide some kind of description of the main features of these three phases. In the succession of efforts designed to achieve equality of educational opportunity, the first phase occurs at the point where it is hoped that this goal can be achieved by affording children free access to all schools in their localities. Hence, the policy emphasis is placed upon free schooling, at least to the end of the compulsory period, and possibly on the admission of all children to a common secondary school with elements of a common curriculum. Furthermore, a good deal of importance is placed upon providing equality of facilities between schools in various parts of the educational jurisdiction—between urban and rural schools and between schools in high- and low-income areas of the cities. In the words of the OECD examiners, "the belief was that this approach would suffice to open to all children—even those from the submerged social groups—access to schools that would lead on to further opportunities, and that this would be the way to remove inequalities and injustices." However, they go on, "in most countries, these hopes were not realized. Most of these children were not able to succeed in the traditional programs of the schools, or showed themselves so little interested in them that they dropped out at the end of the period of compulsory schooling, or sometimes even earlier" (OECD, 1976:38).

The failure of free access to schooling to provide equality of educational opportunity for socially disadvantaged children led many jurisdictions to look more closely at the exceptional complexity of inequality. In particular, they came to realize that the foundations for inequality of opportunity in the school are set in the preschool years, when children develop the various behavioural and linguistic skills which later become vitally important to the process of learning within the school. Hence, the recognition that many socially disadvantaged children —with the members of certain racial and ethnic minorities prominent among them —are often ill prepared through early socialization to meet the demands placed upon them by the educational system (not to mention the fact that some children from low-income families may, even in our prosperous society, arrive at school without adequate nourishment or clothing) led to the second policy phase, prominent during the 1960s, which emphasized preschool education and remedial measures through compensatory education and, in some cases, placed more stress on practice-oriented courses and improved counselling. In other words, while in phase 1 the educational facilities were made available and the children were supposed to take advantage of them, in phase 2 the school was perceived as a posi-

tive agent for social reform, combatting those patterns of social and economic inequality which arise in countries such as Canada and the United States where there are wide variations in the distribution of income and styles of life.

I shall delay a description of the movement from the second to the third policy phase until later in this paper. Here, I wish to concentrate, for the moment, on the educational outcomes of this second phase, because they are linked to the element of disillusionment with educational equalization policies referred to earlier. In their review, the OECD examiners throw light on the matter when they note that "even the most comprehensive [phase-2] program of in-school efforts has not alone sufficed to eliminate the many-sided forms of disadvantage and inequality of opportunity that children experience" (p.39). More specifically, while there is certainly not universal agreement on the relative effectiveness of many phase-2 programs, some educators have been discouraged to find that the mental gains and improvements in scholastic achievement, which have been the goals of the provision of remedial and compensatory education to socially disadvantaged children, have either not been achieved or, where achieved, have not been maintained during the subsequent years of normal schooling. As a consequence of this apparent inability of the educational system to combat the impact of environmental inequalities (even when the children are "caught young"), much of the early optimism has tended to vanish in a cloud of accusations and counteraccusations, of arguments and controversies, and of downright ideological pamphleteering, all of which have had as their major foci either the supposed benefits and deficits of particular compensatory programs or, more generally, the supposed failure of the educational system as an agent for major social reform. Two sets of sociological explanations for the limited success of many phase-2 programs are worth reviewing here, because of their relevance to an understanding of the enormous complexities of the interrelationship between educational system, student, and external social environment.

SOCIOLOGICAL EXPLANATIONS

I will combine the first set of sociological explanations under the heading of "arguments for equality of condition." Briefly, these arguments run as follows: that the major socialization agency which influences children during their early years is the family, and even in later years children seem to be more influenced by family, and possibly by neighbourhood and by mass media, than they are by the school. Since families may be very rich or grindingly poor, live in mansions or slums, include parents with university degrees or with little education, the differential impact of these variations in living and learning conditions on both opportunities and preparedness for learning is sufficiently great to limit severely the effect of the school (which, after all, only takes students for a few hours each day) as an agency of social equalization. The school is, in fact, attempting to compensate for disadvantaged environments, which continue to exert a far more powerful and long-term influence than the school itself is able to do (Carnoy and Levin, 1976:1-20; Karabel and Halsey, 1977:230,241). Furthermore, it is well to note here the comment of the American sociologist Christopher Jencks that even within the school setting, reformers have very little control over those aspects of school life which really affect children. In his

words, "reallocating resources, reassigning pupils and rewriting the curriculum seldom change the way teachers and students actually treat each other minute by minute" (1973:255). In other words, it is the intimate classroom relationships between students and teachers which play a major part in determining whether disadvantaged children are likely to take advantage of learning situations.

Now, the policy ramifications associated with this set of explanations tend to be very broad and somewhat controversial. We may, however, outline briefly a further related argument of some sociologists and educationalists, one with which I confess to having some sympathy. Thus, if we accept that some of the major inequalities of educational opportunity between children in our society arise from prior inequalities of condition—that is, major inequalities in income, power, and prestige—then it does not seem particularly effective or logical to use the school as an institutional device to remedy some of the negative effects of these inequalities upon the academic performance of school children unless we also place a major emphasis on reducing the inequalities of conditions in our society through progressive income redistribution measures and similar devices. After all, so the argument continues, if we can eradicate poverty and achieve a greater equality of income at a level which permits decent living conditions for all, then presumably the educational system will confront a less formidable range of environmental inequalities among children than currently exists, and will, therefore, be able to concentrate more effectively on coping with those inequalities which persist. But then again, it would follow reasonably from this viewpoint that if we do not make major efforts to achieve a greater equality of income and living conditions, and attempt instead to rely on the resources of the school, not only do we stand to be branded as hypocrites for our unwillingness to seek to remedy the economic determinants of educational inequalities at the source but also we are bound to fail in our school-related measures because of the primacy of family and neighbourhood in the process of socialization.

These are arguments with which, as I say, I have some sympathy. I should however, make it clear here that not even the most idealistic of their proponents would believe that the achievement of a greater degree of economic equality in society would eradicate all major environmental variations between social groups, nor would they wish necessarily to advocate that these social and cultural variations should be eradicated. To take a case in point, one is bound to recognize in Canada the existence of substantial cultural variations between racial and ethnic groups, and these variations would probably continue to have a major influence on their young members' attitudes toward the value of education, and hence on students' levels of academic performance, even in circumstances where there existed a high level of equality in incomes and overall living conditions.

Turning now to the second set of sociological explanations, which I shall describe here as "the Marxist perspective," these really arise as an extension of misgivings, expressed by many members of the "equality of condition" school, about the equalizing role of the educational system. In a nutshell, there is a growing body of educational literature of a Marxist orientation, emanating mainly from universities in Britain and the United States, which argues essentially that the educational systems of Western industrial countries are little more than institutional tools of social control whereby the dominant social classes in these countries both maintain and legitimate the transference of their power from one generation to the next (see Bowles and Gintis, 1976; Dale et al., 1976; Carnoy, 1974). Given this viewpoint, it follows that liberal measures designed to equalize educational opportunities are not likely to have much impact, no matter how idealistic and well-motivated educational reformers may be, because the main purpose of schools is to maintain the social, political, and economic conditions which favour capitalist development and capitalist exploitation. Furthermore, so the argument goes, the educational system will continue to be largely a tool of the existing capitalist social order—that is, it will be incapable of having much impact upon class inequalities until the capitalist system gives way to some more socially just form of society.

Now, the uncomfortable feature of this point of view is that it can produce a good deal of hard evidence to demonstrate the importance of the role of the educational system as an agency for the intergenerational continuity of class position and class privilege. Thus, to take just a couple of examples, Marion Porter, John Porter, and Bernard Blishen, in their survey of Ontario high-school students carried out in 1971, show quite clearly how family background plays a role which is just about as important as measured intelligence in influencing students' choice of high-school program and their ultimate educational plans (Porter, Porter, and Blishen, 1975). At the time of their survey, bright working-class children in Ontario were far more likely to enrol in the four-year programs terminating in grade 12 than were bright middle-class children (who were much more likely to opt for the five-year programs); and they were much less likely to expect that they would go on to university, even in instances where they aspired to continue their studies at the university level. Similarly, in a recent study which looks at the social consequences of the expansion of higher education in the United States, Peter Scott shows that even the substantial provision of post-secondary educational opportunities for a wide range of talents in that country has by no means eliminated the substantial proportionate underrepresentation of lower-class and racial-minority youth at American institutions of higher learning (Scott, 1975). In the light of such evidence, one can perhaps gain some consolation from the fact that these patterns of class inequality are to be found within the educational systems of all societies, be they based on politico-economic doctrines that are capitalist, socialist, or communist. However, while the proponents of the Marxist argument cannot be faulted on this score—because they generally make it quite clear that their vision of the just society does not resemble the social systems of existing communist and socialist states—they can perhaps be criticized both for their tendency to fit the educational system too neatly to the prevailing economic order (a viewpoint which effectively denies the possibilities of significant change occurring within the system) and for their frequent oversimplification of the major differences in the social forces and social ideologies which have moulded educational systems in various Western industrial countries. After all, England, Sweden, Canada, and the United States would all be defined as countries with capitalist economies; but how can one explain away, by reference to capitalist patterns of class domination, the high emphasis on openness and equality found in Swedish and U.S. education, and more recently in the structure of Canadian education, in contrast to the traditional emphasis on selectivity and academic elitism which is dying so hard in English secondary education?

These then are some of the major types of explanations given for the limited impact upon educational opportunities of various forms of phase-2 programming. It could hardly be claimed that they provide a very optimistic prognosis for the future role of the educational system as an instrument of social reform. Indeed, the more extreme "equality of condition" and Marxist arguments confront us with something of a dilemma, because if the educational system is inevitably limited in its impact on children's learning potential by the continuation of major environmental inequalities and inequalities in the distribution of power, then it would seem illogical to continue to spend money on increasingly sophisticated programs designed to enhance the mental and scholastic capacities of disadvantaged children. It might also seem illogical to plan major new strategies for the future, since they would appear to be likely to fail for the same kind of reasons. However, such a line of argument is rather defeatist in the sense that it appears to this author to be more reasonable to argue—as indeed do many proponents of the "equality of condition" line—that what *should* be taking place in our society is a two-pronged attack on both inequality of condition and inequality of opportunity, with the schools continuing to strive against those physical and mental outcomes of environmental inequalities which limit learning potential and dampen ambition. Furthermore, it should be recognized that there are many aspects of the pursuit of equality of educational opportunity through the schools—for example, in fostering the educational participation of immigrant children or in countering discrimination on the basis of sex—where the major policy emphasis is not so much on compensatory education as on the devising of programs designed to overcome difficulties imposed by differences in language and culture. In the case of these kinds of programs and policies, the role of the school in the process of equalization would appear to be quite fundamental.

PHASE 3—LIFELONG EDUCATION

To this point in the paper, most of our discussion about equality of educational opportunity and measures taken to foster it has centred around providing programs and services for young people of what is termed "school age." This is quite natural in light of the fact that most phase-1 and phase-2 equalization policies have been aimed at children and adolescents. However, it has been the limited success of these policies, combined with some reassessment of the definition of what constitutes equality of educational opportunity, that has led some countries—with Canada among them—to move on to the third phase in the pursuit of educational equality to which I referred earlier. This phase, in the words of the OECD examiners, is particularly characterized by "the recognition that the right to equality of educational opportunity should not remain confined to the short period of childhood and youth, but should be a lifelong recurrent principle, aimed at catching up on lost chances, and at opening up new opportunities" (p. 39). In other words, while we will undoubtedly continue to combat the impact of environmental inequalities on the educational opportunities of young people, the field of battle is now being extended to the provision of new educational opportunities to adults of all ages.

The educational ideas and concepts which lie behind this third phase of the pursuit of equality of educational opportunity appear to be particularly attractive. What the principles of "recurrent" or "lifelong" education stress is the elimination of institutions and programs which are dead ends and which block the further educational progress of students. What the principles encourage is the belief in education as a lifelong process, so that although a student may drop out of the educational system at the age of 16, he or she is not thereby permanently labelled and stigmatized as a drop-out but rather as someone who may wish—and hence should be provided with the opportunity—to drop back into the system (at age 20 or 30 or in later life) on a part-time or full-time basis. The particular attraction of many recurrent and lifelong education policies—evident, for example, in the establishment of adult high schools in Denmark, in the wide provision of facilities for correspondence education for adults in many countries, and in the formation of such institutions as Britain's Open University and, on a far smaller scale, Athabasca University in Alberta, both of which provide degree-level education almost solely through modes of distance learning—is that not only do they facilitate reentry to the educational process of numbers of people who were denied adequate educational opportunities in their youth but also, by de-emphasizing the traditional attitude that education is something which happens between the ages of four and 24 (and mostly between the ages of six and 16), such policies help to take some of the burden of combatting the external causes of school failure off the beleaguered institutional shoulders of the existing primary and secondary schools. People at least have the opportunity to try again.

As already mentioned, Canada has embarked upon this third phase of policies for educational opportunity—indeed, the OECD examiners cite as its precondition "an open-ended educational system that has eliminated institutions and curricula that are dead ends" and believe that Canadian educational systems have come a long way along this road through the development of flexible principles of operation which avoid "writing off" young people as failures (p. 39). What then is the way ahead? Well, from this writer's perspective, it lies along the route outlined in the reports of two provincial education commissions which were published during the same *annus mirabilis*—1972— and which have been described, by a non-Canadian educationalist, as offering "two instances from 'advanced' democratically based societies of detailed proposals for educational systems based on patterns of recurrent learning" (Molyneux, 1974:119). These commissions—the Commission on Post-secondary Education in Ontario and the Commission on Educational Planning in Alberta—were concerned with far broader policy issues than those linked directly to educational opportunity, but in Molyneux's words "the time has come to invest [the individual student] with considerable choice in deciding when, where, and how he will seek to learn. Such choice has long been a hallmark of the elite in various societies. Alberta and Ontario are significant in seriously proposing to make the traditional privilege a universal opportunity and in regarding it as a social necessity." These are brave words, and it is more than a little disillusioning to recognize that the practical impact of the reports on educational policy-making in this country appears, so far at least, to have been very limited. However, there can be little doubt that the substantial increase in the variety of modes and channels of learning which these reports propose would, if instituted, facilitate the task of educational equalization—although, to stress a point made earlier, only the most idealistic or the most naïve would believe that educational reform, unless accompanied by greater equality of condition, can successfully achieve its desired goals.

ULTIMATE LIMITATIONS

Within the foregoing thoughts, the main thrust of this paper is completed. It is possible, one supposes, that at some future time there may be a series of phase-4 educational equalization policies added to those of phase 3, but I would hesitate to guess what the pursuit of such policies might entail. However, the very thought of such a possibility leads me to conclude on a cautionary note by making reference to the cynical comment of a social philosopher, whose name I cannot now recall, to the effect that the only really effective way of ensuring true equality of educational opportunity in a society would be to ensure that all children undergo surgery for the severing of the frontal lobes of their brains. The point that he was trying to make with this comment is that while the achievement of equality of educational opportunity is clearly a valued end, there are limits to the kinds of means one can use to achieve that end—limits which are imposed by the potential conflict between the proposed means and other ends and conditions of existence which are of equal or greater value. Thus, for example, one supposes that class and ethnic differences in early socialization in the family could be largely eliminated by taking all babies from their parents and placing them in state creches. Such a practice might indeed reduce the impact of an unequal external environment on the educational opportunities of children, but there are few people in Canada who would argue that, in this case, the pursuit of the desired goal was worth such drastic means.

REFERENCES

Alberta
1972   *A choice of futures.* Report of the Commission on Educational Planning. Edmonton: Government Printers.

Bowles, F.
1965   "Educational opportunities and political realities." Paper No. 2. New York: Academy for Educational Development.

Bowles, S., and H. Gintis
1976   *Schooling in capitalist America.* New York: Basic Books.

Carnoy, M.
1974   *Education as cultural imperialism.* New York: David McKay.

Carnoy, M., and H. Levin, eds.
1976   *The limits of educational reform.* New York: David McKay.

Dale, R., G. Esland, et al., eds.
1976   *Schooling and capitalism: A sociological reader.* London: Routledge and Kegan Paul, and The Open University Press.

Gilbert, S., and H. McRoberts
1975   "Differentiation and stratification: The issue of inequality," in *Issues in Canadian Society,* ed. D. Forcese and S. Richer. Scarborough: Prentice-Hall Canada.

Jencks, C.
1973   *Inequality: A reassessment of the effect of family and schooling in America.* New York: Harper Colophon.

Karabel, J., and A. H. Halsey, eds.
1977   *Power and ideology in education.* New York: University Press.
1977   *Educational research: A review and interpretation.*

Molyneux, F.
1974   "International perspectives," in *Recurrent education,* ed. V. Houghton and F. Richardson. London: Ward Lock.

Ontario
1972   *The learning society.* Report of the Commission on post-secondary education in Ontario. Toronto: Ministry of Government Services.

Organization for Economic Cooperation and Development
1976   *Review of national policies for education: Canada.* Paris, Ont.: OECD.

Pike, R.
1975   "Excellence or equality: A dilemma for higher education," *The Canadian Journal of Higher Education,* 5:69-75.

Porter, M., J. Porter, and B. Blishen
1975   *Does money matter?* Toronto: Institute for Behavioral Research, York University.

Scott, P.
1975   *Strategies for post-secondary education.* London: Croom Helm.

13. Changing Patterns of Educational Inequality

Neil Guppy
Paulina D. Mikicich
Ravi Pendakur

In this paper we address the question of historical changes in Canadian educational inequalities. In particular, we focus on the influence of social origin upon educational attainment (see Cuneo and Curtis, 1975; Porter et al., 1982). There has been no systematic assessment of whether the relationship between origin and attainment has altered over the course of this century. To address this issue, we present cohort data on the extent to which students from differing social backgrounds, as measured by father's occupation and parental education, have unequal probabilities of school attainment.

Sociologists focussing on inequality in Canada present very different views concerning possible *changes* in the relationship between social origin and schooling. On the one hand, certain writers perceive a reduction in levels of educational inequality in Canada. Hunter (1981:74-75) notes that "a general upgrading in the educational qualifications of the Canadian population" has been accompanied by "a progressive reduction in the level of educational inequality" (see also Harp, 1980:231; Harvey, 1977:10-11). On the other hand, several analysts have concluded that inequalities in schooling continue—that "ascriptive factors . . . have not diminished in importance and indeed seem to be persistent and patterned obstacles which . . . limit actual [educational] achievement" (Himelfarb and Richardson, 1982:305; see also Marchak, 1981:27-28). The latter view is stated even more emphatically by Forcese (1980:95), who contends that "formal education is a cause of persistent and *increasingly* rigid stratification" (our emphasis).

One of the striking features of this disagreement is the lack of any systematic em-

Reprinted with some revisions from *The Canadian Journal of Sociology*, vol. 9, no. 3 (Summer 1984), pp. 319-31. Reprinted with permission.

pirical investigation that would support or undermine either view. Any solid conclusions about trends in educational inequality should be based on data which cover extended time periods; however, to date, trend studies have been rare, have not always employed national data and have been restricted to short time-spans of less than a single decade (e.g., Hunter, 1981; Harvey, 1977).

Methodological differences among studies and diverging claims about what is happening over time to educational inequalities can also be found in the comparative international literature. Boudon (1974:53), for example, concluded that "Western societies are characterized by a steady and slow decline of inequalities in educational opportunities." Conversely, Halsey, Heath, and Ridge (1980:205) maintained that in the United Kingdom "school inequalities of opportunity have been remarkably stable over the 40 years which [the] study covers." These divergent conclusions probably reflect, among other things, differences inherent in the countries studied and in the methodologies used.

The purpose of this paper is to conduct a systematic analysis of the historical changes in Canadian educational inequalities. Using a national survey, we determine the extent to which students from differing social origins have unequal probabilities of school success. More importantly, we consider the ways in which this relationship has changed in Canada since early in this century. Our interest centres, then, on the three-way interaction between origin, cohort, and schooling—does the relationship between social origin and educational attainment vary systematically for different cohorts?

As we have shown, the Canadian literature contains two differing hypotheses with respect to this question. Some writers (Himelfarb and Richardson, 1982; Marchak, 1981; Forcese, 1980) maintain that educational inequalities have persisted so that the impact of social background on educational attainment has continued—a "constant effects" hypothesis. Others (Hunter, 1981; Harp, 1980; Harvey, 1977) suggest that across time the strength of the relationships between origin and attainment has weakened—a "diminishing effects" hypothesis.

DATA AND METHODS

In order to assess these two hypotheses, we chart the educational attainments of Canadians from different social origins grouped into *birth* cohorts spanning a 40-year period (1913-52).

The data for the analyses are drawn from the 1973 Canadian Mobility Study conducted by Boyd et al. (1977). The study focussed on males and females over the age of 17 who were not full-time students (a constraint which we discuss below). The final sample consisted of 44 868 respondents. We restrict our attention to a subset of this larger sample by focussing on birth cohorts composed of respondents between the ages of 20 and 60 and eliminating anyone receiving part of their education outside of Canada.

We employ the following strategy to operationalize our variables. Our first measure of social origin is based on father's occupation (when the respondent was 16), which we have collapsed into four categories: farmers, blue-collar, white-collar, and professional/managerial (prof/man) workers. Parental education, our second indicator of social origin, is a three-valued measure based on whether neither parent, one parent, or both parents completed high school. We assess historical trends by examining the educational attainments of people from four birth cohorts: 1913-22, 1923-32, 1933-42, and 1943-52. Towards the end of the analysis we further subdivide the cohorts to provide greater detail.

In our initial analysis we use high-school completion rates as our measure of educational attainment. However, because the three-way interaction of origin, cohort, and schooling varies for different measures of educational attainment, we also employ other indicators of school survival and achievement. It is important to consider, for example, whether over time socio-economic inequalities have diminished at the high-school level while remaining constant at post-secondary levels.

DATA ANALYSIS

Table 13-1 presents findings on the percentage of respondents completing high school by social background and birth cohort. As shown in this table, high-school comple-

tion rates have risen across the four cohorts from 37.1 percent to 67.5 percent. Furthermore, high-school completion rates have increased for each socio-economic category. Completion rates have remained the highest for the prof/man strata, increasing from 71.6 percent to 84.9 percent. For those from farming backgrounds the rates have changed from 24.0 percent in the first cohort to 58.8 percent in the last cohort, the largest percentage increase over time for any occupational category.

It could be argued that our measure of social origin is inadequate. For this reason, parental education is used as an alternative gauge to assess the influence of social origin upon high-school completion (see Table 13-2). For the three categories of parental education, high-school completion, in all but one case, increases over the four cohorts. As anticipated, the likelihood of a respondent completing secondary school is higher when both parents are also high-school graduates. Thus, using two different measures of social origin, we find that the general relationship between family back-

TABLE 13-1 Percentage of respondents who have completed high school by father's occupation and birth cohort.

	Birth cohort				
Father's occupation	1913-22	1923-32	1933-42	1943-52	Row totals
Professional/managerial	71.6 (385)	70.6 (445)	79.8 (615)	84.9 (1 230)	79.0 (2 675)
White-collar	57.9 (256)	61.3 (294)	64.9 (412)	73.4 (811)	66.6 (1 773)
Blue-collar	35.4 (746)	37.8 (990)	47.8 (1 390)	63.2 (3 003)	49.5 (6 129)
Farm	24.0 (442)	27.5 (465)	41.7 (556)	58.8 (772)	36.2 (2 235)
Column totals	37.1 (1 829)	40.5 (2 194)	52.6 (2 973)	67.5 (5 816)	(12 813)

ground and educational attainment has weakened over time.

Both Tables 13-1 and 13-2 suggest that egalitarian influences have increased for socio-economic disparities between high-school completion rates. However, we need to assess whether this pattern holds for higher levels of schooling. In order to do so, we replicated the analyses presented in Tables 13-1 and 13-2 for respondents who reported some attendance at university.

Table 13-3 shows the percentages of respondents with some university experience by origin and cohort. On the whole, the

TABLE 13-2   Percentage of respondents who have completed high school by parental education and birth cohort.

		Birth cohort			
Parental education	1913-22	1923-32	1933-42	1943-52	Row totals
Both parents completed high school	80.4 (344)	78.8 (380)	88.8 (545)	88.9 (1 299)	86.0 (2 567)
One parent completed high school	59.6 (364)	61.0 (489)	70.9 (749)	81.1 (1 564)	72.0 (3 166)
Neither parent completed high school	29.0 (1 157)	32.3 (1 327)	41.9 (1 699)	56.9 (3 100)	41.4 (7 283)
Column totals	37.1 (1 865)	40.7 (2 196)	52.3 (2 993)	67.5 (5 963)	(13 017)

TABLE 13-3   Percentage of respondents with some university experience by social origin (father's occupation) and birth cohort.

		Birth cohort			
Father's class	1913-22	1923-32	1933-42	1943-52	Row totals
Professional/managerial	25.5 (137)	27.3 (172)	38.1 (294)	35.1 (508)	32.8 (1 112)
White-collar	12.0 (53)	16.9 (81)	18.6 (118)	19.1 (211)	17.4 (463)
Blue-collar	7.3 (154)	6.3 (166)	11.6 (337)	12.1 (574)	9.9 (1 231)
Farm	5.8 (106)	6.6 (111)	9.7 (129)	12.0 (157)	8.1 (502)
Column totals	9.1 (450)	9.8 (530)	15.4 (878)	16.8 (1 450)	(3 308)

percentage of respondents reporting some university attendance steadily increases over the four cohorts. It is nevertheless important to note that the disparities are far stronger at this level of education than was the case for high-school completion.

In contrast to employing differing levels of educational experience, Table 13-4 presents results using completed years of education as the dependent variable. Furthermore, in order to provide a finer breakdown of results, the birth cohort variable has been divided into eight rather than four intervals.

This table shows that for all strata, average years of education have increased over the 1913 to 1947 period. In addition, disparities continue to exist across the cohorts. Up until 1937 there appears to have been a slight increase in the difference between the mean years of schooling for the prof/man and farm categories (see the bottom row of Table 13-4). This contrasts with the results for the last three cohorts, where this difference is declining. However, the figure of 1.62 for the 1948-52 cohort appears suspiciously low. Consider that for the other seven cohorts the figure for average years of education increases for the prof/man category (as expected), yet drops for the last cohort. This is probably due to sampling underrepresentation.

DISCUSSION AND CONCLUSIONS

Our results indicate that the relationship between social origin and educational attainment has weakened over time. We hasten to stress that social origin continues to exert a strong influence on levels of schooling, although the impact has declined through this century. However, even here we must be cautious because, while origin plays a decreasingly important role in high-school

completion, this decline is far less apparent with respect to post-secondary education. When we measure educational achievement as the probability of attaining some university experience, we find the effect of social origin has, at best, diminished only moderately over time (cf. Goyder, 1980). Furthermore, as noted above, our results do not take into account ethnic, regional, or other differences where educational inequalities could have remained constant, increased, or decreased.

The general patterns of our findings are inconsistent with the results of Halsey, Heath, and Ridge (1980) for males in the United Kingdom, where they found remarkable stability in school inequalities. Their results suggested that educational reforms had done little to equalize educational opportunities, possibly because of the influence of the strong "private" school sector in the British system.

In following Halsey, Heath, and Ridge (1980), our analysis has focussed upon the cumulative impact of social advantage or disadvantage. As such, we have provided an overall portrait of disparities, but we have not endeavoured to pinpoint the effects of social origin on each of the many transitions embedded in the educational system. That is, we have noted that large socio-economic disparities exist at the post-secondary level, but we have not examined exactly how this has come about. For example, students from blue-collar backgrounds may be underrepresented at university as a consequence of their failure to complete high school, their enrolment in high-school programs which prevent immediate transition to university, their decision not to pursue a university education even though eligible, or some combination of these and other factors.

Two final questions must be raised. First, is the gradual reduction, but not elimination, of educational inequality a trend or

TABLE 13-4 Average years of schooling completed by social origin (father's occupation) and birth cohort (five-year intervals).

| | Birth cohorts | | | | | | | | | |
Father's class	1913-17	1918-22	1923-27	1928-32	1933-37	1938-42	1943-47	1948-52	Row totals
Professional/managerial	12.17*	12.31	12.31	13.22	13.86	13.98	14.37	13.60	13.46
	(255)	(262)	(291)	(326)	(316)	(447)	(620)	(790)	(3 307)
White-collar	11.42	11.29	11.99	11.94	11.70	12.61	12.84	12.86	12.30
	(202)	(208)	(220)	(239)	(248)	(290)	(401)	(582)	(2 596)
Blue-collar	9.52	9.78	9.96	10.24	10.70	11.17	12.15	12.05	11.02
	(933)	(986)	(1 115)	(1 336)	(1 261)	(1 522)	(2 122)	(2 494)	(11 769)
Farm	8.73	8.85	8.90	9.62	10.15	10.83	11.61	11.98	9.95
	(819)	(824)	(826)	(747)	(621)	(645)	(639)	(626)	(5 746)
Column totals	9.71	9.87	10.07	10.59	11.08	11.69	12.51	12.42	11.24
	(2 209)	(2 280)	(2 465)	(2 655)	(2 471)	(2 961)	(3 904)	(4 471)	(23 417)
Mean difference (Prof./man − farm)	3.44	3.46	3.41	3.60	3.71	3.15	2.76	1.62	

*The top figure is the average number of years of schooling and the bottom figure is the number of people whose years of schooling were averaged.

merely an historical anomaly soon to disappear? Second, while the influence of origin on years of schooling may have waned in recent years, is it also the case that the impact of social background on the acquisition of academic credentials has diminished?

With respect to the first question, our results do not suggest a gradual, uniform reduction in educational inequalities. In fact, it appears that no reduction whatsoever occurs in the socio-economic differences in years of schooling attained until the cohort of 1938-42 is considered; a cohort that entered high school after World War II. The reduction in inequality *may* thus be interpreted as a consequence of educational reforms introduced in the 1950s and 1960s. Many of these reforms, such as student aid and open learning environments (for the importance of the latter see Richer, 1974), were beneficial to working-class children. However, many of the reforms are now being withdrawn or sharply curtailed as governments react to the social and economic climate of the early 1980s. Should this process continue, the long-term result of such retrenchment could be a return to the levels of educational inequality witnessed earlier

in this century—a process which may enhance the importance of cultural capital as a vehicle of social reproduction (Bourdieu, 1977).

With respect to the question of academic credentials, we must stress that our work suggests that inequalities have reduced in terms of both general level of schooling attained and years of schooling completed. We do not, however, demonstrate that the importance of social background on the acquisition of scholastic credentials has diminished. For example, it is quite conceivable that although individuals from farm or blue-collar backgrounds are attaining ever higher levels of education, they may still be disproportionately underrepresented in selected educational streams which yield more valuable sets of credentials (e.g., professional schools, graduate schools, etc.). Furthermore, if general college and university degrees become increasingly ineffective tickets for occupational and income attainment (see Goyder, 1980), then these professional or graduate degrees will likely prove to be of increasing importance as channels of intergenerational mobility for those from less privileged backgrounds.

REFERENCES

Boudon, R.
  1974   *Education, Opportunity, and Social Inequality.* New York: John Wiley.

Bourdieu, P.
  1977   "Cultural reproduction and social reproduction," in *Power and Ideology in Education,* ed. J. H. Karabel and A. H. Halsey, pp. 487-511. New York: Oxford University Press.

Boyd, M., J. Goyder, F. Jones, H. McRoberts, P. Pineo, and J. Porter
  1977   "The Canadian National Mobility Study," *Canadian Studies in Population,* 4:94-96.

Breton, R.
1970 "Academic stratification in secondary schools and educational plans of students," *Canadian Review of Sociology and Anthropology*, 7, no. 1:17-34.

Cuneo, C., and J. Curtis
1975 "Social ascription in the educational and occupational status attainment of urban Canadians," *Canadian Review of Sociology and Anthropology*, 12, no. 1:6-24.

Forcese, D.
1980 *Canadian Class Structure*. Toronto: McGraw-Hill Ryerson.

Goyder, J.
1980 "Trends in the socioeconomic achievement of the university-educated: a status attainment model interpretation," *Canadian Journal of Higher Education*, 10, no. 2:21-38.

Halsey, A., A. Heath, and J. Ridge
1980 *Origins and Destinations: Family, Class, and Education in Modern Britain*. Oxford: Clarendon Press.

Harp. J.
1980 "Social inequalities and the transmission of knowledge: the case against the schools," in *Structured Inequality in Canada*, ed. J. Harp and J. Hofley, pp. 219-46. Toronto: Prentice-Hall Canada.

Harvey, E.
1977 Accessibility to post-secondary education," *University Affairs* (October): 10-11.

Himelfarb, A., and J. Richardson
1982 *Sociology for Canadians: Images of Society*. Toronto: McGraw-Hill Ryerson.

Hunter, A.
1981 *Class Tells: On Social Inequality in Canada*. Toronto: Butterworth.

Marchak, P.
1981 *Ideological Perspectives on Canada*. (2nd ed.). Toronto: McGraw-Hill Ryerson.

Pineo, P., J. Porter, and H. McRoberts
1977 "The 1971 Census and the socioeconomic classification of occupations," *Canadian Review of Sociology and Anthropology*, 14, no. 1:91-102.

Porter, J., M. Porter, and B. Blishen
1982 *Stations and Callings: Making it Through the Ontario Schools*. Toronto: Methuen.

Richer, S.
1974 "Middle class bias of schools—fact or fancy?" *Sociology of Education*, 47, no. 4:523-34.

C: Education

14. Trends in Participation in Higher Education by Gender

Sid Gilbert
Neil Guppy

Educational systems in Canada have experienced enrolment fluctuations that may be characterized broadly as historical growth and contemporary decline. Two of the major factors in these fluctuations are the size of the various school age cohorts (6-13 years of age for elementary school grades, 14-17 for secondary grades, and 18-24 for post-secondary education) and the participation rate or the percentage of each group, regardless of the absolute size of the group, choosing to undertake a particular level of education.

The post-World War II baby boom and higher participation rates were responsible for the great expansion of elementary and secondary enrolments up to 1970. Since then, and despite increased participation or retention rates, elementary-secondary enrolment has steadily declined. For example, the percentage of 14- to 17-year-olds in

school increased from 84 percent in 1980-81 to 90 percent in 1984-85, yet total enrolment declined. The rate of deline, however, is levelling off.

At the post-secondary level, despite a shrinking cohort of 18- to 24-year-olds, enrolment continues to rise because of increasing participation. The percentage of 18- to 24-year-olds undertaking a post-secondary education increased from 19.8 percent in 1980-81 to 23.7 percent in 1984-85.

Hidden behind this broad characterization is a significant difference in the educational participation patterns for women and for men at the post-secondary level. Historically women and men have averaged similar years of schooling (Boulet and Lavallée, 1984:27), although this resulting equality occurs for very different reasons. A minimum school-leaving age has ensured that everyone receives some formal education, but while women have been more likely than men to complete high school, fewer women have traditionally continued on to

An original essay written especially for this volume.

163

post-secondary education. In other words, the male average obscures much greater variability in their participation. On average, men are more likely than women either to drop out of high school or to continue on to post-secondary studies.

More recently, however, the participation of women in post-secondary education has mushroomed. Women have always dominated in post-secondary non-university institutions because prior to the 1970s the training of nurses and teachers was done completely outside the university context. Even with the integration of nursing and education into the university curriculum, the majority of full-time community college students are women.

Women have also always composed the dominant fraction of students studying part-time. This part-time participation is especially marked for women over 30, as this age cohort constitutes the majority of women who study part-time at university (Boulet and Lavallée, 1984).

Taking enrolments as a measure of participation, more women than men have attended post-secondary courses throughout the 1980s. However, simple head counts using the numbers of women and men at college or university are not entirely accurate. Students drop out or transfer to other schools in midstream (while others register late), causing enrolment figures to fluctuate depending on exactly when the count is taken (Gomme and Gilbert, 1984). A more stable measure of participation is afforded by considering students who successfully graduate.

Based on the number of undergraduate and first-professional degrees awarded in successive years from 1970 through to 1986, Figure 14-1 graphically displays the growth of women's participation in university programs. As the figure shows, women's receipt of university degrees has risen rapidly in the last 15 or so years, and especially between 1973 and 1979 when the number of women earning degrees increased by some 15 000. The growth has been so dramatic that women have, since 1982, received the majority of undergraduate degrees conferred. Similarly in community colleges women continue to receive more degrees and diplomas than do men.

This pattern does not hold for university post-graduate programs, however. With more and more students choosing to pursue graduate-level work, men still receive a disproportionate share of Masters and Ph.D. degrees. In 1984-85 men were awarded 60 percent of all Masters degrees and 75 percent of Ph.D. degrees, although the participation of women had increased at this level as well.

It is important, though, to consider the historical period within which women's participation has grown. At the same time that women became the majority of graduates in colleges and universities, the standards of post-secondary education have come into question. Over a period when women's participation rose sharply, there emerged a growing concern that excellence had been eroded (for example, Bercuson, Bothwell, and Granatstein, 1984). Also coincident with the increasing participation of women in colleges and university has come a period of financial restraint (see Decore and Pannu, 1986). Finally, other research has pointed to a declining economic value in degrees and diplomas relative to the 1960s (for example, Goyder, 1980).

Debate will continue for some time as to whether women's growing participation is causally connected to these changes, or whether there is merely a correlation in time between these events. However that controversy is resolved, it remains a fact that the so-called crisis of higher education has come as women have finally attained much greater access to college and university campuses.

Figure 14-1 is helpful in illustrating that women students have played a crucial role in the continuing expansion of the post-secondary population, but what the graph masks is continuing gender-tracking in the fields of study women and men pursue. In the last few decades different patterns of participation are apparent in different fields of study. As Figure 14-2 reveals, some areas have seen movement toward a more balanced distribution of women and men (for example, law). In other areas, however, gender-tracking has become more pronounced over time (for example, education). The latter process of the increasing concentration of one sex in any particular field occurs only in areas where women have traditionally been in the majority. That is, women are moving into areas that men have historically dominated

FIGURE 14-1   Undergraduate degrees by gender

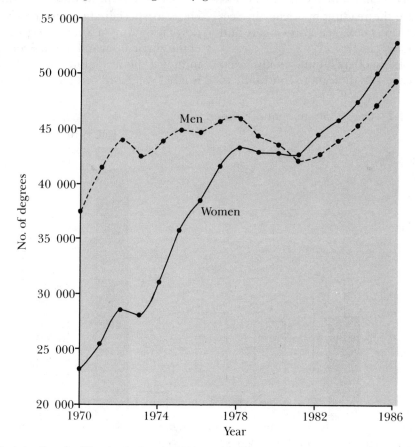

Source: Statistics Canada, *Education in Canada, 1985,* cat. no. 81-229.

(even engineering), but men have not been increasing their relative participation in traditionally female-dominated areas of study. The pattern of women entering traditional male areas of specialization has operated to break down historic patterns of segmentation, but the intensification of women's involvement in certain selected "female streams" has had exactly the opposite effect.

This educational streaming by sex does not begin at the post-secondary level. Differences between women and men in course enrolments can also be found at the high-school level (Gaskell, 1985:46). However, at the lower levels of education, differences between males and females are much less marked (see the reading by Richer in Section III of this book; see also Gilbert and Gomme, 1987:210-13).

Gaskell (1985) offers an informative overview of the reasons thought to contribute to this pattern of sex differences in programs of study. At the individual level, she suggests that family support and personal attitudes about traditional gender roles will influence decisions about field of study. Factors such as aptitude, achievement, and personality characteristics are much discussed in the general literature, but there is little empirical evidence to support any of these as adequate explanatory factors for gender segregation in education. (Evidence on performance differences at various levels of education is discussed in Gaskell, 1985; Gilbert and Gomme, 1987; Guppy, Vellutini, and Balson, 1987.)

Also important to understanding differences in specialization are the characteristics of programs of study. The actual content of the curriculum and the classroom climate influence how comfortable and successful women will be in certain areas of study. At

FIGURE 14-2   Degree attainment of women (%)

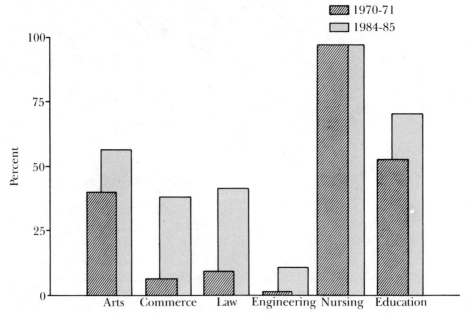

Source: Statistics Canada, *Education in Canada, 1985*, cat. no. 81-229.

the program level, Gaskell also highlights the social processes of guidance, recruitment, selection, and support networks as important forces determining the study streams women and men pursue. Finally, the links to the labour market are crucial: "one of the major barriers to women entering non-traditional programs has been that neither they nor their teachers and advisers are convinced that they will be employed at the end of [the programs]" (Gaskell, 1985:52). This latter point illustrates how the gendered division of labour wherein there are "men's jobs" and "women's jobs" feeds upon itself by promoting gender-tracking in education and job training programs.

The interplay between these personal factors and program characteristics operates to define how educational choices are made. The options and constraints women and men face have changed in some areas such as commerce and medicine, although strict gender segregation has been maintained in other areas (for example, nursing).

Another aspect concerning the issue of sex differences in educational participation may be illustrated by examining teachers instead of students. It is not just that more female students take university courses in education, social work, or nursing. These students are also much more likely to have women as professors than are students enrolled in courses in biology, law, or medicine.

The differentiation in fields of teaching parallels the pattern of gender differences in student fields of study. The two interact with one another, of course, with the female instructors serving as role models for undergraduate women who then become experts in the same selected areas as their mentors, thus helping to perpetuate the initial gender divisons.

Within the teaching faculty there is also a hierarchical form of differentiation. Professors in the university setting pass through a series of ranks in their teaching and research careers. Incoming members of the profession begin as instructors, lecturers, or assistant professors. They may then advance through the ranks to associate, and, ultimately, full professorships.

Women and men occupy very different positions in this hierarchy (see Table 14-1). First, while the majority of university students are now women, in 1984-85 only 17 percent of university faculty were female.

TABLE 14-1 Women and men in university teaching.

	% Female 1970-71	% Female 1984-85	Salary gap 1984-85 (F -M)
Faculty by rank			
Full professor	3	6	− $3 045
Associate professor	8	15	− 1 617
Assistant professor	14	28	− 1 429
Lecturer	29	48	− 2 433
All faculty	13	17	− 8 433

Source: Statistics Canada, *Teachers in Universities*, cat. no. 81-241, pp. 19, 56-57.

Second, women faculty tend to be concentrated in the lower ranks of the university teaching profession, with men dominating in the upper spheres. For example, in 1984-85 almost one of every three faculty members was a male full professor compared to only one in 50 faculty members who were female full professors. Third, in Canadian universities women earned an average of $8433 less than men, and even after salary differences within ranks were considered, women earned less than men (for example, women lecturers earned $2989 less than men of the same rank).

Certain of these differences among university faculty have been changing over time. For example, in 1970-71, 13 percent of faculty members were women, so there has been a modest growth of 4 percent in the number of females teaching at Canadian universities. Among professors, the percentage of females has risen from 3 percent in 1970-71 to 6 percent in 1984-85. On the salary scale, the overall gap has remained fairly steady (after taking inflation into account), although in the 1970s Boyd (1979) reported that women fell further behind. So while some change has occurred, the direction has not always been favourable to women, and certainly the magnitude of change has been very modest.

As an example of one of the professions, university teaching does not present a particularly rosy picture of change for women. Marshall (1987) has shown that between 1971 and 1981 female representation in male-dominated professions grew from 11.4 percent to 18.6 percent. This is a significant swing in a decade, but the progress pales in comparison to women's surging participation in and graduation from college and university over the same period. Neverthe-

less, comparisons of change in terms of students versus faculty members are complicated by two key issues; the first concerns how long it takes for changes to work their way through the educational system and the second relates to the absence of advancement in periods when growth in the educational system is curtailed.

International comparisons reveal that the Canadian patterns of participation by women and men in higher education are broadly similar to experiences in other countries. Among students, Canada has one of the highest participation rates for women of any country in the world (Moore, 1987:24). Among faculty, the percentage of women teaching in Canadian universities (17 percent) is roughly comparable to what is found in other countries, being slightly higher than in the U.K. (13 percent) and slightly lower than in the U.S. (24 percent).

The trend in participation in higher education by sex conveys a mixed message. Propelled by such social forces as the women's movement and the changing economic labour markets of the 1970s and 1980s, the balance of women and men in college and university programs has equalized. And among educational streams leading to some of the better-paying professions (for example, law, medicine) women's participation has dramatically increased. Nevertheless, some areas of study remain an almost exclusive haven for women (for example, nursing). Post-graduate training in the university is still dominated by men, and among faculty members women have yet to attain equal representation. Progress toward a more equitable distribution of opportunities for women and men has occurred, but the pace of change remains slow in certain areas of education.

REFERENCES

Bercuson, David, Robert Bothwell, and Jack Granatstein
1984   *The Great Brain Robbery: Canada's Universities on the Road to Ruin.* Toronto: McClelland and Stewart.

Boulet, Jac-André, and Laval Lavallée
1984   *The Changing Economic Status of Women.* Ottawa: Economic Council of Canada.

Boyd, Monica
1979   "Rank and Salary Differentials in the 1970s: A Comparison of Male and Female Full-time Teachers in Canadian Universities and Colleges." Association of Universities and Colleges of Canada.

Decore, A. N.
1984   "Vive La Différence: A Comparison of Male-Female Academic Performance," *Canadian Journal of Higher Education,* 14, no. 3:35-58.

Decore, A. N., and R. S. Pannu
1986   "Educational Financing in Canada 1970-71 to 1984-85: Who Calls the Tune, Who Pays the Piper?" *Canadian Journal of Higher Education,* 16, no. 2:27-49.

Gaskell, Jane
1985   "Women and Education: Branching Out," *Towards Equity.* Ottawa: Economic Council of Canada.

Gilbert, Sid, and Ian Gomme
1987   "Education in the Canadian Mosaic," in *An Introduction to Sociology* (2nd ed.), ed. M. Rosenberg et al. Toronto: Methuen.

Gomme, Ian, and Sid Gilbert
1984   "Paying the Cost: Some Observations on the Problem of Post-secondary Student Attrition," *Canadian Journal of Higher Education,* 14, no. 3:95-100.

Goyder, John
1980   "Trends in the Socioeconomic Attainment of the University Educated: A Status Attainment Model Interpretation," *Canadian Journal of Higher Education,* 10, no. 2:21-38.

Guppy, Neil, Susan Vellutini, and Doug Balson
1987   "Women and Higher Education in Canadian Society," in *Women and Education: A Canadian Perspective,* ed. J. Gaskell and A. McLaren. Calgary: Detselig.

Marshall, Katherine
1987   *Who are the Professional Women?* Ottawa: Statistics Canada, Cat. #99-951.

Moore, Kathryn, A.
1987   "Women's Access and Opportunity in Higher Education: Toward the Twenty-first Century," *Comparative Education,* 23, no. 1:23-34.

Statistics Canada
Annual *Education in Canada.* Ottawa: Statistics Canada, Cat. #81-229.
Annual *Teachers in Universities.* Ottawa: Statistics Canada, Cat. #81-241.

C: Education

15. Reform Strategies for Education

Stephen Schecter

Schools contribute to inequality by reproducing, via a hidden curriculum and social
structure, the class structure of contemporary capitalism. This paper focusses on the
legitimation or ideological functions of the
school as a social institution which maintains political order in the widest sense and
provides a properly qualified labour force
for the owners of capital. It then discusses
the need to situate reform movements within this overall framework, in the hope that
an insight into the history and contradictions of school reform will open up the possibilities for strategies of change that will
help undermine, rather than reinforce, inequality in Canada. The latter half of this

paper addresses some of the issues involved
in realizing such strategies.

SCHOOLING, SCHOOL REFORM, AND INEQUALITY

Out of the long debate over the relationship between schooling and inequality has
emerged the understanding that schools do
not so much produce as reproduce the class
structure of capitalism. Their crucial role
lies not in determining future school attainment or economic success—the constella-
tion of class forces does that—but in legitimating the inequality and alienation that
are characteristic of the wider social order.
This distinction may seem a fine one, but its
implications for strategies of school reform
are serious.

The dominant discourse surrounding
school reform in the past decade and a half
focussed on giving more schooling to a
greater number of people. Schools were
seen as the major social institution deter-

Revised from Stephen Schecter, "Education and
Inequality: Some Strategic Considerations," in
Allan Moscovitch and Glenn Drover (eds.), *In-
equality: Essays on the Political Economy of Social
Welfare.* Reprinted by permission of the author
and University of Toronto Press. © University of
Toronto Press 1981.

mining the eventual allocation of resources in Western industrial countries. This viewpoint was buttressed by the statistics which indicated a strong association between higher incomes, post-secondary education, and higher-status occupations, an association which was explained in terms of the sophisticated technology required by citizens in those societies. People were poor, therefore, because they lacked the skills necessary for succeeding in modern times. If we want to reduce inequality, so the argument ran, we will have to supply more of these skills to these people, which means giving them more schooling. To the extent that there exist financial or cultural barriers to doing so, we will have to devise programs to overcome them.

The use of education as a means to overcome inequality has proved to be false on nearly all counts. Despite the association between education, income, and occupation, very little of future economic success is actually explained by school attainment; and very little of what schools do seems to affect the latter. More money, smaller classes, and a host of other panaceas might make politicians or parents feel better, but they do not seem to make students stay in school longer. . . .

As in earlier periods, the key to understanding current school reforms lies in the role schools play in legitimating the changing class structure of capitalism. On the one hand, schools instill those values which justify the workings of the general social order and especially the subordinate position in which members of the working class eventually find themselves. Schools must provide workers in the different strata of the capitalist work hierarchy with those attitudes and behaviour patterns commensurate with their occupational destinies. As economic growth continuously transforms the organi-

zation of work, the socialization tasks imposed on schools change accordingly. In the period since the end of the Second World War, the principal transformations in the work structure of Canadian capitalism have been the massive integration of women into the work force, a generalized deskilling of jobs in the monopoly sector, and an increase in the new middle classes, or petite bourgeoisie. The expansion of post-secondary education, especially at the community college level, must be seen as an attempt to prepare those individuals slotted to occupy the middle management posts of both the public and private sectors with the necessary combined attributes of personal initiative and corporate or state loyalty. At the same time the content of ideological legitimation for the subordinate members of the occupational hierarchy also changes. Technology and democratization woven around the idea of upward social mobility became the main themes of school reform, resulting in the ideology and practice of progressive education at the elementary and secondary levels. In actual practice, special classes, refined streaming, and polyvalent high schools were new techniques to prepare those youngsters headed for dead-end positions in the workplace to acquiesce to their own subordination. . . .

NON-REFORMIST REFORM

Any attempt to develop strategies around the issue of schooling that will push society in the direction of greater equality must first unburden itself of the myths that have hitherto informed school reform efforts. The most important myth is that which locates the source of our society's inequality in the structure of our schools instead of in the institutional fabric of capitalism. The second myth is that egalitarianism, as opposed to simple meritocracy, is not only desirable but also possible. The meritocratic conception of equality was the premise upon which progressive schooling relied; yet the kind of equality it presaged only meant ensuring equal access to inequality. Class divisions were accepted as the inevitable functional concomitant of the division of labour in a technologically complex society. This premise has had incredible legitimating force, for it builds structured inequality into its very conception of equality in terms of a seeming social determinism, obscuring the possibility of altering existent social relations.

The use of ability to explain social success reinforces individual conceptions about the natural order of things and the position each person occupies. Schools play a key role in this process since they have claimed a monopoly on defining ability and have elaborated a series of practices to measure it. The fact that IQ does not have a determinant effect on future life chances for most people does not diminish the belief that intelligence explains class position. On the contrary, not only does IQ provide a legitimizing rationale which has the advantage of not being amenable to social change; it also turns people's subordinate position in the class structure into a weapon, which they then turn on themselves. Not only are people thrown the question: "If you're so smart, why aren't you so rich?"; they are also given the converse explanation: "If you're not rich, you're obviously not so smart." . . .

A movement for school reform which seeks to address the problem of inequality in our society must therefore recognize at the outset that the problem is rooted in the very nature of capitalism and will only be overcome with the overthrow of capitalism by a workers' movement committed to socialist democracy. Furthermore, the key articula-

tion between contemporary schooling and inequality lies in the legitimation role which schools assume under capitalism. This legitimating role is assured not only by the formal content of schooling but also by its hidden curriculum.

It is true that much of the formal curriculum is class-based, sexist, and discriminatory toward non-dominant peoples, such that students from socially subordinate groups find school even more alienating than does the general student body. It is also true, however, that the more subtle legitimating mechanisms of schools are even more effective. Grading, streaming, standardized tests, obligatory attendance, hierarchical social relations, credentials, uniform and irrelevant curricula are all means of making school unpalatable and boring to most, while simultaneously fostering the myth that schooling is essential to economic success. Thus students who decide not to proceed to post-secondary levels are resigned to a subordinate position in the class structure and are made to feel that the fault is their own. The division between manual and intellectual labour, which monopoly capitalism has deepened, is further reinforced, thereby depriving working-class people of those tools which would enable them to pierce the ideological domination of capital.

Bowles and Gintis have described the means by which schools carry out these legitimation functions in terms of the correspondence principle: each level of the school hierarchy is governed by a certain behaviour and set of values corresponding to the comportment and attitudes that will be required of workers at the corresponding level of the job hierarchy. Such characteristics as autonomy, self-direction, outspokenness, and critical judgment are highly prized by teachers at the upper end of the school ladder (community colleges, universities), while passivity, conformity to norms, and internalization of externally imposed rules are more rewarded at the bottom rungs of the school system (elementary and secondary grades). It is not surprising then that high-school graduates are destined to perform routine, deadening jobs in the corporate and state apparatuses. These are jobs that require little initiative and an already instilled inclination to accept an organization of work, in both its technical and social aspects, giving these workers little room for creativity and control.

The graduates of community colleges and universities, on the other hand, are slotted to fill the gamut of control and surveillance jobs in our society, tasks which require the capacity for initiative and rule determination without, of course, challenging the wider system on which the entire hierarchy rests. Hence the almost brutal rupture in the passage from high school to community college which many students experience. Hence, too, the maintenance throughout the educational system of an underlying social structure that is hierarchical and authoritarian, even if the relations of authority become progressively masked as one ascends the scale.

In this sense, the social structure of the school corresponds to the social structure of the wider society and, through its own social structure of hierarchy and control, reproduces those social relations which reinforce the system of inequality outside it. Within the classroom, students at any level remain subordinate to the teachers, and within the educational system itself, teachers remain subordinate to a whole battery of surveillance and control personnel, running from principals to district superintendents, to school commissioners, ministry of education officials, and government ministers.

It is this elaborate system of social control

which accounts for much of that bureaucratic interference and red tape which seems to so many teachers and parents as simply rules-for-rules'-sake. Yet that red tape serves a very functional purpose. It ensures that the socialization tasks of schools get carried out, while alternatives become difficult to imagine and even harder to execute. Teachers learn that they are not allowed to experiment without first getting the approval of their superiors, just as workers are not allowed to use equipment without the authorization of foremen or introduce technological changes into factories without the approval of industrial engineers. Young children learn that they are not allowed to go to the bathroom without asking the teacher's permission, just as workers cannot go to the toilet except during designated breaks. High-school students learn that they are free to the extent that they conform to the often unstated, but nonetheless omnipresent, lines of control, much as young workers learn that they are free to the extent that they submit to the hard and soft discipline imposed in the social and industrial factories of contemporary capitalism.

A radical school reform movement in Canada must therefore hit out at both the hidden and overt curricula and combine an alternative school structure with a relevant curriculum that is linked to a class-based analysis of that society. One of the major weaknesses of the free school movement lay precisely in its failure to develop a class-based strategy. The absence of the class dimension isolated the free school movement and left it as an enriching experience for the sons and daughters of the professional middle class but without an impact on the working class, whose daily life and future prospects made such experiences seem remote and irrelevant.

In the last analysis, the experience was not totally irrelevant, for the challenge posed by the free school movement struck at the very heart of the legitimating functions of contemporary education. A non-hierarchical, truly individualized, student-oriented learning process makes for autonomous, critical human beings, the very opposite of what is required by corporate capitalism and of what is elicited by dominant school practices. In offering non-repressive learning environments, free schools indicated that an alternative to the existing system was possible, and also affirmed that the kind of alternative social order envisaged was libertarian, in contrast to the authoritarian character of existing socialist societies.

Important as these contributions were, however, they remained partial, for in the absence of a class perspective, relevant education in the free school movement too often reflected the relatively privileged class position of the students and their parents. The oppression of the dominant social order and the need for collective action to counter it tended to get submerged in the emphasis on individual growth, as though schools could be liberated in a society that remained repressive. . . .

OBSTACLES TO CHANGE

The first obstacle to change is the wearing effect of daily life under capitalism, which tends to grind most people down and reinforce a sense of powerlessness. This situation is in turn reinforced by their ideological subordination to the dominant value system, whose hold is many faceted: an acceptance of the inevitability of the given social order, submission to the expertise of authorities; family relations which tend to reproduce the authoritarian and repressive nature of capitalist work relations and, hence, those

of school relations as well; and attempts to find individual ways out within a psychological dynamic that tears people apart. Such ideological subordination not only makes working-class people prey to the counterattack of the dominant class, for example, by branding teachers' strikes as narrow and selfish, or attempts at school reform as revolutionary; it also makes the political mobilization of the working class difficult.

As well, there are all the tactical considerations. Where, for example, does an individual, especially a working-class parent, start? What issues does he or she raise first, and with whom, even within a revolutionary strategy of school reform? Does not the separation of manual and intellectual labour make it likely that the leadership of these movements will initially fall into the hands of the new petite bourgeoisie, thus reproducing within the reform organizations the very relations which the movement aims to abolish? The predominance of the professional middle classes which seems to characterize struggles outside the workplace also opens up these struggles to eventual reformist or social-democratic practice. The state itself has already undertaken measures to encourage this tendency through decentralization programs, which result in the appointment of powerless consultative bodies designed to contain potential protest. School-parent committees and community health clinics are two such examples.

The class position of teachers is equally problematic. Attempts to link teachers' struggles with struggles of other workers and with working-class parents in the community have been characterized by considerable corporatist ideology and by practices which reflect the ambiguous class position of teachers. On the one hand, teachers perform the dirty work of the education system, and their position within the organization thus resembles that of workers within corporations—relatively little autonomy and increasing pressures towards proletarianization. On the other hand, they carry out important political control functions, internalize many aspects of the dominant ideology, and receive relatively higher wages in recognition of their role.

These obstacles are not an exhaustive list of the pitfalls confronting revolutionary attempts to organize around the issue of schooling. They are indicative of some of the general strategic problems facing a revolutionary strategy based on non-reformist reforms.

Despite these obstacles, such a strategy seems to offer the only viable alternative under today's conditions that at the same time attempts to implement in daily practice those principles of socialist democracy which render it a counter-model to capitalism: the critique of capitalism as an alienating ensemble of social relations; the redefinition of the democratic transformation of the social relations of production and reproduction; the abolition of the social and sexist division of labour; the creation of autonomous worker organizations that would subsequently become the sovereign political institutions of the emerging socialist society; and the recognition, in practice, of the independent contribution to the revolutionary struggle made by diverse attempts to organize around the multiple contradictions of capitalism. Massive democratic mobilization is at the very core of such a strategy and gives it the character of historical necessity, in the multiple sense of that term. Only such a strategy recognizes that the contemporary political situation of the Western working class requires working through and transcending bourgeois political institutions, that the political strength to push through these reforms and strengthen workers' autonomous organizations demands mass mobilization, and that such strategic

principles are alone compatible with the revolutionary project.

Between the possibility and the realization of this historical necessity lie a number of obstacles, such as those already described, which are only insurmountable to the extent that one forgets the dialectical and contradictory nature of capitalism and, indeed, of all social life. In the first place, movements with a revolutionary thrust, organized both around the workplace and outside it, have emerged in the past, and though they have suffered defeat, one can learn from past mistakes; the future need not be a repetition of the past. Theory is important here as is the creation of political networks which would help people working in and around schools to continue to evaluate collectively their experiences. In the second place, capitalism is itself in crisis, rent with contradictions. Social-democratic reformism is one possible outcome to this crisis, but not the only one. The unity between state workers and clients, though far from realized, is proceeding to some extent. The very fiscal crisis which produced increased state confrontation with teachers has also made an alliance between teachers and parents a practical possibility. The class position of teachers is not a static relationship but a dynamic one which responds to the social pressures around it. The very real constraints on the political radicalization of certain social strata, such as teachers', should not blind one to possible alternatives.

Discussion of strategy questions always seems to end on a note of dissatisfaction or of "unfinished business" suspended in the air. This quality reflects the very nature of revolutionary struggle. It reflects, too, the fact that theory is only effective when linked to political practice, and that the analysis of struggle, though necessary and long overdue, can serve only as a guideline to the tactics required by specific, concrete situations. In these hard times, perhaps beginning to discuss these issues is sufficient and signals the existence of an alternative to the misery and inequities of daily life under capitalism. Schools are especially important in this regard because they deal with the very real lives of people who are our inheritors and, thus, pose both the hope and the necessity of making that alternative a reality. Just as important, they are central to any effort which seeks to overcome the basic inequalities of our society.

---

16. Recommendations on Access to Post-secondary Education

Robert M. Pike

The expansion of Canadian post-secondary education during the past 25 years has increased the absolute chances of university and college attendance for all segments of the population. This expansion has been particularly associated with the increased participation of women in university and college studies. It has also been a democratizing factor to the extent that the community-college sectors have provided new educational opportunities for working-class youth, although, in contrast, the university systems have, despite their growth, remained disproportionately the preserve of the middle and upper-middle classes. For their part, provincial governments were willing to fund the expansion while they believed that significant economic returns would result from it, but during the past 10 years a certain

disillusionment with the "human capital" thesis, combined with a desire to control public spending, has encouraged the pursuit of policies of financial constraint. These policies have resulted in a series of measures, including tuition fee increases and enrolment limitations, which pose some threat to accessibility. The recent decision of the federal government to reduce the scale of its transfer payments to the provinces may increase the rigour of financial constraint in future years.

On this somewhat gloomy note, we must conclude—as has Jean-Yves DesRosiers, an economist with the Quebec Ministry of Higher Education and Science—that, with the large amounts already invested in Canadian higher education, "it is foolish to delude oneself into believing that the governments will yet again add substantial amounts, or to think that changing the source of funds (federal instead of provincial) will increase the level of resources and lead to better results . . .[;] financial constraints are here to stay" (DesRosiers, 1986: 11-12). This being the case, it is important

Revised from Robert M. Pike, "Social Goals and Economic Constraints: Issues of Accessibility to Canadian Higher Education During the 1980s," in *Education Research and Perspectives* (December 1986) pp. 32-39.

to consider the possible future directions of those public philosophies and policies which bear upon accessibility, and which are themselves influenced by expectations of continued constraint. Some evidence of the likely directions can be found in certain recommendations of three recent government reports, two provincial and one federal, all of which attempt to chart preferred future scenarios for higher education. The reports are those of the Commission on the Future Development of the Universities of Ontario (commonly known as the Bovey Commission) presented in 1984, the report to the government of Nova Scotia of the Royal Commission on Post-secondary Education (1985) and the report of the federal government's Royal Commission on the Economic Union and Development Prospects of Canada (1985) which is commonly referred to as the Macdonald Commission. All of these reports comment upon the linkage between accessibility and post-secondary financing, although only a small part of the Macdonald Commission's work was devoted to the subject of education. In the limited space available here, we will concentrate just on one set of their recommendations—those pertaining to tuition fees and student financial aid—which throw a particularly clear light on current thinking about accessibility and the future funding of higher education. The focus is primarily upon the university sector.

STUDENT TUITION FEES AND UNIVERSITY FINANCING

Student tuition fees are a significant source of funding for Canadian universities, although fee increases have traditionally been restricted by the provincial governments in order to facilitate financial access to higher learning. Concern that this "low tuition fee" policy is now under pressure, as evidenced in some recent rises in the costs of tuition, is

not, however, a concern which is evident in any of the commission reports. On the contrary, all three reports recommend financial measures which would shift a higher proportion of the costs of university education on to students and their parents. Thus, the Bovey Commission suggests that university tuition fees should gradually be increased from their levels at 16.1 percent of system basic operating income in 1983-84 to a point where they contribute 25 percent of operating income. The Nova Scotian Commission recommends that university tuition fees should rise over a five-year period until they constitute 50 percent of instructional costs (which are less than operating costs) and calculates that this recommendation, if introduced in 1983-84, would have increased fees from $1275 to $2175 per annum. Finally, the Macdonald Commission, in a radical recommendation which is intended primarily to increase institutional variety and foster academic excellence (but also stimulate some "desirable" fee inceases), suggests that the provincial governments should cease to regulate fees which would be set instead by the different universities in response to enrolment demand. The probable outcome of this particular recommendation, so the Macdonald Commission hopes, would be that some Canadian universities would provide an acceptable "no-frills" education for the mass of average students, and that others would offer a more intensive, higher-level (and, presumably, more expensive) education for those who are exceptionally able.

It is a trifle ironic that all of the commission reports couple these recommendations for tuition fee increases with affirmations of the principle of accessibility, and notably with "the essential factor that low-income students who are academically qualified not be excluded from the system by financial barriers" (Macdonald Commission, 1985,

2:750). How do they propose, therefore, to cover the increased educational costs of such needy students? The universal answer is the coupling of the tuition fee increases to new income-based contingency loan plans (which would, in the Nova Scotian case, replace the province's existing non-repayable bursary program). These income-based loan plans would provide loans to students during the course of their education and, unlike present student loan programs in Canada, would gear repayments to a student's ability to pay after having completed his or her education. Thus, because of the "income contingent" element, a graduate with a low income would pay back less each month than one with a high income, and, ultimately, loans to graduates on very low incomes would probably never be fully repaid. Such income-based repayments, to quote the Bovey Commission report, "do not impose a burden on earnings when the graduate is least able to repay." However, "from the general public's viewpoint, such a plan reduces the taxation burden for those persons who do not participate directly in the university system. From a government viewpoint, the plan can be set up so that it does not add to government indebtedness" (Bovey Commission, 1984, appendix 4).

As the above quotation indicates, an emphasis on loan assistance is an attractive policy during a period of financial constraint. So also is the "user-pay" orientation of increasing tuition fees although, in the case of the three reports, the obvious purpose of using such increases to raise revenue is bolstered by a series of interlocking social and economic arguments which are designed to provide a broader level of justification than simply that of raising money. The four main arguments which appear in one or another of the reports (but not necessarily all of them) are as follows: first, that tuition fees as a proportion of university revenue have

fallen considerably since the 1940s, and it is now desirable, especially during a period of economic constraint, that this trend should be reversed; second, that increased revenue from tuition fees will give universities a greater measure of financial freedom from government control; third, that the personal benefits, in terms of general satisfaction and economic remuneration, which accrue to university graduates are sufficiently high to warrant an increased initial investment by them and their parents; fourth, that free-tuition and low-tuition schemes unfairly subsidize the middle- and upper-income groups at the expense of the lower-income groups because it is the former groups which are overrepresented in the university system. Not all of these arguments are equally convincing as a case for increased tuition (see below), but, taken together, they do reflect a major shift in ideology since the educational expansion of the 1960s. At that time the benefits to the society of a substantial output of graduates were considered to be sufficiently high to give low-educational-cost policies a priority over any arguments which gave primacy to personal returns. In contrast, the Nova Scotian report probably sums up the prevailing official sentiment in its observation that "while graduates assuredly benefit society through their skills and knowledge, they receive commensurate—some would argue more than commensurate—personal remuneration" (Nova Scotia Commission, 1985:136).

THE GROWTH OF THE "USER-PAY" ORIENTATION AND ACCESSIBILITY

The bottom line on the above arguments is that they provide the rationale for university tuition fee increases (and related shifts in costs to the "consumer" through increased loans to cover these increases) which, as we have seen, has so far been singularly lacking in Canadian government actions to restrain the growth of higher education costs. Some of these arguments—notably the third and fourth—will undoubtedly be familiar to those readers who have followed the seemingly endless debates on the pros and cons of free tuition in Australian higher education. However, the federal government in Australia appears to be currently committed to free tuition despite its apparent lack of effectiveness in promoting access to university for children from low-income families. In Canada, on the other hand, the recommendations for increased fees and more loan assistance are essentially a rejection of the principle of free or low tuition as a means of facilitating accessibility. The grounds for this rejection are, indeed, well expressed by the Canadian economist David Stager, in a discussion paper on accessibility which he wrote for the Bovey Commission. Stager cites the lack of change in the composition of the Australian post-secondary population following the abolition of fees as evidence that free- and low-tuition schemes are inefficient ways of promoting enrolment increase and access to higher education. His own preference seems to be for an income-based contingent loan plan because it "eliminates any financial barriers to further education without producing undesirable distribution effects that arise from low-cost tuition and other subsidies to university education" (Stager, 1984:31). In other words, relatively high tuition fees, combined with a liberal loans policy, ensure that lower-cost subsidies will be received by those wealthy students who do not need them.

It is hard to gainsay Stager's argument that low or free tuition "is unlikely to change the composition of university enrolment very much because tuition represents only a minor part of the cost, and because so many other factors are influencing a student's decision" (Stager, 1984:29). On this score, we have already noted that the expansion of higher education and the development of various financial aid programs for needy students did little to diminish class differentials in access to Canadian university education during the 1960s and 1970s. However, there is another side to the coin—namely, that it is not necessarily appropriate to argue for new policies solely on the basis of past experience. That is, because past policies such as regulated tuition fees and bursary aid to students failed to democratize university education, it does not necessarily follow that new policies which would raise tuition fees and lead students into increased indebtedness (albeit on the grounds that such action reduces subsidies to wealthy students) will not lead to a measure of social regression in access to the universities. We cannot be sure, of course, that such will be the case, but it is certainly a possibility. As a researcher for the Ontario Federation of Students has noted in reference to the Bovey Commission's suggestion for increased fees, "the decision of whether to go to university is basically made in grade 8. A lot of parents who are unemployed or carrying a heavy mortgage are going to look at the higher tuition and say, "I'm sorry, you can't go!" (Balnis, 1985).

For reasons such as this, it is not possible for a sociologist to be entirely comfortable with proposed policies which claim to maintain financial accessibility while increasing the 'user-pay' element in Canadian university education. However, for the same reasons, it may be equally uncomfortable for governments in many provinces to adopt such policies *formally* because they are potentially in conflict with the political rhetoric of "universal financial accessibility" as an important social goal. Predictions of the future are therefore hazardous, although two of them are reasonably safe bets. The first is that tuition fees will continue to rise, either by a process of upward drift or through formal policy commitment, as governments seek additional sources of funding. The second is that the federal Macdonald Commission's recommendation for complete deregulation of tuition fees will not be acceptable to the provincial governments. Recommendations on education emanating from federal bodies are usually studiously ignored at the provincial level (one might say "as a matter of principle") and this one, by allowing universities to charge what the market could bear, would lead to the complete restructuring of the Canadian university system. The ultimate outcome of fee deregulation would probably be the creation of a number of elite private universities on the American model. This outcome would appeal to some—though not too many—Canadians including, incidentally, the unnamed President of a Nova Scotian university who recently called for the establishment in Canada of a "small, private, expensive, world-class, undergraduate college" with very high entrance standards (Nova Scotia Commission, 1985:2).

CONCLUSIONS

During the late 1960s and early 1970s, Canada spent a higher proportion of its GNP on education than any other member of the Organization for Economic Co-operation and Development. One outcome of this generosity was the creation of a series of systems of mass post-secondary education in which the emphasis was placed upon "giving students a chance" to prove their abilities within the systems rather than upon early academic selection at the high-school level. However, in recent years, the high economic costs of mass post-secondary education have been perceived as a heavy burden upon Cana-

dian governments. The various economic policies and commission recommendations which we have reviewed in the paper, in relation specifically to their impact upon access, are obviously in considerable measure attempts to limit the size of the burden.

Because the central focus of this paper has been the impact of financial constraint on accessibility policies and processes, it is inevitable that some major concerns which bear upon accessibility, but which are as much "academic" as they are "economic," have received short shrift. Two such concerns should be mentioned in this conclusion. The first is the existence of a widespread criticism to the effect that the main emphasis in Canadian higher education has been on minimum standards and universal accessibility rather than on building universities which are world-renowned centres of excellence. A. W. Johnson (1985) is one perceptive analyst of the Canadian university system who supports this criticism, and it also emerges in the Macdonald Commission's desire for more institutional variety between the universities. In the Bovey Commission report, too, a recommendation that Ontario universities should be allowed by the provincial government to reduce their enrolments between 4 and 8 percent without penalty is seen by the Commissioners as "a modest reduction in accessibility" in order to enhance excellence and adaptability. The recommendation, which is patently controversial, would allow universities which succeed in obtaining substantial research funding from federal research councils to have a greater "corridor of insensitivity to enrolment changes" than those which obtain a lower level of funding.

The second concern is one which the universities and colleges have themselves studiously ignored until recently: namely, that Canadian post-secondary education is not only costly to finance but also wasteful of human resources. Such waste is shown in the form of high withdrawal rates: indeed, as many as 50 percent of those students who enter Canadian universities do not remain to complete their programs of studies. This is one academic cost which, it might be argued, could be substantially reduced by more strenuous early selection and higher university admission standards. However, greater selectivity at, or prior to, the point of admission to a university or college also carries its own cost in the possibility that some

from participation in post-secondary studies by the more rigorous selection process. Thus, which of the two alternatives—early selection and low rates of withdrawal from advanced studies or late selection and high rates of withdrawal—is the better one? A consideration of this question might be informed by an examination of the economic costs of each alternative, but ultimately the final conclusion must be grounded, as in all similar decisions, in the dominant values of the wider society.

REFERENCES

Balnis, Richard
    1985   *Toronto Star,* February 2, p. A9.

DesRosiers, Jean-Yves
    1986   "Post-secondary Education in the Renegotiation of Fiscal Arrangements between the Federal Government and the Provinces," *Canadian Journal of Higher Education,* vol. 16-1.

Johnson, A. W.
    1985   "Giving Greater Point and Purpose to the Federal Financing of Post-secondary Education in Canada." Ottawa: Secretary of State.

Macdonald Commission
    1985   "Report of the Royal Commission on the Economic Union and Development Prospects of Canada." Ottawa: Supply and Services Canada.

Nova Scotia Commission
    1985   "Report of the Royal Commission on Post-secondary Education." Province of Nova Scotia: Halifax.

Ontario Commission
    1984   "Ontario Universities: Options and Futures." Report of the Royal Commission on the Future Development of the Universities of Ontario. Province of Ontario: Toronto.

Stager, David
    1984   "Accessibility and Demand for University Education." Discussion paper prepared for the Commission of the Future of Universities of Ontario. Toronto.

FOR FURTHER READING

Anisef, Paul, Norman Okihiro, and Carl James. 1982. *Losers and Winners: The Pursuit of Equality and Social Justice in Higher Education.* Toronto: Butterworths. Reviewing issues of accessibility and equality of educational opportunity, this text uses 1976-81 census data to monitor trends in access to higher education. The book combines an interesting review of literature with an insightful data analysis.

Clark, Warren, Margaret Laing, and Edith Rechnitzer. 1986. *The Class of 82: Summary report on the findings of the 1984 National Survey of the Graduates of 1982.* Ottawa: Supply and Services. A Statistics Canada report surveying the class of 1982 by following up on people who graduated from community college or university. Among many issues, the report touches on earnings, job satisfaction, occupation, and migration.

Gaskell, Jane, and Arlene McLaren, eds. 1987. *Women and Education: A Canadian Perspective.* Calgary: Detselig. This collection of articles focusses on the experiences of women in education. One of the many strengths of the volume is the historical breadth which most papers achieve.

Livingstone, David. 1985. *Social Crisis and Schooling.* Toronto: Garamond Press. The link between social classes and educational policies is the focus of this book. Using data from Ontario, combined with a Marxist theory of education, this text provides a sustained examination of the contemporary social crisis and its impact on education.

Statistics Canada. *Education in Canada: A Statistical Review.* This annual publication presents the most recent figures on enrolments, graduates, teachers, education finance, and educational attainment.

Wotherspoon, Terry, ed. 1987. *The Political Economy of Schooling.* Toronto: Methuen. This volume brings together a set of articles addressed to the current mandate of education in capitalist societies. Examining the Canadian situation, the authors draw out the place of education and its historical role in Canadian society, emphasizing in particular how schools contribute to socially structured inequalities.

ASCRIPTION AND SOCIAL INEQUALITY

A. ETHNICITY AND RACE

B. GENDER

C. AGE

D. REGION

Introduction

A growing consciousness about the rights of all citizens was signalled by the adoption in 1948 of the Universal Declaration of Human Rights (a United Nations initiative). Human rights burst onto the political agenda. Propelled by Martin Luther King and other Black leaders, the U.S. civil rights movement drew attention to the plight of Blacks. As the civil rights movement advanced in the 1950s and 1960s, the promotion of equality in human rights across various linguistic, ethnic, racial, or religious groups was increasingly considered. The expanding consciousness also encompassed social movements based on equal rights for groups defined by gender, nationality, ethnicity, regionalism, and physical disability.

Many of the civil rights grievances of these disadvantaged groups were long-standing, with, for example, the struggles of women and aboriginal peoples having had a tortuously long history. But in the late 1940s and early 1950s, following a world war in which millions had died battling racist ideology, a new thrust of human energy focussed on promoting and advancing opportunities of oppressed people. The racial bigotry of fascism had been crushed at great cost, and a world sensitized to the brutality of human hatred was more accommodating to the idea that there should be equal opportunity, regardless of ascriptive group membership.

Perceiving a maturing of industrial capitalism in the post-war era, some social thinkers came to believe that the political fault lines of society, in the past often based on territory, religion, race, and ethnicity, would dissolve as democratic freedoms and economic opportunities flourished. With economic prosperity would come political modernization. An era of equal opportunity would ensue, where merit and effort would determine the distribution of social resources. Traditional social cleavages would pale in the face of a growing *meritocracy* where competence, achievement, and motivation would determine individual life chances.

In sharp contrast to this modernization view, other social thinkers foresaw growing conflict across social class lines. Rather than a maturing of capitalism, these theorists saw a period of monopoly capitalism wherein a class of wealthy owners prospered at the expense of others. The gap between the rich and the poor would widen, they believed. As a consciousness of class interests grew, the eclipse of traditional cleavages would result and class antagonism would obliterate old hostilities. The significant fault line of modern society, now, would be based on class interests grounded in the differential ownership of private property. Previous conflicts across religious, racial, or regional groupings would be forgotten.

Neither of these two perspectives has served us particularly well in understanding the most recent social movements which have dominated the Canadian political scene. Neither view fits closely with the facts. The women's movement, the quest for aboriginal self-government, the rise of Quebec nationalism, the revival of ethnic solidarity—these are all phenomena whose emergence, and magnitude, were not anticipated by theorists of class antagonism or political modernization. Expressions of group rights were taken up with vigour and dedication by people from a diversity of class backgrounds in a variety of "modern" countries.

At the core of any of these particular movements is a collective membership based on *birthright*. The Black civil rights movement or the women's movement involves people sharing a group definition based on attributes with which one is born. Sex and race are not attained or achieved, they are determined at conception and individuals have no say in the matter. These *ascribed attributes* are important to the extent that others treat them as socially significant. Others react to us, make judgements about us, and generally orient themselves to us on the basis of a variety of these ascribed features which include sex, race, age, ethnicity, and region.

It is not just a process of social differentiation that is at work here, but also invariably a hierarchical structure of dominant and subordinate groupings. The degree and the strength of this hierarchy vary across societies, but inequality based on ascription is a common feature of many known societies; ascriptive attributes are correlated with different scarce rewards: income, power, prestige. This is the context—the "vertical mosaic" as John Porter (1965) labelled the phenomenon of ascriptive inequality in Canada—within which various social groups have rallied to press for increased human rights.

In Canada these social movements have found expression in an array of formal agencies and organizations including the Assembly of First Nations, the National Action Committee on the Status of Women, the Canadian Human Rights Commission, and the National Advisory Council on Aging. Government policy initiatives in such areas as multiculturalism, bilingualism and biculturalism, non-traditional job training for women, and regional development have reinforced these movements.

ETHNICITY AND RACE

The aims of these various movements have not gone uncontested. As social policies emphasizing affirmative action, employment equity, positive discrimination, and comparable worth have been formulated as remedies to injustices suffered by various social groups (Abella, 1984), questions about the need for such reform measures have been forcefully raised.

In the first article in this subsection, Conrad Winn shows how affirmative action programs are aimed at compensating for alleged discriminatory practices against ethnic minorities. His concern is with the contemporary profile of Canada's "vertical mosaic," examining it and asking in the process how unequally distributed are income, education, and mobility opportunities for members of different ethnic groups. Affirmative action, Winn feels, is premised on the existence of *sharp* differences across ethnic groups in the distribution of income, education, and mobility opportunities. Only a modest degree of structured inequality is equated with ethnic and racial origin, according to Winn's data. For this reason, among others, Winn is very pessimistic about the utility of affirmative action policies as a method of uncoupling ethnic origin and social inequality.

While he believes that affirmative action programs may not be efficient policy tools if applied in some "broad brush" approach, Winn is careful to allow that discrimination *is* an issue in Canadian society. The historical evidence reveals a litany of discriminatory acts in Canada from Black slavery to Chinese head taxes to Japanese internment.

Discrimination is not merely some historical remnant. In the second selection in the subsection on race and ethnicity, Frances Henry and Effie Ginzberg demonstrate that there were explicit and undeniable processes of discrimination in hiring practices in a Toronto sample of job interviews. Using an experimental design where job applications were made in person, they measured the extent of preferential hiring for Whites relative to Blacks. Not content with this single indicator, they altered the design to incorporate job searches by telephone and examined the success rates of different "audible" minorities. On the basis of these two types of evidence, they calculate a discrimination ratio of 3:1 indicating that racial minorities suffer substantial handicaps (relative to the dominant White majority group) in their ability to find employment.

Henry and Ginzberg's work is masterful in demonstrating the very direct forms which discrimination still takes in Canadian society. Other, more subtle forms of discrimination also occur in the Canadian labour market. Word-of-mouth hiring procedures, the use of irrelevant job qualifications, biased screening techniques, and systematic misinformation are all examples of more disguised forms of preferential treatment.

Native people have occupied a marginal position in Canada for several centuries. As Judge Rosalie Abella (1984:33) reported in her Royal Commission, "it is not new that their [Native people's] economic conditions are poor. Study after study has documented the facts." What is less often realized, Abella continues, is that

> their economic plight has taken its inevitable toll on social conditions. Native people are angry over the disproportionate numbers of native people who drop out of school, who are in prison, who suffer ill health, who die young, who commit suicide. They are saddened by the personal, communal, and cultural dislocation of their people.

Palmer Patterson, in our selection on Native-White relations, traces the history of "dislocation" that has beset the Native peoples of Canada. He documents the imperialist encroachment on North America of European nations in pursuit of riches from the resources of this continent. For several centuries Native people have been placed in an increasingly dependent position, with their protests over land claim settlements or their calls for greater self-determination going unheeded. More recently, while these old demands remain unresolved, a new Canadian constitution has been signed which does *not* contain material on the aboriginal rights of this indigenous population. Aboriginal self-government remains as a basic demand of the Native peoples.

Issues of group survival have also been prominent among Francophone Canadians who have often feared the assimilationist forces of a dominant English-speaking population. Our selection from Robert Bourbeau traces recent trends in what he calls linguistic mobility, the phenomenon of language transfer measured by determining the proportion of people with a given mother tongue (that is, language first learned and still understood) who now report using a different language in their home. The task he sets himself is the examination of French-language use both inside Quebec and in the rest of Canada.

One of the reasons that research such as Bourbeau's is so important is that language is at the heart of cultural identity. Historically, French Canadians have suffered economically from their position in Canada, although, as we will see later in a selection from Douglas Baer and James Curtis (Section IV), this may be changing. Inequality has, however, been related to language group; and, in a manner parallel to what Native peoples have known, the French Canadian cultural heritage often has been caught up in structured inequality through discrimination based on facility in the English language.

The issues of racial discrimination and ethnic group inequality are combined by Evelyn Kallen in our final reading in this subsection as she studies the concept of "multiculturalism." She addresses the different meanings that have been applied to the term *multiculturalism*—the multi-ethnic composition of Canada's population, the federal government policy on ethnic diversity, and the conception of Canada as an ethnically stratified mosaic. She pays particular attention to the implications of these meanings for policy and government programs. She sees a recent trend toward greater ethnic fragmentation, wherein ethnicity is a significant fault line across which conflict increasingly occurs in this country.

GENDER

We turn next to a second ascriptive factor of increasing salience in Canada, gender. The disadvantaged position of women in Canadian society has become one of the dominant issues of political struggle. Here are some examples of the disadvantages: women working full-time, year round, earn on average about 60-65 percent of what men earn; they are concentrated in a small number of occupations; and they have little power and responsibility in the jobs they do hold. Nevertheless, women's participation in the paid labour force has risen dramatically in recent decades. Various estimates now suggest that if we include the unpaid labour of housework, which largely remains the chore of women, it is a fact that women do a disproportionate amount of all work in contemporary society. One startling set of estimates places the proportion of the world's work done by women at about two thirds, for which women receive approximately one tenth of the income, and women own only about 1 percent of all property (Eichler, 1985).

Controversy surrounds the theoretical approaches one might take in attempting to sort out the different experiences of women and of men in the modern world. We begin the subsection on Gender with an excellent overview, written by Eileen Saunders, of various theoretical approaches to the study of women. After providing succinct discussions of three traditional perspectives—conservatism, feminism, and Marxism—she sketches in the outline of a newly emerging theoretical alternative, socialist feminism.

One issue which each of these theoretical perspectives treats in different ways is the process of socialization. The more conservative approach sees the different roles that women and men play in society as *functional* for the preservation of the social order, stressing in particular that there is a social imperative of women and men to internalize appropriate sex-role learning in order to contribute to the social integration of society. Conversely, the socialist feminist approach, which also addresses socialization, sees the process more as *social control* where, via the "politics of exclusion," women find that their access to certain rewards and opportunities is constrained or limited by definitions of what is right and proper, what is appropriate behaviour, for women.

This theme of differential socialization is pursued by Stephen Richer in his selection on sex-role differentiation in children's play. Using a field study where patterns of cross-sex play interaction were observed in both a day care and a camp setting, he found little reluctance on the part of either girls or boys to play with one another. This shows, he argues, that children must *learn* sex-segregated patterns of behaviour; these are not natural imperatives of "bonding" tendencies. His research suggests that children begin to exhibit patterns of sex-segregated interaction when they enter the formal education system, implying that perhaps the school experience lies at the heart of the sex-typing of women's and men's roles.

While Richer's research demonstrates that young children, whether boys or girls, are willing to "play house," the next selection by Meg Luxton shows, based on interviews at two points in time, that in the adult world the work of household chores remains overwhelmingly the responsibility of women. There is in the adult home, she shows, a gendered division of labour that is crosscut with different power dynamics between wives and husbands. Luxton's approach to this complex transformation of the responsibilities of women and men in the home relies on insights from feminist and socialist perspectives, and aptly illustrates many of the theoretical concerns outlined by Saunders.

Not only is it in the home that patterns of work are changing, but also in the paid labour force. Liviana Calzavara, in our final selection in the subsection on gender, reviews the trends in the employment opportunities of women in Canada between 1930 and 1985. She pays particular attention to comparisons between women and men in employment rates, in earnings, and in occupational segregation. Additionally, she returns to some of the issues addressed earlier, in the paper by Winn concerning discrimination and affirmative action. She highlights the policy initiatives of pay equity and equal employment legislation.

The section on gender shows that over the last few decades some progress has been made toward greater opportunities for women. As detailed earlier (Gilbert and Guppy), women now constitute the majority of students at college and university, and throughout the 1980s more women than men have received bachelor degrees from Canadian universities. Enrolments in professional faculties, most notably law and medicine, have increased dramatically for women. Nevertheless, a series of occupational niches exist in which few women find employment. The Canadian parliament is one place where women are conspicuous by their under-representation—in 1987 only 27 of the 282 seats in the federal House of Commons were occupied by women. So, while some progress has been evident, women continue to organize and struggle to expand their opportunities and rewards.

AGE

Sex and ethnicity are but two ascribed attributes which have served to unite people around social issues. Age is a third. Consider this. Is it reasonable to have a minimum wage policy that specifies that people under a certain age, often 16, 17, or 18, should be paid at a lower rate than people a few days or months older? Should workers be forced out of the labour force once they reach age 65, even if they are willing and capable of continuing to work? Age discrimination is an issue which, especially in the last decade, has received increasing attention and which has become a rallying point for social protest. One particularly dramatic incident occurred in 1985 when Canadian pensioners organized to oppose successfully legislation proposed by the Mulroney government to reduce pension benefits for seniors.

Joseph Tindale provides a general review of issues related to age and social inequality. He begins by outlining recent theoretical approaches to the study of age and social inequality. He then describes links between age and inequality by examining, for example, the connection between income and age, the impact of seniority systems in organizations, and the ongoing debate over mandatory retirement.

Economic disadvantage and old age are given detailed attention in the next excerpt from a publication of the National Council of Welfare. Emphasis is placed on the risk of poverty that is faced by most elderly people, and most especially elderly women. More than a million elderly people in Canada have so little income that they qualify for the Guaranteed Income Supplement, a federal government initiative introduced as an antipoverty program. With the aging of Canada's population, the current inadequacy of our old age income system, whether via public or via private pensions, is in need of dramatic reform.

REGION

The last subsection on ascription shifts our attention from individual attributes to the community and regional contexts in which Canadians live. At first glance it might seem odd to include *region* in a section on ascription. After all, people can choose to move from region to region. Region of residence could be viewed as an achieved or attained status, since it is subject to individual choice in a way that ascribed characteristics like gender or race are not. Nevertheless, there clearly are ascribed aspects to the region variable that should be recognized. Region of birth, for example, is not a matter of personal choice and, moreover, it is a good predictor of a person's ultimate place of residence. That is, people who are born in a particular region often stay in the same locality during their adult life, because of the strong community allegiances, regional identities, and social ties that tend to arise in early life and that constrain people to stay where they are, in spite of pressures or opportunities to go elsewhere.

Region has lasting effects on people's life chances for at least two reasons. First, Canadians have developed stereotypes about regional personality traits—"rednecks" from the West, "laid-back" Vancouverites, or "unsophisticated" Newfoundlanders, for example. Certain expectations are formed and judgements are made, on the basis of whether someone is a "city slicker" or a "country bumpkin." Second, and more importantly, inequalities of reward and opportunity are also structured by the communities in which Canadians live. The regional disparities of the country reinforce many of the differences in income, occupation, and education discussed in the section on the socio-economic bases of inequality.

We begin our consideration of regional differences with Ralph Matthew's discussion of explanations for the regional economic differences which permeate Canadian society. Issues of history and policy are emphasized. It is argued that a broad historical perspective is necessary for an adequate theoretical account of the way regional development policies have tended to favour central regions at the expense of more peripheral areas.

It is this theme of economic dominance by metropolitan centres that is taken up by Keith Semple in his consideration of the social organization of corporate activity in Canada. Describing regional differences on both urban-rural and centre-periphery dimensions, Semple shows how the concentration of corporate wealth has come to favour certain specific urban systems in very particular regions of the country. Semple also returns to themes of earlier readings by showing the prominent role of foreign urban centres in the control of the Canadian economy.

Finally, the concluding paper on region, written by Ingrid Bryan, directly assesses questions of employment and income differences across the Canadian provinces. After reviewing the evidence, the author proceeds to examine both theoretical analyses and policy initiatives, the former designed to explain, and the latter to ameliorate, the rather sharp regional differences her data reveal.

While none of these readings on regionalism directly addresses the question of regional alienation, each underscores the conditions upon which regional discontent or, more properly, hinterland discontent is based. The regional composition of the federal House of Commons is but one of many indicators of the degree to which regional issues are central to power struggles in Canada. Provincial premiers have made careers out of Ottawa-bashing, and Western separatists have found support, particularly in Alberta.

It is instructive to conclude this introduction by considering the very different bases of separatist sentiment in Western Canada and in Quebec. In British Columbia and the Prairie Provinces, the dispute with Central Canada has been largely a series of confrontations over economic issues; much of the fuel for Western separatism comes from the strongly held belief that Westerners were not receiving their fair economic share. In Quebec, too, economic issues were important to the separatist thrust but, unlike in the West, language, culture, and religion were also felt to be threatened.

This should remind us that the degree to which ascriptive factors coalesce with or crosscut one another is an empirical question. For example, socio-economic inequalities, coupled with the ascriptive factors of ethnic affiliation and region, were the key base for the separatist movement in Quebec.

The central concern of this section is the degree to which social inequalities are related to ascriptive factors. Despite those optimistic social commentators who predicted the eclipse of ascriptive influences on inequality, either through modernization or through revolution, it is apparent that life chances continue to be affected greatly by race, ethnicity, sex, age, and region. We are still a long way from the elimination of ascriptive inequalities.

REFERENCES

Abella, Rosalie S., ed.
    1984   *Equality in Employment.* Ottawa: Supply and Services.

Eichler, Margrit
    1985   "Applying Equality to Employment," in *Equality in Employment,* ed. R. S. Abella. Ottawa: Supply and Services.

Porter, John
    1965   *The Vertical Mosaic.* Toronto: University of Toronto Press.

17. *The Socio-Economic Attainment of Visible Minorities: Facts and Policy Implications**

Conrad Winn

INTRODUCTION

"Affirmative action" and "visible minorities" are ambiguous, euphemistic terms. Affirmative action is normally a euphemism for an act of compensatory discrimination whose purpose is to augment the employment or promotion rates of a target, or beneficiary, group. Affirmative action can be used to galvanize or motivate the members of target groups, to provide them with more training opportunities, and/or to provide them with proportionately more jobs and more senior postings.[1] This essay focusses

on quota hiring rather than special efforts to motivate or train because quota hiring raises more complex ethical, empirical, and political issues. Quota hiring is more likely to cause a public stir than other compensatory or preferential actions because quota hiring entails the definite transfer of measurable benefits. Quota hiring is more likely to be perceived than special educational efforts as a transfer of benefits without regard to merit. Quota hiring is especially apt to cause a backlash if it is not based on a moral imperative which is widely shared and on empirical evidence which is widely respected.

This essay seeks to contribute to a discussion of affirmative action for ethno-racial minorities by enumerating and assessing certain premises which underlie the portrait of the economy and society upon which the case for affirmative action is or could be based. Some of these premises are assumptions which can be inferred from the writing

Revised from Conrad Winn, "Affirmative Action and Visible Minorities: Eight Premises in Quest of Evidence," in *Canadian Public Policy—Analyse de Politiques*, vol. 11, no. 4 (December 1985). Reprinted with permission.

of advocates of affirmative action, for example from the Abella Royal Commission Report (1984) on *Equality in Employment.* Some of the premises are not easily inferred from the work of the affirmative action advocates but are nonetheless examined because, if true, they would buttress the argument for affirmative action, and, if untrue, would weaken it.

TESTING PREMISES

Premise 1 is that income and occupational differences among ethno-racial groups are much greater than income differences within these groups. If true, this premise would strengthen the argument for hiring on the basis of ethnicity without regard to regional origin, social class, and/or other intra-group differences. But, if it is false, the intellectual and moral arguments for ethno-racial affirmative action would be weakened.

The census of Canada contains information on ethnicity and economic achievement, but this information is not normally published except by special request and at considerable cost. The Multiculturalism Directorate of the Secretary of State Department permitted the author to examine its census tables for a sample of 16 ethno-racial groups in 1981: Jews, Czechoslovaks, Japanese, Finns, Indo-Pakistanis, Russians, Yugoslavs, Koreans, Spaniards, Ukrainians, Chinese, Filipinos, Portuguese, Blacks, Greeks, and Indochinese. The ratio of mean incomes for the highest (Jews) and lowest income earners (Indochinese) was 2.5. The mean income of the Indochinese was substantially less (28 percent less) than that of the second-lowest group, the Greeks. The low Indochinese income is largely explained by the preponderance of recent immigrants in this group. The mean income among those Indochinese born in Canada

TABLE 17-1 Incomes of selected ethnic groups, 1971, ranked and in sextiles.

Jewish	1st
Asian	1st
Italian	1st
Other Eastern European	2nd
Other Southern European	2nd
British	2nd
Other Central European	3rd
Scandinavian	3rd
Polish	3rd
Ukrainian	4th
German	4th
Hungarian	4th
Netherlander	5th
All other	5th
Russian	5th
Belgian and other Northern Western Europeans	6th
French	6th
Native Indian and Inuit	6th

Source: Adapted from Richmond and Kalbach, *Immigrants and their Descendants*, Table 11-12, based on means, family heads, aged 35-44, 1971 Census.

was seventh highest among the Canadian-born members of the 16 groups.

If the Indochinese are treated as a special case, the resulting ratio of mean incomes of the highest and lowest (Greek) ethnic earners is 1.8. None of the ethno-racial groups experience income differences between regions less than 1.8. For example, Japanese make five times more in Newfoundland than in Nova Scotia. Blacks earn two-and-one-half times more in New Brunswick than in Nova Scotia. Every group also displays marked income differences between social classes. The university graduates in all but one ethnic group earned at least 1.8 times more than the grade-school leavers in their own group. Among immigrants, university graduates earned as much as three-and-one-half times more than grade-school leavers. The essay will argue below that the presence of large income differences within individual ethnic groups ought to be a consideration in the development of government policy.

A virtual corollary of premise 1 is the related premise that so-called "majority" Whites and "visible minority" non-Whites are each homogeneous and their internal differences minor. If indeed Whites and visible minorities were internally homogeneous and different from each other, this fact would strengthen the case for affirmative action for visible minorities. But, if this were untrue, the concept of visible minority might need to be replaced with a new concept, for example that of "disadvantaged ethnic group." Census data are publicly available on the mean incomes of samples of ethnic groups in 1971 and 1981. Table 17-1 shows the rank order of incomes of 18 ethnic groups according to the 1971 census, grouped in sextiles. Table 17-2 shows the rank order of incomes of 16 ethnic groups according to the 1981 census, grouped in quartiles. The particular groups listed in Tables 17-1 and 17-2 are categories for which income data happen to be available.

Neither the 1971 nor the 1981 data present convincing evidence that the incomes of non-White groups or low-prestige White groups are necessarily at the bottom. Asians are the second-highest income earning category in 1971 while Japanese are the third-highest earners in 1981. In 1971 Asian Canadians earned 8 percent more than the British, 13 percent more than the average Canadian, 24 percent more than the French, and twice as much as the Natives. In 1981 the Japanese placed in the top quartile, earning one-fifth more than the median group in the sample and almost twice the income of the Indochinese. In the United

TABLE 17-2 Incomes of selected ethnic groups, 1981, ranked and in quartiles.

Jewish	1st
Czechoslovak	1st
Japanese	1st
Finnish	1st
Indo-Pakistani	2nd
Russian	2nd
Yugoslavic	2nd
Korean	2nd
Spanish	3rd
Ukrainian	3rd
Chinese	3rd
Filipino	3rd
Portuguese	4th
Black	4th
Greek	4th
Indochinese	4th

Source: Mean male incomes, 1981 Census; computed from tabular data made available by the Multiculturalism Directorate.

States, Japanese also occupy a high spot, behind Jews and Americans originating in India and just ahead of Chinese.[2]

The 1981 dataset allows a comparison of the incomes of seven non-White groups. Indo-Pakistanis rank fifth out of 16, while Koreans rank eighth. Chinese, Filipinos, and Blacks rank 11th, 12th, and 14th. A per capita income of only $40 extra per year would place Black incomes above Portuguese and hence above two White groups. Only Indochinese incomes are very low. Greeks earn 39 percent more than the Indochinese. The Indochinese probably earn more than Native people, for whom comparable data were unavailable.

The majority Whites are just as heterogeneous as the non-Whites. The 1981 sample shows that Whites are just as likely to be in the top quartile as in the bottom. The

1971 sample includes high-status White groups and hence permits a comparison of Whites of high and low ethnic prestige. According to the ethno-racial logic of affirmative action, the ethnic group with the highest prestige, people of British ancestry, would earn very high incomes. However, British incomes are lower than the incomes of four low-status ethnic categories—Jews, Italians, "Other Eastern European," and "Other Southern European." Scandinavians, Germans, Netherlanders—all high-prestige northern European groups—earn average or below average incomes. The earnings of the British group are only 4 percent above the national average. In 1971 in the English-speaking provinces, those of British ancestry earned less than average incomes and hence constituted a have-not group.

Premise 2 is that Canadian society is substantially immobile with the result that individuals and groups are unable to improve their relative economic position without government intervention. If true, this premise would greatly strengthen the argument for government intervention to improve the occupational and income positions of members of the visible minorities. But, if it is untrue, the argument for affirmative action would be undermined. The Abella Royal Commission asserts that Canada is essentially immobile, that the occupational progress of visible minorities and other target groups "remain[s] unjustifiably in perpetual slow motion" (p.4).

There is indeed immobility at the very top, among the interlocking directorates of the corporate world. However, boardroom immobilism is fundamentally a problem of leadership, not of income distribution. Below the boardroom, Canada appears to have experienced a considerable degree of ethnic social mobility and especially a considerable rise in the relative positions of

non-White and low-status White groups. Tables 17-3 and 17-4 present the mobility scores for the 1971 and 1981 groups, respectively. A group's mobility score equals its income rank among the foreign-born minus its income rank among the Canadian-born. A plus score indicates that a group's mean income position has increased between the foreign-born generation and Canadian-born generations as compared with other groups. A minus sign indicates a relative decline in rank.

Comparing the rank order position of ethnic groups between foreign- and Canadian-born generations is an imperfect measure of ethnic social mobility. It does not

TABLE 17-3 Mobility of ethnic groups, 1971, direction and number of rank changes.

Italians	+ 13
Other Southern European	+ 12
Asian	+ 11
Other Eastern European	+ 11
Ukrainian	+ 4
Polish	+ 2
Jewish	0
Hungarian	0
Native Indian and Inuit	0
Other Central European	− 3
British	− 4
All other	− 4
Scandinavian	− 5
German	− 7
Netherlander	− 7
Russian	− 7
Belgian and Other Northern and Western European	− 7
French	− 10

N.B. Mobility score = rank among foreign-born − rank among Canadian-born members of same group.
Source: Family heads, aged 35-44, 1971 Census, adapted from Table 11-2, Richmond and Kalbach, *Immigrants and Their Descendants.*

take into consideration the different skills brought into the country by the first generation of each ethnic group, nor does it take into consideration inter-ethnic differences in age distribution. Because the datasets are based on only two census years, 1971 and 1981, the mobility scores do not reflect mobility changes in the more distant past. For example, recent influxes of immigrants from the Pacific rim are well-educated; the Chinese workers imported to construct the railroad in the nineteenth century were not. Jewish immigrants who come to Canada today are highly educated; those who came from Russia during the Czarist period were not. However, in the absence of very long-term, large-sample raw panel data, the mobility scores of Tables 17-3 and 17-4 are useful information.

Table 17-3 (1971) shows that 15 out of 18

TABLE 17-4 Mobility scores of ethnic groups, 1981, direction and number of rank changes.

Indochinese	+	9
Filipino	+	6
Russian	+	6
Japanese	+	4
Korean	+	4
Black		0
Chinese		0
Jewish		0
Ukrainian		0
Finnish	−	1
Spanish	−	1
Czechoslovak	−	2
Portuguese	−	3
Greek	−	5
Yugoslavic	−	8
Indo-Pakistani	−	9

e.g., Indochinese income rose from 16th rank among foreign-born to 7th rank among Canadian-born (16 − 7 = + 9).

groups changed ranks. All the upwardly mobile groups are low-prestige White groups or Asians. All the high-prestige White groups—the British, Scandinavians, Germans, and "Belgian and other Northern and Western European"—experienced downward social mobility. British and other immigrants from northern Europe often arrive with greater skills. Because the British and northern Europeans come from high-income countries, they have the possibility of bringing greater financial assets. British and other northern Europeans begin with the additional advantage of cultural similarity and ethnic prestige. But these advantages did not enable the European groups, as a whole, to sustain their relative position in successive generations. Low-prestige and largely unskilled Italian immigrants and other southern Europeans rose greatly as did Asians. Indeed, Asians and Italians rose to second and third rank positions, respectively (Table 17-1). "Other Eastern European," Ukrainian, and Polish groups also increased their relative position. Not one Protestant ethnic group increased its relative position in a land where the most prestigious faiths are Protestant and where the work ethic is considered to be Protestant.

Table 17-4 (1981) presents mobility scores for a somewhat different sample of ethnoracial groups. Those groups which appear under their own names or under broader classifications in the two tables do not necessarily display exactly the same mobility behaviour. For example, Russians declined in rank according to the 1971 data but rose in the 1981 data. The two most salient patterns emerging from Table 17-4, as from Table 17-3, are a high degree of mobility among all groups and a high degree of upward mobility among low-prestige groups. Twelve of 16 groups experienced a change in rank. The seven non-White groups in the sample of 16 were greatly overrepresented among the upwardly mobile groups. Of the five ethno-racial groups which displayed upward mobility in the 1981 dataset, four were non-White: the Indochinese, Koreans, Japanese, and Filipino. The Russians were the only upwardly mobile white group. Blacks and Chinese experienced no change in rank. Six of the seven downwardly mobile groups were White.

In historical perspective, the present incomes of Japanese and Jewish Canadians are remarkable considering the discrimination in college admissions, housing, and employment which prevailed against these groups until after World War II and which persists in some sectors of the economy today. The meteoric rise of Italians (in the 1971 dataset) is remarkable considering the low skills which they brought with them from southern Italy, their relatively recent arrival, and the traditionally low prestige of their group in Canadian society.

Overall, the scores in Tables 17-3 and 17-4 provide no empirical support for the premise that Canadian society is immobile and that visible or low-prestige groups cannot make economic progress. The data suggest that Canadian society is indeed mobile.[3] The precise mobility scores for individual groups should be treated with caution because they may reflect peculiarities of age distributions. For example, the downward mobility score of the Indo-Pakistanis is misleading because it does not take into consideration their recent immigration to Canada and hence the small proportion of the Canadian-born members of the Indo-Pakistani group who are in the older, high-earning age groups. An Indo-Pakistani mobility score based on 1991 or 2001 census data would probably not display a minus sign.

Premise 3 is that inequalities in income and occupational status are evidence of racist behaviour by employers. The advocates of affir-

mative action rarely assert unambiguously that occupational inequality is unequivocal evidence of discrimination. But they place great emphasis on occupational inequality as a justification for affirmative action. According to the Abella Commission, differences in unemployment rates and incomes should be understood as "'social indicators' of job discrimination. They can also be characterized as systemic discrimination [sic]" (p.15). The Commission Report emphasizes that the Canadian judicial system need not demonstrate discriminatory conduct by an employer in order to require the employer to adopt a program of preferential hiring. To require an affirmative action program, it is sufficient for the courts to observe occupational differences among groups. The stated policy of the Canadian government toward the hiring of women and Natives is that departmental criteria for appointment and advancement must be changed or fully justified to the central agencies once departments discover that the success rate of a beneficiary group is less than 80 percent of the success rate of the most successful group.[4]

Racism, the essay argues later, does affect economic achievement in a number of complex ways. However, a large portion of inequalities are explained by differences in region or location, differences in immigration status, and differences in education and other job qualifications. The fact that British Columbians earn much more than Newfoundlanders is unrelated to racism. The fact that first generation immigrants are often low-income earners is not primarily, if at all, a matter of racism either. Immigrants from different countries arrive with different language abilities, job skills, and capital. Non-British immigrants often arrive with fewer of the requisites for occupational achievement than become available to their Canadian-born children. Thus, Asian Montrealers earn 56 percent more if they are native- rather than foreign-born.[5]

Economic achievement reflects job qualifications including education. Different ethno-racial groups exhibit different propensities or tastes for acquiring education. In the United States, Black income earners and heads of families earn less than their White counterparts, but this difference is substantially attributable to different amounts of formal education. Some categories of Blacks actually earn more than Whites with comparable education. Before affirmative action, Black Ph.D.s earned more than White Ph.D.s with similar professional records, while Black female college graduates earned more than their White sisters.[6]

Hispanics earn lower average incomes than "Whites" and are classed as beneficiaries under affirmative action in the United States. However, the rate of return on schooling is actually higher for Hispanics than for Whites. Employed Hispanics earn percent increases of 5.2 and 11.9 for each year of high school and college, respectively, as compared to 4.4 and 9.8 for Whites.[7] By emphasizing skilled jobs, affirmative action augments the already existing advantage of educated Blacks and Hispanics over uneducated Blacks and Hispanics and over Whites, educated or not.

In the particular case of Blacks, the rate of return for employed grade-school leavers is low as a result of historical racism in education. In the antebellum south, "free" Blacks were forbidden by law from receiving education. For generations after the end of slavery, Black schools were penalized by state governments so that a Black who attended a predominantly Black southern school had to graduate from grade 12 in order to spend as many days in class as a White graduating from grade 8. When Blacks, Whites, and Hispanics are compared with respect to test measures of academic achievement, the rate of return for Black school leavers is lower than for Hispanics, but higher than for Whites.

The 1981 census data on Canada show striking differences in the propensity for education among ethnic groups. Table 17-5 shows that the members of the most widely educated group, the Filipinos, are 12 times more likely to have experienced some college education than the least educated, the Portuguese. If education rather than racism predicts income, we should expect the highest and lowest income earners as shown in Table 17-2 to be among the best and least educated as shown in Table 17-5. Indeed, the three highest-income earners—Jews, Czechs and Japanese—are the three most widely educated. Yet education is not a perfect predictor of income. Only one of the

TABLE 17-5 Propensity for higher education, selected ethnic groups, males.

(% ever attended college/university)

1. Filipino	60
2. Korean	57
3. Jewish	54
4. Chinese	34
5. Japanese	33
6. Indochinese	33
7. Scandinavian*	30
8. Czechoslovak	29
9. Indo-Pakistani	29
10. English*	28
11. Spanish	27
12. Black	26
13. Russian	24
14. Ukrainian	19
15. Finnish	18
16. Italian*	18
17. Yugoslavic	17
18. Native*	17
19. Greek	14
20. Portuguese	5

Sources: Asterisk indicates "Quality of Life" Survey, 1979 (N = 3500 approx.); Otherwise, 1981 census.

three lowest-income earning groups, the Greeks, are at the bottom of the educational heap.

A rudimentary test of the rate of return on higher education is possible by examining data displayed in Tables 17-6 and 17-7. Table 17-6 presents data on the mean incomes of Canadian-born male university graduates in each of 15 ethnic groups. The mean incomes of males who have at least one university degree are presented in order to control for the impact of gender and educational qualification. In a hypothetical world in which formal educational qualifications were equally worthy of merit, in which all ethnic groups displayed the same distributions of age and experience, and in which ethnicity had no earning power, the mean incomes of university graduates would be the same across ethnic groups.

Table 17-6 presents data on the proportion of the Canadian-born members of each ethnic group who have at least some college education. The census does not distinguish between university graduates with first and subsequent degrees, although different degrees have different earning power. In the absence of such information, it is reasonable to infer that ethnic groups with the widest exposure to university education also have the highest proportion of members with advanced degrees. Hence, one could expect

TABLE 17-6 Rates of return for higher education and educational propensity, selected ethnic groups, males: Canadian-born.

Group	Income rank	Mean incomes, university graduates	College propensity rank*	Age-earning rank**
Jewish	1	32 235	1(58%)	5(21%)
Russian	2	30 073	9(22%)	1(27%)
Korean	3	28 210	3(33%)	10(2%)
Japanese	4	28 202	4(30%)	2(25%)
Finnish	5	27 350	10(21%)	6(20%)
Yugoslavic	6	26 366	7(25%)	7(10%)
Czechoslovak	7	26 074	5(23%)	3(22%)
Greek	8	25 670	8(25%)	9(4%)
Ukrainian	9	24 936	11(20%)	4(2%)
Indochinese	10	24 783	6(25%)	−(NA)
Chinese	11	24 370	2(35%)	8(6%)
Black	12	24 085	13(16%)	−(NA)
Portuguese	13	22 244	14(9%)	11(1%)
Filipino	14	20 749	12(17%)	12(1%)
Indo-Pakistani	15	13 186	15(3%)	−(NA)

* Percent ever attended college in parentheses.
** Percent 35-54 years old in parentheses.
Source: 1981 Census tables produced for Multiculturalism Directorate.

inter-ethnic variation in the earning power of university graduates to co-vary with the educational propensity of the ethnic groups. Table 17-6 presents data on the proportion of each group in the high-earning 35-54 age category. One could expect ethnic groups with many members in the 35-54 age category to experience higher mean incomes than ethnic groups with few people in this age category.

Table 17-7 presents data similar to that in Table 17-6, but only for the foreign-born. Tables 17-6 and 17-7 treat the native- and foreign-born separately in order to control for the effect of acculturation.

Table 17-6 shows that Canadian-born Jews, Russians, Koreans, and Japanese have the highest rate of return on university education whereas Blacks, Portuguese, Filipinos, and Indo-Pakistanis have the lowest. On the basis of their propensity for education, Jews, Koreans, and Japanese would be expected to have high rates of return on education, and they do. On the basis of educational propensity, the Russians ought to have low rates of return. But Russians have high rates of return at least in part because they have the highest proportion of members in the high-earning, 35-54 age group. In spite of their second rank in college propensity, the Chinese rank only 11th in earning power, at least in part because of their

TABLE 17-7   Rates of return for higher education and educational propensity, selected ethnic groups, males: foreign-born.

Group	Income rank	Mean incomes, university graduates	College propensity rank*	Age-earning rank**
Czechoslovak	1	32 214	7(33%)	4(38%)
Jewish	2	31 106	3(47%)	10(24%)
Finnish	3	26 788	12(14%)	6(33%)
Yugoslavic	4	25 837	10(15%)	2(48%)
Russian	5	25 297	8(33%)	11(15%)
Ukrainian	6	24 936	11(14%)	12(15%)
Greek	7	24 492	13(12%)	1(51%)
Chinese	8	24 015	5(34%)	8(30%)
Black	9	22 191	9(27%)	– (NA)
Indo-Pakistani	10	22 108	5(37%)	– (NA)
Japanese	11	22 094	4(44%)	7(33%)
Korean	12	20 576	2(57%)	3(41%)
Indochinese	13	20 062	6(34%)	– (NA)
Portuguese	14	19 762	14(5%)	5(37%)
Filipino	15	19 332	1(61%)	9(29%)

*   Percent ever attended college in parentheses.
** Percent 35-54 years old in parentheses.
Source: 1981 Census tables produced for Multiculturalism Directorate.

age distribution. Only 6 percent of Canadian-born Chinese are 35-54 years old; as many as 21 and 25 percent of Jews and Japanese are in this age category. Overall, four non-White groups out of six are ranked among the top half with respect to educational propensity, but only two non-White groups are ranked among the top half of earners from educational investments.

The apparently greater difficulty of non-White groups in transforming educational propensity into high rates of return on education suggests the possibility of racism at work. However, other interpretations cannot be ruled out. The preceding rudimentary analysis may not have measured education and age with sufficient precision or considered all necessary extraneous variables. One study of Chinese and Japanese Canadians found no remaining income differences between these two groups once educational, age, and other differences were controlled statistically.[8]

Table 17-7 shows that foreign-born Canadians, especially non-Europeans, have an enormous difficulty transforming educational propensity into income-earning investments. Six of seven non-White groups are ranked in the top half with respect to college exposure, but no non-White group ranks in the top half with respect to rate of return. This discrepancy suggests the possibility that racism or ethnocentrism affects the earning power of the foreign-born. However, other interpretations of the data are possible. In the absence of valid information on the objective worth of the presumably foreign qualifications of the foreign-born, it is difficult to offer a conclusive explanation. The possibility that the formal educational qualifications of many Asians are objectively less useful in the Canadian economy is compatible with the fact that the only non-White foreign-born group able to achieve as high rank in earnings as in college

propensity is the Blacks, who were presumably educated in Anglo-American institutions. Blacks ranked ninth in college propensity and ninth in earnings (Table 17-7). The fact that immigrant Blacks transformed college propensity into earnings more effectively than other non-Whites is also compatible with the hypothesis that some foreign-born Asians may have done poorly because of insufficient language skills. Indeed, the three highest-earning foreign-born non-White groups—Chinese, Black, and Indo-Pakistani—are the ones most likely to have good English language skills and to have been trained in Anglo-American institutions.

In the absence of better data and better analysis, the following preliminary conclusions seem reasonable. On the basis of the ethnic income data in Tables 17-1 and 17-2, it is evident that non-Whites generally do not earn appreciably less than Whites. The notable exceptions to this are the Indochinese and Native Indians and Inuit. On the basis of the ethnic mobility data in Tables 17-3 and 17-4, it is evident that non-Whites are gaining considerable ground as compared to Whites. The data on rates of return for higher education in Tables 17-6 and 17-7 suggest that non-Whites, especially foreign-born Pacific-rim Asians, have difficulty translating educational propensity into earning power.

The fact that non-Whites are able to gain on or surpass Whites in income has no bearing on and does not contradict other kinds of research evidence that non-Whites encounter racist barriers to occupational success.[9] The evidence of racism and the evidence of economic success can be reconciled in various ways. One can take the view that Canadian-born non-Whites are able to make use of cognitive and other skills so as to neutralize the effects of anticipated discrimination. One can also take the view that racism is a matter of culture and not just physiognomy. The greater income difficulties of foreign-born than of Canadian-born non-Whites suggest the possibility that racism may be targetted against strange accents and habits and not just strange faces. An alternative interpretation is that foreign-born non-Whites experience income difficulties because it is difficult for them to anticipate and cope with racist barriers before having mastered the host language and culture.

A virtual corollary of premise 3 is the related premise that racist attitudes in a society cause economic losses to the outcast group and that these economic losses rise linearly as a function of the intensity of antipathy. In fact, the general relationship between racism and inequality is probably much more complex. Intensely racist attitudes and behaviour probably do deprive the outcast group of so many possible economic transactions that its relative income declines. But moderate racism may increase the incomes of the members of the pariah group by bringing a defence mechanism into play. Barred from prestigious and secure occupations, they may work harder at less prestigious occupations and extract higher revenues. At a minimum, the members of outcast groups have a greater requirement to live in expensive neighbourhoods in order to protect their children from physical assault. At a maximum, the members of threatened minorities require some capital accumulation in the event of social unrest or flight. Their sense of vulnerability may go part way toward explaining the educational and therefore income achievements of Jewish and Japanese Canadians.

Premise 4 is that the cultural or psychological capacity of victimized groups is not an important factor affecting inequality. For example, the extensive discussion of education in the Abella Royal Commission Report pinpointed the responsibilities of the federal government, provincial governments, educational authorities, and teachers, but did not explore the roles of parents, families, and communities. Yet, families influence the subsequent educational and occupational achievements of children more than do schools.[10] Occupationally successful ethno-racial groups, whether pariahs or prestigious, are able to transmit to successive generations a sense of history, a positive sense of collective self-worth, and a willingness to make sacrifices for achievement. Successful groups teach their young to delay marriage, to plan parenthood, and to make other personal and family sacrifices for educational and economic advancement. People who delay procreation and have fewer children have more time to pursue studies and more time to develop income-earning skills. It is no accident that the most successful ethno-racial groups have low birth rates and hence proportionately fewer people in the younger age groups. Among Canadians as a whole, 42 percent are aged 24 or younger according to the 1981 census. Among Natives, the proportion is more than 60 percent. Among Jews and Japanese, the proportion is 32 percent.

The cultural capacity of groups is ignored by proponents of affirmative action because they apparently believe that inequality is largely or entirely explained by current discrimination. The economic performance of Black North Americans of West Indian and North American origin presents some evidence that current discrimination is an insufficient explanation of economic performance. If contemporary racial discrimination were exclusively important and cultural capacity were a factor of no significance, North American-born Blacks would earn the same as or slightly more than North American Blacks born in the West Indies. Yet the incomes of West Indian immigrants are much higher. According to United States income data, which are more detailed than Canadian data, West Indian Blacks earn close to the national average. The children of West Indian Blacks improve relative to nth generation American Blacks and earn more than Anglo-Saxons. (Sowell, 1978: 44.) Like successful White groups, West Indian Blacks in the United States have relatively low fertility rates. (Sowell, 1981:16.)

Tables 17-6 and 17-7 show that Black immigrants to Canada rank ninth among 15 foreign-born groups in terms of rate of return on higher education, while Canadian-born Blacks rank only 12th. The relative rate of return on higher education is greater for foreign-born Blacks partly because of their greater propensity for higher education. The fact that 27 percent of the foreign-born have been to college, as compared to only 16 percent among the native-born, suggests that the foreign-born are more likely to possess advanced degrees.

However, different propensities for college provide only a partial explanation. Black immigrants not only rank higher than native Blacks in their respective categories, but Black immigrants actually earn more than their Canadian-born counterparts. Although immigrants normally earn less than the native-born, the reverse is true among Blacks. West Indian immigrants with college education earn $2000 more annually than their native-born counterparts. West Indians with primary-school education and those with secondary-school education also earn more. Irrespective of education, foreign-born Blacks earn one-and-one-half times more in Nova Scotia, home of a long-standing Black community. In neighbouring New Brunswick, the foreign-born earn three-and-one-half times as much as the native-born.

Advocates of "equality of results" need to be aware of differences in cultural capacity,

not in order to "blame" the less equal and therefore do nothing, but in order to be effective. In their zeal, the proponents of affirmative action may do harm to the very people for whom they wish good. For example, a federal government pilot project providing preferential admission to law school for Natives produced a high rate of failure because realistic assessments of cultural capacity were not made.[11] Natives with insufficient academic preparation were expected to excel when Whites with the same background would not be expected to do so. Quota hiring of Natives in the public service has resulted in a high rate of complaints against Native employees.[12] The quota hiring of Natives has probably done little to improve ethno-racial relations or Native self-images. Native communities require much more basic forms of assistance than quota hiring to management positions. Native communities need whatever assistance is necessary to enable them to transmit history and pride to school-age children. They also need assistance to sustain full employment. Traditional public works programs contribute more effectively to full employment and therefore widespread self-esteem than the quota hiring of senior managers.[13]

Premise 5 is that it is an administratively simple procedure to identify and reward subjugated minorities. Administrative costs and ramifications should normally be considered in the course of evaluating any proposed government policy. If true, the premise of administrative simplicity would strengthen the argument for affirmative action. If it is untrue, the argument for affirmative action would be weakened, and alternative government instruments would need to be considered seriously.

It is exceedingly difficult to identify even in principle which groups should be rewarded, than to identify the members of these beneficiary groups in practice, and to devise a scheme which benefits the right groups. U.S. affirmative action practices provide a good illustration of the moral and empirical arbitrariness of including some groups but not others. American Blacks have a moral claim to special efforts on their behalf because of the effects of slavery, because of the heightened racism of the U.S. government as employer at the beginning of this century, and because of their depressed incomes. No equivalent moral claim can be made on behalf of Hispanics although Hispanics are officially classed as disadvantaged along with Blacks. Given that Hispanics are included, it is unclear why Italians, Greeks, and other low-status Europeans are not also included. In Canada, Natives and Nova Scotia Blacks, a special case, have a defensible claim to compensation on the basis of history. However, it is not clear that East Indian immigrant professionals of high-caste origin should be treated preferentially. Nor is it evident that Japanese Canadians, already successful, should be guaranteed their quota of senior management positions.

Even if it were possible to reach a consensus about which ethno-racial groups should receive preferential treatment, it would be difficult to identify the members of these groups. It would be a geneological nightmare. In the case of intermarriage, governments would need to determine how many grandparents would qualify a candidate for preferential hiring. Governments would need to determine the kinds of evidence which candidates would be required to submit to prove that they genuinely qualified for privileged treatment. Rules would be required to decide whether a candidate qualified if only one grandparent belonged to the certified disadvantaged group but he/she had married within the group. Even in the absence of financial incentives to belong to one ethno-racial group rather than another, people are not entirely sure about what group they belong to. A survey conducted by the U.S. Census showed that a significant minority of respondents changed their racial classifications in questionnaires only months apart. The consistency rate was 94 percent for Blacks and 79 percent for Hispanics ("Spanish total").[14] The Canadian government would need to devise tests for use in classifying semi- and poly-racials and other candidates with ambiguous racial memberships.

The introduction of financial incentives would affect the ethno-racial identities of people. For example, the presence of affirmative action for Natives in the United States resulted in a large increase in self-identifying Natives in census responses. (Glazer, 1983:198.) Canada does not yet have a large number of people who have reclassified themselves as Native. But our federal government does have difficulty getting an accurate measure of the precise quota of jobs to which Natives have a rightful claim under the logic of affirmative action. Federal government documents on personnel matters assert that 4 percent of Canadians are Natives and hence that 4 percent of federal government jobs should go to Natives.[15] According to the Public Service Commission, fewer than 1.5 percent of federal jobs are actually held by Native people.[16] Federal Departments are under pressure to augment their Native complements. However, the 1981 census of Canada shows that Natives, broadly defined, constitute 2 percent, not 4 percent of the Canadian population. Moreover, the 2 percent figure from the 1981 census overestimates the availability of Natives for employment because the Native population is so much younger than the rest. In Canada, the working population is normally between 20 and 65 years old. According to the 1981 census, the Native share of the work age population is actually 1.5 percent, almost identical to their share of federal posts before preferential hiring. For reasons which were never made clear, the Natives' 1.5 percent share was somehow considered evidence of underrepresentation and discrimination by the government *qua* employer.

Premise 6 is that quota hiring benefits equally all members of a given beneficiary group. The moral impetus in favour of affirmative action comes in substantial measure from the occupational and income disadvantages of the most disadvantaged members of potential beneficiary groups. Few people would advocate quota hiring to insure that minority groups are better represented in the boardrooms of the nation, but many would support affirmative action in order to reduce unemployment and augment average incomes among low-income groups whose members are held back in their occupational progress by racial discrimination.

In practice, quota hiring is more apt to benefit the upper strata of a given ethno-racial group than the middle and, especially, than the lower strata. The favouring of the upper strata results from the fact that affirmative action is best suited to filling positions which require credentials, even if lower credentials are required from members of the beneficiary group. The upper strata of beneficiary groups are also favoured because employers opt to pay a premium to the best-qualified members of a government-designated group in order to avoid the risk and cost of terminations.[17] The lowest strata are not easily helped by affirmative action because so many of the lowest-skilled jobs are found in establishments which are too small to undertake programs of quota hiring.[18]

Data on mean incomes, social mobility, and rates of return on higher education are sometimes less useful indicators of need than unemployment rates and incomes for the less educated. According to the census and other data, the low-status members of three groups require particular attention: Native people, Indochinese, and Blacks. Native people undoubtedly have the lowest incomes and highest unemployment rates, apparently as high as 50 percent in some areas of the country. At 8.5 percent, Indochinese have the second highest rates of unemployment. The unemployment among Indochinese is striking because they inhabit the low-unemployment regions of the country. The mean income among Indochinese males with less than grade 9 is only $5000, less than half the earnings of Blacks with the same education.

On the basis of census data, low-income Blacks deserve special attention, too, albeit less than Natives and Indochinese. The unemployment rate among Blacks is 7.4 percent. The Black unemployment rate is higher among the Canadian-born than among immigrants (9.5 percent vs. 5.5 percent), and high in Nova Scotia (9.4 percent). The unemployment rate among the other ethno-racial groups is 5 percent or lower. Blacks are a special case because the plight of their low-status members is not readily apparent from overall data on mean incomes, mobility, and rates of return on higher education, especially among immigrants.

Blacks are bipolarized in class status; they are overrepresented both in high-income, high-status and in low-income, low-status jobs. Blacks experience satisfactory rates of return for higher education but low rates of return for high school or trade certificates. Low rates of return for low-status Blacks are especially marked in Halifax and Montreal. Affirmative action (i.e., quota hiring) for

Blacks would provide unneeded advantages for upper-status Blacks, would provide no direct benefits to low-income and unemployed Blacks, and would accentuate existing inequalities within the Black community.

CONCLUSION

Affirmative action is motivated by the commendable goal of a universalist society free of ethno-racial discrimination. However, affirmative action, more particularly quota hiring, can do harm. The logic of affirmative action depends on a series of premises about society and the economy which have not been satisfactorily defended with evidence and which the essay argues are largely untrue.

Racists and the White advocates of affirmative action are motivated by completely different considerations, but they do have one characteristic in common. Both tend to treat the members of pariah or victimized groups as if they were alike. Both tend to identify pariah groups by their physiognomy rather than by their experience. The case for affirmative action for non-Whites is sometimes predicated on the assumptions that non-White groups are equally victimized or disadvantaged, that they are disadvantaged in the same ways, and/or that the groups are internally homogeneous and classless.

The income data presented in this essay show a considerable heterogeneity among Whites and non-Whites, some success among non-Whites, and some very specific situations calling for intervention. Two visible minorities, Japanese and Koreans, and one identifiable minority, Jews, earn high incomes largely as a result of high propensities for college education (1981 census).

According to 1971 census data, Asians experience high incomes and high upward mobility. According to 1981 census data, four out of five upwardly mobile ethno-racial groups are Asian; five out of six downwardly mobile groups are European.

The income problem most widely shared by non-Whites is a low rate of return for investments in higher education among those born abroad. European-born college graduates earn more than non-Whites born abroad. The low rates of return for non-White college immigrants may be explained by academic training unsuited to the Canadian economy or by language or cultural difficulties. These non-racial explanations for the income problems of foreign-born non-Whites gain some plausibility from two facts: Chinese, Blacks, and Indo-Pakistanis earn higher incomes than other non-White, foreign-born, university graduates, and Canadian-born non-Whites do appreciably better than their co-communalists born abroad.

Three groups merit special economic attention: Native people, Indochinese, and Blacks, in descending order of need. Native people and Indochinese experience the lowest incomes and the highest rates of unemployment. Blacks earn more than Greeks and virtually the same as Portuguese. Black mean incomes are satisfactory because of the concentration of Blacks in some high-status professions and because of the esprit of middle-class West Indian immigrants. However, low-status Blacks experience serious economic problems as evidenced in high unemployment rates, especially in Nova Scotia and among the Canadian-born.

As a result of the economic, educational, and cultural heterogeneity among and within the ethno-racial groups, affirmative action will not assist the groups which need assistance the most and will not assist the deserving members within a given group. Affirmative action increases the rates of return for the best educated without delivering benefits to the least educated. Affirmative action does not respond directly to the problem of racist attitudes.

Affirmative action for visible minorities is attractive in part because it serves the needs of politicians and interest group leaders. Political leaders favour programs such as affirmative action which offer both fiscal and output illusions. Unlike the case of public

works or training programs, the costs of quota hiring are hidden from view, buried in payroll budgets and unmeasured inefficiencies. Public works and training programs would take years to achieve ethnic catch-up. Helping just one specific group such as the East Indian farm workers of B.C. would require wide-ranging changes in labour law, unemployment insurance, the housing code, and pesticide regulations. Affirmative action offers the illusion of terminating inequality by fiat.

NOTES

*Tom Workman was research assistant on this project thanks to a GR-6 from the Graduate Office. A thank you to Dhiru Patel and Ben Teitelbaum, Multiculturalism Directorate, for making available 1981 census tables on ethnic incomes. Also, special thanks for their advice to Julia Zackon, André Blais for *CPP*, and the assessors. None of these people are responsible for the interpretation offered in this essay.

1. For an overview of affirmative action in a Canadian context, see Weinfeld (1981). For recent comparative overviews, see Weiner (1983) and Jain and Sloane (1981). For a discussion of women, see Winn (1985).

2. An unpublished secondary analysis of U.S. census data reportedly concludes that Americans of Indian origin are the highest earning ethnic group. Analysis by Manoranjan Dutta, reported in *India Calling* (May 4, 1984: 12). For other U.S. ethnic income data, see Table 2 in Thomas Sowell, "Weber and Bakke, and the Presuppositions of 'Affirmative Action' " in Block and Walker (1982).

3. For other evidence of ethnic income mobility, see Darroch (1979); Richmond and Kalbach (1980); Richmond and Verma (1978); and Reitz et al. (1982). On the basis of empirical analysis, Richmond and Verma reach the following conclusion: "Most remarkable are the high median incomes of the Canadian born with one or two foreign-born parents. . . . Particularly notable are the high rankings of the Jewish, southern European, and Asian groups among the Canadian born with two foreign-born parents. All three groups were among those with comparatively low "entrance status" and historically speaking, have experienced considerable prejudice and discrimination in Canada" (p.30).

4. Public Service Commission (1983:10). See also Winn (1985).

5. Calculated from Table 11.12 in Richmond and Kalbach (1980).

6. Sowell (1982:71); (1975:18-20); (1981:23). For evidence that U.S. Blacks and Whites with the same reading habits earned the same income as early as 1969, see Freeman (1976, ch.4). See also Freeman (1973); Hall and Kasten (1973); and Glazer (1983, ch.10).

7. Sowell (1981:22), adapted from Eric Hanushek, "Ethnic Income Variations," in Sowell (1978).

8. Peter S. Li, "Income Achievement and Adaptive Capacity: An Empirical Comparison of Chinese and Japanese in Canada," Canadian Sociology and Anthropology Association paper, 1979; reproduced in Ujimoto and

Hirabayashi (1983). Several studies of White groups have shown that occupational inequality among these groups is largely explained by educational differences. See Raynauld et al. (1969); Tepperman (1975); and Darroch (1979).

9. For contemporary evidence of racism, see the many situation reports commissioned by the Multiculturalism Directorate and especially Henry and Ginzberg (1985).

10. For evidence that a cultural predisposition toward education is a better predictor of educational attainment than aptitude or money, see Jencks et al. (1972:141).

11. Lance W. Roberts. "Understanding Affirmative Action," in Block and Walker (1982:147-82, passim).

12. The leading affirmative action department, the Canada Employment and Immigration Commission, observes that "indigenous employees . . . are experiencing proportionately more of 'less than satisfactory' performance ratings." The difficulties of Native employees may have been related to their lesser educa-

tional and employment backgrounds. According to CEIC, "Indigenous employees' entry status tends mainly to be from unemployment and no employees indicated more than five years of prior experience before entering the Public Service." Source: June, 1982 submission to senior management, CEIC, pp.74-75.

13. For empirical evidence of the impact of employment on self-esteem and other states of mind and body, see Joint Economic Committee, U.S. Congress (1976) and Canadian Mental Health Association (1983).

14. Johnson (1974), referred to in Nathan Glazer (1983:198).

15. See PSC periodical, *Dialogue* (March 1984), p.10.

16. Ibid.

17. For a discussion of this point and some empirical evidence, see Sowell (1982:54-56).

18. See note 10 for references on the high rates of return for educated minority group members.

REFERENCES

Abella, Judge Rosalie Silberman
    1984   *Report of the Commission on Equality in Employment.* Ottawa: Supply and Services.

Block, W. E., and M. A. Walker
    1982   *Discrimination, Affirmative Action and Equal Opportunity.* Vancouver: Fraser Institute.

Canadian Mental Health Association
    1983   *Unemployment.* Toronto: CMHA.

Chacko, Thomas I.
    1982   "Women and equal employment opportunity: Some unintended effects," *Journal of Applied Psychology,* pp. 119-23.

Darroch, A. Gordon
    1979   "Another look at ethnicity, stratification and social mobility in Canada," *Canadian Journal of Sociology,* pp. 1-25.

Franks, C. E. S.
    1984   "The public service in the north," *Canadian Public Administration,* pp. 229 ff.

Freeman, Richard B.
    1976   *Black Elite.* Toronto: McGraw-Hill.

    1973   "Changes in the labor market for black Americans, 1948-1972," *Brookings Papers on Economic Activity,* pp. 67-120.

Garcia, Luis T., et al.
    1981   "The effect of affirmative action on attributions about minority group members," *Journal of Personality,* pp. 427-37.

Glazer, Nathan
    1983   *Ethnic Dilemmas, 1964-82.* Cambridge: Harvard University Press.

Hall, Robert E., and Richard A. Kasten
    1973   "The relative occupational success of blacks and whites," *Brookings Papers on Economic Activity,* pp. 781-797.

Henry, Frances, and Effie Ginzberg
    1985   *Who Gets the Work: A Test of Racial Discrimination in Employment.* Toronto: Urban Alliance on Race Relations and the Social Planning Council of Metropolitan Toronto.

Jain, Harish C., and Peter J. Stone
    1981   *Equal Employment Issues: Race and Sex Discrimination in the United States, Canada and Britain.* New York: Praeger.

Jencks, Christopher, et al.
    1972   *Inequality: A Reassessment of Family and Schooling in America.* New York: Basic Books.

Johnson, Charles E., Jr.
    1974   "Consistency of Reporting of Ethnic Origin in the Current Population Survey." U.S. Bureau of the Census Technical Paper, 31 (February).

Li, Peter S.
    1979   "Income achievement and adaptive capacity: An empirical comparison of Chinese and Japanese in Canada." Canadian Sociology and Anthropology Association paper.

Public Service Commission of Canada. Personnel Psychology Centre
    1983   "Adverse impact on employment opportunities" (December).

Raynauld, A., et al.
    1969   "La répartition des revenus selon les groupes ethniques au Canada," quoted in *Book III,* Royal Commission on Bilingualism and Biculturalism. Ottawa: Queen's Printer.

Reitz, Jeffrey G., et al.
    1982   *Ethnic Inequality and Segregation in Jobs.* Toronto: Centre for Urban and Community Studies, University of Toronto.

Richmond, Anthony H., and Warren E. Kalbach
    1980   *Factors in the Adjustment of Immigrants and their Descendants.* Ottawa: Supply and Services.

Richmond, Anthony A., and Ravi P. Verma
    1978   "Income inequality in Canada: Ethnic and generational aspects." *Canadian Studies in Population.*

Sowell, Thomas
    1975   *Affirmative Action Reconsidered.* Washington: American Enterprise Institute.

    1978   *Essays and Data on American Ethnic Groups.* Urban Institute.

    1981   *Markets and Minorities.* New York: Basic Books.

    1982   "Webber and Bakke, and the Presuppositions of 'Affirmative Action'," in Block and Walker (1982).

Tepperman, L.
    1975   *Social Mobility in Canada.* Toronto: McGraw-Hill.

Ujimoto, V., and G. Hiranayashi, eds.
    1983   *Visible Minorities and Multiculturalism.* Toronto: Butterworths.

U.S. Congress. Joint Economic Committee
    1976   *Estimating the Social Costs of National Economic Policy,* Paper 5, Volume 1. Washington: U.S. Government Printing Office.

Weiner, Myron
    1983   "The political consequences of preferential policies: A comparative perspective," *Comparative Politics,* pp. 35-52.

Weinfeld, Morton
    1981   "The development of affirmative action in Canada," *Canadian Ethnic Studies,* pp. 23-39.

Winn, Conrad
    1985   "Affirmative action and women: More than a case of single justice," *Canadian Public Administration* (Spring).

18. Racial Discrimination in Employment

Frances Henry and Effie Ginzberg

Until the publication of our report *Who Gets the Work?* efforts to demonstrate that there is racial discrimination in the Canadian employment arena have been limited to census data analysis, personal reports of victims of discrimination, and attitude studies. Each of these three types of research is limited in its capacity to prove that discrimination based on race is actually the cause of discrepancies in income and access to employment. Critics, sceptics, and racists have easily been able to doubt the presence of racial discrimination in view of weaknesses inherent in these indirect measures of discrimination. *Who Gets the Work?* sought to test directly for the presence or absence of discrimination in the Toronto labour market through the process

of field testing—a quasi-experimental research technique.

For the first time in Canada, a study tested racial discrimination in employment by actually sending individuals, White and Black, to apply for advertised positions in order to find out if employers discriminate by preferring White to non-White employees. We believe we were successful in proving definitively that racial discrimination in Canada affects the employment opportunities of non-White Canadians. Whites have greater access to jobs than do equally qualified non-Whites.

Our study was guided by two questions. One, is there a difference in the number of job offers that White and Black applicants of similar experience and qualifications receive when they apply to the same jobs? And two, are there differences in the ways in which White and Black job applicants are treated when they apply for work? Both questions were tested by two procedures: *in-person testing* and *telephone testing*.

An original article based on research first reported in the authors' *Who Gets the Work?* (Toronto: Urban Alliance on Race Relations and the Social Planning Council of Toronto, 1985).

DEFINING DISCRIMINATION

Discrimination can take place at any point in the employment process. It may exist in such areas as recruitment, screening, selection, promotion, and termination. At the level of employee selection, for example, discrimination against non-Whites can take place when job applicants are called to the initial interview. To the extent that the employer's staff or the other employees themselves practise discrimination, either as a result of racial attitudes of the interviewer or because of instructions to screen out non-Whites as a matter of company policy, non-Whites will not get beyond the initial screening of job applicants. Similarly, in terms of promotion policies, non-Whites may be hired at lower levels, but their promotion to the upper ranks is effectively stopped by discriminatory barriers to mobility. For example, the employer may believe that the other employees will not accept a non-White as their supervisor.

Discrimination in employment can be intentional as well as inadvertent. Employers may not realize that their practices and policies have the effect of excluding non-Whites. The use of standard tests of personality or intelligence to select employees places certain minority groups at a disadvantage since they come from cultures other than the one for which the tests were designed. Recruiting through in-house word-of-mouth techniques often excludes minority applicants since they do not hear about available positions. Requiring Canadian experience and education can effectively eliminate non-Whites, many of whom are immigrants, from job opportunities even though such experience is not necessary to successful job performance.

Thus, there are numerous types of discrimination and numerous ways in which discrimination can be carried out. Our study concentrated essentially on the entry point and/or the selection procedure. In this study, the dynamics of discrimination are studied as discriminatory practices occur, that is, when a job seeker either makes an inquiry on the phone or comes in person to be interviewed. It is at this point that the applicant can run into a prejudiced employer or "gatekeeper" who either presumes that non-Whites are not desired or merely acts according to company policy. The telephone inquiry is particularly crucial at this stage since it is often the first approach made by the job applicant. An individual can be screened out, that is, told quickly and efficiently either that the job has already been filled or that the applicant's qualifications are not suitable. In all likelihood, the applicant will not know that he or she has been the victim of discrimination.

For the purposes of this study, we defined discrimination in employment as those practices or attitudes, wilful or unintentional, that have the effect of limiting an individual's or a group's right to economic opportunities on the basis of irrelevant traits such as skin colour rather than an evaluation of true abilities or potential.

IN-PERSON TESTING

In the in-person testing, two job applicants, matched with respect to age, sex, education, experience, physical appearance (dress), and personality, were sent to apply for the same advertised job. The only major difference between our applicants was their race—*one was White and the other, Black*. We created four such teams: one junior male, one junior female, one senior male, and one senior female. The younger teams applied for semiskilled and unskilled jobs such as gas station attendant, bus boy, waitress, and clerk and sales help in youth-oriented stores. The senior teams applied for positions in retail management, sales positions in prestigious stores, and waiting and hosting positions in expensive restaurants. The senior team members were, in fact, professional actors. Applying for middle-class type jobs meant that they would be required not only to present a sophisticated image but also to participate in a fairly demanding job interview. Professional actors, we believed, would be more convincing in playing the many roles required for this project. The résumés of the team members were carefully constructed to be as alike as possible. In order to further control possible biases, the staff of testers was changed several times so that no individual personality could account for the results.

The younger teams were composed of high-school and university students who would normally be applying for the same types of jobs that they applied for in the testing situation. Since we were not testing for sex discrimination and did not want this type of discrimination to account for any of our results, the male teams were sent to traditionally male jobs and the women went to jobs traditionally associated with women's work. In some types of jobs, for example waiter/waitress, both men and women were acceptable. Men and women were sent to such jobs but never to the same job. Each tester had a different résumé for the various types of positions that he or she was applying for, so each member of the senior female team, for example, carried several résumés, one for a secretary, another for a retail sales assistant, a third for a dental technician, etc. Each résumé contained the names of references supplied by business people and

friends who had agreed to support our research. Our applicants could thus be checked out by a potential employer who could obtain a reference for the applicant. In actuality, only two employers ever called for references.

RESEARCH PROCEDURE

Each evening, a listing of jobs would be selected for the next day from among the classified advertisements. Some types of jobs were excluded such as those involving driving, where licences could be checked. Jobs which required highly technical skills were also excluded.

The testers were instructed either to go to a certain address or to phone for an appointment. They used standard Canadian accents when phoning since we did not want them to be screened out over the phone. The testers would arrive within approximately one half-hour of each other so that there was little chance that a job had been legitimately filled. In most cases the Black applicant went first. After their interviews the testers completed a summary data sheet especially designed for this project in which they wrote down the details of their treatment and the kinds of information they had been given. Their résumés listed telephone numbers which were in actuality lines connected to the research office. Call-backs for second interviews or with offers of employment were received and recorded by the researchers. On-the-spot offers to the field testers were accepted by them. In the case of call-backs and on-the-spot offers, employers were phoned back, usually within an hour, and informed that another position had been accepted, in order to make sure that the employer could fill the vacancy as soon as possible.

RESEARCH RESULTS: THE IN-PERSON TEST

In three-and-one-half months of field testing, the testers were able to apply for 201 jobs for a total of 402 individual applications.

For our purposes, racial discrimination in employment was tested in two ways. First, was an offer of employment made to one of the applicants, both applicants, or neither applicant? Second, during the interview, were there any differences in the treatment of the two applicants? The following tables present the numerical results.

Blacks received fewer job offers than Whites. Of a total of 37 valid job offers, 27 went to Whites, 9 to Blacks, and in one case both were offered the job. There were an additional 10 cases where both were offered jobs, but these were for commission sales which involved no cost to the employer. Our overall results therefore show that *offers to Whites outweigh offers to Blacks by a ratio of 3 to 1.*

We had thought that the nature of the job might influence whether Blacks or Whites would be hired. Only Whites received offers for managerial positions or jobs as waiters and waitresses or hosts and hostesses in the restaurant trade. A Black was offered a job in the kitchen when he had applied for a waiter's job!

As noted above, the second measure of discrimination was whether differential treatment had occurred during the interview. Table 18-2 presents the results.

Blacks and Whites were treated differently 36 times and in all cases but one the White applicant was preferred to the Black. The ways in which differential treatment took place provide a great deal of insight into the nature of discrimination and its subtleties.

TABLE 18-1 Offer of a job versus no offer.

	Number	%
Both offered job	10	5.0
White offered job; Black not	27	13.4
Black offered job; White not	9	4.5
No offer to either	155	77.1
Totals	201	100

TABLE 18-2 Treatment of applicants.

	Number of Cases
Treated the same	165
Treated differently	36

Differences in treatment were sometimes very blatant, as the following examples show.

1. Mary, the young Black tester, applied for a sales position in a retail clothing store and was told that the job had already been taken. Sylvia, our White tester, arrived a half-hour later and was given an application form to fill in and told that she would be contacted if they were interested in her.

2. In a coffee shop Mary was told that the job of cashier was taken. Sylvia walked in five minutes later and was offered the job on the spot.

This pattern occurred five times. Another

form of differential treatment was as follows: the Black was treated rudely or with hostility, whereas the White was treated politely. This occurred 15 times.

3. Paul, our White tester, applied for a job as a waiter. He was given an application form to fill out and an interview. He was told that he might be contacted in a week or so. Larry, the Black tester, was also given an application form and an interview. But as the Manager looked over Larry's résumé, he asked Larry if he "wouldn't rather work in the kitchen."

4. Applying for a gas station job, the White tester was told that there were no jobs at present but that he could leave a résumé. The Black tester was told that there were no jobs, but when he asked if he could leave a résumé, he was sworn at: "Shit, I said no didn't I?"

Another form of differential treatment occurred when the wage offers to Blacks and Whites were different. There were two occasions where the Black tester was offered less money than the White tester for the same job. On a few occasions, derogatory comments were made about Blacks in the presence of our White testers. The Blacks being referred to were our own testers!

These results indicate that Black job seekers face not only discrimination in the sense of receiving fewer job offers than Whites but also a considerable amount of negative and abusive treatment while job hunting. The psychological effects of such experiences became evident in the feelings expressed by the research staff. The Black staff felt rejected and some doubted their own ability: "I was beginning to wonder what was wrong with me and why Jean [the White tester] was so much better than me."

In sum, the findings of the in-person test reveal that in 48 job contacts, or 23.8 percent of the cases, some form of discrimination against Blacks took place. These findings indicate that Blacks and Whites do not have the same access to employment. *Racial discrimination in employment, either in the form of clearly favouring a White over a Black, even though their résumés were equivalent, or in the form of treating a White applicant better than a Black, took place in almost one-quarter of all job contacts tested in this study.* When we examine the results of telephone testing, we will see that this pattern of discrimination occurs again and, if anything, more clearly and strongly.

RESEARCH RESULTS: THE TELEPHONE TEST

We have all had the experience of calling for a job and being told that the job has been filled. We experienced a twinge of disappointment but we rarely felt the need to ask ourselves seriously if we had been told the truth. Members of minority groups have good reason to question whether they have indeed been told the truth. Our study tested this by having callers phone numbers listed in the classified employment section of the newspaper to present themselves as job applicants.

In total, 237 job numbers were phoned. Each job was called four times, once by someone with no discernible accent (apparently a White-majority Canadian), once by someone who had a Slavic or Italian accent, once by a Jamaican-accented caller and finally by a person with a Pakistani accent. Many different jobs were called ranging from unskilled labour, secretarial, and service, to skilled trade, to managerial. To exclude sex discrimination, callers did not cross traditional sex-role categories. Men were of the same age, education, number of years of job experience, and so on for each type of job. Callers were "older" for jobs requiring more experience and maturity. A profile was provided for each of the callers for each type of job so that they had a secretarial profile, a managerial one, one for waitressing and so on. Jobs to be called were selected from among those that had not appeared in the newspaper the previous day; they were all new jobs. Callers within each sex were given identical lists of jobs to call on the next day and were instructed to begin their calls from the top of the list and proceed in order down the list. All callers were to begin the calling at the same time so that the time span between callers would be minimized. All callers were instructed to use standard English, full sentences, and correct grammar so that the lack of language would not be a discriminating factor against them.

In the telephone testing, discrimination was said to occur when one caller was told that the job had been filled while another caller was told that the job was still available. Discrimination was also said to take place when one caller-applicant with a certain set of qualifications was screened out and told that he or she did not qualify although other callers with the same qualifications were told that they did qualify and were invited to apply. Another form of discrimination was identified as occurring when callers were treated differently from one another in that some and not others were screened to see if they had the experience the employer sought. It has been argued that screening some applicants and not others is not necessarily discriminatory. However, if there is not systematic discrimination present, then we would expect all racial or immigrant groups to be subject to the same proportion of screening.

Results of this procedure were that in 52 percent of all jobs called there was some form of discrimination present. Either one of our testers was told that the job was filled when another tester was told that the job was open, or one of our testers was treated differ-

ently in that he or she was screened while another was not.

There were nine instances where our accented callers were told that they did not qualify for the job even though they presented the same experience and qualifications as the White-majority callers. Needless to say, the White callers were told by these same nine employers that they qualified and were invited to apply. In addition, the employers did not perceive the need to screen all of the four minority-accented callers to the same degree. Employers who treated callers differently, that is, the 123 employers who discriminated in some way, never screened non-accented callers. Italian- or Slavic-accented callers were screened 5 percent of the time and the two non-White minority callers received three times as much screening as the Whites, on between 15 percent and 20 percent of all their calls.

Minority-accented callers did not receive the same information about the status of the job as did Whites. Forty-eight percent of the jobs were closed to Blacks and 62 percent were closed to Pakistanis in that the employers told them that the job was filled when the non-accented caller was told that the job was available. Statistical analysis revealed that there were significant differences in the treatment and the type of information that Whites and non-Whites received about work. The Toronto employers discriminated against immigrants in general but to a significantly greater degree against non-White immigrants.

The results of our telephone testing demonstrate that to secure 10 potential job interviews a White Canadian has to make about 11 or 12 calls. White immigrants have to make about 13 calls. Racial minorities must work harder and longer since they must make 18 calls to get 10 potential job interviews. Clearly there are differences in what Whites and non-Whites are being told over the phone about the availability of work in Toronto. And, as noted in the in-person testing, discrimination does not end when a job interview has been obtained.

A RATIO OF DISCRIMINATION

An Index of Discrimination was developed by combining the results of the in-person test and the telephone testing to demonstrate the degree of discrimination experienced by equally qualified persons prior to actual employment. On the phone, Blacks were told that the job was closed to them 20 percent of the time whereas the job was closed to Whites only 5.5 percent of the time. In the in-person test, Blacks experienced discrimination in some form in 18.3 percent of their job contacts. If these figures are translated into the actual chances of having success in the job search, the figures become even more revealing. Blacks have a 64 percent chance of getting through a telephone screening, which means that they can secure 13 interviews out of 20 calls. But their chances of actually getting a job *after* an interview are only about 1 in 20. White applicants, on the other hand, are able to pass through screening very successfully, 87 percent of the time. They can achieve an interview in 17 out of 20 calls. Out of these 17 interviews they manage to receive three offers of employment. *The overall Index of Discrimination is therefore 3 to 1.* Whites have three job prospects to every one that Blacks have.

CONCLUSION

The results of this study clearly indicate that there is very substantial racial discrimination affecting the ability of members of racial minorities to find employment even when they are well qualified and eager to find work. This study examined discrimination only at the very early stages, or entry level, of the employment process. Once an applicant is employed, discrimination can still affect opportunities for advancement, job retention, and level of earnings, to say nothing of the quality of work and the relationships with co-workers.

The findings also support the results of other types of studies done in Canada. We know that indirect measures of discrimination, such as those which reveal income disparities between Whites and non-Whites, all come to similar conclusions: non-Whites in this country are discriminated against. Our studies suggest that discrimination is more widespread than has been thought. Employment discrimination appears not to be the result of a few bigoted employers; there is a system-wide bias against hiring non-Whites. The systemic nature of the discrimination implies that attempting to change the behaviour or the attitudes of individual discriminators will not address the problem. What is required is redress at the system level in order to remove the barriers to the employment of non-Whites so that all Canadians, regardless of colour, can achieve to their full potential.

A: Ethnicity and Race

19. Trends in Language Mobility Between French and English

Robert Bourbeau

STUDYING LINGUISTIC MOBILITY

Now that the initial data of the 1981 census are available, our purpose here is to update the 1971 results and try to discern some recent trends in linguistic mobility, first in Quebec and subsequently in the rest of Canada. This examination becomes all the more interesting by reason of the fact that during the 1960s there was a great deal of debate about the future of the two principal language groups in Canada. That decade also witnessed the passage of various language laws, particularly in Quebec. These factors should be borne in mind in any interpretation of the changes revealed by the 1981 census data.

Revised from Robert Bourbeau, "Canada's Language Transfer Phenomenon," *Language and Society*, 11 (autumn 1982), pp. 14-22. Reprinted with permission.

The Canadian census is the principal source of information on the linguistic characteristics of individuals. These characteristics are revealed by responses to three types of questions: the first refers to present practice (language spoken in the home); the second concerns past practice, in other words the first language learned and still understood (mother tongue); and the third deals not with practice but rather with knowledge of the two official languages in Canada, English and French.

We shall deal here with the first two concepts, mother tongue and language spoken in the home. By comparing the two, we shall be able to assess the language transfer phenomenon (abandonment of the mother tongue in favour of another language). The question dealing with the language spoken in the home was asked for the first time during the 1971 census (one out of every three households), and again during the 1981 census (one out of every five households).

Using the 1971 and 1981 census data, we shall first determine the comparative degree of language transfers for each of the three major language groups: Francophones, Anglophones, and Allophones.[1]

We shall then try to establish an index for the overall linguistic mobility rate, which is the proportion of people with a given mother tongue who state that they use a language other than their mother tongue in the home. This rate is affected by two variables: the intensity of the transfer risk, and the period of exposure to such a risk.

In order to isolate the intensity of this phenomenon the age and birthplace of individuals have to be known. Since we do not currently have a detailed breakdown of the 1981 data, we shall present an overall index that reflects the behaviour of several generations in terms of linguistic mobility. Despite its limitations, this index reveals the major trends of linguistic mobility. We shall use it to provide an overview of such movements in a given time-span, as well as regional variations in linguistic mobility in Canada.

QUEBEC: CHANGES IN LINGUISTIC COMPOSITION SINCE 1971

Since 1971 the linguistic composition of Quebec has changed quite significantly. The 1976 census had already provided some data on the new trends of this composition, and these have been confirmed by the 1981 census (Table 19-1).

In Quebec, the proportion of persons whose mother tongue is French has increased since 1971 and was 82.4 percent in 1981. This is about the same proportion as in 1951. Since 1971 the English mother tongue group has continued to decline in

TABLE 19-1 Population distribution (in %) by mother tongue and language spoken in the home.

Quebec 1971-81

Mother tongue

Year	English	French	Other	Total
1971	13.1	80.7	6.2	100.0
1976*	12.8	81.1	6.1	100.0
1981	11.0	82.4	6.6	100.0

Language spoken in the home

Year	English	French	Other	Total
1971	14.7	80.8	4.5	100.0
1981	12.7	82.5	4.8	100.0

*The 1976 data have been adjusted to make them comparable with those of 1981 (based on Linda Demers and John Kralt, upcoming publication).
Source: Statistics Canada, *Census of Canada*, 1971, 1976, 1981.

size: in 1981 it represented 11 percent of the total population of Quebec, a drop of 2.1 percent from 1971. This reduction in relative terms was accompanied by a reduction in absolute numbers: from 789 200 to 706 100. There are reasons to believe that the slight increase in the number of Anglophones reported in the 1976 census is invalid and linked to changes in the mother tongue reported during that census mainly by the third language group. The relative size of this group grew from 6.2 percent to 6.6 percent between 1971 and 1981.

Analysis of the population composition by language spoken in the home reveals roughly the same trends: an increase in the proportion of Francophones (from 80.8 percent to 82.5 percent), a decline in the proportion of Anglophones (from 14.7 percent to 12.7 percent), and a slight increase in the proportion of Allophones (from 4.5 percent to 4.8 percent). Since the non-Francophones are concentrated largely in the Montreal area, it is possible to examine the recent evolution of the linguistic composition in this area (Table 19-2). Variations in the linguistic composition between 1971 and 1981 are even more pronounced in this area, even if the same trends are evident. The relative size of the Anglophone population dropped by 3.3 percent, while the proportion of Allophones increased by 1.1 percent. The population composition by language spoken in the home evolved in a similar manner.

Are these variations in the linguistic composition of Quebec and the Montreal area significant? Compared with the variation found in previous censuses, the changes

TABLE 19-2 Population distribution (in %) by mother tongue and language spoken in the home.

Montreal census metropolitan area 1971-81

Mother tongue

Year	English	French	Other	Total
1971	21.7	66.3	12.0	100.0
1976*	22.2	67.0	10.8	100.0
1981	18.4	68.5	13.1	100.0

Language spoken in the home

Year	English	French	Other	Total
1971	24.9	66.3	8.8	100.0
1981	22.0	68.6	9.4	100.0

*Non-adjusted data, not comparable with those of 1981.
Source: Statistics Canada, *Census of Canada,* 1971, 1976, 1981.

during the 1970s are certainly much more striking.

One should not forget, however, that any change in this composition is a reciprocal phenomenon and that at least one of the language groups experiences some change as a result. Between 1951 and 1971 the French group experienced a reduction in its relative size and this was a cause for considerable anxiety; today, however, that anxiety is focussed on the decline in the Anglophone population.

Revival of Language Groups

What is the reason for these recent changes? Changes in the linguistic composition of a region result from different mortality rates, birth rates, linguistic mobility, and migration of each of the three major language groups.

With respect to mortality and birth rates, everyone agrees that, notwithstanding the continued gap that exists between the language groups (high mortality rate of Francophones and high birth rate of Allophones), these phenomena no longer play a determining role in changes in linguistic composition, particularly since 1971.

Nevertheless, different rates of migration and linguistic mobility are exerting a growing influence. For the 15-year period subsequent to 1966, immigration to Quebec outweighed emigration from the province.

This situation was less disadvantageous to Francophones than to Anglophones, who are greatly overrepresented not only among new arrivals (40 percent), but even more so among those leaving the province (65 percent) (particularly interprovincial migration). Migration is thus very largely responsible for the reduced number of Anglophones in Quebec, especially since 1971, in terms of mother tongue composition and the language spoken in the home. Linguistic mobility also had a major impact on the linguistic composition of Quebec, at least until 1971; the attraction of English was such that the Allophones rejected French. Francophones were also in a slightly negative situation vis-à-vis their linguistic exchanges with Anglophones. This, at least, was the picture of linguistic mobility revealed by the 1971 census, the principal results of which now follow.

Language Transfers

Table 19-3 shows a comparison of language transfers based on 1971 census data.

These data indicated that the language transfers were largely advantageous to Anglophones; more than 96 percent of the net transfers went to this group. Francophones were also in a slightly positive position,

mainly because of their net gains from the Allophone group; however, the French group was in a net loss position in its exchanges with the English group (49 100 − 73 500 = − 24 400). The vigorous linguistic mobility of Allophones was largely beneficial to the Anglophone group; 71 percent of all transfers made by Allophones were toward English.

In the Montreal area, the situation was much the same except that it was even more favourable to Anglophones, who benefited from 98 percent of the net transfers. Moreover, approximately three quarters of all transfers from the Allophone group went to the English group.

These phenomena spawned a great deal of interest and anxiety in Quebec. With a view to slowing down the assimilative trend of English, the authorities instituted a number of political measures. This is understandable to the extent that linguistic mobility is the demolinguistic phenomenon

TABLE 19-3 Comparative language transfers.

Quebec 1971

| | Mother tongue | | | |
Transfers	English	French	Other	Total (gains)
Toward English	—	73 500	84 400	157 900
Toward French	49 100	—	34 600	83 700
Toward other languages	9 800	6 400	*	16 200
Total (losses)	58 900	79 900	119 000	257 800
Net transfers (gains–losses)	+99 000	+ 3 800	− 102 800	

*This comparison does not show the transfers that took place between groups whose mother tongue was neither English nor French.

Source: John Kralt, *Languages in Canada, Profile Studies, Census of Canada,* 1971, Cat. 99-707, 1976.

which, in our society, is most subject to direct political intervention.

After much criticism was expressed about the Act to Promote the French Language in Quebec (Bill 63), which sought to provide everyone with free choice in language of education, the Government adopted the Official Language Act (Bill 22), which limited access to English schools to those who had "a sufficient knowledge" of English. Bill 22 was in turn replaced in 1977 by the Charter of the French Language (Bill 101) which, in the chapter dealing with the language of education, reserved access to English schools solely for children of whom at least one parent had received his or her primary education in English in Quebec; this legislation also contained a number of transitional measures and exceptions. Given the widespread debate surrounding the adoption and implementation of these legislative measures, everyone eagerly awaited the 1981 census data on linguistic mobility. Did

the context of the 1970s modify the trends observed in 1971? Table 19-4 shows comparative language transfers based on 1981 census data.

This table shows that in 1981 language transfers once again worked largely to the advantage of Anglophones, who increased their net gain by more than 15 000 during the preceding 10-year period; by contrast, the French group, which is much larger, increased its net gain by only 4600 during the same period. It would therefore appear that English maintained its strong attraction, but that the situation of French remained stable. In terms of language transfers with the English group, the Francophone situation is the same as in 1971 $(82\ 135 - 106\ 365 = -24\ 230)$: thus, there has been no increase in the net loss since 1971. Language transfers among Allophones still weighed heavily in favour of the Anglophone group, but a slight decline in the proportion of transfers toward English

TABLE 19-4   Comparative language transfers.

Quebec 1981

| | Mother tongue | | | |
Transfers	English	French	Other	Total (gains)
Toward English	—	106 365	101 625	207 980
Toward French	82 135	—	46 565	128 700
Toward other languages	11 625	13 940	*	25 565
Total (losses)	93 760	120 305	148 190	362 255
Net transfers (gains–losses)	+ 114 230	+ 8 395	− 122 625	

*See note, Table 19-3.
Source: Statistics Canada, *Census of Canada*, 1981.

was recorded (69 percent in 1981 instead of 71 percent in 1971).

In the Montreal area, similar trends were revealed. Exchanges between the French and English groups were slightly less disadvantageous to the French group in 1981 than in 1971; Francophone net losses went from −20 200 to −18 505. On the other hand, among Allophones who made a language transfer, a slightly lower percentage adopted English (74 percent in 1971 and 72 percent in 1981).

In sum, these changes were minor when compared with what some people had expected. Are they in fact surprising? Not really. It is quite normal that, despite language legislation favouring French, particularly Bill 101 which has been on the statute books since 1977, very little change was recorded in 1981.

Charter of the French Language

It should be understood that the Charter's provisions relating to language of education cannot be very effective in the short term because they do not directly affect the phenomenon of language transfer. Instead, they affect one of the related mechanisms, the choice of children's language of education. Moreover, given the transitional measures provided for in Bill 101, this legislation had very little direct influence in the short term. It is only when children have passed through the entire education system that the law will show its full effect. In the coming years, we shall probably see a greater decline in the proportion of students in English schools. Bill 101 will thus have slowed the assimilative trend of these schools. The effect of this aspect of Bill 101 on the language spoken in the home is still very difficult to determine. Anglophones and Allophones may have a better knowledge of French, but they will continue to speak English in the home. In order for French to attract newly arrived non-Francophones, other factors will have to encourage the use of the language, particularly in the workplace.

So far, it could be said that the Charter has had more effect on migration than on linguistic mobility; during the period 1976-81, more people with English as their mother tongue left Quebec for other provinces (131 500) than during the period 1971-76 (101 500); moreover, less people arrived from other Canadian provinces (25 200 as opposed to 41 300 in 1971-76). However, the same trends have been noted among both Francophones and Allophones and they may be as much related to economic conditions as to the language legislation. It is possible that the Charter may have had a temporary effect upon migration by hastening the departure of some Anglophones, particularly those who are unilingual; here we base ourselves on the results of a recent study which shows that the emigration of Quebec's Anglophones, which was higher than average between 1977 and 1979, has returned to normal since 1980, even though Bill 101 is still with us and even though some provisions of this legislation, not in effect in 1977, have now come into force. As for the decline in immigration to Quebec, it is once again difficult to separate the effects of the Charter from those of other socio-economic factors.

CANADA OUTSIDE QUEBEC: CHANGES IN LINGUISTIC COMPOSITION SINCE 1971

Outside Quebec, the 1981 data show that Francophones are still losing ground despite the fact that their numbers are increasing. The French mother-tongue group now represents only 5.3 percent of the population outside Quebec, and the group for which French is the language spoken in the home is even smaller (only 3.8 percent of the population outside Quebec). The size of the English group has once again increased; 79.3 percent of the population outside Quebec has English as their mother tongue, and 88.1 percent use English in the home. The size of the Allophone group has also declined but to a lesser extent than the French group. The progressive erosion of the French-speaking minority outside Quebec is explained in large part by linguistic mobility. It is interesting to follow changes in this phenomenon by comparing the results of the 1971 and 1981 censuses.

Language Transfers

In 1971 the English group benefited from language transfers with other groups, and had net gains of 1 379 800 persons; by contrast, the French group experienced net losses of − 250 400 despite certain net gains in its exchanges with Allophones (+ 3200).

In 1971 it was found that 93.4 percent of all Canadians outside Quebec who did not use their mother tongue in the home had adopted English. This percentage dropped slightly in 1981: 92.1 percent of all transfers were toward English. Moreover, in 1981, transfers from English to French were double those recorded in 1971 (40 385 as opposed to 20 200). Although this phenomenon is marginal, we should understand the source of this new support for the French group. The increase in transfers from English to French is found in every province, but most particularly in Alberta, British Columbia, New Brunswick, and Ontario, four provinces that accounted for 90 percent of all "new transfers" since 1971.

Since these provinces are the preferred destinations of people leaving Quebec, it is not impossible that a portion of these new transfers may be more apparent than real, and may be more directly linked to migration.

Despite this new support for the French group, the net losses of Francophones continued to increase during the period 1971-81, growing from − 250 400 to − 261 600. In 1981, Francophones lost slightly more vis-à-vis Anglophones (− 253 600 to − 264 250) and gained a little less vis-à-vis Allophones (+ 3200 to + 2640).

By way of summary, we shall now examine the overall linguistic mobility rate in order to show the changes that have occurred since 1971 and to demonstrate the regional variations of this phenomenon (Table 19-5).

PROGRESSION OF LINGUISTIC MOBILITY

It should first be noted that the overall linguistic mobility rate has increased since 1971 in every region and for every language group (except for Allophones outside Quebec, for whom fewer have opted for French). This growth in the linguistic mobility of Francophones outside Quebec should not surprise us, given the many socio-economic changes that have taken place (education, urbanization, and industrialization), all of which increase the risks of such mobility. By contrast, however, the significant increase in the linguistic mobility of the English group in Quebec is surprising. A number of phenomena other than a higher propensity to adopt French may explain these variations. The overall linguistic mobility rate does not in itself reveal the reasons for this complex situation

TABLE 19-5 Overall linguistic mobility rate (in %)* by mother tongue.

Canada and Regions 1971-81

	Mother tongue					
Year	English Mobility rate toward:		French Mobility rate toward:		Other Mobility rate toward:	
Regions		Other		Other		
	French	languages	English	languages	English	French
1981						
Canada	0.8	0.8	6.6	0.3	47.4	1.6
Quebec	11.8	1.7	2.0	0.3	23.9	10.9
Montreal area	8.6	2.1	3.3	0.6	25.2	10.0
Canada less Quebec	0.3	0.7	32.8	0.3	51.1	0.2
1971						
Canada	0.5	0.7	6.0	0.2	45.8	1.4
Quebec	6.2	1.3	1.5	0.1	22.7	9.3
Montreal area	4.3	1.6	2.6	0.2	23.1	8.2
Canada less Quebec	0.2	0.6	29.6	0.2	49.3	0.2

*Proportion of persons of a given mother tongue who stated they use a different language in the home.
Source: Statistics Canada, *Census of Canada*, 1971, 1981.

For example, by comparing the 1971 and 1981 data, we see that there is a significant increase in the overall linguistic mobility rate of Anglophones in Quebec toward French. The rate appears to double in this period. Lachapelle and Henripin established that the definitive linguistic mobility of the English group (that of persons over 35 years of age) increases from generation to generation; from 7 percent for the generations of 1911-16 to 11 percent for the generations of 1936-41.

However, the overall rate for all genera-tions, including those under 35 years of age in 1971, was only 6.2 percent. It may appear that, with an overall rate of 11.8 percent in 1981, the mobility of the English group has increased among the younger generations. This may be so, but we should not ignore the selective effects of migration which, particularly for the Anglophones of Quebec whose number declined by 10 percent between 1971 and 1981, has a much smaller effect on persons of English mother tongue who either have adopted French or are at least bilingual.

Two other factors may also explain this phenomenon in Quebec; the aging population and the increased number of marriages to Francophones, given the weaker presence of Anglophones over time.

Table 19-5 reveals the major differences in linguistic mobility between Quebec and the rest of Canada. The mobility of Anglophones is much greater (approximately 40 times) in Quebec than outside that province, and more particularly outside the Montreal area. The opposite is, of course, true for the French group, whose propensity for adopting English is 16 times greater outside Quebec, just as it is much greater in Montreal. In the case of Allophones, mobility toward English is twice as great outside Quebec than within the province, where one out of four Allophones adopts English while one out of 10 adopts French.

CONCLUSION

We have provided a summary description of linguistic mobility in Quebec and in the rest of Canada. We have omitted mention of a number of quite particular regional situations, both within and outside Quebec. Moreover, we have concentrated our attention on transfers between the French and English groups, even though transfers toward other groups, particularly outside Quebec, appear to be not insignificant (approximately 100 000 in 1981). This aspect of linguistic mobility in Canada, as well as a number of other results presented above, should therefore be clarified and explained with the help of other appropriate variables. Nevertheless, we have brought out some of the trends revealed by the preliminary results of the 1981 census as they relate to the linguistic characteristics of individuals.

NOTE

1. Term used in Canada to designate those whose mother tongue is neither English nor French.

---

20. Native-White Relations

E. Palmer Patterson

Europeans first visited North America in their quest for fishing grounds. By the late seventeenth century they had penetrated into the northern half of the continent in search of furs. Over several centuries and across half a continent, many kinds of individual and group relations between Native people and Whites were established. The situations of contact changed over time, the pattern of change from South to North and from East to West reflecting the movement of Europeans. The Beothuk and the Micmac were among the first Indians of Canada to meet the Europeans. The Beothuk, a small group, were treated as enemies and as wild animals to be destroyed. They responded with resistance and flight. Most were killed or died off as a result of economic, social, and physical disruption of their lives. The

Revised from "Native-White Relations," *The Canadian Encyclopedia,* vol. 2 (Edmonton: Hurtig, 1985), pp. 1225-26. Reprinted courtesy of *The Canadian Encyclopedia.*

Micmac, however, became allies and partners of the French.

Peaceful and friendly relations, linked to common goals such as the fur trade, were maintained when they suited the needs of the parties involved. These ties sometimes led to marriages and personal friendships and to greater cultural understanding. When there was no basis for co-operation and material aid, there was likely to be competition, friction, and violence. Prejudices and stereotypes were aggravated and reinforced by economic conditions and the desire by the Whites to acquire more and more Indian land.

The fur trade, at which the Native people were adept because of the nature of their economy and technical skills, dramatically affected the organization of Indian societies. In exchange for pelts, the Europeans offered new, decorative, and often useful goods, e.g., weapons and utensils that were longer lasting and more efficient than some of the Native people's own stone, bone, wood, and hide artifacts.

Like the Indians, the Inuit generally received the Europeans with an initial attitude of curiosity and cordiality. The Inuit had their earliest European contact with explorers (in the sixteenth century) and whalers (by the early eighteenth century). Inuit hunted food for the whalers and were hired as sailors and harpooners, and they traded pelts for European goods. European diseases, introduced first by whalers, spread among the Inuit in epidemic proportions. By the late nineteenth and early twentieth centuries whalers had depleted the whale population, first in the eastern Arctic waters and then in the western Arctic. By this time the Inuit in those areas had become dependent on European trade goods.

The experience of each people that came into contact with the Europeans was unique, but the overall effect of such contact was similar. The technology and economy of Native culture began to change even before face-to-face contact had taken place, because the items that the Europeans traded frequently preceded the Europeans themselves. Native people moved from their aboriginal territory to pursue the pelt-bearing animals, and this altered their economy and sometimes led to conflict with the previous occupants of an area. Native people also became overspecialized in their economic dependence on the fur trade and European goods, neglecting their aboriginal technology and in some cases their traditional food base. When the fur trade moved deeper into the interior, it left the Native people dependent upon European goods and upon new forms of employment, e.g., as canoeists, mercenaries, food suppliers, guides, and translators. As the traditional economic base deteriorated, many Native people became destitute. At the same time, disease decimated their populations. The Huron and the Petun populations were reduced by 50

percent in one decade (1630s) as a result of epidemics. The Haida on the Queen Charlotte Islands declined from a population of about 8000, in the early nineteenth century, to about 800 by the late nineteenth century.

From the mid-seventeenth century to the late nineteenth century, this population decline led many Europeans to believe that Native people would disappear. The autonomy of the Native people first in the economic and technological spheres, then in the social, political, demographic, religious, and even artistic spheres, was increasingly eroded as the Indians moved from a position of collaboration and partnership with the fur traders to a condition of dependence and then subjection. Missionaries, messianic religions, and revitalization movements contributed to or reflected the collapse of traditional systems of social and religious organization. Cultural survival was sought in Indian-based religions, some of which borrowed and adapted elements of Christianity. Responses to the missionary appeal varied among Native people from acceptance to rejection; some Native people believed the power of the newcomer might be drawn upon the Indians.

By the middle or late nineteenth century, relations between Indians and Europeans had entered a new phase because hundreds of thousands of Europeans had settled in the Maritimes and in central Canada. The new dominant economy—agriculture—pushed the Indians to the sidelines and backwaters of social and economic life. In the same year as the Royal Proclamation of 1763, Pontiac organized an armed resistance of more than a dozen tribes in the Ohio Valley and Great Lakes area against the British takeover from the French after the Seven Years' War and the encroachment of British Colonial settlers across the Appalachian Mountains. Tecumseh, like Pontiac, tried to resist White settlements; his alliance with the British was intended to help achieve this goal, but after the War of 1812 the Great Lakes Indians were no longer important military or economic allies. As the European population became a larger and larger majority, European culture came to dominate North America.

The Royal Proclamation gave the imperial government the sole right to alienate lands from the Indians and initiated the procedure of signing land-surrender treaties between the British and Indians in North America. In the late eighteenth and early nineteenth centuries there followed, in Upper Canada [Southern Ontario], a series of land-surrender treaties that confined Indians to small holdings and made large tracts of land available to settlers. Indians were relieved of their lands, through treaties of land surrender, through designation of reserves, and through expropriations of reserve lands. In the Maritimes, Quebec, most of British Columbia, the Yukon, and parts of the northern territories, where treaties were not signed, the Indians were nevertheless obliged to give up large areas of land. It is very doubtful that Indians and Whites had the same understanding of the land surrender treaties. In most Indian cultures, land was not regarded as a commodity that could be bought and sold. Evidence from Indian testimony shows that Indians understood these agreements to be matters of sharing, of friendship, of mutual respect, and not final and irrevocable sales of land. On the European side, however, these treaties were regarded as legal purchases of land, with attending obligations such as the provision of annual payments, farm supplies, medical aid, and so forth.

Throughout the nineteenth century federal legislation shaped the life of Native peo-

ple. In 1876 the Indian Act was passed, consolidating previous legislation and more clearly defining and confining the Native people. Public and legal affairs of status Indians were governed by successive amendments and a new Indian Act in 1951. Bands were assigned reserve lands, which constituted the remains of the vast homelands once held by the Native people. These reserves were to be training grounds for assimilating the Native peoples into the general society. At the same time the Indians were to be removed from the influences that were judged "undesirable" and submitted to controlled culture change toward "civilization" and self-sufficiency.

Like the Indians of the Prairie provinces, the Métis also experienced the effects of the flood of European settlers. Their efforts to resist this threat resulted in the Red River Rebellion and the North-West Rebellion. Their resistance was crushed after brief outbreaks of war and their political leader, Louis Riel, was convicted of treason and executed (1885). In the late twentieth century, paralleling some of the more recent Indian movements, the Métis have begun to reassert their identity.

From the early nineteenth century, government has pursued a policy of encouraging the assimilation of the Native people. European colonizers regarded Indian culture as "backward," "stagnant," "primitive," and "inferior" to European culture. The policy of assimilation would, it was thought, remedy the situation. Indians who seemed to accept programs for cultural change were seen as "progressives"; those who resisted were "conservatives." The enfranchisement system removed an Indian from this group; in exchange for citizen status and voting privileges, Indian status was lost. In the late nineteenth century and early twentieth century Indian administrators interfered increasingly in the everyday affairs of reserve life. Indian landholdings came to be seen as an impediment to "progress" and "development," and this justified the expropriation of reserve lands, especially those close to urban settlements.

To ensure their own survival, Indian leaders have frequently made compromises with the Europeans. Crowfoot expressed his appreciation for aid given the Blackfoot and signed Treaty No. 7 (1877) as a means of further protection. Chief Herbert Wallace, a Port Simpson Tsimshian of the early twentieth century, credited the missionaries with assisting the Indians to understand better their own land claims and land rights. At that time the Nishga renewed their land protest with the Nishga Petition (1913). By the late twentieth century some of the most acculturated Indian leaders had also become the most insistent critics of the poor treatment accorded Indians and advocates of greater concern for the survival of Indian traditions as well as political and economic rights. The White Paper of 1969, which threatened Indian survival, and to which Indian spokesmen such as Harold Cardinal responded vigorously, changed the course of Indian protest.

The 1970s witnessed a great upsurge in Indian activity and media awareness of Indian affairs. The 1969 White Paper was successfully beaten down by the response of Indians and friends of the Indians. Numerous books by and about Indians appeared. Harold Cardinal, already mentioned, wrote *The Unjust Society* and *The Rebirth of the Canadian Indian. The Fourth World,* by George Manuel and Michael Posluns, was another important work of this period. Native artists and poets received wide attention.

The National Indian Brotherhood, embracing status Indians across Canada, was formed and became very active. It was recognized by the United Nations and through the 1970s worked with the federal government to improve Indian conditions. Research into Indian rights of all kinds was more heavily subsidized. Local and provincial Native organizations, including Indians, Métis, and Inuit, were organized or revived. A new, young, vigorous Indian leadership emerged, influenced by national and international issues. Band governments received more financing, and attention was turned to making reserves economically viable where possible. In the mid-1970s Dene action blocked the Mackenzie Valley pipeline.

Pan-Indianism has been fostered to a degree by the meeting of peoples of various tribes and cultures in the cities and as a result of a common language, residential schools (before the second half of the twentieth century), and increased physical mobility. One of the most exciting adaptive possibilities lies in the Northwest Territories where, unlike most of Canada, Native peoples constitute the majority of the population.

Since 1971, the year the Inuit national organization, the Inuit Tapirisat of Canada, was formed, Inuit have also made a greater effort to gain control over their own affairs. Leaders have emerged from among a generation of younger people more familiar with the culture of southern Canada, but determined to preserve and develop Inuit land and culture.

The repatriation of the Canadian Constitution in the early 1980s had an important impact on Indians and other Native peoples. After much debate, the Constitution granted "aboriginal rights," though undefined, and designated status Indians, Métis, and Inuit, aboriginal peoples. Suspicion and mistrust have continued to characterize the attitude of many Native peoples. The failure of Constitutional conferences to settle the question of self-government renewed suspicions and contributed to ruptures within Indian organizations. The threat of increased provincial participation in Indian affairs was viewed with great misgiving. The status of the Territories, where so many aboriginal people live, remained a sore point. The continuing rejection by British Columbia of Indian land claims was repeatedly reflected in the news headlines.

Indians, Métis, non-status Indians, and Inuit gained greatly in organizational and legal sophistication and effectiveness over the decades of the 1970s and 1980s. The need for these skills continues.

The Native people, though socially, culturally and economically exploited by centuries of relations with non-Natives, have survived as a people. They now demand greater control of and participation in all the spheres of public affairs that govern them.

21. Multiculturalism as Ideology, Policy, and Reality

Evelyn Kallen

INTRODUCTION

In the current Canadian context, the concept "multiculturalism" is widely used in at least three senses: (1) to refer to the "social reality" of ethnic diversity; (2) to refer to the federal government policy, designed to create national unity in ethnic diversity; and (3) to refer to the ideology of cultural pluralism underlying the federal policy.

THE IDEOLOGY OF MULTICULTURALISM

Isajiw (1981) has recently examined multiculturalism as a set of social values. He has

Revised from Evelyn Kallen, "Multiculturalism: Ideology, Policy and Reality," *Journal of Canadian Studies*, vol. 12, no. 1 (Spring 1982), pp. 51-63. Reprinted with permission.

argued that multiculturalism, as a value, can provide a basis for a new kind of universalism which legitimizes the incorporation of ethnic diversity in the general structure of society. Historically, he points out, universal values of modern societies were predicated on the shift from ascribed to achieved criteria for evaluation, and, concomitantly, on complete detachment from particularistic ethnic ties. Integration of individuals into the state collectivity was conditional on total disengagement from ethnicity and fragmentation of ethnic identity.

Today, however, this kind of universalism is losing relevance and validity. For one thing, Isajiw argues, people are questioning the legitimacy of the universalistic ideal of inclusion in the face of continuing ethnic exclusion. Thus, ethnic discrimination has rendered the old universalism invalid in the minds of many Canadians. Also, people are questioning the value of assimilation to post-modern, technological culture, which offers little in response to expressive identity needs. Finally, Isajiw points out that the collective needs of members of ethnic collectivities have changed over the generations. People are coming to the realization that their own personal dignity is bound up with the collective dignity of their ethnic community. Recognition of one thus necessitates recognition of the other.

Given these considerations, what is the meaning of multiculturalism as a set of universal social values? Isajiw suggests that it is threefold: (1) it gives positive recognition to the collective identity of all ethnic communities; (2) it can legitimize multiple identities; and (3) it can become institutionalized as a political value.

THE REALITY OF MULTICULTURALISM: UNDERLYING ASSUMPTIONS

As a model for reality, the mosaic ideology is predicated on a national goal of one nation/many peoples/many cultures. The mosaic ideal is rooted in the assumption that members of all ethnocultural collectivities are both able and willing to maintain their ethnocultural distinctiveness. This assumption implies that all ethnic collectivities are characterized by high levels of ethnocentrism, but that they also are willing to adopt a "laissez-faire" (live and let live) stance towards ethnocultural collectivities whose values and lifeways differ markedly from their own. Following from this, the mosaic model assumes that levels of prejudice and discrimination between ethnic collectivities are low enough to allow mutual tolerance. Third, the mosaic model assumes a rough equivalence in the distribution of power among the various ethnic collectivities, so that no one population can assume dominance and

control over others. Finally, this model assumes that members of the different ethnic collectivities in society will mutually agree to limit and control the extent, spheres, and nature of interaction between them. Thus, processes of acculturation and assimilation will be (mutually) restricted by the interacting ethnic units.

Given these assumptions, interethnic relations within the mosaic society would take the form of ethnic segmentation (Breton, 1978). Each ethnic collectivity would be institutionally complete and ethnocultural distinctiveness (cultural pluralism) would be maintained through separate ethnic institutions (structural pluralism). As an outcome of cultural and structural pluralism, every citizen's identity would become hyphenated, i.e., ethnic-national, with equal weights on both sides of the hyphen. With regard to human rights, the society would recognize both the individual human rights of all its citizens and the collective cultural rights of all its ethnic collectivities. Given the basic assumption of equality of opportunity, the social position attained by individual citizens within a mosaic (as within a melting-pot) society would be a function of their demonstrated individual talents, capabilities, and skills, on the one hand, and of the way in which these attributes are culturally valued, on the other. Ethnicity would not provide a criterion for differential personal evaluation or for positional attainment in public life. Ethnicity would, however, provide the recognized basis for collective rights, in that all ethnic collectivities within the society would be guaranteed the freedom to collectively express their religious, linguistic, and cultural distinctiveness.

The most important variable here is the relative weights assigned to "unity" and "diversity." The importance of ethnic *diversity* is reflected in the sphere (or spheres) in which collective (ethnocultural group) rights may be guaranteed. Should the mosaic take the form of pluralism in the public sector, then ethnocultural rights could be guaranteed through political representation, economic (occupational) control in specified area(s), recognition of linguistic rights, and (in its most extreme form) territorial (regional/local) autonomy. The latter form of pluralism provides the basis for *nationhood* based on the geographical separation of ethnic collectivities sharing language, culture, and territory. If viable for all ethnic groups, this kind of pluralism could lead to multinationhood—a multinational society within a common political (federal) administrative framework. In the latter kind of society, the national group rights of all ethnic collectivities would be recognized.

Within the Canadian context, the myth of the mosaic was not (initially) conceptualized in "nationhood" terms for populations other than the charter groups (English and French). Rather, as applied to (later) immigrant ethnic collectivities, the mosaic model relegated cultural and structural pluralism to the private sphere of life. Within the public sector, individual citizens would be accorded equal societal opportunities without reference to ethnic classification. But, with regard to collective (ethnocultural group) rights, the public sector was envisaged as an Anglo or Franco cultural monolith, thus attainment of social positions within the sphere of secondary institutions would be predicated on required acculturation to prevailing Anglo or Franco norms and practices.

THE CANADIAN MOSAIC AS GOVERNMENT POLICY

The impetus for Canada's multicultural policy lay in the negative response of immigrant ethnic minorities to the model of bi-lingualism and biculturalism which underscored the efforts and reports of the "Bi and Bi" Commission in the 1960s. Reacting against the idea of a policy which would relegate non-English and non-French Canadians to the status of second-class citizens, spokesmen for the (alleged) "Third Force" of immigrant ethnic collectivities demanded equal treatment. Spearheaded by Ukrainians, the demands of the other ethnic groups gave rise, in 1969, to Book IV of the *Report of the Royal Commission on Bilingualism and Biculturalism*: "The Cultural Contribution of the Other Ethnic Groups." This document contains 16 recommendations for the implementation of an official government policy of multilingualism and multiculturalism designed as a model of integration for immigrant ethnic collectivities.

Then Prime Minister Trudeau's announcement of a multicultural policy for Canada, on October 8, 1971, was the official response of the federal government to the recommendations contained in Book IV. On this occasion, Mr. Trudeau made it clear that although the government endorsed the "spirit" of Book IV, it did not support the position, implicit in its recommendations, that language and culture are indivisible. The federal government rejected the notion that multiculturalism necessitates multilingualism and proposed that the multicultural policy be implemented within a bilingual framework.

The Prime Minister emphasized the fact that under the newly introduced policy the preservation of ethnic identity is a *voluntary* matter, both for the individual and for the group. The funding of multicultural programs would therefore be directed *only* toward those ethnic groups whose members *express a desire* to maintain their ethnocultural heritage and who can demonstrate a *need for support* in their efforts to maintain their ethnic distinctiveness. Similarly, Mr.

Trudeau recognized the right of each individual to be *free to choose* whether or not to maintain his or her distinctive ethnic identity.

Unlike the ideal model of cultural pluralism which assumes that every individual and group desires to maintain a distinctive ethnic identity and heritage, the Canadian policy of multiculturalism gives recognition to the fact that some people will, inevitably, find greater human affinities *outside* their ethnic group than within it. Thus, while the policy legitimates the right of each immigrant ethnocultural community to maintain its distinctiveness, it also gives recognition to the right of individuals to *choose* whether or not to value maintenance of ties and loyalties to their particular ethnic group, and it supports the right of individuals to participate fully in Canadian society, independent of their (actual or assumed) ethnic classificaiton. The *voluntary* nature of maintenance of ethnic ties, loyalties, and identities under the multicultural policy protects the *individual* rights of members to dissent or dissociate themselves freely from the collective values of their ethnic origin group.

The federal government's policy statement on multiculturalism (House of Commons *Debates*, October 8, 1971) sets forth four objectives:

1. The Government of Canada will support all of Canada's cultures and will seek to assist, resources permitting, the development of those cultural groups which have demonstrated a desire and effort to continue to develop a capacity to grow and contribute to Canada, as well as a clear need for assistance.

2. The Government will assist members of all cultural groups to overcome cultural barriers to full participation in Canadian society.

3. The Government will promote creative encounters and interchange among all Canadian cultural groups in the interest of national unity.

4. The Government will continue to assist immigrants to acquire at least one of Canada's official languages in order to become full participants in Canadian society.

The first policy objective seeks to encourage ethnocultural diversity through support of those ethnic groups which have demonstrated a desire to develop as distinctive cultural entities. Scholars who support this objective (for example, Burnet, 1975; 1976; 1978) tend to view ethnic collectivities in expressive, rather than instrumental terms. They conceptualize the primary function of ethnic communities as one of providing people with havens of security, places where they can escape from the alienating workaday world of post-technological society. Ethnicity provides a sense of group belongingness and rootedness, i.e., a focus for ethnic identity and cultural continuity.

One line of argument put forward by scholars who oppose this policy objective (notably, the late John Porter, 1975; 1979) is that encouragement of ethnic diversity and cultural distinctiveness fosters (implicitly, if not explicitly) ethnic separation, enclavement, and retention of traditional values. Ethnic particularism, in turn, perpetuates the vertical (ethnic) mosaic by creating barriers to upward mobility in post-industrial society which is predicated on universalistic norms. In this view, government encouragement of ethnic diversity legitimates the proliferation of particularistic value differences among Canadians and thus impedes the development of national unity. Further, some critics have argued, the (original) exclusive focus of the policy of multiculturalism on the other ethnic groups, i.e., immigrants, contributes to ethnic divisiveness rather than national unity among Canadians. Specifically, Canadian scholars have argued that the artificial separation of the three categories of Canadian ethnic collectivities (immigrants, charter population, and indigenes) for political purposes—endorsed and reinforced by the multicultural policy—represents the age-old Colonial technique of divide and rule utilized by majority ethnic elites to guarantee and perpetuate their ascendancy (Kallen, 1978; Peter, 1979).

A second line of argument against the first policy objective (i.e., maintenance of ethnocultural distinctiveness) is that there are *no* relevant cultural differences among Canada's immigrant populations other than minor differences in tastes (e.g., food preferences) which neither warrant nor require a multicultural policy in order to be maintained (Brotz, 1980). Members of all of Canada's ethnic collectivities, Brotz argues, aspire to the same "bourgeois-democratic" way of life, with the exception of the (already transitional) way of life of those indigenes in reservations who continue to be engaged in a pre-industrial hunting and gathering economy (1980:43).

The expressive emphasis of the first multicultural policy objective, particularly as implemented in programs featuring "ethnic exotica" has come under sharp criticism by Canadian academics and other scholars (Wilson, 1978; Bullivant, 1981; Peter, 1979). Bullivant argues that this exclusive focus on the *expressive* (roots/belongingness) function of ethnicity deflects attention away from the *instrumental* (corporate group interests) side of ethnic collectivities as politically- and/or economically-oriented survival blueprints or designs for living intimately connected with an ethnic group's life chances. Peter (1979) goes even further than Bullivant in his criticisms of both the first and the fourth multicultural policy objectives. He argues that the "we" (Canadian society)/ "they" (ethnic collectivities) syndrome, which assumes that Canadian society somehow exists *independently of* (and prior to) the ongoing interaction between the ethnic collectivities which compose it, relegates the role of minority ethnic groups to that of contributors of quaint customs/upholders of primordial identities, while at the same time it denies them a political and economic reality in Canada. Peter contends that the Multicultural/Bilingual Policy is a policy of appeasement and containment of the conflicting demands made by the other ethnic groups (immigrants), on the one hand, and by Quebeckers, on the other.

With regard to the second and third objectives of the multicultural policy statement, Canadian scholars appear to be far more unified in their positive support. The second policy objective of multiculturalism seeks to overcome cultural barriers to full participation in Canadian society; the third seeks to promote creative encounters and interchange among all of Canada's ethnic groups. Both of these objectives appear to be designed to reduce racial/ethnic discrimination, to protect the fundamental human rights of members of immigrant ethnic collectivities, and to foster Canadian unity.

Canadian scholars generally evince strong support for these two policy objectives. They also point out that the policy *rhetoric* does not correspond with programs of implementation at the level of social *reality*. Indeed, the weakest and most neglected part of multicultural programs implemented under the policy has been in this area (Hughes and Kallen, 1974; Kelner and Kallen, 1974; Kallen, 1978; Burnet, 1975; 1976; 1978).

Probably the most contentious aspect of the multicultural policy is reflected in its fourth objective, i.e., linguistic assimilation of immigrants into one of Canada's two official language communities (English and French). The bilingual framework of the policy accords official recognition only to the linguistic rights of the founding peoples, while the linguistic rights of immigrant ethnic minorities are neither recognized nor guaranteed. From the viewpoint of the Third Force, multiculturalism, in the sense of maintenance of viable ethnocultural communities, is meaningless without multilingualism (Yusyk, 1964). Scholars who favour this perspective—the position adopted in the recommendations of Book IV of the Report of the Commission on Bilingualism and Biculturalism—contend that, where numbers warrant, regional guarantees for the protection and recognition of *non*-official as well as official minority languages should be afforded. In direct opposition to this view is the position put forward by the staunch Francophone supporters of bilingualism and biculturalism (Bourassa, 1971; Rocher, 1976). Proponents of this view argue that the constitutional protection of the special status of the French in Quebec places them in a unique position in Canada as one of the two founding *nations*. By virtue of this special status, they argue that in public life their language and culture should be expressed and recognized throughout Canada equally with that of the English. Both arguments—for multilingualism/multiculturalism and for bilingualism/biculturalism—are predicated on the assumption that "living" cultures and "living" languages are inextricably linked. As models for reality, however, the former position more closely approximates an egalitarian mosaic ideal for a multiethnic society, while the latter enshrines the dominant status of the (alleged) charter groups.

THE MULTICULTURAL MOVEMENT: MOSAIC AS SOCIAL REALITY

As an ethno-political movement, the multicultural movement may be conceptualized as a movement for social reform spearheaded by immigrant ethnic minorities in a collective effort to achieve the goal of an egalitarian Canadian mosaic.

The multicultural movement arose from the discontent of non-English and non-French immigrant ethnic minorities with their alleged status as second-class citizens under the terms of reference of the Royal Commission on Bilingualism and Biculturalism. At this time, discontent with the biculturalism goal focussed on the notion of the two founding races—a term of reference which confuses race and culture—used by the Royal Commission to refer to the English and French charter groups in Canada. This notion, it was argued, relegated all other peoples and cultures to minority status within Canada. In a similar vein, objections were raised against the goal of bilingualism as interpreted by the Commission to mean the languages of the English and French, and as later enshrined in the Official Languages Act (1969).

The earliest and the most powerful spokesman for the multicultural movement was Senator Paul Yuzyk, who, in his first speech in the Canadian Senate on May 3, 1964, put forward the idea of a Third Force —a coalition of all non-English and non-French ethnic collectivities in Canada. Yuzyk clearly articulated the *instrumental* goal of the movement when he argued that the Third Force (then) represented almost one third of the Canadian population, and as a united organizational force they could hold the balance of power between the English and French.

The *expressive* goal of the multicultural movement soon became evident in demands for a Canadian (mosaic) nation based on a policy of multiculturalism and multilingualism. Spearheaded largely by Ukrainian spokesmen such as Yuzyk, the movement was (at least covertly) supported even in its early stages by representatives of other long-resident immigrant ethnic collectivities, such as Jews, and later by a variety of newer immigrant populations including

Italians, Armenians, Portuguese, Greeks and others.

The majority response to the conflicting demands of the Third Force, on the one hand, and of the French Canadian nationalists who supported a model of English/French bilingualism and biculturalism, on the other hand, was represented in the compromise policy of multiculturalism within a bilingual framework. Minority ethnic protest against the terms of the policy, since its inception, has indicated clearly that it has not satisfied the demands of either of the constituencies (French or "other" immigrants) whose claims it sought to address. Just as proponents of bilingualism and biculturalism argue that the latter necessitates the former, proponents of the multicultural movement continue to argue that language and culture are indivisible; therefore multiculturalism is meaningless without multilingualism. While the early proponents of the multicultural movement focussed on fundamental human rights, especially the right of equal access of all ethnic groups to political, economic, and social power, spokesmen for a variety of ethnic organizations over the years have increasingly come to make demands based on collective minority (cultural and linguistic) rights.

MULTICULTURALISM, MINORITY RIGHTS AND EDUCATION

Spokespersons for the multicultural movement have long criticized the federal multicultural policy for its avoidance of the educational implications of the multicultural ideal through the political strategy of shifting the burden of responsibility to the provinces. Because public education is a provincial matter, the federal policy has conveniently sidestepped this critial issue.

In response to early protest against the focus of multicultural programs on folk art and museum culture, as opposed to living languages and ethnocultures, multicultural programs were expanded so as to offer limited support to *private*, supplementary, minority ethnic schools. But proponents of the multicultural movement continued to argue that failure to provide support for maintenance of language and culture in *public* institutions—in primary and secondary schools, and in community colleges and universities as well as in public broadcasting and other media—perpetuates the minority status of the other ethnic groups (Burnet, 1981:31). From the viewpoint of the multicultural movement, the present policy continues to violate the collective minority rights of non-English and non-French ethnic collectivities.

MULTICULTURALISM AND RACIAL DISCRIMINATION

Another position put forward under the rubric of the multicultural movement focusses on the second multicultural policy objective, i.e., that of combatting racial discrimination. Spokespersons for visible minorities such as Chinese, West Indians and South Asians have argued that early programs of implementation under the multicultural policy did not place nearly enough emphasis on eradicating racism in Canada.

In response to this position, in 1975, the (then) Minister of Multiculturalism, the Honourable John Munro, declared a shift in program emphasis from language and culture to group understanding. The subsequent change in focus of multicultural programs toward combatting prejudice and discrimination sparked a number of important researches in the area, notably the national survey of ethnic attitudes carried out by

Berry et al. (1977) and a study of racism in Toronto (Henry, 1977), among others. While these academic studies provided important documentation on the nature and extent of racial/ethnic prejudice and discrimination in various parts of Canada, they were not designed primarily to alleviate the negative social and personal consequences of these phenomena for those Canadians found to be most disadvantaged by them, i.e., for visible minorities. It was the various spokespersons for visible minorities who took up the cause of racial discrimination and, under the rubric of multiculturalism, began to press for greater protection (particularly through fairer practices of law enforcement) for their fundamental human rights. For these minorities, the fight against racial discrimination takes precedence over the fight against cultural discrimination so earnestly pursued by the proponents of multilingualism and multiculturalism under the same multiculturalism rubric.

Most recently, in response to the political implications of state funding of ethnic organizations in Canada, criticism of the policy of multiculturalism has come to focus on the syndrome of "state policy as state control" (Kallen, 1981; Anderson and Frideres, 1981). At the level of social reality, it is argued, government funding of minority ethnic organizations legitimated under the multicultural policy represents a major technique of dominant management of minority ethnic demands. For state funding bodies are controlling agencies: the dominant fund-giving agency sets the terms (conditions) under which funds are allotted, selects the recipients, and oversees and regulates the process through which the funds are distributed and expended. Government funding of minority ethnic organizations thus allows (indeed facilitates) government (and, indirectly, dominant) intervention in

minority affairs. Through this subtle (and sometimes not-so-subtle) process the ethnic minority is kept in a dependent position, and minority ethnic protest is contained and diffused. Further, insofar as ethnic minorities must compete against each other for the same scarce resource (multicultural program grants), ethnic divisions gain in strength and salience.

The implications of ethnic group competition and factionalism for the future of the multicultural movement are manifold. For the tension between the competing and ofttimes conflicting interests of internal lines of division has impeded the instrumental thrust of the multicultural movement as a multiethnic coalition in Canada. Nevertheless, at present, the multicultural movement continues to flourish, despite its many vociferous critics. Over and above the competing and conflicting demands of its internal factions, the movement provides a recognized, legitimate forum for minority ethnic protest. Further, as Isajiw (1980) has pointed out, the multicultural *policy* has given ethnic collectivities a legal basis for making claims on public policy and public funds. Thus the policy, despite its (alleged) limitations, provides an important legitimating mechanism for minority claims based on ethnic group demands for recognition of their collective dignity and collective rights.

The evidence presented in the foregoing discussion indicates that the concept of multiculturalism is inherently problematic at all levels of analysis, i.e., as a set of universal social values (ideology), as federal policy, and as an ethno-political movement (social reality).

At the level of values, the assumptions of the mosaic ideology pose at least three sets of problems with regard to its potential for implementation. First, as an egalitarian ideology, the mosaic assumes relative symmetry of political, economic, and social power among the constituent ethnic units in the society. What this assumption implies is that the mosaic ideology is inappropriate where there are vast disparities in power between ethnic collectivities. Before the mosaic model could be implemented in an ethnically stratified society like Canada, for example, a major redistribution of power between ethnic units would have to occur. Secondly, the mosaic ideology assumes that all ethnic units in the society are equally desirous and capable of developing and maintaining distinctive ethnocultures. This aspect of the ideology does not take into account the possibility that ethnic units may differ in the degree to which their members desire to maintain ethnic distinctiveness and in the degree to which they have the demographic, economic, and institutional resources which would enable them to do so. While no society can legislate or otherwise ensure any population's desire to remain culturally distinctive, measures can be taken to facilitate this end, if so desired.

Third, the mosaic ideology assumes that, through tolerant interethnic relations involving the full and equal participation in public life of members of all ethnic communities, a common, national culture and identity would be created. Further, the common national consciousness so created (it is assumed) would be equal in strength to the particular ethnic consciousness of each of the country's citizens. This third set of mosaic assumptions is even more problematic than the first two, on several counts. First, it fails to indicate the specific nature of the common, national culture which emerges in the society. Whose cultural norms, legal and ethical standards, institutional forms and language(s) would govern the conduct of public life? Except in its most radical (multi-nationhood) interpretation. what the mo-

saic ideology *really* assumes in public life is an empirically, highly improbable melting pot. A second set of inherent problems arises from the internal contradiction between the objectives of ethnocultural distinctiveness, on the one hand, and full and equal participation in public life, on the other. Here, the long-accumulated evidence from the study of ethnic relations clearly demonstrates that maintenance of ethnic distinctiveness requires geo-ethnic segregation and restriction on participation in public life, while the development of national consciousness and commitment requires extensive ethnic interaction through full and equal participation in public life.

Clearly, as an ideology of ethnic integration, the mosaic model poses formidable problems of implementation in the current Canadian context. The next question, then, concerns the extent to which the adaptations to the mosaic model built into the federal government's multicultural policy have improved its applicability to the reality of Canada's multicultural society. First, with regard to the variable nature of the desire of ethnic units to maintain distinctive ethnocultures, the policy statement deviated from the mosaic ideology by making it clear that this was a *voluntary* matter, both for the individual and for the ethnic collectivity. Second, with regard to the contradiction between the objectives of maintenance of ethnic distinctiveness, on the one hand, and full and equal participation in Canadian society, on the other, the policy statement adopted a compromise position which posited a clear division between public and private life sectors and which relegated maintenance of distinctive *minority* ethnocultures entirely to the private sphere. Further, the policy guaranteed equal opportunities for all citizens, regardless of ethnic classification, in public life. Third, with regard to the necessity for culturally specific norms, institutions, and language(s) in public life, the policy statement again deviated from the mosaic model: it explicitly offered bilingualism (English and French) and implicitly assumed (parallel) biculturalism. The latter aspects of the multicultural policy are inherently problematic as they clearly negate the egalitarian ethos of the mosaic ideology. What is probably most problematic, however, is that the multicultural policy says nothing and does nothing (to paraphrase Bullivant) about existing racial ethnic inequality in Canada. Thus the long-term effects of structural racism, such as the "welfare colonialism" of Canada's indigenous peoples, and the virtual absence of representation among Canadian elites of visible minorities is nowhere addressed in the multicultural policy statement.

REFERENCES

Anderson, A.B., and Frideres, J.S.
    1981   *Ethnicity in Canada: Theoretical Perspectives.* Toronto: Butterworths.

Berry, J.W., R. Kallin, and D.M. Taylor
    1977   *Multiculturalism and Ethnic Attitudes in Canada.* Ottawa: Ministry of Supply and Services Canada.

Bourassa, R.
    1971   "Objections to multiculturalism," Letter to Prime Minister Trudeau in *Le Devoir,* November 17, 1971.

Brotz, H.
    1980   "Multiculturalism in Canada: A Muddle," *Canadian Public Policy,* 6 (Winter): 4-16.

Bullivant, B.M.
    1981   "Multiculturalism—Pluralist Orthodoxy or Ethnic Hegemony," *Canadian Ethnic Studies,* 8, no. 2:1-22.

Burnet, J.
    1975   "Multiculturalism, immigration and racism," *Canadian Ethnic Studies,* 7:35-39.
    1976   "Ethnicity: Canadian Experience and Policy," *Sociological Focus,* 9, no. 2:199-207.
    1978   "The policy of multiculturalism within a bilingual framework: A Stock-taking," *Canadian Ethnic Studies,* 5, no. 2:107-13.
    1981   "The social and historical context of ethnic relations," in *A Canadian Social Psychology of Ethnic Relations,* ed. R.C. Gardner and R. Kalen, pp. 17-35. Agincourt: Methuen.

Canada, Parliament
    1960   *Canadian Bill of Rights.* Act passed by the Parliament of Canada and given force of law on August 10, Ottawa.

Canada, Parliament, Special Joint Committee on the Constitution
    1981   *Constitution Act.* Proposed resolution respecting the constitution of Canada, Ottawa.

Case, F. I.
1971   *Racism and National Consciousness.* Toronto: Plowshare Press.

Douglas, R.A.S.
1979   Cited in "Working paper for a conference on minority rights," by J. Leavy. Paper presented at York University, Downsview, October.

Glickman, Y.
1976   "Organization indicators and social correlates of collective Jewish identity." Ph.D. dissertation, Department of Sociology, University of Toronto.

Henry, F.
1977   *The Dynamics of Racism in Toronto: A Preliminary Report.* Downsview: York University.

House of Commons Debates
1971   Statement of Prime Minister Trudeau, October 8.

Hughes, D.R., and E. Kallen
1974   *The Anatomy of Racism: Canadian Dimensions.* Montreal: Harvest House.

Isajiw, W.W.
1980   Report of a Conference on Minority Rights, York University, February 29. Sponsored by the Canadian Human Rights Foundation.
1981   "Social evolution and the values of multiculturalism." Paper presented at the Ninth Biennial Conference of the Canadian Ethnic Studies Association, October 14-17, in Edmonton, Alberta.

Kallen, E.
1978   *An Evaluation of the Visiting Professors and Visiting Lecturers Programme* (Canadian Ethnic Studies). Report submitted to the Multicultural Directorate, Department of Secretary of State, Ottawa, August.
1981   "Academics, politics and ethnics," *Canadian Ethnic Studies*, 8, no. 2:112-23.
1981   "The semantics of multiculturalism." Paper presented at the "Consciousness and Inquiry" Conference, March 29-April 1, at the University of Western Ontario, London, Ontario.

Kelner, M., and E. Kallen
1974   "The multicultural policy: Canada's response to ethnic diversity," *Journal of Comparative Sociology*, 22:21-24.

Peter, K.
1978   "Multicultural politics, money and the conduct of Canadian ethnic studies," *Canadian Ethnic Studies Association Bulletin*, 5:2-3.
1979   "The myth of multiculturalism and other political fables." Paper presented at the Canadian Ethnic Studies Conference, October 11-13, in Vancouver, B.C.

Porter, J.
1965   *The Vertical Mosaic.* Toronto: University of Toronto Press.
1975   "Ethnic pluralism in Canadian perspective," in *Ethnicity: Theory and Experience*, ed. N. Glazer and D. Moynihan, pp. 267-304. Cambridge, Mass.: Harvard University.
1979   "Melting pot or mosaic: Revolution or reversion?" in *The Measure of Canadian Society*, pp. 139-62. Toronto: Gage.

Rocher, G.
   1976   "Multiculturalism: The doubts of a francophone," in *Report of the Second Canadian Conference on Multiculturalism,* by Canadian Consultative Council on Multiculturalism, pp. 47-53.

Royal Commission on Bilingualism and Biculturalism
   1970   *The Cultural Contributions of the Other Ethnic Groups, Book IV.* Report of the Royal Commission. Ottawa: Queen's Printer.

Wilson, J.
   1978   "Come, let us reason together," in *Black Presence in Multi-Ethnic Canada,* ed. V. D'Oyley. Toronto: O.I.S.E.

Yusyk, P.
   1964   Senatorial Address, May 3. Ottawa.

FOR FURTHER READING

Asch, Michael. 1984. *Home and Native Land*. Toronto: Methuen. After examining the meaning of aboriginal rights as used by various interest groups, Asch turns to the question of political rights and assesses how the current impasse in Native land claims and self-government might be resolved. An excellent, readable account of a major Canadian issue.

Bienvenue, Rita, and Jay E. Goldstein. 1985. *Ethnicity and Ethnic Relations in Canada* (2nd ed.). Toronto: Butterworths. This collection contains many useful research articles on "ethnicity and ethnic relations," "ethnic differentiation," "ethnic inequalities," "prejudice and discrimination," and "conflict and change."

Breton, Raymond, Jeffrey G. Reitz, and Victor Valentine. 1980. *Cultural Boundaries and the Cohesion of Canada*. Montreal: The Institute for Research on Public Policy. This book is made up of an introductory chapter which describes the ethnic composition of Canada followed by three chapters on French-English relations, the non-charter groups, and Native peoples. Each lengthy chapter presents detailed information on the contemporary situation for the minority groups and tests theories on intergroup relations. The volume also gives consistent attention to the social policy implications of the findings and theories.

Driedger, Leo, ed. 1987. *Ethnic Canada: Identities and Inequalities*. Toronto: Copp Clark Pitman. This collection of 21 articles presents a good overview of issues of ethnic inequality including: the social standing of ethnic and racial groupings, ethnicity and collective rights, ethnic stereotypes, discrimination, and affirmative action.

Kallen, Evelyn. 1982. *Ethnicity and Human Rights in Canada*. Toronto: Gage. In this book the author expands on the issues addressed in her article above. The concepts of ethnicity and race are analysed, as is government policy on these phenomena. The book's focus is upon the rights of ethnocultural groups and how they are recognized and protected. Changes in these regards over time are emphasized, including the implications of the Constitutional Act of 1982.

Ponting, Rick, ed. 1986. *Arduous Journey. Canadian Indians and Decolonization*. Toronto: McClelland and Stewart. This reader contains 18 essays documenting the struggle of Canadian Indians toward self-determination.

Porter, John. 1965. *The Vertical Mosaic: An Analysis of Class and Power in Canada*. Toronto: University of Toronto Press. This is Canada's classic study of the relationship between ethnicity on the one hand and attainment of occupational status, income, and educational status on the other hand. No volume approaches this one in dealing with these relationships over earlier decades. Also discussed is the question of how difficult it was for minority group members to achieve positions in the elite, and why it was difficult.

B: Gender

22. Theoretical Approaches to the Study of Women

Eileen Saunders

At first glance, the profusion of analytical work on women might seem confusing or bewildering. However, in spite of this apparent diversity, it is possible to classify the attempts of social scientists to make sense of the current situation of women into three major approaches. This classification is based on the different ways each approach defines the problem to be analysed, and then explains the "problem" in question. The *conservative approach* focusses on sex differentiation, and argues that differentiated sex roles can be explained by the contribution this differentiation makes to the maintenance of social order. The *feminist approach* argues that sex differentiation also results in inequality in the relations between the sexes, and argues that this situation is largely a

Revised from Eileen Saunders, "Theoretical Approaches to the Study of Women," in Dennis Forcese and Stephen Richer, eds., *Social Issues: Sociological Views of Canada* (Scarborough: Prentice-Hall Canada, 1982) pp. 218-35. Reprinted with permission.

consequence of cultural values and ideologies. The *Marxist approach* agrees with the feminist that differentiation and inequality go hand-in-hand, but locates the explanation of this relationship at the level of class analysis.

It is important then to appreciate how each approach defines and explains the emergence and persistence of the patterns of social relations between men and women. Moreover, it is necessary to determine the implications for social change in each approach. Only then will we be able to evaluate the scientific contribution each is able to make to our ability to understand the contemporary position of women in Canadian society.

CONSERVATISM

The thrust of the *conservative* approach is on the *imperative* nature of sex differentiation. There are three variants of conservatism: the biological, the psychological, and the sociological. Their common link, in spite of their different conceptions of the nature of the imperative in question, is the retention of a static conception of the relation between the individual and society, and an evolutionary or gradualist approach to social change. While we will focus particularly on the sociological approach, a brief discussion of the other two views serves as a useful backdrop.

The *biological* and *psychobiological* arguments are deterministic views which posit a *natural* basis for sex inequality. The thrust of research in the biological tradition has been on the anatomical, genetic, and hormonal differences between males and females. The psychobiological stream has focussed on psychological differences in such areas as skill, aptitude, attitude, temperament, and other characteristics which are viewed as related to biological differences. Both positions have come under a great deal of criticism in recent years for their tendency to *assume* a direct link between biology and behaviour.

The critiques levelled against the *biological argument* can be classified into three general categories. First, there is the failure of the various assumed relationships between biology and behaviour to "stand up" in cross-cultural comparisons. We know, for example, that the assumed correlation between hormonal levels at certain periods in the female menstrual cycle and emotional states such as tension, anxiety, or irritability does not exist in many other cultures (see Bardwick, 1971:27-33). This indicates that emotional fluctuations during hormonal cycles are to a large extent *learned* rather than innate behaviour.

A second problem is the tendency to ignore or downplay the impact of cultural patterns on a particular sex difference. Margaret Mead, for example, found that in Arapesh culture, the lack of emphasis on strenuous work for *either* sex decreased the differences in somatotype—particularly muscular build (Mead: 1935). In other words, there *is* some social capacity to affect sex differences through cultural practices.

Finally, a taxonomy of particular biological sex differences in no way serves as an explanation for the differential social *evaluation* of these differences. To argue that women, for biological reasons, perform tasks associated with the family sphere cannot in itself lead us to an understanding of how differential rewards and values are attached to the different tasks.

Very similar objections are raised against the psychobiological approach to sex inequality. To illustrate this, we can point to the classic position in the psychobiological tradition: the work of Sigmund Freud. Infamous for his view that "anatomy is destiny," Freud attempted to tie the unequal social treatment of the sexes to sex differences in personality patterns which emerge as a response to physiological differences. The cornerstone of his argument is the assumption that "penis envy" in the female child necessarily persists into adulthood in the form of feelings of inferiority, passivity, and an unhealthy "superego." The implication is that the psychological inferiority of women is translated into inferior social status.

The major problem with the Freudian position is that it cannot be tested. The assumption, for example, of an innate faulty female superego is not open to question, given that Freud sees the latter as part of the unconscious aspect of personality. Moreover, even those assumptions which are testable have been shown to lack empirical support; e.g., the role of phallic gratification in personality development (see Nielsen, 1979:106).

A related problem, and one shared by the biological variant of conservatism, is Freud's attempt to use an invariant to explain a variant. Anthropological research has shown that female role behaviour *has* varied from one culture to another. (For a review of this literature, see Quinn, 1977; Friedl, 1975; Reiter, 1975.) Therefore the attempt to reduce the origin of female behaviour to an invariant or universal psychobiological make-up simply is inadequate. It just is not able to explain the cross-cultural fact of diversity. It is largely for this reason that sociologists have attempted to locate the explanation for sex differences in terms of social factors.

The *sociological* variant of conservatism shifts the explanation of sex differentiation from a *natural* imperative to a *social* imperative. The classic illustration of this position is the *Functionalist* framework of analysis.

The basic theme in functional analyses is that society is an integrated and relatively stable system composed of interdependent parts or elements. Social order exists when the different parts of a society are integrated, or in equilibrium. However, because these parts are interdependent a change in any one will have consequences for the system as a whole. Social change, in this context, becomes the adaptive adjustment process whereby the equilibrium of the system is reconstituted. The major concern of the functionalists is thus to discover the *function* or contribution which each social element makes to the needs of the system, to social integration, and to societal equilibrium.

Functionalist analysis begins with the assumption that the origin and the persistence of differential sex roles can both be explained by reference to the contribution these differences make to the maintenance of social stability. In other words, functionalists attempt to explain sex-role patterns by reference to the *invariant social needs* which necessitate a particular form of sex-role arrangement. This analysis of *functional neces-*

sity is assumed to hold true for both pre-industrial and industrial societies, although specific features of the sex-role pattern may vary.

Functionalists have argued that, in early hunting and gathering societies, sex-role differentiation was a consequence of two basic survival requisites: reproduction and subsistence. They argued that the mobility of the female was restricted due to the lengthy period of dependence of her children for nursing, care, and protection. Because of the lack of cultural or technological alternatives (e.g., bottle-feeding, prepared foods, etc.) the female was unable to share in the major subsistence activities with males. This is particularly the case with hunting, which required long periods of absence from the community. The sexual division of tasks and labour which emerged was thus a *complementary* division of interdependent roles along sex lines, rather than a stratification or ranking by sex. Moreover, it was a division of labour which met basic survival requisites and thus ensured the stability and persistence of the society.

A similar analysis is employed by functionalists who examine the persistence of a sexual differentiation in modern industrial societies. Two key assumptions are retained:

1. the complementarity of sex roles and positions; and
2. the functional necessity of sex-role differentiation.

An important example of this type of analysis is the work of Talcott Parsons. Parsonian functionalism, while sharing the basic principles of general functionalist analysis, also served as benchmark in the orientation of sociological research toward sex roles. It attempts to understand the position and role of women in industrial society in terms of their relationship to the *family institution.*

Parsons begins with an attempt to discern the relationship between the kinship structure and the occupational structure of modern societies. Social status is assumed to stem from both structures; one is *ascribed* (given) a status through membership in a particular family unit, and one *achieves* (earns) a status through differential participation in a hierarchial occupational system. The essential element in the nuclear family form is the emotional bond, between both husband and wife, and parent and child. The defining element in the occupational structure, on the other hand, is the competition ethic between participants for the unequal rewards attached to differentially evaluated positions. The dilemma in modern society, argued Parsons, is the possibility of destabilizing the nuclear family through the presence of a competition structure external to the family. In other words, if husband and wife engage in occupational competition external to the family, the solidarity of the family structure would be threatened. The resolution of the dilemma for Parsons is the evolution of an internal structure for the nuclear family which is adapted to the functional imperatives of the occupational system. Sex-role differentiation is essential to that structure, if kinship competition is to be avoided.

The internal structure, sustained by cultural norms prescribing family relationships, is based on a division between *instrumental roles* and *expressive roles.* Instrumental roles are those defined as achievement- and task-oriented and related largely to occupational behaviour outside the family. Expressive roles are those defined as emotionally oriented and related largely to integrative behaviour within the family. Parsons argues that women are logically more suitable for the latter, given their biological tie to childbirth and nursing, roles which already include expressive components. Instrumental roles are therefore best suited to males who do not have a "pre-established" relationship to the familial role.

Parsons argues that the effect of the sex-role segregation is to contribute to the stability of the family institution directly, and thus to the welfare of the entire social system indirectly. The positive aspects of this structure are highlighted by Parsons:

> There are perhaps two primary functional aspects of this situation. In the first place . . . it eliminates any competition for status, especially as between husband and wife. . . . Second, it aids in clarity . . . by making the status of the family in the community relatively definite and unequivocal. (Parsons, 1954:192)

It is important to point out that Parsons does not consider the fact of sex-role differentiation as evidence for the presence of sex-role inequality. Quite the opposite; Parsons posits an egalitarian relationship between males and females for several reasons:

1. Marriage, he argues, is necessarily an egalitarian relationship, given the fact that the social status of the wife is identical to her husband's through status ascription to the family unit.
2. The housewife has *functional equivalents* to compensate for her segregation from occupational achievement. He argues that such equivalents exist in the form of the "glamorous" female, the "humanistic" volunteer, or the "good companion" roles.
3. For females who reject the expressive role, there exists an equal opportunity structure in the occupational system. Thus, those women who are unequal in this context are assumed to be the products of *individual* failure to seize opportunity.

In keeping with the overall functionalist focus on order and stability, Parsons defines non-traditional sex roles as dysfunctional or threatening to the total system. It is in this context that he introduces the functional necessity of the nuclear family form. The family is more than a mere agency for reproduction, in his scheme; it is the principal agency for assuring the continuation of social norms, and values, and patterned relationships, via its role in the primary socialization of children. In addition, it serves an important role as a "cooling-out" agency, an arena where tension derived in the occupational sphere may be diffused. Thus the functional significance of the nuclear family is ultimately found in its performance as an integrating agency, as an institution which reaffirms and recreates the cultural order in each succeeding generation.

Social change in Parsonian functionalism occurs as an adaptive response to an alteration in the relationship between elements in the total system. In his later work, there emerges an assumption that certain changes in the industrial structure of modern societies would bring about a gradual equalization in sex-role behaviour. Essentially the argument is that sex-role segregation will ultimately become increasingly *dysfunctional* given changes in the occupational system which result in a demand for increased female participation. In a context of role equalization, persisting sex inequality would be seen as a consequence of the individual failure of particular women to seize educational, economic, legal, and political opportunities.

In summary, functionalism is a framework which argues that differentiation by sex is functionally related to the needs of the system at a particular stage of evolution. Segregation of males in the labour process and females in the family in modern society serves a stabilizing function, while equality of opportunity in the labour process serves as a protective mechanism against the possibility of inequality. Because change is an evolutionary process, there is little need for an interventionist politics to redress sex-role differences.

Evaluation

There are several arguments one can raise against the sociological variant of the conservative paradigm. First, the major impact of Parsonian functionalism is to direct the focus of sociological research on women to the relationship of women to the family. Because functionalism assumes that the primary position and role of women is within the family unit, it generally ignores the role women play in the paid labour force. Moreover, a functionalist discussion of the female role in the family is usually couched in normative terms. In other words the "effective" role of the housewife and mother is conceptualized largely as a socializing role having little utilitarian value in an economic sense. Second, equality of opportunity is too often assumed rather than demonstrated. Parsons, and functionalists who followed in his wake, often choose to ignore various forms of opportunity restriction such as discrimination in employment, channelling of career aspirations, and the differential socialization of the sexes in the family. There are institutionalized forms of sex discrimination which functionalist theory does not and cannot address.

Third, Parson's assumption of an egalitarian structure within the family seems to be based more on a North American conception of romantic love than a realistic appraisal of status differences between husband and wife. One cannot ignore the possibility that the instrumental, or income-earning, role of the male may place him in a position of greater control within the family. Functionalist theory is not able to account for the possibility of a hierarchy of power in the family unit. This is also true of the functionalist conception of "alternative roles" for women which are deemed to be *functional equivalents* to the male occupational role. Given that social status in Western industrial societies derives from occupational achievement, it is difficult to discern how being a "good companion" to one's husband is equivalent in terms of derived social and interpersonal reward.

Fourth, the functionalist focus on sex differentiation rather than sex inequality ignores the fact that social rewards, and the power to control those rewards, attach to the differentiated positions in a critically different manner. Thus the social structuring of the roles men and women play goes beyond mere specialization in tasks. There is also a differentiation in reward and status which is necessarily involved.

Fifth, the functionalists fail to pursue the question of whether there is a link between the female role in the family and the female role in the labour force. Instead, they argue that the family serves as an "allocating agency" for placing women in the occupational hierarchy. It is her family status, not her gender, which is seen as the determinate factor in the process (see for example Parkin, 1971:14-16). This is a questionable argument, one which is open to empirical test. We will return to this issue in the following sections.

Finally, one must question the functionalist assumption that sex-role differentiation is an *integrative* mechanism ensuring social stability. Functionalist theory in general is an *order-oriented* analytical framework seeking to demonstrate the functional contribution of each societal element to social order. Thus, in order to "prove" the functionality of sex-role differentiation, it is necessary to *posit* an ideology of equality of opportunity

and an egalitarian family structure. Such a position leads functionalism into the dilemma of ignoring or explaining away the inequalities which do in fact exist between the sexes. As a result, integration remains an assumption in functionalist theory and serves to mask the issue of whether sex-role differentiation may in fact translate into sex-role inequality.

FEMINISM

Feminism is an analytical framework which emerged as a counterpoint to the conservative position. While different feminists disagree on the type of intervention necessary to effect change, they all focus on the exclusion and discrimination of women in the distribution of socially valued resources such as marketable skills, wealth, prestige, and power. The issue then for feminism is more than sex differentiation; it is sex inequality. The explanatory thrust of the feminist argument focusses on *ideological factors* in the culture of a society, factors which serve to justify the exclusion and subordination of women.

A key concept in feminist analysis is *patriarchy*, a term which first received popular exposure in the work of K. Millet (1969). Though often used loosely in the literature, patriarchy essentially refers to a hierarchial system of power in which males possess greater economic and social privilege than females. This differential power is reflected in differential sex roles. Explicit in a feminist position is the insistence that patriarchy is a universal feature of all known societies.

Sex inequality is located in the relationships between males and females; these relationships are thought by feminists to be the manifestation of a cultural system which defines women as inferior to men. In other words, once patriarchy emerges, it is maintained and reproduced through an ideological system which justifies inequality. The *original basis* for the emergence of patriarchy lies in the importance of biological differences in size, strength, and relation to reproduction between the sexes in early pre-industrial societies. The male's biological "advantage" allows him to take control of the important resources in society such as food, land, weapons, and implements of production. More importantly though, according to feminist theory, the economic and social rewards which this control allows are maintained through the cultural definition of appropriate sex roles. Thus, the persistence of male privilege, or patriarchy, is ensured through the emergence of a culture which defines men as superior. As a result, while biological differences are now no longer as important in a technological industrial society, the preservation of male privilege continues because of the persistence of a "patriarchal ideology." This is not to suggest that sex inequality is apparent only in the realm of ideas, attitudes, and values. Rather, feminist theory argues that the exclusion of women from access to economic or social power can only be understood by reference to the role of ideology. They argue that ideology has replaced biology as the determinant in the reproduction of sexism.

Feminist work has focussed on two areas of inquiry: the role of the family as a mechanism in transmitting patriarchal ideology, and the role of various socio-economic institutional practices in excluding women from equal opportunities with men.

Essentially, feminists share with functionalists a conception of the nuclear family as a socializing agency. Where they differ is in their conception of the content and conse-quence of such socialization. Functionalists argue that family socialization allows for the integration of the individual into a stable, consensual culture. Feminists, on the other hand, claim that the role of family socialization is to reaffirm and justify the pattern of segregated, unequal role differentiation. It does this largely through the creation of what Millet calls a *psychic structure* for women which is very different from that of men. The psychic structure for women is predicated on an image of the female as passively related to her social world. De Beauvoir conceptualizes this relation as a dichotomy between male as subject of action and female as object of action (De Beauvior, 1952). The consequences of the differential psychic structure are felt on several levels: women develop a different temperament than men, they have inferior self-images, and channel their motivational aspirations toward different role behaviour. Essentially the argument is a restatement of the "self-fulfilling prophecy" notion which is so popular in socialization research. In other words, if a culture defines men and women differently, and organizes its socialization practices on that assumption, then the consequence is the objective difference in the status of men and women. But the primary level of explanation is the realm of cultural attitudes and expectations which both sexes are socialized into accepting. Because the institution of the family is the first and most important source of cultural ideas, its role in transmitting and reproducing patriarchy is crucial.

As indicated earlier, another body of feminist research focusses on institutional practices which reinforce a patriarchal system. Again, these practices are assumed to be manifestations of cultural beliefs about women. The unity of this approach lies in the attempt to demonstrate how the consistent ideology of women as being different from men in temperament, skill, and attitude is translated into practices which exclude women from access to institutional positions. For example, Reuther (1974) has argued that the ideological association of the male image with divinity figures in various religions has supported the official exclusion of women from participation in certain levels of the religious hierarchies. Therefore, the fact of male control of theological decision-making is maintained through ideological support which defines theology as a male preserve.

The feminist consensus regarding a definition of the problem is unfortunately not reflected in feminists' approach to a solution to the problem. The feminist framework is polarized at the level of intervention strategy between views which can be loosely called liberal feminism and radical feminism.

Liberal feminism is predicated on the assumption that the social system is "reformable," that patriarchy can be eliminated within the parameters of society as it now exists. This approach retains a classic conception of liberal democracy as a *meritocracy,* a system providing equal opportunity to achieve unequal rewards. In this view, the problem is to "restore" the meritocracy so that women can compete equally with men. Given equal opportunity, all individuals can rise or fall to their own level of merit, rather than have their mobility predetermined by their gender. Thus, intervention for liberal feminists is directed largely toward the occupational sphere and involves the removal of cultural attitudes about gender which impede equal opportunity. In positing equal opportunity as their goal, they focus their attack on both the socialization process which transmits patriarchal beliefs and the legislative process which permits particular discriminatory institutional practices. Thus liberal feminists would argue, for example,

in favour of content regulation of educational texts or the broadcast media in order to control sexist images. At the same time they would lobby for the enforcement of equal pay legislation to prevent wage discrimination at work. Actually the two levels of intervention are interrelated in that it is assumed that if one can expose myths about working women through reeducation (e.g., the assumption that women only work for "pin money"), the justification for unfair employer practices is necessarily removed. Liberal feminism, then, does not question the premise of hierarchial positions and rewards in society; what it questions is the distribution of those positions and rewards on the basis of gender.

Radical feminism shares with liberal feminism a belief that effective change must involve an alteration in cultural ideology. However, they disagree on the nature of intervention. Radical feminism does not place particular emphasis on the occupational discrimination of women; the latter is dealt with as merely one manifestation of a deeper problem. In radical feminist strategy, the psychic structure formed in family socialization is defined as the key target of attack. Consequently, the family institution is defined as the major agent in the reproduction of inequality. the implication for strategy then involves an attempt to restructure the family institution in order to strip it of its patriarchal form. There are some radical feminists who suggest this be accomplished on an individual basis, primarily using the technique of "consciousness-raising." The latter is conceived of as a process whereby individual women, through dialogue with others, come to see the patriarchal form and roots of their own "psychic structures" and come to translate that new-found awareness into attempts to regain control over their own development. It is essentially an individual, voluntaristic model for change.

There are other radical feminists, however, who question the very existence of heterosexual marriage and the family institution. They argue that the contemporary form of the family is premised on a dependency relationship between the male and the female, a dependency which is personified even at the level of sexuality: hence, they believe the elimination of sex inequality requires the abolition of monogamous marriage and the nuclear family. Once the family institution is destroyed, patriarchy as a power system will collapse.

What emerges in the latter version of radical feminism is a conception of a fundamental alteration in society as we know it, rather than a reform in certain elements of society as liberal feminism suggests. Moreover the model of change moves from an individual to a collective level and questions the very basis of hierarchical privilege. As Firestone argues, a hierarchical society breeds a "power psychology" (1970:12) which is at the root of all forms of oppression against women, children, ethnic groups, etc. Thus a challenge of power psychology in its sexist form implies a challenge to its basis: hierarchical society. Radical feminism of this type has not yet clarified its image of an alternative form of society to modern capitalism other than to suggest socialism is not the solution. Moreover, as a political strategy, it shies away from violent confrontation, arguing that a revolutionary is in reality a teacher who will use the power of ideas to provoke radical change.

Evaluation

In summary, feminism is a framework which assumes the universality of patriarchy and attempts to explain it by reference to ideological factors. There are several problems inherent in this approach, both at the level of explanation and of intervention. First, there is a tendency toward biological determinism in the explanation of the origin of patriarchy. It is assumed that biological differences universally hindered the female in her access to participation in, or control over production in early societies. However, anthropological studies indicate that the productive role of women in many hunting and gathering societies equaled and sometimes surpassed that of men.

A second, and more serious, problem is the characterization of patriarchy as a universal system of power. On the one hand, this analysis fails to specify how patriarchy changes in form from one historical period to another; for instance, sexism in feudal societies cannot be simply equated with sexism in modern capitalist societies (Mitchell, 1971). Thus, to treat patriarchy as an ahistorical, autonomous system of male power ignores its specific features in particular periods. On the other hand, the feminist conception of patriarchy as a system of male power over females ignores the differential relationship particular groups of men and women have to patriarchy. In other words, not all men benefit equally from patriarchy as feminist theory would suggest; often, a particular class of men benefits more than others (e.g., male employers of cheap female workers). In the same vein, not all women suffer equally under patriarchy. Particular groups of women may have more access to status and reward than others (e.g., middle- and upper-class women). To simply portray the contradiction as lying between men as a group and women as a group is to mask the actual contradictions in status which exist *within* each sex group. This "glossing" of the problem is reflected in particular strategies for intervention. For example, legislation directed at equal opportunity to compete ignores the fact that different strata of women, depending on their class background, bring different resources to the labour market. In addition, consciousness-raising may be more of a middle-class luxury. For many women, it is the lack of basic life necessities which is their most immediate concern.

A third and related problem is the primacy of ideology in feminist analysis. To argue that patriarchal ideas create particular structural conditions for women ignores the possibility that patriarchal ideas may emerge as a consequence of and support to particular material conditions. In other words, the belief that women are not as "valuable" workers as men in the labour market may be the result of the necessity to maintain a relatively cheap labour pool. We shall see in the following discussion how Marxists make this argument in reversing the causal sequence of sex inequality.

Finally, feminism fails to analyse the specific links *between* the female role in the family and the female role in the labour market. They are treated as two separate dimensions of inquiry, other than to suggest patriarchal ideology shapes females status in each sphere. It is necessary to inquire whether the structure of the family institution at a given point in history is related to the structure of the labour market. In this way one could investigate whether female entrance into the occupational sphere is shaped by factors in women's familial position. The failure to tie these two spheres of female participation analytically is reflected in the polarization of feminist theory strategically. On the one hand you have liberal feminists fighting for reform of institutions on a piecemeal basis through legislative lobbying, educational content regulation, rights within unions, political representation, and other such changes. On the other hand you have radical feminists focussing on inequality in the family through improved birth control rights, contractual marriage, or ultimately abolition of marriage. The fatal flaw

is their failure to analyse and deal with the interdependence between these various manifestations of sex inequality.

MARXISM

Marxism is a theoretical framework which focusses on the relation between the way a society organizes production and the ideologies which develop to protect the class interests of those who control production. In this context, Marxism argues that the position of women reflects the class relations which emerge within a capitalist form of production. For Marxists, these relations *exploit* the female, as a worker in the labour force and *oppress* her as a form of property in the family institution. Her exploitation, according to Marxism, has no specific features outside of the general mechanisms which exploit all workers, and her oppression or powerlessness in the family is determined by factors in capitalist society which are external to the family institution. Thus, Marxist analysis sees the female as simply one more victim of capitalism, and the material conditions which are perceived to underlie her "victimization" are seen as identical to those which underlie exploitation in general.

Because Karl Marx himself wrote very little on the *origin* of sex inequality, it is necessary to go to the work of his friend and theoretical collaborator Frederick Engels for the classic Marxist position on the emergence of women as a subordinate group. Engels' argument, presented in *The Origin of the Family, Private Property and the State,* is essentially that the original subordination of women is historically tied to the emergence of *private property* in agricultural and herding societies (allowed for in the transition from a subsistence to a surplus form of society). The monogamous family, and the isolation of women to guarantee sexual exclusivity, evolved as means to ensure the "legitimate" heirs. Thus the notion of *patriarchy* came to be defined as a relationship reflecting a property relation between husband and wife in the context of the family. In other words, it refers to the fact that the husband controlled the existence and disposal of property in the family.

The important point in Engels' analysis is his claim that earlier forms of society—such as hunting and gathering—were sexually egalitarian and that it was only the emergence of private property which led to a subsequent subordination of the female role. The existence of a sexual division of labour or specialization in tasks in early societies was never questioned by Engels. Instead, he argued that while men and women performed different types of subsistence labour, the absence of production-for-exchange precluded an unequal relationship between them. The crucial step, for Engels, was the development of resources for production which allowed *production-for-exchange* in addition to *production-for-use*. Male tasks tended to be located in the sphere where production resources expanded—e.g., irrigation of land: hence, their labour became part of production-for-exchange. Female tasks, on the other hand, tended to be located in the sphere where production resources were stabilized—e.g., preparation of food for consumption: hence their labour remained part of production-for-use. In Marxist terms they did not receive an *exchange value* (e.g., a wage) for their work. What Engels was attempting to describe was the emergence of a break between two types of labour spheres and the segregation of sexes to different spheres. Moreover, he claims that this break created the condition necessary for the subordinate role of women: their exclusion from participation in "valued" production.

In the industrial transition to early factory capitalism, this break was retained and solidified as a break between a *public sphere* of production and a *private sphere* of the family. This is because the production process was removed entirely from the household locus, and the family (and any labour performed within its boundaries) became a secondary institution which merely reflects the economic relations of production. For Marxists the family is now *epiphenomenal;* its form is a reflection of the material conditions of capitalism. In other words, it is part of the superstructure of society. It performs an essential role for capitalism by being the institution for the appropriation and transmission of private property. Moreover, the female role in the family is argued to be a consequence of women's lack of access to participation in public production, and thus lack of control over property. This is important in informing Marx's conception of patriarchy in capitalism. When Marx made reference to patriarchy, he defined it as a particular relationship of household production whereby the household head owned or controlled the resources of production and organized the labour power of its members (McDonough and Harrison, 1978). For Marxists, patriarchy as a power relationship involving subordination of women to men has no meaning or existence apart from its base in the family institution. More importantly, it is possible, in Marx and Engels' terms, to postulate the disappearance of patriarchal relations *within* a capitalist society. As proof, they refer to the absence of patriarchy among working class or "proletarian" families. They argued that the development of capitalism had led to the increased entry of working class women (and children) into the labour force. Consequently, their role in the family altered to reflect their role in social production; equal exploitation in production supposedly provoked non-oppressive relations in the family. Thus, the patriarchal treatment of women as property is characteristic of the "bourgeois" family, not the proletarian.

> The proletarian is without property; his relation to his wife and children has no longer anything in common with the bourgeois family relations. (Marx and Engels, 1970:25)

The specific Marxist "map" for *intervention* aimed at changing sex inequality is tied to a larger conception of the kind of social change necessary in capitalist society. Since capitalist relations, not men, are defined as the "enemy," consequently capitalist society must be the target of intervention. The model of change suggested by Marxist theory is one of revolutionary alteration in the basic structures of society. Specifically, it calls for a transformation at the level of organization of production whereby class ownership of the means of production is abolished and replaced by a socialist or collective organization of production. The thesis is that the seizure of economic control, at the level of production, by a previously subordinate proletariat class will lead to a transformation in all other social spheres, including the political, the judicial, and the ideological. Marxists posit three specific strategic factors as being necessary to "equalize" the position of women. First, there must be a large-scale entrance of women into the social production labour force. Second, the labour now performed by the housewife in the sphere of the family (caring for children, provision of meals, maintenance tasks such as laundering, etc.) must be transferred to the sphere of social production. Third, the capitalist *form* of the family must be abolished through the elimination of its *raison d'être:* private property. To repeat, in Marxist theory these interventionist policies are linked to the overall pro-

gram of a transition from capitalist to socialist society.

Evaluation

In summary, Marxist analysis redirects our focus to several major issues defined as crucial to the subordinate role of women. To begin, Marxism directs attention to the historical link between *variability* in female status and changes in the form of production in a society. Second, Marxism focusses on patriarchy as a *specific* power relation vested in the family structure. Finally, the Marxist conception of household, or domestic, labour (i.e., production-for-use performed usually by the wife in the context of the family institution) involves a recognition of the "alienating" nature of such work, particularly when the woman is also engaged in wage labour in the public sphere. Thus their argument that:

> The emancipation of women will only be possible when women can take part in production on a large social scale and domestic work no longer claims anything but an insignificant amount of her time. (Engels, 1951:11)

What needs to be questioned is whether the analytical framework of Marxism can fully account for an understanding of sexual inequality. There have been several critiques raised against this position.[1]

One of the more serious flaws in the Marxist argument is its assumption that increased female entrance into public production would bring about an objective equalization in sex status. As we will see more clearly in the following section, one fact which is clear from recent research is the persistence of objective difference in social reward along sex lines *despite* the increased labour force participation of women. What seems to be more important than the entrance of women into the labour force is the *context of entrance.* In other words, it is essential to investigate whether women go into different sectors of the labour market and, if so, what the economic characteristics associated with those sectors actually are. The failure of Marxism to deal with this area of inquiry stems from the absence of any theory regarding *sexual division of labour.* In Marxism, the sex division exists *between* the public and private spheres of labour: there is no conception of it existing both between and *within* the two spheres. As a result, one cannot use Marxist theory to account for the fact that men and women do different and differentially evaluated tasks both in the family and in the public labour force. Moreover, it does not permit one to question whether there is a *link* between female labour in the private sphere and the public sphere.

This relates to a second problem in Marxist analysis. The family sphere is analytically divorced from the economic sphere; there is no theory of the family other than a conception of it as a product of relations in the production process. Labour performed in the family is defined as unproductive in that it creates no value for the capitalist class. The family's main role is characterized as a property institution. This approach conceals, on the one hand, an inquiry into the link between household labour and capitalism and, on the other hand, an analysis of the ideological function of the family. There is recent analytical work which suggests that the labour of housewives *does* provide essential services for capitalism and not just the family unit. Housewives not only provide a new generation of workers through biological reproduction; they also supply capitalism with a continued source of daily labour power through their care and maintenance of the male worker (see Benston, 1969). In other words, the domestic work of women in the home frees the male to devote his energy to creating profit for the capitalist in his public labour.

The ideological role of the family is important in considering whether a particular cultural definition of the family serves certain class interests. For example, if women are defined as dependent on males economically and psychologically in the family, could this provide the labour force with an individual who, when she does seek work, is easier to manipulate (i.e., less militant or more likely to accept low wages). These are important questions, and require investigation in a variety of areas. The problem is that Marxist theory does not offer the analytical tools for even formulating the questions.

Finally, there are aspects of the Marxist definition of patriarchy which require consideration. It is a definition based on property relations; one which assumes that the basis for patriarchy will erode as more women enter the work force. Moreover, patriarchy is conceptualized as residing solely in the family institution. The problem with this approach is its failure to address the role of particular conditions and ideologies outside the family which specifically oppress women as a group. This critique relates back to the problem of a sexually segmented labour force. In other words, if women enter the labour force along the lines of a sexual division of labour (whereby males' jobs are economically and ideologically "superior"), then the basis for her lack of control in the family will *not* be eroded. Recognition of this *dual* nature of female inferiority—lack of control both in the family and outside it—could point to a reworking of the definition of patriarchy.

Thus, Marxism essentially reduces the female problem to women's inability to work or have access to property resources. Consequently, Marxism sets up an "*a priori* symmetry" between feminism and socialism as political movements, without ever demonstrating a real basis for the unity (Mitchell, 1971).

ALTERNATIVE THEORETICAL APPROACHES

We are left with the question of where do we go from here? Obviously, I cannot fully provide an answer here, but I do feel there are certain theoretical and conceptual options which might go a long way toward realizing a stage where we are at least asking the right questions in our research on women.

I am arguing that the traditional alternatives are inadequate as they now stand. However, there exists the possibility of drawing on the contributions of two analytical frameworks, Marxism and feminism. Moreover, analytical work which expresses a foundation in these two traditions has emerged in the past decade. Referred to in the literature as "socialist feminism" or "feminist materialism," this work is still very much in its formative stage as a framework.[2] Nevertheless, its theoretical mandate is clear: to establish the interrelationship of a capitalist mode of production and structures of sex inequality (see, for example, Kuhn and Wolpe, 1978).

The thrust of their work is twofold, and focusses on:

1. the relationship of patriarchal relations to historical modes of production; and

2. the relationship of the organization of the household to the organization of production.

The analytical roots of socialist feminism lie within both feminist and Marxist traditions. Their links with feminist analysis are reflected in the attempt to explain patriarchy as a system of sexual power which cuts across the family sphere *and* the public sphere. However, while socialist feminists recognize the importance of patriarchal ideologies in sustaining power, they reject the ahistorical primacy this concept occupies in feminist analysis. The analytical links with Marxism are found in the focus on the *material base* of inequality and on the *historical variability* of status. Moreover, there is a recognition of the importance of domestic, or household, labour as a form of production, as is suggested by contemporary Marxist arguments. The points of departure from Marxist analysis are found in a reworking of the concept of patriarchy and a reanalysis of the interaction of the family institution and social production.

The ideological support for the particular expression of the sex division of labour is found in the "social construction of gender" (Young, 1978:125). In other words, it involves the socializing process through which symbolic structures frame the acquisition and internalization of the attitudes and behavioural expectations embedded in sex roles.

The conceptualization of the sex division of labour as the systematic allocation within, or exclusion from, production processes is sufficiently broad to allow for the consideration of both the family and the productive spheres. In other words, socialist feminists would ask whether women are allocated solely to production-for-use in particular periods; whether they are excluded from particular types of production-for-exchange in other periods; and, finally, how sex criteria are used in varying periods as a basis for allocation and exclusion.

The argument is not that sex subordination is a necessary constant consequence of a sex division of labour. Rather, the primary question is how the *particular* operation of this division, in conjunction with other relationships (e.g., capitalist relations of production), can intensify or restrict power differentials between men and women. A related question is how economic conditions in various historical periods can intensify or restrict the operation and emphasis of a sex division of labour. This is precisely where socialist feminist analysis goes beyond previous explanatory frameworks; it offers a basis for investigating the *interplay* of political economy and patriarchy.

Socialist feminism is not simply a synthesis of Marxism and feminism. Rather, it attempts to go beyond the limitations or inadequacies of each and to develop new insights into the phenomenon of sex subordination.

Socialist feminists reconceptualize patriarchy as a set of historically situated relations of sex subordination within the overall organization of production and symbolic structures. As a force in history, patriarchy interacts with other sets of relationships within varying modes of production. Socialist feminist analysis is not as concerned with

the penultimate issue of the *origin* of subordination in early societal forms; rather it deals with the question of the *expression* and *maintenance* of sex subordination in various periods. This is because dominance and subordination are historically-specific concepts; they make sense only in the context of the prevailing social arrangements.

Thus, in order to investigate the expression and maintenance of patriarchy, one must look at both its material and ideological forms. Socialist feminism argues that the material expression of patriarchy is the *sex division of labour,* and that it is supported ideologically by particular *cultural values and beliefs* regarding sex roles. The sex division of labour has two levels of appearance (Young, 1978:125).

1. It is a systematic *allocation* of individuals to positions in the process of production on the basis of sex criteria.
2. It is a systematic *exclusion* of individuals from positions in the production process and social relations at large on the basis of sex criteria.

NOTES

1 It should be noted that while there is some support for his *general* account, there is considerable disagreement among anthropologists as to the evolutionary sequence Engels posits.
2 It is generally agreed that J. Mitchell's book

Woman's Estate (1971) was the first serious attempt to rework Marxist theory on women through a redefinition of the materialist basis of sex inequality. The most intense period of theoretical work, however, has been since 1975.

REFERENCES

Barwick, J.
  1971   *The Psychology of Women.* New York: Harper & Row.

Benston, M.
  1969   "The Political Economy of Women's Liberation," *Monthly Review,* 21, no.
          4:13-27.

Engels, Frederick
  1951   *The Woman Question.* New York: International Publishers.
  1972   *The Origin of the Family: Private Property and the State,* ed. E. Leacock. New York:
          International Publishers.

Firestone, S.
  1970   *The Dialectic of Sex.* New York: Bantam Books.

Freud, Sigmund
  1933   "Essay on Femininity," *New Introductory Lectures on Psychoanalysis.* New York:
          W.W. Norton & Co.

Marx, Karl, and Frederick Engels
  1970   *The Communist Manifesto.* New York: Pathfinder Press edition.

McDonough R., and R. Harrison
  1978   "Patriarchy and Relations of Production," in *Feminism and Materialism,* ed.
          A. Kuhn and A. Wolpe. Boston: Routledge and Kegan Paul.

Mead, Margaret
  1935   *Sex and Temperament.* New York: Mentor.

Millet, K.
  1969   *Sexual Politics.* New York: Avon Books.

Mitchell, J.
  1971   *Woman's Estate.* New York: Pantheon.

Nielson, J.
  1979   *Sex in Society: Perspectives on Stratification.* Belmont, California: Wadsworth.

Parkin, F.
  1971   *Class Inequality and Political Order.* St. Albans, England: Paladin.

Parsons, Talcott
  1954   *Essays in Sociological Theory.* New York: Free Press.

Reuther, R.
  1974   *Religion and Sexism.* New York: Simon and Schuster.

B. Gender

23. Sexual Inequality and Children's Play

Stephen Richer

The problem of sexual inequality has been the catalyst for much social science research in the last two decades. The research, however, has predominantly focussed on status and income attainment among adults, where the major ideological premises maintaining such inequality are already in place (e.g., Armstrong and Armstrong, 1975). My conviction is that in order to fully understand the dynamics of the reproduction of sexual inequality, one must consider those early stages of social development that characterize very young children. Indeed, the parallels between the inequality manifested in such phenomena as so-called "male bonding" (Tiger, 1969) and labour market segmentation (Armstrong and Armstrong, 1978), and the sex-segregated play of boys and girls, are striking. What this evokes is a process of increasing vertical differentiation of the sexes, begun in childhood and strengthened and maintained throughout the life cycle.

This particular paper summarizes what we know about early childhood interaction according to sex, goes on to present some primary research data on cross-sex play (a key, I shall argue, to any assault on structured sexual inequality), and concludes with some suggestions for further work.

SEX AND CHILDREN'S INTERACTION

Sexual inequality is a phenomenon which is manifested at every phase of the life cycle. A crucial phase, however, is early childhood, where the taken-for-granted world of meanings about males and females is initially formed. A quick perusal of the literature on children's play reveals a world very early segregated into that of boys and girls. First, boys' activities differ from those of girls. Various studies of young children reveal boys play-

Revised from the article of the same name in *The Canadian Review of Sociology and Anthropology*, vol. 21, no. 2 (May 1984) pp. 166-80. Reprinted with permission.

264

ing more active games while girls for the most part played house or school, and were typically involved in more sedentary types of activities (Richer, 1979). In general, boys monopolize physical, competitive, outdoor, and team games, while girls tend towards less physical, solitary, or dyadic activities in an indoor setting (Schwartzman, 1978; Sutton-Smith, 1972; Richer 1982a, 1982b).

Different activity interests and/or play styles thus coincide with segregated play. Even when children are forced into joint activities, however, or when there are no opportunities for expressing acitivity interest, sexual differentiation is conspicuous. For example, games involving an explicit selection of classmates (like Farmer in the Dell) invariably produce an inordinate amount of same-sex choices. Further, sex-segregated eating groups at lunchtime are the norm, as are sexually homogeneous classroom seating arrangements (Richer, 1979).

The above facts about children's play imply only a horizontal differentiation of the sexes, mainly according to interest. This is not the case, however. The differentiation is accompanied by a hierarchical component, in that both boys and girls evaluate boys' activities and boys in general more positively than they do girls and girls' activities. As I summarized it elsewhere (Richer, 1982a):

> . . . A recurring negation of girls by boys was manifested in the phenomenon of "girl germs." Among the children we observed, a boy coming into physical contact with a girl was the occasion for the enactment of an activity which can be described, with some apology to ethnographers, as a purification ritual. The only way to prevent one from catching girl germs was for the stricken boy to cross his fingers as soon as possible, preferably while still in contact with the girl. The fact that the expression "boy germs" was never used by the girls, and that in

general they made no effort to challenge the girl germs label, is evidence, I believe, of the very early acceptance of both sexes of a hierarchical division between males and females.

As intimated earlier, then, we have a striking isomorphism between the very early vertical differentiation in children's play and the situation among adults of occupational segregation in the labour market. The issue which concerns me is how this seemingly closed cycle might be overcome through a restructuring of children's play. The assumption is that if boys and girls can be brought together in play situations, many of the stereotypes held by each sex about the other might be weakened. It seems to me that at least three basic questions must be explored to this end: (1) Are there already some activities in which boys and girls play together? (2) Under what conditions does such play occur? (3) Exactly when in the life cycle does sex-segregated play emerge?

These questions led me to a systematic review of the play literature. What little material I was able to find on cross-sex play confirmed the rarity of this phenomenon; play in a wide range of societies is largely sex-segregated. Further, on those occasions when the sexes *are* observed together, it is typically to engage in some variant of what I shall call courtship activity. Virtually all the major play ethnographies describe at least one game of this sort, played by children from seven to 16 years of age (see Sutton-Smith, 1972). The most common type is a chasing game, in which girls chase boys and kiss them when they are caught. If the boy is caught, a kiss can be given by one or several girls. In a variant of this, several boys might themselves catch one of their number and bring the typically wildly resisting boy to the girls to be kissed. Indeed, the boys often assist in this process by holding their peer down so that he can more easily meet his fate. (The image evoked is that of a sacrificial offering.) It is striking that boys rarely do the chasing, and that when they do it is to push or pull hair rather than to kiss. This is yet another indicator of the greater value seemingly attached to boys by girls than by boys to girls.

Such games clearly perpetuate traditional sex-role relationships, both because they reinforce the notion that males are more desirable than females, and because they implicitly suggest that the major impetus for cross-sex interaction is some kind of sexual activity. The idea that boys and girls play together without this sexual component seems a foreign one in that very little non-courtship cross-sex play is evident, either from the play literature or from my own observations. Figure 23-1 illustrates the point (the circle represents all play activity).

That is, most children's play is sex-segregated, and when they do play together the predominant activity is some form of courtship game. My interest is in the very small triangle of cross-sex, non-courtship play. These activities transcend the sex-differences manifested in the two other types of play. If it were possible to isolate the condi-

tions under which it occurred, we would gain much needed insight into the factors related to the perpetuation of sexual inequality among children. At the same time, as suggested earlier, research might be done into the evolution of sex-segregated play itself. At what age does this typically occur and what factors appear important in this process?

In order to address these questions we observed three groups of children—one older group and two preschool groups. The former was the group of 20 camp children alluded to earlier (ranging in age from six to 14). Thirty hours of participant observation was carried out in the camp, with each day of the week covered at least once. Our observation focussed mainly on instances of cross-sex play. When one such instance was observed a complete description of the event was secured. We eventually organized these descriptions around three variables we believe central to understanding cross-sex play: the activity involved; the social setting (i.e., when and where the activity occurred); and the sex-age composition of the play group.

The other two groups were utilized in

FIGURE 23-1   Types of play

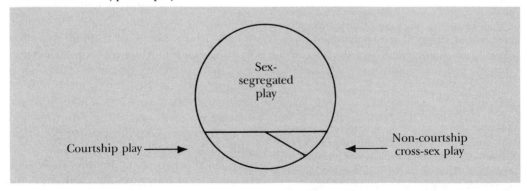

order to trace the evolution of sex-segregated play. Since the literature revealed that this phenomenon is already strongly developed in the first year of public schooling (i.e., by the age of four to five), we observed two groups of three- and four-year-olds in day-care settings. One was a fee-paying centre containing 16 girls and 12 boys from executive and professional families, while the other was a subsidized centre serving largely working class children (14 girls and 13 boys). Each group was observed for a total of six hours. The specific question addressed was the following: Is the sex-segregated play so conspicuous among school children also evident in children not yet in the public system? A well-documented answer to this question should shed some light on the issue of the time at which sex-segregated play begins, as well as helping in speculation on factors related to its emergence.

CROSS-SEX PLAY IN A CAMP SETTING

Our observations in the camp confirmed the pattern of sex-differentiated play intermingled with some courtship activity (teasing, flirting, and some chasing). One incident in particular highlights the power of the segregation norm, particularly among boys. This occurred while teams were being chosen for a morning baseball game. Two boys were captains and both proceeded to select players, choosing only boys (this despite the fact that one of the girls was acknowledged to be a better player than at least half of the boys). When only the girls remained, one of the captains refused to select a girl, a position quickly adopted by his counterpart on the other team. Despite counsellor efforts the game proceeded

without the girls. It should be pointed out, however, that the boys' rejection of girls in competitive and physical activities was partially supported by the girls themselves. By and large the idea of participating in the same game with boys was not an attractive proposition to most girls. A typical pattern showed initial participation followed by withdrawal from the activity. When we queried them on this the reason invariably given was the aggressiveness of the boys: "it's too rough"; or "they play too rough."

A clearly important variable for older children concerning the extent of cross-sex play is thus the type of activity involved. Any physical activity with a strong competitive component is likely to produce little if any cross-sex interaction. Indeed, on the few occasions when we observed cross-sex play, it was almost always associated with either a non-physical activity or a physical activity devoid of competition. Examples of the first are games like monopoly and dominoes (the latter a particular favourite). Popular examples of the second were a simple game of catch, and recreational swimming. The latter produced a fair amount of cross-sex play in the form of splashing and dunking. Activities in which physical strength is irrelevant for participation and/or success thus had the greatest probability of eliciting cross-sex interaction.

Apart from the activity, we also found the setting (i.e., the time and place of the activity) to be of considerable importance. Cross-sex play typically occurred outside the formal camp program, the most common time being between 8:30 and 9:00 in the morning. Although the camp began officially at 9:00 A.M., many parents dropped off their children early on the way to work. Although this time period often produced considerable running around, on some days it became the occasion for relatively quiet talk and the playing of board games in small groups. In sharp contrast to the modal pattern, no sex differentiation was evident, with both boys and girls involved as players in the same game. Further, the typical verbal teasing and sex-based name calling was conspicuously absent. Also of interest was the area in which these games were played—the stage area at the far end of the hall. This was the furthest point from which the staff met every morning to plan the day's program. Indeed, often the children would draw the stage curtain in order to not be visible to the staff.

There was a pronounced difference between this cross-sex interaction that was relatively easy and without self-consciousness and the tension that emerged once the formal program began; the difference was highlighted in the field notes of both observers. Despite the cross-sex interaction characteristic of these pre-camp waiting periods, as soon as the children were assembled in the "morning circle," patterns of sex-segregation emerged, with the boys and girls typically clustered in non-overlapping groups. Why might this be the case? I would suggest that when the entire group of children is assembled, major norms (in this case non-fraternization with members of the opposite sex) become much more likely to be operative, particularly if adults are present. The argument is that deviance is more likely to be overlooked when only a part of the community is present. However, public deviance (that occurring in the presence of everyone) must be dealt with to preserve the "*conscience collective*" (Durkheim, 1893). The significance of the adult presence lies in the fact that the particular norm of sex segregation had *counter-cultural* status in the camp. That is, the counsellors and directors made it quite clear that their general preference was sex-integrated play. This was manifested in

pressure on the children (particularly the boys) to choose members of the opposite sex on their teams and to participate together in activities such as cooking and drama. The children's conformity to their sex-segregation norm in the public sphere thus had a dual consequence—it reinforced a major group norm and at the same time was a symbolic statement of resistance to adult values.

We must point to an exception to this, however. There was one public setting which did not produce the pattern of sex differentiation. When the children played a game as a unit against another unit, the children manifested considerable cross-sex interaction and an absence of boy-girl hostility. We observed two such instances: a baseball game against the counsellors; and a soccer game against another camp. The goal of overcoming an outside group dissolved, albeit temporarily, the internal sex divisions. The old notion that external threat leads to internal cohesion (e.g., Sherif and Sherif, 1953) would appear to have some contemporary currency.

Finally, a third variable which struck us as relevant to understanding cross-sex play was that of age composition. Although sexually mixed activity did occur among all age groups, the most common combination was that of older girls interacting with younger boys. The norm of no playing with girls was undoubtedly most strongly held by the older boys (those aged nine to 14). They were much more likely not only to manifest such behaviour but also to be more tolerant of their younger peers' deviance than they were of their own age-mates. Further, as mentioned earlier, the norm of no playing with boys appeared a defensive reaction by girls to their rejection by the older boys rather than a norm indigenous to the girls' group itself. Indeed, the girls actively solicited the older boys' participation in various activities, only to be met invariably with distinctively negative reactions. For these reasons the younger boys were much more likely to engage in cross-sex play than their older peers.

In sum, these data are useful in three respects: (1) they give us some insight into the conditions surrounding cross-sex play; (2) they provide further support for a large literature confirming the prevalence of sex-segregated play among older children; (3) they imply that any search for the beginning of sex-segregation in the developmental cycle must start with very young children.

BOY-GIRL INTERACTION IN TWO DAY-CARE CENTRES

The object of our observations in these settings was to see if the sex-segregation typical of children from kindergarten on was also characteristic of preschoolers (children three to four years old). The method followed was to take an inventory at five-minute intervals of the sex composition of the group playing in each of the three major day-care areas. These were: the "quiet area" (for reading and working on puzzles); the "house area" (which contained a miniature stove and fridge and a large collection of dishes), and the "activity area," (containing toy trucks, blocks, . . .). In addition to simply counting the number of children of each sex in the three areas, it was also noted whether there was any interaction, and whether these were same- or cross-sex interactions.

An interaction was operationally defined as any returned verbal communication or any instance of participation in a common task (e.g., doing a puzzle together, building a bridge together, etc.). Each centre was observed for six hours on six randomly selected days in a three-week period. In addition to these data, the four female teachers in each centre were briefly interviewed regarding their perception of the extent of cross-sex play and sex-segregated play in their particular group.

RESULTS

The rather unambiguous finding indicated neither a clear horizontal differentiation in play patterns nor any indication at all of a vertical differentiation by sex. My conclusion is based on the general observation that boys and girls displayed no reluctance whatsoever to play with one another. Boys were found dressing up and playing "doctor" or "cook" with the girls, just as the girls were found in the activity area building with blocks or driving the trucks.

Even when a particular area was being monopolized by the girls or by the boys, as occasionally was the case, there was never any evidence of exclusion based on sex. For example, on one occasion a group of girls was busily engaged in playing "Daddy is sick" in the house area. One of the girls had an adult male hat on, and was lying in obvious discomfort on two pillows. Two other girls, dressed in women's clothes, were attending her, while a third was on the phone to an imaginary doctor. Two boys entered the area and proceeded without incident to join in the drama, one playing the doctor and the other the ambulance driver. Similarly, when four boys were converting the truck into an imaginary spaceship, two girls who wished to ride along were invited to do so.

Horizontal differentiation along sex lines was virtually non-existent. The same is the case for vertical differentiation. Not once in 12 hours of observation did sex-based name calling occur or rejection of one child by another on the basis of sex. Indeed, the instances of rejection observed were predominantly intra-sex, e.g., two boys not permitting another boy to enter their "star wars spaceship." Children were certainly picked by others as "best friends," and rejected by others as "not my friend," but this process had nothing whatsoever to do with sex. All of the teachers spoken to indicated that they could not recall more than one or two instances of such sex-based acceptance or rejection among the preschoolers cared for over the previous several years. As one teacher put it, "they like or dislike one another for what they do, not because of who they are."

The story-time observations confirmed this, as did the more formal data on cross-sex interactions. During story time each teacher would read to a group of six or seven children. Particularly interesting in these sessions was the extent of sex clustering in the seating patterns (since these were voluntary, they would indicate, I suggest, the presence of any recurrent intra-sex preferences). The children, however, displayed no such tendencies. For example, the following seat-ing arrangement, taken from a story session in the subsidized centre, was quite typical:

GBGBBGB
TB

That is, boys and girls sat close together and exhibited no propensity for sex-based clustering. This also held true of snack and lunch-time periods.

The important finding is the considerable amount of cross-sex interaction in which the children are engaged. Fully 44 percent of all the interactions in the fee-paying centre and 45 percent in the subsidized centre are cross-sex interactions.

In sum, then, the data are quite inconsistent with those typically reported for school-aged children. The overall conclusion must be a virtual absence of both horizontal and vertical sex differentiation at this level.

DISCUSSION

I have in effect presented two sets of data which speak to the issue of sex differentiation. The first, based on older children, gave us some insight into the conditions under

FIGURE 23-2 Typology of activities

		Reward structure	
		Competitive	Co-operative
	Physical	1	3
Dominant type of interaction			
	Non-physical	2	4

which cross-sex play of the non-courtship variety tends to occur. If we combine the two dimensions we alluded to earlier—competitive-co-operative and physical-non-physical—we have a simple and possibly useful typology of activities, as expressed in Figure 23-2.

The cells distinguish fairly well the traditionally male from the traditionally female activities. Cell 1 contains most of the commonly played male-dominated North American sports, including baseball, football, and hockey; cell 2 includes many of the popular board games (checkers, monopoly etc. . . .) played by both sexes. It is this type of game which appears most consistently to yield cross-sex interaction. Our observations with regard to the counsellor-camper baseball game as well as the inter-camp soccer match give us some reason to believe that games typical of cell 3 may work to dissipate internal divisions within a group. Although the competitive dimension was still present *between* the teams, the intra-team co-operation required in these games, and its subsequent dissolution (albeit temporary) of sex divisions, makes the development and dissemination of games embodying a group rather than an individual goal appear worthwhile (e.g., Orlick, 1978). Because they retain the physical dimension, they are not likely to lose the boys, and their co-operative nature might well appeal to girls typically disconcerted by interindividual competitive activity involving boys. As for cell-4 activities, our observations give little hope that they will be accepted, particularly by the boys. Much unlearning is required in order to enjoy these games, and it has been my experience that older boys are simply too well socialized into the competitive ethnic and physical culture of North American male society to give such activities a reasonable chance. Nevertheless, one could have these in mind as perhaps a long-term objective.

More concretely, what one could attempt with school children is a gradual movement from cell 1 to 2 to 3. Certainly type-2 and type-3 games can be introduced as part of the school curriculum, reducing the inordinate emphasis currently placed on cell-1 type activities. Further, our research indicates the advisability of introducing these in as informal a fashion as possible, preferably through the children themselves, and in small groups rather than in such units as classrooms or grades.

Let me turn now to the data I presented on the preschoolers. The conclusion of most general import here is that sex differentiation, both its horizontal and vertical manifestations, appear to be *learned* phenomena. That we found virtually no evidence for their existence among children three to four years old, combined with our already existing knowledge that older children undoubtedly exhibit such patterns, is inconsistent with any arguments to be posited concerning innate or genetically based interests or "bonding" tendencies. Further, it appears that this learning coincides with the beginning of formal schooling. Kindergarten children exhibit such patterns while preschoolers do not. This suggests to me that young children are socialized by their older schoolmates and school-aged siblings with regard to "appropriate" male-female behaviour. The school experience itself, through various processes, further reinforces these norms. As I have pointed out in an earlier paper, teachers' differential interaction with boys and girls, as well as their use of sex as a basic organizational device, increases the tendency of children to see their world as a sex-stratified one (Richer, 1979). Also, I would suggest that as school progresses, boys are increasingly forced to *confront* the school as a group; the boys thereby differentiate themselves both from the school and from the girls, who exhibit considerably greater compatibility with the social demands of public education. This process of male confrontation is well documented in the literature, and it is manifested in the greater deviance of boys and in their poorer academic performance (Boocock, 1980).

REFERENCES

Armstrong, H., and P. Armstrong
  1975 "The Segregated Participation of Women in the Canadian Labour Force, 1941-1971," *Canadian Review of Sociology and Anthropology*, 12:370-84.
  1978 *The Double Ghetto.* Toronto: McClelland and Stewart.

Boocock, Sarane
  1980 *Sociology of Education*. Boston: Houghton Mifflin.

Durkheim, Emile
  1893 *De la division du travail social.* Paris: F. Alcan.

Gilmore, J.
  1966 "Play, A Special Behaviour," in *Current Research in Motivation,* ed. R. N. Haber, pp. 343-55. New York: Holt, Rinehart.

Goldberg, Philip A.
  1968 "Are Men Prejudiced Against Women?" *Transaction,* 5:28-30.

Mackie, Marlene
  1979 "Gender Socialization in Childhood and Adolescence," in *Childhood and Adolescence in Canada,* ed. K. Ishwaran, pp. 136-60. Toronto: McGraw-Hill Ryerson.

Markle, Gerald E.
  1974 "Sex-Ratio at Birth: Values, Variance and some Determinants, "*Demography,* 11:131-42.

Newell, W. W.
  1903 *Games and Songs of American Children* (expanded version). New York: Dover.

Orlick, Terry
  1978 *Winning Through Cooperation.* Washington: Acropolis Bks.

Richer, Stephen
  1979 "Sex-Role Socialization and Early Schooling," *Canadian Review of Sociology and Anthropology,* 16 no. 2: 195-205.
  1982a "Sex-Role Socialization: Agents, Content, Outcomes and Relationships." Forthcoming in K. Ishwaran, *The Canadian Family.*
  1982b "Sex-Role Socialization Outcomes as Manifested in Children's Drawings." Unpublished manuscript, Carleton University.

Schwartzman, Helen B.
  1978 *Transformations The Anthropology of Children's Play.* New York: Plenum Press.

Sherif, M., and C. W. Sherif
    1953   *Groups in Harmony and Tension.* New York: Harper.

Sutton-Smith, B.
    1972   *The Folkgames of Children.* Austin: University of Toronto Press.

Tiger, Lionel
    1969   *Men in Groups.* New York: Random House.

B. Gender

24. *The Gendered Division of Labour in the Home*

Meg Luxton

When I first got a job, I just never had any time, what with looking after the children and the housework. But now my husband has started to help me. He cooks and picks up the kids and is even starting to do other stuff! What a difference! Before, I used to feel like the second hand on the clock—you know, always racing around. Now, with his help, it feels like there are two hands for the clock—his and mine—so I get to stop occasionally.

More and more married women with young dependent children are employed outside the home. Studies conducted in the early and mid-1970s suggested that when married women took on paid employment, their husbands did not respond by increasing the amount of time they spent on domestic labour. These studies reached the general conclusion that married women were bear-

Reprinted from Meg Luxton, "Two Hands for the Clock: Changing Patterns in the Gendered Division of Labour," *Studies in Political Economy*, 12 (Fall 1983), pp. 27-44. Reprinted with permission.

ing the burden of the double day of labour almost entirely by themselves (Hartmann, 1981).

Underlying women's double day of labour is the larger question of the gendered division of labour itself. The gendered division of labour, and particularly women's responsibility for domestic labour, have been identified as central to women's oppression in the capitalist societies as a whole, and specifically to women's subordination to men within families (Rapp, 1978; Barrett, 1980; Barret and MacIntosh, 1983). Women's changing work patterns have posed sharply questions about domestic labour—What is actually being done in the home? Is it sufficient? Who is actually doing it? Who should be doing it? This in turn has raised further questions about the existing unequal power relations between women and men.

In the paid labour force, some women's groups, particularly within the union movement, have organized campaigns centred on such specific issues as equal pay and equal access to jobs. Their efforts are a challenge to the existing divisions of work between women and men (for example, see Gallager, 1982; Field, 1982). Such changes in the definition and distribution of women's work raise the question of whether or not attitudes toward the gendered division of labour in the family household are also being challenged. Has there been any comparable redefinition of men's work roles? And further, has there been any redistribution of work inside the family household? As women learn to drive electrohauls, shovel muck, and handle the heat of coke ovens, are men learning to change diapers, comfort an injured child, or plan a week's food within the limits imposed by a tight budget?

A recent Gallup poll on the sharing of general housework is suggestive. The poll, conducted across Canada in August 1981, reports that during the years 1976 to 1981, Canadians changed their opinions substantially about whether husbands should share in general housework. When asked the question, "In your opinion, should husbands be expected to share in the general housework or not?" 72 percent responded "yes" in 1981 as compared with 57 percent in 1976. Only 9 percent (11 percent of all men and 7 percent of all women) replied that men should not share the work.

However, changes in attitudes do not necessarily indicate changes in behaviour. The Gallup poll goes on to suggest that there has apparently been little change in what husbands do. It also implies that women and men disagree on the extent to which men are helping regularly. In 1976, 44 percent of men polled said they helped regularly with housework, while in 1981, 47 percent said they did. By contrast, in 1976, 33 percent of women polled said men regularly helped while in 1981, 37 percent of women polled said men regularly helped (Canada Institute of Public Opinion, 1981).

FLIN FLON REVISITED

In 1976-77 I investigated women's work in the home through a case study of 100 working-class households in Flin Flon, a mining town in northern Manitoba (Luxton, 1980). Five years later, in 1981, I carried out a follow-up study to discover whether or not changes had occurred over the preceding five years. As Flin Flon is a small, fairly remote, single-industry town, it is not a Canadian pace setter. Changes occurring in Flin Flon probably indicate more widespread developments. While this case study does not dispute the finding of earlier studies (that when married women get paying jobs they continue to do most of the domestic labour), it does suggest that the situation is considerably more complex than had previously been perceived. It illustrates some of the factors underlying the emergence of the different patterns of attitudes and behaviours reflected in the Gallup poll. It also shows that in some working-class households, important changes in the division of labour are beginning to occur, as women exert pressure on their husbands to take on more domestic labour.

In the first study I interviewed women of three generations. The first generation set up households in the 1920s and 1930s, the second in the 1940s and 1950s, and the third in the 1960s and 1970s. With just a few exceptions, women of the third generation were the ones with young children under the age of 12. Just over half the women interviewed had held paid work outside the home for some period after their marriage. None of them, however, had worked outside the home while their children were young. Most had worked for pay before their children were born, but then had not worked for pay again until the children were of school age. Regardless of whether or not they held paid jobs outside the home, these women identified themselves primarily as housewives and considered domestic labour their responsibility. They generally maintained that they did not expect their husbands to help with domestic labour. Those few men who did some work were praised as wonderful exceptions.

In the follow-up study I sought out only women of the third generation and was able to locate 49 of the original 52. In striking contrast to the previous study, I found that these women, all of whom had children 12 years of age or less, were for the most part working outside the home for pay. Over half of these women had preschool children, and 19 had had another baby between 1976 and 1981. Despite their continued child care responsibilities, 44 women had full-time employment. Of these, 14 said they would prefer to be in the home full-time; nine said they would prefer part-time work; and almost half (21) said they were satisfied with the situation they were in. Four women had part-time paid work. Of these, two were satisfied while one wanted, but had not yet been able to find, a full-time paid job. One wanted to return to full-time domestic labour, but could not afford to quit her job. Only one woman was still working full-time in the home and she said she was there by choice.

What emerged from the interviews was that regardless of whether or not they wanted to be employed, these women were changing their identification of themselves as being primarily housewives. As one of the women who was working for pay full-time, but who wished she could stay at home, put it:

I am a housewife. That's what I always wanted to be. But I have also been a clerk for four years so I guess I'm one of those working mothers—a housewife, a mother and a sales clerk.

Given the demands of their paid work, these women were forced to reorganize their domestic labour in some way. Both interviews and time budgets showed that the attitudes women have towards their work responsibilities (both paid and domestic) affect the way they reorganize domestic labour. A key factor was the extent to which they were willing to envisage a change in the gendered division of labour inside the family household.

Labour force participation did not necessarily reflect their approval of "working mothers." In 1981 all of the women were asked what they thought about married women who had dependent children and who worked outside the home. Seven flatly opposed it under any circumstances, although all of them were in that situation. Nine did not think it was right for them personally, although they felt such a decision should be made on an individual basis. Eight women said it was fine if the woman needed the money, although they opposed mothers working outside the home for any other reasons.[1]

In contrast, over half of the women interviewed (25) maintained that mothers with dependent children had every right to work outside the home if they wanted to. Many of them (14) went further and argued that it was better for mothers to be working outside the home. For these women, economic need was only one of several valid reasons that women would take paid employment.

There was a direct correspondence between the attitudes these women expressed toward paid employment for mothers and their views on the gendered division of labour in the home. All of the women were asked who they thought should be responsible for domestic labour. Their responses show three distinct strategies in balancing the demands of domestic labour, paid employment, and family. I have identified these distinct positions, based on their conceptualization of appropriate gender relations, as follows:

1. separate spheres and hierarchical relations;
2. separate spheres and co-operative relations;
3. shared spheres and changed relations.²

Separate Spheres and Hierarchical Relations

Seven respondents (14 percent) advocated a strict gender-based division of labour. They flatly opposed women working outside the home because doing so would both violate women's proper role and detract from their ability to do domestic labour. These women argued that men, as males, were breadwinners and were "naturally" also household or family heads. Women were to be subordinate to their husbands—this was described by several women as "taking second place to my husband." They argued that women's wifely duties included acquiescence in relation to their husbands' demands and putting their families' needs before their own. These women maintained that they themselves held paid jobs outside the home only because their earnings were crucial. They intended to stop work as soon as the "emergency" was over.

They insisted that their paid work must never interfere with their ability to care for their husbands and children or to run their households. Because they assumed that domestic labour was entirely women's responsibility, they did not expect their husbands to help. They maintained that boy children should not be expected to do anything at all around the house and argued that they were teaching their girl children domestic labour skills, not because the mothers needed help,

but as training for the girls' future roles as wives and mothers. Accordingly, these women sustained the full double day of labour entirely by themselves.

To deal with the contradiction between their beliefs and their actions, these women worked even harder at their domestic labour. In what appears to be a rigorous overcompensation, they actually raised their standards for domestic labour. They were determined to behave as though paid work made no difference to their domestic performance. Many of them insisted, for example, that every evening meal include several courses made from scratch as well as homemade desserts.

As a result, these women set themselves up in a never-ending vicious circle and ran themselves ragged. Their fatigue and resulting irritability and occasional illnesses only served to convince them that their original prognosis was correct: paid employment is bad for women and harmful to their families.

Separate Spheres and Co-operative Relations

Seventeen women (35 percent) said that women and men are different. Each gender moves in a separate sphere, and marriage, in uniting a woman and man, requires co-operation between the two spheres, with each person pulling his or her own weight. These women considered it acceptable for women to "help out" by earning money when necessary but, they argued, women's real work was in the home.

There were two identifiable currents within this general position. Nine women advocated full-time domestic labour for themselves though they agreed that might not be the best option for all women. These women maintained that they should not be working outside the home because they thought it interfered with their family responsibilities. While they were more flexible in their attitudes than those in the first group of women, they argued generally for the maintenance of the gendered division of labour. Particularly in their childrearing attitudes and behaviour, they adhered to a strict notion that boys should not be expected to engage in domestic labours while girls should be encouraged to do so.

Like the first group of women, these women also did most of the domestic labour on their own. Their way of trying to cope with the enormous strain this created, however, was to ease up their standards for domestic labour. They were much more willing to purchase "convenience foods" or to eat in restaurants. They talked about doing less around the house and about feeling vaguely disappointed that they could not keep their place nicer. They were, however, prepared to accept that they could not work outside the home and continue to do full-time domestic labour as well.

Taking a slightly different approach, eight women stated that paid work was acceptable for women with children, if the woman's income was necessary for her household economy. While these women also indicated that they were in favour of maintaining a traditional gendered division of labour, they often engaged in contradictory practices. They would argue that domestic labour was women's work, but in day-to-day activities they frequently asked their husbands to lend a hand, and they all expected their boy children as well as the girls to learn and take on certain domestic tasks.

To a large extent, it appears that the discrepancy between their beliefs and their behaviour lies in an experienced necessity. Unlike those who argued for hierarchical relations, these women were unwilling to become "superwomen." They acknowledged

the pressures on them and were willing to ask for help. The extent to which they asked for, and received, assistance varied from household to household. In most cases, children had assigned chores such as washing the dishes or setting the dinner table which they were expected to do on a regular basis. Husbands were not assigned regular jobs but were usually expected to "lend a hand" when they were specifically asked.

Toward Shared Spheres and Changing Relations

Twenty-five women—just over half the sample (51 percent)—stated that regardless of necessity, women with young children had the right to paid employment if they wanted it. For them, wives and husbands were partners who should share the responsibilities for financial support and domestic labour. They supported the idea of changing the division of labour and in practice they were instituting such changes by exerting increasing pressure on their husbands and children to redistribute both the responsibility for, and the carrying out of, domestic labour. As it is these women who are challenging the existing ideology and practice of the gendered division of labour, and especially the place of women and men in the family home, I want to look more closely at the changes they have enacted in the last five years.

A REDISTRIBUTION OF LABOUR TIME

While the women who argued for separate spheres were defending a gendered division of labour within the household, statements made by the third group reflected the trends indicated in the Gallup poll. When these 25 women were asked in the 1976 study if they thought husbands should help with domestic labour, most agreed that they did not expect their husbands to do anything, although six said their husbands actually did help. By 1981, however, they unanimously insisted that husbands should help out and all said their husbands did some domestic labour on a regular basis.

An examination of time budgets for these households shows that men have in fact increased the amount of time they spend on domestic labour. By themselves, the figures seem to be quite impressive; men increased their domestic labour time from an average of 10.8 hours per week in 1976 to 19.1 hours in 1981—an increase of 8.3 hours.

By contrast, in 1976 full-time housewives spent an average of 63 hours per week on domestic labour while women working a double day spent an average of 87.2 hours per week working, of which 35.7 hours were spent on domestic labour. In 1981 women doing both jobs averaged 73.9 hours per week of which 31.4 hours were spent on domestic labour. This is a decrease of only 4.3 hours per week. While one would not expect a direct hour for hour substitution for one person's labour for another, there is a discrepancy between the increase in men's work and the relatively insignificant reduction in women's work. Women on an average were spending 12.3 hours a week more than men on domestic labour. Furthermore, there is a discrepancy between the women's insistence that domestic labour should be shared equally and the actual behaviour of household members. These discrepancies generate considerable tension between wives and husbands—tension which reflects the power struggle inherent in the redistribution of domestic labour.

WOMEN AND MEN'S DOMESTIC LABOUR

The women who want their husbands to be more involved have developed a variety of strategies and tactics with which to get the men to take on more work. These range from gentle appeals to fairness or requests for assistance to militant demands for greater (or equal) participation. In a few cases women discussed the situation with their husbands and they mutually agreed on a sharing of tasks that both partners considered fair and reasonable. In the majority of cases, however, negotiations appeared to be out of the question. Instead the couples seemed locked into tension-generating, manipulative power struggles.

For the women, the impetus to change comes first from the pressures of their two jobs. It is fuelled further when they compare their experiences with those of their husbands. Some contrasted their own working time at home with their husband's leisure time.

> I come home from work dead tired and I still have to cook and be with the kids and clean up. And he just lies around, drinking beer, watching TV and I get so mad, I could kill him.

Others compared the standards their husbands expected from their wives with those the men held for themselves. They noted that when living alone, some men kept their households immaculately clean; others lived in a total mess. Whatever their standards for themselves, when the women were around, men changed their behaviour, altered their expectations and pressured the women to meet male standards.

> When my husband is on his own, he's quite happy to live in a pig sty. Mess doesn't bother him. But the minute I get back he insists that he can't live in the house unless it's spotless.

Before we were married he lived on his own and his place was so clean and tidy. But as soon as we got married, he somehow never felt he could clean up. It was all up to me.

Despite the obvious interest these women have in redistributing domestic labour, and despite their motivating anger, there are numerous forces operating which make it difficult for women to insist that their spouses actually share the work.

Because inequalities in the division of labour are based on male power, when women demand equalization of the work, they are challenging that power. Some women were afraid that if they pushed for more male participation, they would provoke their husbands' anger and rage. At least one woman said her husband had beaten her for suggesting he help with domestic labour.

While there is evidence to suggest that when women have paid employment they increase their own power in marriage, all of these women earned considerably less than their husbands. As a result, the men retained economic power (breadwinner power). Men can also use their greater earnings as a justification for not doing domestic labour. They often argued that with their earnings they discharged the responsibility to the household. Under present circumstances it is up to the individual women to initiate changes in the patterns of domestic labour. For many, economic dependency makes it difficult to challenge their husbands.

Furthermore, the actual task of getting men to do domestic labour is often difficult. If women want their husbands to begin doing domestic labour, they must be prepared to take responsibility not only for overcoming male resistance but also for helping men overcome both the accumulated years of inexperience and the weight of traditional assumptions about masculinity. Generally, the women assumed that their husbands were unfamiliar with domestic labour and therefore neither knew what needed doing nor had the necessary skills to carry out the work. Taking on this training of resisting and unskilled workers is often in itself an additional job.

When men do start doing domestic labour, women begin to lose control. Domestic labour has traditionally been the one sphere of female control and power. For most women, the kitchen is the closest they ever come to having a "room of one's own." It is difficult for many women to relinquish this, particularly if they are not compensated for that loss by gains made elsewhere —for example in their paid work. While the women were uniformly pleased that their husbands had increased their contribution, they were troubled by the way domestic labour was being redistributed.

MEN AND DOMESTIC LABOUR

That men increase the amount of time they spend on domestic labour does not in itself convey much about changing work patterns. Most significantly, it was still assumed that women were primarily responsible for domestic labour and that men were "helping out." When women do domestic labour they often juggle several tasks at once. One of the ways that men have increased the amount of time they spend on domestic labour is by taking over some of that simultaneous work. Many women reported that their husbands were willing to watch the children while the women prepared dinner or did other household chores. While such actions obviously relieved some of the pressures and tensions on women, they did not reduce the amount of time required of women for domestic labour.

Often when men (and children) took on certain tasks, they ended up generating even more domestic work. A number of women indicated that their husbands cooked, but when they did so they seriously disrupted the orderliness of the kitchen, emptying cupboards to find something and not putting things back or using an excessive number of dishes in the preparation. Another commonly cited example was that when men agreed to look after the children, they actually paid more attention to their visiting friends or the TV. Unattended, the children ran "wild" through the house so that when the woman returned she had to spend a great deal of time tidying the house and calming the children. Further, many women pointed out that getting their husbands to do domestic labour required a considerable amount of their time and energy. Sometimes, women argued, it took more work to get the man to do the work than it did to do the work themselves.

Furthermore, men tended to take over certain specific tasks which had clearly defined boundaries. They did not take on the more nebulous, ongoing management tasks and they rarely took responsibility for pre-task planning. For example, a number of men did the grocery shopping on a regular basis but they insisted that the woman draw up the basic list of things needed. Some men would do the laundry, if all the dirty clothes were previously collected and sorted and if the necessary soap and bleach were already at hand.

A recurring theme throughout the interviews was that men preferred jobs that involved working with machinery. A number of men were willing to do the vacuuming because they enjoyed playing with the vacuum cleaner. One woman described how her husband had refused to cook until they purchased a food processor. After that he was forever reading the recipe book and planning new techniques for meal preparation. Several women noted that their husbands had increased their participation in meal preparation after they bought microwave ovens.

The redistribution that is occurring is selective. The husbands tend to take the path of least resistance. The trend has been for men to take on those tasks that are the most clearly defined, or sociable and pleasant ones, while leaving the more ill-defined or unpleasant ones to the women. Repeatedly women noted that their husbands had taken on reading the children a bedtime story and staying with them until they fell asleep, thus "freeing" the women to wash the dishes and tidy the kitchen. Men were often willing to feed their infant children or take older ones to the park, but on the whole they would not change soiled diapers or wash their children's hair. They would wash the dishes but not the kitchen floor or the toilet. One man would vacuum the living room rug but refused to do the stairs because they were too awkward.

One of the most significant tranformations of men's involvement in domestic labour has been in the area of child care. While most fathers have always spent some time with their children, particularly with older children, increasingly they are doing more of the day-to-day caregiving, especially with younger children. Perhaps the most significant change of all has been with the birth process itself.[3] In 1976 only four out of 25 men had been present at the birth of at least one of their children. However, of the babies born between 1976 and 1981, 10 of the 19 new fathers had been present at the birth (and only two of these were of the original four). The wives indicated that they felt very strongly that having their husbands involved in the birth also drew the men into the whole process of pregnancy, child birth, and infant care. Men who were willing to attend the birth were subsequently more inclined to get up at night with the baby, to take over certain feedings and to be generally more involved with their small babies.

Despite this very promising shift, women were still responsible for overall child care. All 25 women said it was up to them to arrange day care for their children when they worked outside the home. If the child care arrangements fell through on any particular day, it was the woman who had to get time off work to stay home, although this can in part be explained by her lower pay and in part by his unavailability when underground.

Furthermore, men "babysat" their own children—something that women never did. The implication of this typical reference was that the children were the responsibility of the mother, and the father "helped out." This attitudinal difference was often carried out in behaviour as well. Women repeatedly described situations where men would agree to watch the children, but would then get involved in some other activity and would ignore the children. As children grew up, they learned from experience that their mothers were more likely to be helpful, and so they would turn to the woman rather than the man for assistance, thus actively perpetuating the traditional division of labour.

The ambivalent and often reluctant way in which these men have moved into domestic labour reflects a combination of valid reasons and invalid excuses. In "The Politics of Housework," Pat Maindari describes with biting sarcasm the various forms of male resistance developed in response to a wife's attempt to share housework:

(Husband): "I don't mind sharing the work, but you'll have to show me how to do it."
Meaning: I'll ask a lot of questions and you'll

have to show me everything every time I do it because I don't remember so good. And don't try to sit down and read while I'm doing my jobs because I'm going to annoy the hell out of you until it's easier to do them yourself. (Mainardi, 1970)

Flin Flon women described various forms of male behaviour that were obviously intended to resist attempts to draw them into domestic labour. The majority of resisters took a subtle approach (passive resistance) similar to the ones satirized by Maindari. One woman described how their kitchen sink was directly in the centre of the kitchen counter. Normally the draining board sat on the left-hand side and the dirty dishes were stacked on the right. Her husband maintained he was unable to do the dishes as he was left-handed and the sink was designed for right-handed people. Some women talked suspiciously of the way household machinery "broke down" when their husbands tried to use it. Several women told of incidents where their husbands agreed to do the work but then repeatedly "forgot" to do it, complained when the women "nagged" them about it, and finally told the women to do it themselves if they did not like the way the men did it. One man explained his position quite clearly:

Look, I'm not interested in doing stuff around the house. I think that's her job, but since she's working she's been on my back to get me to help out so I say "sure I'll do it." It shuts her up for a while and sometimes I do a few things just to keep her quiet. But really, I don't intend to do it, but it prevents a row if I don't say that.

For men to take on domestic labour meant that they had to give up some of the time they had previously spent on their own enjoyments. Within certain limits this may not be much of a sacrifice, but at some point a man's increasing involvement in domestic labour starts eroding his ability to engage in other activities he values highly. There is a substantial difference between washing dishes and watching TV, and in having to come home early from drinking with one's mates at the pub because one has to cook dinner.

Because the majority of men have, until recently, not been expected to do domestic labour, they have not been taught either implicitly, the way girls learn via their dolls and play kitchens, or explicitly, through "helping" mother or in home economics classes. As a result, they often lack knowledge and are unskilled and awkward. Working at a job for which one is ill-prepared often generates feelings of anxiety, inadequacy, and incompetence which are easily translated into a generalized reluctance to continue the job.

Some men expressed a willingness to do domestic labour but they were afraid that if it were publicly known that they did "women's work," they would be subjected to teasing and ridicule. One man, for example, quite enjoyed doing the vacuuming. However, there were no curtains on the windows, so the interior of the house was visible from the street. As a result, he did the vacuuming on his knees so that no one would see him! Other men were willing to do tasks inside the house but steadfastly refused to do those tasks that were "women's work" outside in public (hanging washing on the line, for example).

CONCLUSION

This case study suggests that changing patterns of paid employment are creating a crisis in the way labour is currently distributed and accomplished in the family household. It illustrates the ambiguities reflected in the Gallup poll findings and shows that these ambiguities arise from serious problems in the way domestic labour is changing. It also suggests that ideologies of "family" are very strong and play a central part in the way most people organize their interpersonal relationships and their domestic lives.

Because people tend to evaluate their experiences in light of existing social explanations and ideologies, the response of Flin Flon women can be set in a broader context. The three perspectives expressed reflect ideologies which are currently prominent.

Those women who put forward a "separate spheres and hierarchical relations" position were defending the traditonal conservative view which locates women inside the family, subordinates women's interests to men's, and places priority above all on the preservation of the breadwinner husband/dependent wife nuclear family.

Because the beliefs these Flin Flon women held conflicted directly with the activities they engaged in, they were compelled to mediate the contradiction. Their attempts to defend a strict gendered division of labour forced them deeper into the hardship of the double day. Their actual experiences highlight the conditions under which support for right-wing "pro-family" reform movements is generated, for in their opinion, it is their paid work that creates the problem.

Those women who argued for "separate spheres and co-operative relations" were expressing a classic liberal view of appropriate female/male relations in the family. This "different but equal" perspective echoes the maternal feminism of some early twentieth-century theorists. It is also found in many sociologists of the family such as Young and Wilmott, who argue that marriages are now symmetrical or companionate (McLung, 1915; Young and Willmott, 1973).

Those women who argued for "shared spheres and changing relations" were expressing contemporary feminist views which hold that the existing gendered division of labour is a major factor in women's oppression. In challenging the way work is divided in the home, they are questioning the existing relationships between women and men, and between children and adults. Discussing existing family relationships, Hartmann (1981: 379) has argued that "Because of the division of labour among family members, disunity is thus inherent in the 'unity' of the family."

This study suggests that a large-scale social transformation is occurring as traditional patterns are eroding and new ones are emerging, but to date the change has been acted out on the level of the individual household, and may, in the short run, be intensifying family disunity. What emerged from these interviews was the total isolation both women and men felt. Women involved in active, collective organizing to change the division of labour in the paid workforce have the women's liberation movement, the trade union movement, Status of Women committees, and sometimes the law and other organizations or institutions, such as the Human Rights Commissions, to back them up. In contrast, women challenging the gendered division of labour in the home do so on an individual basis. Similarly, there is a complete lack of social and material support for men with regard to domestic labour. Very few unions have won paternity leave, for example, so it is very difficult for new fathers to get time off work to be with their new children. This makes it very difficult for men actually to take equal responsibility for their infants.[4] Accordingly, any man who takes on domestic labour places himself at odds with current social practices. It takes a certain amount of self-confidence and courage to do so.

As a result, the majority of respondents implied that they considered that the changes in their domestic division of labour were specific to their individual households. They perceived these changes not as part of a large-scale transformation in the patterns of work and family life, but as a personal struggle between them and their spouse. Such a perception only exacerbated the tensions between women and men.

As material conditions change and new ideologies emerge, many individuals and families are floundering, trying to decide what they want, how to get it, and most problematically, how to resolve conflicts between various possibilities and needs. There are currently no social policies or clear-cut, developing social norms to provide a context in which individuals can evaluate their own actions. Instead, there are several contending ideologies and related social movements, such as the "pro-family" movement and the women's liberation movement (Harding, 1981). While these movements articulate positions on what female/male relations should entail, they rarely organize to provide support for women to achieve the desired end. The current situation is thereby generating a great deal of confusion and often pain and interpersonal conflict, especially between women and men.

Finally, this study demonstrates that until the exclusive identification of women with domestic labour is broken, there is no possibility of achieving any kind of equality between women and men. If the necessary labour is not redistributed, women end up with a dramatically increased work load. Unlike earlier studies, the findings of this research suggest that, despite all the problems, some working-class women are contesting male power and challenging male privilege and some men are responding by assuming more responsibility for domestic labour.

NOTES

This paper reports the results of research carried out in Flin Flon, Manitoba in 1981. All the quotes cited in the paper without references are from interviews conducted as part of that research.

The article is a revised version of a paper presented at the Canadian Sociology and Anthropology Association meeting in Ottawa in 1982. For critical comments I am grateful to Margaret Benston, Pat Connelly, Heather Jon Maroney, Pat Marchak, Ester Reiter, Harriet Rosenberg and Wally Seccombe.

1. The problem here, however, lies in trying to determine what constitutes economic need. All of these women (24) maintained that they were working outside the home for economic reasons, because their families needed the money. In all likelihood, this is true. However, it may be that these women, like most employed housewives who have been studied, also have non-economic reasons for accepting paid employment. Economic necessity is a more socially legitimated reason and some of these women may be dealing with the contradictory feeling they have toward their family obligations and their pleasure in employment by convincing themselves and others that they are only working because they "have to."

2. There were no obvious sociological factors that might explain the differences in opinion and behaviour. While a large-scale survey might reveal correlations between these different strategies and such factors as political or religious affiliation, ethnicity, and husbands' attitudes, at least among this group of women, and given the available data, no such patterns emerged.

It is also important to point out that while these three approaches are typical, they are not the only available options. Some women have fully egalitarian relations with the men they live with; others live alone or with other women.

A creative strategy was developed by one couple (not included in the study). The man worked a 40-hour week in the mines; the woman was a housewife. They determined mutually what work she was responsible for during a 40-hour week. She did child care while he was at work, as well as heavy cleaning and certain other chores. The rest of the domestic labour—child care, cooking, cleaning, laundry, shopping—they divided equally between them. As a result, each worked a 40-hour week at their own work and shared all remaining labour.

3. It seems to me that the involvement of men in the actual birth of their children is of enormous significance—something which has not yet been appreciated, or studied.

4. In Québec the unions of CEGEP teachers have won paternity leave. This has made it possible for some men to take equal responsibility for infant care.

REFERENCES

Barrett, Michelle
    1980   *Women's Oppression Today.* London.

Barrett, Michelle, and Mary MacIntosh
    1983   *The Anti-Social Family.* London.

Canadian Institute of Public Opinion
    1981   *The Gallup Report,* pp. 1-20. Toronto (October 7).

Field, Debbie
    1982   "Rosie the Riveter Meets the Sexual Division of Labour," in *Still Ain't Satisfied: Canadian Feminism Today,* ed. Maureen Fitzgerald, Connie Guberman, and Margie Woolf. Toronto.

Gallager, Deirdre
    1982   "Getting Organized in the CLC," in *Still Ain't Satisfied: Canadian Feminism Today,* ed. Maureen Fitzgerald, Connie Guberman, and Margie Woolf. Toronto.

Harding, Susan
    1981   "Family Reform Movements: Recent Feminism and its Opposition," *Feminist Studies,* 7, no. 1 (Spring):57-75.

Hartmann, Heidi
    1981   "The Family as the Locus of Gender, Class and Political Struggle; The Example of Housework," *Signs,* 6, no. 3 (Spring):377-86.

Luxton, Meg
    1980   *More than a Labour of Love: Three Generations of Women's Work in the Home.* Toronto.

Mainardi, Pat
    1970   "The Politics of Housework," in *Sisterhood is Powerful,* ed. Robin Morgan, pp. 449-51. New York.

McClung, Nellie
    1915   *In Times Like These.* Toronto.
    (1972)

Rapp, Rayna
    1978   "Family and Class in Contemporary America: Notes Towards an Understanding of Ideology," *Science and Society,* 42 (Fall):278-301.

Young, Michael, and Peter Willmott
    1973   *The Symmetrical Family.* London.

B. Gender

25. Trends and Policy in Employment Opportunities for Women

Liviana Calzavara

How much progress have women in the labour force made in the past 50 years? There are some indicators, such as the rate of labour force participation, the visibility of women in traditionally "male" occupations, and the introduction of equal pay and equal opportunity legislations, that may suggest that meaningful progress has been made. This report documents the nature of the progress by using data from existing studies on Canadian women in the labour force.

WOMEN IN THE LABOUR FORCE—THE PAST 50 YEARS

Labour Force Participation

Rate of participation Women's labour force participation has grown rapidly dur-

ing the last 50 years. For example, 22 percent of women were in the labour force in 1931 compared to 53 percent in 1983 (see Table 25-1). The fastest growth occurred between 1961 and 1971, with an 11 percent increase in labour force participation in the 10-year period. The majority of Canadian women 15 years and over are now in the labour force.

While the participation rate of women of all ages has increased, growth has been greatest for women between the ages of 25 and 64. In 1951, 25 percent of women aged 25-34 and 20 percent of women 35-64 were in the labour force. By 1971 participation of the 25-34 age group had increased to 45 percent; and for the 35-64 age group, to 42 percent.

Most analysts agree that the increase in women's participation rate (since the 1950s)

Revised from Liviana Calzavara, "Trends in the Employment Opportunities of Women in Canada, 1930-1980," in R. S. Abella, ed., *Equality in Employment: A Royal Commission Report* (Ottawa: Supply and Services, 1985). Reproduced with permission of the Minister of Supply and Services Canada.

TABLE 25-1 Labour force participation rates of men and women in Canada, selected years, 1901-1986.

Year	Men	Women
1901	88 %	16 %
1911	91	19
1921	90	20
1931	87	22
1941	86	23
1951	84	24
1961	81	29
1971	76	40
1980	78	50
1983	77	53
1986	77	55

Source: The figures for 1901-1971 are from Morley Gunderson, "Work Patterns," in *Opportunity for Choice*, ed. Gail Cook (1976), Table 4-1. They are based on census data. The 1980 and 1983 figures are calculated from the Statistics Canada survey *The Labour Force*.

has been mainly the result of the growing number of married women entering the labour force. The participation rate for married women has increased from less than 4 percent in 1941 to 36 percent in 1971. There are many factors that account for the increased participation of women (and married women in particular), but most analysts agree that wages are a principal incentive. The changing standard of living and inflation have caused more married women to seek paid employment. It has been established that the lower the husband's income the more likely it is that the wife will participate in the labour force. As more marriages dissolve, more and more women must rely on wages as their major source of income (Boyd, 1977). Accompanied by this financial push, women have been drawn into the labour force by the results of technological changes (such as better birth control meth-

ods, better domestic technology, and more cheaply produced consumer goods). These changes have made it possible for women to take on dual jobs (work at home and in the labour force). Women have also been drawn into the labour force as a result of the growth in demand for female workers. Armstrong and Armstrong (1983:32-33) argue that the industries experiencing the greatest growth in terms of job creation have been those that traditionally hired many women and many part-time workers.

Rate of unemployment The large increase in women's labour force participation may be interpreted as a sign that they have been accepted into the labour force. It can also be interpreted as more women trying to find work, for the labour force figures include workers who are employed and those who are seeking work.

Are there sex differences in the rates of unemployment and, if so, are they improving? When the Royal Commission on the Status of Women asked that question in 1970, it found that women's rate of unemployment was lower than that of men, suggesting that women were generally more successful than men in finding work. More recent figures show that the situation has changed. Between 1946 and 1970 the male rate of unemployment was consistently above the female rate.

The consistently lower rates of unemployment among women are partly explained by the occupational distribution of women. Women were predominantly found in "service-producing" industries (transportation, storage, communications, trade, finance, insurance, real estate, recreation, business and personal services, public administration). Men tended to be found in "goods" industries (agriculture, forestry, fishing, mining, quarrying, oil wells, manufacturing, construction, utilities). Between 1946 and 1966 the service industries experienced a faster growth rate of employment than the goods industries.

By 1971 women's rate of unemployment had approached and surpassed that of men (see Table 25-2). As of December 1980, the rate of unemployment for men was 6.9 percent to 8.4 percent for women. The reason for this change remains unclear. It may be that the growth of the "service-producing" industries has slowed down.

Part-time employment While there has been an increase in the number of women participating in the labour force, much of this increase results from women working on a part-time basis. Between 1966 and 1980 the proportion of women in the labour force increased by 12 percent and the proportion employed full-time increased by 6.5 percent. According to Armstrong and Armstrong (1983: 65-66, 234, 249), 17 percent of Canadian women worked part-time in 1966 compared to 3 percent of men. In 1980, 24 percent of the women and 6 percent of the men worked part-time, an increase of 7 percent for women and only 3 percent for men. The figures over the 14-year period indicate that the proportion of women working part-time is increasing, and at a faster rate than that for men.

An issue is whether this greater rate of increase in part-time work for women is a sign of greater underemployment among women or a greater preference to work only part-time. The answer is not readily available. Some evidence suggests that fewer women than previously take part-time work from preference. The percentage of women who took a part-time job because they did not want to work full-time has decreased from 46 percent (in 1975) to 42 percent (in 1980). The percentage who took a part-time job

because they could only find part-time work increased from 11 percent (in 1975) to 17 percent (in 1980). Other figures show that women are still more likely than men to accept part-time jobs because they do not want full-time work. In 1980, 42 percent of women but only 16 percent of men said they worked part-time because they did not want full-time jobs. The majority of women who prefer part-time work are married.

Whether by preference or need, the increase in part-time employment among women means that more of them are in a segment of the labour force that is subject to

TABLE 25-2 Unemployment rates by sex, 1966-1986.

Year	Unemployment rate		Women as percent of unemployed
	Women	Men	
1966	3.4%	3.3%	31.8%
1967	3.7	3.9	31.4
1968	4.4	4.6	31.8
1969	4.7	4.3	35.1
1970	5.8	5.6	34.7
1971	6.6	6.0	36.8
1972	7.0	5.8	39.1
1973	6.7	4.9	42.6
1974	6.4	4.8	42.6
1975	8.1	6.2	43.2
1976	8.4	6.4	44.2
1977	9.5	7.3	44.1
1978	9.6	7.6	44.8
1979	8.8	6.6	46.1
1980	8.4	6.9	44.8
1981	8.3	7.0	45.0
1982	10.9	11.1	40.9
1983	11.6	12.1	40.7
1984	11.4	11.2	42.7
1985	10.7	10.3	43.5
1986	9.9	9.4	44.1

Source: Pat Armstrong and Hugh Armstrong, *A Working Majority* (1983), Table 1. Based on Labour Force Survey data.

greater exploitation. Part-time workers receive lower rates of pay, fewer fringe benefits, and less job security.

Earnings of Women and Men

Most analysts agree that earnings are perhaps the single most important indicator of labour market progress, since earnings reflect both the nature of labour force participation (unemployment, part-time work) and occupational distribution.

Time-pattern of earnings differentials Studies that look at the pattern of earnings differentials without adjusting for differences in work-productivity factors (education, training, labour force commitment) indicate that there were and still are large gaps in the earnings of men and women in Canada. For example, in 1911 the average wage of employed women stood at 53 percent of the average male wage (Phillips and Phillips, 1983:25). By 1979 the average earned income of women who worked a full year was 63 percent of men's full-year earnings, while the average annual income of all women (including part-time workers) was only 51 percent of the male average. Full-time working women in 1979 earned 63 percent of what men earned. The average annual earnings for women working full-time in 1979 were $11 741, compared with $18 537 for men (Armstrong and Armstrong, 1983). If one looks at all women (full-time and part-time workers) the gap has actually decreased between 1971 and 1979 from 50 percent to 51 percent.

It appears that there has been some slight improvement in the relative wages of women working full-time, especially between 1971 and 1979. At this point, it is not clear whether this represents only a short-term fluctuation or a continuing trend. The introduction of equal pay legislation (first enacted in 1951) has not had a dramatic effect on the wage gap. The unadjusted differences show that women who are full-time workers still earn 65 cents for every dollar earned by men (1987). This does not represent much progress from the 53 cents women earned in 1911.

Productivity differences or discrimination While most analysts agree on the historical existence of a wage gap, they disagree on the actual size of the gap and its causes. Some argue that it is a result for the most part of differences in men's and women's work-productivity. Women are paid less because they have fewer skills, less training, and less work experience: these factors should be taken into account when trying to explain the gap. Others argue that the entire gap reflects discrimination against women; that those controlling for productivity factors ignore past discrimination, which has kept women's productivity lower. A number of empirical studies have been undertaken recently to determine the extent of the earnings gap when adjustments are made for aspects of productivity.

Two basic methods have been used to measure levels of earnings discrimination. The "sampling" approach compares the earnings of men and women holding identical jobs within the same establishment and having equal qualifications, performance, and work hours. While conceptually more appropriate, this approach is operationally less feasible because of the difficulty of finding men and women who meet those criteria. The approach most often used is the "adjustment" approach. The female-to-male gross earnings ratio is computed, and net differences are then obtained by adjusting for differences in work-productivity factors. The unexplained differences that result are said to reflect discrimination.

Gunderson (1982) provides a good review of some of the Canadian studies that use these two methods.

Females in Canada typically earn 50-80 percent of what males earn. When productivity adjustments are made, women typically earn 80-90 percent of what males earn.

If one argues that all of the earnings difference reflects discrimination, then women earn 20-50 percent less than men because of present and past discrimination.

If one argues that productivity differences are the result of choice (and if one makes appropriate adjustments), women earn 10-20 percent less than men as a result of discrimination.

Net earnings differentials between men and women employed in the same occupation, within the same firm, are much lower, but women still earn a little under 10 percent less than men.

Even a conservative approach to estimating earnings discrimination indicates that Canadian women with the same level of productivity, and those who do the same work in the same firm, still earn anywhere from 10 to 20 percent less than men.

It is argued that one of the main reasons women earn less than men (even after adjusting for productivity differences) is that women are concentrated in a small number of low-wage occupations. Overcrowding in these occupations further serves to keep the wages low. There is some evidence to substantiate the claim that some desegregation of occupations would reduce the earnings gap. For example, case studies of men and women in the same occupations and firms show that both the unadjusted ratio and the adjusted ratio of female-to-male earnings are much higher.

Another factor that helps to reduce the earnings gap is unionization. According to White (1980), unionization significantly improves women's earnings and decreases the earnings gap between men and women. White looked at 20 office occupations and found that the average difference between men's and women's wages was 10 percent for unionized workers and 17 percent for nonunionized workers.

The one factor that should have resulted in a rapid narrowing of the earnings gap is equal pay legislation. As noted earlier, this has resulted in a slight narrowing of the gap but not a significant one. Most analysts feel that equal pay legislation has had little impact on the earnings gap for a number of reasons. The restrictive nature of equal pay legislation makes it applicable only where both men and women are employed at the same job in the same firm. Therefore the legislation does not apply to the large number of women in segregated occupations. There are loopholes that allow employers to claim that wage differences are due to differences in seniority, experience, merit. The existence of the earnings gap between men and women who work at the same job, in the same firm, after adjusting for productivity differences, confirms that the legislation is not being enforced.

Occupational and Industrial Distribution

One of the main reasons for the existence of the earnings gap between women and men is attributed to the occupational segregation of women. Women's earnings are lower because they are concentrated in lower-paying jobs (Armstrong and Armstrong, 1983). The wages in these occupations remain low because the supply of labour relative to demand has been greater. Equal pay for equal work legislation has not been effective because of the differences in the occupational distributions of men and women.

Time-patterns of occupational and industrial segregation Gunderson's (1976a:111-18) analysis of women's distribution in occupational and industrial categories from 1901 to 1971 provides a systematic view of what has been happening to Canadian women. For each census year, Gunderson calculated a coefficient of variation that indicates the extent to which women are evenly distributed across the occupational categories. The smaller the coefficient the more even the distribution. He found that from 1901 to 1971 there was a consistent decline in the coefficient. For example, in 1901 it was .985, in 1931 it was .792, and in 1971 it was .577. The corresponding coefficient for men during the same period has remained roughly constant at .30.

However, the evidence also suggests that there are still high levels of segregation within the occupational categories, as well as high levels of segregation if one looks at the industries within which these occupations are located. In 1980, more than one third of female workers (35 percent) were employed in clerical occupations (compared with 6 percent of men). Eighteen percent were in service occupations (compared with 10 percent of men); and of these most were in low-paying service sub-categories (such as cooking, cleaning, caring for children, hairdressing, waiting on tables) rather than the more highly paid protective services (such as firefighters, police). Nineteen percent of women were in professional occupations (compared with 13 percent of men) but mostly in lower-paid professions (such as teaching and nursing). Very few are in higher-paid professions (such as doctor, lawyer, or engineer). More than 72 percent of women in 1980 were employed in clerical, professional, and service occupations (Armstrong and Armstrong, 1983) (see Table 25-3).

TABLE 25-3 Occupational distribution of labour force by sex, 1971 and 1980 (percentages)

	1971		1980	
Occupation	Men	Women	Men	Women
Managerial	5.5	2.0	9.5	4.9
Professional	10.0	17.8	12.9	19.0
Clerical	7.6	31.6	6.3	34.6
Sales	10.0	8.4	10.4	10.4
Service	9.2	15.1	10.1	18.1
Primary	9.8	3.7	8.5	2.8
Blue-collar	40.5	10.6	42.3	10.2
Not stated	7.4	10.8	—	—
All occupations	100.0	100.0	100.0	100.0

Sources: Figures for 1971 are from M. Gunderson, "Work Patterns," in *Opportunity for Choice*, ed. G. Cook (1976), Table 4.6 (based on census figures). Figures for 1980 are from P. Armstrong and H. Armstrong, *A Working Majority* (1983), Table 5.

Choice or discrimination Are women concentrated in clerical, service, and sales occupations by choice or as a result of discrimination? This is another major debate in the literature which, unlike the productivity or discrimination debate (when explaining earnings differentials), has received very little systematic empirical analysis. Therefore we cannot even say, as we could with earnings differences: if you take the "choice" position, "x" amount of occupational segregation is explained by discrimination. It is not clear how much of "choice" is the result of past discrimination which has kept women from obtaining the necessary qualifications and support to compete in traditionally "male" occupations.

BARRIERS TO EQUAL OPPORTUNITY: DISCRIMINATION, PRODUCTIVITY DIFFERENCES, CHOICE

A number of theories attempt to explain why the differences exist, either in terms of women's preferences and lower productivity, or in terms of discriminatory behaviour on the part of employers, unions, and co-workers. The statistical information on women's position in the Canadian economy is interpreted differently, depending on the observer's theoretical point of view. To some, the differences reflect women's preferences and choices. To others, they reflect the constraints faced by women. Unfortunately, too few empirical studies have attempted to collect evidence on the sources of the differences. The work of those who have identified and documented some of the barriers is so recent that the issue of changes in the barriers over time has not been addressed.

Theoretical Explanations for Differences

The theoretical explanations can be divided into two camps: those that assume that discrimination exists and try to explain who discriminates and why; and those that assume that differences are not the result of discriminatory behaviour. The first three theories presented attempt to explain discrimination.

Personal prejudice or aversion model   According to this model, individuals are prepared to pay a cost in order to avoid associating with members of a disfavoured group, in this case, women. The cause of discrimination is seen as personal prejudice or aversion toward women. According to this theory (developed by Gary Becker), employers are prepared to pay a premium or sacrifice profits in order to avoid hiring women. Similarly, discriminatory employees will be prepared to accept a lower wage to avoid employment with such minorities, or require higher wages if they must work with them. Discriminatory clients will prefer to pay higher prices to avoid dealing with the disfavoured group.

This theory sees discrimination as economically irrational and costly. It therefore predicts that discrimination is likely to persist only where market structures are monopolistic. In competitive market structures, employers would be unable to compete with non-discriminatory employers. According to this theory, discriminatory behaviour reduces the income both of those who discriminate and those who are discriminated against.

Monopoly-power model   The monopoly-power model is based on the belief that it is possible for majority groups to gain at the expense of the disadvantaged group. In this model, discrimination is seen as a way for some workers to obtain and maintain control over jobs in order to ensure job security and higher income. Both overt and covert exclusion methods are used to reduce the labour supply. Trade unions, and more specifically craft unions and professional associations, have been known to attempt to influence pay and working conditions by limiting the available supply of labour. The supply of labour can be limited by such tactics as licensing the occupation, restricting the numbers allowed to enter, and using informal hiring.

Dual segmented labour market model
Economists have identified the existence of, at minimum, a dual labour market. A primary market is composed mainly of prime-aged, white males who are concentrated in stable jobs which are high-paying, offer on-the-job training, and allow for internal mobility. A secondary market is composed mainly of youth, coloured workers, and women who are concentrated in low-paying, unstable jobs which offer no skill development and no prospects for advancement. Confinement to the secondary job market not only does not allow workers to invest in further human capital but actually adversely affects work habits, thereby making workers less motivated and less committed to the labour force.

Radical economists argue that capitalists deliberately segment labour markets in order to divide workers and maximize their profits. By excluding women from "men's" jobs, employers cause women to be overcrowded into a small number of occupations. The increased supply of labour (relative to demand) depresses wages in the secondary market; and the large, cheap supply of female labour can be used as a threat to keep men in the primary labour market from demanding higher wages.

Human capital model Human capital theory explains earnings and occupational distribution differentials in terms of differences in the productive capacity of men and women. The greater one's productivity, the higher one's earnings. In order to increase one's productivity, individuals invest in education, training, and experience in the labour force. The earnings differentials of men and women merely reflect the fact that men have made higher levels of human capital investment (i.e., have more education, more training, and more labour force experience).

Preference or choice model There are those who argue that women are segregated in particular occupations because they choose to be. Most women choose jobs on the basis of their being complementary with household activities and child-raising. They therefore look for jobs with flexible hours, or for part-time work, so that they can combine their household responsibilities with participation in the paid labour force. Childbearing and care of family members who are ill has meant that some women prefer jobs that allow them to leave and reenter the labour market easily.

Some women may not apply for certain jobs because they have lower productivity than the job requires, or at least believe their productivity to be lower. They may also feel that some jobs are not "women's" work.

These five approaches indicate the number of possible explanations for differences in the employment opportunities of men and women. Where discrimination is identified as a cause, reasons for discriminatory behaviour are attributed variously to prejudice or misinformation, higher profits, higher wages, job security; potential sources of discrimination include employers, clients, co-workers, and trade unions.

Documentation of Barriers

The brief survey of theoretical approaches indicates that the causes and sources of discrimination and the causes of differences are numerous and interconnected. No doubt all are at work simultaneously to produce the differences documented above. In this part of the section some of the barriers that women face are discussed. An attempt is made to provide some empirical evidence for the existence of each barrier, and how important it may be in explaining the position of women in the Canadian economy.

Education and experience Inadequate education and training are often mentioned as one of the barriers deterring women's advancement in the labour force. It has been repeatedly verified that education and experience explain a large percentage of income and status differences among individuals and groups (Gunderson, 1976a). In general it appears that women with higher levels of education are more likely to participate in the labour force, are less likely to be unemployed, and have a smaller earnings gap.

It has also been argued that current productivity differences result partly from past discrimination or pre-labour market commitments. Through socialization women have been conditioned not to invest in productivity since their primary role is seen to be outside the labour force. Education systems have conditioned and channelled women into fields of study (such as arts, education, nursing) that lead to "women's" jobs. As of 1971, enrolment figures show an increase in the number of women enrolled in traditionally male-dominated fields of study (such as law, medicine, commerce), but total female enrolment remains small (Robb and Spencer, 1976).

Labour force commitment It is sometimes argued that women do not do as well as men in the labour force because women are not as committed to their jobs. Because of their primary commitment to household responsibilities: (1) women restrict their productivity investment; (2) they apply for the kinds of jobs that accommodate part-time work, higher turnover rates, and high levels of absenteeism; (3) employers are less likely to invest in training women; (4) women are less likely to acquire as much labour force experience as men.

Evidence indicates that married women, women in their middle years who are raising children, and women with low levels of education have weak labour force commitment. Women with these characteristics are precisely the ones who suffer the greatest earnings gap (Gunderson, 1976a). The gap is least for women who are young and single, precisely those who are most committed to the labour force and have fewer family responsibilities.

While the reasons for the weaker labour force commitment may be seen as originating from prior discrimination, the fact that it is a factor in explaining some of the earnings differences indicates that women must either overcome the constraints that keep some women weakly committed to the labour force or accept the lower commitment as part of the reason for the differences which exist.

Lack of equitable division of labour in the household and absence of childcare facilities One of the major sources for the weaker labour force commitment of some women is the lack of equitable division of labour in the household and the absence of childcare facilities. Being married and having children entails costs and benefits. Household responsibilities and child-rearing influence one's occupational choice, length of time in the labour force, and nature of labour force participation (full-time versus part-time work). What is discriminatory about the situation is the fact that the cost of being married and especially having children is much greater for working women than for working men (Cook, 1976:1-12). Married women who work full-time in the labour force work more hours each week (in the home and labour force combined) than their husbands. Working mothers are faced with guilt and emotional strain, for society still finds it unacceptable for mothers of young children to work outside the home.

Social attitudes—sex-typing of jobs and roles   Social attitudes can be a powerful source of discrimination. Society's expectations of the roles that men and women should play are usually based on past trends and patterns. Sex stereotyping starts very early in the home and is reinforced in children's books and in schools. The presence of increasing numbers of women in the labour force and in non-traditional jobs should help to change and reinforce new expectations and attitudes about women's role in the labour force.

Attitudes change as new role models are created. The fact that women entering the labour force are still segregated in traditionally "women's" jobs helps to perpetuate the existing sex-typing of occupations. While some may feel that the sex-typing of occupations is based on biological and temperamental differences between men and women, there is overwhelming evidence that sex-typing of occupations is purely cultural. (Report of the Royal Commission on the Status of Women, 1970:79).

The sex-typing of occupations leads women to obtain training in traditionally female-dominated fields of study and employers to exclude them from male-dominated occupations. The perpetuation of occupational segregation in turn reinforces sex-typing. This is a vicious cycle that keeps women in low-paying, "women's" occupations. In order to break the cycle, women must be allowed into traditionally male-dominated jobs.

Given their relative newness in the labour force and limited occupational representation, women face "statistical" discrimination. That is, women entering the labour force for the first time are judged by employers on the basis of the record of other working women. Given that until recently most women were not committed to the labour force, have been concentrated in jobs with low lev-els of responsibility, and have had less training and experience, they have a reputation as being less productive than men. Until the stereotypes of working women are updated, women will not have an equal opportunity.

Systemic discrimination   Overt discrimination, of the door-slamming variety, is just one of the possible manifestations of discrimination. A more common and less visible form is "systemic" discrimination, a product of employment practices and systems (see Jain and Sloane, 1981). It frequently exists even when there is no intent to discriminate. But whether intended or not, hiring practices and job-assignment/promotion practices can bar women from equal access to employment opportunities.

The extent to which systemic barriers actually affect the hiring, job-assignment, and remuneration of women is difficult to assess, given that the reasons for decisions are not made public. There is therefore very little evidence on which to assess the seriousness of each possible barrier. At this point, it is important to identify these potential barriers in order that their workings can be investigated.

Hiring mechanisms

Women of equal ability to men may be unable to compete for specific jobs because they are unaware of their existence. Firms that recruit by word of mouth (informal hiring channels) attract workers similar to those already employed in the firm. Informal recruitment perpetuates existing occupational segregation (Calzavara, 1982). This is especially harmful for women since they are segregated in a small number of low-paying jobs. While it is no longer legal to show sex-bias in job advertisements, some firms have turned to employment agencies who will (illegally) screen job candidates on the basis of sex.

Job-assignment and promotion

Once hired, women may face discrimination with respect to the level at which they are hired, the rate of wage increase, and the rate at which they move up through the organizational hierarchy. These decisions, like the decisions to recruit and hire, are subject to the same kinds of discriminatory barriers.

POLICY IMPLICATIONS

Documentation has been presented showing that there are differences in the employment opportunities of men and women. While changes over the last 50 years show that occupational segregation is lessening, and that the wage gap has narrowed slightly, the existing differences are still quite large. The change that has occurred since the introduction of equal employment legislation and equal pay legislation has not been dramatic. Some even argue that the legislation has had no impact on the rate of change. The differences between women and men are still large enough and costly enough to warrant some prompt action.

Policies Aimed at Labour Supply

Education and training   Women should be encouraged and helped to acquire the education and training that will allow them to compete on equal terms with men. When identifying the barriers, it becomes clear that adjusting for productivity differences reduces the income gap between men and women. A comparison of the educational qualifications of men and women indicates that a lower proportion of women have uni-

versity degrees, and that most of those are held in traditionally female-dominated fields. Since it appears that this situation may result from both discriminatory practices and social attitudes, solutions must address both sources.

Labour force commitment   Remove some of the attitudinal and structural barriers that lower some women's labour force commitment. The section on barriers showed that women with characteristics associated with lower labour force commitment (middle years, low education, and especially raising children) fare poorly in the labour market. Women suffer greater costs than men when they combine marriage and labour force participation. Most analysts attribute the greater costs to the unequal division of household work and women's responsibility for childcare. In order to reduce the burden that lowers some women's labour force commitment, a number of things can be done (Cook and Ebert, 1976).

Family roles can be redefined (through campaigns geared to alter sex-stereotyping of roles). Husbands can be encouraged to share more equitably in the performance of household tasks.

Restructure working conditions in the labour force to facilitate part-time work and shorter work weeks. Make these changes practical alternatives rather than a sign of lack of labour force commitment, which penalizes the worker.

Government and employers should be encouraged to provide childcare support and extend present support by providing more childcare facilities and more subsidization of care.

Policies Aimed at Demand for Labour

Some of the barriers that result from the demand side of the labour market (employers) can be reduced by a combination of improvements to present legislation, affirmative action programs, and campaigns to change social attitudes and update stereotypes.

Equal pay legislation   Documentation was presented in an earlier section showing that at the very least 10-20 percent of the wage difference between men and women is a result of discrimination. Equal pay legislation in Canada was first enacted in 1951. Employers are required by law to give men and women workers equal pay for equal work within the same establishment, although there are specific exceptions under which differences in wages are allowed by the legislation; these include seniority, experience, and merit. The legislation has had little effect on the wage gap. Critics have pointed out a number of problems with the legislation which make it ineffective.

Its major problem lies in its restrictive nature. It applies only to women and men who do the same or similar work within the same establishment. Given the differences in the occupational distribution of women and men, the law does not apply to two thirds of working women—women who are employed in jobs with few or no male co-workers.

In order to make the legislation more effective, all government jurisdictions should adopt the equal-value standard. That is, male and female workers should receive equal pay for work of equal value. This would make the legislation applicable to all workers and reduce some of the negative side effects of the present legislation.

Equal employment legislation   In 1964 equal employment legislation was enacted prohibiting discrimination in the areas of hiring, promotion, and conditions of work.

Some jurisdictions also make an effort to reach discrimination in recruitment (prohibit discriminatory job advertisements and job descriptions, prohibit trade unions and employment agencies from screening applicants on the basis of sex).

While basically sound, equal employment legislation should be made more effective by modifications to the way in which it is enforced. At present, complaints may be initiated only by the persons aggrieved. If an employee complainant cannot be found, there is no case. To set the case in motion, the employee must have knowledge of the legislation, the ability and resources to use it, and the motivation to take action against her employer not knowing whether she will win.

Despite the suggested improvements in the equal pay and equal employment laws, legislation by itself is unlikely to eliminate discrimination. Jain and Sloane (1981:74) point out that: (1) legislation is limited in scope; (2) it must be effectively implemented; (3) the evolution of law and legal principles is a slow process; and (4) it is aimed at law-abiding employers and does little to restrain lawbreakers.

Affirmative action   Besides broadening legislation, enforcing it more thoroughly, and imposing more severe penalties, governments and employers should engage in positive efforts to encourage training, recruitment, and career development through affirmative action.

Affirmative action is a comprehensive attempt to remove some of the past and present employment discrimination that women face. This goal is achieved through a series of stages. The first stage is to examine the work force in an establishment and obtain data on the positions held by men and women, their salaries, rates of promotion, and other relevant information which can be used to assess women's status. The second stage is to review personnel practices to identify systemic discrimination (in recruiting, hiring, promotion, etc.) and to set up strategies aimed at removing any discrepancies in the workforce. The third step involves setting targets (or quotas) and timetables for overcoming identified inequalities. The fourth step is to set up a monitoring and evaluation system to assess progress. Affirmative action can be achieved on a voluntary basis, through government incentives (contract compliance), or made mandatory.

Affirmative action, especially if it can be achieved on a voluntary basis or through contract compliance (where government makes it a condition for securing funding or government contracts), would provide women with an opportunity to make up for past discrimination. Affirmative action may be the only chance women have to free themselves from occupational segregation and all its negative side effects.

Those women who choose to remain in traditionally "female" occupations will not find affirmative action helpful. What they require is a new wage system whereby wages are determined by the skills and experience necessary to do the work.

Changes in attitudes If people are to change their behaviour voluntarily and/or comply with imposed legislation, a fundamental change in social attitudes toward the role and abilities of women is necessary.

Government and private agencies can initiate a media campaign designed to inform and educate individuals, especially employers. Such a campaign would attempt to alleviate sex-stereotyping of roles and jobs.

Implementation of laws and policies indirectly serves to change attitudes by recognizing, amplifying, and sanctioning discriminatory behaviour.

Governments can influence attitudes by acting as model employers. If women are given the chance to show what they can do, their performance in the public sector can serve to change and reinforce the new attitudes in the private sector.

REFERENCES

Armstrong, Pat, and Hugh Armstrong
  1983   *A Working Majority: What Women Must Do For Pay.* Ottawa: Information Canada.

Boyd, Monica
  1975   "English-Canadian and French-Canadian attitudes towards women: Results of the Canadian Gallup Polls," *Journal of Comparative Family Studies,* 6:153-69.
  1977   "The status of immigrant women in Canada," in *Women in Canada,* ed. Marylee Stephenson. Don Mills, Ontario: General Publishing.

Calzavara, Liviana
  1982   "Social Networks and Access to Job Opportunities." Ph.D. Thesis. Department of Sociology, University of Toronto.

Canada, Royal Commission on the Status of Women in Canada.
  1970   *Report.* Ottawa: Queen's Printer.

Cook, Gail
  1976   "Opportunity for choice: A criterion," in *Opportunity for Choice,* ed. Gail Cook. Ottawa: Information Canada.

Cook, Gail, and Mary Eberts
  1976   "Policies affecting work," in *Opportunity for Choice,* ed. Gail Cook. Ottawa: Information Canada.

Gunderson, Morley
  1975   "Equal pay in Canada," in *Equal Pay for Women,* ed. P. Pettman. London: MEB Books.
  1976a "Work Patterns," in *Opportunity for Choice,* ed. Gail Cook. Ottawa: Information Canada.
  1976b "Time-pattern of male-female wage differentials: Ontario 1946-1971," *Industrial Relations/Relations Industrielles,* 31:57-71.
  1982   "The male-female earnings gap in Ontario: A Summary." Research Branch, Ontario Ministry of Labour.

Jain, Harish, and Peter Sloane
  1981   *Equal Employment Issues.* New York: Praeger.

Philips, Paul, and Erin Phillips
  1983   *Women and Work: Inequality in the Labour Market.* Toronto: James Lorimer.

Robb, Leslie, and Byron Spencer
  1976   "Education: enrolment and attainment," in *Opportunity for Choice,* ed. G. Cook. Ottawa: Information Canada.

Statistics Canada
  Annual *The Labour Force.* Catalogue No. 71-001.

White, Julie
  1980   *Women and Unions.* Ottawa: Supply and Services Canada.

FOR FURTHER READING

Abella, Rosalie S., ed. 1984. *Equality in Employment: A Royal Commission Report.* Ottawa: Supply and Services. Judge Rosalie Abella conducted a Royal Commission in the early 1980s examining the position of women, visible minorities, Native Indians, and the physically disabled. The findings of the Commission provide a detailed account of inequality in modern Canada, and her policy ideas highlight many of the parallel circumstances facing disadvantaged groups in this country.

Armstrong, Pat, and Hugh Armstrong. 1984. *The Double Ghetto: Canadian Women and Their Segregated Work* (2nd ed.). Toronto: McClelland and Stewart. An examination of the work women do, the social constraints that restrict their options, and the impact of work on women's consciousness. The book offers a systematic examination of women's unequal position in Canadian society.

Eichler, Margrit. 1985. "And the work never ends: Feminist contributions," *Canadian Review of Sociology and Anthropology,* 22, no. 5:619-44. This essay reviews the historical development of feminist scholarship in Anglophone sociology. It provides an ample bibliography of feminist studies and a careful review of a plethora of salient issues faced by women and men in contemporary Canadian life.

Mackie, Marlene. 1983. *Exploring Gender Relations: A Canadian Perspective.* Toronto: Butterworths. Oriented around the question of what it means to be female or male in modern Canada, this book examines relations between women and men. Among the many issues examined are family patterns, gender socialization, structured inequalities, and prospects for change.

Wilson, Suzanne. 1986. *Women, the Family and the Economy* (2nd ed.). Toronto: McGraw-Hill Ryerson. Women's experiences in family, work, and public life are reviewed. This is a basic introduction to a range of material dealing with Canadian women.

C: Age

26. *Income, Pensions, and Inequality in Later Life*

Joseph A. Tindale

INTRODUCTION

The consideration of age in analyses of structured social inequality in Canada is a relatively recent phenomenon. In one of the first treatments of this question, Myles (1980) examined the manner in which the state influences the distribution of resources to elderly persons. Prior to this, gerontological researchers focussed on micro and individualistic concerns. The situation has changed dramatically over the last decade. Increasingly researchers have considered the aged as cohorts, or age groups, as well as individuals. It is also recognized now that age, class, gender, and/or ethnic group interests interact and are sometimes in conflict with each other as well as with more individual priorities (Marshall and Tindale, 1978-79; Tindale and Marshall, 1980).

It is not possible in the space allotted a

single chapter to survey all possible dimensions of the age and inequality question. Attention will therefore first be focussed on providing an overview of the development of gerontological theory as it relates to questions of inequality. The interpretive perspective, and particularly its macro contributions, will then be applied to what is probably the most fundmental component of age and inequality: the relationship between income and later life.

THEORETICAL PERSPECTIVES

Gerontology is a relatively young interdisciplinary field of study. Its theoretical foundations draw on a number of disciplines, principally sociology and psychology. The North American roots stretch back to the 1920s (Cole, 1984), although substantial theory development did not emerge until the 1960s with the formulation of disengagement theory by Cumming and Henry

An original essay written especially for this volume.

(1961). And while this early theoretical work did not specifically address questions of inequality, the failure to ask such questions reflects the starting assumptions of disengagement theory and its links to structural-functional systems theory (Parsons and Shils, 1951).

Disengagement theory rests on a central assumption of individual and societal mutuality in the passive withdrawal of individuals from the central work and family roles of adulthood. In assuming this, the theory is functionalist in terms of subordinating the interests of individuals and groups to the dominant demands of the larger society. As such, the theory serves better as a description of the status quo than as an explanation of the way in which people actually negotiate their ongoing place in the community (Marshall and Tindale, 1978-79).

The construction of a model for disengagement did serve the purpose of formally articulating what had until this time been a vague debate among researchers about whether older persons were better off staying active or disengaging from their communities following departure from primary social roles (Rose, 1968). The critics of this theory (Marshall and Tindale, 1978-79) have made the point that disengagement theory and its intellectual siblings—activity theory (Lemon, Bengtson, and Peterson, 1972) and continuity theory (Atchley, 1971)—all share essentially the same assumptions of individual passivity and value consensus. These theoretical models cannot, therefore, be considered alternatives to each other. Activity and continuity theory are but thematically consistent revisions of the disengagement model.

These individualistic theories can be profitably contrasted with age-stratification and modernization models. These latter models are inclined toward a more structural or organizational focus and away from an exclusively individualistic orientation. Nonetheless, while the focus is on larger groups of older persons, typically cohorts, the theoretical assumptions remain consistent with the status quo.

The age-stratification theorists (Riley, 1976; Foner, 1978; Foner and Kertzer, 1978) have sought to extend micro theorizing by concentrating on cohorts of persons whose movement through the life span and across time is analysed by a process they term *cohort flow*. They have also introduced conflict into their analysis, through a consideration of the possibilities for intergenerational tension following from political squabbling over scarce social and economic resources as an aging population gradually begins to act in a politically cohesive manner (Foner, 1974).

The conceptualization of cohort flow by age-stratification theorists has facilitated methodological advances in the effort to separate age (maturation) effects from cohort (birth groupings) effects and period (environmental) effects. The attempted movement from a micro (individual) to a macro (cohort) focus, and from consensus to conflict, should be appreciated. However, the actual contribution of age-stratification research to an understanding of inequality in age relations is limited by the fact that the substantive focus is still individual in its impact. Individuals are allocated roles along an age hierarchy based on their birth date. They are expected to conform to these in keeping with societally shared values. The conflict, when it exists, is between generations over scarce resources, and does not take into account differential interest between classes of people that may intersect or override age interests (Tindale and Marshall, 1980).

Modernization theory, in some respects quite similar to the age-stratification thesis, caught the imagination of researchers (Fischer, 1978; Achenbaum, 1978; Graebner, 1980; Quadagno, 1982) in a manner reminiscent of the disengagement/activity debate. The issue was whether or not modernization theorists (Cowgill and Holmes, 1972; Cowgill, 1979) were accurate in their assertion that the status of the aged in any society is inversely related to the level of modernization of that same society.

The shortcomings of micro and macro normative theorizing have spawned a series of efforts to construct what has been termed *interpretive theory* (Marshall and Tindale, 1978-79; Tindale and Marshall, 1980). The central characteristics of interpretive theorizing are directly opposite to those found within the traditions of disengagement theory, age-stratification theory, or modernization theory. Theory developed within the interpretive perspective is supportive of inductive thinking, does not assume shared values, accounts for the possibility of conflict between individuals and groups of differential interest, is historical in outlook, and encourages the use of qualitative methods (Marshall, 1980).

Interpretive theorizing has been developed in both micro and macro contexts such that interpretive theorists do not seek to construct theories of aging which are universal in application. Instead, attempts have been made to apply contemporary theories, i.e., symbolic interactionism and conflict theory, to particular age-related settings. Theory development along these lines has demonstrated a rich potential for the emergence of a strong interpretive paradigm in gerontology.

The best micro-level examples of this application of existing theory to gerontological settings are derived from symbolic interactionist work in the tradition of Mead and Goffman. In a purely theoretical vein, Chappell and Orbach (1986) have delineated a Meadian process of socialization to old age, where one tries on roles in a dynamic fashion quite different from the passive socialization to roles that Rosow (1974; 1976) writes of, or the societally determined allocation to age-graded roles described by the age-stratification theorists (Riley, 1976; Foner, 1978).

Spence (1986) talks about adult development as *career* in a symbolic interactionist framework that is similar to that applied by Tindale (1980) to the maintenance of identity by old men on skid row. In describing adult development in terms of career, Spence is also combining the traditionally psychological term *development*, with the sociological understanding of *career*. This kind of social psychology suggests the combination of the two base disciplines, sociology and psychology, in a way that the term would lead one to expect but which in fact rarely happens. Social psychologists are increasingly combining developmental psychology and symbolic interactionist concepts in a manner consistent with the assumptions of the interpretive perspective. Ryff (1986) has done so with regard to the construction of self-concept, as has Norris (1987) in her discussion of social identity in later life.

The theory-building process at the macro level in gerontology has followed a similar path to that of the micro-level theorizing. The consensus-model precursors to the political economy of aging theorizing are age-stratification theory and modernization theory. From there have evolved various attempts to account better for social conflict among individuals and groups as they seek what they perceive to be their fair share of existing social resources.

For example, Tindale (1987) examined the effect of student enrolment declines and government budgetary restraint on age-group relations among Ontario secondary-school teachers. As enrolments declined and as funding for the school system tightened, tensions generated by age and class arose with respect to jobs and income. He found that the age and work experience concept of seniority was being invoked by teachers as a gatekeeper for access to job opportunities. Teachers are in a middle-class profession, and while they experience considerable day-to-day autonomy on the job, they are unable to control the general conditions of their work. Teachers, for instance, have control over the specific timing and approach taken to the material they convey. However, it is the government and not the teachers who decides the question of hiring levels.

When the Ontario government applied budgetary restraint, the school boards were required to reduce the supply of teachers. They did this, with the reluctant co-operation of the Ontario Secondary School Teachers' Federation, by declaring that the criterion for job security would be seniority. Junior, and most often younger teachers, were declared redundant and let go without regard to ability. The result was that age tensions between younger and older teachers were exacerbated as the teachers turned on each other in an internal struggle to protect jobs and incomes. This occurred because the federation was unable to resist the external authority of the provincial government. The increased age tensions might well have been worse had it not also been the case that many junior teachers were no more eager than the older, more senior teachers to replace seniority with some other criterion for job tenure. The dynamics of these job conditions illustrate a situation in which age and class location interact to link an individual's biography to the social context within which he or she lives.

A focus on the macro relationship between social class and relative access to work and retirement opportunities is being developed by researchers working within the political economy perspective. This work is akin to the micro interpretive work in that theory-building is still relatively embryonic and relies on borrowing concepts from existing theory and testing to see how applicable they are to populations of older persons. Estes, Swan, and Gerard (1982) and Walker (1981) entitle their papers "Towards a Political Economy of Aging" and "Old Age," respectively. In this kind of work, social class is the predictor variable where the quality of life for the elderly is the outcome variable.

The work of Townsend (1981), Neysmith and Edwardh (1984), and Myles (1984) complements that of Estes and colleagues and Walker in that their focus is on the ways in which social dependency is constructed through class relations and on the intervening efforts of the state to try and moderate structured social inequality with the intervention of social policy. Each of these analyses would suggest that it is the conditions associated with class location and gender, as well as their cumulative impact across the life course, which creates inequality in later life. As such, social policy which is targetted only at older persons will not affect such fundamental social inequality. It must be content with a minor redistribution of resources and the partial replacement of lost earnings for older workers when they retire.

In reviewing the emergence of theory in gerontology, the argument has been made that micro and macro interpretive models are best equipped to explain conditions of inequality across the life span. Theory which views individuals as negotiating their own situation within the opportunities and constraints afforded them by their class location and community resources can provide a framework for understanding why so many older persons are disadvantaged in later life. It is a combination of class, gender, and age effects. In what follows, the interpretive perspective will be applied to the issues of work, income, and retirement.

INCOME INEQUALITY ACROSS THE LIFE SPAN

The companion chapter on age in this volume, based on a National Council of Welfare report (1984), reviews much of the relevant material related to poverty and poverty trends among the elderly. As a result, this chapter will take that material as a complementary given and concentrate on the importance of considering income across the life span, the implications of this for sources and levels of income, and the relationship between income and wealth as one's family matures.

It was suggested in the theory review that later-life differences in social condition are a function of class and gender biography across the life span. This is well illustrated in Table 26-1 where family income by age and gender is shown for the year 1984. Incomes for male-headed families accelerate faster and reach higher levels than is the case for females. And while there is a slight lag in the peaking of income for females relative to males, the more important point to note is that the decline in income, while consistently downward for both male- and female-headed families after the peak, is slower for females than for males. Indeed, beyond age 70 there is only a negligible difference be-

TABLE 26-1 Average income for Canadian families headed by males and females, 1984.

Age	Males	Females
<or = 24	$ 25 806	$ 11 508
25-34	35 659	15 452
35-44	42 377	21 343
45-54	45 122	26 273
55-59	41 754	27 276
60-64	34 164	25 676
65-69	31 031	25 460
>or = 70	23 940	23 353
>or = 65	25 753	23 991

Source: Calculated from Table 8, p.59 in Statistics Canada, *Income distributions by size in Canada 1984* (Ottawa: Minister of Supply and Services Canada, 1986).

tween the two. The near absence of wages as an income source beyond age 70, contrasted to their continuing presence in the 65-and-older figures, and the corresponding reliance on pensions, have a levelling effect. This is because pensions replace only a portion of pre-retirement income, and the government pensions of Old Age Security and the Guaranteed Income Supplement—unlike wages—are not gender biased.

Table 26-1 refers only to income; had wealth also been calculated, the figures would have been considerably higher. The principal source of wealth other than income held by most Canadians is their homes. The incidence of home ownership jumps from 12 percent for those families and individuals where the head is under age 24 to 53 percent where age of head is 25-34 years (Statistics Canada, 1977). That incidence increases right through to the cohort of those aged 45-54; this parallels linear increases in income and wealth. After age 54 all three begin to fall off.

The income lost through retirement and partially replaced by pension and investment income is largely derived from public sources. In 1981 (National Council of Welfare, 1984) non-poor couples and individuals received 43.5 percent and 31.2 percent respectively of their income from public sources. Poor couples and individuals relied on public source's considerably more, 93.2 percent and 86.8 percent respectively. It is apparent that were it not for public sources of retirement income, many couples and individuals who are not now poor would be. What are these public sources of later-life income and how did they evolve to their current levels?

INEQUALITY AND SOCIAL POLICY: THE CASE OF PENSIONS

In 1982 the Ministries of Finance and Health and Welfare noted in the green paper they released on pension reform that "the foundation for all retirement income is the federal Old Age Security Pension." Its emergence can be traced back to 1927 when the federal government initiated a plan funded equally by the federal and provincial governments. This paid beneficiaries a maximum of $20.00 a month, provided they were at least 70 years of age, could pass a means test, and had resided as British subjects in Canada for at least 20 years. This minimal annuity was first substantially revised with the passing of the Old Age Security Act (OAS) in 1951. The enactment of this legislation eliminated the means test, increased the benefit levels, and relaxed the residency requirement. By the mid 1960s the monthly benefit had been increased to $75.00, but even so it was becoming abundantly clear that many Canadians would

need substantially more if they were to avoid poverty. As a result of these conditions, the income-tested Guaranteed Income Supplement (GIS) was introduced in 1967. By 1970 the age of eligibility had been gradually lowered to 65. In 1973 the OAS and the GIS were indexed to the Consumer Price Index on a quarterly basis. And in 1975 the Spouse's Allowance (associated with the GIS) was introduced to provide for persons widowed between the ages of 60 and 64 whose spouse had been over the age of 65 (Special Senate Committee on Retirement Age Policies, 1979). It has also now become available to spouses between the ages of 60 and 64 where the living spouse's retirement income is minimal. Given Canadian age-at-marriage patterns and traditional conditions differentiating male and female working incomes, in most cases the beneficiaries are women (Tindale and Neysmith, 1987).

The figures in Table 26-2 clearly indicate the basic income available to the Canadian aged living in Ontario at the end of 1986. Canadians over 65 years of age and satisfying a minimum residency requirement received $303.64 per month in OAS benefits. If they essentially had no other visible income, they would also be entitled to a monthly GIS payment of $360.87 as a single person, or $235.03 per person as part of a couple. Some provinces also add to this package with a provincially administered income supplement program. Ontario, for example, has a program called the Guaranteed Annual Income Supplement (GAINS), where the maximum individual payment is $83.00. Both the GIS and GAINS payments are reduced by $1.00 for every $2.00 of non-government income up to the threshold of eligibility. Thus, as one's income increases beyond the minimum threshold, these income-tested supplements are reduced accordingly until they disappear.

TABLE 26-2 Pensions (maximum) available to Ontarians.

Non-contributory pension plans: pension source	*July 1987*	
	Individual	*Person as part of couple*
OAS	$ 303.64	$ 303.64
GIS	360.87	235.03
GAINS	83.00	83.00
Total per month	747.51	621.67*
Total per year	8 968.08	7 460.04**

*$ 1 243.34 per couple
**$14 923.68 per couple
Source: Figures are calculated from those provided by officials in the GAINS office, July 1987.

These public, non-contributory pension sources provide an income that is very near poverty line cut-offs (Tindale and Neysmith, 1987). As such, these are minimum income assistance programs and do not constitute the adequacy levels more often associated with income security programs (Myles, 1986). To achieve an income that moves one beyond a subsistence level, older persons must be eligible for benefits derived from one or more contributory pension plans. Public plans like the Canada/Quebec Pension Plan (C/QPP), private employer plans, and personal annuities are included in this group.

These plans merit further examination because the pension reform debates that have raged around them for the past decade throw the economic side of age and inequality into stark relief. As Table 26-3 illustrates, coverage in the private and the public spheres increases with growth in earning levels. In the public sector, almost everyone earning more than the Average Industrial Wage (about $23 000) was covered. In 1979,

49 percent of males and only 30 percent of females in the private sector were covered. For both genders those at the highest income levels are covered to a lesser degree than those in the middle income levels because the former are more likely to be self-employed where their surplus income is invested elsewhere, in RRSPs for example. Those least likely to be covered, men or women, are those receiving 1.5 times the average wage (Health and Welfare Canada, 1982).

Coverage also increases with age. It increases sooner in the public sector: 48 percent coverage in the public sector at age 18-24 as against almost no coverage for this age cohort in the private sector. This is important because the period of time one has to wait until point of pension contribution eligibility has an impact on the level of pension credits one will be able to accumulate.

The factors of earning level, gender, and age interact at both the micro and the macro level. Individuals combine age and gender attributes with their class location as they

TABLE 26-3   Distribution by employment income of CPP/QPP, RPP and RRSP contributors.

Males in the private sector, 1979

Employment income range	No. of CPP/QPP contributors	Registered pension plan contributors as % of CPP/QPP contributors			Estimated members of non-contrib. Plans as % of CPP/QPP contributors	Total Pension plan members as % of CPP/QPP contributors
		without RRSP's	with RRSP's	Total		
$1 – $7 499	816 948	5.3	0.3	5.6	5.2	10.8
$7 500 – 14 999	1 361 808	16.9	2.2	19.1	17.8	36.9
$15 000 – 22 499	1 344 501	26.7	6.8	33.5	31.2	64.7
$22 500 – 29 999	530 439	25.7	14.6	40.3	37.5	77.8
$30 000 +	276 710	20.7	24.2	44.9	41.7	86.6
Total	4 330 415	19.1	6.2	25.3	23.5	48.8

Females in the private sector, 1979

Employment income range	No. of CPP/QPP contributors	Registered pension plan contributors as % of CPP/QPP contributors			Estimated members of non-contrib. Plans as % of CPP/QPP contributors	Total Pension plan members as % of CPP/QPP contributors
		without RRSP's	with RRSP's	Total		
$1 – $7 499	1 471 273	5.1	0.3	5.4	2.0	7.4
$7 500 – 14 999	1 280 218	27.5	4.6	32.1	12.1	44.2
$15 000 – 22 499	265 999	45.0	11.4	56.4	21.3	77.7
$22 500 – 29 999	28 206	23.4	25.1	48.6	18.4	66.9
$30 000 +	8 760	8.7	19.3	28.0	10.6	38.6
Total	3 054 440	18.1	3.3	21.5	8.1	29.6

Source: Health & Welfare Canada, *Pension Plan Coverage by Level of Earnings and Age 1978 and 1979* (Ottawa: Government of Canada, 1982), Tables 1, 4.

negotiate personal futures which offer them the best chance of maintaining independence as they move into later life. The negotiations these individuals are engaged in take place across the life span as personal biographies are constructed within the pa-rameters permitted by social conditions. As such, income insecurity in later life will be a widespread phenomenon until such time as the structural inequalities between men and women and between income groups are substantially moderated.

Progress made in reducing the ranks of the poor (National Council of Welfare, 1984) has been limited to males. The reasons for this include the traditional role strain between mother and worker, and the differences in earnings between men and women. In the mid 1960s women earned 58 cents for every dollar earned by men doing similar work. Today the 58 cents has grown slightly to 66 cents (Tindale and Neysmith, 1987).

In its final report, the Parliamentary Task Force on Pension Reform stated that they did not think Canadians wanted them to upset the fundamental status quo inherent in our three-tiered pension system. The task force saw themselves as having to face two issues (Martin Matthews and Tindale, 1987). The first of these involves the degree to which the government was willing to move on some long-standing inequities in the treatment of women in their role as workers, and more importantly as family caregivers.

The second issue requires a choice to be made between directing subsequent pension reforms to either the public or the private sector. At stake are very large pools of capital created by pension contributions. Encouraging employer plans or RRSPS as opposed to expanding the C/QPP or the public non-contributory plans has huge implications in terms of where these contribution pools will develop and how accessible they will be to private and public investment borrowers.

The task force (1983) made a decision to concentrate their reform recommendations on gender issues, and to preserve the status quo with respect to the balance between public and private pension plans. In so doing they opted to reproduce in later life the inequality that the pension plan eligibility and contribution structure helps to create among younger working persons. In

refusing to improve the benefit structure of the C/QPP from 25 percent to 50 percent of the Average Industrial Wage, the task force members were repudiating the recommendations made by many labour and other non-governmental organizations in their submissions to the task force.

While improvements to public-sector pension benefits were not recommended, the task force did assert the need for the elimination of some of the most transparent pension inequities facing Canadian women. It was recommended that survivors' benefits be guaranteed at the 60 percent level, pension credits be split in the event of marriage dissolution, improvements be made to the spousal allowance, and a C/QPP-like pension for homemakers be set up (Martin Matthews and Tindale, 1987).

This parliamentary task force was a Liberal creation. The Progressive Conservative government which took office in the fall of 1984, approximately nine months after the final report was submitted, has had an uneven track record in terms of its response to these recommendations. The government has several times attempted to erode public pensions benefits, has succeeded in enhancing private pension benefits for those wealthy enough to take advantage of them, and has publicly proclaimed some relatively minor but nevertheless noteworthy changes to the C/QPP and employer-sponsored occupational pension plans (Tindale and Neysmith, 1987).

In the winter of 1984-85 the federal government published a discussion paper which focussed on the possibility of terminating the universality feature of the Old Age Security pension benefit. This flew in the face of the Prime Minister's election promise to hold the OAS universality as a "sacred trust." The public raised a loud hue and cry with the result that the government reasserted their promise not to tamper with universality.

A second foray against public pensions was mounted in the 1985 spring budget. It included a provision to partially de-index the Old Age Security benefit from its full tie to the Consumer Price Index. There very quickly emerged a grass roots social movement to protest any budget provision which would make older Canadians more vulnerable to the ravages of inflation. This loose coalition of older individuals and seniors' groups received public support from organized labour, the women's movement, and antipoverty groups. This alliance is consistent with the "middle class incorporation" thesis (Myles, 1986), which argues that the inclusion of the middle class in social welfare programs ensures their vocal support when such programs come under attack.

However, while the federal government has not been successful in reducing the Old Age Security benefits, they have enriched the private pension investment opportunities of the well-to-do. This same May budget which failed to undercut the inflation protection on the old age security pension, did manage to raise the ceiling on contributions to Registered Retirement Savings Plans (RRSPs). These are retirement annuity plans that persons with disposable income often invest in because they provide a tax deduction on the annual contribution and relatively low-taxed pension benefits paid out when one is older. The budget lifted the ceiling on contribution from $5500 to $15 000 and reduced the proportion of income that could be annually invested to 18 percent from 20 percent (Myles, 1986). The senior citizens who were vulnerable to the potential erosion of inflation protection on the OAS are also the people who are least likely to be in a position to take advantage of these changes in the RRSP regulations (Tin-dale and Neysmith, 1987).

In late 1985 and early 1986 the federal government engaged in negotiations with the provinces that have resulted in some reforms being made to the Canada/Quebec Pension Plan and employer-sponsored pensions. As of January 1, 1987, contributors to the C/QPP have been able to begin receiving their pension benefit anytime between their 60th and 70th birthdays. This represents a flexibility that was not previously available when benefits began at 65. The benefit level is adjusted accordingly depending on when in this period an individual retires. Also commencing at this time, contribution rates, presently set at 3.6 percent per year shared equally by the individual and his or her employer, will be increased by 0.2 percent per year for each of the next five years, culminating in a contribution rate of 4.6 percent. The rate will then be increased by a further 0.15 percent per year between 1992 and 2001 when the contribution rate will have increased to 7.6 percent (Tindale and Neysmith, 1987).

This implementation of changes to the C/QPP was supposed to parallel a set of reforms to private plans. And while the legislation has been passed, as of early 1987 the provinces had not been able to adjust fully their bureaucratic machinery. As a result, the anticipated changes in the private sector have been slower than expected in coming on stream. The anticipated changes include guaranteed survivors' benefits at 60 percent of the original, two-year vesting as compared to the former 10 years, and credit-splitting of pension contributions between spouses in the event of marriage breakdown.

These changes, while welcome, neither solve the inequities faced by women nor place private employer plans on an equal footing with the C/QPP. Credit splitting is eliminated when a former spouse remarries and, more importantly, there are no provisions in these reforms to include mandatory inflation protection. However, at least in one province, Ontario, legislation has been passed to provide inflation protection on employer plan benefits at 60 percent of inflation up to an annual rate of 8 percent. Further, these reforms are of no value to persons employed in firms where no occupational pension is offered, and they do not begin to address the question of inequality that is rooted in class location and which merely becomes more visible in later life.

LATER-LIFE: PRIVATE TROUBLES AND PUBLIC ISSUES

Gerontological issues often tend to be defined in individualistic terms divorced from their larger social context (Mills, 1959). When pension benefit levels are considered, it is in the context of some amorphous aggregate called *the aged*. The age-stratification theorists (Riley, 1976; Foner, 1974; 1978) look for conflict between age strata based on cohort differences. They do not look for intra-generational differences, (i.e., class location) and ask whether they might override age interests. Neither do they make a convincing case that because a cohort of people happen to be born at the same time, they will necessarily share the same social interests. The reason these questions are not asked is that the assumption of the age-stratification theorists and government theorists when they respond to the "grey vote" is that societal values are shared in a consensual fashion approximating equilibrium.

However, at the same time as the government talks about the needs of the elderly, it acknowledges differences among them,

when arguing for the elimination of universality in pension benefits, because not all of the aged "need" the Old Age Security cheque each month. Does this constitute recognition of structured social inequality? No, it does not. Rather, it reflects a liberal view that some individuals, through meritorious work and thrift, are well prepared for retirement. Others, for want of the same characteristics, are not prepared and must be subsidized by the state. This is the same argument that provides welfare to the non-aged. This is the view of the rugged individualist expressing a market ethos (Macpherson, 1962; Bryden, 1974).

A macro-based and interpretive perspective on later life suggests an alternative explanation and direction for social change. This is the view that has guided the preceding discussion of income and pension reform. There are differences in income that are age related and these are predictable across the life span. Depending on which part of the life cycle one is examining, age-related income differences can serve to either minimize or maximize differences which are first of all class and gender based.

The individualist viewpoint, the aging-as-a-social-problem perspective, reproduces in later life that which precedes it. It is for this reason that age-based policies are flawed. At the same time, if need is defined only in individual terms, then need-based policies with their income/means testing attributes attached are just as severely flawed. This dilemma of choice between age and need exists because, in this country, policy is defined in individualistic terms; if collective thinking occasionally held the upper hand, the situation might be different.

The example of mandatory retirement and the Canadian Charter of Rights and Freedoms can serve to illustrate this point. Traditionally in Canada employers in most provinces have been able to terminate employees for no other reason than their age if they were younger than 15 or older than 65. Unemployment of this sort has been termed mandatory retirement. The passing of the Constitution Act, which encompasses the Charter, seemingly forbade such policy. Section 15 of the Charter (1982:15) guarantees "equal benefit of the law without discrimination and, in particular, without discrimination based on race, national or ethnic origin, colour, religion, sex, age, or mental or physical disability." However, Section 1 of the Charter declares that the Charter's rights and freedoms are "subject to such limitations as are shown to be justified in a free and democratic society" (1982:2). Mandatory retirement has been considered justifiable discrimination by some employers.

As a result, a small group of university professors facing mandatory retirement from their respective universities have gone to court in Ontario to argue that justifiable-discrimination interpretation abrogates their constitutional rights under the Charter. As of March 1987 the Supreme Court of Ontario has denied the claim of the professors and ruled in favour of the universities. The professors have appealed this decision to the Supreme Court of Canada and the case was scheduled to be heard in May 1987.

As it stands now the plaintiffs in this case are a small group of individuals. They are not presenting a class-action suit. However, under Canadian common law the Supreme Court decision will set a precedent that should determine policy for all Canadian employers.

The Charter, if it is upheld in this regard, denies discrimination on the basis of age and gender among other attributes. In so doing it requires an employer to show just cause when firing an employee. However, it takes each case on its individual merit and does not ask whether there is something in the social organization of work that has implications for particular collectivities unrelated to any ascriptive attributes.

In short, social class location is considered an achieved status and not in need of protection. In fact, it is those persons who are least able to control their work situation who are most likely to be vulnerable to employer regulations such as mandatory retirement. Individualistic legislation creates opportunity for individuals to challenge discriminatory regulations. The result is that people who are vulnerable to unemployment because they do not control the work process are forced to support mandatory retirement as one of only a very few avenues offering hope of employment for them.

People such as the professors who have gone to court are in quasi professions where they exercise autonomy over day-to-day responsibilities. However, on the issues that count—hiring, firing, salary and benefits—this control is greatly reduced (Tindale, 1987). Mandatory retirement simply brings this lack of control into the spotlight. If it is only viewed as persons being denied their individual rights, then one is presented with a public issue (one's place in the work process) being paraded as a private trouble (a wronged individual).

CONCLUSION

Throughout this chapter the intention has been to maintain a focus on the ways in which the issue of structured inequality interacts with age. Theory development, proceeding from earlier normative theories to the interpretive modelling currently dominating the field, has been couched in terms of the effectiveness with which each theory contributes to an understanding of inequality issues. The argument was made that an interpretive perspective, drawing on political economy approaches to the interaction of class, gender, and age, is the best conceptual vehicle available for analysing the empirical phenomena of later life.

The theoretical point was illustrated by delineating the sources of income most typically relied upon by older persons. In the course of doing this it became clear that the economic circumstances of old age are structured by people's earlier personal biographies and the social location they work in. This relationship becomes more visible in old age when the ability of people's work career to sustain them through retirement is tested.

Social policy is organized public intervention in the private course of peoples' lives. Policy in this country targets individual characteristics for reward and punishment (private troubles). To the degree that this is the case, the implications of structured social inequality (public issues) are ignored. This was illustrated in the nature of pension reform with its attendant concern for individuals who need safety nets. A further example was provided by showing how mandatory retirement, a creation of the social organization of work, is dealt with as a question of individual rights, a process that obscures the causes of forced retirement.

Inequality due to age, as with other forms of structured inequality in Canada, will remain so long as the social world is organized and policy created along individual dimensions. When the relationship between the individual and his or her social location is recognized, when they are seen as being integral to each other, then perhaps policy and planning will more adequately respond to the conditions *class* and *gender* as they are made more severe in old age.

REFERENCES

Achenbaum, W.
  1978   *Old Age in the New Land.* Baltimore: Johns Hopkins University Press.

Atchley, R. C.
  1971   "Retirement and Leisure Participation: Continuity or Crisis?" *The Geron-tologist,* 11:13-17.

Bryden, K.
  1974   *Old Age Pensions and Policy-Making in Canada.* Montreal: McGill-Queen's University Press.

Chappell, N. L., and H. L. Orbach
  1986   "Socialization in Old Age: A Meadian Perspective," in *Later Life: The Social Psychology of Aging,* ed. V. W. Marshall, pp. 75-106. Beverly Hills: Sage.

Cole, T. R.
  1984   "The Prophecy of Senescence: G. Stanley Hall and the Reconstruction of Old Age in America," *The Gerontologist,* 24:360-66.

Cowgill, D. O.
  1979   "Aging and Modernization: A Revision of the Theory," in *Dimensions of Aging,* ed. J. Hendricks and C. D. Hendricks, pp. 54-67. Cambridge, Mass.: Winthrop.

Cowgill, D. O., and L. D. Holmes
  1972   *Aging and Modernization.* New York: Appleton-Century-Crofts.

Cumming, E., and W. H. Henry
  1961   *Growing Old: The Process of Disengagement.* New York: Basic.

Estes, C., J. Swan, and L. Gerard
  1982   "Dominant and Competing Paradigms in Gerontology: Towards a Political Economy of Ageing," *Ageing and Society,* 2:151-64.

Fischer D.
  1978   *Growing Old in America.* New York: Oxford University Press.

Foner, A.
  1974   "Age Stratification and Age Conflict in Political Life," *American Sociological Review,* 39:187-96.

Foner, A. and D. Kertzer
  1978   "Transitions over the Life Course: Lessons from Age-Set Societies," *American Journal of Sociology,* 83:1081-104.

Government of Canada
  1982   *The Charter of Rights and Freedoms: A Guide for Canadians.* Ottawa: Minister of Supply and Services Canada.

Health and Welfare Canada
  1982   *Pension Plan Coverage by Level of Earnings and Age 1978 and 1979.* Ottawa: Government of Canada.

Lemon, B., V. Bengtson, and J. Peterson
    1972   "An Exploration of the Activity Theory of Aging: Activity Types and Life Satisfaction Among Inmovers to a Retirement Community," *Journal of Gerontology,* 27:511-523.

Macpherson, C. B.
    1962   *The Political Theory of Possessive Individualism: Hobbes to Locke.* London: Oxford University Press.

Marshall, V. W.
    1980   "No Exit: An Interpretive Perspective on Aging," in *Aging in Canada: Social Perspectives on Aging,* ed. V. W. Marshall, pp. 51-60. Toronto: Fitzhenry and Whiteside.
    1987   "Social Perspectives on Aging: Theoretical Notes," in *Aging in Canada: Social Perspectives,* (2nd ed.), ed. V. W. Marshall, pp. 39-59. Toronto: Fitzhenry and Whiteside.

Marshall, V. W., and J. A. Tindale
    1978-79   "Notes for a Radical Gerontology," *International Journal of Aging and Human Development,* 9:162-75.

Martin Matthews, A., and J. A. Tindale
    1987   "Retirement in Canada," in *Retirement in Industrialized Societies: Social, Psychological and Health Factors,* ed. K. S. Markides and C. L. Cooper, pp. 43-75. Sussex, Eng.: John Wiley & Sons.

Mills, C. W.
    1959   *The Sociological Imagination.* New York: Oxford University Press

Myles, J. F.
    1980   "The Aged, the State, and the Structure of Inequality," in *Structured Inequality in Canada.* ed. J. Harp and J. R. Hofley, pp. 317-342. Scarborough, Ont.: Prentice-Hall Canada.
    1984   *Old Age in the Welfare State: The Political Economy of Public Pensions.* Boston: Little, Brown.
    1986   "Public Policies for the Elderly in Canada." Unpublished paper.

National Council of Welfare
    1984   *Sixty-five and older: a report by National Council of Welfare on the incomes of the aged.* Ottawa: Minister of Supply and Services Canada.

Neysmith, S. M., and J. Edwardh
    1984   "Economic Dependency in the 1980s: Its Impact on Third World Elderly," *Ageing and Society,* 4:21-44.

Norris, J. E.
    1987   "Psychological Processes in the Development of Late-Life Social Identity," in *Aging in Canada: Social Perspectives* (2nd ed.), ed. V. W. Marshall, pp. 60-81. Toronto: Fitzhenry & Whiteside.

Parliamentary Task Force on Pension Reform
    1983   *Pension Reform.* Ottawa: Minister of Supply and Services Canada.

Parsons, T., and E. A. Shills
     1951   *Toward a General Theory of Action.* New York: Harper Torchbooks.

Quadagno, J.
     1982   *Aging in Early Industrial Society: Work, Family, and Social Policy in Nineteenth Century England.* New York: Academic.

Riley, M.
     1976   "Age Strata in Social Systems," in *Handbook of Aging and the Social Sciences*, ed. R. Binstock and E. Shanas, pp. 189-217. New York: Van Nostrand Reinhold.

Rose, A. M.
     1968   "A Current Theoretical Issue in Social Gerontology," in *Middle Age And Aging: A Reader in Social Psychology,* ed. B. L. Neugarten, pp. 184-189. Chicago: University Press.

Rosow, I.
     1974   *Socialization to Old Age.* Berkeley: University of California Press.
     1976   "Status and Role Change Through the Life Span," in *Handbook of Aging and the Social Sciences,* ed. R. Binstock and E. Shanas, pp. 457-482. New York: Van Nostrand Reinhold.

Ryff, C. D.
     1986   "The Subjective Construction of Self and Society: An Agenda for Life-Span Research," in *Later Life: The Social Psychology of Aging,* ed. V. W. Marshall, pp. 33-74. Beverly Hills: Sage.

Special Senate Committee on Retirement Age Policies
     1979   *Retirement Without Tears.* Ottawa: Minister of Supply and Services Canada.

Spence, D. L.
     1986   "Some Contributions of Symbolic Interaction to the Study of Growing Old," in *Later Life: The Social Psychology of Aging.* ed. V. W. Marshall, pp. 107-23. Beverly Hills: Sage.

Statistics Canada
     1986   *Income Distributions by Size in Canada 1984.* Ottawa: Minister of Supply and Services Canada.

Tindale, J. A.
     1980   "Identity Maintenance Processes of Old Poor Men," in *Aging in Canada: Social Perspectives,* ed. V. W. Marshall, pp. 88-94. Toronto: Fitzhenry & Whiteside.
     1987   "Age, Seniority and Class Patterns of Job Strain," in *Aging in Canada: Social Perspectives* (2nd ed.), ed. V. W. Marshall, pp. 176-192. Toronto: Fitzhenry & Whiteside.

Tindale, J., and V. Marshall
     1980   "A Generational Conflict Perspective for Gerontology," in *Aging in Canada: Social Perspectives,* ed. V. W. Marshall, pp. 43-50. Toronto: Fitzhenry & Whiteside.

Tindale, J., and S. Neysmith
     1987   "Economic justice in later life: A Canadian perspective." A manuscript forthcoming in *Social Justice Research.*

Townsend, P.
    1981   "The Structured Dependency of the Elderly: Creation of Social Policy in the Twentieth Century," *Ageing and Society,* 1:5-28.

Walker, A.
    1981   "Towards a Political Economy of Old Age," *Ageing and Society,* 1:73-94.

27. Sixty-Five and Older: Profiles and Policies

National Council of Welfare

INTRODUCTION

In 1982, for the first time since low-income statistics have been collected, the poverty rate for families headed by elderly Canadians dipped below the poverty rate for families led by persons under 65. An estimated 11.7 percent of aged families had incomes below the low-income line, compared to 14.2 percent of non-aged families.

Traditionally old age has brought a high risk of poverty, so from the viewpoint of elderly families this is an encouraging statistic. However the 11.7 percent figure applies to all families headed by persons 65 and older: a distinctly different picture emerges

when we compare the sexes. The poverty rate for families led by aged men was an estimated 10.2 percent in 1982 (one in 10) but 24.6 percent of families headed by elderly women (one in four) were below the low-income line.

Moreover the large and rapidly growing group of unattached elderly Canadians (i.e., those who live alone or in a household where they are not related to other members) faces five times the risk of poverty of aged families: an estimated 57.7 percent of the unattached aged lived on low incomes in 1982. Again, women are worse off than men; 60 percent of unattached elderly women are poor as opposed to 49 percent of aged men.

The lesson is clear. No single statistic or simple statement can adequately characterize the economic condition of the diverse and expanding population of elderly Canadians.

Reprinted from National Council of Welfare, *Sixty-five and Older* (Ottawa: National Council of Welfare, February 1984). Reprinted with permission.

DEMOGRAPHICS: THE AGED BOOM

Most Canadians have heard that the "baby boom" of the 1950s has given way to an "aged boom" in the 1980s. Less well known, however, is the remarkable size and pace of growth in the elderly population.

An Aging Canada

At the turn of the century this country's 271 201 aged made up only 5 percent of the total population. By mid-century their numbers had passed the one-million mark and their share of the population had risen to 7.8 percent. The 1981 Census counted 2 360 975 people 65 and older, or 9.7 percent of all Canadians. The most recent estimates, for June 1983, put the elderly at 2 496 500—10 percent of the population.

The elderly are forecast to reach 3.5 million or 12 percent of the population in 2001. By the year 2031 there will be in the order of 6.6 million aged men and women who will account for about 20 percent of all Canadians—double their current proportion (see Table 27-1).

Women

Another striking trend is the rapidly expanding population of elderly women. In 1901 women accounted for 48.8 percent of persons 65 and older. Their proportion increased to 49.2 percent in 1951, 51.5 percent by 1961, 55.2 percent in 1971, and 57.2 percent in 1981. By 2001, six in every 10 aged Canadians will be women.

The numerical increase in elderly women has been marked. While the number of aged men rose from 138 913 in 1901 to 1 010 850 in 1981—a 628 percent increase—the population of elderly women went up even more,

from 132 288 to 1 350 125, for a 921 percent increase over 80 years.

The pace of growth in the ranks of elderly women has been accelerating in recent years. The number of women 65 and over rose by 17 percent between 1971 and 1976 and by 20 percent from 1976 to 1981. Elderly men also increased in numbers, but not as much as women—12 percent from 1971 to 1976 and 15.5 percent between 1976 and 1981.

Marital Status

Another significant difference between elderly men and women—one that, as we shall see later, has a lot to do with their unequal economic positions—is that most men are married whereas most women are single.

Six in 10 elderly women are single, whereas three in every four aged men are married.

TABLE 27-1   Number of aged Canadians and their share of the population, trends and projections, 1901 to 2051.

	Number of aged	Aged as a percentage of the population
1901	271 201	5.0%
1911	335 317	4.7
1921	420 244	4.8
1931	576 076	5.6
1941	767 815	6.7
1951	1 086 273	7.8
1961	1 391 154	7.6
1971	1 744 405	8.1
1981	2 360 975	9.7
1991	2 985 900	11.1
2001	3 504 000	12.0
2011	4 074 100	13.1
2021	5 379 200	16.4
2031	6 644 400	19.6
2041	6 539 400	18.9
2051	6 388 200	18.2

The proportions of never-married and divorced persons are similar for both sexes. However the percentage of widows (49 percent of all aged women) far outweighs that of widowers (14 percent).

The living arrangements of elderly men are very different from those of women, again because women tend to outlive men. Most aged men (72 percent) live in their own families, whereas the majority of elderly women (58 percent) do not. A sizeable group of aged women (32 percent) lives alone, and another 13 percent with relatives. A larger percentage of elderly women than men lives in collective dwellings (10.4 percent versus 6.6 percent).

The growth in the aged who live alone—most of them women—is a development with major economic and social implications. In just 20 years, the proportion of Canadians 65 and over living alone has doubled (from 12 percent in 1961 to 24 percent in 1981). The number and percentage of elderly women living on their own have been increasing rapidly. At last count 434 640 women—32 percent of all elderly women—lived alone, compared to 131 070 men (13 percent of aged men).

The elderly living alone will continue to increase for some time to come. The aged population as a whole will expand until well into the next century, and a growing number who are widowed, unmarried, or divorced prefer to live on their own rather than with a friend or relative or in an institution. In addition, the proportion of elderly women living alone will continue to rise at a faster pace than that of men.

The Dependency Burden

Canada's aged are not just growing in numbers. They are also forming an ever-larger proportion of the population. Their share doubled from 5 percent in 1901 to an estimated 10 percent in 1983, and will double again to 20 percent by the year 2031.

Some observers have drawn pessimistic conclusions from the demographic trends, warning that by sheer weight of numbers the future aged will overwhelm the retirement income system, health care, social services, and other sources of support. They foresee a bleak future in which retired Canadians will gobble up more and more of society's resources and place an intolerable burden on the working population.

This doomsday scenario has elements of truth, but it is exaggerated and incomplete. A closer look at the statistics shows that the aging of Canada's population is neither as precipitous nor permanent as some alarmists would have us believe.

A decrease in the aged after 2031 will occur as the baby boom generation that swelled their ranks begins to die off. Because the baby-boomers are not reproducing as prolifically as their parents, there are now comparatively fewer children than in the past. Today schools are closing because there are not enough youngsters to fill them; by the middle of the next century we may well witness a shortage in clients for old age homes built for the baby boom elderly.

The dependency argument hinges on the fact that the elderly are increasing faster than the population of working age. The rise in the "old-age- dependency ratio"—the number of aged relative to the number of persons of working age—is often cited as evidence of the mounting burden of the elderly on society.

The old-age-dependency ratio has increased over time. In 1901 the ratio was 10.1, which means there were 10 aged persons for every 100 of working age. The ratio dipped slightly to 8.8 in 1911 but has risen steadily ever since. Today there are 17 elderly Canadians for every 100 between 20 and 64, and the ratio is projected to be 32.5 by the middle of the twenty-first century. A generation from now, the aged will be substantially larger relative to the working age population.

We still have about 30 years before the ratio of the aged to those of working age begins its rapid ascent—valuable time that can and must be used to improve the pension system and prepare for the increased demand on housing, health care, social services, and other provisions for the elderly. There will be a critical 20-year period between 2011 and 2031, but the situation will begin to ease thereafter.

The decline in the total dependency ratio —the young and old combined relative to the working age population—is no cause for complacency. The aged account for about three times as much public spending as young persons on a per capita basis, largely because the over-65s consume a larger slice of income security and health care budgets. Per capita spending on the aged will grow in future as a result of their increasing pressure on the health system and anticipated improvements in government programs and services.

HOW POOR ARE CANADA'S AGED?

An astonishing number of this country's aged are poor. In 1981, by conservative estimate, 604 000 elderly citizens—415 000 women and 189 000 men—were below the poverty line. One aged Canadian in four lives on a low income.

The Risk of Poverty

In 1982 an estimated 98 000 elderly families—11.7 percent of all those headed by a person 65 or older—had incomes below the poverty line. The risk of poverty is much greater for the unattached elderly: 57.7 percent, or 422 000, were poor. In fact the unattached aged are five times more likely to be poor than the aged in families (see Table 27-2).

Elderly Canadians traditionally have run a greater risk of poverty than those under 65. In 1982, for the first time since low-income statistics have been published, the poverty rate for families with aged heads (11.7 percent) was lower than the figure for families with non-aged heads (14.2 percent). However the unattached elderly continue to face much higher odds of living below the poverty line than the non-aged unattached; 57.7 percent of unattached individuals 65 and over were poor in 1982, as opposed to only 30.9 percent of those under 65.

Women Poverty is more common among elderly women than among elderly men. One quarter of families headed by women over 65 were low income in 1982, compared to only one tenth of those led by elderly men.

Unattached elderly women—most of them widows—outnumber unattached men in their age group by over three to one. They also face a higher risk of poverty. In 1982, an estimated 60.4 percent of unattached elderly women were poor, compared to 48.9 percent of unattached men 65 and older.

The older aged Increasing age raises the risk of poverty for elderly Canadians who are unattached. While the incidence of poverty among unattached men and women aged 65–69 is high—50.2 percent were poor in 1981—it is even higher for those 70 years and older—61.6 percent, the highest low-income rate of all age groups in 1981. The large majority of elderly unattached persons below the poverty line—close to eight in 10—are over 70 years of age.

Poverty Trends

There has been considerable progress against poverty among the aged. However the reduced risk of poverty has benefited elderly men more than women, and families more than the unattached aged.

In 1969, 41.4 percent of families with elderly heads were poor, but by 1982 the rate had fallen to 11.7 percent—a substantial drop of 72 percent. In comparison, the poverty rate for families led by persons under age 65 went from 17.7 percent in 1969 to 14.2 percent in 1982, a decline of only 20 percent (see Table 27-3). In 1969 the 262 000 low-income families with elderly heads made up 26 percent of all poor families; by 1982 there were only an estimated 98 000 poor aged families and they represented just 10.7 percent of all families under the poverty line.

The recent trend in poverty among elderly families is very favourable. In 1979, 21.9 percent of families with aged heads were below the low-income line. Their poverty rate fell to 14.2 in 1980, remained virtually the same (14.5 percent) in 1981, and then registered another significant decrease to an estimated 11.7 percent in 1982.

There has been more modest though welcome progress against poverty among unattached Canadians 65 and over. Their poverty rate went from 69.1 percent in 1969 to 66.3 percent in 1979, declining steadily thereafter to an estimated 57.7 percent in 1982. On the other hand, the low-income rate for non-aged unattached individuals is much the same today (30.9 percent at last count) as it was in 1969 (31.6 percent).

When we compare the poverty rates for aged men and women, however, a different picture emerges. Table 27-4 shows that the considerable decline in the risk of poverty for elderly families in recent years applies to those led by men but not women. The incidence of poverty among families headed by aged men dropped sharply from 21.8 percent in 1979 to 13.3 percent in 1980, 12.9 percent in 1981 and an estimated 10.2 percent in 1982. Yet the poverty rate for families led by elderly women actually increased from 22.2 percent in 1979 to 24.6 percent in 1982.

TABLE 27-2 Low-income families and unattached individuals, by age and sex of head, preliminary estimates, 1982.

	Aged		Non-aged	
Families	*Poverty rate*	*Number*	*Poverty rate*	*Number*
female head	24.6%	21 000	48.2%	307 000
male head	10.2	77 000	9.9	507 000
total	11.7	98 000	14.2	814 000
Unattached individuals				
female	60.4	337 000	32.2	297 000
male	48.9	85 000	29.7	300 000
total	57.7	422 000	30.9	597 000

TABLE 27-3 Trends in poverty rates, aged and non-aged families and unattached individuals.

	Families		Unattached individuals	
	Aged	*Non-aged*	*Aged*	*Non-aged*
1969	41.4%	17.7%	69.1%	31.6%
1979	21.9	11.8	66.3	30.3
1980	14.2	11.9	61.5	30.6
1981	14.5	11.6	58.7	29.4
1982	11.7	14.2	57.7	30.9

As a result, the poverty gap between families headed by elderly men and by elderly women has widened in recent years. In 1979 the risk of poverty was much the same for families headed by men and by women 65 and older. By 1982 families led by aged women were two-and-a-half times more likely to be poor than families led by aged men.

The poverty rate remains very high for unattached elderly Canadians—49 percent for men and 60 percent for women. Again, however, men have enjoyed more progress than women, so the poverty gap between them has increased.

THE INCOMES OF THE ELDERLY

Not all elderly Canadians are poor, by any means. However most are concentrated on the lower rungs of the income ladder. Aged women fare particularly poorly.

Levels of Income

The median income of families headed by elderly persons is estimated at $16 967 for 1982. This amount represents just 58 percent of the median income $29 246 for all families and only 47 percent of the estimated $35 930 for families with heads in the prime earning years of 45 to 54.

In 1982 the median income of unattached individuals 65 and over was $7458, which represents 66 percent of the median income of $11 369 for all unattached individuals and only 39 percent of the median income of $19 055 for those aged 35–44. The median income of the unattached aged actually fell below the poverty line in 1982.

Most unattached elderly Canadians are women, and their incomes are lower than those of aged men. In 1981 the median income of unattached women 65–69 was $6876, as opposed to $8026 for unattached men in that age group. The median income for unattached women 70 and over was $6395, compared to $6921 for unattached men over 70.

The adage "two can live as cheaply as one" has been supported by studies which conclude that a single person's living costs are about two-thirds those of a couple. Yet in 1982 the median income of unattached elderly Canadians was only 44 percent of that for families with heads in the same age bracket. Clearly the unattached elderly are considerably worse off financially than aged families.

THE OTHER SIDE OF INCOME

Canada's elderly do not live by money alone. Many possess wealth (chiefly their homes) and enjoy services and subsidies that bring them a better standard of living than the income data might indicate. One study claims that the total income of the aged population would be some 30 percent greater if the value of non-money sources of income and unreported cash gifts were taken into account.

Nor do the statistics presented earlier recognize the greater demands made upon the incomes of Canadians of working age, particularly those with children to support. Most elderly persons do not work and so do not have to pay Canada or Quebec Pension Plan contributions, unemployment insurance premiums, union dues or professional association fees, commuting costs and other employment-related expenses.

It is true that an exclusive focus on money income paints a one-sided and overly pessi-mistic portrait of the aged. However we must weigh carefully other factors that affect their economic situation.

Elderly Canadians do not share in non-cash sources of income equally, any more than they all have adequate money incomes. Non-aged families and individuals also have available a wide range of health and social services and other subsidies and in-kind benefits. Even so the non-money income received by the elderly does not fully make up for the money income gap that separates them from younger people. Nor do senior citizen discounts for buses and movies, occasional gifts from children, subsidized rents, social services, and the other benefits bestowed by government and the voluntary and private sectors fully compensate for the very low incomes on which many thousands of elderly Canadians—particularly those who live on their own—must live.

Shelter Costs

The most prevalent form of wealth held by elderly Canadians is their homes. Over three quarters of families with heads 65 and older own their accommodation, as do 40 percent of aged unattached individuals. In

TABLE 27-4 Trends in poverty rates, aged family units by sex of head.

	Aged families		Aged unattached individuals	
	Female head	Male head	Women	Men
1979	22.2%	21.8%	68.8%	58.6%
1980	21.2	13.3	65.4	51.9
1981	24.7	12.9	62.2	48.4
1982	24.6	10.2	60.4	48.9

comparison, 71.6 percent of families led by persons under 65 and only 19.5 percent of non-aged unattached individuals count a home among their possessions. The equity the elderly have built up in their homes is their major asset, accounting on average for close to half of their net worth.

Not only do many senior citizens own their own homes, but the large majority of those who do have paid off their mortgage. Eighty-six percent of elderly homeowners who head families and 90 percent of those who are unattached do not have to make monthly mortgage payments. Among homeowners under the age of 65, by contrast, 36 percent of family heads and just under half of unattached persons do not carry a mortgage. As a result. the shelter costs of elderly homeowners tend to be lower than their non-aged counterparts, who also have had to contend with high interest rates when renewing their mortgages in recent years. Some economists believe the value of imputed rent on owner-occupied houses and condominiums should be counted as a form of non-money income.

It is not just the well-off elderly who are homeowners. Six in 10 low-income aged family heads own their home, as do one in three unattached individuals who are over 65 and under the poverty line. Most poor elderly homeowners have paid off their mortgage.

Since so many senior citizens own their homes free and clear of debt, they obviously can get by on less income than the average Canadian who must make rent or mortgage payments each month. However there are also expenses incurred in running a house or condominium—utilities (heat, electricity, and water), insurance, property taxes, maintenance and repairs—that can put a strain on the budget of elderly homeowners, espe-

cially the large number with modest incomes. The price of fuel, water, and electricity increased by 103 percent from 1977 to 1982, exceeding the 63 percent rise in the overall cost of living. The cost of household operations went up by 80 percent, home insurance premiums by 61 percent, and repair costs by 54 percent during the same five-year period.

As a result, some elderly Canadians find themselves in the anomalous situation of being "house rich and cash poor." Their most valuable asset puts a roof over their heads, but at the same time brings additional operating costs that take a hefty bite out of their modest incomes. Unanticipated expenses—such as replacing a worn roof or fixing faulty plumbing—are particularly worrisome for elderly homeowners and can force them to sacrifice on other basic expenditures. Keep in mind that their homes are older than average and may require more frequent and costlier repairs, especially if the aged are unable to do the work themselves.

Understandably, many elderly homeowners do not relish the prospect of selling the home they spent so many years buying. Even if they decide to sell, they then must face the prospect of finding affordable rental accommodation—a scarce commodity in many Canadian communities. In any case, the term "house rich" is a bit of an exaggeration, since homes owned by the elderly tend to be older and fetch a lower price on the housing market. Trading their principal asset for cash would provide at best a temporary solution to the income problem of many elderly homeowners, and could prove to be a short-sighted decision that left them no better off in the long run.

The shift from owned to rented accommodation is particularly marked among aged households headed by women; 68 percent were homeowners and 32 percent were renters in 1961, but by 1976 approximately half owned and half rented. The percentage of elderly women renters is almost double that of aged men.

Though some aged homeowners have trouble making ends meet, in general the elderly who own their own homes tend to be better off than those who rent. Elderly renters have lower incomes than those who own their own homes. Nearly half of aged renters devote 25 percent or more of their income to housing, compared to only one quarter of elderly homeowners.

TRENDS AND PROSPECTS

The economic position of elderly men and their wives has improved considerably over the past two decades. Unfortunately the same cannot be said for the large and growing group of elderly women who head families or live on their own.

The cornerstone of Canada's retirement income system is the federal Old Age Security program, popularly known as "the old age pension." Parliament passed legislation in 1951 establishing a program of monthly payments to all persons 70 years and older; since 1970 the age of eligibility has been 65. The program currently pays $263.78 a month to all elderly Canadians.

A second major federal program, the Guaranteed Income Supplement, was enacted in 1966 to serve elderly Canadians who have little or no income other than Old Age Security. The maximum monthly benefit is now $265.60 for a single person and $204.86 for each spouse in a couple. In 1975 the Spouse's Allowance was created to help lower-income couples in which one spouse is over 65 and the other aged between 60 and 64; if the older spouse dies, the younger

spouse continues to receive the Spouse's Allowance until age 65. The maximum Spouse's Allowance is $468.64 a month.

Ottawa and the provinces added a second tier to Canada's retirement income system in 1966 with the Canada Pension Plan (Quebec set up a parallel plan, the Quebec Pension Plan, at the same time). Every Canadian between the ages of 18 and 65 who is in the paid labour force, whether an employee or self-employed, is a member of the Canada Pension Plan or Quebec Pension Plan. The maximum monthly retirement pension for 1984 is $387.50. The plans also pay a disability pension, a pension to the surviving spouse and children, and a lump-sum death benefit.

The provincial governments also contribute to the income of their aged residents through various income supplement programs and tax subsidies. All three levels of government, along with the voluntary and private sectors, offer a wide range of services and subsidies which help defray the extra costs that accompany old age and stretch elderly Canadians' limited dollars.

Despite these developments, Canada's retirement income programs neither prevent poverty among all the elderly nor adequately replace pre-retirement income. The problems with the pension system are not the subject of this study, but they can be summarized in brief.

The Old Age Security and Guaranteed Income Supplement together guarantee an income above the poverty line for some elderly couples, but leave many couples and all aged singles (most of them women) below the low-income line. In their present form, the Canada and Quebec Pension Plans can make only a limited contribution to retirement income because they replace only one quarter of insurable earnings up to a level that is still below the average wage. The failings of private pension plans are glaring: most working Canadians are not covered by them (especially lower-wage earners and workers in the private sector) and the minority who do belong typically receive meager pensions that are not adequately protected against inflation. Private pensions contribute only about 11 percent of the income of the aged.

Half of elderly Canadians—more than 700 000 women and 500 000 men—have so little retirement income that they qualify for the Guaranteed Income Supplement, an antipoverty program originally intended to serve what was supposed to have been a dwindling number of impoverished pensioners. Many Canadians who are middle-income earners during their working years undergo a serious drop in income after they retire. The gap between the haves and have-nots yawns wide among the elderly: a minority enjoy comfortable retirement incomes from savings, investments, and private pension plans, while the majority have to get by on low or modest incomes obtained mainly from government programs.

Canada's retirement income system serves least adequately the very group—elderly women who are widowed or unmarried—that is growing fastest. By 2001, six in 10 aged Canadians will be women, most of them living alone. Without major reforms to our pension system, the majority of Canadian women will continue to face an old age limited by low income.

FOR FURTHER READING

Canada, Senate, Special Senate Committee on Youth. 1986. *Youth: A Plan of Action.* Report of the Special Senate Committee. Ottawa. Based on written briefs and oral testimony from Canadians concerned about young people, this report provides an overview of the special problems facing young Canadians. The plan of action consists of 26 recommendations to alleviate the problems of Canadian youth.

Dryden, Ken. 1984. *Report of the Ontario Youth Commissioner.* Toronto: Government of Ontario. This is a brief report examining problems facing young Canadians, including issues of employment opportunities.

Marshall, Victor, ed. 1987. *Aging in Canada: Social Perspectives* (2nd ed). Toronto: Fitzhenry and Whiteside. As a collection of essays, this volume covers a wide range of topics related to aging. While focussing mainly on the elderly, the book provides one of the best overviews of aging in Canada.

McDaniel, Susan. 1987. *Canada's Aging Population.* Toronto: Butterworths. This text provides one of the best overviews of the causes and the consequences of Canada's aging population. The book combines the strengths of demography and of sociology to provide up-to-date coverage.

Myles, John. 1984. *Old Age in the Welfare State.* Toronto: Little, Brown and Company. An excellent book examining the economic and political structure in which our aging population grows. Its use of international comparisons makes this one of the best books dealing with aging.

28. *Issues in Regional Development*

Ralph Matthews

. . . The present pattern of regional economic differences in Canada was not preordained but has been created. That pattern has been created since Confederation, and is the product of political, economic, and social forces operating in this country. . . . It is therefore useful to begin this analysis with a brief look at how these disparities occurred.

ORIGINS OF REGIONAL DISPARITY

It is clear that economics played a major role in Confederation. Though it is now easy to regard the Maritimes as having always been

Revised from Ralph Matthews, *The Creation of Regional Dependency* (Toronto: University of Toronto Press, 1983), pp. 99-117. Reprinted by permission of the author and University of Toronto Press. © University of Toronto Press 1983.

poor and the central area as always developed, that is not historically accurate. Before Confederation, Nova Scotia and New Brunswick had engaged in a lively and highly profitable trade in fish, timber, ships, and even mineral products with Great Britain, the United States, and the West Indies (Acheson, 1977; Naylor, 1975). In contrast, central Canada was at a disadvantage. Cut off from the sea when the St. Lawrence was frozen, its supplies and few staple exports had to go overland via New York and Boston. . . . If the central region of British North America were to develop it needed its own railway to the sea. Confederation was of obvious economic benefit to central Canada for it would provide a direct land route to the sea for that railway. The leaders of the maritime provinces were unable to see equal benefits for their territories and steadfastly opposed confederation. By the 1860s, however, they had been convinced that their traditional trade with the north-east United States would be unaffected by confederation and that the proposed railway would give their industries access to the largely unindustrialized regions of Montreal and Quebec. Thus, Confederation became a reality.

However, as Hutcheson (1978:38) points out, Confederation was only one stage in a long-range plan for the development of British North America from sea to sea. Canada had to expand westward quickly, for American settlers were already threatening to spill northward into the north-west. To expand westward would require an influx of population to fill up the west, the development of an economic base to supply it, and a railway to import goods to western settlers and bring out their agricultural produce. The post-Confederation government of John A. Macdonald had to develop policies not only to encourage immigration, but also to develop the economy of the new country so that it could sustain the cost of railway construction both east and west. Accordingly, regulations were passed favouring the immigration of Central Europeans. To take care of the economic needs of the country a "National Policy," which placed tariffs on imported American goods and culminated in the Tariff Act, was passed in 1879. Its purpose was to cut off the flood of American goods into Canada, to encourage the development of Canadian industry, and to provide income for the construction of the railway from the tax revenue. In retrospect, this tripartite combination of confederation, immigration, and taxation established the pattern of regional specialization and regional economic disparity which still exists.

Confederation originally had little effect on the pattern of trade or on the economy of the Maritimes (Acheson, 1977:91), but the economic structure was altered substantially by the imposition of Canadian tariffs and by retaliatory measures taken by the Ameri-

cans. Merchants and industrialists in the Maritimes were largely cut off from one of their major markets and sources of supply. In additon, in the 1870s a decided slump in the market for ships and ships' spars affected almost one third of New Brunswick's exports and a sizeable portion of Nova Scotia's trade (Acheson, 1972:3). Ironically, the tariffs originally renewed prosperity in the maritime region. With improved rail links the maritime merchants and industrialists became the only suppliers for the whole central Canadian market, as there were comparatively few industries in Ontario and Quebec. Industrial growth was accompanied by the development and expansion of financial institutions throughout maritime Canada. Almost every town had its own savings bank which would finance local merchants who wished to construct new or expand existing manufacturing operations. In this period three of the six current national banks in Canada were formed in Halifax. . . .

Maritime underdevelopment followed quickly in the 1890s, however. The Maritimes were at the end of a 2000 mile rail supply line to the new markets in Central Canada. As long as there was little industry in the centre of the country, this did not matter. But one of the goals achieved by the tariff policy was the development of industry in Ontario and Quebec. . . . The result was a series of failures in Atlantic industry and, by the early decades of the twentieth century, the dominant industrial power had shifted to Montreal and Toronto.

A similar shift occurred in financial power. As industries in the Atlantic region collapsed, they undermined the community banks which simply were not large enough or diversified enough to withstand the economic shock. Many simply folded. Moreover, Naylor (1975:1) documents that those banks which did survive were bought out by the growing financial groups in Central Canada. Economic control thus shifted west also and the headquarters of the major banks were moved to Central Canada. . . .

As the Maritimes declined in economic well-being, the centre of the country flourished, in part because of the entrepreneurial activity of its business and commercial elite. The commercial elite of Montreal and, to a lesser extent, Toronto were also those most directly involved in railway construction and in banking. In addition, many were actively involved in federal and provincial politics, some being part of Macdonald's government (Berton, 1972). Under such circumstances, it was understandable that the state became the instrument of the dominant class. Banking policy, railway policy, and tariff policy all increased the wealth of those in economic and political power in Central Canada.

Yet the "National Policy" did not work entirely as had been planned. Comparatively few Canadians in Central Canada became directly involved in industrialization. To fill the vacuum and circumvent the tariff, American industrialists began to build plants in Canada. . . . Most American industrial investment was in Central Canada partly because that was where the major untapped market was and partly because it was closer to American operations in upper New York (Chorney, 1977:126).

Thus the Tariff Act of 1879 not only undermined the industrial base of the Maritime provinces, but also established the branch plant phenomenon characteristic of so much Canadian industry today. By locating primarily in Quebec and Ontario the branch plants contributed to regional industrial disparity. Ray calculated that 45 percent of American-controlled manufacturing employment in the 1960s was within 100 miles of Toronto, 64 percent within 300 miles, and 83 percent within 400 miles. He

also calculated that, if American-controlled manufacturing employment had the same distribution as Canadian-controlled employment, there would be an increase of approximately 20 percent in employment in the Atlantic Provinces (Ray, 1968).

The western region of Canada was intended to serve as the economic hinterland. The policy of encouraging immigration from Central Europe ensured that the prevailing social elite would not include residents of the west. Without a background from one of the two "charter groups" of English and French, newcomers would find it difficult to reach the corridors of economic power. The fact that they were isolated in small communities some 2000 miles from the seats of power did not improve their chances.

If Canada were to fulfil its "national dream" of stretching from sea to sea, however, the railway had to be built and the west had to contribute to the cost. While the railway became the means whereby western agricultural produce came east for milling and shipment, it also increased the economic well-being of Ontario and Quebec merchants. As the means of shipping goods manufactured in Ontario and Quebec westward, it increased the economic well-being of Ontario and Quebec producers, giving them a further edge over their competitors in the Maritime Provinces. . . .

This overview raises the issue of the continuing effect of historical patterns and social structures on Canada's regional structure. The current pattern of regional differences and disparities was created in the process of making Quebec and Ontario economically strong. If that pattern persists today despite 50 years of programs aimed at changing it, one must surely ask if these two provinces still benefit so greatly because they use their power and influence to frustrate any such programs. . . .

THE CHANGING VALUE ORIENTATION OF REGIONAL DEVELOPMENT POLICY

. . . Canada's regional development policy began with Confederation and was effectively established with the imposition of the Tariff Act of 1879. These developments were not seen as regional development policies, and the pattern of regional development and regional underdevelopment which they created was not necessarily a deliberate goal. In contrast, during the last 50 years the federal government has attempted to find ways to eliminate at least the most extreme regional disparities. These efforts began in March 1935 when the Prairie Farm Rehabilitation Act was passed in an attempt to alleviate the growing plight of western farmers. . . . The Prairie Farm Rehabilitation Act provided limited funds to farmers to keep small farms operating. In 1948 a similar program was established to open new farmland in the maritime provinces under the Maritime Marshlands Rehabilitation Act (Buckley and Tihanyi, 1967:ii). It is clear that both programs placed a high value on *rural development.*

Similar values were incorporated in a more ambitious program begun under the Agricultural Rehabilitation and Development Act passed by the House of Commons in June 1961. This was the first attempt at formulating a comprehensive regional development policy for Canada (Daniels, 1981:56). ARDA focussed on "land use" projects designed to "salvage lands as agriculture retreated from marginal areas" (Buckley and Tihanyi, 1967:18). . . .

In the mid-1960s these programs came under close scrutiny from economists. In a study commissioned by the Economic Council of Canada, Buckley and Tihanyi were highly critical of the land development strat-egy of ARDA and its predecessors. . . . Their report outlined two ways of promoting per capita economic growth in any area. The first was assistance with "development projects" and the second, described as "labour force adjustment" and later simply as "adjustment," incorporated measures designed to encourage the movement of population out of underdeveloped areas (Buckley and Tihanyi, 1967:17). . . .

Buckley and Tihanyi's analysis was not the only basis for an attack on existing regional development policies. In the 1960s the growth-pole theory expounded by Perroux and Hirschman was gaining a considerable following among regional planners in Canada. That theory was clearly antithetical to rural development, arguing that regional economic growth can be stimulated best by establishing large "master" industries in underdeveloped regions. Such industries were seen as capable of altering the whole pattern of economic relationships within the region by developing strong links with the suppliers of raw materials and services on the one hand and with those outlets receiving the products on the other. It was assumed that one of the advantages of building a master industry was that it would encourage many users of its product to establish in the underdeveloped region as well. . . . Thus there is a decided orientation in favour of urban development in the growth-pole theory that is the antithesis of the orientation towards rural development found in ARDA. As a result, the principles of growth-pole theory informed all Canadian regional development planning from 1965 through the next decade.

In 1965 the federal government established the Fund for Rural Economic Development (FRED), in many ways a compromise between old techniques of development and new growth-pole theories.

The focus remained on rural development but there was a decided emphasis on rural adjustment as well that involved farm consolidation and the assisted migration of "surplus" population from rural areas. The FRED program was undoubtedly the most comprehensive and systematic effort in regional planning and development ever undertaken in Canada. . . . Unfortunately, by the time that much of the planning had been accomplished, federal policy had changed and the FRED program was cancelled. . . .

The cancellation of the FRED program coincided with the election of Pierre Elliott Trudeau as prime minister of Canada in 1968. Trudeau moved regional planning into the political arena in that same year. His campaign platform had rested largely on two promises. In Quebec, he informed his audiences that, if elected, he would introduce measures to provide French-speaking Canadians economic and social equality with English Canadians throughout the country. In much of the rest of the country, he argued that regional disparities had the same potential to divide the country as did the more publicized division between French and English and he declared that, if elected, he would make an effort to rectify them (Phidd, 1974:174). Shortly after his victory, Trudeau established the new Department of Regional Economic Expansion (DREE). There can be little doubt that DREE policy was based on the growth-pole theory of development. Early statements outlining its programs and goals referred to three related programs: infrastructure assistance, industrial incentives, and social adjustment (Francis and Pillai, 1972:46). All three were to take place in "special areas" selected by the department in co-operation with the provinces (Francis and Pillai, 1972:54-55). These "special areas" were selected primarily in the belief that certain centres within underdeveloped regions could be

made attractive to industry once "substantial improvements have been made to the infrastructure and social services currently available in them" (Francis and Pillai, 1972:54). Between 1970 and 1973, 23 areas were identified as "special areas" entitled to special assistance (Daniels, 1981:57). The areas were large and included all of the island portion of Newfoundland, much of the Atlantic Provinces, almost all of Quebec, much of eastern and northern Ontario, and a substantial portion of the western provinces. . . .

Obviously, DREE programming favoured urban growth and industrial development. In addition to infrastructural development to make selected centres attractive, industries would be attracted by direct cash grants to encourage them to set up operations or expand existing plants in the "special areas.". . .

With its focus on industrialization and urbanization, DREE programming was the embodiment of the growth-centre strategy. Canadian regional development policy had made a 180-degree turn from 1930 to 1969. Moreover, its dominant consideration was economic development, and relatively little effort was spent in examining the social structure and social vitality of the areas affected by DREE programs.

By the mid-1970s DREE policies were beginning to receive considerable criticism. It was suggested that the Liberal party had used DREE programs to reward industries for partisan financial support (Phidd, 1974: 185-88). DREE was also accused of paying industries to close old plants in industrial areas and open new ones in underdeveloped areas, without any net gain in jobs. David Lewis, the New Democratic Party leader made such criticisms the basis of his campaign book (1972). However, by far the most criticism came from the provincial governments. DREE's cost-sharing infrastructural assistance programs placed a heavy burden on the provinces, many borrowing money to take advantage of available DREE funds. Furthermore, the industrial incentives program was a source of irritation because it operated without any direct provincial involvement. Perhaps because of this, most special area agreements had been allowed to lapse by 1975, and DREE programming began to take another tack.

After 1974 the general thrust of DREE policies centred on greater co-operation with the provinces and decentralization of administration. DREE worked out "General Development Agreements" (GDAS) with each of the provincial governments except Prince Edward Island where the massive FRED program was still in effect. Those agreements still fostered DREE policies of infrastructural development, but provincial departments of economic development were involved in identifying the services they most needed, their location, and explicit development strategies to exploit economic opportunities. In addition, DREE decentralized its operations to the extent that two thirds of its staff worked outside Ottawa in the "underdeveloped" regions themselves (Daniels, 1981:58). Both measures were clearly intended to meet objections that DREE policies and programs were out of touch with provincial government objectives and provincial needs.

ALTERNATIVE PROPOSALS FOR A "NEW" CANADIAN REGIONAL DEVELOPMENT STRATEGY

. . . Canada's regional planners . . . during the past two decades have had an opportunity to apply their theories in an attempt to reduce Canada's regional economic disparities. They have based their plans primarily on a combination of neo-classical economic theory and the growth-centre strategy. It now seems legitimate to examine whether the evidence indicates that they have been successful.

In 1971, shortly after DREE programs began, Newfoundland had an unemployment rate of 8.4 percent. Seven years later it had risen to 16.4 percent. Indeed, with the exception of Alberta, all Canadian provinces had higher rates of unemployment in 1978 than in 1971. More significantly, the poorer provinces which had received most DREE funding had the greatest increases (McAllister, 1980:39). If regional disparity is thought of in relative rather than in absolute terms, there has been virtually no alteration in the way in which provinces are ordered in terms of unemployment. Throughout the past 50 years, the Atlantic Provinces have consistently had the highest unemployment rates, followed by the Prairie Provinces, British Columbia, Quebec, and Ontario. The only notable exception to this has once again been Alberta, where recent developments in the oil industry reduced unemployment rates in the late 1970s.

There is some evidence that the gaps in income levels among the provinces are narrowing, however. Ontario and British Columbia, which in the 1930s had per capita disposable income up to 30 percent higher than the national average are now only about 10 percent above it. The Prairie Provinces which have had levels as low as 30 percent below the national average are now generally slightly above it. The Atlantic Provinces, despite 30 years of regional planning, have been able to raise the relative position of their incomes only about 15 percent and remain some 20 percent below the national average (Daniels, 1981:56). While this trend is certainly in the right direction, one must question if it represents any fundamental change. The narrowing gap may be simply the result of the massive transfer payments made by DREE and other agencies to the underdeveloped regions and may not reflect any fundamental change in economic well-being. It is also possible that the narrowing gap reflects the deteriorating economic well-being of the provinces of Ontario and Quebec rather than any improvement in the poorer provinces. . . .

A number of regional development experts have suggested alternatives to DREE programs and policies. In a critical but constructive look at DREE and the alternatives to it, McAllister (1980) suggests that DREE failed largely because of bureaucracy and because no clear and accepted goals were formulated for it by federal politicians. He argues that it is necessary to specify clear goals (figures) with respect to income, participation rates, and unemployment rates. In addition he advocates ending the federal "poker game" with the provinces. He argues that once federal financial goals and programs have been established, the provinces should be directly involved in their implementation (1980:19-21). The most significant aspect of McAllister's analysis is his call for "regional self-sufficiency" rather than "the extreme positions of either 'small is beautiful' or 'big is beautiful'" (1980:19). Here McAllister clearly sets himself apart from the growth-pole theorists while also trying to distance himself from the perspective of Schumacher (1975) and his followers who advocate small-scale technological development as the solution for underdeveloped areas. To achieve regional self-sufficiency, McAllister argues, it is necessary to abandon "centralist Canadian protectionist policies no longer appropriate as they may once have been" (1980:41). In short, he is attacking the program of tariff protection which was partly responsible for the current

pattern of regional disparities. Yet McAllister hedges his bets, warning that "care must be taken not to go 'whole-hog' into a freer trade approach" (1980:41). As McAllister sees it, what is needed is regional specialization in terms of the mainstream sections: fisheries, wheat production, key transport nodes, and so on. In addition, he makes a strong case for encouraging smaller-scale activities: "The regions of Canada might be prudent to concentrate much attention on the welfare of small farms, small businesses and the semi-subsistence activities that people can fall back on in times of inflationary pressures. Such activities can provide a far more socially meaningful and economically productive cushion than broad social programs such as unemployment insurance or family allowances" (1980:41).

In many ways McAllister's position is typical of that of an economist from an underdeveloped region. He wants to use central capital but have local influence, to throw off certain protective tariffs which benefit central regions and expand export trade in the resources produced by the peripheral regions. He wishes to build up small-scale local economic acitivity not only to employ more people in these labour-intensive activities but also to provide security in the fluctuating world of staples markets. Yet it would be unfair to dismiss his argument simply because it is more or less what might be expected from a local advocate. Indeed, it is probably the best discussion of regional disparity in Canada written by an economist. McAllister's call for a reduction of centralist protection policies shows his grasp of the role which they play in hindering the development of Canada's peripheral regions. His advocacy of regional specialization shows his recognition of the importance of local resources in any strategy of regional development. In contrast, growth-pole theory advocates the introduction of enterprises with little or no resource base in the local region and which must compete with similar operations elsewhere for both their supplies and their markets. Small industries do not have to rely on a distant market for their customers and have the advantage of being closer to the local market than any external competitors. Though their product runs may be small and thus their manufacturing costs higher, that is often offset by lower transportation costs. Finally, McAllister is one of the few orthodox economists who appears to recognize the importance of social factors and "socially meaningful" work.

An alternative position is reflected in the work of Daniels which is more in line with the "transfer dependency" position. Like McAllister, Daniels recognizes DREE's failure to reduce regional disparities, but his proposed alternatives differ substantially from McAllister's. Rather like the military leader of antiquity who put to death the messenger who brought bad news, Daniels questions the indicators used to establish if regional disparity has been altered, asking if the problem of regional disparity can "be viewed realistically in terms of these classical indicators" (1981:58). He does not, however, suggest what indicators might be used in their stead. Daniels bases his approach to regional disparity on a theory of adjustments that must be made if transfers are absent: "It is a simple matter of arithmetic. If a region has a declining share of output, in the absence of compensating transfers, accommodating adjustments must take place" (1981:60). These adjustments will involve changes in income, the labour market, and/or demographic factors. . . .

If regional development policy involves adjustments, Daniels is aware of opposition to using migration as the "adjustment" to

solve regional disparity. He notes that "the idea of increased mobility may be simply unacceptable from a human, social, and political point of view" and declares that his own proposal does not advocate that solution (1981:61). On the other hand, migration does seem to dominate his attention and he argues that, if other adjustment processes are precluded, "such net migrations must occur," and he calls for "the reduction of barriers to interregional mobility as an important element of regional policy" (1981:61). Indeed, he adds that if migration is ruled out because of human, social, and political factors, "the encouragement of a 'stay option' will force pressure back on labour market adjustment . . . unemployment rates will rise further, and especially if transfers are tied explicitly to such rates through say, unemployment insurance schemes, more income will flow into the lagging region, thus ameliorating the aggregate circumstances in the area" (1981:61). Though he may deny it, this certainly seems to be an argument for using migration as the major adjustment. . . .

REGIONAL DEVELOPMENT POLICY FROM A DEPENDENCY THEORY PERSPECTIVE

Dependency theory attributes the economic underdevelopment of peripheral regions in a developed society to an historical pattern of social relationships in which developed regions exploit underdeveloped ones. Underdeveloped regions are exploited for natural resources, labour, and even the capital required for their own exploitation (Mandel, 1973). Resources are sent outside the underdeveloped areas for refining, reducing local economic gains. Even if they are refined locally, economic control of local industry usually rests outside the area and the bulk of the profit still leaves the underdeveloped region. The surplus of local labour in underdeveloped regions usually ensures that natural resources can be obtained at minimal labour cost, while this labour pool also benefits manufacturing industries located outside the region. This labour can be drawn in during times of economic expansion and returns home when times are tight. Political leaders, local businessmen, and ordinary citizens frequently purchase goods and equipment manufactured in the economic centres. This ensures a region's continued economic dependency, for such acquisitions reduce the amount of local capital available to finance economic growth.

Underdevelopment is not simply the process of one region exploiting another, however, but *also* a process in which a dominant class, located for the most part in the developed region, comes to exploit the underdeveloped region. Even then, this process does not occur simply through the direct action of the dominant class. Rather, the process of regional subordination and exploitation is actually mediated through the actions of an elite group within the underdeveloped region itself. This group thus serves as a "bridgehead" for the exploitation of the underdeveloped region (Galtung, 1971).

It is possible to examine Canadian regional development policy to see if it effectively reduces the dependency of the underdeveloped regions or if it, instead, increases that dependency. In any such analysis, the focus is on whether the exploitation of underdeveloped regions for their resources, labour, and capital is increased or decreased by regional development policy, and on the interests being served by existing policies. At issue is whether Canadian regional develop-

ment policies counteract the historical pattern of regional and class exploitation or whether they simply reinforce it. It is noteworthy that Hodge, the director of the School of Urban and Regional Planning at Queen's University, has described Canadian regional development planning as "colonialism" pursued with an eye to exploiting rural and hinterland areas to serve the needs of metropolitan ones (1975:87-94). However, Hodge's statement considers only part of the problem with Canadian regional development policies. Such policies do not just serve metropolitan interests over hinterland ones, but also operate in the interest of the dominant class in both the hinterland and the metropolitan areas. A central feature of DREE policies has been the attempt to provide the infrastructural facilities required by industry as well as incentives to private investors in those industries. Particular efforts have been directed toward giving such incentives to investors from outside the underdeveloped region. However, as we have seen, these outside interests have historically played a central role in the process of underdeveloping Canada's peripheral regions. Thus, DREE regional policies have been directed at assisting those interests that have helped create regional underdevelopment in the first place and benefit most from it. Such a strategy of development fails to deal with the underlying structural conditions which create regional underdevelopment. Until a policy able to counterbalance the power of these dominant interests is in place, it is extremely unlikely that the pattern of regional inequality in Canada will be altered appreciably.

When industries come from outside an underdeveloped region, the basic aim of the owners is to remove wealth from the area rather than to increase the wealth and benefit the living conditions of those who live there. The fact that some will benefit by employment in the new plant has to be weighed against the cost of lengthening dependency and a future in which economic power and decisions remain outside local regional control.

Of course a number of local industries and entrepreneurs also receive and benefit from industrial incentive grants. Such grants benefit the region more for they allow capital to be built up within the local area. Certainly this has advantages over giving funds to outside corporations. However, it should not be overlooked that many such firms are engaged in resource exploitation, and the grants subsidize the export of resources from the region rather than encouraging local development. . . .

The evidence just presented indicates that ultimately DREE programming increased the dependency of underdeveloped regions on outside interests and led to further exploitation of local resources, labour, and capital, exacerbating the problem it was intended to alleviate. It could, of course, be argued that simply because regional development incentives benefit the rich does not mean that they necessarily hurt the poor. An argument can be made that jobs are provided and that the total society benefits from stimulating the local economy. Though Marxists sometimes think in zero-sum terms when it comes to class relations (Poulantzas, 1978:117-19), it is at least worth considering whether in fact regional development policies do benefit everyone—even if not equally.

There is some evidence, however, that even in the short run, few workers benefited from the program offered by DREE. Woodward indicates that DREE subsidies favoured assistance for machinery and equipment, a policy "inconsistent with the department's primary objective—employment" (1974:162-3,

173). If that is true, DREE programming offers relatively little employment to the large unemployed labour force of peripheral regions. To be successful, the growth-pole model requires that industry be technically efficient in order to overcome the additional costs involved in transporting its goods to market. Such technical efficiency may be antithetical to a policy aimed at promoting employment.

PROSPECTS FOR REGIONAL DEVELOPMENT POLICY

There are several conflicting schools of thought within social theory about the relation between the state and the ruling class. Poulantzas contends that a unified capitalist class controls the state structures and uses them for its own purposes (1978). In contrast, Miliband argues that there is at least some degree of "elite pluralism" where competing elite groups at least ensure that there are some elements of countervailing power within the capitalist system. However, both theorists also qualify their positions. Poulantzas points out that some social policies make it possible for certain dominated classes to usurp some of the *economic* power of the dominant class as long as its *political* power remains inviolate (1978:193), while Miliband argues that in spite of divisions among elite groups, together they still constitute a dominant class within the capitalist system. Miliband contends that, even under "bastard forms of socialization" the bias involved in the operation of the modern state ensures that capitalist interests automatically benefit from state intervention (1969:72).

Both approaches must lead one to question if regional development policy will ever be able to reduce regional disparities in Canada. According to both analyses, a successful policy for eliminating regional disparity is impossible within the present economic system because it must inevitably benefit some ruling class. In Canada, as in most industrial societies, that class is clustered in the central or metropolitan area of the country. Poulantzas' statements leave open the possibility of developing policies to raise the economic if not the political well-being of the working class in underdeveloped regions. This may potentially be possible. However there is little evidence to suggest that past or present policies have been successful in doing so. Indeed, the historical and contemporary evidence suggests that regional development policy in Canada has favoured the dominant class in both the underdeveloped and the developed regions.

If the pattern of regional development policies has been to favour the central regions over peripheral ones and the interests of capital over labour, it is important to consider the conditions under which this pattern is likely to change. Marxists argue that change will come only when the historical forces of capitalism have run their course and the revolution of the working class has occurred. There is little evidence that such a social and political revolution is likely to disrupt Eastern and Western Canada in the near future, however. An alternative theory of the conditions needed to effect change can be found in Gans (1972). Gans examines the persistence of poverty despite our belief that it is harmful to our society and despite endless programs aimed at either eliminating or reducing it. He contends that if any aspect of a social system persists, it must be functional in some way to society. He does not, however, adopt the usual functionalist position that society is essentially a monolithic entity in which all parts must contribute to the functioning of the whole. Rather, he argues that it is possible for certain generally undesirable elements of social structure to persist if they benefit the more powerful interest groups in society. He argues that poverty has persisted because it benefits those who hold economic and political power in society and, moreover, he argues that it will not likely be eliminated until "alternatives" are found to replace it. Gans examines its various social, cultural, and political functions only to find that no apparent functional alternatives exist (within a capitalist system) for some of the main economic and social functions of poverty. The implication for regional development policy is that any policies will likely remain unsuccessful until they are directed at reducing the role played by regional disparity in maintaining the well-being of the central regions and their dominant classes.

While both Marxists and Gans suggest that it is unlikely that any regional development policies (short of revolution) will ever totally alter the pattern of regional economic disparity in Canada, there are certainly ways to improve the relative position of underdeveloped regions. It is necessary first to reject the growth-pole and master industry approach to regional development and any policy based on it. Such approaches inherently favour the central and dominant interests. Second, any approach based on a pattern of "adjustment" by migration is unacceptable not only because it is too socially disruptive and unpopular, but also because there is reason to believe that it will not work. Change in the pattern of regional disparity in Canada must occur through policies designed to eliminate the historic pattern of the dependency of the peripheral regions. Protectionist policies which favour central regions over peripheral ones, perpetuating underdevelopment, must be eliminated. Deliberate attempts must be made to enhance the economic self-sufficiency of underdeveloped regions by developing local resources and industries which will satisfy local needs. In this way underdeveloped regions can have an economic advantage in production and begin to reduce their economic dependency and the constant drain of scarce capital. Finally, and most important, is the need for employment. Efforts should be made to promote labour-intensive rather than technologically efficient industry. The fundamental goal of regional development policy should be regional self-sufficiency, not industrialization and urbanization. Yet there is little evidence that the federal government will ever adopt such guidelines to regional development. If it is not forced to do so by the provinces, our peripheral regions are doomed to a future of underdevelopment perpetuated by our regional development policies.

REFERENCES

Acheson, Thomas W.
  1972   "The National Policy and the Industrialization of the Maritimes, 1880-1910," *Acadiensis*, 1: 3-28.
  1977   "The Maritimes and Empire Canada," in *Canada and the Burden of Unity*, ed. David J. Bercuson, pp. 87-104. Toronto: Macmillan Co. of Canada.

Berton, Pierre
  1972   *The National Dream: The Great Railway, 1871-1881.* Toronto: McClelland & Stewart.

Buckley, Helen, and Eva Tihanyi
  1967   *Canadian Public Policies for Rural Adjustment: A Study of the Economic Impact of A.R.D.A., P.F.R.A., and M.M.R.A.* Economic Council of Canada Special Study no. 7. Ottawa: Queen's Printer.

Chorney, Harold
  1977   "Regional Underdevelopment and Cultural Decay," in *Imperialism, Nationalism and Canada*, ed. John Saul, pp. 85-107. Toronto: New Hogtown Press.

Daniels, Mark
  1981   "The Birth and Shaping of Regional Policies," *Policy Options*, 2: 55-61.

Francis, J. P., and N. G. Pillai
  1972   *Regional Development and Regional Policy: Some Issues and Recent Canadian Experience.* Ottawa: Department of Regional Economic Expansion.

Gans, Herbert J.
  1972   "The Positive Functions of Poverty," *American Journal of Sociology*, 78: 275-89.

Hodge, Gerald
  1975   "Regional Planning: Where It's At," *Plan Canada*, 15: 87-94.

Hutcheson, John
  1978   *Dominance and Dependency: Liberalism and National Policies in the North Atlantic Triangle.* Toronto: McClelland & Stewart.

Lewis, David
>   1972 *Louder Voices: The Corporate Welfare Bums.* Toronto: James, Lewis and Samuel Co.

McAllister, Ian
>   1980 "How to Re-make DREE," *Policy Options,* 1: 39-43.

Mandel, Ernest
>   1973 *Capitalism and Regional Disparities.* Toronto: New Hogtown Press.

Miliband, Ralph
>   1969 *The State and Capitalist Society.* London: Quartet Books.
>   1973 "Poulantzas and the Capitalist State," *New Left Review,* no. 82.

Naylor, Tom
>   1975 *The History of Canadian Business, 1867-1914,* 2 vols. Toronto: James Lorimer & Co.

Phidd, R. W.
>   1974 "Regional Development Policy," in *Issues in Canadian Public Policy,* ed. G. Bruce Doern and Seymour Wilson, pp. 166-202. Toronto: Macmillan Co. of Canada.

Poulantzas, Nicos
>   1978 *Political Power and Social Classes.* London: Verso Editions.

Ray, D. Michael
>   1968 "The Spacial Structure of Regional Development and Cultural Differences: A Factoral Ecology of Canada, 1961." Paper presented at the annual meeting of the Regional Sciences Association, November 8.

Schumacher, E. F.
>   1975 *Small Is Beautiful: Economics as if People Mattered.* New York: Harper & Row.

Woodward, Robert S.
>   1974 "The Capital Bias of DREE Incentives," *Canadian Journal of Economics,* 7: 162-73.

D: Region

---

29. Urban Dominance, Foreign Ownership, and Corporate Concentration

R. Keith Semple

INTRODUCTION

This paper investigates regional inequalities and urban dominance in the distribution of corporate ownership and control of the Canadian economy. Corporate control is exerted over the various regions within the Canadian economy by decision-makers associated with corporate headquarters located in a system of international, national, and regional urban centres. Control within the system has both domestic and foreign components that are constantly changing over time. These interrelated dynamic components complicate any analysis of Canadian regional inequalities (Semple, 1985a; 1985b).

In Canada, the trend toward increased corporate size and power has been accelerating since the late 1950s and is associated with a maturing economic structure, mod-

An original essay prepared especially for this volume.

ern technological developments, and an unprecedented wave of mergers and acquisitions. For Canada and Canadians the increasing power of giant corporations is both a blessing and a source of concern. Corporations provide jobs and security, are technological innovators, and have the monetary resources and administrative skills to undertake the risky and costly developments so necessary to Canadian growth and well-being. However, their extensive power is not well understood, is concentrated in a few key metropolitan centres, and has increasingly come under the influence of foreign investors and entrepreneurs (Semple, 1977b). The regional and national corporate system is complicated further by powerful federal and provincial Crown corporations. At present one or two huge corporations dominate virtually every subsector of the Canadian economy. This power is concentrated in the hands of senior executives located in the major centres of the nation and in foreign centres abroad. The analysis that follows examines the relative levels of urban dominance of the various financial and non-financial sectors of the Canadian economy, as well as the relationship between urban dominance and foreign ownership.

THE NATIONAL ECONOMY

This study assigns the top Canadian corporations, as of 1985, to a headquarters centre and to one of six sectors of the economy. As is customary, the largest corporations in the finance, real estate development, and utility sectors are measured by the size of their assets, and those in manufacturing, service, and resources by the size of their revenues (Semple, 1973).

The Financial Sectors

Table 29-1 provides a detailed breakdown of the largest 268 financial corporations, with over $890 billion in assets under their control. The top 70 banks, with over $428 billion, form the largest financial subsector. The large "schedule A" Canadian banks, which control over 90 percent of these assets, and the more than 60 "schedule B" foreign banks have their headquarters in Toronto or Montreal. Herein lies the single largest component of financial and geographical power in Canada. This financial power, more than any other factor, accounts for the dominance of Toronto and, to a lesser degree, Montreal over the Canadian economy. Diversified finance is the second-largest subsector, with the top 50 corporations in this field having assets in excess of $122 billion. Included here are Toronto and Montreal corporations, such as Trilon and Power Financial, which account for just over one half of the assets of this subsector. In addition, there are Crown corporations like Canada Mortgage and Housing and the Al-berta Treasury Branches that give Ottawa and Edmonton much of their financial clout. The top 27 life insurance companies constitute the next-largest subsector. Toronto, which houses the headquarters of Sun, Manufacturers, Canada, Confederation, and Crown Life, controls over 60 percent of the national market. Trust companies, the fourth-largest subsector, are concentrated in Montreal. The industry leader, Canada Trust, is controlled by Imasco and controls over $21 billion in assets. Virtually all the remaining trust companies are directly or indirectly controlled by a few investment conglomerates, which in turn trace their ownership to a few powerful families like the Reichmanns, Bronfmans, and Belzbergs. The numerous credit unions form the smallest subsector. Collectively, these member-run institutions are found throughout the country and in most important centres. These organizations have the most dispersed level of corporate power, although some concentration does occur in the provincial credit union centrals. By far the most important group of this kind in Canada is the Quebec City-based Confédération des caisses populaires Desjardins du Québec, a $22.5-billion member-owned federation of credit unions.

The last two subsectors are utilities and real estate developers. The top 25 corporations included in the utility subsector either generate electrical power or transport oil and gas by pipline. Provincial crown corporations, such as Saskatchewan Power, Bruncor, Hydro Québec, and Ontario Hydro, dominate this sector. These utilities are headquartered in their respective provincial capitals or major commercial centres and by law have a spatial monopoly over their respective regions. Thus, Canada has effectively decentralized energy provision and transmission. Unlike in other sectors, no

TABLE 29-1 Total assets of financial, utility, and development corporations in Canadian cities in 1985 in millions of dollars.

			Top 70	Top 50	Top 27	Top 26	Top 40	Top 25	Top 30	Top 268		
Rank	City	Region	Banks	Diversified finance	Life insurance	Trusts	Credit unions	Utilities	Real estate	Total	Percentage of total	Total foreign
1	Toronto	Central	218 021	33 627	67 918	2 970	2 287	33 452	26 475	384 732	43.00	40 873
2	Montreal	East	206 192	31 404	8 533	38 284		30 176	102	314 691	35.18	32 293
3	Quebec City	East		4 450	6 548	385	23 651			35 034	3.92	
4	Ottawa	Central		22 287	3 709		486	267	2 377	29 126	3.26	3 709
5	Edmonton	West	106	21 409		1 775	593	2 013	2 500	28 396	3.17	
6	Vancouver	West	4 515	3 749		509	3 792	12 853	1 308	26 726	2.99	1 102
7	Winnipeg	West			10 801	118	462	4 689	611	19 923	2.23	
8	Calgary	West				912	607	11 294	4 673	17 486	1.95	860
9	Stratford	Central				8 706				8 706	0.97	
10	Kitchener	Central			7 588					7 588	0.85	
11	Halifax	East		555	1 512	3 537	164	1 433	118	7 319	0.82	
12	Regina	West					1 406	2 820	35	4 261	0.47	
13	Fredericton	East						2 820		2 820	0.31	
14	St. John's	East						2 457		2 457	0.26	
15	Saskatoon	West				69	938			1 007	0.11	
16	Hamilton	Central		626		107	208			941	0.11	477
17	London	Central		685					144	829	0.09	685
18	Barrie	Central		470						470	0.05	
19	Victoria	West					410			410	0.05	
20	St. Catharines	Central					327			327	0.04	
21	Chilliwack	West					188			188	0.02	
22	Steinbach	West					163			163	0.02	
23	Kelowna	West					149			149	0.02	
24	Trail	West						139		139	0.02	
25	Swift Current	West					135			135	0.02	
26	Red Deer	West					132			132	0.01	
27	Prince Albert	West					129			129	0.01	
28	Lloydminster	West					121			121	0.01	
29	Nelson	West					121			121	0.01	
30	Moose Jaw	West					88			88	0.01	
Others				29					54	168	0.02	
	Total domestic		428 834	122 533	106 609	57 372	36 557	104 498	38 379	894 782	100	
	Total foreign		30 234	10 412	16 311	21 570		860	612			79 999
	Percentage foreign		7.1	8.5	15.3	37.6	0.0	0.8				8.9

one centre dominates the industry. Consequently, this sector provides an example of an intermediate level of corporate concentration, with national dispersion but regional concentration. The last subsector is uniquely Canadian and comprises the top 30 real estate development corporations. Three of the largest are Olympia and York of Toronto (the largest company of its type in the world), Trizec of Calgary, and Cadillac Fairview of Toronto. The latter city dominates the Canadian urban system by directing or controlling the equivalent of 70 percent of the skyscraper and shopping plaza developments.

For the largest 30 cities in the financial, utility, and real estate sectors, the urban decision-making hierarchy is divided in Table 29-1 into three major decision-making regions: Central, West, and East. The Central region controls almost half (48.6 percent) of the assets in this sector, the East 40.5 percent, and the West 11.1 percent. Of the eight cities that the Central region includes, Toronto is clearly dominant, accounting for $385 billion of the $433 billion in this region. Ottawa is a distant second, at $29 billion, followed by Stratford, Kitchener, Hamilton, London, Barrie, and St. Catharines. In the East region there are five key cities involved in the finance-utilities-real estate sector and here, as well, one city dominates. Montreal accounts for $315 of the $362 billion in assets in the East region, with Quebec City well back at $35 billion, followed by Halifax, Fredericton, and St. John's. Finally, there is the West region. where 17 cities control only about $100 billion in assets in finance, utilities, and real estate. This amount is fairly widely dispersed, with Edmonton the largest centre, closely followed by Vancouver, Winnipeg, and Calgary. Regina is next, with the remaining 12 cities well behind the top four in this region (Martz

and Semple, 1985). In summary, over 75 percent of all the assets in the financial, utility, and real estate sectors are controlled from corporate head offices located in Toronto and Montreal, the two dominant centres in the financial hierarchy. The importance of all other centres declines rapidly after these two cities.

The Non-Financial Sectors

Toronto, the largest city within the Canadian urban system, also dominates the manufacturing, service, and resource sectors. Tables 29-2, 29-3, and 29-4 illustrate that Toronto-based corporations account for the largest percentage of ownership in manufacturing (53) and in services (34), as well as the second-largest in resources (46), for an overall average of 44.1 percent. Toronto dominates seven of the nine manufacturing subsectors, with corporations such as GM and Ford in transportation machinery, Canada Packers in food, CIL in chemicals, CGE in electrical products, IBM in machinery, Procter and Gamble in miscellaneous manufacturing, and Bata in textiles. Toronto also dominates four of the eight service subsectors and one resource subsector, with companies such as Westons in retailing, Honda in wholesale and distributing, McDonalds in miscellaneous service, Royal Insurance in professional services, and Noranda in mining. Montreal dominates six of the subsectors, with Alcan in metals, Domtar in forest products, C.P., C.N., and Air Canada in transportation, Bell Canada in communications, Canada Cement Lafarge in construction, and Co-opérative fédérée du Québec in co-ops. Montreal ranks second overall, with 22.5 percent of the total revenues. Calgary-based resource corporations control over $37 billion of revenues and now outstrip Toronto, for the first

TABLE 29-2   Total revenues of manufacturing corporations in Canadian cities in 1985 in millions of dollars.

			Top 50	Top 70	Top 50	Top 55	Top 55	Top 60	Top 50	Top 60	Top 25	Top 475		
Rank	City	Region	Transport machinery	Food	Metals	Forest	Chemical	Electrical	Machinery	Misc. mfg.	Textiles	Total	Percentage of total	Total foreign
1	Toronto	Central	39 768	12 593	6 937	5 257	9 688	11 795	9 396	4 755	3 312	103 501	53.02	72 279
2	Montreal	East	2 878	12 390	10 145	6 244	3 328	817	1 024	1 463	1 276	39 565	20.27	12 133
3	Vancouver	West	1 273	277	120	7 643		37		1 400	87	10 873	5.56	2 731
4	Windsor	Central	7 249		31		84					7 364	3.77	7 333
5	Hamilton	Central	925	91	2 643	234	649	784	284	145		5 755	2.95	3 120
6	London	Central	557	2 426		506				414		3 903	2.00	302
7	Ottawa	Central	255	18	965	107	425	717	962	103		3 552	1.82	1 140
8	Calgary	West		1 551					55	1 812		3 418	1.75	102
9	Kitchener	Central	328	648			672	154		72	71	1 945	1.00	891
10	St. Catharines	Central	465	113	104	501	62		10	77		1 332	0.68	860
11	Sarnia	Central					1 290					1 290	0.66	1 290
12	Sault Ste. Marie	Central			1 176	78						1 254	0.64	
13	Edmonton	West		750	43					192	180	1 165	0.60	180
14	Florenceville	East		1 023								1 023	0.52	
15	Winnipeg	West	182	75	58	63	20			252	46	696	0.36	449
16	Kamloops	West				561						561	0.29	500
17	Halifax	East	100	454								554	0.28	
18	Saskatoon	West		376				60				436	0.22	
19	Brantford	Central			95		76		139		118	428	0.22	76
20	St. Georges Beauce	East				330						330	0.17	
21	Peterborough	Central	74	242								316	0.16	316
22	Prince George	West					310					310	0.16	160
23	Regina	West			304							304	0.16	
24	St. Thomas	Central	179						73	51		303	0.16	303
25	St. John's	East		298								298	0.15	
26	Cambridge	Central						50	119		119	288	0.15	119
27	Guelph	Central						247	41			288	0.15	150
28	Woodstock	Central	13						227		33	273	0.14	
29	Kingsley Falls	Central					266					266	0.14	
30	Kitimat	West					236					236	0.12	
	Others			706	547	669	682		349	316	115	3 384	1.73	1 083
	Total domestic		54 246	34 031	23 195	23 005	16 976	14 661	12 679	11 062	5 357	195 212	100	
	Total foreign		50 057	11 534	6 153	5 245	11 044	5 745	9 792	5 009	938	105 517		54.0
	Percentage foreign		92.3	33.9	26.5	22.8	65.1	39.2	77.2	45.3	17.5	54.0		

TABLE 29-3 Total revenues of service corporations in Canadian cities in 1985 in millions of dollars.

			Top 60	Top 50	Top 65	Top 70	Top 70	Top 30	Top 90	Top 40	Top 475		
Rank	City	Region	Retail	Trans-port	Commu-nication	Whole-sale	Misc. service	Co-ops	Professional service	Construction	Total	Percentage of total	Total foreign
1	Toronto	Central	30 362	2 095	10 644	8 101	4 967	638	7 304	1 422	65 533	33.96	20 387
2	Montreal	East	9 926	25 459	16 744	2 881	1 282	3 212	1 255	3 154	63 913	33.12	4 627
3	Winnipeg	West	10 259	796	398	4 466	5 371	1 748	658	97	23 793	12.33	5 638
4	Vancouver	West	1 736	916	95	6 154	657	350	262	457	10 627	5.51	3 965
5	Calgary	West	324	1 025		1 228	300	2 164		557	5 598	2.90	421
6	Ottawa	Central		217	503	74	3 167		84		4 054	2.10	
7	Edmonton	West	221	518	1 314	81	80	305		1 193	3 712	1.92	174
8	Regina	West	92		423			2 023	268		2 806	1.45	
9	Saskatoon	West	82			334		1 831			2 247	1.16	
10	Hamilton	Central		556		537	230			226	1 549	0.80	836
11	Stellarton	East	908					114			1 022	0.53	
12	Quebec City	East						190	546	140	876	0.45	
13	Granby	East						759			759	0.39	
14	Victoria	West							714		714	0.37	
15	London	Central	144	40	19	259	186		40		688	0.36	255
16	Guelph	Central					79		544		623	0.32	79
17	Kitchener	Central	299						312		611	0.32	
18	Halifax	East		107	310		80	93			590	0.31	80
19	Moncton	East		191				287			478	0.25	
20	Cornerbrook	East								328	328	0.17	
21	Drummondville	East				275					275	0.14	
22	Saint John	East			243						243	0.13	
23	Red Deer	West					71	169			240	0.12	
24	Rimouski	East						225			225	0.12	
25	Sault Ste. Marie	Central		200							200	0.10	
26	Blenheim	Central				185					185	0.10	
27	Thetford Mines	East				183					183	0.09	
28	St. John's	East	42		136						178	0.09	
29	Kelowna	West						171			171	0.09	42
30	North Bay	Central		130							130	0.07	
	Others			140	51		53	148		55	447	0.23	
	Total domestic		54 395	32 390	30 880	24 758	16 532	14 427	11 987	7 629	192 998	100	
	Total foreign		11 360	570	1 925	13 098	2 634		3 905	3 012			36 504
	Percentage foreign		20.9	1.8	6.2	52.9	15.9		32.6	39.5			18.9

time in the country's history (Semple and Smith, 1981). Corporations such as Shell, Gulf, and Petro-Canada underline the premier rank of Calgary, not only in the petroleum subsector but also in the resource sector. Nationally, in all sectors, Calgary ranks third, with 10.1 percent of the revenues. Vancouver ranks fourth, with the headquarters of MacMillan Bloedel, Core-Mark, and Mitsubishi Canada and 5.4 percent of the total. Winnipeg ranks a close fifth at 5.3 percent, with Canada Safeway and Cargill. Ottawa ranks sixth (1.7), with Canada Post and the Royal Canadian Mint; Windsor seventh (1.6), with Chrysler; Hamilton eighth (1.5), with Dofasco and Navistar; Edmonton ninth (1.1), with PCL Construction, and London tenth (1.0), with John Labatt. Other cities in descending order of importance are Regina (0.7), with the Saskatche-

wan Wheat Pool, Saskatoon (0.7), with Federated Co-operatives, and Saint John (0.6), with the Irving Group.

The pattern of control in the non-financial sectors can also be examined with respect to the three key regions: Central, East, and West. The Central region, with its many Ontario-based corporations, is responsible for more revenues than the West and East combined. Toronto ranks at the apex of the national urban hierarchy and dominates the central region subhierarchy. Other notable centres include Ottawa, Windsor, Hamilton, and London, followed by Kitchener, Sault Ste. Marie, St. Catharines, and Sarnia. The Eastern region has a dual hierarchical structure dominated by Montreal, with lesser centres in Saint John, Halifax, and Quebec City. Stellarton and Florenceville represent two small centres

TABLE 29-4 Total revenues of resource corporations in Canadian cities in 1985 in millions of dollars.

Rank	City	Region	Top 100 Petroleum	Top 50 Mining	Top 150 Total	Percentage of Total	Total foreign
1	Calgary	West	37 588	202	37 790	45.55	11 797
2	Toronto	Central	21 621	14 958	36 579	44.09	16 684
3	Vancouver	West	458	3 191	3 650	4.40	105
4	Saint John	East	2 210		2 210	2.66	1 110
5	Montreal	East		743	743	0.90	426
6	Saskatoon	West		423	423	0.51	20
7	Cornwall	Central	400		400	0.48	
8	Edmonton	West	169	110	279	0.34	77
9	Ottawa	Central		271	271	0.33	
10	Regina	West	161	57	218	0.26	
11	Thetford Mines	East		115	115	0.14	
12	Quebec City	East	20	80	100	0.12	
	Others		174	10	184	0.22	88
	Total domestic		62 081	20 161	82 962	100	
	Total foreign		27 118	3 189			30 307
	Percentage foreign		43.7	15.8			36.5

housing the Sobey and McCain empires. The West is not dominated clearly by any one city, except that Calgary appears to have the potential to be a second-level decision-making centre. Vancouver and Winnipeg are also of importance, followed by Edmonton, Regina, and Saskatoon. Victoria and Kamloops are now beginning to develop and take their place in the urban hierarchy.

TRENDS IN URBAN DOMINANCE

Dominance in the urban system is related to the degree of business control which emanates from each of the components in the system. On the one hand, control can be decentralized and emanate from a system of local centres dominated by local corporations making decisions over local economies. On the other hand, control can be centralized and emanate from one major centre dominated by a number of large multinational corporations making decisions over the entire economy. From the previous discussion it is evident that the Canadian economy is highly centralized. Many of the largest multinational corporations are headquartered in a handful of large centres, particularly Toronto, where they make decisions that affect everyone. The important task arising from this observation is to determine trends in the spatial concentration of decision-making. Is there a tendency for regional inequalities to increase when decision-making is concentrated in the hands of a few large corporations headquartered in a national centre (Semple and Phillips, 1982)?

This section examines trends in urban corporate dominance in Canada over the past decade. There are essentially two ways in which dominance can increase or decrease. One way involves the rapid growth of corporations at one level in the decision-making hierarchy at the expense of corporations at other levels, while the second way involves the actual or perceived movement of corporate headquarters among the various levels in the urban hierarchy. For example, if the largest centres in the nation's heartland are growing more rapidly than lower-level centres in the periphery, and if existing corporations in the regions are transferring their executive offices to the centre, then urban dominance increases. Let us focus attention on real and perceived corporate-headquarters moves. There are three ways in which moves can occur. The first involves closing a headquarters in one town and reopening in another. The second involves the merger of two corporations or the acquisition of one by another, where the headquarters of the companies are in two distinct centres prior to the merger but in one centre afterwards. The third way involves corporate births or deaths. The births may be newly incorporated businesses and the deaths may be bankruptcies. The processes that encourage corporate moves, mergers, births, and deaths either increase or decrease urban dominance. For example, dominance is encouraged when large regional firms decide to participate more fully in the national economy by moving their headquarters, say from Halifax to Toronto, in order to take advantage of face-to-face contacts with multinational decision-makers. Mergers and acquisitions quite often achieve the same goal. At the same time, deregulation of business activity may encourage foreign corporations to incorporate in domestic national centres, and an economic recession may hit small regional firms harder than large national companies, resulting in the bankruptcies of the small firms (Semple and Green, 1983; Semple, Green, and Martz, 1985).

Consider, for example, the corporate-headquarters moves of the financial, utility, and development sectors for the period 1976-86. Toronto, already the largest financial centre in the country. gained the most due to corporations' moving, merging, acquiring, or establishing new headquarters in that city. Toronto gained almost $50 billion in assets this way, while also losing over $20 billion, for a net gain of approximately $30 billion. London, a large regional centre, lost over $18 billion, the largest net loss. A highly celebrated move involved the Sun Life Assurance transfer from Montreal to Toronto, due to the perceived instability of Quebec and the growing international potential of Toronto. An even larger transfer involved the acquisition and merger of Canada Trust of London and Canada Permanent Trust of Toronto by British-controlled Imasco of Montreal. Another significant event involved new banking regulations, which permitted the incorporation of schedule-B foreign banks in Canada. For the most part these new banks located in Toronto. A few French-language banks located in Montreal, while some Asian banks located in Vancouver. The 1981 recession forced the bankruptcy of the Northland and Commercial banks of Calgary and Edmonton. An interesting financial move occurred when Victoria and Grey Trust of Lindsay merged with National Trust of Toronto and set up a legal corporate head office in Stratford. Overall, it is evident that the movement of financial corporate headquarters over the past decade favours the already dominant urban centres of Toronto and Montreal and hurts the regional centres of Calgary, Edmonton, and London. The trend is clearly toward more dominance and greater decision-making inequality.

We can also consider corporate-headquarters moves for the manufacturing, service, and resource sectors. From 1976 to 1986, Calgary made the largest net gains, while Toronto, Montreal, and Vancouver showed the largest net losses. Calgary continued to consolidate its position as the petroleum corporate headquarters centre of Canada. Most domestic corporations have their headquarters in Calgary and, during the past few years, the international companies have acknowledged Calgary as the oil capital. Corporations like Shell Canada and Gulf Canada moved their headquarters from Toronto. British Petroleum and Petrofina, as the result of mergers and acquisitions, moved from Montreal, while Chevron Canada consolidated its Vancouver operations in Calgary. A second basic trend in this decade was the movement of foreign resource and manufacturing firms out of Montreal to the cities of Toronto, Calgary, and Vancouver. Among the movers were the European petroleum firms, Ultramar, BP, and Petrofina. Another group included numerous American and British manufacturers: Allied Chemical, CIL, Cyanamid, Standard Brands, Benson and Hedges, Consolidated Foods, Robin Hood Multifoods, Cadbury-Schweppes, Canadian Vickers, and Genstar. A third basic trend involved gains by Toronto and Montreal at the expense of mainly regional centres. Toronto gained from such centres in Southern Ontario as Windsor (Green Giant); Chatham (Libby McNeil Libby); London (Commonwealth Holiday Inns); Woodstock (Eaton Yale); and Cambridge (Dresser). Toronto also gained from towns in Northern Ontario and the West, including: Sudbury (Cochrane-Dunlop); Fort Frances (Boise Cascade); and Calgary (Burns Foods). Montreal gained from Toronto (Maple Leaf Mills, GTE Sylvania); Ottawa (Loeb); Vancouver (B.C. Air); London (Air Ontario); Gander (Eastern Provincial Airlines); and from smaller Quebec centres like Temisca-ming (Tembec). A fourth trend saw Japanese-based corporations move from Vancouver to Toronto (for example, Yamaha and Simitomo). These trends show some regional centres like Calgary becoming dominant in particular sectors of the economy, while other dominant cities like Montreal struggled to maintain their positions of power at the expense of other cities.

In summary, the movements in the financial sectors appear to be reinforcing the dominance of Toronto as the national financial centre, while relegating Montreal to the role of a regional centre. A more complicated pattern is evolving in the non-financial sectors. Calgary has established itself as the petroleum centre of Canada and Toronto has become the dominant headquarters for manufacturing, while Montreal is challenging Toronto for dominant position as a centre of consumer services such as transportation and communication.

URBAN DOMINANCE AND FOREIGN CONTROL

Dominance in the urban system refers to the degree of corporate control that emanates from an urban centre. This control may be domestic or foreign. This section focuses attention on foreign control. Tables 29-1, 29-2, 29-3, and 29-4 document the level of international ownership of each of the financial and non-financial subsectors of the economy. Foreign ownership percentages ranged from very low levels in credit unions (0.0), utilities (0.8), and transportation (1.8), to very high levels in chemicals (65.1), machinery (77.2), and transportation machinery (92.3). The current level of foreign ownership in the financial sector amounts to almost $80 billion, or 8.9 per-

cent of the total. Over $76 billion is concentrated in Toronto and Montreal in banking, diversified finance, and trust companies. Extremely small amounts are associated with Ottawa and Vancouver and there is almost nothing elsewhere. Foreign control is reinforcing the already dominant positions of Toronto and Montreal. Continued internationalization of the financial industries, along with federal and provincial deregulation, should enhance the positions of these two cities.

Foreign ownership in the non-financial sectors is much higher than in the financial areas. In 1985 over 36 percent of the revenues generated by the top 1100 corporations ($170 billion of $464 billion) was controlled by foreign-based multinational corporations. This is the largest level of foreign ownership for any developed country and has been the subject of much discussion by Canadians. Of more significance is where the ownership is concentrated in the urban system. It is evident that Toronto holds a commanding position in the nation economy. This position must be kept in perspective, however, by taking into account the level of foreign penetration. As Table 29-2 indicates, the proportion of Toronto's revenues accounted for by foreign firms, based in countries like the United States, the United Kingdom, Japan, the Netherlands, and Germany, is actually larger than for domestic firms. Consequently, the largest urban revenue pool in Canada in 1985 was the over $190 billion which we may designate as the Toronto foreign pool. The real decisions concerning this pool are made outside the country. Put into perspective, this block of money is larger than the entire Western or Eastern domestic block. Montreal, on the other hand, has a much smaller foreign component, which means that its domestic component actually rivals Toronto's in the

TABLE 29-5 Total revenues and assets by the largest foreign corporations in millions of dollars* by sector, region, and city for 1985.*

1 Non-financial

	City		Country													
		U.S.A.	U.K.	Japan	Nether-lands	Ger-many	Swit-zerland	France	New Zealand	Sweden	South Korea	Italy	Aus-tralia	Other	Total foreign
West	1 Calgary	6 063	287	1 600	4 270									100	12 320
	2 Vancouver	2 040	594	3 023		90	98		853				103		6 800
	3 Winnipeg	5 721	51		197					118					6 087
	4 Kamloops	500													500
	5 Edmonton	354	77												431
	6 Saskatoon							20							20
Subtotal		14 678	1 009	4 623	4 467	90	98	20	853	118			103	100	26 158
Central	1 Toronto	88 373	8 523	7 321	727	2 606	1 138	183		312	169		16		109 368
	2 Windsor	7 333													7 333
	3 Hamilton	3 109	774			73									3 956
	4 Sarnia	1 290													1 290
	5 Ottawa	927	213												1 140
	6 Kitchener	672				219									891
	7 St. Catharines	860													860
	8 London	517	40												557
	9 Guelph	229													229
Subtotal		103 310	9 550	7 321	727	2 898	1 138	183		312	169		16		125 624
East	1 Montreal	10 919	2 906	221	61	533	851	1 453				161		81	17 186
	2 Saint John	1 110													1 110
	3 Halifax									168					168
	4 St. John's		42												42
Subtotal		12 029	2 948	221	61	533	851	1 453		168		161		81	18 506
Grand total		130 017	13 507	12 165	5 255	3 521	2 087	1 656	853	598	169	161	119	181	170 228
Percentage		76.35	7.93	7.14	3.09	2.07	1.23	0.97	0.50	0.35	0.10	0.09	0.07	0.11	100

(continued)

TABLE 29-5 *Continued*

								Country							
		U.S.A.	U.K.	France	Japan	Swit-zerland	Italy	Ger-many	Hong Kong	Israel	Luxem-bourg	Nether-lands	South Korea	Other	Total foreign
II Financial, utility, developers															
West	1 Vancouver				393				664				65		1 102
	2 Calgary	860													860
Subtotal		860			393				664				65		1 962
Central	1 Toronto	27 664	4 756	353	2 627	2 426	1 069	851		432		253	144	298	40 873
	2 Ottawa	3 709													3 709
	3 London	685													685
	4 Hamilton	477													477
Subtotal		32 535	4 756	353	2 627	2 426	1 069	851		432		253	144	298	45 744
East	1 Montreal	312	27 875	3 620							373			113	32 293
Subtotal		312	27 875	3 620							373			113	32 293
Grand total		33 707	32 631	3 973	3 020	2 426	1 069	851	664	432	373	253	209	411	79 999
Percentage		42.13	40.79	4.97	3.77	3.03	1.34	1.06	0.81	0.54	0.47	0.32	0.26	0.51	100

* Sectors I and II in revenues and assets respectively.

non-financial sector. Still, the Montreal foreign block is the largest single block of revenue in the East. The combined industrial towns of Southern Ontario also contain a foreign block of just over $15 billion and this pool is larger than the domestic block. These facts underscore the high level of foreign involvement in Canada's non-financial sectors.

As Table 29-5 indicates, the high concentration of foreign ownership in the Canadian urban system is overwhelmingly American. The American share of foreign ownership in the non-financial sectors is 76.4 percent, with 51.9 percent of this located in Toronto. The United Kingdom is second, at 7.9 percent, but is now rivalled by Japan, with 7.1 percent. New Zealand and South Korea are also making their presence felt. In the financial sectors, American-based corporations account for 42.1 percent of foreign assets but are followed closely by the United Kingdom with 40.8 percent. The United States concentrates 82.1 percent of its holdings in corporations headquartered in Toronto, while the United Kingdom concentrates 85.4 percent in Montreal. Hong Kong's involvements are primarily in Vancouver.

FUTURE PROSPECTS

The basic problem faced by Canada in the 1990s, as in the past, appears to be the need for domestic corporations to expand to the point where they can simultaneously serve the national interest and successfully compete in a multinational setting. That is, corporations in Canada have to be large enough to meet the costly demands of innovation and foreign competition, to overcome the disadvantages of serving a small and spatially dispersed national market, and to run a successful business with an adequate level of profitability. These conditions imply that one way for Canadian corporations to meet contemporary challenges successfully is to expand until they achieve a commanding market position within the domestic economy. In this position, they would be able to control enough wealth and power to protect themselves and the domestic market from foreign inroads and control. It appears that for the foreseeable future, however, Canada's economy will be characterized by even fewer and more geographically concentrated corporate locations. This spatial concentration will occur in the largest cities and, as a result, the existing corporate cities will play an even more dominant role in the affairs of the nation. It is also possible that foreign investment will expand at an even greater rate, especially in the fastest growing sectors and subsectors. This could occur because foreign investors tend to concentrate investments only in those sectors of the economy and in those selected commercial centres with the greatest economic advantages and political stability. Hence, these investments will also be directed by corporations with headquarters located in the largest and most viable Canadian corporate centres.

REFERENCES

Green, M. B., and R. K. Semple
    1981   "The Corporate Interlocking Directorate as an Urban Spatial Information Network," *Urban Geography,* 2:148-60.

Martz, D. J. F., and R. K. Semple
    1985   "Hierarchical Corporate Decision Making Structure within the Canadian Urban System: The Case of Banking," *Urban Geography,* 6:316-30.

Semple, R. K.
    1973   "Recent Trends in the Concentration of Corporate Headquarters," *Economic Geography,* 49:309-18.
    1977a   "Regional Development Theory and Sectoral Income Inequalities," in *Geographical Horizons,* ed. J. Odland and R. N. Taffe, pp. 45-63. Dubuque, Iowa: Kendall Hunt.
    1977b   "The Spatial Concentration of Domestic and Foreign Multinational Corporate Headquarters in Canada," *Cahiers de géographie de Québec,* 21:33-51.
    1985a   "Quaternary Place Theory: Toward a Spatial Model of Decision Making Activity," *Journal of Modeling and Simulation,* 16:217-24.
    1985b   "Toward a Quaternary Place Theory," *Urban Geography,* 6:285-96.

Semple, R. K., and M. B. Green
    1983   "Interurban Corporate Headquarters Relocation in Canada," *Cahiers de géographie de Québec,* 27:389-406.

Semple, R. K., M. B. Green, and D. J. F. Martz
    1985   "Perspectives on Corporate Headquarters Relocation in the United States," *Urban Geography,* 6:370-91.

Semple, R. K., and A. G. Phipps
    1982   "The Spatial Evolution of Corporate Headquarters within an Urban System," *Urban Geography,* 3:258-79.

Semple, R. K., and W. R. Smith
    1981   "Metropolitan Dominance and Foreign Ownership in the Canadian Urban System," *Canadian Geographer,* 25:4-26.

30. Regional Inequalities and Economic Policy

Ingrid Bryan

In few other countries has the regional distribution of income reached such a level of importance as it has in Canada. In Canada the income differential between provinces and regions has always been large, perhaps because of the sheer size of the country and the variations in population, climate, and culture. The persistence of the differential has been the source of continual conflict. At times the National Policy has been blamed, as it is alleged to have favoured the industrial heartland of Ontario and Quebec to the detriment of the outlying provinces whose inhabitants were forced into a lower standard of living. The railways have also been a favourite target for criticism. The most recent source of inequality (and envy) is the unequal distribution of energy resources across the country.

Revised from Ingrid Bryan, "The Rich and the Poor: The Provinces," in *Economic Policies in Canada,* 2nd ed. (Toronto: Butterworths, 1986), pp. 195-211. Reprinted with permission.

REGIONAL DISPARITIES IN INCOME AND EMPLOYMENT

A region is defined as a geographic area which is essentially homogeneous in one or more respects. In Canada, regions are usually identified with provinces, even though large provinces such as Ontario and Quebec are too large to be treated as single regions. It is also common to group the provinces into five regions: the Atlantic Provinces (the three Maritime Provinces and Newfoundland), Ontario, Quebec, the Prairie Provinces (Manitoba, Saskatchewan, and Alberta), and British Columbia. The whole of northern Canada should also be treated as a separate region.

The most common measure of regional disparity is per capita personal income. According to this measure, in 1982 people in Alberta were the richest and those in Newfoundland the poorest (see Table 30-1). It is interesting to note that whereas in 1960 and 1970 people in Ontario had the highest in-

TABLE 30-1 Personal income per capita, by province, 1950, 1960, 1970, and 1982.*

Province	1950	1960	1970	1982	1982 $/capita
Newfoundland	50.9	55.5	63.4	66.8	8 580
P.E.I.	55.1	56.9	66.5	69.3	8 894
Nova Scotia	74.4	76.4	77.5	78.6	10 090
New Brunswick	70.2	68.1	72.0	71.9	9 229
Quebec	85.9	87.2	88.7	93.6	12 021
Ontario	121.2	117.8	118.4	107.8	13 842
Manitoba	101.4	99.4	92.9	93.4	11 987
Saskatchewan	83.3	89.2	72.4	96.4	12 372
Alberta	100.6	99.8	99.3	109.2	14 025
B.C.	124.9	115.3	108.8	107.6	13 811
Yukon and N.W.T.	—	105.7	94.6	101.4	13 014
Canada	100	100	100	100	12 839

Source: Department of Finance, *Economic Review*, April 1984, Reference Table 16. Reproduced by permission of the Minister of Supply and Services Canada.
* As a percentage of personal income per capita at the national level.

come per capita, in 1982 Ontario was in second place, having been superseded by Alberta. Table 30-1 also suggests that regional disparities have decreased since 1950. In 1950, B.C.'s per capita income was almost 2.5 times higher than that in Newfoundland, whereas in 1982 Alberta's was 1.6 times higher than B.C.'s.

However, if, instead of per capita incomes, unemployment rates are used as a standard of comparison, the gaps appear to have increased. For example, in 1966 (Table 30-2) the unemployment rate was 2.4 percent in the Prairie Provinces and 5.4 percent in Atlantic Canada. In 1983 the rate was 9.7 percent in the Prairies and 15.0 percent in Atlantic Canada, a difference of over 5 points. This disparity may indicate that had it not been for the generous federal transfer payments in the form of equalization payments

and federal financing of health and education, the gap in personal income may well have been larger.

TABLE 30-2 Unemployment rate by region, 1966, 1970, 1975, and 1983.

Region	1966	1970	1975	1983
Atlantic	5.4	6.2	9.8	15.0
Quebec	4.1	7.0	8.1	13.9
Ontario	2.6	4.4	6.3	10.4
Prairie	2.4	4.9	3.9	9.7
British Columbia	4.6	7.7	8.5	13.8
Canada	3.4	5.7	6.9	11.9

Source: Department of Finance, *Economic Review*, April 1984. Reference Table 32. Reproduced by permission of the Minister of Supply and Services Canada.

CAUSES OF REGIONAL DISPARITIES

Many explanations have been given for regional disparities, but there is little agreement. The Senate Committee on Government Policy and Regional Development wrote in 1982:

> . . . far from being a mature field of study with well-established theories and a substantial body of empirically tested "facts," regional development theory is, at best, only partially formed. In particular, the theoretical explanations we heard during the course of our examination seem to lack the ability to explain adequately, if at all, the existing pattern of regional development in Canada. And few of our witnesses reached anything resembling general agreement as to the causes of regional, or for that matter national, economic growth. (Standing Senate Committee, 1982:27)

Our survey shall concentrate on the role in regional development of factors such as natural resources, market size, transport costs, spatial immobility, and low productivity.

Natural Resources

It is obvious that natural resources can be an important determinant of a region's prosperity—particularly if the resource is oil—but the lack of a marketable resource does not necessarily lead to low regional income. At the international level, the OPEC countries are rich; however, so are Switzerland and Japan—countries almost entirely lacking in resources. Copithorne (1979) has shown that if the value of primary production per worker is used as a proxy for measuring natural resource endowments, the four poorest provinces and the four western provinces have larger resource endowments than the most industrialized provinces. Newfoundland, which is one of the poorest provinces, is by any measure a resource-rich province; it is the largest producer of iron ore in Canada, and yet in 1978-79, the revenue forecast from mining and royalty taxes was expected to be less than the revenue generated from tobacco taxes.

One reason why mineral resources appear to have so little effect on a region's prosperity is the poor linkages generated from mining. In a study on the impact of minerals on economic development in Canada, McCulla and Stahl (1977) found that compared with other industries, both backward and forward linkages in mining were very modest, the reason being that most minerals are exported in raw form. For these reasons, the income and employment multipliers were among the lowest of all industries.

Transportation Costs, Market Size, and Aggregate Demand

Transportation costs and the size of the market for a region's products are sometimes given as explanations for regional disparities. Firms that service only a regional market may not be able to achieve economies of scale and therefore low cost, and if transportation costs into the region are less than the cost disadvantage, the firms are forced to pay low wages to survive. Similarly, if a firm sells to outlying regions, it has to absorb the transportation costs in order to compete, which again may mean low wages for the employees. Lower wages are usually associated with lower incomes.

Comparatively little work has been done on the effect of transport costs on regional income. Casas and Kotowitz (1976) demonstrated, using a theoretical model, that transportation subsidies are unlikely to raise regional income in a poor area; that is, the theoretical link between transportation costs and regional income is tenuous. This seems to have been confirmed by empirical work. McRae (1981) found that for most industries, transportation costs are of little consequence as a barrier to competition. Norrie and Percy (1983) in their simulation study of the effect of freight rate reform on the western economy found surprisingly modest effects on regional incomes.

A related factor is the lack of urban centres in the poorer areas. Urban size appears to have a positive influence on income and productivity because of economies of scale in transportation and distribution and also because of agglomeration economies. Sources of supply may be concentrated and therefore cheaper and quicker to obtain. Industry can get cheaper services because of economies of large-scale production. The supply of electricity is a good example. Hydro rates are far higher in the Atlantic Provinces than in Ontario and Quebec, the reason being the high cost of transmission over large, sparsely populated areas.

The importance of aggregate demand in determining regional income was emphasized by the Economic Council of Canada (1977). Unless compensated for by large government expenditures, small markets will lead to low aggregate demand and therefore low income for a region. A related factor is the regional impact of stabilization policies. A recession affects poor people disproportionately in the sense that they are usually the first to be out of work. This is also true for poor provinces. An analysis of unemployment data for 1953-75 demonstrates that a 2 percent increase in the unemployment rate in Canada as a whole implies a 3.7 percent increase in the Atlantic region, 2.6 in Quebec, 1.3 in Ontario, 1.7 on the Prairies, and 1.9 in B.C. (Economic Council

1977:98). This means that stabilization policies should take into consideration the specific needs of the different regions in order to overcome the bias shown to Ontario, for example, which benefits the most during periods of fiscal expansion.

Regionally differentiated stabilization policies are not without problems. Because of the mobility of capital, the Bank of Canada cannot maintain different interest rates in different parts of the country. Government expenditure and taxation policies are already regionally differentiated because of the operations of the automatic stabilizers (a region with high unemployment automatically receives more unemployment insurance payments; a rich region automatically pays more taxes). A regionally discriminatory taxation policy would probably not be politically feasible, unless the provinces themselves shouldered a larger responsibility for fiscal policy-making. Ontario has used sales tax cuts as a stabilization measure, but increased involvement by the provinces in this area would require a surrender by the federal government of some tax room. There is also some doubt as to the efficiency of provincial fiscal policies because of the substantial economic interdependence between the provinces and the concomitant presence of large leakages. Substantial co-ordination would be required (Maxwell and Pestieau 1980:46-59).

Spatial Immobility

Spatial immobility has often been used as an explanation of persistent regional disparities. According to neo-classical theory, market wages are determined by the intersection of the demand and supply curves for labour. The demand for labour is determined by the productivity of labour (the marginal revenue product of labour). Low regional wages therefore imply low productivity of labour (and high productivity of capital). Assuming there are no obstacles to the movement of labour and capital, labour will move from low-wage to high-wage (high-productivity) areas, and capital will move to low-wage areas where the marginal product of capital is high. Given that regional disparities still exist, it must mean that there are obstacles to the mobility of labour and capital, in the form of high transport costs, lack of information, or even federal transfer payments which keep wages and services artificially high in poor regions and therefore retard the migration flows, and have therefore interfered with the normal adjustments of the market. Courchene (1981) claims that transfers and various regional policies have resulted in a policy-induced regional equilibrium which is inefficient.[1] As an illustration of inefficient policies he uses the decision to extend unemployment insurance in the off-season to self-employed Newfoundland fishermen. The change in policy resulted in more fishermen, smaller than optimum-size boats, and lower returns.

Many studies on migration (for example, Courchene, 1971; Vanderkamp, 1980) confirm that people migrate in response to economic factors. Migration alleviates the problems of a region when there is a sudden decline in an important regional industry. Low wages and unemployment will cause people to move, which in turn may alleviate unemployment and raise wages for both the migrants and the people left behind. However, these results do not necessarily mean that migration always has a beneficial effect on regional income, nor that insufficient migration means persistent regional disparities. According to a study by the Economic Council (1977:179), net outmigration from the Atlantic region has been substantial. Indeed, between 1951 and 1971, 15 percent of

the population migrated without any appreciable effect on unemployment or incomes in the Atlantic Provinces. There may be several explanations for this. In the first place, it is not necessarily the unemployed or the workers in low-productivity employment who move. Most studies show that it is the young and the educated who migrate (Courchene, 1970; Economic Council, 1977:176), leaving behind an older, less-educated population—a mix that will not lessen regional income disparity. Migrants can bring with them technology, capital, education, as well as their own labour—factors which tend to increase per capita income in the receiving region and reduce it in the giving region (Polese, 1981). Second, as labour moves out, the size of the local market declines, a factor which further depresses local industries. This can lead to a downward spiral: the more people leave, the more the industry will become depressed, so that a region could become depopulated without having achieved income inequality. Third, migration adversely affects the provision of local services; as the tax base becomes eroded, the community can no longer afford good schools and municipal services.

Productivity

Productivity is usually regarded as the main determinant of prosperity. According to recent studies done for the Economic Council, differences in productivity are of major importance in explaining income differentials. Output per worker (labour productivity) varies greatly between the provinces. For example, between 1970 and 1973, labour productivity in Prince Edward Island was only 60 percent of the national average, whereas productivity in Alberta, British Columbia, and Ontario was 114 percent, 110 percent, and 104 percent, respectively (cf. Auer, 1978).

Productivity differences may be explained by differences in industrial mix. If a province has a large proportion of service industries (which traditionally have low productivity) and a low share of manufacturing industries (which traditionally have high productivity), its average productivity will be low. A study by Auer (1978) shows that industrial mix explains only 20 percent of productivity differences among the provinces—with the exception of Prince Edward Island and Saskatchewan where it accounts for more. The remaining productivity differences can be explained by productivity differences within the same industry. For example, a B.C. cow gives 12 000 lbs. of milk per year, an Ontario cow 9 000 per year and a Quebec cow 7 000 per year. A worker bottling soft drinks in Ontario turns out 50 000 bottles per year, whereas a worker in Nova Scotia turns out 30 000 per year. Similar differences exist in some services. Federal offices handling family allowance and old-age pension cheques accomplish more work in one part of the country than in another.

The causes of these and similar productivity differences are difficult to document. Theorists claim that productivity differences can be attributed to differences in the amount of capital per worker, in technology and the amount of human capital per worker, and in management skills. Differences in the quality of labour exist, with differences in education being the most prominent. Alberta has the highest proportion of university graduates and Newfoundland the lowest. British Columbia has the highest proportion of high-school graduates. The quality of management varies as well. In a 1970 survey, 32 percent of Canadian managers held university degrees, but the provincial averages varied from 18 percent in Newfoundland to 37 percent in Alberta (ECC, 1977:75). There is also some evidence that the adoption of new technology is slower in the Atlantic Provin-

ces; for example, they trail behind the others in the use of computers.

Which of these factors (labour quality, management, and technology) is the most important in explaining productivity differences has not been determined. However, the quality of labour, management, and technology tend to go hand in hand in promoting a high-productivity, future-oriented industrial structure.

The evidence presented above suggests that a good regional policy should aim to promote efficiency in the movement of goods in the local and national markets; it should aim to upgrade the quality of the labour force and of management in the poor regions; and it should actively promote the dissemination of new technology. The policy should also aim to facilitate the migration of labour in those areas where unemployment reaches crisis proportions. The next section gives an account of Canada's past and present regional policies.

REGIONAL POLICY IN CANADA: AN OVERVIEW

The 1957 Royal Commission on Canada's Economic Prospects was possibly the first public inquiry to consider the regional dimension of income (Brewis, 1978). Later a Special Senate Committee on land use found that rural poverty was a serious problem, with a large proportion of farmers, particularly in Eastern Canada, earning an income barely above subsistence level. The committee recommended the establishment of a national land use policy which would designate certain areas as rural or agricultural, and other areas to be used for other purposes. Subsequently, the federal government introduced the Agricultural Rehabilitation and Development Act in 1961 with the intention of alleviating rural poverty. The main emphasis was on soil and water conservation and land use conversion, with financing split equally between the federal and provincial governments. This program was expanded in 1965 in the Agricultural and Rural Development Act (ARDA), which was followed in 1966 by the Fund for Rural Economic Development (FRED). FRED was to provide additional funds to selected areas in need of assistance. Funds would be forthcoming after the federal and provincial levels of governments had agreed to a basic development program for the region. In 1962 the Atlantic Development Board was set up to inquire into measures and projects for promoting growth and development of the Atlantic Provinces. Subsequently the Board received funds to develop growth projects, funds which were mainly used for the development of infrastructure (roads, for example). In 1963 the Area Development Agency (ADA) was formed to provide incentives for firms to locate in specific regions, mainly through tax concessions. In 1965 the program was modified to include capital grants (the Area Development Incentives Act or ADIA).

The provincial governments also entered into a large variety of different development programs with little or no co-ordination. For this reason the Department of Regional Economic Expansion (DREE) was established in 1969. Its terms of reference are to ensure that growth is widely dispersed across Canada and that employment and income projects in slow-growth regions are brought up to the national average. Most of the existing programs were transferred to DREE. Special areas were demarcated for attention; specifically, the development of infrastructure, primarily highways and streets, with secondary importance given to water and sewer systems.

ADIA was replaced by a new Regional Development Incentives Act (RDIA) which was to stimulate industrial expansion in designated areas. The designated areas included all provinces except Alberta and British Columbia, and Southern Ontario. Incentives in the form of grants were to be given either for expansion or modernization of existing facilities, or for starting new ventures. The only industries which did not qualify for grants were pulp and newspaper mills and oil refineries. Grants for modernization contributed up to 20 percent of eligible capital costs, and for a new plant and equipment up to 25 percent of eligible capital costs; other grants paid up to 30 percent of the wage bill in the Atlantic Provinces (15 percent in other designated regions). Since early 1974 there has been increased provincial participation through General Development Agreements (GDA) signed with each province except P.E.I.

With all these changes, there is a bewildering array of programs. They can be classified into four major areas: (1) aid to private industry through RDIA and GDA; (2) aid to the public sector in urban areas outside the Atlantic Provinces through the Special Area program to the Atlantic Provinces, through the Atlantic Development Board; (3) aid to the public sector in rural areas (FRED, ARDA, GDA); (4) various manpower and research programs. Total expenditures in the fiscal year 1983-84 amounted to $481.7 million, with the largest share going to infrastructure (Canadian Tax Foundation, 1984:249). On a per capita basis, Prince Edward Island has been the largest recipient, followed by New Brunswick and Newfoundland.

The RDIA program has been subject to substantial criticisms for its terms of reference (Usher, 1975) and for its capital bias (Woodward, 1974a; 1974b; 1975). According to the RDIA, no grant is to be given if it is probable that the facility would have been established without the grant. The grant should not be larger than is necessary to bring forth the investment in the region—an extremely difficult principle to follow. It is also an unusual principle in public finance, for normally a person is subsidized for doing something regardless of whether the person would do it without a subsidy. The principle would operate in the same way as one restricting family allowance to children who were conceived only because of the allowance (Usher, 1975).

In assessing the effectiveness of RDIA, a few words of caution should be added. First, even if the program has added more firms to an area, it may have rendered other investments unprofitable because the new firm(s) could have increased wages and rents in the area; therefore the next effect of the program might be negligible. Second, competition from subsidized firms could displace or reduce investments by firms already established. Third, firms that need to be "bribed" to invest in an area may be less likely than other firms to reinvest, and therefore the long-term benefits of subsidized investments may be small.

There have been three studies of the effectiveness of RDIA in generating additional investments in the designated areas. Springate (1972) did a survey of 31 firms that had received grants from DREE. In particular, Springate tried to find out the extent to which the availability of a grant affected the location, timing, and size of a project. Only 30 percent of the larger firms—compared with 45 percent of the smaller firms—indicated that the RDIA grant was critical. In 1972-73 the Atlantic Development Council's survey of 51 firms that had received assistance found that 60 percent of the firms thought the RDIA grant was instrumental (ECC, 1977:161-62). These two surveys may suffer from considerable bias, however. The Springate survey was based on unstructured

subjective interviews, and it appears that many of the interviewed executives did not want to convey an impression of relying on government aid. For this reason they could have understated the importance of government aid. The ADC survey was more objective, but unless the questions were carefully phrased, it could also have been subject to bias.

The Economic Council (1977:156-68) tried another approach and looked at the annual births of establishments by industry in the Atlantic region. If the "birth rate" increased significantly after the location grants became available, the grants had worked. It was found that 25 percent of the DREE-supported firms located in the area because of the grant, 41 percent did not, and for the remaining 34 percent, it was impossible to come to any conclusion either way.

Usher (1975) claims that a cursory examination of manufacturing investment trends in the Atlantic Provinces before and after the inception of the grants program shows that the large grants could not have had any appreciable effects on the overall level of investments. Similarly, overall employment in the Maritime Provinces does not show any appreciable increases after the program was initiated. These observations, of course, do not prove that the program has not worked, since in its absence it is possible (but not likely) that both investments and employment would have declined. It can therefore be concluded that no study has been able to demonstrate how effective RDIA has been.

The other criticism of RDIA was that despite the fact that the program gives subsidies to labour as well as to capital, the program has a capital bias in the sense that the grant benefits capital-users more than labour-users. The bias can be determined by comparing the wage/rental ratio before and after the use of a grant (rental being an estimate of the payments to capital). If a grant leads to an increase in the effective wage-rental ratio, the grant encourages firms to adopt more capital-intensive methods than they would have done otherwise. Woodward (1974a; 1974b; 1975) has demonstrated that the RDIA grants do indeed display this bias.

In 1982 the federal government announced a major reorganization of departments involved in regional policy. No single department would have sole responsibility for regional policies. DREE was merged with the Department of Industry, Trade, and Commerce to form a new Department of Regional Industrial Expansion (DRIE). The Ministry of State for Economic Development was extended to include regional aspects of policies and was renamed Ministry of State for Economic and Regional Development. The incentive program operated by DREE was reassigned to DRIE, while the GDA program was to be phased out. Funds previously assigned to GDA were shifted to a new regional fund, designed to support special initiatives. The federal government also stated its intention to encourage megaprojects as a tool in regional development and to increase its presence in regional development.

The changes were apparently made for several reasons (Savoie, 1984). One was that under the GDA program the federal government received little credit for in many cases substantial cash contributions. Second, it was widely believed at the time that energy-related megaprojects on the East Coast and on the Prairies would shift the focus of activity away from Central Canada and therefore would lessen regional disparities.

Apart from regional policies, the federal government has manpower policies designed to encourage mobility through relocation grants to labour, transport policies which subsidize the transport of some goods in and out of some provinces, and fiscal transfer policies (equalization payments, established program financing). The relocation grant program, even though it is quite generous, is not particularly effective. For example, in the 1974-75 period, 50 000 jobs were filled each month, only 1000 of which fell under the mobility program (ECC, 1977:180). The program accounted for only 2 percent of vacancies filled and less than 5 percent of migrants who moved in Canada. It is possible that many unemployed workers do not know of its existence.

No discussion of federal aid to poorer provinces would be complete without a discussion of equalization payments. The problems which led to equalization payments first surfaced in the 1930s during the depression (Lewis, 1978). The depression led to the collapse of economic activity in many parts of the country. The fall in tax revenues, together with the fiscal stress caused by the high-debt burden and relief payments to the destitute, led to almost insurmountable difficulties for some of the provinces. In response, taxes were raised and the federal government stepped in with grants. A royal commission was appointed to investigate dominion-provincial relations (the Rowell-Sirois Commission). The commission's report in 1940 recommended that the provincial governments retreat from the personal and corporate tax fields (and death duties), which should instead be taken over by the federal government in return for which it would give grants or transfer payments to the provinces. The recommendations were not implemented but the provinces surrendered temporarily (until 1962) their rights to levy income and death taxes in return for cash transfers from the federal government.

The present arrangement dates to the 1982 amendments of the Federal-Provincial Fiscal Arrangements and Established Programs Financing Act of 1977. The purpose of equalization payments is to guarantee citizens in all provinces of Canada equal access to public services. The basis for the payments is a five-representative-province tax yield from each revenue source on a per capita basis, against which is calculated the tax yield of each province on a per capita basis. If the provincial per capita tax yield exceeds the five-province per capita tax yield, no equalization payment is due. If, however, the provincial yield is less than the national yield, the province is paid the difference times the population.

SUMMARY AND CONCLUSIONS

The causes of regional disparity are elusive. The brief survey presented here showed that the presence of natural resources, transportation costs, and spatial immobility probably cannot explain the large differentials existing at present. More important factors are the size of the market for a region's prod-

ucts, and productivity. It was shown that productivity differences between the provinces are substantial; the Economic Council tentatively attributes these to differences in technology and in the skills of labour and management. If the analysis is correct, regional policies should aim to improve productivity through the upgrading of skills and technology.

The survey of regional policies in Canada showed that little attention has been paid to productivity. Instead, the major emphasis has been on moving labour out of poor regions and/or moving capital (industry) in. An example of the latter approach is the policies administered by DRIE. It was shown that these policies have not been effective, on the basis of which it can be argued that regional policies should be more people-oriented in the sense that more money should go to the very poor in a region, and conscious efforts should be made to improve their skill levels. More emphasis should be given to management and technology in determining a region's welfare.

NOTES

1. The Economic Council of Canada in its 1982 report took a different view of the efficiency of transfer payments, based on work by Broadway and Flatters (1982). It was argued that if Alberta's oil wealth resulted in lower taxes for Albertans, people would be induced to migrate to Alberta, but for the wrong reasons. Migration to Alberta would in this case not equalize incomes but rather dissipate resource rents. The Council therefore argued that transfer payments to poor provinces were necessary to offset this inefficiency so that no policy-induced migration would take place. Dales (1983) takes issue with this view, pointing out that it goes against the general theory of the second best. One of the results of the general theory of the second best is that two wrongs do not necessarily result in one right.

REFERENCES

Auer, L.
1978   *Regional Disparities of Productivity and Growth.* Ottawa: Supply and Services.

Broadway, R. W., and F. Flatters
1982   "Efficiency and Equalization Payments in a Federal System of Government: a Synthesis and Extension of Recent Results," *Canadian Journal of Economics,* 15:613-34.

Brewis, T. N.
1978   "Regional Development in Canada in Historical Perspective," in *Regional Economic Policy: the Canadian Experience,* ed. N. H. Lithwick, pp.215-30. Toronto: McGraw-Hill Ryerson.

Canadian Tax Foundation
1984   *The National Finances, 1983-84.* Toronto: Canadian Tax Foundation.

Casas, F. R., and Y. Kotowitz
1976   *Transport Subsidies and Regional Distribution Policies.* Ottawa: Canadian Transport Commission.

Copithorne, L.
1979   "Resources and Regional Disparities," *Canadian Public Policy,* 5:181-95.

Courchene, T. J.
1970   "Interprovincial Migration and Economic Adjustment," *Canadian Journal of Economics,* 3:550-76.
1981   "A Market Perspective on Regional Disparities," *Canadian Public Policy,* 7:506-19.
1983   "Canada's New Equalization Program: Description and Evaluation," *Canadian Public Policy,* 9:458-76.

Dales, John H.
1983   "Distortions and Dissipations," *Canadian Public Policy,* 9:257-64.

Economic Council of Canada
1977   *Living Together: A Study of Regional Disparities.* Ottawa: Supply and Services.
1982   *Financing Confederation: Today and Tomorrow.* Ottawa: Supply and Services.

Lewis, Perrin
1978   "The Tangled Tale of Taxes and Transfers," in *Canadian Confederation at the Crossroads,* ed. Michael Walker, pp. 39-109. Vancouver: The Fraser Institute.

Maxwell, J., and C. Prestieau
1980   *Economic Realities of Contemporary Confederation.* Montreal: C. D. Howe Institute.

McCulla, D., and J. E. Stahl
1981   *Quantitative Impact of Minerals on Canadian Economic Development: A Partial Analysis.* Ottawa: Energy, Mines and Resources.

McRae, J. J.
1981   "An Empirical Measure of the Influence of Transportation Costs on Regional Income," *Canadian Journal of Economics,* 14:155-63.

Norrie, Kenneth H., and Michael B. Percy
  1983   "Freight rate reform and regional burden: general equilibrium analysis of western freight rate proposals," *Canadian Journal of Economics,* 16:325-50.

Polese, M.
  1981   "Regional Disparity, Migration and Economic Adjustment: A Reappraisal," *Canadian Public Policy,* 7:519-26.

Savoie, D. J.
  1984   "The Toppling of DREE and Prospects for Regional Economic Development," *Canadian Public Policy,* 10:328-38.

Springate, D. J. V.
        "Regional Development Incentives Grants and Private Investments in Canada." Unpublished PhD thesis, Harvard University, Grad. School of Business Administration.

Standing Senate Committee on National Finance
  1982   *Report on Government Policy and Regional Development.* Ottawa: Supply and Services.

Usher, Dan
  1975   "Some Questions About the Regional Development Incentives Act," *Canadian Public Policy,* 1:557-76.

Vanderkamp, J.
  1968   "Interregional Mobility in Canada: A Study of the Time Pattern of Migration," *Canadian Journal of Economics,* 1:595-608.

Woodward, R. S.
  1974a   "Effective Location Subsidies: An Evaluation of DREE Location Subsidies," *Canadian Journal of Economics,* 7:501-10.
  1974b   "The Capital Bias of DREE Incentives," *Canadian Journal of Economics,* 7:161-73.
  1975   "The Effectiveness of DREE's New Location Subsidies," *Canadian Public Policy,* 1:217-30.

FOR FURTHER READING

Brym, Robert J., ed. 1986. *Regionalism in Canada*. Toronto: Irwin. Among the topics considered in this reader are regional differences in policies, ideology, and the nature of attitudes and values. Some papers also focus on the special concerns of individual regions such as British Columbia and Newfoundland.

Coffey, William, and Mario Polese, eds. 1987. *Still Living Together*. Halifax: Institute for Research on Public Policy. This book considers recent trends and future directions in regional development in Canada. Regional differences in income distribution, economic development, technological change, state policy, and various other issues of relevance to regional inequality are addressed.

Gibbins, Roger. 1982. *Regionalism: Territorial Politics in Canada and the United States*. Toronto: Butterworths. The principal concern of this book is to outline the nature of territorial political cleavages in both Canada and the United States. In Canada, the problems of federal-provincial relations, territorial political representation, and regional differences in political attitudes and political culture are some of the topics that have impications for understanding regional inequalities.

Matthews, Ralph. 1983. *The Creation of Regional Dependency*. Toronto: University of Toronto Press. This monograph is concerned with how regional inequalities have been established and maintained during the process of Canada's development. The historical bases for regional dependency and the government's involvement in the patterning of regional inequalities are given considerable attention.

Phillips, Paul. 1982. *Regional Disparities* (2nd ed.) Toronto: Lorimer. This is a compact analysis of economic and structural inequalities among Canada's major regions. Questions about the impact of regionalism on Confederation and rebuilding the economy with a new national policy are also examined.

Section IV

THE STATE AND SOCIAL INEQUALITY

Introduction

In the opening chapter of this volume it was pointed out that, in recent years, *the state*—the various elements of government or the political system—has become a major focus of discussion and analysis among students of social inequality. At several points throughout the book we have found evidence of this focus. We have also seen that some analysts believe the state should use its legislative and judicial powers to do more to reduce or alleviate significant social inequalities.

There are numerous areas where government decision-making, policy creation, and formal regulation could conceivably be implemented to achieve such changes. In our section on ownership in Canada, for example, we touched on the prospects of state intervention to lessen corporate concentration and ownership centralization in the economy. In other earlier sections we also examined articles on such questions as establishing government programs to redistribute income or increase educational accessibility and opportunity. Under the section on social ascription, several questions concerning state activities were reviewed. Included here were papers on the possibility of generating a more effective policy on multiculturalism, the prospects for government action to enhance women's employment opportunities, the state's role in helping the aged, and the government's strategies to transform the structure of regional inequality in Canada. In virtually all important areas, then, the state has the formal capacity, if not always the concerted will, to alter fundamentally the key bases and patterns of inequality in modern societies. The full recognition of this official authority has not always been acknowledged by writers in the field of inequality, nor have the other major powers of the modern state. These include the power to use coercive force through the police or the military to gain its goals, and its power to gather information about and place under surveillance groups and individuals.

With all of these formal mechanisms of control at its disposal, we might expect the state structure to have done more to transform the overall contours of society and, in particular, the pattern of inequality. Of course, there is no doubt that the various levels of government in Canada have exercised their powers in this manner at different times. As some of our selections suggest, there is reason to believe as well that, in some cases, these efforts have met with success.

Nevertheless, many of these initiatives seem on balance to have taken place within serious constraints, since the state is an integral part of a system in which certain private interests tend to have an inordinately strong influence on not only the political means of power but also the economic and ideological mechanisms of domination. In other words, the relatively advantaged interest groups in our society—the propertied class, the wealthy or affluent, the well-educated, males, and urban dwellers, to name a few—have historically been able to dominate with some regularity the activities of the state. One factor in this process has been the disproportionate nomination of people with these backgrounds to the candidacies of major political parties and their eventual election to key political offices within governments.

There is another fundamental constraint on the state's activities that is evident in capitalist societies and that may often limit the ability or the will of the state leadership to transform the structure of inequality. This restriction concerns the heavy dependence of governments on the private business economy for generating wealth and, ultimately, the funds for the government's own operation. This assertion may be disputed by those who contend that the state has far too much control over the economy itself, through the growth of government-owned or government-funded enterprises such as Canadian National or Petro-Canada.

Much of the evidence to be found in the selections included in this section of the book indicates, however, that government intervention and control within the Canadian economy are only moderate, especially compared to the situation in the economies of other industrialized nations. Instead, it can be argued that the state, given its dependence for its operating revenues on the taxation of both business profits and the wages of workers employed by private enterprises, is often unable to control abuses of economic power by large-scale corporations and their owners. This argument is plausible to the extent that state leaders, most of whom are essentially sympathetic to the basic principles of capitalism in any case, must balance their responsibilities to the electorate at large with their desire to maintain a profitable capitalist economy and the crucial source of state funding it represents.

These are the kinds of issues and concerns that the papers in this section address. The first article, by Wallace Clement, provides an outline and an historical overview of the Canadian state's involvements in a range of developments since the 1930s. Clement's primary concerns centre on government activities pertaining to the consolidation of large-scale capitalism over time, the increased presence of foreign ownership in the Canadian economy, and efforts by disadvantaged groups—particularly workers, women, and the less powerful regions of the country—to improve their situation within Canada as a whole.

The second paper on the state takes as its central focus the idea of human rights and the responsibility that government must take as the guarantor and enforcer of these rights in Canadian society. Alan Cairns and Cynthia Williams touch on a range of policy concerns for the state, all of which are tied to major bases for inequality in Canada. These include such issues as gender and the rights of women, the recognition of ethnic, linguistic, and racial minorities in public policy decisions, and federal-provincial debates over the rights and jurisdictions of different regions.

The third article in this set is by Neil Guppy, Sabrina Freeman, and Shari Buchan and deals with the question of political representation. This paper is important for documenting the point raised earlier, which is that certain influential interest groups have had considerable success in dominating the principal political offices within the Canadian state. More specifically, the article provides evidence that people from privileged class or socio-economic backgrounds, as judged by their occupational statuses, are considerably more likely than other Canadians to be elected to parliament and to be appointed cabinet ministers within the federal government. Moreover, this pattern has held for an appreciable period of time, including the past two decades.

The fourth selection on the Canadian state, written by John Fox and Michael Ornstein, addresses the question of personnel overlaps between the state leadership and those individuals who are in control of Canada's largest businesses. This paper offers information for the period after World War II and reveals that many of the officials who have headed royal commissions, crown corporations, and other major government organizations have also held comparable positions with the largest private-sector business enterprises. These connections, or interlocks, are sufficiently numerous for the authors to conclude that the state's powers are not entirely independent of the interests of big business; nevertheless, the links are not extensive enough to support any claim that Canada's major corporations really control the state or its activities in some complete sense. Rather, a partnership involving these two related but distinct spheres of power seems to be at work in the Canadian context.

While Fox and Ornstein consider interlocks among those who run the government and those who direct the private economy, John Calvert's paper on the state looks at the link between the state and the economy in another way. In this concluding paper, Calvert examines the claim that governments have made serious incursions into owning or administering the nation's economy, so much so that, according to some critics, the state has undermined the capitalist system and created major economic problems for all Canadians. Calvert's findings are that the Canadian state's role in the economic structure has been exaggerated and that any responsibility government has for business crises may stem from too little, not too much, intervention. His conclusions raise questions about the real capacity of the state to generate policies to redistribute wealth to the disadvantaged, to expand social services for those who require them, and so on, as long as these programs are not in the interests of large-scale business owners or other powerful groups.

The research presented in this section leads to the conclusion that the state and its branches have considerable legal authority to shape or transform the structure of inequality in Canadian society. However, many of the potential initiatives that could be introduced to reduce inequalities and improve the quality of life for all people may be blunted by conflicting goals and interests and by the relative success of privileged factions in occupying strategic state offices or influencing important state decisions.

31. The State and the Canadian Economy

Wallace Clement

Canada's past 50 years begin and end with depressions, albeit of significantly different sorts. Between these depressions there was a tremendous industrial expansion during and after World War II, an intensification of resource exploitation, and major changes in the structure of the labour force. The experience of the 1930s and subsequent struggles created a net of social services designed to catch the fall-out of unemployment, although the scale of demand on the state in the early 1980s threatens to burst the net. This paper explores changes in the organization of capital, labour, and the state over the past 50 years in Canada, locating these social structural changes within the context of major social movements, such as nationalism, unionization, and women's struggles. These have been a turbulent 50 years, and it

Revised from Wallace Clement, "Canada's Social Structure: Capital, Labour, and the State, 1930–1980," in Michael Cross and Gregory Kealey, ed., *Modern Canada 1930–1980s* (Toronto: McClelland and Stewart, 1984), pp. 81-101. Reprinted with permission.

will only be possible here to outline some of the most significant trends rather than provide detailed investigations of any specific developments.

THE DEPRESSION

The 1930s was a period of consolidation, concentration, and retrenchment for the Canadian economy. Ironically, as British capital withdrew and U.S. direct investment declined, there was consolidation of the U.S. foothold in Canadian industry. Many small manufacturers failed and more established firms intensified their hold on core industries. Basing his analysis on the Royal Commission on Price Spreads, Lloyd G. Reynolds found that Canadian monopolies fared well during this period, earning rates of return at 12.2 percent annually, while competitive industries were folding (Reynolds, 1975:60-61). Leading the merger movement were Canadian financial capitalists. The larger firms, especially in automobiles and related products, gasoline, machinery, tobacco, electrical products, and aluminum, were U.S. branch plants, many of which had been induced into Canada by a combination of restrictions on exports from the United States in response to the Hawley-Smoot tariff of 1930 and the introduction of British Imperial Preference in 1932. Resource extraction, the cornerstone of Canada's exports, was severely curtailed; the wheat market had collapsed, pulp and paper was slashed to 53 percent of capacity, and mineral exports dropped by over 60 percent (Creighton, 1970:200-201).

While resource extraction was located in the hinterland, new industrial capacity was becoming increasingly concentrated in Central Canada, particularly manufacturing firms controlled in the United States. Of U.S.-controlled manufacturing plants in 1931, 66 percent were in Ontario, 16 percent in Quebec, and only 18 percent in the other provinces (compared to all manufacturing, which was 42 percent in Ontario, 31 percent in Quebec, and 27 percent elsewhere) (Marshall *et al.*, 1936:222).

As might be expected, given the economic conditions, the trade union movement experienced "virtual disintegration" during the depression, especially large industrial unions in mining, textiles, clothing, and building trades (Jamieson, 1968:214). There was resistance led mainly by left-wing unions organized through the Workers' Unity League (WUL). By the mid-1930s the centre of strike activity shifted to Ontario and Quebec, away from the West and British Columbia, as struggles for union recognition followed the development of such heavy industry as steel, automobiles, machinery, chemicals, meatpacking, and clothing and textiles (and away from resource-centred struggles).

The depression radically altered the terrain of Canada's social structure. Canadian workers were pressed into seeking security through representation in industrial unions,

facilitated by the growing concentration of industry into fewer, more centrally located companies in the industrial heartland. The fact that these unions were directed from the United States mirrored the growing presence of U.S. branch plants, and often for similar reasons. The U.S. organizations were more developed than those in Canada, possessing the necessary start-up funds and expertise. Both were welcomed into Canada by their respective constituencies as shortcuts to creating an industrial structure.

THE SECOND WORLD WAR

Although the depression had induced the Canadian state to take a more active role in the economy, such as creating the Canadian Wheat Board in 1935 (only to lapse and have to be reinstated in 1943) and the Bank of Canada in 1935 (effectively nationalized in 1938), it was the Second World War and carry-over to the Korean War that would dramatically alter Canada's social structure. World War II had its main impact on manufacturing; by 1943, 60 percent of employees in manufacturing were working on war materials (Firestone, 1958:214). The Korean War's main impact was on resources; the U.S. government's Paley Report (*Resources for Freedom*) identified Canada as the major source for 12 of 22 key resources it required for industrial supremacy, thus leading to an intensification of U.S. investment in Canadian resources (Clark, 1979). By the end of the period, Canada's manufacturing and resource sectors had been dramatically transformed. In 1946, 35 percent of Canada's manufacturing was foreign-controlled, shifting to 50 percent by 1953 and by 1957 to 56 percent; corresponding increases in mining and smelting were from 38 to 57 to 70 percent (Rosenbluth, 1961:206).

C. D. Howe, the most powerful minister in

the King and St. Laurent administrations, was at the heart of Canada's industrial restructuring. Using broad powers under the War Measures Act, Howe created the War Supply Board and Department of Munitions and Supply, which operated autonomously from Parliament. These agencies would transform the profile of Canada's social structure in a very short period. Twenty-eight Crown corporations were created, and inducements were offered to private capital through special fast write-offs for capital expenditure. Three quarters of the $700-million government expenditure on plants was for Crown corporations, the rest was private; $500 million in tax credits and depreciation went to private companies, plus expenditures of $800 million on defence construction, aside from purchases of supplies (Department of Reconstruction and Supply, 1949). The War Assets Corporation, created in 1943, transferred facilities to private capital best able to use it. To say it "sold" these assets would be too strong since no "market" as such was cultivated.

Employment in manufacturing had doubled from 1939 to 1943, declining somewhat in 1946, and reaching the 1943 peak of one million again in 1950. During the war this restructuring occurred without the benefit of foreign capital (Pentland, 1968:197). The rapid rise of foreign ownership occurred as these assets were being sold off following the war and during the expansion surrounding the Korean War, as will be discussed in the next section.

In terms of labour, according to Stuart Jamieson, World War II and its immediate aftermath were a "continuation" of forces established in the late 1930s with a series of unionization and recognition strikes (Jamieson, 1968:276). Full employment and labour shortages accompanied unprecedented demand for production, while recognition strikes were settled under government pres-

sure, peaking in 1943. These strikes were concentrated in manufacturing (steel, autos, aircraft, and textiles) and mining. The war brought conditions favourable to labour's organizing but it also brought emergency wartime powers, through the War Measures Act of 1939. This made the federal government the centre of labour attention since it had the power to limit wages and restrict the right to strike. These measures were met by intense union opposition, causing the government to pass PC 1003 in 1944, granting "workers' rights to organize, certification of collective bargaining units, and compulsory collective bargaining" (Jamieson, 1968:294), thus reducing strike levels, at least temporarily, until controls were finally lifted late in 1947.

One feature of the labour force during the war was the rapid mobilization of women into paid labour. Ruth Pierson has argued that "Canada's war effort, rather than any consideration of women's right to work, determined the recruitment of women" (Pierson, 1977:125). The consequence was, of course, that once the war ended women were expected to return to the home, having served their role as a reserve army of labour. There were few immediate effects in the women's labour force; as Pierson observed: "If women took jobs previously held only by men, they were generally regarded as replacing men temporarily" (Pierson, 1977:145). There were long-term effects, however, as the women's movement in the 1970s was able to point to wartime work by women as demonstrating the capacities of women for "men's work" with considerable success.

POST-WAR RECONSTRUCTION

Following World War II there was a brief economic slowdown in 1949 and 1950, with expansion accompanying the Korean War and another recession from 1957 through to the early 1960s. C. D. Howe continued to be the prime mover in the federal state. His ongoing initiatives from the Department of Reconstruction and Supply were folded into the Department of Trade and Commerce, which he headed from 1948 to 1957. From these central institutions, Howe actively sought foreign investment; between 1946 and 1960, $1.1 billion was granted in deferred taxes to foreign-controlled companies in Canada (Bothwell and Kilbourn, 1979:238). The Massachusetts-born Liberal was instrumental in encouraging the import of U.S. industry, telling a Boston audience in 1954 that "Canada has welcomed the participation of American, and other foreign capital in its industrial expansion. In Canada, foreign investors are treated the same as domestic investors" (Wolfe, 1973:120). In the 1950s Canada's economy was turned increasingly toward its continental neighbour. Internally the focus was on transportation networks, including the three giant projects of the 1950s: the Trans-Canada Highway (1950), the Trans-Canada Pipeline (1952), and the St. Lawrence Seaway (1954), which featured both shipping and hydro power.

Post-war expansion by the state also included increased social assistance and service activities, such as the Unemployment Insurance Commission, the Department of Health and Welfare, and Central Mortgage and Housing Corporation, as well as a tremendous growth in the Department of Labour. Much of this state expansion was to accommodate demands made by organized labour. From 16 percent in 1940, the proportion of the non-agricultural labour force organized into unions increased to 29 percent by 1949 and levelled off at 34 percent by 1955. By the mid-1950s, most readily organized manufacturing industries were unionized.

Labour proved willing to strike in the relatively prosperous 1950s. Strikes were common in extractive industries (forest products, fishing, and mining), manufacturing (especially automobiles in Ontario and textiles in Quebec), construction, and particularly transportation. There was a national railway strike of both the Canadian Pacific and Canadian National in 1950. Again in 1957 there was a railway strike over technological change.

In Quebec, as elsewhere in Canada, there was a resource rush following the war, concentrated on cheap hydro power used to stimulate pulp and paper production, aluminum smelting, and the chemical industry. Quebec's Hydro Electric Commission was established in 1944 but complete nationalization was delayed until 1963 (Ontario Hydro had been founded in 1905). Mining was important to rural Quebec: asbestos (Eastern Townships), iron ore (Ungava), plus copper, gold, and zinc (Rouyn-Noranda). In Montreal, manufacture of clothing, textiles, and tobacco was most important.

Unions in Quebec had a particularly difficult struggle. Maurice Duplessis, in power most of the 1936-60 period, opposed all but the tamest of unions. In 1954 he passed a law to decertify any union that "tolerated Communists," and was the central figure in the now-famous Asbestos Strike in 1949. Duplessis had the Labour Relations Board decertify the asbestos unions and declared the union leaders to be "saboteurs" (Beausoleil, 1964:152-53). This strike marked a coming of age for Quebec labour; it was now a force to be reckoned with in Quebec's development. The struggle was difficult: during the Asbestos Strike, 1973 strikers were arrested, yet support was given by a wide spectrum of society ranging from the church to Quebec public opinion and the labour movement in other provinces.

RISE OF THE PROVINCES

Beginning in 1949, but gaining considerable momentum in the post-OPEC world of the early 1970s, there was a tremendous expansion of energy extraction in Alberta. Controlled by the already dominant multinational oil companies, this expansion was directed from abroad and was highly vulnerable to international forces. It did, nonetheless, create in its wake a rash of construction, exploration, and service activities that served as an accumulation base for smaller, provincially based capitalists (Richards and Pratt, 1979), who would identify with the Lougheed regime in the 1970s. This tended to be "quick-fix" capital, demanding tremendous labour during construction but being very capital-intensive in its operation. The economy relied on continuous expansion for job creation, while the state relied on resource rents to fund its commitments.

The other province undergoing tremendous growth during the 1960s was Quebec. Its growth was mainly in state service activities involving social welfare, health, and education. The Liberal regime ventured into the economy in a limited way through Hydro-Quebec, Société générale de financement (SGF), and Sidérurgie québécoise (SIDBEC), but with limited success. According to K. McRoberts and D. Posgate, "the only instance of outright nationalization was the case of Hydro-Quebec; here Quebec was merely following a precedent long established by other provinces. . . . The autonomy of American and English-Canadian corporations remained intact" (Posgate and McRoberts, 1980:111). While Hydro-Quebec did become the province's largest employer, SGF and SIDBEC were failures in the 1960s, although in the 1970s SGF was somewhat successful in assisting small- and medium-sized Francophone capital.

Quebec and Alberta, joining Ontario's already dominant position among the provinces, represented an unprecedented growth of political power to challenge Ottawa. It was, to quote Pentland, "a decline of national authority and a rise of aggressive provincialism" (Pentland, 1968:259). A combination of provinces seeking out multinational corporations to locate branch plants within their boundaries and intensified resource exploitation caused both interprovincial rivalry and federal-provincial conflict. Provinces were required to meet the increasingly costly demands for social services, and, to satisfy these expenses, they sought to expand their provincial revenue bases.

Growth of state activities had significant implications for the state as an employer. In 1967 federal civil servants gained the right to bargain through the Public Service Staff Relations Act, and provincial government workers, especially in Quebec, also expanded their rights to bargain. While the union movement had stabilized at 1.5 million workers between 1956 and 1964, these new unions added 500 000 members between 1965 and 1968, giving the union movement its first shot in the arm since World War II. The 1960s experienced a wave of "new" strikers: state workers (in hospitals and schools, especially) and newly organized clerical, service, and sales workers (especially in Quebec).

According to Pentland, "the most novel and revealing feature of the labour militancy of the 1960s was the frequent revolt of union membership against their leaders" (Pentland, 1968:382). Members began to question, through their actions, not only their leadership but the state itself: "The propensity of workers to defy legal restrictions which they considered to be unjust was another striking aspect of militancy in the 1960s" (Pentland, 1968:383). An important illustration was the national wildcat strike by postal workers in July and August of 1965.

During the 1960s the first rumblings of concern about the effects of automation were heard, and early signs of structural unemployment emerged. Expansion of the state and service sectors was creating new demands for clerical labour as women were pulled into the paid labour force in increasing numbers. The late 1960s also began to display two forms of nationalism, one in Quebec and another in English Canada. Nationalism had long been evident in Quebec, primarily of a conservative, defensive nature (*survivance*) to protect the rural people from the non-Catholic, industrial world. In the 1960s an assertive nationalism based on the right to self-determination (*indépendentiste*) began to emerge. English-Canadian nationalism was also something that had existed before, primarily in terms of maintaining loyalty to Mother England, and was most prominent during the two world wars. The new nationalism was a response to the perception of domination by the United States and the loss of Canadian sovereignty. The branch plant was the primary economic expression of foreign control while dependence upon resource exports at the expense of indigenous manufacturing became a concern for those who feared jobs would be lost during difficult economic times.

STAGNATION AND CRISIS

By the 1970s the labour movement in Canada had a new shape. Although still a dominant force in industry, international unions were no longer the only principals in labour struggles. National unions had grown with the increase in state workers. The three largest public-service unions could claim a third of the CLC membership.

The labour movement as a whole is under attack in the 1980s. Public-sector workers, whether federal or provincial, are being compelled to bear the brunt of state overexpenditure. Industrial workers are bearing the costs of a distorted economy where foreign-controlled automobile companies impose massive layoffs and resource firms geared to export do the same.

The economic crisis of the late 1970s revealed fundamental weaknesses long endemic to the Canadian social structure: resource dependence and branch plant manufacturing. Resource workers based in such externally dominated activities as mining, forest products, and fishing have been subject to international markets and major fluctuations in the demand for the products of their labour. Aside from these cyclical changes in demand, there has been a constant tendency to make these activities more capital-intensive, thus decreasing labour requirements and displacing those traditionally engaged in resource extraction. Herein lies a major source of regional unemployment and unrest in the current period.

The implications of job loss extend to the very structure of the labour movement itself, undercutting its ability to represent workers. The United Steel Workers of America, for example, has been particularly hard hit because of its membership in mining and the steel industry; its membership is down to 125 000 from 200 000 only a few years earlier.

In manufacturing the hardest hit has been the automobile industry. This industry is based entirely on branch plants and is intimately tied to the United States through the Auto Pact agreement. Automobiles represent about 10 percent of Canadian manufacturing and 80 percent of the end-product exports from Canada to the United States. In the 18 years the Auto Pact has been in place, Canada has accumulated a $41-billion deficit with the United States, including $5 billion in 1982. This means Canadians have been consuming more cars than they have been producing, consequently shifting jobs to the United States. In 1980, 23 200 Canadian auto workers were laid off. Not only have jobs been sacrificed through the Auto Pact, but the quality of the jobs as well. J. J. Shepherd, vice-president of the Science Council of Canada, reports that the U.S. automobile labour force contains 8 percent skilled workers and 43 percent semiskilled (leaving 49 percent unskilled); in Canada, only 2 percent are skilled and 23 percent semiskilled (leaving 75 percent unskilled) (Shepherd, 1978:7). In 1982 Canadian members of the UAW led their U.S. counterparts in an important strike against concessions.

The most important strike in the 1970s, however, was the 1978-79 battle by Inco workers in Sudbury. Its significance rests not only with the fact that it was the largest strike in Canadian history measured by days lost, lasting eight-and-a-half months and involving 11 700 workers, but it came at a time when capital (reinforced by the state) was attempting to roll back workers' rights. Unlike the disastrous strike of 1958, when community leaders turned against the strikers and the union was left in disarray, the people of Sudbury and the national labour movement gave their support. Finally, after 261 days, the settlement represented a victory for Inco workers and was symbolic of the general resolve of Canadian workers not to retreat (Clement, 1980:322-31).

White-collar workers have not been immune from the crisis. In 1982 General Motors cut 500 salaried jobs, as did MacMillan Bloedel and Eaton's; also, Gulf cut 400 and Inco 320, to list but a few examples (*The Globe and Mail*, 1982:11). Cuts such as these have induced white-collar workers to unionize, even outside the state sector. As clerical work becomes increasingly automated and

routinized, the potential for unionization expands, particularly for women. The proletarianization of white-collar work makes possible greater working-class solidarity, but the struggle will be difficult because of legislative barriers, employer resistance, and various unions competing for the same workers.

By the end of the 1970s the labour movement had reached 40 percent of all non-agricultural workers, a significant increase from the 34 percent it had at the beginning of the decade or the 30 percent it appeared to have stagnated at in the 1960s. As the labour movement expanded its power, however fragmented in terms of national direction, the state responded with policies designed to moderate that power. Both the federal and provincial governments frequently used back-to-work legislation throughout the 1970s to force government workers, who had only gained the right to strike in the late 1960s, to end their strikes. The Anti-Inflation Program of 1975-78 empowered the Anti-Inflation Board to roll back collective agreements to conform to wage guidelines in both the public and private sectors. In 1982 the Public Sector Compensation Restraint Act imposed mandatory "6 and 5" percent increases, for the following two years suspending the right of federal workers to bargain or strike. The largest provinces followed suit for their employees, with Quebec imposing the most severe cutbacks.

DIRECTIONS OF CHANGE

Labour shortages during World War II reinforced the power of the working class, which in turn permitted some working-class demands to be accomplished in the 1950s and 1960s. These had the effect of expanding the welfare role of government and creating a dynamic new category of workers, themselves placing demands on government revenues as they insisted on and received recognition. Both federal and provincial governments became important employers and purveyors of increasingly expensive services (Armstrong, 1977). During the current economic crisis government revenues have declined and expenses increased; particularly heavy were payments on foreign debt, which reached 18 percent of the Gross National Product in 1980.

In its rush to stimulate investment, the federal government presses for megaprojects in energy, and the provinces press for intensified resource extraction. These are inherently unstable answers. The construction these policies induce (when they work at all) provides a "quick fix," but there are few long-term jobs in these capital-intensive activities, and the concessions offered to entice foreign capital depreciate the value of the resource rents. The spiral is one of increasing dependence and insecurity of employment.

Like the union movement, the other major social movements of the 1970s have been less than successful. Regionalism as a social, political, and economic phenomenon continues to reflect the uneven development of the country. Provincialism has increased as the provinces continue to struggle with the federal government over scarce resource rents and overextended financial responsibilities. English Canadian nationalism has made limited gains: there is a watered-down Foreign Investment Review Agency, and Petro Canada is now a major actor in the petroleum field (but foreign ownership still stands at 75 percent). There can be little pleasure for nationalists in the fact that foreign control of manufacturing slipped back to 48 percent since the major reason has been deindustrialization, the very fear that prompted nationalists in the first place.

Branch plants are leaving behind empty shells, not a vibrant industrial base. All levels of government are once again courting foreign investors.

The impact of the women's movement may well have been the most subtle and far-reaching of all. Out of economic necessity women are entering the labour force at a rapidly increasing rate. By 1980 over 50 percent of women were in the labour force, accounting for 40 percent of the entire employed labour force. Women, nevertheless, continue to experience higher rates of unemployment, greater part-time work, and lower incomes than men (Armstrong and Armstrong, 1983). The proletarianization of clerical, sales, and service work has had its greatest impact on women who were recruited in large numbers into these activities during the 1960s and 1970s. Increasingly, teachers, nurses, and insurance and bank workers are turning to unionization as the pay levels and content of their work fail to correspond to the privileged image of white-collar work. Labour force segmentation means, however, that there tend to be gender-segregated unions. Through newer unions, like CUPE, such women's issues as paid maternity leave, child care, and equal pay for work of equal value are placed on the agenda. Patriarchal attitudes and practices, however, persist among many male unionists, and calls can still be heard for women to "return to the home so men can have a job."

The upper echelons of the Canadian economy have been immune to most of the major social forces of the post-war era. Neither the women's movement nor Québécois nationalism has gained ground in the economic elite, nor has regional representation changed greatly. The one consequential force has been foreign ownership, although its penetration has not served to dislodge the cornerstones of corporate power. Large Canadian capitalists, rather, have entered into an unequal alliance with foreign capital, thus reinforcing the strength of each (Clement, 1977).

Throughout the past half-century capital has engaged in a multitude of control practices, often working hand-in-hand with government policies designed to facilitate capital accumulation "in the national interest." During the 1930s repression was the order of the day—work camps and the Regina Riot. During World War II there was heavy reliance on an ideology of unity in the face of adversity (spiced with a heavy dose of long overdue concessions to labour). The immediate post-war period relied on practices of conciliation and liberalized labour legislation designed to bring labour into a national partnership, on the condition that labour keep its own house in order and eliminate "extreme" elements. In the boom of the 1960s, prosperity and immigration reigned until the crisis of the 1970s forced the state to both cut immigration and place wages under controls. As in the 1930s, coercion has once again become the order of the day, but this time less physical and more legislative. Unemployment, wage controls, and regressive labour laws discipline the labour force. Under these conditions the labour movement is directly challenged, even its most wage-conscious sectors. More unified than ever, labour has never been more directly challenged. Its response will be the key to charting the 1980s.

Canadian society remains a fractured, distorted formation. There is a dynamic tension between capital and labour, with the state becoming an increasingly direct actor in the relationship—mediating on behalf of capital and itself as an employer.

REFERENCES

Armstrong, Hugh
1977   "The labour force and state workers in Canada," in *The Canadian State: Political Economy and Political Power,* ed. Leo Panitch. Toronto: University of Toronto Press.

Armstrong, Pat, and Hugh Armstrong
1983   *A Working Majority: What Women Must Do for Pay.* Ottawa: Supply and Services.

Beausoleil, Gilles
1974   "History of the strike at Asbestos," in *The Asbestos Strike,* ed. Pierre Elliott Trudeau. Toronto: James Lewis and Samuel.

Bothwell, Robert, and William Kilbourn
1979   *C. D. Howe, A Biography.* Toronto: McClelland and Stewart.

Clark, Melissa
1979   The Canadian State and Staples: An Ear to Washington. M.A. thesis, McMaster University, Hamilton.

Clement, Wallace
1977   *Continental Corporate Power: Economic Linkages Between Canada and the United States.* Toronto: McClelland and Stewart.
1980   *Hardrock Mining: Industrial Relations and Changes at Inco.* Toronto: McClelland and Stewart.

Creighton, Donald G.
  1970   *Canada's First Century, 1867-1967.* Toronto: Macmillan of Canada.

Department of Reconstruction and Supply
  1949   *Encouragement to Industrial Expansion in Canada.* Ottawa.

Firestone, O. J.
  1958   *Canada's Economic Development, 1867-1953.* London: Bowes and Bowes.

Jamieson, Stuart
  1968   *Time of Trouble: Labour Unrest and Industrial Conflict in Canada, 1900-1966,*
          Study #22. Ottawa: Task Force on Labour Relations.

Marshall, Herbert, Frank A. Southard Jr., and Kenneth W. Taylor
  1936   *Canadian-American Industry: A Study in International Investment.* New Haven:
          Yale University Press.

McRoberts, Kenneth, and Dale Posgate
  1980   *Quebec: Social Change and Political Crisis.* Toronto: McClelland and Stewart.

Pentland, H. Clare
  1968   *A Study of the Changing Social, Economic and Political Background of the Canadian
          System of Industrial Relations.* Ottawa: Task Force on Labour Relations.

Pierson, Ruth
  1977   "Women's emancipation and the recruitment of women into the labour force
          in World War II," in *The Neglected Majority: Essays in Canadian Women's History,*
          ed. Susan Mann Trofimenkoff and Alison Prentice. Toronto: McClelland and
          Stewart.

Reynolds, Lloyd G.
  1940   *The Control of Competition in Canada.* Cambridge, Mass.: Harvard University
          Press.

Richards, John, and Larry Pratt
  1979   *Prairie Capitalism: Power and Influence in the New West.* Toronto: McClelland
          and Stewart.

Rosenbluth, Gideon
  1961   "Concentration and monopoly in the Canadian economy," in *Social Purpose for
          Canada,* ed. Michael Oliver. Toronto: University of Toronto Press.

Shepard, J. J.
  1978   "Slam the brakes on auto parts' vicious circle?" *The Globe and Mail,* November
          21, p.7.

Wolfe, David
  1973   Political Culture, Economic Policy and the Growth of Foreign Investment in
          Canada. M.A. thesis, Carleton University, Ottawa.

32. *The State and Human Rights*

Alan Cairns and Cynthia Williams

Government has a more powerful presence in our day-to-day life than at any earlier time in Canadian history. Individuals and groups turn to governments with increasing frequency for the satisfaction of an ever-expanding array of wants and desires. In recent decades there has been a noticeable trend for these demands to be expressed in the language of citizen rights.

The worldwide concern with human rights since 1945 owes much of its existence to the efforts of the United Nations and its agencies. The 1948 Universal Declaration of Human Rights set the stage for a post-war politics premised on the obligation of governments to guaranteee and enforce an unprecedentedly wide range of citizen rights.... Pronouncements, declarations,

and conventions of the United Nations have further elaborated and expanded notions of both individual and collective citizens' rights and have contributed to the pace and direction of domestic public policy in many Western countries. The International Year of Women declared by the United Nations in 1975 precipitated an intensive review of the status of women in Canada and a flurry of government policies to enhance the equality of women. It also provided a focal point for the activities of women's groups and served to activate and reinforce a consciousness of "women's rights" in the broader public. The same is true of the more recent United Nations years of the handicapped and of youth, among others.

The United Nations initiative on human rights in the 1948 Universal Declaration reflected the world's abhorrence at human rights violations in Nazi Germany during the 1930s and 1940s and the oppression of colonized peoples around the world. But, as longtime human rights advocate John Humphrey (1970:47) has noted, the concern with protecting human rights survived

Revised from Alan Cairns and Cynthia Williams, *Constitutionalism, Citizenship and Society in Canada* (Toronto: University of Toronto Press, 1985), pp. 30-41. Reprinted by permission of the authors and University of Toronto Press. © Minister of Supply and Services Canada, 1985.

well beyond these immediate and arresting post-war concerns, to address such issues as the right to collective bargaining, the equality of women, equal pay for work of equal value, and an end to all forms of discrimination.

United Nations conferences and meetings have focussed international attention on the human rights claims of various groups. The third United Nations Conference on Women, held in the summer of 1985 to commemorate the tenth anniversary of the United Nations International Year of Women, was one such occasion. Three thousand delegates representing 159 countries attended the official conference, while another 12 000 representatives of non-governmental organizations conducted a more informal "Alternative Forum '85." The events, stretching over a three-week period, were covered by 1500 media representatives.

In such ways, the human rights concerns of the United Nations have been relevant to domestic circumstances in developed as well as less developed countries. The international jurisprudence on alleged violations of UN guarantees argued before the International Court of Justice has also on occasion had a profound effect on domestic national governments.

The American civil rights movements in the 1960s and its spinoff social movements also had a powerful demonstration effect throughout the Western world and especially in Canada. The unprecedented interventions by the U.S. government in matters of school integration, educational opportunities, and affirmative action programs, and through a host of social policies, seemed to show how successful governments could be in changing attitudes and advancing equality. The manifold impact of international human rights initiatives on Canadian expressions of rights consciousness was reflected in Canadian preoccupations and realities.

The increased interaction of citizen groups and governments has been discussed in the context of the newly politicized self-consciousness of individuals and the politicization of an increasingly broad array of human activities and identities. Drawing on the rhetoric of human rights, citizen groups have sought to employ the state for their own advancement. Turning to government for the protection and enhancement of an ever-expanding array of interests, groups have refined a popularized language of citizen rights which demands active government intervention and state-directed social engineering as the means of securing the promises of human rights.

Groups have enjoyed considerable success in expanding discussions of human rights and in securing positive government responses through a wide range of public policies as well as through the legal and constitutional validation of various rights claims. The success of one group spreads quickly to another. This is perhaps nowhere clearer than in recent equality claims and demands for programs to achieve a government-directed redistribution of opportunity. As political scientist Jill McCalla Vickers (1983:53-54) has argued, equality aspirations are contagious.

We know from historical evidence that women in the nineteenth century in the United States came to a consciousness of their inequality by applying the analysis of slavery and racial inequality to their own situation. A similar process gave shape to the contemporary women's movement in North America when affirmative action legislation aimed at blacks was seized on as a tool for achieving more equality for women. . . . Nor has the contagion been limited to the level of analysis and ideology. Modes of organizing and instruments of correction also spread from group to group. Hence, individual competence tests which will certainly emerge to ascertain whether individual retirees should or should not continue to enjoy the right to work where mandatory retirement provisions are declared discriminatory may well also be transferred to the context of deciding when individual young people may gain the right to be treated as adult persons rather than as members of a "protected" group with very limited equality rights. Similarly, affirmative action mechanisms are already being transferred from the context of women's aspirations for equality to the context of the handicapped.

As Vickers confirms, the language of rights is an expansive language, easily molded to the aspirations and demands of a broad range of interests. In addition, the language of rights is a powerful political resource, as claims garbed in the language of citizen rights have an aura of moral righteousness that is disruptive to normal processes of political discussion.

Governments in Canada have also contributed to the recent popularizing of a language of citizen rights, viewing rights as a powerful tool for shaping society. State elites have their own agenda, derived from their visions of desirable futures. The recognition of citizen rights has been a means of achieving these visions. Prime Minister John Diefenbaker believed the 1960 Bill of Rights could symbolically affirm his vision of "One Canada," educating all Canadians to the pan-Canadian rights of citizenship. The 1960 Bill of Rights emphasized racial and ethnic equality, matters on which the prairie Prime Minister of German descent had strong views. He believed the possession of citizen rights could be a cornerstone of Canadian citizenship and would underpin a strong sense of national unity....

The federal/provincial controversy leading up to the Charter of Rights and Freedoms in 1982 illustrated the high stakes involved for the governments of Canadian federalism. While the federal government hoped to strengthen a pan-Canadian identity and secure a non-territorial, pan-Canadian bilingualism, the Quebec government believed that its own provincial Charter of Rights had established an effective code of human rights guarantees. The debate over which rights would be guaranteed often veiled a more fundamental point at issue: which level of government would benefit most from a national Charter of Rights? In the end, the Charter reflected the difficulty of resolving this issue. The restrictions of mobility rights and the inclusion of a general override provision respecting fundamental, legal, and democratic rights were the cost of securing sufficient provincial support for the project as a whole to succeed. Special provision was also made respecting the application of language rights in Quebec.

Whether in response to pressures from the international arena and citizen demands or in pursuit of government objectives, the recognition of citizen rights through legislation has had an increasingly significant effect on the self-definitions of communities in Canada. For better or for worse, every recognition of a right carries with it an altered sense of community and of what membership in the community entails.

Legal frameworks live in a symbiotic relationship with society. They are not immutable simply because they are legislated. Viscount Sankey's characterization of the Canadian constitution as a "living tree" is as true of the Canadian constitution in 1985 as it was in 1930.

At least as powerful as its capacity to adapt to changing circumstances, however, is the stability and continuity which a constitutional framework provides by establishing parameters within which orderly change can occur in a political community. Constitutions articulate the rules and procedures for the conduct of government and the terms and conditions on which a people agree to live with one another in a political community. In this sense, a major change in the constitutional framework, such as was introduced in Canada in 1982, can be expected to have an equally profound change on the nature and meaning of membership in the national community.

The implementation of the Charter signals a profound change in the Canadian constitutional system of government, in our political culture, and in citizen-state relations. The long-run consequences of the Charter as a third pillar of Canadian constitutionalism, taking its place alongside parliamentary government and federalism, are not predictable in detail. However, expectations are high among potential "users" that the Charter will have a profound and positive effect on the status, legitimacy, and goals of particular sets of interests. Women's groups, for example, have recently organized an umbrella association to assist in education and litigation of Charter issues that will advance the equality of women.

The Charter's effect will not be limited to the interests of particular groups who use it for their own purposes. As the third pillar of constitutional government in Canada, the Charter will have a transforming effect on the general conduct of politics and indeed on the very nature of consensus and understanding that underpin constitutional government in Canada.

In the limited space at our disposal, we will not undertake a detailed analysis of the historical evolution of the theory and practice of citizenship rights in Canada. Instead, we propose a selective look at basic trends in the protection of fundamental citizen rights to single out features of the changing system of Canadian constitutional government that appear to have special relevance to our focus on citizenship and community.

To the Fathers of Confederation, comfortable with their received British political tradition and wanting to differentiate themselves from their neighbours to the south,

the idea of an entrenched Charter of Rights, like the related concept of popular democracy, had negligible appeal. The principle of parliamentary supremacy presupposed that political executives and legislators could and should be trusted, that a constitutional monarchy—in which freedom resided in tradition, the common law, and practice which had produced the rights of British subjects —was preferable to the American arrangement in which rights resided in the people. Furthermore, the Canadian Fathers were not creating a new polity based on a revolutionary repudiation of past traditions or of the mother country. With the unavoidable exception of federalism, the principal characteristic of the political rearrangement of the British North American colonies in 1867 was continuity. Canada, as the preamble to the British North America Act stated, was to have a constitution "similar in principle" to that of the United Kingdom. Confederation was the handiwork of practical politicians with limited predilections for theorizing about the rights of citizens. Moreover, the new central government was given immense nation-building responsibilities for which constitutionally entrenched rights could only have been perceived as an unnecessary restraint on executive leadership.

The limited citizen rights explicitly guaranteed in the 1867 constitution were responses to circumstances specific to British North America and thus were not subsumed in the traditional "rights of Englishmen" implicit in the new constitution. The Fathers of Confederation guaranteed the continuation of certain minority denominational education rights existing in Canada at the time of Confederation (Section 93) and guaranteed (in Section 133) the continuation of English and French in the Parliament of Canada and the Legislative Assembly of Quebec. Section 121, the precursor of modern notions of protecting rights in the economic union, guaranteed that no tariffs would be levied on the movement of goods across provincial borders. Democratic rights to vote in regular free elections were not explicitly guaranteed, although they were clearly understood to be a part of both the English and the British North American practice of government. Provisions were included guaranteeing the powers of the popularly elected House of Commons and the principles of representation, as well as the five-year maximum life of any Parliament. But again, these guarantees were not expressed as the rights of individual citizens, as would have been the case if Confederation had taken place a century later—or in the United States a century before. Instead, they were a code of guarantees that could be deduced from the limitations placed on the supremacy of parliaments.

The Fathers of Confederation did not view the individual citizen as the source of political legitimacy. The dominant principle guiding the work of the constitution makers in 1867 was responsible government under a constitutional monarchy, modified in the Canadian case to accommodate a system of federal government. Their approach did not imply an indifference to rights, but rather the assumption that their evolution and protection required no special institutional arrangement or guarantees outside the British tradition.

The 1867 arrangement for protecting the rights of citizens appears to have been generally accepted in the post-Confederation period. A constitutionally guaranteed code of rights did not have wide appeal or public support until the mid-twentieth century. Although there were scattered precursors such as the social-democratic CCF in the 1930s, the erosion of support for parliamentary supremacy and advocacy of entrenched citizen rights can be dated from World War II. In the post-war period, the perception of

what a right is, which rights should be protected or fostered, and how, changed significantly as public opinion, organized group effort, changing intellectual currents, and the developing purposes of governments all converged to produce a radically new political environment.... A steady if discontinuous evolution in public opinion and elite responses since World War II has caused support for the entrenchment of rights to grow, culminating in the Charter of Rights and Freedoms in 1982.

The differences between the 1960 Bill of Rights and the 1982 Charter reveal the time-bound character of rights-consciousness. The 1960 Bill of Rights was primarily concerned with individual legal rights, the growth of the administrative state, and violations of the rule of law. It did not address social rights; paid no special attention to language rights, aboriginals, or multiculturalism (the word was not in common usage at the time); and lacked the equivalent of Section 15(2) of the Charter, which invites affirmative action on behalf of disadvantaged groups. In addition, it was not entrenched and did not apply to the provinces. The inadequacies of the Canadian Bill of Rights, due partly to judicial philosophies hostile to an activist role for courts and partly to the increasing sense that its clauses could not end discrimination even if they were given full effect, became relevant fodder for the next stage of discussion. On the one hand, the 1960 Bill of Rights further accustomed Canadians to a language of rights and the idea of a constitutional document for their protection. On the other hand, the shortcomings of the Bill of Rights contributed to efforts to replace it by a stronger, more comprehensive document.

A major change since the 1960 debate on the Diefenbaker Bill of Rights related to support for entrenchment. Although under some pressure from the CCF and others to entrench the civil liberties guarantees in the

1960 Bill, the Diefenbaker government was unwilling to wait for the unlikely agreement of the provinces to the project and, believing entrenchment only at the federal level had no effective meaning, therefore proceeded with simple legislation.

Several developments in the 1960s and 1970s contributed to changed thinking about entrenchment. The demonstrated weaknesses of the 1960 Bill of Rights, and the general unwillingness of the courts to approach it as other than a piece of simple legislation, led many to the view that constitutional entrenchment was necessary if a Canadian Bill of Rights was to be an effective check on parliamentary supremacy. Discussions on constitutional reform that began in 1967 in response to emerging Quebec nationalism also focussed attention on the inclusion of individual language rights guarantees in the Canadian constitution. The federal government began to view a constitutional charter or bill of rights as the centrepiece of a federal strategy to counter powerful centrifugal forces in Canadian federalism.

The constitutional recognition of citizen rights in the 1982 Charter demonstrated the interplay and convergence of government efforts to shape conceptions of political community in Canada, and the demands and pressures exerted by mobilized, organized citizens able to adapt notions of fundamental citizen rights to the particular interests they represented. The federal government found a welcome and powerful ally in the citizen groups appearing before the Joint Committee on the Constitution in 1980-81.

Ottawa's skillful cultivation of a broadly based public civil rights constituency during the hearings of the Special Joint Committee on the Constitution in 1980-81 . . . finally secured the entrenchment project. Though by no means unanimous, there was widespread support for an entrenched Charter of Rights and Freedoms by the early 1980s and for the view that entrenchment was a useful and appropriate constraint on parliamentary majorities.

Premier Sterling Lyon of Manitoba was the strongest opponent of entrenchment, on the grounds of its general interference with parliamentary supremacy, although the 1978 constitutional position of the British Columbia government had also strongly supported parliamentary supremacy. Other premiers objected to entrenchment of specific subjects, most notably Quebec Premier René Levesque's strong opposition to minority language education rights—as part of his general opposition to a Charter binding on the provinces. In the House of Commons, the overwhelming majority of MPs, including leaders of opposition parties, favoured entrenchment.

Some of the premiers argued that entrenchment would hinder each government's ability to pursue legislation *on behalf* of minority interests, but such objections were met through special "notwithstanding" provisions of the Charter, such as the general override power (Section 33), the affirmative action clause respecting equality rights (Section 15(2)), and the limited power to override mobility rights guarantees (Section 6(4)).

In terms of constitutional principles, the general override provision (Section 33) was a concession to both parliamentary government and federalism. It permits governments to pass laws over matters within its jurisdiction that are inconsistent with the Charter's guarantees of legal, democratic, and fundamental rights when those governments believe such actions are warranted in their community. Limiting such overrides to a five-year period, however, ensures that the Charter provisions are the "normal" state of affairs. The burden of justifying departures from the Charter provisions is placed squarely on the shoulders of those who would so legislate, subject to the mechanisms of parliamentary approval.

As with most examples of social change, it is easy to overstate the extent of institutional innovation heralded by the arrival of the Charter of Rights and Freedoms. Federalism and parliamentary government, and the traditions of citizenship they have imparted, remain the primary historical referents for Canadians; these two principles have underlaid the institutional basis of the Canadian constitutional order for over a century, during which time the very conception of Canadian citizenship emerged. But these traditional notions no longer enjoy a monopoly. They must now jostle with notions of citizenship expressed in the guarantees of the Charter. The citizen has a new status as a bearer of rights. Government activities must be consistent with Charter guarantees. Parliamentary supremacy has been curtailed.

The Charter has changed the constitutional status of citizen rights. In the past the dominant view was that legislative powers in Canada were exhaustively distributed between the two levels of government and that within their respective spheres of legislative competence, the federal and provincial legislatures were supreme. By the late 1950s, through a number of *causes célèbres,* the Supreme Court of Canada had taken the view that provincial legislatures had very circumscribed powers to legislate respecting civil liberties. Only a few judges suggested, however, that some rights and freedoms were beyond the authority of the federal government by virtue of the preamble to the 1867 Constitution Act.

This constitutional arrangement has changed with the Charter. With it has changed the constitutional status of the Canadian citizen, who no longer need rely on the consent of one of the two levels of government for the protection or guarantee of fundamental rights and freedoms. On the contrary, through successful appeals to the Charter of Rights, citizens will be able to make authoritative claims against certain government actions previously under the legislative jurisdiction of that level of government. The Charter is now part of the fundamental law of the land and Section 1 states unequivocally that the Charter is not subject to simple parliamentary override but only to limitations that are "demonstrably justified in a free and democratic society."

The Charter has thus given Canadian courts an enhanced role in the constitutional order. Important as federalism remains, many issues of civil and human rights which were formerly decided by the courts on the basis of spheres of federal or provincial legislative competence will henceforth be decided on the basis of the Charter of Rights and Freedoms. Speaking recently to the Canadian Bar Association, Chief Justice Brian Dickson (1985) spoke to the Court's response to its new role:

> Canadian courts, including the Supreme Court of Canada, have accepted the new responsibility which has been thrust upon them by the Parliamentarians. They recognize the vital role they will play in determining the kind of society Canada is and will become under the *Charter.* . . . At the same time the judiciary have assumed a greater prominence in determining how the fabric of Canadian society is to be woven and cut.

It is too early to tell how openly the courts will embrace an activist policy role through their new responsibilities as guardian of the constitutional rights of citizens, although it is already clear that the Charter will not suffer the same fate as the Canadian Bill of Rights in the hands of the judiciary. Undoubtedly, the role the courts define for themselves under the Charter will have a long-term effect on the eagerness with which others will seek authoritative court decisions. Would-be reformers may find that the

Charter is more effectively used as a reference in discussion and negotiation with other political actors than it is as positive law in the hands of the judiciary. In either case, however, as the experience of the first three years has amply demonstrated, the Charter now figures prominently in discussions of Canada's constitutional order.

Citizens now will participate directly in shaping the constitutional order, using the Charter of Rights and Freedoms as a springboard for advancing various claims on government. The opportunity to use the Charter as a way of placing issues on the political agenda was apparent to many groups during the discussions and negotiations leading up to its final approval.

Burt (1985) . . . discusses the organization of women's groups around the issue of constitutional reform, as they realized the opportunities to advance discussion of women's rights in the context of constitutional equality guarantees. Similarly, the fact that women have organized the Legal Education and Action Fund, to ensure that women use the Charter to achieve equality and other rights, suggests that the interest group activity first organized around the content of the Charter will continue to influence its interpretation and impact.

As was clear from the range of groups appearing before the Joint Committee on the Constitution, the Charter has given a new prominence to certain interests and cleavages in Canadian society. In the process, it altered the balance of competing citizen identities. The Charter was an integral part of federal government efforts in the late 1970s to stem the forces of centrifugalism that were popularly perceived as threatening Canadian national unity. The language rights and personal mobility rights in the Charter were only the most obvious efforts to arrest the forces of balkanization by directly challenging some provincial programs and poli-

cies already in place. More subtle in effect is the Charter's appeal to non-territorial identities of citizens—race, ethnicity, gender, age, and others. The Charter draws attention to identities and cleavages in Canada that cut across regionalism and may in the long run generate pan-Canadian identities and a more nationally-based political discourse.

The emergence of strong political identities based on ethnicity, race, gender, and age in turn generates pressure on political elites to ensure that these identities are appropriately represented in the institutions of government. Recent efforts by federal and provincial governments to increase the visibility of women and ethnic minorities by appointments to high-profile positions are evidence of the governmental response. The Supreme Court of Canada will be prone to these same pressures. As the Charter of Rights and Freedoms attaches new legitimacy to various citizen identities, there will be mounting pressure for the Court to become more socially and politically representative. Justices may become increasingly conscious of their special responsibility to particular subgroups in society which they may be taken to "represent." For example, in reflecting on whether to accept an appointment to the Supreme Court of Canada, Madame Justice Bertha Wilson has said; "I knew if I were asked there wasn't a choice—too many women were counting on me."

The belief that a national code of rights guarantees would aid in the consolidation of pan-Canadian identities underlay the federal government's strategy of nation-building through the Charter. In the end, the necessities of political negotiation with the provinces resulted in a number of provisions that moderated this pan-Canadian thrust. The general override clause, permitting all legislatures to pass laws that could conflict with the fundamental legal or equality guarantees, has already been invoked on a blanket basis by the Government of Quebec. As a consequence, in that province discussions of these rights have focussed on provisions of provincial legislation, reinforcing the symbolic presence of the province as guarantor of fundamental rights and freedoms—contrary to the objectives of the federal government through the national Charter of Rights and Freedoms. Similarly, the special provision exempting Quebec from the minority-language education rights guarantees of Section 23(1)(a) until acceded to by the Quebec legislative assembly or government demonstrates to Canadians that at least until such consent is granted, these language rights remain under provincial jurisdiction in that province. Other provisions moderating the nationalizing thrust of the Charter were agreed to by the federal government as a cost of securing approval for the project as a whole....

What these developments illustrate is that a constitution does not just establish the machinery and instruments of government. It also embodies and reflects the values and beliefs of a political community, and the terms and conditions on which its members have agreed to live with one another and

in relation to the state. While constitutions must adapt to evolving circumstances over time if they are to survive, the notion of a "living constitution" at best tells only half a story. Over time, constitutions shape and mold a people as much as they are shaped and molded by one. Constitutions embody the highest principles and ideals of a political community, linking the past with the present and future, breathing life into and giving form to the very conception of citizenship.

Under the 1867 Constitution Act, Canadians were to be a parliamentary and a federal people, under the Crown of the United Kingdom. The "rights of the Englishman" were part of the British heritage of Canadians. In the journey "from colony to nation" citizen rights were subject to the division of powers and to the self-restraint of cabinets and legislative majorities. This arrangement changed in 1982, when the twinned principles of Canadian constitutional government were made a triumvirate—parliamentary government, federalism, and the Charter of Rights and Freedoms. In the process the very basis for determining Canadian citizenship has been changed....

REFERENCES

Burt, S.
    1985   "Women's issues and the women's movement in Canada since 1970," in *The Politics of Gender, Ethnicity and Language in Canada.* Toronto: University of Toronto Press.

Dickson, B.
    1985   Address to the Mid-Winter Meeting of the Canadian Bar Association. Edmonton, mimeo.

Humphrey, J.
    1970   "The world revolution and human rights," in *Human Rights, Federalism and Minorities,* ed. A. Gotlieb. Toronto: Canadian Institute of International Affairs.

Vickers, J. M.
    1983   "Major equality issues in the eighties," *Canadian Human Rights Yearbook.* Ottawa: University of Ottawa.

33. Economic Background and Political Representation

Neil Guppy, Sabrina Freeman, and Shari Buchan

As an elected assembly, parliamentary government rests on the principle of representative democracy. Only a small fraction of the population has no voice in selecting representatives, and the vast majority of Canadians are themselves eligible to seek office. But while most people can vote, those who serve remain a select group.

Historically, democratically elected representatives have come from privileged backgrounds. Commenting on political recruitment, Weber (1946:94) pointed to the elite status of lawyers and argued that "since the French Revolution, the modern lawyer and modern democracy absolutely belong together." In Canada, Porter (1965:392) remarked that this direct tie between the legal profession and politicians had "increased

over time" in the federal cabinet. Ward (1950: 133), however, reported a growing diversity of occupational representation in the Canadian parliament since Confederation, although in 1945 the legal profession still held "approximately one third of the total membership in the House."

Contemporary evidence reveals that lawyers have not preserved their one-third share of parliamentary seats. By the late 1960s only 26 percent of members in the federal House had legal training, and this trend of declining representation continued through to the early 1980s when only 20 percent of parliamentarians had backgrounds in law (based on Chief Electoral Reports). This apparent erosion of the strong unity between lawyers and elected officials in Canada not only runs counter to Weber's observation, but also raises several questions concerning the democratization of parliament.

Building on a tradition of research (e.g., Marsh, 1940; Ward, 1950; Porter, 1965; Presthus, 1973; Forcese and de Vries, 1977; Ogmundson, 1977; Olsen, 1980; and Fox and Ornstein, 1986), we use federal election in-

Revised from Neil Guppy, Sabrina Freeman, and Shari Buchan, "Representing Canadians: Changes in the Economic Backgrounds of Federal Politicians, 1965-1984," *Canadian Review of Sociology and Anthropology,* vol. 24, no. 3 (August 1987) pp. 417–430. Reprinted with permission.

formation from the last two decades to chart patterns of change in the direct economic representation in federal Canadian politics. Specifically, we ask, have the economic backgrounds of parliamentarians become more heterogeneous, reflecting a widening or democratizing of the economic interest groups in the House of Commons? Our data include information on both candidates and elected members. We also assess possible changes in the economic backgrounds of Cabinet Ministers.

To examine these questions we rely on information from official reports of the Chief Electoral Office for the seven elections between 1965 and 1984. "Occupation" listings were provided by all candidates completing nomination papers (N = 8673, excluding by-elections). We follow Forcese and de Vries (1977) in taking this information at face value. Between 5 and 10 percent of candidates do not participate in the paid labour force. In the "occupation" category on the official nomination paper they would list such statuses as student, housewife, and retired. For 49 candidates no useable "occupation" information was listed (e.g., no listing, "Thinker", "Dilettante"). Missing data occur mainly among candidates from fringe parties (e.g., Rhinoceros Party).

Occupation was coded into broad socioeconomic categories following Pineo, Porter, and McRoberts (1977:98). The six categories, including a residual category for those not in the paid labour force, are as follows: (1) business owners, self-employed professionals, and top-level executives or managers; (2) employed professionals, middle managers and executives; (3) other white-collar workers; (4) blue-collar workers; (5) farmers; and (6) others (including students, retirees, housewives).

We contrast the pre-election careers of all political candidates with comparable distributions of the general population. This required some method of generating equivalent information on occupational distributions for each electoral period. Following Forcese and de Vries (1977) we use Census information as our source and report the distribution of the total population according to the sixfold classification noted above for 1961, 1971, and 1981.

METHODS AND AN ILLUSTRATIVE EXAMPLE

Our central interest is in examining changes in the democratization of parliament. We accomplish this by comparing the occupational distribution of the general population with the pre-political careers of federal candidates and elected MPs. To illustrate our strategy we continue a theme of Weber, Marsh, Ward, and Porter by concentrating on the legal profession.

In 1965 only a fraction of the Canadian population (approximately 0.1 percent of people aged 18 and over) were members of the legal profession (judges, magistrates, lawyers, and notaries). However, in the 1965 election 143 candidates had legal backgrounds (14.1 percent of all candidates) and 66 law professionals were elected (24.9 percent of all elected members). Among candidates, members of the legal profession were overrepresented by a factor of 141 and as elected MPs they were overrepresented by a factor of 249. Lawyers were not only overrepresented, but as Aberbach, Putnam, and Rockman (1981) maintain, the disproportion increases as the focus shifts from candidates to elected officials.

By 1981 there were 36 105 practicing law professionals constituting just under 0.2 percent of Canadians over the age of 17. The proportion of candidates with law backgrounds seeking office in 1984 had declined to 8.6 percent (from 14.1 percent in 1965). The proportion of elected lawyers had also dropped relative to 1965, and now stood at 16.3 percent (down from 24.9 percent). Individuals with backgrounds in law were still overrepresented as candidates (by a factor of 43) and in parliament (by a factor of 81.5), but over the two decades their dominance had declined. In sum, the overrepresentation of legal professionals was greater among MPs than candidates in both elections although the size of the disproportion had diminished.

The law example illustrates our general procedure of analysis and also highlights the main complexity which our strategy encounters. There are two dimensions of change involved in considering representation. The first concerns the growth or decline in the numbers of people in any of our six categories. The second involves growth or decline among either candidates or MPs. Since these processes of growth and decline can work in tandem or in opposition, we need a direct, summary measure of over- or underrepresentation.

A direct measure of representativeness comes from dividing the percentage of candidates or elected representatives by the corresponding percentage for the general population (at equivalent time periods). For example, in the 1960s, 56.1 percent of elected officials were in the owner/self-employed professional category, compared to only 4.7 percent of the general population. These percentages correspond to an overrepresentation by a factor of 11.9 (56.1/4.7). Expressed in an alternate manner, these elected officials were represented 11.9 times more frequently than would be expected given the general population distribution. These ratios of candidates or elected officials relative to the general population appear in parentheses in Table 33-1. The size of these numbers directly summarizes the degree of over- or underrepresentation relative to the distribution of the general population.

RESULTS

We begin by assessing the socio-economic status (SES) backgrounds of politicians and examining whether there has been any democratization in economic representation in the last two decades. The overall pattern of democratization shows that *for candidates* there is a very small change toward greater representativeness over time. The percentage of candidates from the first two categories shows this slight decline (from 69.7 percent in the 1960s to 67.3 percent in the 1980s). The reason is that more fringe party candidates are running and these candidates are more likely to come from the lower four SES categories. Whereas 79.6 percent of all candidates ran for major parties in the 1960s, this had declined to 57.7 percent by the early 1980s. Furthermore, in the 1980s, 81.1 percent of major party candidates but only 48.4 percent of other candidates came from the top two SES categories.

For *elected* MPs exactly the reverse occurs, as they have become less representative of the general population. In the 1960s, 77.3 percent of MPs came from the top two SES categories, a percentage which increased by 7.0 points in the 1970s and by a further 3.6 points in the 1980s. Therefore, while candidates for federal political office are coming to represent more widely the Canadian populace, over the past two decades elected MPs have increasingly come from selective economic backgrounds.

We now assess five central research questions, each of which concerns the degree to which the federal government provides democratic representation of people from different economic and social backgrounds.

TABLE 33-1 Occupational distributions for the general labour force, for political candidates, and for elected officials over three time periods.*

Occupation categories	General population**			Political candidates			Elected representatives		
	1960s	1970s	1980s	1960s	1970s	1980s	1960s	1970s	1980s
Owners/Self-employed professionals	4.7%	5.6%	6.9%	46.1% (9.8)	39.4% (7.0)	36.2% (5.2)	56.1% (11.9)	54.4% (9.7)	52.7% (7.6)
Professionals/middle managers	9.1	10.3	12.6	23.6 (2.6)	28.3 (2.7)	31.1 (2.5)	21.2 (2.3)	29.9 (2.9)	35.2 (2.8)
Other white-collar	18.2	19.5	22.3	11.3 (0.6)	13.0 (0.7)	12.1 (0.5)	7.9 (0.4)	4.6 (0.2)	3.0 (0.1)
Blue-collar	17.1	18.0	20.1	8.0 (0.6)	7.6 (0.4)	7.5 (0.4)	3.2 (0.2)	2.7 (0.2)	1.2 (.06)
Farm	4.8	3.5	2.6	7.0 (1.5)	5.0 (1.7)	4.1 (1.6)	9.8 (2.0)	7.3 (2.1)	6.6 (2.5)
Other	46.2	43.2	35.5	3.9 (.08)	6.6 (.15)	9.0 (.25)	1.7 (.04)	1.1 (.03)	1.2 (.03)
TOTAL Column %	100.0	100.0	100.0	100.0	100.0	100.0	100.0	100.0	100.0
Number	11.1m	13.9m	18.6m	1 974	3 733	2 917	529	810	562
I of D***	.72	.73	.76	.71	.74	.74	.62	.61	.59

*The three time periods incorporate the following elections: 1960s—1965 & 1968; 1970s—1972, 1974 & 1979; 1980s—1980 & 1984.

**These general population *estimates* refer to individuals 18 years of age and over, and come from census data for 1961, 1971, and 1981.

***I of D = Index of Diversity: high values mean greater diversity (spread) across categories.

Source: For political candidates and elected officials, occupation data is from Chief Electoral Reports. For the general labour force, the occupation data come from the Canadian Census.

The "law of increasing disproportion"

According to this law (Aberbach, Putnam, and Rockman, 1981), political candidates are disproportionately from high SES positions, elected officials are even more disproportionately from high SES backgrounds, and Cabinet Ministers are yet again more disproportionately from high SES origins. There is good support in our findings for this claim. Among the highest SES group, candidates in the 1980 period were overrepresented by a factor of 5.2 while elected officials were overrepresented by a factor of 7.6. This greater disproportional representation also holds for the two earlier periods, although the magnitude of overrepresentation is weakening more quickly for candidates (from 9.8 to 5.2—a 47 percent change) than for MPs (from 11.9 to 7.6—a 36 percent change). In the second highest SES category, the rule holds in 2 out of 3 cases and is very close to support in the third instance.

The only major exception among the lower four SES categories occurs for farmers. While the relative number of farmers in the general population has declined, consistently farmers have been overrepresented among both candidates and elected officials. However, since many of these individuals are probably farm owners, they *may* more accurately be classified as coming from among the ranks of a well-to-do farming elite.

Differences by political party

One theme in Canadian political commentary is the "tedious similarity" (McLeod, 1965:3) among the major parties. We assess this claim by cross-tabulating political party and the pre-political occupations of candidates and elected officials (Table 33-2).

For candidates, an NDP-other split can be shown by partitioning the chi square (of 524.8) for the entire table into two compo-

TABLE 33-2   Pre-political backgrounds of candidates and elected members by major political party.

Background categories	All candidates				Elected representatives			
	Lib	PC	NDP	Total	Lib	PC	NDP	Total
Owners/Self-employed professionals	56.8%	56.9%	30.5%	48.2%	57.1%	56.7%	34.5%	54.7%
Professionals/Middle managers	27.5	23.3	37.4	29.3	32.2	21.6	48.0	29.0
Other white-collar	5.9	7.2	11.9	8.3	4.8	4.8	6.2	4.9
Blue-collar	1.8	2.6	9.5	4.6	2.0	1.6	6.2	2.2
Farm	5.8	7.8	4.2	6.0	2.6	14.0	3.4	7.8
Other	2.1	2.2	6.5	3.6	1.3	1.3	1.7	1.4
TOTAL Column %	100.0	100.0	100.0	100.0	100.0	100.0	100.0	100.0
Number	1898	1900	1863	5661	836	820	177	1833
I of D*	.59	.61	.74		.57	.61	.64	

*I of D = Index of Diversity: high values mean greater diversity (spread) across categories.

nents (see Blalock, 1979:297-99). A first component is formed by comparing Liberal with Conservative candidates. The chi square is 17.1 and suggests relatively little major difference. A second component comes from comparing NDP candidates to those in the other two parties, and yields a chi square of 509.5 showing this to be the major contrast. Among candidates, the NDP nominates decidedly more people from outside the two SES categories.

For elected MPs, there is also a contrast between the NDP and the other two parties. Successful NDP candidates most often come from the employed professional and middle-management ranks (48.0 percent), although owners and self-employed professionals are heavily represented (34.5 percent). This contrasts with the pattern of the Liberals and Conservatives. But for the other two parties a much sharper difference exists among elected officials than was the case for their candidates. Although for both these parties elected officials tend to come from the top two SES categories, MPs from farming backgrounds are much more likely to be found in the Tory caucus than among Liberal MPs.

Another key difference between the parties is the degree to which their respective candidates and MPs reflect the diversity among Canadians. While no party perfectly represents the general backgrounds of all Canadians, the NDP nevertheless come the closest, but only with respect to candidates. Notice that New Democrat MPs are as likely as Liberals or Conservatives to come from the top two SES categories. A comparison of the Index of Diversity scores along the bottom row of Table 33-2 clearly depicts this pattern.

There have also been changes over the past two decades in the recruitment patterns of the major parties. For the Liberals and NDP, in the 1980s more candidates and more MPs came from employed professional or middle-management positions. However, for MPs, this change has opposite sources in the two parties. In the 1960s just over 25 percent of NDP MPs came from blue-collar or lower-white-collar backgrounds, but in the 1980s this representation had eroded to less than 4 percent. For the Liberals, the major change occurred among MPs from the top executive or self-employed professional ranks who, although now holding 50 percent of Liberal seats, had in the 1960s held over 63 percent of their seats.

For the Progressive Conservative party, change has been somewhat less dramatic. Almost one in four Conservative MPs had occupational backgrounds in farming in the 1960s, but this has declined to just under one in 10 in the most recent elections. Some of this apparent decline in the relative fortunes of Conservative MPs from agricultural backgrounds has come because of the party's success in non-agricultural areas. Nevertheless, there are fewer Conservative farmers in the House in the 1980s than during the late 1960s.

Table 33-1 reveals that over the last two decades candidates have become marginally more representative of the Canadian population but that MPs are increasingly from the top two SES categories. Controlling for party and examining the representativeness of MPs in the last two elections, the NDP have a greater proportion of their MPs from the top two SES categories (56 of 61 MPs—91.8 percent) than do the Tories (267 of 313—85.3 percent). While the Conservatives have held their base among Western farmers, the more recent NDP success has been in urban ridings where their professional members have been elected. Over the last two decades, the greater selectivity in the backgrounds of all MPs is primarily a consequence of the growing professional representation among successful NDP candidates.

Regional differences

Given the manufacturing industries of central Canada and the resource bases of the rest of the country, differences in regional representation might not be surprising. However, the most notable feature of regional comparisons is the remarkable consistency in the dominance of the top SES categories, with the only major exception coming in the larger farm representation from the West. Among candidates, Quebec has a somewhat distinctive profile with an underrepresentation in farming and an overrepresentation in the "other" category (as a consequence of greater student participation in federal politics). For MPs, the West is the region of difference, largely due to the agricultural representation. Marsh's (1940:418) early finding of Quebeckers' "marked preference" for lawyers is not supported in more recent elections. Among MPs,

lawyers predominate in the Atlantic Provinces (30.7 percent) and in Ontario (25.9 percent). His other finding, however, that in the West electors choose lawyers as political representatives less often, is borne out in the more recent data. Among Western MPs only 14.5 percent have legal backgrounds. Of Quebec MPs, 20.5 percent have legal training.

Gender differences

We turn next to the issue of whether or not the increasing participation of women has introduced any change in the economic representativeness of candidates and MPs. Table 33-3 shows gender differences in pre-political careers of both candidates and MPs. While female candidates are more representative of the Canadian population than their male counterparts (compare the Index of Diversity scores), women MPs are a more

TABLE 33-3 Pre-political backgrounds of candidates and elected members by gender.

Background categories	All candidates		Elected representatives	
	Women	Men	Women	Men
Owners/Self-employed professionals	20.9%	42.1%	35.7%	55.1%
Professionals/ Middle managers	31.5	27.8	54.3	28.1
Other white-collar	13.8	12.2	2.9	5.1
Blue-collar	12.0	7.2	1.4	2.5
Farm .	0.8	5.7	0.0	8.1
Other	21.1	5.1	5.7	1.1
TOTAL Column %	100.0	100.0	100.0	100.0
Number	901	7 222	70	1 831
I of D*	.78	.72	.57	.61

*I of D = Index of Diversity: high values mean greater diversity (spread) across categories.

select group with 90 percent coming from the top two SES categories (versus 83.2 percent for men). While women candidates better represent the general population distribution, women MPs do not. Not only is it "the higher, the fewer" with respect to the national political participation of women (Bashevkin, 1985; cf. Kopinak, 1985), but also "the fewer, the higher" in terms of women and SES. This finding appears to reflect a double standard wherein women must demonstrate greater achievement than men in the economic arena before they can succeed at the polls (see Carroll, 1985:66-70 for a U.S. comparison).

Cabinet representation

One final area in which the issue of representativeness has always been acute as in the composition of the federal Cabinet. Dawson (1948) and Smith (1985) have articulated the theme of Cabinet representativeness, noting that many believe a good Cabinet must represent the key sectoral interests that crosscut Canadian society. But while there appears to be a consensus that geographic interests must be balanced in Cabinet, the evidence suggests no strong conviction that diverse economic interests also need incorporation. In fact, while heterogeneity characterizes regional representation, homogeneity describes economic background.

Porter (1965) and Olsen (1980) have shown that Cabinet ministers come overwhelmingly from one or two key occupational groups. As Table 33-4 indicates, the majority of Cabinet members come from legal and/or corporate backgrounds. Although the representation of lawyers has declined over the three time periods shown in the table, their places have been filled by other professionals from either business, the public service, or education. While in more recent governments Cabinet members come from a wider range of occupations, those occupations are

TABLE 33-4 Pre-political occupations of federal cabinet ministers for three time periods.

| | *Time period* | | |
Occupations	*1940-1960**	*1961-1973***	*1974-1984****
Lawyers	61.6%	40.6%	35.1%
Business/Executive	18.6	27.1	26.7
Farmer	5.8	7.3	6.9
Physicians	2.3	1.0	0.0
Public/Armed service	5.8	7.3	13.7
Teachers/Academics	4.7	11.5	13.0
Journalists/Broadcasters	0.0	4.2	3.8
Labour union leaders	0.0	1.0	0.8
Skilled tradesmen	1.2	0.0	0.0
TOTAL Column %	100.0	100.0	100.0
Number	86	96	131

Notes: *From Porter (1965:391-392).
**From Olsen (1980:27).
***From Canadian News Facts (various issues) and Chief Electoral Reports (various elections).

still overwhelmingly professional in nature. Cabinet ministers come almost exclusively from the top two SES categories depicted in Table 33-1, and thereby reflect the third tier in the "law of increasing disproportion". Furthermore, at least in the most recent period, there was virtually no difference between Conservative and Liberal governments in the occupational representativeness of their respective Cabinets.

DISCUSSION AND CONCLUSIONS

A long traditon of social science investigation has examined the representativeness of Canadian politicians (references above). That research tradition has been motivated by the question of how politicians differ from the public they govern. We have focussed on the economic dimension of political representation and provided new information for the last two decades. In addition to updating existing knowledge, we have examined a series of specific research questions.

Our results show two diverging patterns of representativeness. For candidates, there is a modest increase in the diversity of economic backgrounds. The major reason for this is the growth of fringe parties participating in the electoral process. In addition, the growing participation of women has contributed to a broader representation of political candidates.

For MPs, there has been a growing homogeneity of economic background. Over the two decades we examined, the percentage of parliamentarians coming from the top two SES categories has grown from 77.3 percent to 87.9 percent. One of the most striking findings here is that a substantial portion of that increase comes from members of the NDP. What makes this finding even more startling is its distinctiveness vis à vis other electoral communities. For example, Aberbach, Putnam, and Rockman (1981:82) note that "while the secular conservative parties are bastions of those with upper-status backgrounds, the left wing especially seeks people from lower-status backgrounds to present to the electorate." The absence of this pattern in Canadian federal politics may contribute to the explanation of the relative lack of class voting in this country (Horowitz, 1966).

With respect to Aberbach, Putnam, and Rockman's (1981) "law of increasing disproportion," we found that for candidates, MPs, and Cabinet Ministers respectively, the higher SES groups were increasingly overrepresented. We did note, however, that this law appears to be weakening. When comparing men and women in federal politics this law has been reexpressed by Bashevkin (1985) as "the higher, the fewer." Men, and higher SES groups, are grossly overrepresented in politics.

Regional representation by SES does not appear to differ. In the Cabinet, regional representation is carefully balanced, although economic interest groups are not equally represented in this powerful body.

Reflecting on earlier findings, previous commentators (e.g., Marsh, 1940; Ward, 1950; Porter, 1965) have been quick to note that "there is no essential reason why a Parliament should be an exact microcosm of the occupational structure. . ." (Marsh, 1940: 423). This view would seem to represent the majority opinion among political observers. Fewer political analysts have noted that "there is no essential reason" that a highly specialized and privileged fragment of Canadians should represent the views of an economically diverse population.

Marchak (1981:67-68) suggests that the economic composition of Parliament is important to the question of whether or not "government is an independent institution representing everyone equally. . . ." She argues that since politicians come overwhelmingly from upper SES backgrounds, they could not represent the views of the total population, even if they were willing to do so.

The logic of this position rests not on "interest group representation" but on social perspective. As Porter (1965:391) makes the case:

> If we accept Mannheim's persuasive argument that a person's beliefs about social reality are shaped by the social milieu to which he [or she] has been exposed, we can see that the definitions of reality which provide the framework for making political decisions depend much on the social background and life experiences of politicians. The predominance of some occupational groups and people of one class background means that limited perspectives are brought to bear on public issues.

Whether or not one accepts the force of this position, the fact remains that the homogeneity of economic background on which the argument rests has become even more concentrated since Porter's remarks. Evidence contrary to what we have found would have seriously weakened this position.

When we consider voting, a review of the historical record shows the increasing political integration of the working class and women. However, with regard to direct economic representation, no significant broadening of participation has occurred. In fact, over the last 20 years federal politicians have come increasingly from the highest SES circles. While lawyers are now less involved in politics than Weber (1946:94) foresaw, it remains the case that a privileged economic elite and modern parliamentarians "absolutely belong together."

REFERENCES

Aberbach, Joel, Robert Putnam, and Bert Rockman
    1981   *Bureaucrats and Politicians in Western Democracies.* Cambridge: Harvard University Press.

Bashevkin, Sylvia
    1985   *Toeing the Lines: Women and Party Politics in English Canada.* Toronto: University of Toronto Press.

Blalock, Hubert
    1979   *Social Statistics.* New York: McGraw-Hill.

Carroll, Susan
    1985   *Women as Candidates in American Politics.* Bloomington: Indiana University Press.

Chief Electoral Office
    various years *Report of the Chief Electoral Officer.* Ottawa: Minister of Supply and Services, Cat. # SE 1-1.

Dason, R. M.
    1948   *The Government of Canada.* Toronto: University of Toronto Press.

Forcese, Dennis, and John de Vries
    1977   "Occupation and Electoral Success in Canada: the 1974 Federal Election," *Canadian Review of Sociology and Anthropology,* 14, no. 3:331-40.

Fox, John, and Michael Ornstein
  1986 "The Canadian State and Corporate Elites in the Post-War Period," *Canadian Review of Sociology and Anthropology,* 23, no. 4:481-506.

Horowitz, Gad
  1966 "Conservatism, Liberalism, and Socialism in Canada: An Interpretation," *Canadian Journal of Economics and Political Science,* 32, no. 2.

Kopinak, Kathryn
  1985 "Women in Canadian Municipal Politics: Two Steps Forward, One Step Back," *Canadian Review of Sociology and Anthropology,* 22, no. 3:395-410.

McLeod, John T.
  1965 "Party Structure and Party Reform," in *The Prospect of Change: Proposals for Canada's Future,* ed. A. Rotstein. Toronto: McGraw-Hill.

Marchak, Pat
  1981 *Ideological Perspectives on Canada* (2nd ed.). Toronto: McGraw-Hill.

Marsh, Leonard
  1940 *Canadian In and Out of Work.* Oxford University Press.

Olsen, Dennis
  1980 *The State Elite.* Toronto: McClelland and Stewart.

Ogmundson, Rick
  1977 "A Social Profile of Members of the Manitoba Legislature 1950, 1960, 1970," *Journal of Canadian Studies,* 12, no. 4:79-84.

Pineo, Peter, John Porter, and Hugh McRoberts
  1977 "The 1971 Census and the Socioeconomic Classification of Occupations," *Canadian Review of Sociology and Anthropology,* 14, no. 1:91-102.

Porter, John
  1965 *The Vertical Mosaic.* Toronto: University of Toronto Press.

Presthus, Robert
  1973 *Elite Accommodation in Canadian Politics.* Cambridge: Cambridge University Press.

Smith, David E.
  1985 "The Federal Cabinet in Canadian Politics," in *Canadian Politics in the 1980s* (2nd ed.), ed. M. Whittington and G. Williams. Toronto: Methuen.

Ward, Norman
  1950 *The Canadian House of Commons: Representation.* Toronto: University of Toronto Press.

Weber, Max
  1946 "Politics as a Vocation," in *From Max Weber: Essays in Sociology,* ed. H. Gerth and C. Wright Mills. New York: Oxford University Press.

34. The Canadian State and Corporate Elites

John Fox and Michael Ornstein

Central to the theoretical debate about the capitalist state is the nature of the relationship between the state and the capitalist class. Aside from formal and informal communication between capitalists and state officials,

Revised from John Fox and Michael Ornstein, "The Canadian State and Corporate Elites in the Post-war Period," *Canadian Review of Sociology and Anthropology*, vol. 23, no. 4 (November 1986), pp. 481-506. Reprinted with permission. The research in this paper is based on data collected for the project on Canadian capital in the post-war period, directed by William Carroll and the authors of this paper and generously supported by the Social Sciences and Humanities Research Council of Canada. The authors wish to express their appreciation for research assistance to Mahbub Ahmed, Lucille Covelli, Ada Donnelly, Aloma Mendoza, Alejandro Rojas, Alex Roman, Greg Stockton, and Rod Wheeland. Peter Meiksins and two anonymous CRSA reviewers provided helpful comments on an early draft of this paper. The authors thank Marian Steggerda, Maureen Pereira, and Anita Citron for typing the manuscript of this paper.

this relationship is facilitated by career mobility between corporations and the state and by the involvement of corporate management in state institutions, including commissions, task forces, and the boards of state enterprises, universities, and hospitals. While we recognize the structuralist claim that the character of state institutions embodies the domination of capital and that this domination is not reducible to career mobility and organizational involvements, we believe that empirical analysis of these mechanisms has significant implications for understanding the state.

This paper examines the ties between capital and the state in Canada between 1946 and 1977. On the corporate side, we shall study the largest Canadian corporations, law firms, and securities dealers, and the major Canadian business policy organizations. State institutions studied include the federal and provincial cabinets, deputy ministers, the boards of the largest federal and provincial crown corporations, the governor general and lieutenant governors, the Senate, the highest courts, and the boards of major universities and hospitals. In each year of the study, all of the occupants of the designated positions were identified. Since many positions considered were full-time jobs and in certain cases there were legal restrictions on simultaneously holding some pairs of positions, our analysis includes capital to state links involving individuals who occupied corporate and state positions at different times.

THEORIES OF THE STATE AND PRIVATE CAPITAL

The most important empirical research on the links between capital and the state was created in the course of the long-running debate between pluralist and radical theorists of contemporary capitalism. While the pluralists characterized modern capitalist societies in terms of competition for power among a variety of social and political groups (for example, see Dahl, 1961; 1967), the radicals argued that however widespread the appearance of political conflict, some groups were almost always able to get their way (Mills, 1956; Domhoff, 1967; 1970; 1972; 1974; 1979). In most of the radical formulations, big business and the military establishment were seen as the dominant groups. The radicals also argued that the most powerful groups could prevent debate over fundamental issues which would change the balance of power from ever reaching the political arena (Merelman, 1968). Obviously the pluralists had a strong interest in finding relatively weak relationships between capital and the state since the existence of strong relationships would undermine their claims that no one group is politically predominant. Conversely, the radicals needed to show that these relationships were strong.

For the most part these radical critics of pluralism have not put forward a more complete alternative position and, while it is tempting to see the radical arguments as confirmation of a Marxist approach, no such interpretation is warranted. Although capitalist domination may be insured by capitalists' direct involvement in the state apparatus, Marx (1968) himself does not see bourgeois hegemony as *requiring* their direct participation.

Precisely how capitalist domination of the state is assured is the key point of dispute in the well-known debate between Ralph Miliband and Nicos Poulantzas. In his seminal *The State in Capitalist Society* (1969), Miliband draws attention to the participation of capitalists in government and to the patterns of social mobility that assure that state elites are drawn from the "upper and middle class" (p. 60). This position is commonly labeled "instrumentalist" (but, see Carnoy, 1984: 104ff) and is often caricatured as total business domination of the state. It is worth quoting Miliband's own, more modest claim: "Notwithstanding the substantial participation of businessmen in the business of the state, it is however true that they have never constituted, and do not constitute now, more than a relatively small minority of the state elite as a whole" (1969:59).

In debating Miliband in the *New Left Review* (Miliband, 1970; 1973; Poulantzas, 1969), Nicos Poulantzas sets out his "structuralist" position (also see Poulantzas, 1973). He emphasizes that the very structure of the state embodies the assumption of bourgeois rule and that the character and role of the state is thus not dependent on the class composition of the state elite.

Within Marxism, there is actually a much earlier and even stronger instrumentalist theory of the state. In the various versions of "state monopoly capitalist" theory, as formulated by sections of the Third International, state monopoly capitalism is usually treated as a distinct stage of capitalism characterized by the fusion of monopoly forces with the bourgeois state to form a single mechanism of economic exploitation and political domination (Jessop, 1982:32).

Of course, this perspective also suggests that we should observe strong connections between capital and the state.

Although Miliband and Poulantzas were central in initiating far more intensive analysis of the capitalist state, important aspects of *both* their positions have achieved a general acceptance. Contemporary Marxist theorists address a series of questions that transcend the instrumentalist-structuralist dichotomy. In particular, Marxists have sought to specify what it is about the structure of state apparatuses that is inherently capitalist, to understand how the relatively "unpolitical" class of capitalists comes to adopt a coherent position on issues transcending individual capitalists' interests, to develop an understanding of ideology beyond the idea of its reflecting the self-evident interest of a class, and to demonstrate precisely how policy is made in a capitalist state faced with conflicting class interests (Laclau, 1975; Jessop, 1977; 1982; Block, 1977; Offe, 1984).

Canadian Marxists have tended to characterize the relationship between the state and capital in instrumentalist terms. Leo Panitch's argument is typical:

We . . . immediately note a particularly striking characteristic of the Canadian state—its very close personal ties to the bourgeoisie. Whatever the merits of Poulantzas' contention that the most efficient state is that with the least direct ties to the dominant class, it is rather an academic point as applied to Canada . . . John Porter's demonstration of the degree of co-optation from business to government and exit from cabinet to business makes the very concept of an autonomous political elite in Canada a highly tenuous one. . . . (1977:11-12)

We believe that the evidence used to support an instrumentalist approach is misleading. First, two examples often cited to support state connections to capital are not necessarily relevant to analysis of the contemporary Canadian state. Nineteenth- and early twentieth-century railway promoters' successes in gaining state financing and land grants do not offer a model for current relationships between capital and the state. (See Naylor, 1972; Clement, 1975; Myers, 1914; Macdonald, 1975; McNally, 1981.) Similarly, the recruitment of prominent capitalists to the wartime federal bureaucracy is not an appropriate model for the present-day civil service. (Granatstein, 1982).

A second major problem in much of the work on business-state relations is the failure to distinguish recruitment of businessmen into state positions from movement in the opposite direction, which confuses processes with two very different implications. High levels of business recruitment of former politicians and bureaucrats by no means signify corporate domination of the state. Clement's (1975:46) argument for increasing interpenetration is based only on movement from state elites into corporate positions. Olsen (1980:129) shows that there is *no* change in the proportion of state elites from elite backgrounds (comparing his data from 1961-73 to Porter's data for 1940-60); he finds that 15.1 percent of state elites had a "previous elite in family" and an additional 22.4 percent came from families including the "owners of substantial businesses, judges and prominent members of the bar, [and] directors of large but not dominant corporations." Porter's corresponding figures were 16.4 percent and 24.0 percent.

By advancing these criticisms we do not intend to take the structuralist position in the debate with instrumentalism, nor to argue that capital has no influence on the Canadian state. We simply want to argue that the policies of the Canadian state reflect its role as a capitalist state, not a peculiarly Canadian instrumentalism. The mechanisms producing state policies friendly to capital reflect the structure of the state and the implicit threat of an "investment strike by capital." Still there is a great deal more conflict and instability in the system than is easily explained by instrumentalism. How, for example, are we to account for the former Liberal government's National Energy Policy which, even after some modification under pressure from the oil and gas industry, clearly represented the preference of *no* significant fraction of Canadian capital (Watkins, 1983)?

Our own expectation in approaching these data falls somewhere in the middle of the theoretical positions already discussed. The complete or even majority domination of state institutions by corporate elites entails serious drawbacks to effective government. The transparency of its domination by capital would make such a state an easy target of political attack and would hinder attempts at legitimation. Business-dominated institutions would face difficulties in formulating public policies with the necessary minimum of co-optation to avoid the buildup of massive opposition from workers and their organizations. A cabinet made up entirely or mostly of businessmen would have difficulty in reconciling conflicts within a capitalist class disunited by sectoral differences in their vulnerability to import competition, need for external markets, and rates of pay. More independent state managers can better reach effective compromises among conflicting capitalist groups and formulate policies that successfully accommodate the demands of workers and independent commodity producers.

We do not claim that the personnel of the capitalist state are recruited entirely from outside the ranks of big capital or that complete independence of the state would be optimal for capital. A limited but direct representation of bourgeois interests in the state gives capital an effective voice and provides for liaison between capital and the state. So long as business interests are a minority within the highest councils of the state, the business presence can be defended against political attack.

In principle, a state without ties to its capitalist class could serve the interests of that class, just as corporations could function without a network of directorate interlocks linking boards and executives. Nevertheless, the presence of the interlocks and the representation of capital within the state both serve the interests of capital. That is precisely why ties between capital and the state exist in practice, even if they are not necessary in theory.

DATA AND METHODS

Our data collection was based upon samples of *organizations* in the different institutional sectors. Names and periods of service of the executives and directors of the selected organizations, as appropriate to the particular type of organization, were recorded. In some cases the way to proceed was obvious (for example, listing the members of the federal cabinet is not problematic), but in other cases we had to make judgments about which organizations to select under the constraint of limited financial resources. For the corporations, universities, and hospitals it was necessary to decide where, along a continuum of influence and size, to divide the organizations included from those not included in the sample. That problem is further complicated by the longitudinal character of the study, since some of the organizations selected at one time might not have been included in the sample had it been selected at another time.

Due to changes in the sizes of corporations over time, numerous mergers, lack of consistent and easily accessible financial data for the early years of the study, and the need to compare corporations for which the appropriate measures of size were not the same, selecting the sample of corporations posed the most difficult problem. For the industrial corporations (including manufacturing, transportation and utilities, and resource extraction) rankings by assets were assembled at five-year intervals beginning in 1946. Any corporation ever among the largest 70 was included in the sample. Similarly, any corporation ever ranking among the largest 20 in the financial sector or among the largest 10 in the commercial sector was included in the sample, except that in the first year's ranking fewer than 10 firms existed in magnitude comparable to the largest commercial firms (e.g., Eaton's and The Hudson's Bay Company). Because there was no property development corporation of significant size at the beginning of the postwar period, corporations from this sector were only added in the last years of the study, using a cutoff point of assets equal to the smallest industrial firm in the sample. Because their assets are relatively small compared to their overall influence (exercised by means of major, often controlling, blocks of stock in other firms), selected holding companies were added to the sample (cf. Carroll, 1981). Twenty-six law firms, which were selected on the basis of two or more partners in the "economic elites" defined by Porter (1965:277ff) or Clement (1975: 187ff), were also added to the sample as were nine securities dealers, which were selected on the basis of their being mentioned by Neufeld (1964) and Park and Park (1962).

For the corporate sector, the sample of individuals included board members of the selected corporation and all partners of the selected law and securities firms between 1946 and 1977. In our discussion below, "executives" were board members who held an executive position in the same corporation at some time in the period covered by the study; these executives are often termed "inside directors." Executives who were not board members were excluded from the study. Because the securities dealers and law firms operated as partnerships, the distinction between executives and directors did not apply to them.

The state organizations in this study included several federal and provincial government institutions, and major universities and hospitals. At the federal level, the cabinet, all deputy ministers, major crown corporations, Royal Commissions in the period of study, the Senate, the senior courts, and the governor general were included in the study. At the provincial level, the cabinets, deputy ministers, major crown corporations, and lieutenant governors of all the provinces were included. The universities were ranked by size, and board members of the 20 largest were included in the study; similarly, the 15 largest hospitals were included. Although a number of the universities and hospitals were "private" rather than governmental institutions, they were included in the state sector because of their dependency on state financing and regulation.

In order to measure the impact of business interest groups, we included two categories of organizations. One contained only the Canadian Chamber of Commerce and the Canadian Manufacturers Association, the two most important traditional business interest groups. The other category included seven more recently prominent policy-planning organizations: the Conference Board of Canada, the C. D. Howe Research Institute, the Canadian-American Committee, the Canadian Economic Policy Committee, the Institute for Research on Public Policy, the Business Council on National Issues, the Ontario Research Foundation, and the Fraser Institute.

The data base includes a total of about 23 000 mentions, though of course the number of different individuals is smaller because of overlapping memberships.

In our analysis we examine interlocking between the corporate and state organizations to discover the existence of links between pairs of organizations, whether the result of simultaneous position holding or mobility between them. This analysis fits into an emerging tradition of research on social networks, which is most developed in the area of interlocking between corporate boards. Of course two organizations are said to be linked even if only one person provides a link between two boards each including 30 or more individuals. We focus on whether there is *any* connection, rather than on the strength of the connections between the pairs of organizations.

OVERLAPPING MEMBERSHIPS BETWEEN PUBLIC AND PRIVATE ORGANIZATIONS

Table 34-1 presents the frequencies and densities of intersectoral ties for several categories of state and private institutions. The ties recorded in this table pertain to unique pairs of organizations, and any such pair can contribute at most one tie to the recorded count. For example, a federal crown corporation and a bank that shared more than one director contribute only one to the count of ties between the federal-crown-corporation and financial sectors in the table. Along with contemporaneous ties, Table

34-1 includes ties established over time. The reader should understand that by virtue of holding positions in three or more organizations at one time or moving among several organizations in the course of his or her career, a single individual can be responsible for creating many tied pairs.

The density figures in Table 34-1 were calculated by dividing the number of tied organizations by the potential number of such ties for each pair of institutional sectors. Thus, for instance, the 19 federal crown corporations and 34 financial firms could give rise to at most 19 times 34 or 646 tied pairs of organizations; of these, 166 tied pairs were in fact observed, yielding a density of ties of 166/646 or 257 per 1000, as recorded in the table.

Overall, more than 3300 ties connect the 148 state organizations and 302 private organizations entered in Table 34-1, representing a general density of ties between the state and capitalist sectors of 7.5 percent. All of the categories of private organizations are tied to substantial numbers of state organizations; the ties maintained by capitalist firms are particularly noteworthy, especially those for the manufacturing and financial sectors. Particularly large densities are observed for the financial firms. These findings fit in well with the evidence showing that financial institutions have very large boards and numerous interlocks with other corporations (see Carroll, 1982; Carroll, Fox, and Ornstein, 1981; and Ornstein, 1976) and are generally conceived as occupying a central position in capital. The major business interest groups—the CMA and CCC, and the policy-planning organizations—are also densely linked to the state, which seems appropriate to their mission of assuring state policies that support the accumulation process.

The extent to which specific state sectors

TABLE 34-1 Number and density (per thousand) of tied pairs of organizations between types of public and private organizations, 1946-1976.

State organizations	Corporate organizations												
	Mining	Manu-facturing	Utility	Finance	Invest-ment	Commerce	Property	Securities	Law	CMA & CCC	Policy	Total	Number of organizations
Federal Cabinet	8 (216)	37 (381)	7 (189)	16 (471)	8 (500)	2 (87)	1 (91)	1 (83)	7 (269)	1 (500)	5 (714)	93 (308)	1
Federal bureaucracy	3 (81)	25 (258)	5 (135)	11 (324)	3 (188)	2 (87)	0 (0)	1 (83)	5 (192)	1 (500)	5 (714)	61 (202)	1
Federal Crown Corporation	64 (91)	221 (120)	86 (122)	166 (257)	46 (151)	36 (82)	14 (67)	14 (61)	26 (53)	16 (421)	58 (436)	747 (130)	19
Royal Commission	20 (13)	62 (16)	26 (17)	74 (53)	16 (24)	7 (7)	1 (2)	7 (14)	6 (6)	5 (61)	33 (115)	257 (21)	41
Senate	7 (189)	39 (402)	11 (297)	23 (676)	4 (250)	4 (174)	2 (182)	1 (83)	6 (231)	2 (1000)	4 (571)	103 (341)	1
Courts	0 (0)	2 (10)	3 (41)	5 (74)	0 (0)	0 (0)	0 (0)	0 (0)	6 (115)	0 (0)	0 (0)	16 (26)	2
Governor General	0 (0)	1 (10)	0 (0)	2 (59)	0 (0)	0 (0)	0 (0)	1 (83)	0 (0)	0 (0)	0 (0)	4 (13)	1
Provincial Cabinet	7 (19)	23 (24)	11 (30)	25 (74)	3 (19)	1 (4)	1 (9)	1 (8)	5 (19)	1 (50)	6 (86)	84 (28)	10
Provincial bureaucracy	4 (11)	13 (13)	4 (11)	2 (6)	1 (6)	3 (13)	3 (27)	3 (25)	3 (12)	0 (0)	3 (43)	39 (13)	10
Provincial Crown Corporation	9 (14)	66 (40)	34 (54)	43 (74)	10 (37)	7 (18)	6 (32)	4 (20)	7 (16)	10 (294)	17 (143)	213 (41)	17
Lieutenant Governor	0 (0)	10 (10)	4 (11)	20 (59)	2 (13)	0 (0)	0 (0)	0 (0)	1 (4)	3 (150)	3 (43)	43 (14)	10
University	96 (130)	359 (185)	137 (185)	245 (360)	59 (184)	42 (91)	21 (95)	24 (100)	33 (63)	24 (600)	66 (471)	1 106 (183)	20
Hospital	45 (81)	189 (130)	71 (128)	117 (229)	31 (129)	27 (78)	11 (67)	20 (111)	13 (33)	10 (333)	30 (286)	564 (125)	15
Total	263 (48)	1 047 (73)	399 (73)	749 (149)	183 (77)	131 (38)	60 (37)	77 (43)	118 (31)	73 (247)	230 (222)	3 330 (75)	148
Number of organizations	37	97	37	34	16	23	11	12	26	2	7	302	

Note: First number listed indicates frequency; number in parentheses indicates density.

are tied to private organizations is much more uneven, both as regards the frequencies of ties and their densities. The universities and hospitals maintain many and dense ties with capitalist institutions. In general the federal government is much more strongly linked to big capital than are the provincial governments. Ties between crown corporations and the private sector are especially numerous, while the ties linking the federal cabinet and the Senate to the private sector are particularly dense: the Senate and cabinet are each tied to more than 30 percent of the private organizations included in our study.

Note also that the federal and provincial cabinets are much more strongly linked to capital than are the corresponding bureaucracies: the densities are one-and-one-half to two times greater for the politicians. The implication is that pressure from business is more likely to flow from the cabinet to the bureaucracy, rather than the reverse. This finding lends support, as well, to the idea that liberal policies (such as economic nationalism) have bases of support in the bureaucracy and that business pressure on the cabinet accounts for the erratic history of actual legislation.

Table 34-2, which gives the frequency and density of ties among the private organizations themselves, provides a point of comparison for the data of Table 34-1. In general, ties within the private sector are considerably more prevalent than those between the private and public sectors. In total there are nearly 7600 tied pairs among the 302 private organizations, which represents a density of 16.7 percent, more than double the density of state-to-capital ties (7.5 percent). Particularly large numbers of ties are maintained by the industrial and financial firms, and the density of ties for the latter is nearly double the overall figure. The business interest groups also maintain notably

dense ties with the other private organizations. The general conclusion that emerges from a comparison of Tables 34-1 and 34-2 is that, while the level of integration between the public and the private sectors is lower than that within the private sector itself, intersectoral ties are far from negligible.

Table 34-3 shows how the pattern of ties between categories of public and private organizations changed during the years from 1946 to 1976. This table records frequencies of tied pairs occurring in each of three slightly overlapping 11-year periods: 1946-56, 1956-66, and 1966-76. To avoid awkwardness, we at times refer to these periods as "decades." As in Table 34-1, ties created over time, here within a decade, are combined with contemporaneous ties existing during the same period.

It is apparent from Table 34-3 that the number of ties between public and private organizations increases dramatically from decade to decade: the totals for the decades are 871, 1617, and 1808 ties. This increase is only partly due to the rise in the number of organizations over the time period under study, for the corresponding densities for the three decades (3.2 percent, 4.6 percent, and 6.0 percent, as calculated from Table 34-3) show a similar pattern of change.

Among private organizations, increasing numbers of ties are especially evident for the property-development and policy-planning organizations, whose representation in our study grows over time. Less striking but still noteworthy gains are posted by the mining, investment, and securities categories.

Between 1956-66 and 1966-76 there is a general growth in the numbers of ties linking private organizations to the provincial public sector and to the federal cabinet and bureaucracy. For the cabinet only, this growth between the first and second decades of the study is followed by a dramatic decline in the third decade.

TABLE 34-2 Number and density of tied pairs of organizations between types of private organizations, 1946-1976.

	Corporate organizations											
	Mining	Manu- facturing	Utility	Finance	Invest- ment	Commerce	Property	Securities	Law	CMA & CCC	Policy	Total
Mining	88 (132)											
Manufacturing	422 (118)	834 (179)										
Utility	151 (110)	585 (163)	135 (203)									
Finance	336 (267)	1 074 (326)	432 (343)	264 (471)								
Investment	92 (155)	301 (194)	88 (149)	198 (364)	20 (167)							
Commerce	54 (63)	199 (89)	65 (76)	168 (215)	38 (103)	19 (75)						
Property	28 (69)	72 (67)	31 (76)	66 (176)	17 (97)	22 (87)	5 (91)					
Securities	38 (86)	94 (81)	40 (90)	49 (120)	18 (94)	20 (72)	16 (121)	13 (500)				
Law	53 (55)	140 (56)	51 (53)	113 (128)	22 (53)	24 (40)	24 (84)	4 (13)	32 (98)			
CMA & CCC	19 (257)	108 (557)	34 (459)	53 (779)	9 (281)	9 (196)	1 (45)	5 (208)	5 (96)	1 (1 000)		
Policy	88 (340)	304 (448)	86 (332)	137 (576)	47 (420)	28 (174)	24 (312)	13 (155)	18 (99)	12 (857)	17 (810)	
Total	1 369 (131)	4 133 (168)	1 698 (162)	2 890 (299)	850 (181)	646 (97)	306 (94)	330 (93)	486 (65)	256 (426)	774 (371)	7 593 (167)
Number of organizations	37	97	37	34	16	23	11	12	26	2	7	302

Note: First number indicates frequency; number in parentheses indicates density.

TABLE 34-3 Number of tied pairs of organizations between types of public and private organizations, by period, 1946-76.

Public organization	Period	Mining	Manu-facturing	Utility	Finance	Invest-ment	Commerce	Property	Securities	Law	CMA & CCC	Policy	Total	Number of organizations
Federal Cabinet	46-56	0	2	0	4	1	0	0	0	2	0	0	9	1
	56-66	5	23	4	14	7	0	0	0	3	0	3	59	1
	66-76	2	8	3	2	3	1	1	1	1	0	4	26	1
Federal bureaucracy	46-56	0	2	0	1	1	0	0	0	0	0	0	4	1
	56-66	0	0	1	2	0	0	0	0	2	0	1	6	1
	66-76	0	6	2	1	0	1	0	1	2	0	2	15	1
Federal Crown Corporation	46-56	7	48	31	43	9	11	2	3	3	4	4	165	17
	56-66	14	72	33	80	14	10	0	3	6	3	18	253	17
	66-76	33	120	39	79	25	18	13	5	20	5	35	392	19
Royal Commission	46-56	3	6	7	15	3	1	0	2	3	1	0	41	20
	56-66	7	24	11	41	9	3	0	2	2	3	18	120	24
	66-76	4	11	1	11	1	1	1	1	0	0	6	37	5
Senate	46-56	2	19	7	15	1	1	0	0	4	2	0	51	1
	56-66	5	24	8	20	4	2	0	0	3	2	3	71	1
	66-76	3	22	6	14	2	3	3	0	5	0	4	62	1
Court	46-56	0	0	0	0	0	0	0	0	1	0	0	1	2
	56-66	0	0	1	3	0	0	0	0	2	0	0	6	2
	66-76	0	2	0	1	0	0	0	0	1	0	0	4	2
Governor General	46-56	0	1	0	1	0	0	0	0	0	0	0	2	1
	56-66	0	0	0	2	0	0	0	0	0	0	0	2	1
	66-76	0	0	0	0	0	0	0	1	0	0	0	1	1
Provincial Cabinet	46-56	0	4	4	5	0	0	0	0	2	0	0	15	10
	56-66	0	2	2	6	1	0	0	0	1	1	2	15	10
	66-76	5	17	5	13	2	0	1	1	3	0	4	51	10
Provincial bureaucracy	46-56	0	1	2	0	0	1	0	0	1	0	0	5	10
	56-66	1	1	2	0	0	0	0	0	1	0	0	5	10
	66-76	2	7	0	2	1	0	2	3	1	0	2	20	10

Provincial Crown Corporation													
46-56	2	4	6	5	2	1	0	0	3	1	0	24	10
56-66	0	9	7	11	1	3	0	0	2	3	3	39	14
66-76	5	52	16	28	6	5	6	3	3	5	14	143	17
Lieutenant Governor													
46-56	0	5	3	7	1	0	0	0	0	0	0	16	10
56-66	0	2	1	10	0	0	0	0	—	0	0	14	10
66-76	0	2	0	3	1	0	0	0	1	2	2	11	10
University													
46-56	18	113	34	85	11	14	2	2	12	11	3	305	14
56-66	49	236	83	167	42	23	7	9	14	16	37	683	20
66-76	56	236	80	165	36	28	12	16	21	13	56	719	20
Hospital													
46-56	16	82	33	64	6	9	1	8	6	6	2	233	14
56-66	23	127	50	75	16	16	4	12	2	7	12	344	14
66-76	26	110	33	70	19	18	7	9	7	5	23	327	15
Total													
46-56	48	287	127	245	35	38	5	15	37	25	9	871	111
56-66	104	520	203	431	94	57	11	26	39	35	97	1 617	125
66-76	136	593	185	389	96	75	46	41	65	30	152	1 808	112
Number of organizations													
46-56	28	82	32	32	10	17	2	12	26	2	1	244	
55-66	34	93	33	32	16	22	6	12	26	2	4	280	
66-76	30	91	27	28	14	20	11	12	26	2	7	268	

DISCUSSION AND CONCLUSIONS

There are very substantial links between the state and corporations in Canada. The data on densities of ties demonstrate the pervasiveness of movement from the state to the corporate sector, from corporations to the state, and concurrent membership. Furthermore, there is evidence that the frequency of these interlocks is increasing. The state organizations may be arranged along a continuum of interlocking beginning with the densest ties to universities and hospitals, followed by the federal crown corporations and Royal Commissions, then the provincial crown corporations, the Senate, federal and provincial cabinets; the lowest levels of ties are found for the federal and provincial bureaucracies, the courts, and the governor general and lieutenant governors. Notwithstanding the example of the wartime federal bureaucracy, these data suggest that corporate input into the governmental decision-making is much more likely to occur at the political than the bureaucratic level.

The data demonstrate nothing like a fusion of capital and the state. A comparison of ties between capital and the state with the interfirm links provided by interlocking directorships shows the latter to be more dense by a factor of about two, and exclusion of the hospitals and universities raises the ratio to more than three to one.

There are some obstacles to interpreting our results. Although the radical, instrumentalist Marxist, and state monopoly capital theories lead to predictions of higher levels of mobility and interlocking between capital and the state than the pluralist and structuralist Marxist theories do, no precise boundary between the two groups of theories can be established. Furthermore, while structuralist Marxism directs our attention to factors other than these mechanisms in explaining the character of the state, the existence of moderately high levels of mobility and interlocking is quite compatible with this theoretical approach. And, similarly, only a caricature of the radical, instrumentalist, and state monopoly capital theories would see them as requiring the total domination of state institutions by business.

Whatever its inherent properties as a capitalist state, there is strong evidence of a corporate presence in the state to provide for effective liaison with, though not control by, capital. Even accounting for the Senate as a virtual repository of corporate directors, the links between corporations and the state are not strong enough to permit control by capital. The levels of interlocking within the business community (some of which reflects intercorporate control) are very much greater than the levels of capital-state links. Furthermore, the predominance of mobility *from* state organizations *to* capital suggests corporate efforts to understand and influence a state not under corporate domination. The level of interlocking shown here combines effective communication with sufficient state independence to maintain policy-making processes in touch with what the public will tolerate in the way of direct corporate influence.

Our results do not appear compatible with Panitch's contention that "the very concept of an autonomous [state] elite in Canada is a very tenuous one." In arguing, against the strong instrumentalist theme, we do not intend to suggest that the state is autonomous. The systematic and pervasive connections between the state and corporations are strong evidence against pluralist notions of the state acting as arbiter among contending interest groups. The results support our argument that the Canadian state should be viewed as having a combination of the characteristics ascribed to it by instrumentalism *and* structuralist theory. Miliband's (1983:65) most recent formulation seems appropriate:

> In short, an accurate and realistic "model" of the relationship between the dominant class in advanced capitalist societies and the state is one of *partnership between two different, separate forces,* linked to each other by many threads, yet each having its own separate sphere of concerns [emphasis in original].

REFERENCES

Block, Fred
  1977   "The ruling class does not rule: Notes on the Marxist theory of the state," *Socialist Revolution,* 7, no. 3:6-28.

Carnoy, Martin
  1984   *The State and Political Theory.* Princeton: Princeton University Press.

Carroll, William
  1981   "Capital accumulation and corporate interlocking in post-war Canada." Unpublished doctoral dissertation. York University.
  1982   "The Canadian corporate elite: Financiers or finance capitalists." *Studies in Political Economy,* 8:89-114.

Carroll, William K., John Fox, and Michael Ornstein
    1981   "The network of directorate interlocks among the largest Canadian firms,"
               Canadian Review of Sociology and Anthropology, 19:44-69.

Clement, Wallace
    1975   *The Canadian Corporate Elite: An Analysis of Economic Power.* Toronto: Mc-
               Clelland and Stewart.

Dahl, Robert
    1961   *Who Governs?* New Haven: Yale University Press.
    1967 ·   *Pluralist Democracy in the United States.* Chicago: Rand McNally.

Domhoff, G. William
    1967   *Who Rules America?* New York: Prentice-Hall.
    1970   *The Higher Circles.* New York: Random House.
    1972   *Fat Cats and Democrats.* Englewood Cliffs, N.J.: Prentice-Hall.
    1974   *The Bohemian Grove and Other Retreats.* New York: Harper and Row.
    1979   *The Powers That Be.* New York: Random House.

Granatstein, Jack L.
    1982   *The Ottawa Men: The Civil Service Mandarins, 1935-1957.* Toronto: Oxford
               University Press.

Jessop, Bob
    1977   "Recent theories of the capitalist state," *Cambridge Journal of Economics,*
               1:353-73.
    1982   *Theories of the State.* New York: New York University Press.

Laclau, Ernesto
    1975   "The specificity of the political: the Poulantzas-Miliband debate," *Economy*
               and Society, 4:87-110.

Macdonald, L. R.
    1975   "Merchants against industry: An idea and its origins," *Canadian Historical*
               Review, 56:263-81.

Marx, Karl
    1968   "The Eighteenth Brumaire of Louis Bonaparte," in *Karl Marx and Frederick*
               Engels, Selected Works in One Volume, pp. 95-180. New York: International
               Publishers.
    1976   *Capital, Vol. 1.* London: Penguin.

McNally, David
    1981   "State theory as commodity fetishism: Marx, Innis and Canadian political
               economy," *Studies in Political Economy,* 6:35-63.

Merelman, Richard M.
    1968   "On the neo-elitist critique of community power," *American Political Science*
               Review, 62:451-60.

Miliband, Ralph
    1969   *The State in Capitalist Society.* London: Weidenfeld and Nicolson.
    1970   "Reply to Nicos Poulantzas," *New Left Review,* 59:53-60.
    1973   "Poulantzas and the capitalist state," *New Left Review,* 82:83-93.
    1983   "State power and class interests," *New Left Review,* 138:57-68.

Mills, C. Wright
    1956   *The Power Elite.* New York: Oxford University Press.

Myers, Gustavus
    1914   *History of Canadian Wealth,* Vol. 1. Chicago: Charles H. Kerr.

Naylor, Tom
    1972   "The rise and fall of the third empire of the St. Lawrence," in *Capitalism and the National Question in Canada,* ed. Gary Teeple, pp. 1-41. Toronto: University of Toronto Press.
    1975   *The History of Canadian Business 1867-1914.* Toronto: Lorimer.

Neufeld, Edward P., ed.
    1964   *Money and Banking in Canada: Historical Documents and Commentary.* Toronto: McClelland and Stewart.

Offe, Claus
    1984   *Contradictions of the Welfare State.* Cambridge, Mass.: MIT Press.

Olsen, Dennis
    1980   *The State Elite.* Toronto: McClelland and Stewart.

Ornstein, Michael
    1976   "The boards and executives of the largest Canadian corporations: Size, composition, and interlocks," *Canadian Journal of Sociology,* 1:411-37.

Panitch, Leo
    1977   "The Role and Nature of the Canadian State," in *The Canadian State: Political Economy and Political Power,* ed. Leo Panitch, pp. 3-27. Toronto: University of Toronto Press.

Park, Libbie, and Frank Park
    1962   *Anatomy of Big Business.* Toronto: Progress.

Porter, John
    1965   *The Vertical Mosaic.* Toronto: University of Toronto Press.

Poulantzas, Nicos
    1969   "Problems of the capitalist state," *New Left Review,* 58:67-78.
    1973   *Political Power and Social Classes.* London: New Left Books.

Watkins, Mel
    1983   "The NEP and the left: A commentary on Sher and others," *Socialist Studies* (annual):151-57.

35. Government Policy and Economic Crisis

John Calvert

The most widely discussed view of the causes of Canada's current economic mess is that government policies, and particularly government spending, are to blame. According to this view (whose leading proponent is the conservative American economist Milton Friedman), government has become a millstone on the economy, crushing its ability to operate efficiently (cf. Friedman, 1962; Friedman and Friedman, 1981). The state sector has absorbed too large a share of gross national expenditure. It has choked off business investment and displaced productive private manufacturing from key areas of the economy.

Supporters of this view assert that government taxation has diverted vital investment capital into non-productive service activities. This, in turn, has denied industry the

Revised from John Calvert, *Government Limited: The Corporate Takeover of the Public Sector in Canada* (Ottawa: Canadian Centre for Policy Alternatives, 1984), pp. 11–32. Reprinted with permission.

finances required to modernize in an increasingly competitive international environment.

Government has also been fingered for generating inflation by allowing the money supply to expand too quickly. This is because it has failed to trim spending programs to bring them into line with tax revenues. Instead, it has simply printed more money and increased its borrowing. As a result the money supply has grown excessively, while government debt has skyrocketed. These policies have, in turn, fuelled inflation.

Proponents of the business explanation for our current economic ills also assert that government has established a whole range of "non-productive" social services which we can no longer afford. They argue that these services absorb too much of the nation's resources—both human and material—and place an excessive tax burden on the "productive" private sector. According to this view, the private sector is the engine of economic development and, ultimately, pays for all public services. Thus, if the private sector is squeezed too much, it cannot produce enough to support social services, while still generating the investment capital it requires to survive and grow.

The corporate sector has criticized government for allowing the wages and fringe benefits of public employees to rise too quickly, making the costs of government services excessive. It asserts that wages in the public sector have established an inflationary precedent for private sector workers. As a result, so-called "wage-push" inflation has been on the increase, fuelled by the "unrealistic" demands of overpaid public sector workers.

Government has also been attacked for imposing too many regulations on the private sector. Business interests claim that by so doing it has deterred private firms from making new investments. Government regulations, according to this view, have added enormously to the costs of production and greatly weakened the ability of Canadian firms to compete successfully with their overseas rivals. Regulatory agencies such as the Foreign Investment Review Agency (FIRA) have deterred foreign investors from establishing or expanding in Canada, thus denying us needed economic growth and jobs. And, because they push up the costs of production, government regulations have also forced many Canadian firms to close down or to locate new factories in other countries.

THE BUSINESS REMEDY

Since the mid-1970s there have been increasingly strident demands by business organizations (such as the Canadian Chamber of Commerce and the Business Council on National Issues) that the public deficit be reduced, that spending on social programs

be curtailed and that the size of the public sector be dramatically cut (Beigie, 1980). There has been a call to privatize many services currently provided by government employees. There has been growing pressure to provide more financial assistance to corporations though tax expenditures and subsidies. And there has been vigorous lobbying to repeal many of the regulations that were imposed during the last two decades to protect consumers, workers, and the environment from the excesses of business.

The corporate sector has also been pushing hard to turn the clock back on the way government manages the economy. It has argued that the only way to improve Canada's economic performance is to give the market scope to operate more freely. The corporate sector has demanded an end to the social welfare aspects of Keynesian economic policies, and has pressed vigorously for more government support for business.

The business community has also lobbied for wage controls, especially in the public sector, as a way of cutting labour costs. It has demanded that unions be weakened by taking away their right to strike, and that even more limits and restrictions be placed on collective bargaining.

In short, the corporate solution to our economic malaise is to lower the standard of living of all working Canadians. Workers are blamed for living beyond the country's means and for demanding an unrealistically high level of public services.

IMPLEMENTATION OF THE BUSINESS REMEDY

The plan favoured by the corporate sector has been adopted at the federal level by both the Liberals and Conservatives and by the overwhelming majority of provincial governments. As early as 1975 the federal Liberals had discarded Keynesian policies, which they had followed with varying degrees of commitment during the 1960s and early 1970s. The expansion of social programs was halted. Instead, the goal of economic policy became one of restraining government spending and containing inflation. National income was to be redistributed from wages to corporate profits to provide business with the investment capital it required to rebuild the economy.

New spending restrictions and public sector wage guidelines at provincial and federal levels were established. Collective bargaining in the federal public sector was attacked through the introduction of new bargaining constraints. Back-to-work legislation was resorted to more and more frequently to undermine the effectiveness of public sector strikes and force down public sector wage settlements. Between October 1981 and October 1983 there were 17 separate pieces of legislation attacking public sector workers. More recently federal and provincial governments have used public sector wage controls and outright rollbacks of negotiated wage increases, as in Quebec, British Columbia, and Ontario.

The attack on workers' incomes and the collective bargaining process was only one aspect of the adoption of restraint policies. Another was the reduction of funding for social and educational programs. In 1977 the federal Liberals renegotiated their cost-sharing programs with the provincial governments to limit their financial obligations to fund medicare, post-secondary education, and social services. This decision was a major step toward dismantling the welfare state.

In terms of wider economic policy, the federal Liberals allowed unemployment to rise as a way of dampening consumer demand, in the hope that this would slow the rate of growth of price increases. Simultaneously, the Bank of Canada was allowed to tighten the money supply and raise interest rates.

The short-lived Conservative government of Joe Clark (1979-80) was even more committed to implementing major cutbacks in public and social spending. One of the party's main campaign platforms was "privatization." The proposal of Finance Minister John Crosbie to sell off Petrocan, when combined with the huge price increases granted to the oil companies in the first budget, proved to be the undoing of the Clark government. The corporations had tried to grab too much, too quickly, for the Canadian public to accept.

The return of the Liberals in 1980 did not spell an end to the campaign to dismantle public and social services. While they had been elected on a platform that opposed Clark's policies, they quickly reverted to the restraint policies adopted in the mid-1970s. After the election it became increasingly clear that they still accepted the corporate view that the government's role in the economy should diminish over time.

The federal government's intention to shift resources away from social and public services and toward greater support for corporate interests was restated in the November 1981 budget. Social affairs spending over the next five years was to be kept significantly below the rate of growth of government expenditures. And these expenditures, in turn, were to be kept below the growth of the economy as a whole.

The 1981 budget also lowered the tax rates paid by the highest income groups from 62 percent to 50 percent, expanded the funding available to private corporations under the guise of "economic development," and imposed new taxes on such employee benefits as extended health care plans and dental plans (the latter were eventually dropped) (Calvert, 1982).

The June 1982 budget went even further in its attempt to placate corporate demands. The end result was that the level of income tax paid by wage and salary earners increased at precisely the same time that the social services they used were decreased.

In contrast, the same budget gave investors major tax breaks. At the time it was estimated by the Department of Finance that these tax breaks would shift $875 million from government to investors in 1983, and over $2.8 billion in 1984.

The April 1983 budget provided new tax incentives, subsidies, and public capital spending projects. Business was given $905 million in tax cuts in 1983-84 and $955 million in 1984-85. It also received a $270-million boost for private sector research and development over a four-year period. And $2.2 billion in public investment was approved specifically to shore up the economic infrastructure needed by business to operate profitably in the future.

At the same time new (and more regressive) taxes were imposed on working Canadians. Virtually nothing was done to create jobs for the 1.5 million officially unemployed. And further cuts in social programs and transfers to the provinces were earmarked in the long-term budget forecast.

At the provincial level in 1983, the same pattern of economic policies was also seen. Taxation became more regressive, and social programs were cut back. Wage controls, and in some provinces wage rollbacks, were imposed. Incentives for business were increased, while corporate taxation was reduced or eliminated. In short, the federal and provincial governments have been implementing the business "solution" to our economic malaise for almost a decade. Yet the economic crisis shows no signs of abating.

Thus the question remains: Why is Canada's economy still in a mess? What are the real sources of our economic malaise? The answers to these questions are essential if we are to understand how we got into the present mess and what we must do to get out of it.

IS THE CORPORATE DIAGNOSIS OF OUR ECONOMIC MALAISE SOUND?

It is highly questionable whether the reasons for our present economic woes are to be found in the government sector. A more critical analysis suggests that the crisis flows from the contradictions inherent in the free enterprise, or capitalist, system itself.

This view gains support when we look at what is happening internationally, when we study the fluctuations in the business cycle over the past hundred years, and when we examine, in greater detail, the actual policies followed by the Canadian government during the last two decades.

At the international level, it is clear that all the major industrialized countries are experiencing the same kinds of economic problems. The list includes Japan, West Germany, Great Britain, France, Italy, Sweden, Belgium, Holland, Denmark, and the United States. None of the governments concerned, whether social democratic (as in Sweden and France), or conservative (as in Britain and the U.S.), has found a ready-made solution to these serious economic difficulties (Sweezy, 1978). This suggests that the problem is not simply caused by the growth of the public sector in Canada, but is related to the wider international economic system.

It might be argued that Canada's problems are particularly serious because government in Canada absorbs a higher share of GNP than its counterparts elsewhere. Indeed, as suggested earlier, business interests do assert that the relatively large role played by the government in the economy is responsible for Canada's economic crisis.

Yet the size of the public sector in Canada is smaller than that of most other western industrialized countries. For example, the size of the government sector in Canada in 1981 was *less* than the average of the 13 countries belonging to OECD, the Organization for Economic Co-operation and Development. Only Australia, Japan, and the U.S. had smaller government sectors. Austria, Denmark, France, Germany, Italy, the Netherlands, Norway, Sweden, and the United Kingdom all had larger public sectors.

The present world recession has not singled out those countries with a high share of government involvement in their economies for particularly harsh treatment. It is enlightening to compare the U.S., which has the third-lowest government sector, with Sweden, which has the highest. The U.S. recession has been as severe as Sweden's, inflation has not been significantly lower, and unemployment is far worse. It is a sobering fact that according to the U.S. Bureau of Labour Statistics, the average real wage for workers in the U.S. is now *lower* than it was in 1962. Low government spending is no guarantee of high living standards. Moreover, there is no clear-cut international evidence which demonstrates that the size of the government sector, per se, is necessarily the cause of the economic crisis that Canada now faces.

THE SIZE OF THE PUBLIC SECTOR IN THE CANADIAN ECONOMY

The impact of the public sector in the economy can also be assessed by the number of workers it employs. In January 1984 there were 1 959 000 workers in government services. This figure includes federal, provincial, and municipal levels of government, all Crown corporations, and all public agencies funded or owned by different levels of government.

There are various ways in which the number of public sector workers can be compared to the overall labour force. For example, we can assess employment in the public sector in relation to the number of employed, paid workers in the economy. In January 1984 this total was 9 334 000. Thus the 1 959 000 public sector workers represented 21.0 percent of the employed paid labour force.

Another approach would be to compare public sector employment to the total number of paid workers, both employed and unemployed. This figure was 10 670 000 in January 1984. Using this comparison, the public sector represented 18.4 percent of the paid labour force.

The preceding labour force figures do not include small employers or the self-employed. When these workers are added along with those working in agriculture, Canada's labour force amounts to 10 443 000 excluding the unemployed, and 11 916 000 including all workers. Public sector employment represented 18.8 percent of the former figure and 16.4 percent of the latter.

These figures do little to substantiate the claim that the public sector has gobbled up the economy and squeezed out the private sector. By the broadest definition of who should be included in the public sector and the narrowest definition of the labour force, employment in government services represented barely one fifth of total employment. And, using other wider definitions of the labour force, the percentage of workers in the public sector is substantially smaller.

Another way to assess the size of government in the economy is the amount of capital investment which it absorbs. In 1982 total investment in the Canadian economy according to Statistics Canada was $111.9 billion. Of this, $10.6 billion was accounted for by government departments. This represented 9.5 percent of overall capital investment, compared to 15.0 percent in 1960. Hence, government capital investment has fallen as a proportion of total investment in the economy over the past two decades.

The preceding figures on the share of employment and share of investment by the public sector in the Canadian economy underline the fact that the role of government is far more modest than widely assumed.

THE ROLE OF THE PUBLIC SECTOR IN A MIXED ECONOMY

Attacks on government spending that focus solely on the size of the public sector reveal little understanding of the many ways in which the private sector is assisted by public spending.

First, government establishes the economic infrastructure required to allow business firms to operate profitably. Second, it provides a large market for the products and services of the private sector. Third, it provides needed research for the private sector. Fourth, government absorbs the costs of educating and training the labour force. Fifth, it provides a wide range of services to assist the corporate sector, such as export loan guarantees. Sixth, government subsidizes many corporations directly through literally hundreds of different assistance programs. Seventh, government frequently provides risk or venture capital for private firms, thereby absorbing the risks associated

with new products or industries. At the same time, government allows the private sector to make profits if the products succeed. Eighth, government absorbs the costs of many employee benefits and related services, such as health care, that employers would otherwise have to pay. Ninth, government provides a wide range of police, fire, and other security services that protect the assets of the private sector. Tenth, government provides a framework of legislation which regulates industrial relations and assists employers in managing their work forces.

Several of the preceding points merit further elaboration. Government support for the economic infrastructure, for instance, is one of the key methods of fostering private sector development. State spending on roads, electrical utilities, pipelines, water and sewage systems, land servicing, airports, and a wide range of other facilities is necessary for private corporations to produce and market their goods efficiently. A significant reduction in spending on these services would have the long-term effect of lowering the overall level of efficiency and profitability in the economy. If roads, railways, and port facilities deteriorate, transport costs rise dramatically. This in turn pushes up the selling price of goods. Firms dependent on inefficient transport are less able to compete.

Similarly, if adequate government funds were not allocated to airport construction and to the development of sophisticated air traffic control systems, the growth—and profitability—of private sector aviation would be restricted. Over 70 percent of all airline travel relates to business. Government subsidies to aviation are actually subsidies to virtually all business firms.

To give another illustration, electric utilities in Canada are almost entirely under public ownership, thereby adding to the size of the public sector as a whole. Yet these utilities supply the power needed by private industry, and provide it at rates that are generally lower than private sector utilities south of the border. The availability of cheap electrical power has been used by a number of provinces as a major selling point in their attempts to attract private investment.

Public ownership of electric utilities has not been a burden on business. Rather, the public has provided the enormous amounts of risk capital needed for these investments while the corporate sector has benefited substantially from being able to purchase cheap power.

Another example of public support for private firms can be found in the resource sector. Federal and provincial governments normally provide the infrastructure of new roads, power supplies, port facilities, railways, and many other services needed to open up new mines or forest resources. Indeed, virtually every resource development project undertaken by private companies involves substantial amounts of new public investment—investment which directly contributes to the profitability of the corporations concerned. Yet such investment also raises government spending and increases the share of government in the overall economy.

The same arguments apply to a wide range of other services. While the corporate sector vigorously attacks government spending, it takes for granted the public sector infrastructure which facilitates its profit-making activities.

Critics of the size of government also ignore the direct and indirect effects of public expenditure in providing a market for private sector goods and services. The volume of private sector products purchased by all levels of government is enormous. In many industries, such as defence, government is the only purchaser.

Nor do critics take into account the impact of government spending in raising the overall level of demand within the economy. Such spending stimulates economic growth. The dramatic expansion of all the major economies of the West can be attributed, in large part, to the impact of public demand for a wide range of goods and services.

Even spending on social, educational, and health services has considerable benefit for the private sector. A well-educated and technically trained labour force facilitates efficient production and ensures that the skills required by business are available. An educated labour force is a valuable asset to business, especially in a rapidly changing technological environment. And it is government that pays the costs of this training.

By providing basic medical and hospital services, governments ensure that absenteeism caused by sickness is reduced. And a healthy labour force is more productive. Moreover, by providing public health care, governments reduce the direct costs to corporations of private health insurance schemes.

In short, government expenditures assist the private sector, both directly and indirectly, in numerous ways. Far from being a non-productive burden on the private sector "engine" of production, public enterprises and services absorb many of the expenses which otherwise would have to be paid by private corporations as part of their cost of production.

The preceding considerations suggest that there is no obvious correlation between the size of government and the stifling of private industry, despite the latter's cries to the contrary. Indeed, it could just as logically be argued that a larger government sector, depending on how its funds were allocated, would enhance, rather than hamper, the development of the private sector.

This is not to suggest that the corporations are acting irrationally or against their economic interest when they attack government spending and demand cuts in certain government programs. From the perspective of the corporations, governments are providing too many services to ordinary Canadians and not enough to business. Underlying the attack on "big government" is a desire to *redirect* the activities of government. That the causes of our current economic crisis are being wrongly attributed to government does not alter the fact that the corporations are benefiting enormously from the policies now being implemented.

GOVERNMENT INTERVENTION AND THE BUSINESS CYCLE

Business interests have long claimed that government economic mismanagement has precipitated the current crisis. Yet if we look briefly at the history of capitalism from the eighteenth century to the present, we find that recessions and depressions have occurred regularly. Following a definite historical pattern, referred to as the business cycle, the system has lurched from crises of overproduction to crises of massive unemployment and bankruptcies. Then it starts all over again (Marx, 1867; Mandel, 1980; Gonick, 1978).

The current crisis must therefore be seen in its historical context. It is not a new phenomenon of the free enterprise system, but a recurrence of the pattern of boom and bust that has existed for several centuries. Moreover, this pattern was apparent long before government began regulating the economy in any significant way. To blame government indiscriminately for our present economic problems, while ignoring the

fact that such problems are an integral part of the cycle of capitalist development, is to mistake cause for effect.

One of the basic reasons for government economic regulation in the post-war period was to control the excesses of the business cycle that had led to the Great Depression. To put it more bluntly, government intervention, through both fiscal and monetary policy, was necessary to save the capitalist system from its own excesses. The business interests and conservative economists who are now pushing for less government regulation have a conveniently short memory. Government did not cause the stock market crash of 1929; nor was it responsible for the ensuing depression. Furthermore, it was not the market that ended the Great Depression, but the fiscal policies of Roosevelt and (more importantly) the stimulative effect of government spending as the Second World War began.

History shows that the absence of government intervention is no guarantee that the economy will function smoothly. Quite the contrary: the period since the Second World War has been unprecedented in terms of the length of time during which economic growth advanced without a major depression. This was partly due to the use of Keynesian economic policies and the high level of U.S. government spending on defence. Perhaps most significantly, the period reflected the ability of one government, the U.S., to control and stabilize the international economic system.

This is not to suggest that we can deal with our present crisis simply by returning to the policies of the 1950s and 1960s. But a return to the policies of the 1920s is no answer either. While it is true that the Keynesian solution is exhausted, the reason is not the excessive growth of government, but rather the way in which the capitalist system has developed in recent years. Its basic contradictions have given rise to new pressures, both national and international, which are beyond the ability of national governments to control with conventional fiscal and monetary policies.

To put this another way, the problem is not that government has become excessively large. Rather, the cyclical tendencies of the capitalist system have again become unmanageable. Increasingly, the private decisions of multinational corporations are beyond the ability of any government to control. Fiscal measures that could influence the behaviour of business in the past are now ineffective. Today the corporations have the power to evade such measures or inflict significant retribution against governments attempting to impose them.

Basic decisions concerning the level and direction of investment are increasingly controlled by multinational corporations in conjunction with the banking and international financial systems. These companies view the *world* as their sphere of operations. Consequently, both federal and provincial governments in Canada, at the expense of national economic planning, are being pressured to adopt policies favourable to the multinationals.

If governments fail to provide tax concessions, grants, subsidies, and other assistance demanded by business, the corporations can—and do—turn off the investment tap. With the growing internationalization of the system, it has become much easier for corporations to transfer capital and production to other countries, especially in the Third World, if they do not get their way (Cameron, 1983). Increasingly, federal and provincial governments find themselves in competition with each other, and with foreign governments, in their attempts to attract capital. Under such conditions, it becomes extremely difficult for them to impose the kinds of controls on corporate behaviour that are necessary to regulate the economic system effectively and deal with economic problems faced by the country as a whole.

For example, if governments attempt to control inflation by placing curbs on monopoly pricing practices, they face retaliation from the corporations whose profits are threatened. An investment strike, with all its implications for unemployment and growth, is a very effective method to bring governments to heel.

The reality of our present economic system, then, is not that government has too much control over the economy, but that it lacks the ability to direct economic development. This inability stems not from its incompetence or its inherent inefficiencies, but from its growing vulnerability to pressure from corporate interests.

Federal and provincial governments are now faced with two conflicting pressures. First, there are the increasing demands from business to establish a more favourable investment climate for private capital. Second, there are the continuing demands from ordinary Canadians to maintain the many public services that were established during the 1960s and early 1970s. How can governments provide the cash and other assistance (which business is so anxious to obtain), and still be able to continue paying for these services?

Since the mid-1970s the answer has been clear: social spending is to be sacrificed in favour of policies that will assist the corporate sector.

REFERENCES

Beigie, C
    1980   "Inflation and budgetary deficits." Report of Proceedings of the Thirty-Second Tax Conference. Montreal, Canadian Tax Foundation (November): 8-16.

Calvert, J.
    1982   "MacEachen's disastrous budget: It's a prescription for economic ruination," *CUPE Facts*, 4, no. 2.

Cameron, D.
    1983   "Order and disorder in the world economy," *Studies in Political Economy*, 11 (Summer): 122-24.

Friedman, M.
    1962   *Capitalism and Freedom*. Chicago: University of Chicago Press.

Friedman, M., and R. Friedman
    1980   *Free to Choose*. New York: Harcourt Brace Jovanovich.

Gonick, C.
    1978   *Out of Work*. Toronto: Lorimer.

Mandel, E.
    1980   *Long Waves of Capitalist Development: A Marxist View*. Cambridge: Cambridge University Press.

Marx, K.
    1867   *Capital, Volume I*. Moscow: Progress Publishers.

Sweezy, P.
    1978   "The global crisis," *Monthly Review*, 11 (April).

FOR FURTHER READING

Albert, James, and Allan Moscovitch. 1987. *The Growth of the Welfare State.* Toronto: Garamond. The principal focus in this book is on the increased role of government in the system of social welfare in Canada. The implications of the state's activities for the economic structure and the well-being of the population are of special concern.

Banting, Keith. 1982. *The Welfare State and Canadian Federalism.* Montreal: McGill-Queen's University Press. This book examines the role of state welfare programs, especially those concerned with income security, in structuring the Canadian federal system.

Calvert, John. 1984. *Government, Limited.* Ottawa: Canadian Centre for Policy Alternatives. The central theme of this analysis is that, despite the allegations of growing involvement of government in the Canadian economy, such incursions by the state have been largely constrained by the activities of major corporations. This book argues that government has in fact become increasingly subordinate to private business interests. An alternative strategy for Canada's future economy is proposed.

Olsen, Dennis. 1980. *The State Elite.* Toronto: McClelland and Stewart. This monograph is concerned with outlining and analysing the structure of Canada's state system and the backgrounds of those individuals who occupy the leading roles in Canada's political, judicial, and state bureaucratic machinery.

Panitch, Leo, ed. 1977. *The Canadian State: Political Economy and Political Power.* Toronto: University of Toronto Press. A collection of essays on the state and political power in Canada, this book takes for the most part a Marxist view of the Canadian state and discusses such topics as the state elites and the linkages between the corporate elite, the capitalist class, and the Canadian state.

Section V

CONSEQUENCES OF SOCIAL INEQUALITY

Introduction

The preceding four sections have described the main patterns of social inequality in this country, as featured in social class, income/occupation/education, and social ascription. Various interpretations have been offered of the circumstances leading to the current situation. One of the effects of social inequality, in particular, received considerable attention: the ways in which the struggles between classes or between elites were translated into trends or history. For example, Clement's selection in Section IV suggests how the economic structure of this country has changed as a result of the interplay between capitalists and the state elite. Earlier, his piece in Section I showed how crucial to such developments is the prevailing understanding of what "property" is. This understanding too arose out of past struggles over economic interests and became rooted in the law. It is difficult to describe Canada's socially unequal class and elite relations for very long, without spelling out how history is determined by them. Nearly all of the selections in Sections I and IV attest to this type of result of social inequality.

There is a second important effect of social inequality, though, which was not addressed in Sections I-IV. This is the *consequences for individuals and groups in their lives within a situation of social inequality.* Here the focus is upon how day-to-day living is affected as opposed to how the society is changing, or not changing, with time. By *consequences* we mean any aspects of the experiences, beliefs, and behaviour of individuals that are influenced by differences in social inequality.

Our purpose in Section V is to portray this second type of effect. There is a vast number of such consequences because social inequality touches so many aspects of social life. Thus we cannot pretend to give, in the seven selections in this section, the last word on the consequences of social inequality, but we will provide some enlightening examples. To suggest how broad the range of consequences can be, we would quote Hans Gerth and C. Wright Mills, who once wrote (1953:313) that the consequences of social inequality for individuals "include everything from the chance to stay alive during the first year after birth, to the chance to view fine arts, the chance to remain healthy and grow tall, and if sick to get well again quickly, the chance to avoid becoming a juvenile delinquent . . . and . . . the chance to complete an intermediary or higher educational grade."

Various forms of consequences of social inequality for individuals can be found in any capitalist society for several reasons, but two reasons seem very important. First, the existence of social inequality in the form of economic advantage means that some can "buy" more or "afford" more of the valued aspects of social life, the "life chances" of the society. Some can easily afford to take time off work when they believe their children might benefit from a doctor's examination; others cannot readily afford this. Some can afford to live in the best neighbourhoods, with the

432

best in leisure and educational facilities for their children; others cannot. Some can send their children to the best "finishing" schools, law schools, or medical schools; others cannot. There are many such differences in life chances between "haves" and "have-nots."

Second, because differences in economic advantage involve differences in economic interest, we can expect that, often, some awareness of these interests will develop, and the haves and have-nots will vie with each other about their interests (see Peter Archibald's piece in this section for details on how this takes place). If such pursuit of interests becomes at all pronounced, it can be expected to lead to differences between the haves and the have-nots in the areas of political beliefs and values, behaviour, and opportunities. For the same reason, social barriers between the haves and the have-nots should develop. And these, in turn, may lead to still other differences in beliefs, behaviour, and opportunities. In other words, *subcultures of different ways of thinking and acting* can easily develop out of the interests that surround separate social classes and socio-economic statuses.

There is no easy way of predicting the full details of these subcultures in advance, no way of saying precisely how they will differ in beliefs, behaviour, and opportunity. For an understanding of the prevalence and character of inequality-based subcultures in any society for any particular time period, a careful, large-scale research effort is required. The selections in this section will suggest what a very large task this is and will give examples of appropriate research techniques.

The selections here are limited to *three categories* of consequences of social inequalities: (1) people's differences in *life chances;* (2) their differences in *ways of thinking and behaving* concerning social inequalities; and (3) their differences in *orientation to social interaction.*

We shall first deal with the issue of differences in life chances. We will employ an aspect of "life chances" which involves the toughest of definitions, however—that of life expectancy. This is "toughest" in the sense that life is one of the most prized possessions in Canadian society, and probably *the* most prized possession for a large majority of people. This being the case, using the criterion of life puts our society's patterns of inequality to a tough test. It would clearly cast doubt on the idea that ours is a society of vast equality if we find good evidence that differences in economic circumstances create differences in life expectancy.

Just this pattern has been shown to be true of other countries. Probably the most complete international study of this topic was conducted in the United States by Kitagawa and Hauser (1968) who matched 340 000 death certificates (for deaths occurring during four months in 1960) to the 1960 census records. Using educational attainment level as an indicator of socio-economic status, these researchers found a strong inverse relationship between mortality rates and educational attainment. For example, among white women between the ages of 25 and 64, the mortality rate for those with less than eight years of school was 61 percent higher than for college-educated women. Among white males in this age bracket, the mortality rate for those with less than eight years of school was 48 percent higher than for the college-educated men.

What about Canada? The first selection in this section, by D. J. Wigle and Y. Mao, does not support the supposition that Canadian society has been exempt from this particular consequence of social inequality. Wigle and Mao report that they looked at income levels and death rates for various census tracts in 21 major Canadian cities in 1971 and found markedly better life expectancy levels for areas with higher average-income levels. For instance, they report the sobering finding that males in the highest-income areas had life expectancies 6.2 years greater on average than males in the lowest-income areas.

Wigle and Mao remind us that there is still serious debate concerning precisely what it is about income levels that causes the differences in life expectancies. The answers probably lie in one or more of these differences across the different income levels: people's lifestyles, the healthfullness of their environments, or their utilization of health care.

On the matter of utilization of health care, Wigle and Mao conducted their study in a period immediately following the passing in 1966 of the Medical Care Act which was intended to help equalize access to medical care. Thus, there had not been time for this Act to have an effect upon life expectancy in the population (if there was to be an effect) before the two researchers did their study. It would therefore be very interesting to replicate Wigle and Mao's study for the 1980s and the 1990s. This would let us know whether there has been any change of the income-death rate relationship after several years under the Act. Of course, other factors affecting the relationship may have changed too during this period. It would be difficult to show the effects of the Act by itself. This is yet another indication that searching out the precise causes of the social inequality-life expectancy pattern is a task that will remain with us for some time to come.

The second type of individual and group consequences addressed in this section has to do with differences in *ways of thinking and behaving* in situations of social inequality. Here we can start by recalling Karl Marx's famous observation that it is not the consciousness of men that determines their being, but rather their social being, primarily their relation to the mode of production, that determines their consciousness. We can ask to what extent this view is correct for Canada today. Are the different social classes and social status groups aware of their differences? Do individuals in similar economic positions have similar sets of interests? Do such individuals try to safeguard or promote their interests? Going further, we can ask whether the different classes and status groups develop still other differences in attitudes, values, and behaviour.

Questions of this type, designed to probe the degree and extent of class and status consciousness, or common thinking by classes and strata, raise problems of obvious significance for understanding the dynamic aspect of Canada's structure of social inequalities. For example, class consciousness of common interests has existed at many times and places and has at times led to organized class actions and class struggles that changed the whole structure of societies. But class consciousness does not follow automatically from objective class differences. People may have a class position which differs markedly from that of others without being particularly aware of this difference. Thinking and conduct are not determined merely by objective position in the economic or social order but depend in part upon the way in which people perceive and interpret their social circumstances. For example, socialization through the educational system and the media probably will have some effect upon people's thinking about their class or status position and its meaning. It is likely that these influences lead people of differing classes to have a *common assessment* of the reasons for class differences. Some observers say that much of what is taught in the educational system and via the media is supportive of, or justifies, existing class inequality. The argument is that everyone who will listen is taught that some inequality is a necessary outcome of a capitalist economy, but that this should be tolerated because capitalism is for the common good.

Also, Canadians "carry with them" various achieved and ascribed backgrounds and related sets of experiences at any given point in their lives. A person has, simultaneously, the experiences of a class position, a level of education achieved, an occupation, a certain level of income, an ethnic status, a race, a gender, and an age group. It is therefore difficult to know which of these sets of experiences will influence most the person's perceptions of social inequality. We cannot assume the presence of common class or status thinking, but must investigate how Canadians evaluate and respond to existing differences.

Fortunately, over the past few years there have been some well-developed national-sample surveys of adult Canadians' beliefs about social inequality and political behaviour which have helped us to understand this issue better. William Johnston and Michael Ornstein's study in this section reports on an interesting set of results from one such survey. Their study explored the relationship between social class, defined in the Marxist sense, and three sets of ideological beliefs— beliefs having to do with support for redistribution of income, social welfare expenditures, and support for the labour movement. As would be expected from the class interests involved for each class, the bourgeoisie are shown to have a more right-wing position on these issues, and the working class to have a left-wing position. The bourgeoise was less likely to favour pursuing greater equality through income redistribution and greater social welfare, and they were less supportive of the labour movement. The difference in beliefs between the classes, however, was far from complete. Many members of one class shared in the majority beliefs of the other class, and vice versa.

Johnston and Ornstein go on to show how the attitudes of the working class were strongly affected by a number of aspects of their working conditions. Education and family background proved to be less important factors in explaining dif- ferences in the three types of beliefs.

Moving to the question of whether political behaviour reflects thinking about social inequality, the selection by Ronald Lambert and colleagues shows that sometimes it does, and that currently this occurs more frequently in some areas of Canada than in others. The researchers use another national survey conducted just after the 1984 federal election to ask whether people's own definitions of their social class position (and their occupations, incomes, and education levels) were related to the class leanings of the party they voted for. The survey respondents were asked to define, in terms of whose interests each represented, each of the major parties using a seven-point scale ranging from "for the lower social classes" to "for the higher social classes." Then the respondents' evaluations of the party they voted for on this dimension were linked to informaton on self-class placement and economic background.

There was a positive relationship between economic circumstance and the definition of the party voted for when education and income were the measures (but not when occupation was the measure). The lower the economic status of the respondent, the more he or she was likely to have voted for a party he or she defined as "for the lower classes." This pattern was even stronger when the party definitions were compared to the voter's own definitions of his or her economic circumstances, measured in terms of "upper class" versus "middle class" versus "lower class." Each of these patterns held also for voting in the most recent provincial election.

The provincial-level results were interesting because they showed that residents of British Columbia had, by far, the strongest relationship between economic status and class perception of the party voted for. This suggests that provinces where there are strong militant unions and where parties of the lower class have had some success in reaching power are more likely to have strong class-voting behaviour. Both of these facts are more true of British Columbia than of the other provinces currently. Mobilization of the class interests of the lower classes requires organizational vehicles such as these.

The issue of the effects of social inequalities upon people's political behaviours is taken in a different direction in the selection by Edward Grabb. He studies the influences upon feelings of powerlessness, or the belief that one cannot affect politicians and the government. Grabb reasoned, based on earlier work by Melvin Kohn on the effects of occupations upon conformity, that characteristics of jobs should affect how powerful one feels. If one is relatively free of supervision at work, and if one perhaps even does some supervision oneself, there should be a greater sense of power at work and, by extension, stronger feelings of power in the political arena. People who are closely supervised at work should feel powerless there, and possibly for the same reason powerless in politics. The study also tested the idea that higher education, because it gives a "breadth of perspective" (and, we might add, because it teaches people to feel competent and worthy) should lead to stronger beliefs in one's political power.

Grabb's data, from an area sample of workers in London, Ontario, support both of these views. Both educational status and job control were negatively related to feelings of political powerlessness.

It is interesting to speculate about what these patterns reported by Grabb might mean for the future of political behaviour in Canada. Some argue that, over time, increasing numbers of jobs in this country are becoming more controlled, more closely supervised. Does this mean that there will be a growing portion of the population who feel incapable of influencing politics? There is also a trend toward a higher average-education level for Canadians, as we have seen in an earlier section. This should produce effects in the opposite direction. Does this bode well for stronger feelings of political efficacy and more widespread political involvement among Canadians? Of course, there can be many factors involved here. We will need to have careful trend studies before we arrive at firm answers to these questions.

If living in different socio-economic circumstances shapes one's political beliefs, then we might also expect to find differences in beliefs and values across categories of people defined by some of the *ascribed* statuses that have been discussed in other sections of this reader—the statuses defined by ethnicity, race, gender, and age. There should be differences in ways of thinking correlated with these ascribed statuses because, as we have seen, these statuses too differ in economic circumstances; some groups do well and some not so well (for instance, the English versus the French, the middle-aged versus the aged, and so on). Would we expect any differences between these social groups, though, once we have controlled for the circumstances of income, occupation, and education? Do ascribed-status groups have subcultures that have significance which goes beyond their different make-ups in terms of education, jobs, and income? This is the question that Douglas Baer and Jim Curtis pursued in their French Canadian-English Canadian comparisons. The answer appears to be "yes" in this instance.

Baer and Curtis employed national survey data to show that, contrary to the opposite expectation in the previous sociological literature, French Canadians showed *higher* levels of achievement values than did English Canadians. This held true for six different measures even after controls for socio-economic circumstance.

The previous literature, based largely on social histories of Quebec, contained the hypothesis that French Canadians are *less* achievement-oriented than English Canadians because they place heavier emphasis on family and religious values which should conflict with strong attention to economic striving. Baer and Curtis offer the following alternative interpretation of their surprising French-English differences: The French have higher achievement values than the English because for decades economic success and economic security have been less readily attainable in the French subculture. This being the case, economic achievement has come to have a comparatively higher priority there than in English Canada. Turning the comparison around, English Canadians are more likely to take economic achievement for granted than are French Canadians. Thus, the history of economic differences between French and English in this country appears to have left a residue of differences in achievement values between the two language groups.

The third category of individual and group consequences of social inequality looked at in this section has to do with *effects upon social interaction.* Two selections specify some of the issues here. Peter Archibald's piece describes a Marxian-oriented theory of how interaction between higher-class and lower-class individuals takes place (the theory also applies to interaction between higher-status and lower-status people, and between those with much power and those with little power). Archibald tests his theory by using a sweeping review of results from many other studies. His work leads him to a set of generalizations about interactions between unequals which are based on the principle that such interactions will necessarily involve some interpersonal threat and exploitation. They will involve conflict and coercion, however subtle these may be at times. Archibald goes on to consider alternative theories based on the idea that there is consensus, co-operation, and exchange in interaction between unequals. He allows that these processes may occur occasionally, but they are not the most common forms of interaction between unequals. Interaction based on some form of threat is said to be more common.

The selection by Colin Goff and Charles Reasons provides a case in point for Archibald's theory. Goff and Reasons study material on the incidence of crimes and the character of criminal law to develop a description of two different types of crime, "street crime" versus "suite crime." "Street crimes" are the kinds that we generally hear about in the news—vandalism, burglary, robbery, assault, murder, and so on. These are crimes performed by the economically disadvantaged and the masses. "Suite crimes" are the crimes of the corporate boardrooms and the civil elites. They include such activities as price fixing, failure to maintain safety standards, and violations of human rights. The authors go on to show that suite crimes are as prevalent as street crimes, if not more so, and that they are as likely as street crimes to have victims who suffer financial loss, injury, and sometimes death. Yet suite criminals are often ignored; they are seldom brought before the courts.

How can this suite crime occur and persist? The answer to the first part of the question lies squarely in the theory described by Archibald. The corporate criminals are simply practising the type of social interaction that is common everywhere between unequals; they are "using" the public or the workers, to the extent that they can, for greater financial gain for themselves and their organizations. The answer to the second part of the question (how this can persist) is more complex, as Goff and Reasons show. Part of the answer lies in the ideological purpose (Goff and Reasons use the term "morality") of the criminal law. Much of the law was put in place to serve the interests of business people and the economic elites. Laws have as one of their purposes the maintenance of economic order. This goal appears to take very strong priority in law enforcement. The interests of the public and workers fall a distant second. Heavy law enforcement resources, and clear and easily enforceable laws, are given over to controlling street crimes; and suite crimes are seldom "gotten around to" in these regards.

REFERENCES

Gerth, Hans, and C. Wright Mills
    1953 *Character and Social Structure: The Social Psychology of Social Institutions.* New York: Harcourt Brace and World.

Kitawaga, Evelyn M., and Philip M. Hauser
    1968 "Education Differentials in Mortality by Cause of Death: United States, 1960," *Demography,* 5:318-53.

36. *Income and Life Expectancy*

D. J. Wigle and Y. Mao

BACKGROUND

Historically, William Farr was probably the first person to study systematically the relation between mortality and socio-economic characteristics. Farr, appointed Compiler of Abstracts in the General Register Office of England in 1839, was able to exploit statistics available due to the registration of vital events throughout England and Wales as required by legislation introduced in 1837 (Dorn, 1966). Farr used occupation as an index of social class and analysed mortality by occupation beginning in the census year 1851. Stevenson continued and extended the work of Farr to the analysis of mortality by social class defined by aggregating occupations into five grades (Stevenson, 1923; 1928).

Revised from D. J. Wigle and Y. Mao, *Mortality by Income Levels in Urban Canada, 1980* (Ottawa: Health and Welfare Canada, 1980), pp. 1-46. Reproduced with permission of the Minister of Supply and Services Canada.

A study of mortality by social class in Finland revealed that males in social class 1 had a life expectancy at birth of 67.5 years compared to 60.3 years for males in social class 4 (Nayha, 1977). Kitagawa and Hauser (1973) also analysed life expectancy by social class based on census tract of residence in the city of Chicago and observed that white males in social classes 1 and 5, respectively, had life expectancies at birth of 67.4 and 60.0 years. Thus, there was a social-class differential in life expectancy of 6 or 7 years among males in England, Finland, and the United States.

Analysis of mortality by social class on a national scale was not attempted in Canada until very recently. Billette and Hill (1974), utilized a case-control method based on a random sample of deaths due to selected causes among males 25 to 64 years of age in Canada during 1974. The analysis was based on 2265 case-control pairs which represented 15 percent of the total deaths in the relevant category. Social class was based on the occupation recorded on the death certificate. Men in social class 5 (unskilled occupations, farmers, and labourers) had more than three times the risk of death due to pneumonia, bronchitis, and non-traffic accidents compared to those in social class 1.

PRESENT STUDY

The purpose of this report is to present an overview of the variations of mortality by income level in Canada. The study is based on all deaths which occurred in the 21 census metropolitan areas (CMAS) of Canada during 1971 (the 21 CMAS accounted for 54 percent of the 1971 Canadian population). It was possible to code the address of usual residence to the census tract level for 98.2 percent of the 81 465 deaths which occurred in the CMAS. The address of usual residence for 7.2 percent of the deaths was an institution (hospital or nursing home) and these records were excluded from the analyses; thus, the analyses in this report were based on 91 percent of all deaths.

Census tracts are small permanent census statistical areas which have been established in large urban communities. For the purpose of this study, the most important features of census tracts are that they are quite homogeneous with regard to economic status and living conditions, and detailed data concerning the demographic and economic characteristics of census tract populations are available from the 1971 Census. The index of social class for decedents was based on the median household income of the census tract in which the person usually lived. Ideally, social class would have been assigned using socio-economic information for individuals but this approach would have been much more difficult and costly.

There were 2228 census tracts in the 21 CMAS in 1971 and the median household income of each ranged from $2456.00 to more than $20 000.00. The census tracts were ranked by median household income and divided into approximate quintiles. Mortality and census data by census tract were aggregated into five income levels based on median household income.

INTERPRETATION OF RESULTS

Associations between income level and mortality rates must be interpreted with caution. Income level is correlated with factors such as education, occupation, and lifestyle which can independently contribute to the risk of disease. Chronic disease and disability may cause a decline in income level due to loss of employment or a decline in job status and pay; thus, a relatively low income at the time of death can be a result of disease as opposed to a cause.

Associations between income and mortality should not be interpreted to indicate that income per se directly influences mortality rates. The income level of decedents was assigned using census data for the census tract in which the person maintained a residence at the time of death. Income level should be considered as an approximate indicator of socio-economic status.

LIFE EXPECTANCY BY INCOME LEVEL

Life expectancy is a useful summary indicator of the net effect of a given factor on the risk of death due to any cause. In Figure 36-1, life expectancies at birth are presented for each sex by income level. Life expectancy declined with decreasing income level from 72.5 to 66.3 years in males and from 77.5 to 74.6 years in females. The differences in life expectancy between the highest and lowest income levels were 6.2 years for males and 2.9 years for females. Thus, the importance of income level appeared to be substantially greater for males than females.

The difference in life expectancy between the highest and lowest income levels by sex and age is presented in Figure 36-2. The differential in life expectancy by income level was greater for males than females at all ages. The differential for each sex was maximal at birth, relatively constant up to age 30 and declined rapidly after age 40. The differential was less than one year for females over age 55 and males over age 75.

To put the differential in perspective, the difference in life expectancy at birth between income levels 1 and 5 for males (6.2 years) was more than twice the expected increase in life expectancy if all cancer

deaths could be prevented (2.8 years, Department of National Health and Welfare, 1977). The corresponding differential for females (2.9 years) was equal to that expected if all cancer deaths could be prevented.

CONCLUSIONS

A major question which arises from this type of study concerns the specific aspects of income level which are responsible for increased mortality rates. It is well known that lifestyle, environment, and utilization of health care services all vary by income level. The prevalence of current cigarette smoking was about 30 percent for males in social class 1 in England and Wales but was about 65 percent for males in social class 5 (Office of

FIGURE 36-1 Life expectancy at birth by sex and income level

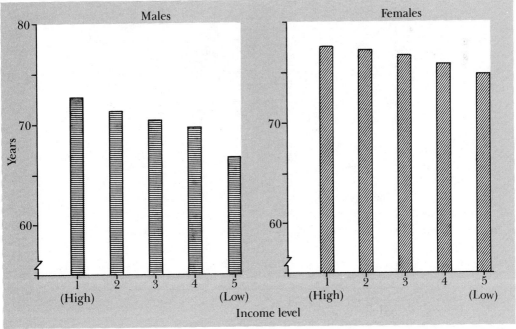

Population, 1978). Less variation was observed for females. Occupation is closely related to income level; persons in lower income levels are more likely to be employed in jobs involving hazardous exposures such as various dusts and fumes. Furthermore, there is the potential for synergistic interactions between lifestyle and occupational risk factors which may involve mainly persons in lower income levels. For example,

workers exposed to both asbestos and cigarette smoking experienced a much higher risk of lung cancer than would have been expected if the two factors were independent (Saracci, 1977). Dietary habits also vary by income level. Analysis of data collected during the Nutrition Canada Survey (1970-1972) indicated that persons in low-income groups consumed lower than recommended amounts of several nutrients (Myres and

FIGURE 36-2   Difference in life expectancy between income levels 1 and 5 by sex and age

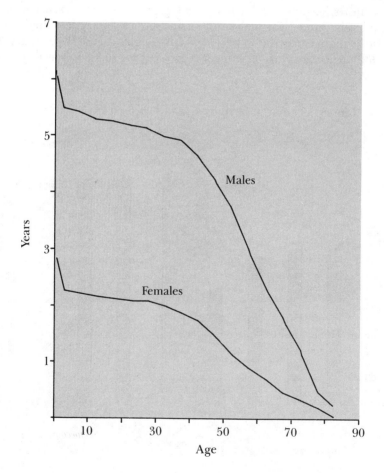

Kroetsch, 1978). However, the role of diet in the differential mortality by income level for various diseases is not yet clear. The accessibility to medical care was equalized in principle for all income levels in Canada with the introduction of the Medical Care Act in 1966. However, utilization of health care services may vary by income level in Canada. For example, a case-control study of cervical cancer in Toronto revealed that women in lower income levels were less likely than women in higher income levels to have undergone cytological screening for cancer of the cervix (Clarke and Anderson, 1979).

RECOMMENDATIONS

Despite the problems which arise in the interpretation of differential mortality by income level, it is clear that Canadians in lower income levels did experience substantially higher mortality rates than persons with higher incomes. It is highly probable that differentials will remain indefinitely unless appropriate control measures are developed and implemented. Given that substantial individual income differences will probably persist for many years, it is important to determine the relative importance of those specific aspects of income level which are related to the risk of premature mortality. Priority should be given to studies designed to provide such information.

There are already some programs which should help to reduce differential mortality by income level or at least prevent an increase in the differential. Examples include educational programs to control smoking, occupational health programs to reduce hazards in the work environment, environmental health programs to reduce hazards in the general environment (e.g., air, water) and health-care-delivery research programs to identify more effective mechanisms for delivery of essential health services. Such programs should be continued and should be assigned high priority for expansion and increased support.

REFERENCES

Billette, A., and G. B. Hill
　　1978　"Risque relatif de mortalité masculine et les classes sociales au Canada 1974," *L'Union Médicale du Canada*, 107:583-90.

Clarke, E. A., and T. W. Anderson
　　1979　"Does screening by 'Pap' smears help prevent cervical cancer?" *Lancet*, 2:1-4.

Department of National Health and Welfare
　　1977　*Cancer Patterns in Canada, 1931-1974*. Ottawa.

Dorn, H. F.
　　1966　"Mortality," in *Chronic Diseases and Public Health*, ed. A. M. Lilienfeld and A. J. Gifford, pp. 23-44. Baltimore: Johns Hopkins Press.

Kitagawa, E. M., and P. M. Hauser
　　1973　*Differential Mortality in the United States: A Study in Socioeconomic Epidemiology*. Cambridge: Harvard University Press.

Myres, A. W., and D. Kroetsch
    1978   "The influence of family income on food consumption patterns and nutrient intake in Canada," *Canadian Journal of Public Health,* 69:208-21.

Nayha, S.
    1977   "Social group and mortality in Finland," *British Journal of Preventive and Social Medicine,* 31:231-37.

Office of Population Censuses and Surveys
    1978   *Occupational Mortality, England and Wales, 1970-72.* London.

Saracci, R.
    1977   "Asbestos and lung cancer: an analysis of the epidemiologic evidence on the asbestos-smoking interaction," *International Journal of Cancer,* 20:323-31.

Stevenson, T. H. C.
    1923   "The social distribution of mortality from different causes in England and Wales, 1910-12," *Biometrika,* 15:382-400.
    1928   "The vital statistics of wealth and poverty," *Journal of Royal Statistical Society,* 91:207-30.

37. Class and Political Ideology

William Johnston and Michael Ornstein

The study of political attitudes among the Canadian general public raises two central issues for Marxist social science. The first question concerns whether an understanding of the class structure—defined on the basis of the relations of production—provides a meaningful insight into political consciousness. Second, presuming an affirmative answer to the first question, it is necessary to identify the experiences that pro-

Revised from William Johnston and Michael Ornstein, "Class, Work and Politics," *Canadian Review of Sociology and Anthropology,* vol. 19, no. 2 (1982) pp. 196-214. Reprinted with permission. The authors gratefully acknowledge the support of the Social Sciences and Humanities Research Council of Canada (grant #S75-0332) and of York University for providing the funds to collect the data employed here and supporting the project staff. This paper forms a part of the research conducted under the Social Change in Canada project, directed by Tom Atkinson, Bernard R. Blishen, Michael D. Ornstein, and H. Michael Stevenson at the Institute for Social Research, York University. The Institute was responsible for the collection of the survey data.

vide the basis for that consciousness. For example, the discovery that working-class people give stronger support to socialized medicine than other classes says something about the current struggle over cutbacks in medical services, but it does not really tell us why workers take the position they do. Excepting perhaps a small, politicized minority, people are not likely to take political positions according to some logical deductions from a knowledge of their class positions. Instead, the conditions of everyday life, perhaps personal needs for social services, experiences while growing up, in school, and at work, and the character of family and social relations provide an experiential basis for political judgements. The problem is then to identify what elements of that complex web of everyday experiences play a central role in forming political attitudes.

This paper focusses on the problem of identifying the experiential roots of class differences in political ideology, using data from a representative sample survey of Canadians. We employ a definition of the class structure of advanced capitalist societies elaborated by G. Carchedi in a recent series of articles (1975a; b; c). As a preliminary step, we establish the existence of class differences in Canadians' views of three related measures of political ideology, labelled support for the labour movement, support for redistribution of income, and support for social welfare measures. The analysis then considers the impact of family background and the characteristics of the work situation on the three measures.

DATA AND METHOD

The Sample

The survey data discussed here were collected as part of the project on "Social Change in Canada" conducted between May and July of 1977, measuring perceptions of the quality of life, personal values, political attitudes, and personal characteristics of 3288 Canadians. Data were obtained in face-to-face interviews with a probability sample of persons 18 years of age and over living in households in Canada, excluding the Yukon and Northwest Territories, residents of the far northern regions of Canada, public and private institutions, and Indian reservations. A multi-stage sampling procedure was used to select the sample. This analysis is limited to the 1787 respondents employed for 20 or more hours per week at the time of the survey.

Defining Social Class

We employ a concept of class developed in the work of Carchedi (1975a; b; c), who proceeds from an examination of the capitalist production process to delineate capitalist relations of production which in turn form the basis for the "economic identification" of

social classes. While recognizing the importance of the ideological and political dimensions of social class, Carchedi's procedure is warranted by his view that classes are ultimately determined by the economic level of a mode of production facilities, control over newly accumulated capital, and control over the labour process.

1. Class is regarded as a set of discrete categories, not as some continuum;
2. individuals are assigned to classes on the basis of their objective characteristics, not their subjective identification; and
3. the primary considerations are the ownership and control of existing production facilities, control over newly accumulated capital, and control over the labour process.

In operationalizing Carchedi's categories, individuals are assigned to social classes on the basis of their responses to two questionnaire items that ascertained their occupations and whether or not they were self-employed. High and middle managers are included in the bourgeoisie, because they exercise real ownership of the means of production, obtain their salaries from revenue (i.e., from surplus value), and perform the function of the global capitalist. The new middle class includes individuals who control and maintain surveillance of the labour process. The petty bourgeoisie contains all the self-employed. The working class includes all employed workers who do not engage in the surveillance or supervision of production. The result is a class structure divided in the following proportions: bourgeoisie 7.7 percent; petty bourgeoisie 13.8 percent; middle class 19.6 percent; and working class 59.9 percent.

Political Ideology

We chose to work with three short scales measuring support for the labour movement, support for redistribution of income, and support for social welfare measures.[1] We were guided in our choice of these scales by our previous research (Johnston and Ornstein, 1979), which suggested that they would be likely to locate existing class differences in political ideology and by our assessment that they related to critical political issues.

The three measures are fairly strongly related: the correlation between support for redistribution and for social welfare is .49; and those two scales have correlations with support for labour of .36 and .37, respectively. The strength of these relations suggests that there is some coherence in the political attitudes of Canadians. The stronger relation between support for redistribution and for social welfare is presumably a function of their both focussing on distributional issues in the sphere of consumption; support for labour relates to the sphere of production.

The Labour Process and the Conditions of Labour

A total of eight measures describing the respondents' work situation are included in the analysis. They are intended to provide a general picture of the objective nature and subjective perception of jobs. They measure the following:[2]

1. the dichotomy between manual and non-manual workers;
2. the dichotomy between a category of skilled workers and the remaining semi- and unskilled work force, also based on the Pineo, Porter, McRoberts categories;
3. trade union membership, a dichotomy;
4. the perceived quality of the work environment (using a 13-item scale);
5. difficulties with hours of work (a four-point scale);

6. whether the respondent often feels he or she is "very tired physically" when finished work, a dichotomy;
7. whether the respondent is often "very tired mentally" after work, a dichotomy;
8. the rate of pay (measured as the logarithm of annual pay).

In additon, a ninth variable, family income (scored as for the rate of pay), is included in this group of variables.

Background Variables

We first selected two conventional measures of characteristics of respondents' families of origin—the education of the respondent's parents and the occupation of his or her father. Educational attainment was measured in years of schooling and occupation with a set of 16 occupational categories (from Pineo, Porter, and McRoberts, 1977) that divides occupations according to levels of skill, the manual versus non-manual distinction, and industry. This detailed occupational categorization had no effect on political ideology, net of the impact of parents' education, and was therefore dropped from the analysis. It would have been better to employ a typology for father's occupation also based on Marxist theory, and it is possible that, measured in this way, father's occupation would have some effect. Unfortunately the present data do not allow us to test this possibility.

The respondent's educational attainment, also measured in years, and family income (actually, the logarithm of its value in thousands of dollars) were also included in the analysis.

DATA ANALYSIS

We begin with an examination of the extent of class differences in the three measures of political attitudes, then proceed to the discussion of what specific factors might account for those differences. Table 37-1 gives the mean scores in each of the four class categories. On the scales of support for labour and support for redistribution, a score of 9 is given to respondents taking the neutral position on all three items; a score of 12 is given to respondents who agree and of 15 to those who strongly agree with every statement; similarly scores of 3 and 6, respectively, would be given to respondents who strongly disagree and disagree with all the statements.

As Table 37-1 indicates, on the scale of support for labour the working class averages 9.8, about a point above the middle of the scale; the petty bourgeoisie and bourgeoisie have almost identical mean scores of 8.4 and 8.3, respectively; and the middle class is right at the centre, with an average score of precisely 9.0. The differences are in the expected direction, but there is nothing like complete polarization on these issues. Class explains 8.8 percent of the variance in support for labour (see Table 37-2, top row). A similar pattern is manifest for support for redistribution, but the overall mean is six-tenths of a point lower—only the working class has an average score above the neutral point. There is another more important difference: the petty bourgeoisie proves to be less conservative than the bourgeoisie on this issue, though still measurably more

TABLE 37-1 Political attitudes by social class.

| | Social class | | | | |
Variable	Working class	Middle class	Petty bourgeoisie	Bourgeoisie	Total
Support for labour					
Mean	9.80	9.00	8.40	8.30	9.40
Standard deviation	1.80	2.00	2.10	2.20	2.00
Difference from mean in standard deviations	.23	−.17	−.48	−.52	.00
Support for redistribution					
Mean	9.30	8.50	8.10	7.60	8.80
Standard deviation	2.10	2.30	2.40	2.50	2.20
Difference from mean in standard deviations	.19	−.16	−.32	−.52	.00
Support for social welfare					
Mean	23.20	21.50	21.00	20.10	22.30
Standard deviation	4.20	4.10	4.20	4.10	4.30
Difference from mean in standard deviations	.21	−.20	−.31	−.52	.00
	(1052)	(350)	(246)	(139)	(1787)

Note: N is in parentheses. Missing values are for: support for labour 24; support for redistribution 6; support for social welfare 3.

conservative than the middle class and considerably to the right of the working class. Overall, there is somewhat less class cleavage than was found in support for labour, and class accounts for 5.3 percent of the variance in support for redistribution. The pattern of support for social welfare is almost identical to that for redistribution. All four mean scores fall between the mid-point on the scale (a score of 17) that would be given to respondents who wanted, on average, "about the same effort" in the eight social welfare areas and the score (25) they would obtain by wanting "more effort" in each area. Class explains 6.6 percent of the variance for this variable. Note that there are no important differences in the standard deviations of the three political variables among the class categories.

The similarity of these findings is hardly surprising, given the strong correlations among the scales. The patterns correspond to the classical conceptions of class interest: the working class and bourgeoisie occupy, respectively, the left and right extremes; the petty bourgeoisie is more favourable to redistribution and social welfare than the bourgeoisie, but equally opposes the extension of trade union rights. The middle class is divided on these issues. It is difficult to say whether the class differences are "large" or "small." There is nothing like total polarization; but, on the other hand, if these results are compared to other studies of the relation between social structure and political attitudes and voting, the differences are substantial, especially in light of the relatively low reliability of the three scales.

TABLE 37-2 Variance in support for labour, redistribution, and social welfare explained by social class, job characteristics, and background (percentages).

Independent variable	Holding constant	Variance explained		
		Support for labour	Support for redistribution	Support for social welfare
Social class	Alone	8.8	5.3	6.6
	Job and income	3.4	0.7*	1.7
	Family background	8.1	4.2	5.6
	Both	2.4	1.0	2.7
Family background	Alone	2.8	5.5	2.7
	Social class	2.1	4.2	2.0
	Job and income	0.6*	1.1	0.1*
	Both	1.0	1.4	0.4*
Job and income	Alone	10.8	11.1	9.4
	Family background	8.6	7.3	6.9
	Social class	5.0	7.1	4.3
	Both	3.9	4.2	3.1
All		14.8	13.8	11.3

*not significant at .05

Labour Process and Conditions of Work

The introduction of the measures of working conditions produces a dramatic decline in the impact of social class on support for labour, indicating that we have succeeded in identifying underlying variables that serve to "transmit" just over half the total effect of class. Class alone explains 8.8 percent of the variance in support for labour, but it raises the total explained variance by only 3.4 percent when the nine measures of working conditions are first entered in the equation (all the variance estimates are in the first column of Table 37-2). The job variables alone explain 10.8 percent of the variance in support for labour, 5.0 percent above and beyond the effect of social class. So, job characteristics not only serve as intervening variables, they have independent effects that cannot be attributed to social class.

An examination of the regression coefficients, in Table 37-3, shows the directions of these effects. First, comparing the coefficients, for the class variables (top four lines, first and fifth columns), the difference between the working class and the bourgeoisie falls from .75 to .46 standard deviations in support for labour. When working conditions are held constant (in column 3), the petty bourgeoisie moves to the right of the bourgeoisie—but the shift is of numerically small magnitude. The relative positions of the four classes do not change substantially from the raw means in Table 37-1.

Taking the effects of occupational characteristics alone, the regression coefficients (Table 37-3, third column, bottom) indicate that support for labour is stronger among workers who

1. hold unskilled and semi-skilled rather than skilled jobs;
2. are members of trade unions—a very strong effect;

3. report being frequently physically tired at the end of a day's work;
4. do *not* report being mentally tired after work; and
5. earn less pay on the job.

It is interesting that the measure of the perceived quality of the work situation, a very reliable 13-item scale, has no idependent effect at all, suggesting that the underlying conditions of work rather than perceptions of satisfaction shape attitudes towards the rights of labour and management. Perhaps perceptions of work are coloured by workers' expectations, which are a function of those underlying physical conditions. Our findings about the effects of physical and mental tiredness is interesting—these two variables obviously contain a mixture of objective and perceptual factors, but we cannot say in what proportions. It is also notable (Table 37-3, bottom row) that family income has no effect on political attitudes, once job conditions are taken into account; nor do problems concerning hours of work have any impact.

The fifth column of Table 37-3 shows what happens to the effects of job conditions, when social class is held constant. There are two dramatic changes—the effect of trade union membership is reduced from .52 to .19 (standard deviations between union and non-union members) and the effect of level of skill disappears. The impact of trade union membership on political attitudes is thus, in large measure, a reflection of class differences. Support for labour cannot be reduced to a simple calculus whereby members support their unions and non-members do not. Finally, a comparison of columns 5 and 6 of Table 37-3 shows that holding social background constant does not alter the impact of job characteristics.

Because of the strong similarity between the measures of support for redistribution and social welfare, they may be discussed

TABLE 37-3 Regression of support for labour, redistribution, and social welfare (all standardized) on social class, class background, job characteristics and income.†

Independent variable	Regression coefficient for support for labour							Regression coefficient for support for redistribution							Regression coefficient for support for social welfare			
	(1)	(2)	(3)	(4)	(5)	(6)	(7)	(8)	(9)	(10)	(11)	(12)	(13)	(14)	(15)	(16)	(17)	(18)
Social class																		
Working class	.23			.22	.16	.17	.19	.16			.16	.07	.08	.21		.19	.12	.13
Middle class	-.17*			-.13*	-.08*	-.08*	-.16*	-.19			-.19	-.01	-.01	-.20*		-.17*	-.09*	-.09*
Petty bourgeoisie	-.48*			-.51*	-.39*	-.43*	-.32*	-.37			-.37	-.23*	-.28*	-.31*		-.35*	-.24*	-.26*
Bourgeoisie	-.52*			-.45*	-.30*	-.30*	-.52*	-.32			-.32	-.06	-.06	-.52*		-.44*	-.23*	-.28*
Background																		
Father's education**		.00		-.01			-.01		-.00		-.01			-.04	-.05			-.04
Mother's education**		-.11*		-.11*			-.10*		-.10*		-.10*			-.06	-.06*			-.04
Respondent's education**		-.09*		-.06*			-.03		-.14*		-.06*			-.11	-.07*			.00
Job and income																		
Manual occupation			.06		-.01		-.03			.11*		.04			.16*		.10	.03
Skilled occupation			-.11*		-.01		.00			-.13*		-.11			-.24*		-.15*	-.07*
Trade union membership			.52*		.19*		.18*			.28*		.22*		.20*	.27*		.19*	.11*
Perceived quality of work**			.00		.00		.00			.00		.03		.03	.17*		-.09*	-.09*
Difficulty with work hours**										.06*		.05*		.06*	.05*			
Physically tired by job			.20*		.22		.19*			.20*		.22*		.19*	.09*		.18*	.17*
Mentally tired by job			-.14*		-.15		-.12*			-.18*		-.18*		-.15*	-.09*		-.18*	-.16*
Rate of pay**			-.12*		-.08*		-.08*			-.15*		-.14*		-.13*	-.11*		-.08	-.08
Family income**			-.05		-.05		-.03			-.09*		-.10*		-.08*	-.06*		-.06	-.04

*Significantly different from zero at the .05 level, for social class, comparison of other three classes to the working class.
†Except for the four class variables, which measure differences from the mean.
**Standardized variable.

together. But first, consider the difference between these two scales and for support for labour. Support for redistribution and social welfare emphasizes differences in levels of consumption and social relations outside the workplace; they do not refer directly to the social relations of production. Therefore, they should be less tied to job characteristics than support for labour and more attached to indicators of social relations and consumption—in this case measured by education and family income (as distinct from rate of pay). By this reasoning they should be less tied to social class itself than was support for labour, because there is considerable overlap in the educational attainment and income levels of the four classes.

The results do little to support these hypotheses. First, jobs play an even stronger role in mediating the relation between social class and support for redistribution and social welfare than they did in the case of support for labour. Social class alone explains 5.3 percent of the variance in support for redistribution, but its effect net of job characteristics is only .7 percent; for support for social welfare the corresponding figures are 6.6 percent and 1.7 percent (see Table 37-2, columns 2 and 3). Furthermore, working conditions (including a rather small effect of family income) have strong effects on the two scores, explaining 11.7 percent and 9.4 percent of the variance, respectively, with no other factors considered. Trade union membership has a stronger effect on support for labour than on support for redistribution and social welfare, but when social class is held constant, union membership has approximately equal effects on all three variables.

Holding social class constant, the effects of a number of features of the job are unaltered. Support for redistribution is a function of the differences between manual and non-manual workers and between skilled and the combination of semi- and unskilled workers, trade union membership, difficulty with work hours, physical and mental tiredness, and rate of pay. All the effects are in the directions observed in the previous analysis of support for labour, except for the effect of mental fatigue. Workers faced with more unpleasant and less remunerative jobs take more left-wing positions.

When job conditions are held constant, a considerable alteration in the positions of the four social classes takes place. On the scale of support for redistribution, there is a remarkable decline in the difference between the two extreme classes, from .71 standard deviations to only .30. Originally the classes are spread out on a continuum from the working class on the left, through the middle class and petty bourgeoisie, to the bourgeoisie on the right. When job conditions are held constant, there is little difference among the working class (which is still on the left), the middle class, and the bourgeoisie. The petty bourgeoisie is farthest on the right, perhaps suggesting their greater fear of being levelled to the condition of the working class—a threat that members of the bourgeoisie are confident they have the political strength to combat. The class differences in support for social welfare strongly resemble those for support for labour. Once more, the insertion of the three background variables does little to change the patterns just described.

Background Effects

The fact that the introduction of statistical controls for class background has little impact on the relation among social class, job characteristics, and political attitudes, means that a political socialization model is not likely to be of much use in explaining the relation between class and ideology. The impact of family background is generally not as strong as that of either social class or jobs. With no other variables held constant, it explains 2.8 percent of the variance in support for labour, 5.5 percent in support for redistribution, and 2.7 percent in support for social welfare (in Table 37-2). These effects are reduced by about one quarter when social class is held constant, by at least three quarters when job conditions are added. With class and job held constant, the values of the explained variance are reduced, respectively, to 1.0 percent, 1.4 percent and 0.4 percent.

The most striking result of an examination of the regression coefficients (in Table 37-3, columns 6, 12, 18) is that educational attainment, of respondent and mother, is negatively related to support for left-wing political positions. Father's education has almost no effect, when the other two variables are held constant. The introduction of controls for job characteristics serves to change the relative importance of mother's and respondent's education: the insertion of job as a control dramatically lowers the effect of respondent's education, but does little to alter the impact of mother's education. This makes sense, for the studies of occupational attainment all reveal much stronger relations between respondent's jobs and their own levels of education than between jobs and their parents' education and occupations. Job conditions mediate the effect of education, as well as that of class, on political ideology.

A comparison of class differences, with and without education held constant, shows that the controls for education, as for job conditions, alter the positions of the petty bourgeoisie and bourgeoisie—the former holding a more liberal position when job and background are held constant (compare columns 1 and 4, 7 and 10, 13 and 16). Thus much more of the evident conservatism of the bourgeoisie can be laid down to other factors—higher levels of education, non-union jobs, higher pay and family income, and so on—than is true for the petty bourgeoisie. This suggests that the class condition of the petty bourgeoisie is an independently conservatizing element, that is absent for other classes, including the bourgeoisie. Still, these differences are of relatively small magnitude. Also, the bourgeoisie category includes both high- and middle-level managers, certainly it does not represent the big bourgeoisie, since it includes almost 8 percent of the working population.

CONCLUSION

In our view, the findings support the arguments that class can be successfully defined on the basis of Marxist categories, that modest class differences in political ideology do exist and are elaborated on the basis of class interest, and that differences in the work situation of the various classes serve to mediate the effect of class on political ideology. The attempt to consider the prior role of social background as a common cause of class and political attitudes was not very fruitful. The implication is that models of political socialization, at least insofar as they are based on parental education and occupation, do not provide adequate explanations of political ideology. The immediacy of the work environment clearly plays a more critical role. The results also cast doubt on the theoretical arguments of Hindess and Hirst and their collaborators that there is a "necessary non-correspondence" between the economic and the political. Still, the extent of the correspondence is quite small.

The more left-wing position of the working class reflects a number of aspects of the jobs they hold, including the distinctions between manual and non-manual work, between skilled and semi- and unskilled jobs, rates of pay, physical and mental tiredness, and trade union membership. In a certain sense, however, our original goal of locating the experiential basis of class differences in political attitudes is retreating as we advance—for these findings pose a new set of questions about the roots of political ideology. If we began by asking what it is about class that leads to differences in political attitudes, we now may wonder what it is about trade union membership, and physical and mental tiredness, that causes them to affect ideology. The items dealing with tiredness raise the most serious problem—since it is not clear to what extent they represent the objective conditions of jobs and to what extent they are measures of individual

differences in perceptions of jobs. We have made progress, but the initial problem is only partly solved.

An interesting by-product of this analysis is the finding that there are aspects of jobs whose effects on political attitudes cannot be traced to underlying class differences. These effects are certainly comparable in magnitude to the class differences. These findings suggest that we inquire into the nature of political differences *within* social classes, rather than account for differences *between* classes. The question then is whether different factors might operate in different classes, or, to put it another way, whether there is interaction between class and the mediating variables.

NOTES

1. Support for labour was measured by summing the responses to the statements:
   a. Workers should have the right to refuse to work in conditions which they consider to be unsafe, until a government inspector assures them that conditions are safe.
   b. During a strike, management should be prohibited by law from hiring workers to take the place of strikers.
   c. Workers should have positions on the board of directors of the organization for which they work.
   The scale of support for redistribution was created by summing the responses to the following statements:
   a. There is too much difference between rich and poor in this country.
   b. The government should provide jobs for Canadians who want to work but cannot find a job.
   c. People with high incomes should pay a greater share of the total taxes than they do now.

   For the two scales above, a card was presented to the respondents containing the following

alternatives: strongly agree (scored 5); agree (4); neither agree nor disagree (3); disagree (2); strongly disagree (1); and no opinion (3). Respondents giving more than one "no opinion" response were not scored on the scale. The mean inter-item correlation was .27 for support for redistribution, and .26 for support for labour—when computed for the entire cross section of the Canadian population (not just the subset of workers analysed here). Support for social welfare was measured by combining the responses to eight items, as measured in the following larger question:

We would like to know how much effort you think government should put into a number of activities. Please choose the answer on this card which comes closest to your opinion about the effort that should be made in each area. Remember that putting more effort into one of these areas would require a shift of money from other areas or an increase in taxes. How much effort should be put into
a. health and medical care
b. providing assistance to the unemployed
c. creating more jobs

d. helping the poor
e. building public housing
f. education
g. helping retired people
h. workman's compensation

The card contained the following alternative responses: much more effort (scored 5); more effort (4); about the same effort (3); less effort (2); much less effort (1). The mean correlation among the eight items is .27 for the entire population.

2. The measurement of the variables is self-explanatory, except as listed below.
b. Supervisory, semi-professional, professional, technical, managerial occupations are all classified in the "skilled" category.
d. This measure is derived from summing the responses to a question that reads: "I am going to read you some statements about jobs. Please tell me how true each one is of your job using one of these answers." [The respondent is handed a card with four responses: very true (scored 4); somewhat true (3); not very true (2); and not at all true (1).] (1) The people you work with are competent and helpful; (2) The pay is good; (3) The physical surroundings are pleasant; (4) The work is interesting; (5) The job security is good; (6) The chances for getting ahead are good; (7) There is an opportunity to develop your skills and abilities; (8) Your supervisor is good at his/her job; (9) The job does not interfere with your personal life and leisure activities; (10) There is the recognition you deserve for your work; (11) You can influence important decisions that are made by your supervisor; (12) There is a great deal of freedom to decide how to do your work; (13) The work you do makes a real contribution to other people.
e. This variable is defined by combining the responses to two items that read as follows:
1. Do you have any problems or difficulties concerning the hours you work, your work schedule or overtime? (a) yes (continue to next question); (b) no (scored zero, next question skipped).
2. How serious are these problems for you? (a) very serious (scored 3); (b) fairly serious (scored 2); (c) not very serious (scored 1).

REFERENCES

Carchedi, Guglielmo
   1975a   "Reproduction of social classes at the level of productive relations," *Economy and Society*, 4, no. 4:361-417.
   1975b   "The economic identification of the state employees," *Social Praxis*, 3, no. 1:93-120.
   1975c   "On the economic identification of the new middle class," *Economy and Society*, 4, no. 2:1-85.

Johnston, William, and Michael D. Ornstein
   1979   "Social class and political ideology in Canada." Paper presented at the Annual Meeting of the American Sociological Association, Boston.

Pineo, Peter C., John Porter, and Hugh A. McRoberts
   1977   "The 1971 census and the socioeconomic classification of occupations," *Canadian Review of Sociology and Anthropology*, 14, no. 1:91-102.

38. Social Class and Voting

Ronald D. Lambert, James E. Curtis, Steven D. Brown, and Barry J. Kay

EARLY STUDIES OF SOCIAL CLASS AND VOTING

The question of the relationship between people's social class positions and who they vote for can fairly be described as a vintage problem in Canadian political sociology. In his 1963 book *Party and Society*, Robert Alford proposed that class voting can be measured by the difference in the levels of support given by the working class and the middle class to left-wing parties or to right-wing parties (Alford, 1963:79-80).[1] The larger the discrepancy between the two social classes in either case, the greater the level of class voting. Another measure is simply the correlation between voters' social-class positions and the left/right orientations of the parties for which they vote. By "left," Alford meant the extent to which par-

ties promote the interests of the working class and work for economic equality in society; by "right," he meant the extent to which parties promote the interests of the middle class and oppose the intervention of government into the market place in pursuit of the goals of economic equality. We accept these conceptions of left/right for the purposes of this paper.

As we shall see shortly, our estimate of the class vote depends on how voters' social class and parties' left/right orientations are measured. On the voters' side, Alford singled out occupation as the preferred indicator of social class; on the parties' side, he relied on the opinions of experts to categorize their left/right orientations. For the latter, the informed opinion of the day located the Liberal and the CCF parties (the CCF is now the NDP, of course) on the left and the Progressive Conservative party on the right.

Having defined and measured what he meant by class voting, Alford (1963:81-84) proceeded to compare Canada with Britain,

An original article prepared especially for this volume.

Australia, and the United States. On the basis of public opinion poll data that was collected between 1952 and 1962, Canada received an average score of 8 percentage points on his index of class voting. This means, in other words, that the spread between working-class and middle-class support for left-wing parties was 8 percent. The comparisons showed 16 percent for the United States, 33 percent for Australia and 40 percent for Britain. In another study, based on surveys covering roughly the same period, Lenski and Lenski (1974:356) reported that Canada ranked lowest out of nine nations in the incidence of class voting.

Canada emerges from these studies, then, as relatively unique among western industrialized nations in its "non-class voting." In an attempt to explain this finding, various authors have argued that Canadians are more susceptible to electoral appeals around non-class issues, such as ethnic and regional concerns. Apart from these general trends, however, Alford detected greater class voting in certain sectors of the Canadian population. The level of class voting was higher in Ontario than in the other provinces, among urban dwellers compared to rural residents, and among Protestants than Roman Catholics. From these results, he predicted that class voting would emerge more clearly in the future because of continuing urbanization, industrialization, and secularization, and because of the gradual breakdown in Quebec's isolation from the rest of Canada.

OGMUNDSON'S EXTENSION OF THE CLASS VOTING STUDIES

A major departure in research on the problem of the class vote was signalled in a series of articles published by Ogmundson in the mid-1970s (Ogmundson, 1975a; 1975b; 1975c; 1976). What was innovative in his work was the use of voters' opinions, in preference to those of experts, to identify the class orientations of the federal parties. In doing so, he challenged the wisdom of classifying the Liberal party as a left-wing party. He posed the following kinds of paradoxes: While experts may believe that the Liberal party favours the left, what are we to make of middle-class people who vote for it, thinking that it is right-wing? And what are we to make of working-class people who vote for the Progressive Conservatives in the belief that it is left-wing? In the minds of some critics, these individuals may be misguided, but it would be short-sighted to dismiss their views out of hand. This was the oversight that Ogmundson wished to correct.

The first of a series of Canadian National Election Studies, this one conducted after the 1965 general election, asked a national sample of voting-age adults about their perceptions of the major federal political parties. In one of the questions, the respondents were shown a seven-point rating scale defined at one end with the phrase "for the working class" and at the other end with the phrase "for the middle class". Ogmundson (1979:805) used this scale because he believed that it captured essentially what Alford and others had in mind when they wrote about the class vote. He was also of the opinion that the idea of social class enjoys greater currency than the idea of left/right among the public. He, therefore, used this scale to measure class voting.

Ogmundson's research yielded a number of interesting findings. The first one was that people tended to perceive the NDP as favouring the working class and the Liberals and Conservatives as favouring the middle class. He argued that the disagreement between voters' and experts' judgments of the Liberal party provides the key to understanding the results of previous studies that showed low levels of class voting in Canada.

Ogmundson measured social class in terms of people's education, income, occupation, and subjective social class. Individuals from the 1965 National Election Study were categorized as either high or low on each of these measures. Education, income, and occupation are self-explanatory measures. For "subjective social class," Ogmundson used the respondents' answers to the following question:

> If you had to pick one, which of the following five social classes would you say you were in— upper class, upper-middle class, middle class, working class, or lower class?

He treated people who answered upper class, upper-middle class, or middle class as "middle class," and people who answered working class or lower class as "working class" (Ogmundson, 1975a:170).

Next, Ogmundson related the information on the respondents' social-class positions and their reported vote in the previous federal election. When the parties' class orientations were defined according to the opinions of experts (that is, Liberal and CCF are "left," or "for the working class"), there was evidence of a *negative* class vote for each of the social-class measures. In the case of income, for example, higher-income respondents were somewhat more likely than lower-income respondents to support parties labelled by the experts as leftist.

The direction of the relationship changed, however, when party orientations were based on the average perceptions of respondents across the country (that is, Liberals and Progressive Conservatives are "right," or "for the middle class"). There was evidence of a positive class vote for each of education, occupation, and subjective social class, but not for income. In the case of subjective social class, for example, people who said they were working class were considerably more likely than those who labelled themselves middle class to support the NDP, Social Credit, or Creditistes. The class vote (percent difference score) was 7.9 in 1965. When Lambert and Hunter (1979:294) repeated his kind of analysis with data from the 1968 National Election Study, the class vote was only slightly higher at 9.1 percentage points.

The presence of a class vote was shown to be even more pronounced when Ogmundson focussed on each respondent's own definition of the class orientation of whichever party he or she supported. Subjective class voting was said to occur, for example, when a person's income level corresponded with the class orientation that he or she attributed to his or her preferred party. In the case of subjective social class, the subjective class vote is entirely relative to each respondent because he or she has defined his or her own social class *and* has defined the class orientation of the party for which he or she has voted. Ogmundson's procedure produced difference scores of 17.6 percentage points in 1965 and 17.1 in 1968 for voters whose social class was subjectively measured (Lambert and Hunter, 1979:294).

PURPOSE OF THE PRESENT STUDY

We will report on data taken from the 1984 Canadian National Election Study or CNES (Lambert, Brown, Curtis, Kay, and Wilson, 1986).[2] Our study departs in several important respects from the previous studies of class voting in Canada. We asked the survey respondents to rate the class orientations of the provincial parties in the provinces where they resided, as well as the three major federal parties. We were therefore able to investigate class voting at the federal level and separately at the provincial level. Our research within selected provinces allows us to test predictions about these provinces in order to test predictions about the regions where class voting should be strongest and weakest. Fortunately, there were sufficient numbers of respondents from the provinces in question for purposes of analysis.

The point of departure for this paper is the assumption that non-class issues frequently override class issues as determinants of the direction of people's votes. For one example, this shows up in regional variations in the party system across Canada. The NDP, which is clearly the principal left-of-centre federal party in Canada (Lambert, 1982:140), is weaker in its voter support in some provinces and stronger in others (Zipp and Smith, 1982). As a result, voters in provinces where the NDP is weak are sometimes discouraged from "wasting" their vote for a party which, it is prophesied, is destined to finish third. Also, working-class voters are less likely to be knowledgeable about the NDP where it is weak, and consequently are less likely to appreciate its relevance for their class interests.

We expected more class voting in the provincial and federal elections in British Columbia where there is a militant trade union tradition and where the NDP has formed the government and is now the official opposition, than in Quebec, where politics has been oriented more to questions of language and ethnicity and where the NDP is weak. We also report results for Ontario in which we expected less class voting than in British Columbia, but more than in Quebec.

In addition, we predicted less federal-level than provincial-level class voting, on the assumption that federal votes are more likely to be solicited on the basis of regional, ethnic, and other loyalties that have little to do with social class. Part of the appeal of the federal NDP in the Western provinces, for example, may be less for reasons of class than as a protest against what is perceived to be Ontario and Quebec's domination of federal politics. In general, however, we assume that the latter factor will not figure prominently in people's thinking about the provincial NDP in each of the Western provinces.

The 1984 CNES measured the respondents' perceptions of federal and provincial party orientation using a seven-point scale whose end-points were labelled "for the lower social classes" and "for the higher social classes." The following instructions were read to the respondents:

> Some people believe that political parties favour particular social classes over other social classes. Here is a scale for describing each of the federal parties. [Respondents were shown a card depicting the scale.] The closer to "1," the more the party favours the lower social classes, and the closer to "7," the more a party favours the higher social classes. [Respondents were then asked:] Where would you place the federal Liberal party on this scale? . . . the federal Progressive Conservative party? . . . the federal NDP? [Respondents were next asked the following:] Now I would like to ask you about the provincial political parties here in [respondent's province of residence was named]. First, how much does the provincial Liberal party favour the lower or the higher social classes? [Respondents were then asked to rate each of the major provincial parties, by name, in their respective provinces.]

This scale differs from the one used by Ogmundson and was used on the assumption that class conflict, if it is perceived, is more likely between the lower and the upper classes than between the lower and the middle classes. However, in order to anchor the findings produced by the new scale in previous studies based on the old scale, the 1984 CNES also asked respondents to rate the three federal parties on the working class/middle class scale. We report on findings using this scale, too.

Our analyses allow us to evaluate simultaneously the effects of different aspects of socio-economic status. Much of the previous research, in contrast, has looked at the relationship between separate dimensions of social class, taken singly, and the class orientations of the parties for which people have voted.[3] At the same time, we distinguish between "objective" measures of social class, such as income, occupation, and education, and our single "subjective" measure, subjective class identification. This is an important distinction because subjective measures are psychologically "closer" to people's perceptions of the parties than are objective measures. By "closer," we mean that social psychological events occurring within individuals, such as which class they identify with, are nearer in time and space to the behaviour we are trying to explain, than are variables such as how much education they have. Thus, the subjective variable should be most relevant to explaining the class vote.

We examined what percentage of people's voting behaviour can be explained by the three objective measures, and then asked how much more of their behaviour can be explained by the single subjective measure. We will speak of these findings in terms of "explained variance."

RESULTS

Relationships Between the New Scale and the Old Scale

Before we turn to the results using the new scale, we will consider the magnitude of the correlations between people's ratings of the federal parties on the old scale (for the working class versus for the middle class) and the new scale (for the lower social classes versus for the higher social classes). The correlations measure the amount of agreement in the relative scores respondents obtain on the two scales. Nationally, the correlation was high, though not perfect ($r = .49$; $p<.001$). It was highest in British Columbia ($r = .69$; $p<.001$), where class politics are presumably most developed, and lowest in Quebec ($r = .31$; $p<.001$). The correlation for Ontario ($r = .54$; $p<.001$) fell in between the correlations for British Columbia and Quebec, as expected.

Provincial Differences in the Strength of Class Voting

Our predictions about the relative strength of provincial-level class voting in the three provinces are supported by the results presented in Table 38-1. The three objective measures of social class explained 16.1 percent of the variance in the provincial class vote in British Columbia; adding subjective social class boosted this figure to 19.8 percent. The lowest level of provincial class voting occurred in Quebec, where the three measures accounted for 2.8 percent and all four measures accounted for only 3.3 percent of the total variance. Ontario fell in between on both counts.

Table 38-2 shows that the highest level of social-class voting at the federal level occurred in British Columbia, with the lowest in Ontario; the level in Quebec fell somewhere in between. The four social-class measures explained 12.0 percent of the variance in British Columbia, 6.9 percent in Quebec, and only 4.0 percent in Ontario.

Provincial versus Federal Class Voting

We expected that class voting would be more pronounced at the provincial level than at

TABLE 38-1 Provincial-level class voting in selected provinces and nationally, using the scale "For the lower social classes" versus "For the higher social classes"[1]

	Quebec			Ontario			British Columbia			National		
	(N)	Unadj.	Adj.	(N)	Unadj.	Adj.	(N)	Unadj.	Adj.	(N)	Unadj.	Adj.
Education												
Elem. & some HS	146	3.95	4.02	221	4.25	4.41	53	3.72	3.97	688	4.10	4.20
HS graduate	130	4.10	4.10	107	3.98	3.98	55	4.03	4.21	453	4.10	4.14
Post-HS	140	4.09	4.08	109	4.48	4.42	60	4.15	3.88	490	4.22	4.21
Degree	64	4.09	3.96	84	4.17	3.83	30	3.48	3.24	288	4.02	3.76
e/b =		.05/.04			.11/.16			.14/.18			.04/.11	
F =		0.17			4.04**			1.87			5.60***	
Income (000s)												
Less than $10	171	3.88	3.89	180	3.98	3.90	80	3.63	3.58	693	3.91	3.90
$10–20	107	3.93	3.94	110	4.36	4.45	33	3.98	4.01	409	4.08	4.09
$20–30	94	4.19	4.16	91	4.20	4.31	25	3.89	3.95	317	4.17	4.20
$30–50	49	4.18	4.18	75	4.61	4.58	35	3.68	3.76	256	4.29	4.30
$50 +	21	4.39	4.40	17	4.36	4.36	14	5.73	5.63	75	4.72	4.74
DK; Refused	39	4.44	4.47	48	4.30	4.23	12	4.03	4.00	168	4.46	4.40
e/b =		.14/.14			.15/.17			.31/.30			.14/.15	
F =		1.63			2.55*			3.12**			7.04***	
Occupation												
Hi white-collar	105	4.14	4.03	134	4.48	4.31	55	3.85	3.82	467	4.24	4.15
Lo white-collar	85	3.98	3.97	98	3.84	3.78	35	4.14	4.09	338	4.04	3.99
Hi blue-collar	124	4.13	4.15	146	4.11	4.09	45	3.99	3.67	486	4.10	4.08
Lo blue-collar	38	3.81	3.83	38	4.52	4.78	15	3.24	3.50	151	4.03	4.14
Farmer	17	4.07	4.03	15	4.52	4.64	2	—	—	93	4.21	4.22
Homemaker	112	4.01	4.09	90	4.30	4.51	45	3.84	4.14	384	4.08	4.21
e/b =		.07/.07			.16/.19			.16/.16			.05/.05	
F =		0.42			3.97**			0.92			0.93	

(continued)

TABLE 38-1 Continued

	Quebec (N) Unadj. Adj.			Ontario (N) Unadj. Adj.			British Columbia (N) Unadj. Adj.			National (N) Unadj. Adj.		
Subjective social class												
Upper-class	51	4.08	4.02	53	4.51	4.65	16	5.28	4.83	176	4.38	4.36
Middle-class	330	4.12	4.11	245	4.50	4.51	95	4.08	4.12	1 040	4.26	4.27
Lower-class	100	3.81	3.85	223	3.87	3.80	87	3.45	3.48	704	3.85	3.84
e/b =		.09/.08			.21/.23			.30/.24			.14/.15	
F =		1.37			11.96***			5.30**			17.78***	
Variance explained =		3.3%			11.2%			19.8%			6.4%	
Variance explained without subjective social class =		2.8%			6.3%			16.1%			4.8%	

[1]The appropriate provincial weights were used for each provincial analysis and the national weights were used for the national analysis. Province was used as a control in the national analysis. "Unadj." = figures unadjusted; and "adj." = figures adjusted to control for the other variables in the analysis.

*Signifies statistically significant at $p<.05$.   **At $p<.01$.   ***At $p<.001$.

the federal level. The results are consistent with this prediction in British Columbia and Ontario, but not in Quebec. The four predictors explained 7.8 percent more variance for provincial politics than for federal politics in British Columbia. The gap was 7.2 percent in Ontario. In the case of Quebec, however, the direction of the difference was reversed; the full set of social-class measures accounted for 3.6 percent more variance federally than provincially. To underscore the latter finding, this means that Quebec respondents said they voted more in line with their social class when they voted federally than when they voted provincially. Of course, it is important to bear in mind that the overall level of class voting in Quebec was relatively low both provincially and federally.

We also found, in separate analyses not reported in Tables 38-1 and 38-2, that a combined subsample of respondents from the Atlantic Provinces scored between Ontario and British Columbia on the level of class voting on both measures (the provinces were combined, and not studied separately, because of the small number of respondents from each province). For example, there was 8.1 percent variance explained by the four social-class measures for the provincial vote, and there was 6.1 percent variance explained for the federal vote. Similar analyses for the three Western provinces (Manitoba, Saskatchewan, and Alberta) combined, yielded levels of class voting between those of Ontario and British Columbia; there was 7.6 percent explained for the provincial-level vote and 4 percent for the federal vote.

Subjective versus Objective Social Class Measures

We can estimate from the figures given at the bottom of Tables 38-1 and 38-2 the increment in the variance explained that is produced by subjective social class. British Columbia is most interesting, of course, because it showed the highest level of provincial and federal class voting. Subjective social class added another 23 percent to the variance explained for the provincial vote; this variable increased the variance explained by another 85 percent for the federal vote in British Columbia. In Ontario, subjective social class added approximately 78 percent to the explanation of the provincial class vote. As we have already noted, the figures were generally low with or without subjective social class in Quebec.

Effects of the Individual Social Class Measures

Looking at the variance explained tells us something about the magnitude of the relationship between the social-class measures and the class vote. However, it does not tell us about the direction of these relationships. We must keep in mind the possibility of the negative class voting pattern reported by Ogmundson (1975b:510; see also Lambert and Hunter, 1979:294) using the Alford procedure for defining parties' class orientations. Tables 38-1 and 38-2 allow us to tell whether there is positive or negative class voting by comparing the class vote for people in each category of income, education, occupation, and subjective social class. Voting scores in the columns marked "unadjusted" give us this information. The columns marked "adjusted" show us whether there were differences in class voting across the categories of a particular social-class measure after controls have been made for the effects of the other social-class measures.

As Tables 38-1 and 38-2 show, subjective social class was a statistically significant predictor (p<.01) in all of the analyses except

for Quebec provincially, and the patterns were as expected. That is, respondents who thought of themselves as belonging to the working class were more likely to report voting for a party which they perceived as favouring the lower social classes than were respondents who claimed a higher class for themselves. As Table 38-1 shows for the national sample, those who defined themselves as "lower class" had a mean score of 3.85 on the party definition question, those who identified with the "middle class" had a mean of 4.26, and those who defined themselves as "upper class" had a score of 4.38.

In general, the effects of subjective social class were higher than the effects for the three objective indicators, as anticipated. And the effects of subjective social class were not appreciably diminished when the effects of the other social-class measures were taken into account.

Income was the most important predictor of voting direction among the three objective measures of social class. The pattern of effects for income, with and without controls, was more or less as expected, although there were some departures from the pattern in Ontario and British Columbia at the provincial level. Respondents with higher incomes were more likely to report voting for parties that they perceived as biased in favour of the higher social classes. For example, in Table 38-1 for the national sample, those with less than $10 000 per year in income scored at a mean of 3.91 on the party definition scale and the means steadily rose with greater income until the category with $50 000 or more in earnings scored at 4.72.

The effects of the other two social-class variables were more noteworthy for their general unimportance and for their irregularity in those cases where they were significant. For example, most of the effect associated with education in the national analysis

TABLE 38-2 Federal-level class voting in selected provinces and nationally, using the scale "For the lower social classes" versus "For the higher social classes"[1]

	Quebec (N)	Unadj.	Adj.	Ontario (N)	Unadj.	Adj.	British Columbia (N)	Unadj.	Adj.	National (N)	Unadj.	Adj.
Education												
Elem. & some HS	157	4.17	4.31	267	4.43	4.55	61	4.00	4.22	787	4.28	4.38
HS graduate	137	4.55	4.56	137	4.36	4.37	68	4.22	4.16	528	4.37	4.38
Post-HS	157	4.15	4.10	180	4.48	4.45	81	4.35	4.25	658	4.29	4.27
Degree	61	4.56	4.28	110	4.32	4.07	35	4.32	4.28	341	4.39	4.18
e/b =		.14/.13			.04/.11			.09/.03			.03/.06	
F =		2.83*			2.10			0.05			1.72	
Income (000s)												
Less than $10	213	4.14	4.14	275	4.37	4.32	101	3.91	3.91	941	4.18	4.16
$10-20	102	4.33	4.38	139	4.29	4.35	47	4.33	4.33	458	4.29	4.34
$20-30	83	4.39	4.37	108	4.42	4.48	31	4.63	4.66	344	4.39	4.43
$30-50	49	4.65	4.64	88	4.72	4.72	35	4.22	4.29	284	4.54	4.54
$50 +	19	4.56	4.41	21	4.38	4.35	15	5.22	4.96	80	4.69	4.66
DK; Refused	45	4.45	4.44	64	4.44	4.41	16	4.10	4.10	207	4.44	4.39
e/b =		.13/.12			.09/.09			.23/.20			.10/.11	
F =		1.14			1.01			1.74			4.32***	
Occupation												
Hi white-collar	109	4.41	4.26	183	4.58	4.55	69	4.14	3.89	569	4.43	4.32
Lo white-collar	73	4.44	4.38	143	4.21	4.20	50	4.42	4.37	418	4.29	4.25
Hi blue-collar	132	4.17	4.23	184	4.32	4.30	60	4.39	4.38	585	4.28	4.29
Lo blue-collar	61	4.25	4.32	54	4.36	4.47	17	3.80	4.05	209	4.16	4.27
Farmer	16	4.48	4.43	16	4.83	4.89	2	—	—	94	4.30	4.37
Homemaker	120	4.30	4.38	115	4.50	4.54	46	4.03	4.38	439	4.34	4.44
e/b =		.08/.05			.11/.11			.12/.14			.06/.05	
F =		0.24			1.56			0.87			0.86	

Subjective social class

Upper-class	60	4.60	4.67	75	4.62	4.68	20	4.95	4.83	226	4.58	4.56
Middle-class	348	4.41	4.39	342	4.54	4.54	125	4.48	4.49	1 272	4.44	4.45
Lower-class	103	3.80	3.82	277	4.19	4.17	99	3.75	3.76	817	4.06	4.05
e/b =			.19/.20			.13/.14			.26/.25			.14/.14
F =			8.58***			5.26**			6.33**			19.24***
Variance explained =			6.9%			4.0%			12.0%			4.1%
Variance explained without subjective social class =			4.3%			2.4%			6.5%			2.5%

[1]See footnote to Table 38-1.
*Signifies statistically significant at p<.05.
**At p<.01.
***At p<.001.

of the provincial class vote was attributable to the differences between respondents who possessed a university degree and those who had any level of education short of a degree. In this analysis, highly educated respondents were more likely than anybody else to support a party that they perceived to favour the lower social classes. Here we have a class vote; but its direction is opposite to what we would expect. This is the only instance of negative class voting in the present analyses.

Results Using the Scale "For the Working Class" versus "For the Middle Class"

To this point, we have presented results using information from the scale "for the lower social classes" versus "for the higher social classes." As we said, the federal parties were also rated on the scale "for the working class" versus "for the middle class" because previous research on class voting has been based on it. Space does not permit presentation of a table containing the results of these analyses, paralleling Table 38-2, but we will note the major findings.

Slightly more variance was explained using the old scale than the new scale in most of the comparisons. The biggest differences occurred in British Columbia where the three objective measures accounted for 11.1 percent of the variance on the old scale, compared to 6.5 percent on the new scale; and all four variables accounted for 17.4 percent, compared to 12.0 percent on the new scale. It is interesting, however, that the subjective and objective social-class measures were less likely to exhibit significant effects on the vote when the old scale was employed. Statistically significant effects were limited to subjective social class in British Columbia and nationally, and to income for Quebec and nationally.

Replication of Ogmundson's Analysis

We mentioned that Ogmundson (1975a; 1975b), as well as Lambert and Hunter (1979), measured each voter's social class simply as low or high on each of occupation, education, income, and subjective social class. The perceived class orientations of the parties were also dichotomized between those that were "for the working class" and those that were "for the middle class." The results that we have reported to this point are based on the social-class variables taken as a set, and with each of these variables measured at more than two levels (that is, low versus high). In addition, we have used the party ratings as seven-point scales, rather than dichotomizing them.

In order to make our findings directly comparable with those reported by Ogmundson (1975a, 1975b) and Lambert and Hunter (1979), we performed some supplementary analyses of the 1984 data, based on dichotomies and analysing the data in the way they did. Using each voter's own opinion of the class orientation of the party for which he or she voted in 1984, there was less evidence of class voting than there was in 1965 and 1968. This was true for each of the two scales for measuring parties' class orientations and for each of the four ways of measuring respondents' social class. It would appear that successful election campaigns, built around the personality of an attractive leader, and not unlike appeals to voters' regional and ethnic concerns, can override the effects of voters' social class. It is worth remembering, however, that the stronger evidence for class voting in 1968 emerged from an election characterized by "Trudeaumania."

DISCUSSION AND CONCLUSIONS

The evidence presented here is generally consistent with our predictions that class voting would be more pronounced in British Columbia than in Quebec and in provincial politics than in federal politics. We believe this pattern reflects the greater polarization of politics along explicitly class lines in British Columbia and at the provincial level. The greater importance of subjective class than of the three objective measures of social class supports the prediction that class consciousness is a significant factor in translating the objective circumstances of people's social class into a subjective class vote. At the same time, however, the finding that income was a significant predictor of the direction of people's vote in British Columbia and, to a lesser extent, in Ontario, points to the material or economic component in the class vote.

On the other hand, there appeared to be less class voting in 1984 than there was in the 1960s. These comparisons were limited, of course, by the fact that they were confined to federal class voting; we know from the 1984 data that class voting at this level was weaker than it was at the provincial level. Comparisons were further limited by the fact that the social-class and party orientation variables were dichotomous, and these variables were looked at one at a time rather than as a set. We also thought that the new scale defined by the phrases "for the lower social classes" and "for the higher social classes" might produce more evidence of class voting than the traditional scale. We were wrong. It may be that the sheer size of the middle class compared to the admittedly puny upper class makes it a more perceptible and meaningful comparison point for working-class voters, thus favouring the working-class/

middle-class contrast as a basis for perceiving class conflict. But this is purely conjectural on our part.

Our final observations have to do with how we should think of the class vote phenomenon. The disciplines of political science and sociology share "joint custody" for this area of study. Not surprisingly, political scientists are more interested in voting behaviour than in social class, which they use to explain voting. Sociologists, on the other hand, are primarily interested in social class and social stratification. The electoral system and voting behaviour have little appeal, as such, for them. Sociologists are more inclined to examine the array of effects associated with social class as a means of understanding the workings of social class; one of these effects happens to be voting choice. Students of social class fit class voting into theories of social class, not into theories of voting.

A consequence of this curious division of intellectual labour, at least among sociologists, has been an exceedingly truncated view of voting behaviour. Political scientists know that voting behaviour is the product of a number of major variables, such as leader and party images, policy issues and party identification. These variables, in turn, are understood to be the products of still other antecedent variables, including, but not limited to, social class. Social class may affect voter choice either indirectly through these intervening variables, or directly.

Seen from the perspective of political science, the question should not be whether there is or is not a class vote, but under what circumstances the electoral effects of social-class variables are most or least likely to appear. The results presented here suggest that class voting is most pronounced in political systems in which political life is cast in class terms, such as British Columbia. It appears to be minimized in systems in which the substance and rhetoric of politics is cast more in non-class terms, as in Quebec. In addition, appeals to regional, ethnic, and other loyalties are more likely to displace social class in federal politics. Thus, class voting is more likely to occur at the provincial than at the federal level. However, since society is not static, we can anticipate changes in the level of class voting following shifts in the bases of social conflict. In Quebec, for example, class voting may become more pronounced in the future if there is a movement in politics away from constitutional issues and toward economic issues. The analysis of class voting will benefit if it is thought of, once again, in terms of voting theory.

NOTES

1. Some sociologists prefer to reserve the concept of social class to refer to people's different relations to the means of production and to use the concept of social stratification to refer to dimensions such as occupation, education, and income, according to which scarce rewards are allocated. It is an accident of the discipline that the concept of class voting has tended to be used in the stratification sense.

2. The sample design of the 1984 Canadian National Election Study was a multi-stage, stratified cluster sample of the electorate, with systematic oversampling of the less populous provinces. The raw sample of 3377 respondents has been weighted (N = 3380) to make it nationally representative in terms of population, age, gender, and urban-rural composition. Each provincial sample has also been

weighted to make it provincially representative. Additional information about the study design appears in Lambert, Brown, Curtis, Kay and Wilson, 1986.

3. The principal statistical procedure used in this paper is called Multiple Classification Analysis or MCA (Andrews, Morgan, Sonquist, and Klem, 1973). This technique is used to examine the relationship between a single predictor or independent variable (for example, income, in this study) and a dependent variable (here, the class bias of the parties for which respondents reported voting), or the relationship between each of a set of predictors and the dependent variable, holding the effects of the remaining predictors constant.

This procedure provides the mean score on the dependent variable for each category with a predictor before and after the effects of the control variables are taken into account. Thus, in Tables 38-1 and 38-2 the figures show where in the range from 1 (for the lower social classes) to 7 (for the higher social classes) the mean response fell for any particular category of respondents. The "adjusted" figures are for analysis with controls and the "unadjusted" figures are the means before controls are taken into account.

This procedure also yields *eta* and *beta* coefficients which, when squared, provide a rough measure of the proportion of the total variance in the dependent variable that is accounted for by each predictor variable (1) without controls (eta) and (2) with controls (beta) for the other predictors.

REFERENCES

Alford, Robert A.
    1963   *Party and Society*. Chicago: University of Chicago.

Andrews, F., J. Morgan, J. Sonquist, and L. Klem
    1973   *Multiple Classification Analysis*. Ann Arbor: Institute of Social Research, University of Michigan.

Lambert, Ronald D.
    1982   "Question design, response set and the measurement of left/right thinking in survey research," *Canadian Journal of Political Science* 16, no. 1 (March):135-44.

Lambert, Ronald D., Steven D. Brown, James E. Curtis, Barry J. Kay, and John M. Wilson
    1986   *The 1984 Canadian National Election Study Codebook*. Waterloo (February).

Lambert, Ronald D., James E. Curtis, Steven D. Brown, and Barry J. Kay
    1986   "In search of left/right beliefs in the Canadian electorate," *Canadian Journal of Political Science*, 19, no. 3 (September):541-63.

Lambert, Ronald D., and Alfred A. Hunter
    1979   "Social stratification, voting behaviour, and the images of Canadian federal political parties," *Canadian Review of Sociology and Anthropology*, 16, no. 3 (August):287-304.

Lenski, Gerhard, and Jean Lenski
    1974   *Human Societies* (2nd ed.). New York: McGraw-Hill.

Ogmundson, Rick
    1975a   "On the use of party image variables to measure the political distinctiveness of a class vote: the Canadian case," *Canadian Journal of Sociology*, 1, no. 2 (Summer):169-77.

1975b   "Party class images and the class vote in Canada," *American Sociological Review,* 40, no. 4 (August):506-12.

1975c   "On the measurement of party class positions: the case of Canadian federal political parties," *Canadian Review of Sociology and Anthropology,* 12, no. 4 (November, part 2):565-76.

1976   "Mass-elite linkages and class issues in Canada," *Canadian Review of Sociology and Anthropology,* 13, no. 1 (February):1-12.

Ogmundson, Rick, and Mary Ng
1982   "On the inference of voter motivation: a comparison of the subjective class vote in Canada and the United Kingdom," *Canadian Journal of Sociology,* 7, no. 1 (Spring):41-59.

Zipp, John F., and Joel Smith
1982   "A structural analysis of class voting," *Social Forces,* 60, no. 3 (March):738-59.

39. Occupation, Education, and Feelings of Powerlessness

Edward G. Grabb

INTRODUCTION

Some of the most interesting and influential research into the consequences of class position and class experience deals with the question of "class and conformity" (Pearlin and Kohn, 1966; Kohn and Schooler, 1969; Kohn, 1969; 1977). This work makes the persuasive argument that certain key characteristics of occupations are crucial for understanding class differences in values, orientations, and perceptions. Two factors in particular are discussed: occupational experiences and educational training.

First, occupational experiences are important mainly with respect to "the conditions of self-direction that jobs provide or preclude" (Kohn, 1969:188). This argument asserts that non-manual jobs, which are generally characteristic of the middle class, entail more active manipulation and freedom from supervision than do the manual occupations typically associated with the working class. The latter involve close supervision, external direction, and minimal individual responsibility (Kohn, 1969:ix-x). A major consequence of this alleged difference in personal control over work is greater conformity to external authority in the working class, and a feeling that personal power and control are limited: "the essence of lower class position is the belief that one is at the mercy of forces and people beyond one's control" (Kohn, 1969:189; cf. Lockwood, 1966:251). In contrast, middle-class people are said to glean from their job experiences a sense that their decisions and actions are consequential, "that self-direction is both possible and efficacious" (Kohn, 1977:xxvi).

The second factor of consequence in this formulation is the level of educational training associated with different occupations. It is generally recognized that middle-class, non-manual positions presuppose more education than do jobs involving manual labour. In the view of Kohn and his associates, this education difference has an impact on the degree of "intellectual flexibility and

Revised from Edward G. Grabb, "Class, Conformity and Powerlessness," *Canadian Review of Sociology and Anthropology*, vol. 18, no. 3 (August 1981), pp. 362-69. Reprinted with permission.

breadth of perspective" of the middle and working classes (Kohn, 1969:188; cf. Gabennesch, 1972). Of course, higher education is no guarantee of a broader perspective; yet, at a minimum, the lower general education level in working-class occupations reduces the probability of exposure to diverse ideas and points of view which would promote such a wider prospect (Kohn, 1969:191). The key consequence of a broader perspective, it seems, is that it militates against the perception of immediate realities as unchangeable and externally defined, against what might be called a "reified" social construction of reality (Berger and Luckmann, 1966; Gabennesch, 1972:862-8). The argument, then, is that those in manual jobs will be less likely to believe they can affect their personal situations: middle-class occupations, on the other hand, produce in the individual a more pronounced sense of self-direction because of the greater educational training such jobs involve and the concomitant broader perspective which that implies.[1]

In addition, it is also the case that higher education is itself a prerequisite for many of those jobs which carry with them the privilege of personal responsibility, freedom, and control. Thus, Kohn views education as having two kinds of effects on subjective perceptions of self-direction: directly, as a consequence of developing a broader perspective; and indirectly, as a result of its impact on the level of job control experienced by the individual in the workplace (Kohn, 1977).

CLASS, CONFORMITY, AND POLITICAL POWERLESSNESS

One of the more intriguing elements of the class and conformity thesis is the claim that it has broad and general implications for understanding the links between social structure and the values, attitudes, and perceptions of individuals. The thesis is portrayed as a "learning-generalization model" in which "the lessons of work are directly carried over to non-occupational realms" (Kohn, 1977:liii). Kohn, for example, has attempted to demonstrate the link between class and conformity in the work world and class differences in parental values in the family setting. (For Canadian research on this topic, see Coburn and Edwards, 1976).

The purpose of this paper is to assess the applicability of the class and conformity thesis in a quite different context: the political sphere. Specifically, this paper examines the extent to which differences in education level and job control account for class differences in feelings of power and the effect on those in political authority. There are some obvious parallels between Kohn's research on external conformity in the working class and a body of research which indicates that working-class people express a relatively low sense of power to influence or change the existing political structure. One recent review of previous research on this topic finds consistent support for this argument, and cites American survey data from the 1950s and 1960s which further confirm the conclusion that socio-economic status is negatively related to subjective political powerlessness (Guest, 1974; see also, Almond and Verba, 1963; in Canada, see, for example, Simeon and Elkins, 1974; Manzer, 1974).

To this author's knowledge, the connections between these two bodies of literature on subject powerlessness have as yet not been demonstrated or even considered. The establishment of such a connection would seem to be a worthwhile extension of Kohn's more general class and conformity hypothesis: that there is "a direct translation of the lessons of the job to outside-the-job realities" (Kohn, 1977:liii). In this case the outside-the-job reality is the political context. If

Kohn's theory is to be extended, we should find, first, that manual workers do exhibit relatively more subjective political powerlessness, and second, that these class differences are partly or wholly explained by differences in educational training and level of job control.

DATA SOURCE AND MEASUREMENT

The data come from an area probability sample survey of 558 London, Ontario, residents. By excluding farmers and those with no stated occupation the number of respondents was reduced to 484. The measures for the four variables considered in the analysis should be briefly discussed. Occupation is dichotomized into manual and non-manual categories as the best approximation to the middle-class/working-class distinction. Educational training is measured simply by the highest level of schooling completed.

To measure the level of job control experienced in the work setting, an index of four items was devised.

1. "Do you feel that you have the power to make decisions about the things that have true importance to your work?" (Yes or no)
2. "Do you have much influence on the way things go at work?" (Yes or no)
3. "Is the speed at which you work controlled mostly by you, your boss, your work group, or the speed of the machinery?" (Categories were grouped into "you" versus all others.)
4. "How much control does your direct supervisor have over your work?" (A great deal, some, not very much, none at all)

An index was computed in a similar manner to measure subjective political powerlessness, this time involving seven items. The seven questions were shown in a factor

analysis to produce a strong one-factor solution, thus suggesting that all seven questions are tapping the same underlying construct. The items are as follows:

1. "I feel that my political leaders hardly care what people like myself think or want." (For all seven questions, the responses were strongly agree, agree, neutral, disagree, strongly disagree.)
2. "There doesn't seem to be much connection between what I want and what my representative does."
3. "Nothing I ever do seems to have any effect upon what happens in politics."
4. "It seems to me that whomever you vote for things go on pretty much the same."
5. "Political parties are so big that the average member hasn't got much to say about what goes on."
6. "The people who really 'run' the country do not ever get known to the voters."
7. "It's no use worrying about public affairs; I can't do anything about them anyhow."

RESULTS

The bivariate relationships among the four variables are shown in Table 39-1.[2] The correlations reveal that each of the six associations is statistically significant, of low to moderate magnitude, and in the expected direction. That is, manual workers are indeed more likely to express feelings of political powerlessness than are non-manuals ($r = -.204$); in addition, education is negatively associated with powerlessness ($r = -.257$), as is level of job control ($r = -.169$). The relationships among the three predictor variables are also consistent with the assumptions of Kohn's model, in that education, job control, and occupational status are all positively interrelated.

The bivariate findings, then, tend to support the view that differences in occupation-related factors may affect class differences in feelings of political efficacy. Both higher education and greater job control seem to be associated more with the non-manual occupations characteristic of the middle class. These factors, in turn, are associated with greater feelings of personal control and participation in the political realm.

These relationships by themselves, of course, are insufficient to establish this conclusion or to test Kohn's model. To accomplish these tasks, we must examine the relationships among all four variables operating simultaneously. Such a procedure will determine to what extent middle-class/working-class (or non-manual/manual) dif-

ferences in powerlessness are attributable to the related effects of education and job control. This produces some interesting results (Table 39-2). It becomes apparent that both education and job control maintain their modest but significant negative effects on subjective political powerlessness. Occupational status, however, has no appreciable impact on powerlessness when the other factors are taken into account. This suggests that *all* of the difference in powerlessness between manuals and non-manuals is a consequence of education and job-control differences. Hence, it does appear that the two factors which Kohn has isolated are the ones which account for class differences in subjective political powerlessness.

TABLE 39-1   Correlations for the relationships between the four variables.*

	Occupation (non-manual/manual)	Education	Job control	Political powerlessness
Occupation	—	.533	.297	− .204
Education		—	.228	− .257
Job control			—	− .169
Political powerlessness				—

*All correlations are statistically significant, p ≤ .001.

TABLE 39-2   Multiple regression of subjective political powerlessness on occupation, education, and job control.

Predictor	Step 1	Step 2	Step 3
Education	− .257	− .231	− .197
Job control		− .116	− .104
Occupation (non-manual/manual)			(− .068)
			N.S. p = .20
Total R^2	.07	.08	.08

DISCUSSION

The findings reported here lend support to two rather distinct bodies of literature: first, they appear to confirm the argument that the characteristics of occupations can have implications for understanding class differences in feelings of personal control, as in the work of Kohn and his associates; second, they further demonstrate the already well-established link between socio-economic status traits, such as occupation and education, and feelings of political efficacy. In this way, our results are significant in demonstrating the convergence of these two independent research traditions in sociology.

Perhaps the most interesting result is that a particular feature of the occupational milieu, namely level of control in the workplace, can have an impact on a phenomenon as far removed from the work world as subjective political powerlessness. This may signify a useful extension or amplification of the class and conformity argument. In addition, it suggests that factors other than the purely socio-economic should be taken into account when analysing class differences in political attitudes.

That education is found to be an important factor in explaining differences in subjective powerlessness is, of course, congruent with both bodies of literature mentioned above. This congruence, however, in a sense poses problems of interpretation, for it is not clear whether the education effect reflects, in Kohn's words, the greater "intellectual flexibility and breadth of perspective" of the middle class or simple socio-economic differences. In other words, it may be that socio-economic advantages closely related with higher education have produced greater *objective* political power, which in turn leads to a greater sense of political efficacy in the middle class. Intellectual flexibility or breadth of perspective, then, would have nothing to do with class differences in subjective powerlessness. In fact, the education effect revealed in these data could be indicative of processes quite distinct from either of these two explanations. For example, it could be that middle-class people, with their more extensive education, have merely received a more thorough exposure to that segment of our liberal democratic ideology which asserts that every citizen does have a say in government. Hence, class variations in this case would be attributable to differential acceptance of the ideology of political participation, rather than to differences in breadth of perspective.

NOTES

1. There are several other interpretations concerning education's effect on values, interpretations which have nothing to do with breadth of perspective. We reserve our discussion of these alternative explanations, however, for the end of the paper.

2. In computing correlation coefficients, occupational status was treated as a dichotomous dummy variable, with non-manuals coded as 1 and manuals as 0. For education, values were assigned to correspond approximately to the mean number of years of schooling represented by each category: "some grade school" = 4; "completed grade school" = 8; "some high school" = 10; "completed high school" = 12; "some university" = 14; "university graduate" = 16; "more than four years of university" = 18. The indices of job control and subjective political powerlessness were, of course, computed using factor score coefficients, and so involved no reclassification. Mean values were substituted for missing responses in all cases.

REFERENCES

Almond, Gabriel, and Sidney Verba
1963   *The Civic Culture.* Princeton: Princeton University Press.

Berger, Peter L., and Thomas Luckmann
1966   *The Social Construction of Reality.* Garden City: Doubleday.

Coburn, David, and Virginia L. Edwards
1976   "Job Control and Child-Rearing Values," *Canadian Review of Sociology and Anthropology,* 13 (August):337-44.

Gabennesch, Howard
1972   "Authoritarianism as World View," *American Journal of Sociology,* 77 (March): 857-75.

Guest, Avery M.
1974   "Subjective Powerlessness in the United States: Some Longitudinal Trends," *Social Science Quarterly,* 54 (March):827-42.

Kohn, Melvin
1969   *Class and Conformity. A Study in Values.* Homewood: The Dorsey Press.
1977   *Class and Conformity. A Study in Values* (2nd ed.). Chicago: University of Chicago Press.

Kohn, Melvin, and Carmi Schooler
1969   "Class, Occupation, and Orientation," *American Sociological Review,* 34 (October):659-78.
1978   "The Reciprocal Effects of the Substantive Complexity of Work and Intellectual Flexibility: A Longitudinal Assessment," *American Journal of Sociology,* 84 (July):24-52.

Lockwood, David
1966   "Sources of Variation in Working-Class Images of Society," *Sociological Review* (new series), 14 (November):249-67.

Manzer, Ronald
1974   *Canada: A Sociopolitical Report.* Toronto: McGraw-Hill Ryerson.

Pearlin, Leonard J., and Melvin Kohn
1966   "Social Class, Occupation, and Parental Values: A Cross-National Study," *American Sociological Review,* 31 (August):466-79.

Rinehart, James W., and Ishmael O. Okraku
1974   "A Study of Class Consciousness," *Canadian Review of Sociology and Anthropology,* 11 (August):197-213.

Simeon, Richard, and David J. Elkins
1974   "Regional Political Cultures in Canada," *Canadian Journal of Political Science,* 7 (September):397-437.

40. Differences in the Achievement Values of French Canadians and English Canadians

Douglas E. Baer
James E. Curtis

THEORIES OF FRENCH-ENGLISH VALUE DIFFERENCES

As Guindon (1978) and Murphy (1981) among others have emphasized, in much of the Canadian social science literature, even recently, there has been the persistent view that the cultural values and beliefs of French Canadians involve placing less emphasis on individual achievement and more emphasis on family and kinship compared with English Canadians. These views on French-English differences have been developed in several descriptive and speculative accounts of the two subcultures and they also have been invoked as interpretations of data on the differential social mobility of French Canadians and English Canadians (compare, for example, Hughes, 1943; Taylor,

1964; Garigue, 1964; Porter, 1965; Auclair and Reed, 1966; Richer and Laporte, 1971; Yackley and Lambert, 1972; Lambert et al., 1972; Beattie, 1975; Kanungo et al., 1976; Nightingale and Toulouse, 1977; Kanungo and Bhatnager, 1978; and Jain et al., 1979.) In the latter studies, the idea that these value differences exist has provided what Guindon has called "soothing explanations" for the lower participation rates of French Canadians in higher management and professional positions in the private sector and in the ownership of large firms.

A careful scrutiny of the literature will show, however, that there is little clear evidence of French-English differences in achievement values, whether for earlier periods or for the contemporary situation. Previous results have been contradictory, and they have not been drawn from representative samples of French Canadians and English Canadians. What support there is for the conventional view has received wide circulation and frequent citation however. Tay-

---

An original article prepared for this volume.

lor's (1964) work is perhaps most widely known among studies from earlier periods. He found in the 1950s that French-speaking owners of businesses were less likely to take risks, had lower aspirations for their businesses, were less inclined to pursue business aggressively, and were more preoccupied with family matters than were English-speaking owners of similar businesses. Taylor suggested that these differences and values had caused French firms to be smaller and to grow more slowly than English firms.

Most writers who have argued the case for the conventional view of French-English value differences have attributed them, in part, to differences in the religious beliefs of the two subcultures. Some have also argued that the value differences result from French Canadians having more traditional kinship structures, or from the lower socio-economic statuses and education levels of French Canadians (compare, for example, Taylor, 1964; Guindon, 1964; Elkin, 1964; Porter, 1965; Kanungo et al., 1976; and Toulouse and Nightingale, 1977). In each case the argument is that something else, family or religion, takes priority over achievement in the lives of French Canadians in a way that it does not for English Canadians.

Guindon (1978) and Murphy (1981) have been among those who have critiqued the conventional view of French-English value differences, and each has offered counter-evidence. Guindon has argued that just prior to and during the Quiet Revolution in Quebec the French Canadian new middle-class and bureaucratic elites shared in the view that the majority of French Canadians had more traditional values than the English, but they preferred to change this and to modernize Quebec society, and they did. "The educational system was completely revamped and modernized. The provincial state took over the leadership from the Church in all spheres of societal life. Catholicism as a set of values and as a set of practices collapsed" (Guindon, 1978:231). Guindon argued that these changes cannot be easily reconciled with the view that French Canadians, at least the French Canadian new middle class, place a comparatively lower value on achievement. He also emphasized that it is difficult, currently, to discern patterns of differences in the size and growth of firms owned by French Canadians as opposed to English Canadians. In each case firms appear to grow especially as a function of "their integration to, or their absorption by, dominant continental corporations," and not as a result of their guidance by management with English versus French backgrounds (Guindon, 1978:22).

Murphy (1981) has emphasized that studies of secondary-school students in the 1960s showed some results which were opposite to those expected from the conventional wisdom. In these studies French Canadian students attached greater importance to the pursuit of work and career and were more likely to say that they would make sacrifices for them than was the case for English Canadian students. Murphy also presented findings on the work orientations of English and French secondary-school teachers in 1965 and 1972, and showed that the French had become similar to the English over time in their views on gaining success through occupations and on the importance of education in attaining higher income. Murphy interpreted these results as follows: The French "gave higher priority to the security of steady work because members of the French community were subject to more risks in a labour market that placed before them special linguistic and cultural barriers not faced by the English" (1981:167).

The facts pointed to by Guindon and Murphy should give pause to advocates of the conventional view. However, it is likely that they will not be entirely compelling because

Guindon's evidence involves indirect measures of values and because Murphy's survey data are not representative of the general adult population of French Canadians and English Canadians. For example, it may be argued that the Quiet Revolution was largely supported by a new middle class whose beliefs and values were not shared equally by other social strata in Quebec and that, therefore, the social change of this period is not a sufficient indicator of the thinking of French Canadians in general. Some will doubt that other social strata shared in the values of the new middle class. Similar arguments on the non-representativeness of the data can be made concerning inferences about French-English differences in values based on responses by teachers and their students (although one would still have to develop explanations of why French Canadian students appear to emphasize career achievement more than their English Canadian counterparts).

The evidence in support of the conventional view has been derived entirely from non-representative convenience samples, however. We lack an appropriate test of the values differences hypotheses, one which employs survey data on the achievement values for national samples of adult French Canadians and English Canadians. Fortunately, this type of data is now available, and it is our purpose to present the findings here.

HYPOTHESES

Our choice for hypotheses was between those implied by the conventional view and those implied by the critical studies of Guindon and Murphy. Because the latter seemed to us to have a somewhat stronger evidential base for the contemporary period, we expected results consistent with the conclusions of these authors. We expected that there would be few if any differences in values between French Canadians and English Canadians. The analyses by Murphy led us to expect that, if there were any differences in achievement values, French Canadians would attach a *greater* importance to achievement than English Canadians. We were aware of the fact that the conventional view might be accurate for French-English differences in periods prior to the Quiet Revolution, while the critical view might best describe the more recent situation. However, only study of representative samples will establish the accuracy of one of the views for the contemporary period.

We considered the following variables as controls in part of our analyses: income, education, community size, frequency of church attendance, age, sex, and number of children. Guindon and Murphy's work suggests that the social change which led to higher levels of achievement values among French Canadians began in, and emanated from, the urban new-middle-class sector of Quebec. This being the case, it is possible that French Canadians most exposed to the changes in this sector are highest in achievement values. Hence, younger French Canadians with higher levels of education and higher incomes and from urban areas may show the highest achievement values. Comparisons of these subgroups with their English counterparts should be most likely to show close similarities in values across French and English subsamples, or *higher* achievement value scores for the French. Sex was considered as a control because French Canadian women have probably had less exposure than men and English Canadian women to the urban new-middle-class sector and may, for this reason, place a lower value on achievement (compare, for example, Cuneo and Curtis, 1975:8ff). Frequency of church attendance was controlled because of Guindon's argument that the Catholic church was a countervailing force for the changes in values among French Canadians. This being the case, we might expect that French Canadians who attend church frequently would be less likely to endorse achievement values and more likely to be high on family orientation than their counterparts who are less involved in the church. Number of children in the family is a potential control because those with large families may place a greater value on the family, and perhaps a lesser emphasis on achievement, and the French Canadians in our sample had larger families than their English counterparts (compare, for example, Cuneo and Curtis, 1975:9ff).

DATA SOURCE

Our analyses employ data from the "Quality of Life Survey" which was conducted in 1981 as part of the "Social Change in Canada Project" at York University. These data were collected from a nation-wide probability sample of 3455 persons 18 years of age or older.

For the purposes of this study, we defined English Canadians as respondents who were born in, and currently live in, a Canadian province other than Quebec, whose mother tongue was English and who spoke only English at home. Similarly, French Canadians were defined as respondents who were born in and currently live in Quebec, whose mother tongue was French and who spoke only French at home. We used these "pure types" out of a concern that our examination of English-French differences might be contaminated by minority-group status or changes in language status (for example individuals who were born with one mother tongue but were primarily speaking the other at the time of the interview).

Six items measuring achievement values were included in the 1981 "Quality of Life Survey." Three of these were positively worded, such that respondents had to agree with the item to express an achievement orientation, while three of the items were negatively worded, such that respondents had to disagree with the item to express an achievement orientation. We were pleased to have both types of items (positively and negatively worded), because it is possible that one language group has a tendency to agree more with questionnaire items in general. Our technique allowed us to check for any problem in this regard.

The value items were introduced with the following statement:

> We would like your opinion about life in general. Please tell me whether you agree or disagree with the following statements using one of the statements on this card (strongly agree; agree; strongly disagree).

Positively-worded items dealing with achievement orientation were as follows:

> Life is most enjoyable when you are trying to achieve some new goal (ACHIEVE).

> You should always try to improve your position in life rather than accept what you have now (IMPROVE).

> A person ought to set goals for themselves which are difficult to achieve (GOALS).

Negatively-worded items dealing with achievement orientation were as follows:

> Unless one learns how to reduce one's desires, life will be full of disappointment and bitterness (REDUCE).

> Those who are always trying to get ahead in life will never be happy (NOT HAPPY).

> When you come down to it, the best thing to do is be contented with what you have since you never know what the future will bring (CONTENT).

FRENCH-ENGLISH DIFFERENCES ON THE ACHIEVEMENT MEASURES

Table 40-1 presents the mean scores for the achievement items for French Canadians and English Canadians. The variables have been recoded so that a higher score indicates agreement with the item (from a score of 4 for "agree strongly" to a score of 1 for "disagree strongly"). The hypothesis that French respondents would be *more* likely to endorse achievement values is supported for *each* of the six measures (at the p < .001 level of significance).

Using a factor analysis procedure which we will not present in any detail here, we found that the six items formed two basic "factors," one involving negatively-worded items (a "remain content" factor) and one involving positively-worded items (an "achievement" factor). The factor patterns for the two language groups were not significantly different, suggesting that the *mea-*

nings of the items were similar for the two language groups. On the achievement factor, French Canadians scored significantly *higher* than English Canadians (t = 6.413), while on the "be content" factor, French Canadians scored significantly *lower* than English Canadians (t = 6.796).

We extended our analysis with the introduction of controls (age, sex, family size, income, education, and church attendance)[1] through the use of multiple regression analysis to determine whether the English-French differences observed in Table 40-1 could be attributed to differences in any of these other factors. This did not appear to be the case. With the controls mentioned, all of the French-English differences observed in Table 40-1 remained significant (at p < .01) and the magnitudes of these differences were approximately the same. The difference between the factor means for the "be content" factor without controls (.221) was very similar to the difference with controls (.224). And the difference between

TABLE 40-1   Mean scores on six achievement items for the two language groups.

Value items	French sub-sample (N=626)	English sub-sample (N=1227)	t-value	probability
REDUCE one's desires	2.533	2.652	3.08	<.001
NOT HAPPY unless try to get ahead	2.266	2.456	6.79	<.001
Life enjoyable when trying to ACHIEVE	3.116	3.017	3.76	<.001
Should try to IMPROVE	3.103	2.847	8.31	<.001
Ought to set GOALS	2.615	2.409	6.50	<.001
Better to BE CONTENT	2.447	2.685	6.41	<.001

Notes: 1. The variables were coded on 4-point scales, with 1 = "strongly disagree" and 4 = "strongly agree."
2. The t-test values are for separate variance estimates since for all variables the variances differed significantly.

the factor means for the "achievement" factor without controls (.145) was similar to the difference with controls for income, age, education, sex, religiosity, and number of children (.123). In both cases, the analysis with controls yielded significant (p < .001) differences in the factor means. The French Canadians were more likely to agree with the items which denote an achievement orientation, and they were less likely to agree with the items stressing the importance of "being content" with what one already has.

EFFECTS OF THE CONTROL VARIABLES WITHIN THE LANGUAGE GROUPS

One of the reasons for our control variables was that there might be more social differentiation in values among French Canadians than English Canadians, with the controls having greater effects among the former than the latter. We were able to test for this pattern. We compared analyses for each language subsample and checked whether the control variables were more strongly associated with achievement values in the French subsample. The results of these analyses are shown in Table 40-2. Only those predictors of the value items which are significant at p < .01 are included in this table. In both subsamples, males scored higher on the achievement factor than females, but income, community size, age, church attendance, and number of children had no effect by themselves in either of the subsamples. Education had a significant effect on the "be content" factor in both subsamples; controlling for income, community size, age, church attendance, sex, and number of children, higher educated individuals were less likely to agree with the idea that one should "be contented with what you have." In both the English and the French subsamples, older people were more likely to agree that one should be content

TABLE 40-2   Comparative influence of background variables on achievement factors.

Dependent variable: Achievement

	Unstandardized		Standardized	
	English	French	English	French
Sex (male = 1; female = 0)	+.053	+.092	+.101	+.174

Dependent variable: Be content

	Unstandardized		Standardized	
	English	French	English	French
Education	−.038	−.034	−.367	−.317
Religiosity − Catholic	+.024	−.101(ns)	+.107	−.045(ns)
Religiosity − Non-Cath.	+.030	−.009(ns)	+.120	−.035(ns)
Age	+.003	+.008	+.149	+.351

Note: All coefficients are significant at p < .01, except for the coefficients for "religiosity" in the French subsample.

with what he or she has (controlling for the other factors mentioned above). This effect was the only effect that seemed more pronounced in French Canada. Finally, religiosity (as measured by church attendance) predicted higher levels of agreement with items in the "be content" factor in English Canada, but not in French Canada.

Overall, the evidence that the control variables have a different effect in English Canada than they do in French Canada does not receive any strong support. A test of statistical significance to determine whether, *in general*, the findings for the two language groups are different yielded results which were not statistically significant.

CONCLUSIONS

The idea that French Canadian culture restrains the French from developing achievement-related interests gains no support whatsoever in our findings. In fact, the findings conform more with Murphy's (1981) suspicion that French Canadians emphasize striving for occupational success even more than their English counterparts. This may result, as Murphy suggests, from French Canadians seeing economic success and security as more problematic following their less successful experience with the workplace, compared with English Canadians.

It could be argued that the conventional view was valid for periods up to recent times. If this is the case, one might expect to find vestiges of the past in the values of a representative sample of adults, with older French Canadians versus older English Canadians displaying values more consistent with the conventional view. Our findings give some slight evidence of this pattern in relation to the "be content" factor. Thus, there is some evidence that the conventional view regarding value differences may have held at an earlier point in time.

NOTES

1. Education was measured using a 10-point scale, ranging from a low of "no schooling" to a high of "professional degree or doctorate." Family income was coded into 18 categories ranging from a low of no income to a high of $100 000 or more. Community size was coded as follows: (1) under 1000 plus rural; (2) 1000-10 000; (3) 10 000-100 000; and (4) census metropolitan area. The respondents' report of their total number of children was used (the interviews did not ask how many of the children still lived at home). The church attendance controls were constructed separately for Catholics and non-Catholics based on responses to a question on how often in the past year the individual had attended church services. The six response options and their codes were: (1) more than once a week; (2) once a week; (3) two or three times a month; (4) once a month; (5) less than once a month; (6) not at all. Catholics were given a score of 6 on the "non-Catholic" variable and non-Catholics were given a score of 6 on the "Catholic" variable.

REFERENCES

Auclair, G. A., and W. H. Read
　　1966　"A cross-cultural study of industrial leadership." Study prepared for the Lurendeau-Dunton Commission, Montreal.

Beattie, C.
　　1975　*Minority Men in a Majority Setting.* Toronto: McClelland and Stewart.

Cuneo, C. J., and J. E. Curtis
　　1975　"Social ascription in the educational and occupational status attainment of urban Canadians," *Canadian Review of Sociology and Anthropology,* 12, no.1:6-24.

Elkin, F.
　　1964　*The Family in Canada.* Ottawa: Vanier Institute of the Family.

Garigue, P.
　　1964　"Change and continuity in French Canada," in *French Canadian Society,* ed. M. Rioux and Y. Martin, pp. 123-37. Toronto: McClelland and Stewart.

Grabb, E.
　　1980　"Differences in sense of control among French and English Canadian adolescents," *Canadian Review of Sociology and Anthropology,* 17:169-75.
　　1981　"The ranking of 'self-actualization' values: The effects of class, stratification and occupational experiences," *The Sociological Quarterly,* 22:373-83.

Guindon, H.
　　1964　"Social unrest, social class and Quebec's bureaucratic revolution," *Queen's Quarterly,* 71:150-62.
　　1978　"The modernization of Quebec and the legitimacy of the Canadian state," in *Modernization and the Canadian State,* ed. D. Glenday, H. Guindon and A. Turowetz, pp. 212-46. Toronto: MacMillan (also in the *Canadian Review of Sociology and Anthropology,* 15:227-45).

Hughes, E.
　　1943　*French Canada in Transition.* Chicago: University of Chicago Press.

Jain, H. C., J. Normand, and R. N. Kanungo
　　1979　"Job motivation of Canadian English-Canadian and French-Canadian hospital employees," *Canadian Journal of Behavioural Science,* 11:160-63.

Kanungo, R., and J. Bhatnager
　　1978　"Achievement orientation and occupational values: A comparative study of young French- and English-Canadians," *Canadian Journal of Behavioural Science,* 10:202-13.

Kanungo, R., G. Gorn, and M. Dauderis
　　1976　"Motivation orientation of Canadian English-Canadian and French-Canadian managers," *Canadian Journal of Behavioural Science,* 8:107-21.

Lambert, W. E., A. Yackley, and R. Hein
　　1972　"Child rearing values of English Canadian and French Canadian parents," in *Social Psychology: The Canadian Context,* ed. J. W. Berry and G. J. S. Wilde, pp. 149-72. Toronto: McClelland and Stewart.

Murphy, R.
    1981   "Teachers and the evolving structural context of economic and political attitudes in Quebec society," *Canadian Review of Sociology and Anthropology,* 18:157-82.

Porter, J.
    1965   *The Vertical Mosaic.* Toronto: University of Toronto Press.

Nightingale, D. V., and J. M. Toulouse
    1977   "Values, structure, process and reactions/adjustments: A comparison of French and English Canadian industrial organizations," *Canadian Journal of Behavioural Science,* 11:160-63.

Richer, S., and P. Laporte
    1971   "Culture, cognition and English-French competition," in *Immigrant Groups,* ed. J. L. Elliott, pp. 141-50. Scarborough: Prentice-Hall Canada.

Taylor, N. W.
    1964   "The French-Canadian industrial entrepreneur and his social environment," *French Canadian Society,* Vol. I, ed. M. Rioux and Y. Martin. Toronto: McClelland and Stewart.

Taylor, D., N. Frasure-Smith, and W. E. Lambert
    1978   "Psychological development of French and English Canadian children: Child-rearing attitudes and ethnic identity," in *The Canadian Ethnic Mosaic,* ed. L. Driedger, pp. 153-68. Toronto: McClelland and Stewart.

Yackley, A., and W. E. Lambert
    1972   "Inter-ethnic group competition and levels of aspiration," in *Social Psychology: The Canadian Context,* ed. J. W. Berry and G. J. S. Wilde, pp. 214-30. Toronto: McClelland and Stewart.

41. Class and Social Interaction

W. Peter Archibald

Sociologists have long been concerned with the ways in which social class impinges upon such characteristics of interpersonal interaction as the amount of interaction which occurs and the symmetry or asymmetry of familiarity and influence patterns. A number of theories have been offered to identify and explain such patterns. The "exchange" theories of Homans (1974) and Blau (1964) represent one such attempt; another is the "expectation states" theory of the Stanford group (Berger, Cohen, and Zelditch, 1972); the work of Goffman (1967; 1959; 1961), an eclectic blending of elements of exchange, functionalism, and conflict, is yet another.

The present paper is an attempt to develop and substantiate a Marxian-oriented theory of micro-stratification phenomena as

an alternative to the above-mentioned approaches. I begin by presenting and substantiating four empirical generalizations extrapolated from Marx's theory of alienation, and then develop a micro-conflict theory consistent with the latter theory to explain these generalizations as well as a number of exceptions to these same generalizations.

THE EMPIRICAL GENERALIZATIONS

For the immediate purposes of this paper, only a few features of Marx's theory of alienation (Archibald, 1974) need to be noted. First, other people constitute one of four objects from which individuals are alienated. Second, an alienated relationship between an individual and an object of orientation is characterized by four features: (1) the individual is detached from, or indifferent to, the object; (2) when he does approach the object, it is for very narrowly defined, egoistic purposes; (3) when he con-

Abridged from W. Peter Archibald, "Class and Social Interaction," *American Sociological Review*, vol. 41, no. 5 (October 1976), pp. 819-37. Reprinted with permission. The author thanks especially John Gartrell for comments on earlier versions of this manuscript.

fronts the object, he does not control it but is instead controlled by it; (4) his orientation toward the object is characterized by certain feelings, among which are (often vague) feelings of dissatisfaction and hostility. The latter feelings need not be conscious, and the crucial indicators of alienation are not consciously expressed attitudes, but overt behavioural orientations. For Marx, the sources of alienation from others centred around class as defined by position in the productive process, and particularly in the distinction between capitalists and workers. The former earn their livelihood parasitically by hiring workers for a wage and appropriating surplus value, and private ownership of the means of production and conscious control of the work process permit them to do so. However, in the empirical generalizations which follow, class differences often entail simply the middle-class/working-class or non-manual/manual distinction. Moreover, the present treatment further extends the scope of the theory by adding Max Weber's concepts of "status" (prestige or honour) and "power" (the ability to control others) as potentially independent sources of alienation from others. Empirically, of course, the three tend to go together.

The Detachment Generalization: Persons of different classes, status, and powers tend to avoid each other

The empirical validity of this generalization is perhaps so obvious that it is forgotten when theories of cross-class interaction are constructed.

In the first place, those of different class, status, and power tend to be physically separated. In work organizations, management tends to have separate maintenance facilities, such as entrances, elevators, washrooms, and cafeterias (Goffman, 1967:110),

their offices tend to be separate from the production area; and they make extensive use of "go-betweens," such as supervisors and foremen, as buffers between themselves and the production staff (Goffman, 1959:149). Similarly, in the wider community one finds a great deal of "residential segregation," a phenomenon that has been statistically documented for Britain (Wilmott and Young, 1960), France (Rhodes, 1969), the United States (Duncan and Duncan, 1955; Feldman and Tilly, 1960; Uyeki, 1964; Laumann, 1966) and Canada (Balakrishnan and Jarvis, 1968; Adler, 1970).[1]

Second, there tends to be a great deal of "social distance" between those of different classes, statuses, and power. Thus even in mixed neighbourhoods, voluntary associations and pubs tend to be frequented by those of the same class (e.g., Wilmott and Young, 1960:97; Lorimer and Phillips, 1971:6). On a more intimate level, high-school cliques tend to follow class lines (Hollingshead, 1949), working-class students tend to be isolated on college campuses (Ellis and Lane, 1967), and the friends and marriage partners of adults tend to be from the same class and status level (Kahl and Davis, 1955; Curtis, 1963; Laumann, 1966; Lorimer and Phillips, 1971:28; Grayson, 1973).

The Means-Ends Generalization: When persons of different class, status, or power do interact, it tends to be on a narrow, role-specific, rather than a personal basis. In short, they "use" each other

That cross-class interaction follows these utilitarian lines has been noted for some time. Of capitalists and workers, for example, Marx (*Capital* 1:195) said there is "'No admittance except on business.'. . . The only force that brings them together puts them in relation with each other, is the selfishness, the gain and private interest of each." Many of the apparent exceptions to the Detachment Generalization seem to follow this pattern. Thus Goffman (1959:199) notes that British upper-class reserve "has been known to give way momentarily when a particular favour must be asked of . . . subordinates," and that North American managers often affect superficial shows of familiarity in order to avert strikes and other incidences of rebellion.[2]

Utilitarian tendencies outside the workplace are evident in the fact that psychiatrists express less desire for leisure time than for professional contact with psychologists and social workers in the mental health field (Zander et al., 1959). Even interaction of the (presumably) most intimate kind seems to follow this pattern, in that older, upper-class men who do not fit the advertising image of handsomeness and marry "down," tend to marry women who do fit the advertising image of female beauty (see Rubin, 1973: 67-68). Apparently upper-class women in the same position sometimes do the same, although more often they remain unmarried (Martin, 1970).

The Control-Purposiveness Generalization: Persons of high class, status, or power tend to (a) initiate activity, (b) make attempts to influence others, (c) actually influence others more than do persons in lower positions

Much of the comparative quantitative evidence for this generalization in relatively less formalized settings has been referred to by Berger et al. (1972). A great deal of support can also be found in the literature on formal organizations.[3] Finally, to this body of evidence one can add Goffman's observation (1961:129-31; 1967:64-65, 74-79) that the pattern for expressions of familiarity is also asymmetrical.

The Feelings Generalization: An element of hostility underlies much and perhaps most interaction between "unequals," and occasionally rebellion occurs

Perhaps the most common expression of hostility on the part of Low persons are such work-group activities as "restriction of output" (Mathewson, 1969) or simply "make-work" when the boss comes by (Goffman, 1959:109). However, during lunch breaks and the like in "back regions," hostility is more openly evident, and perhaps even more evident in actual face-to-face confrontations during strikes (e.g., Doyle, 1974:3; Israel, 1971:225-26). Similarly, in the wider community this conflict is evident in snobbishness and lower-status persons' reaction to it. While such expressions of hostility tend to be more subtle in North America (e.g., Dobriner, 1963:107-8; Lorimer and Phillips, 1971:27-28) than in Europe (e.g., Wilmott and Young, 1960:5-6, 97-98, 119-22), they are nevertheless present.

EXPLAINING THE GENERALIZATION: A THEORY OF INTERPERSONAL THREAT

Let us examine the following set of explanatory principles implied in my review of the literature.

Class, Status, and Power Differences Are Threatening

That those of high position would be *threatened*[4] by those lower than themselves is, perhaps, obvious: while the former's privileges depend upon the continued deference or acquiescence of Lows, such deference and acquiescence is not always assured, as was noted in the feelings generalization. Many and probably most of the "underprivileged" realize that greater equality is in their best interest, as is indicated by the greater importance working-class people place upon equality and government intervention to achieve it (Form and Rytina, 1969; Mann, 1970). Similarly, lower-status professionals covet the greater income, status, and decision-making power of those higher than themselves (Zander et al., 1959). It would be surprising indeed if the privileged were unaware of this and, in fact, as the latter study indicates (Zander et al, 1959:26-30), they *do* seem to be aware of it. In specific encounters with the less privileged these outcomes could be realized in at least two ways: either directly by rebellion on the part of the less privileged—or at least the refusal to acquiesce—or indirectly by a poor "performance" which would discredit one's image as a superior person and hence lessen one's future power over the less privileged.[5]

That those of low position would be threatened by those higher than themselves is also obvious: "stepping out of line" can be and often is sanctioned by the privileged. Some of the sanctions are obvious, for example, the possibility of being fired from one's job or the consequences of the privileged's greater access to institutional support, particularly governmental and legal, for their interests. But again, the coercive element can be more indirect, as with the anticipation of embarrassment if one "messes up" in front of the privileged.[6] One suspects that their low status makes working-class people particularly self-conscious and prone to embarrassment. While they by no means totally accept the social evaluation of personal worth implicit in their status, this evaluation is difficult to ignore, given its institutionalized support. Therefore, particularly in North America where the predominant ideology has stressed individual achievement

and mobility, many working people seem to have an ambivalent evaluation of their personal worth (Kaplan, 1971; Sennett and Cobb, 1972).

It is important to note that this *need not* mean that this ambivalence is accompanied by a high evaluation of the abilities of those higher in status. A worker or other low-status person may feel that his ideas are as good as others', but he may simply lack confidence in his ability to express them because he is self-conscious about his vocabulary or lack of education. Rather than acceptance of status differences, his covert orientation may be resentment.

Ways of Dealing with the Threat

As Goffman (1967:15) suggests with regard to the threat of embarrassment (and this can be generalized to most threats), "The surest way for a person to prevent threats to his face is to avoid contacts in which these threats are likely to occur." *Avoidance as a self-protective strategy* is, thus, a very plausible explanation for the Detachment Generalization. Several astute observers of cross-class interaction have used such a coercion explanation (e.g. Goffman, 1967:70; Adams, 1970:50-51), and "harder" evidence for its validity will be presented below.

Obviously those of different classes, statuses, and powers cannot avoid each other totally for, in a perverse sort of way, they "need" each other; that is, those of high position can maintain their positions only be exploiting those lower than themselves, those of low position must obtain employment from enterprises controlled by the privileged and those who are unemployed are, of course, extremely dependent upon those in higher positions for various forms of welfare. However, given that one must interact with threatening others to some extent, the next best thing is to try to ensure that the interaction is *predictable* (e.g., Goffman, 1961:128; Sampson, 1963). There are several ways of doing this.

First, *one can try to restrict the scope of cross-position activity to highly circumscribed roles*, such as those of boss-worker, and so forth. What Goffman (1961:30) refers to as "rules of irrelevance" are also likely to be invoked; that is, feelings and other personal characteristics of the "back regions" are not focussed upon, officially at least. Literally and figuratively, neither side wants to be "caught with its pants down" (Goffman, 1967:83). The desire for predictability would seem to be a plausible explanation for the Means-Ends Generalization; that is, restricting the number of roles and the scope of activities associated with each role permits one to get some of what one wants from the person in a different class, status, or power position while at the same time minimizing threat.

Second, *adhering closely to the prerogatives these roles give to the privileged* would seem to have the same advantages, for those in low as well as those in high positions. Goffman (1961:128) states this well:

> Adherence to formalities seems to guarantee the *status quo* of authority and social distance; under the guidance of this style, one can be assured that the others will not be able to move in on one. Reversing the role point of view, we can see that adherence to the formalities one owes to others can be a relatively protective matter, guaranteeing that one's conduct will be accepted by the others...

These processes, of course, entail *some* degree of agreement between Highs and Lows, but note that even this modicum of agreement is in the service of self-protection; that is, Lows are *coerced* into upholding the prerogatives of the privileged. This is not to say that there are no secondary satisfactions resulting from conformity. One may, of course, be "patted on the head" for one's performance and, as Goffman also suggests (1961: 128), playing strictly by the rules permits one to justify one's overt behaviour to others and oneself as demanded by the situation, while at the same time denying covert personal involvement in potentially demeaning conduct. Or, to put it another way, "role distance" is only possible if one plays the role in the first place. However, these various secondary satisfactions should be seen for what they are—secondary. They may rationalize one's adherence to the formalities, but one feels little choice about adhering to them. Threat and the desire for predictability thus constitute a plausible explanation for the Control-Purposiveness Generalization.

Finally, one may react to threat, not by overtly conforming to protocol and simply covertly decreasing one's involvement, but by *expressing hostility and, perhaps, rebelling* in an effort to circumvent or change the effects of the class, status, or power structure. However, one would expect this strategy to occur less frequently than the other three in most circumstances, for this is the only reaction of Lows which is against the interest of Highs, and it is therefore *the only one that is subject to punishment*.

While the above theory obviously oversimplifies the processes occurring in cross-position, face-to-face interaction, it receives a fair degree of independent empirical support in the literature.

Thus, for example, having to perform in front of a group of high-status persons has been found to be more anxiety-arousing (as measured by physiological arousal and response latency) than having to perform in front of lower-status persons (Cohen and Davis, 1973). Furthermore, in this particular study, the anxiety produced by the presence of the high-status persons is lower when it is made explicit that observers will evaluate the subject than when the role of the observers is not defined and, presumably, less predictable. Similarly, it has long been observed that persons of low status do not feel free to express hostility toward those of higher status. Worchel (1957) found this to be the case after college students had been provoked by a professor (to cite a case where these results are completely common-sensical), but more recent experiments indicate that similar things occur even in seemingly trivial encounters. Thus, after having experimenters drive either a flashy new Chrysler or a beat-up old Ford to a stop light and remain there after the light had turned green, Doob and Gross (1968) found that 84 percent of the drivers behind the Ford honked their horns while only 50 percent of those behind the Chrysler did so, and that two of the former actually hit the experimental car. Similarly, after having a group of sidewalk discussants who appeared to be either older and middle-class or younger and of lower status block the sidewalk, Knowles (1973) found that passers-by were much more likely to walk through the latter than through the former group. In the latter case, age rather than class may have been the more important factor, but age, like class, often gives one coercive power over others.

Variations in Immediate Threat and the Strategies Used

The present treatment is meant to be more illustrative than definitive, but one can already point with a reasonable degree of confidence to many conditions which appear to increase or modify the aforementioned processes. Two categories of conditions are discussed here: (A) those having to do with features of the class, status, or power structure *external* to the encounter or potential encounter in question and (B) those having to do with the *internal* structure of the encounter.

The external structure   Aside from the degree of inequality and/or mobility in the class, status, or power structure itself, one might expect that *the more the structure is supported by other structures* in a society, whether or not the supporting structure is an institutionalized government, the *less* will be the threat. Hence, there will be fewer reactions to it in *Highs*, but *more* threat and reactions to in *Lows*.

While it is difficult to make cross-societal comparisons, the interpenetration of Canada's economy and polity has been said to be greater than that of the United States (e.g., Myers, 1972). Similarly, the greater insecuri-

TABLE 41-1   Sources of political advice named by Canadians and Americans.

Advisor	Advisee							
	Broadview Riding (Toronto)				Elmira, Ill.			
	P/M	*W.C.*	*SK.*	*S&U*	*P/M*	*W.C.*	*SK.*	*S&U*
Professional/managerial	38%	35%	25%	13%	68%	54%	34%	26%
White-collar	21	31	25	11	14	31	14	22
Skilled	9	3	10	17	8	4	47	25
Semi- and unskilled	32	31	40	59	10	11	5	27

Source: Grayson, 1973.

ty this might produce in Canadian workers presumably would be increased further by the fact that, since World War II, Canada has had one of the highest rates of unemployment among western nations (OECD, cited in Adams et al., 1972:86). Given these considerations, it is interesting to examine Grayson's findings (1973) concerning the occupations of those approached by Canadians and Americans for political advice. Table 41-1 shows that upper-class Canadians are *more* likely than upper-class Americans to say that they consult working-class people, while working-class Canadians are *less* likely to say that they consult middle- or upper-class people. These results are at least consistent with the above proposition; that is, if upper-class Canadians receive more support that their American counterparts from institutions external to encounters with working-class people, they should be less threatened by working-class people and hence avoid them less. Working-class Canadians, on the other hand, should be more threatened by upper-class people and hence avoid them more than their American counterparts do. While there are many problems in interpreting these results, they are intriguing and warrant further research.[7]

Fortunately, the effects of external support for a class or status structure can be examined more carefully in a number of experiments. In a series of games with teams of working-class boys, Thibaut (1950) simulated certain features of class differences by giving some teams (High Class) and not others (Low Class) the exclusive right to do such things as jump on members of the other team. Similarly, in his experiment with college students Kelley (1960) led some teams to think that they had the better job, the differences between the two jobs described being very similar to the non-manual/manual distinction. The findings that (1) the average number of interteam communications when

there were class/status distinctions was almost identical to those in a control condition and (2) that Lows communicated to Highs more than Highs communicated to Lows appear to contradict the Detachment and Control-Purposiveness Generalizations, indicate that the class/status structure in these experiments is unique indeed. That is, all subjects come from the same class outside the laboratory and the experimenter's support for the class/status structure is its *only* basis. It is therefore understandable that Highs, like the *nouveau riche* more generally (Mills, 1956), would be particularly insecure in this situation, and that Lows would be somewhat bolder than usual, although restrained in their expression of hostility because of the experimenter's control. Thibaut (1950:268-70) and Kelley (1960: 787-94) both report that this appears to have been what happened, and this conclusion is supported by the additional findings of Kelley that Highs expressed considerable embarrassment and less criticism of their own jobs to Lows than Lows expressed to Highs. Nor should it be concluded from the latter finding that Lows were necessarily in fundamental agreement with the status structure. While they were more likely than Highs to express confusion about their jobs, they nevertheless tended to "defend its importance and rarely say that it was too easy."

There is some evidence that similar apparent reversals of the Control-Purposiveness Generalization in real life settings occur under conditions analogous to those of the above experiments. Thus Brewer (1971) attributes the fact that management in an insurance company permitted underwriters to communicate upwards to two other conditions, among others. Since the underwriters work with little supervision, monitoring their own reports of their work was simply an efficient means of managing. Second, being more highly educated than their immediate supervisors, the underwriters would more openly resent top-down communication. Similarly, Brewer suggests that the equalization for downward and upward communication in an electrical construction company can in good part be explained by peculiar conditions. Thus because crew leaders were legally required to be union members and were in extremely close, continuous contact with workers, they were particularly susceptible to being "corrupted" by workers. Management therefore not only permitted upward communication from the crew leaders, but also funnelled all downward communication through them in order to co-opt them into the company bureaucracy. Finally, Rosenberg (1962) reports the absence of class differences in participation in a patients' council in a mental hospital; this, however, can be attributed to the fact that this was the explicit intention of the doctors, who had new elections to the council conducted "on a monthly basis" and emphasized that "affiliative skills" rather than "literacy, verbal fluency, and problem-solving ability" were prerequisites for participation. The latter would be expected to lessen the threat of embarrassment for Lows.[8] Reports of relatively low worker participation in workers' councils (e.g., see Mulder, 1971)

suggests that such explicit restructuring of encounters may be a general prerequisite for more equal participation rates.

The internal structure of the encounter
If it is true that predictability is a major concern for the participants of cross-class interaction, then *the less structured or more ambiguous participants' roles or tasks are in the encounter, the greater should be the threat and use of the strategic reactions to it.*

Cohen's (1959) work confirms this. He told female employees of a public utility company that their partner in the experiment was a supervisor from their own company and that the purpose of the experiment was to see whether or not the subject was capable of working with the company's supervisors. The subject and the supposed supervisor performed a word-symbol matching test, but in some cases the supervisor's interpretations and instructions were clear and familiar (Structured), while in others they were vague and unfamiliar (Ambiguous). As one would predict given the above proposition, threat as measured by anxiety, time to complete the task and perceived agreement with, and approval from, the supervisor was greater in the Ambiguous than the Structured condition. The same was the case

TABLE 41-2   Percentages of subjects in the Gerard experiment sending directive notes.

| | Highs | | Lows | |
| | Goal | | Goal | |
Role	Clarity	Unclarity	Clarity	Unclarity
Clarity	58%	71%	58%	46%
Unclarity	50	70	25	8

Source: Gerard, 1957.

when hostility was measured by liking for, and projected anger toward, the supervisor.

Similarly, in an experiment by Gerard (1957), subjects working on a jigsaw puzzle had the job of recording the content of notes which subjects presumably had sent one another. Half thought they were the "boss" with the power to give orders to the others (Highs), while the other half thought they were clerks whose job simply was to record the notes (Lows). Ambiguity was manipulated by (1) whether or not the experimenter described to the subject what his instructions to the rest of the group would be (Role Clarity versus Unclarity) and (2) whether or not the subject was given an alleged record of past groups' performances (Goal Clarity versus Unclarity). Aside from the usual findings that Highs communicated more than Lows, Gerard found other differences in the number of directive notes sent, as shown in Table 41-2. These results indicate that except for one set of comparisons (Role Clarity versus Unclarity for Highs), ambiguity increased the number of influence attempts by Highs and decreased those by Lows.[9]

A second important condition affecting threat and the strategies used against it is *the degree to which an individual is supported by other members of his own class or interest group.* Specifically, one might expect that when the threat from other sources is low, the greater the *number* of persons from one's own class present, the *less* will be the threat. When the threat from other sources is high (e.g., management is attempting to institute a speed-up), one might expect the presence of other members of the lower class to *increase* the likelihood of Lows expressing hostility and rebelling. Also, one would expect that the greater the (observable) *degree of consensus* within one's own class or interest group, the greater the likelihood of reacting to threat by rebelling.

Evidence for these propositions is not definitive, but it is persuasive. Thus, in a partial replication of Kelley's experiment, Cohen (1958:46) found that the number of messages critical of Highs sent by Lows to Highs increased when subjects "felt that they had support from others in their own . . . group for their opinions and ideas." Similarly, after having been provoked by a professor-experimenter, subjects who thought their group was composed of others similar to themselves were more likely to initiate physical activity and express hostility than were subjects who thought their own group was heterogeneous (Pepitone and Reichling, 1960). Certainly there is much evidence that the presence of dissenting models increases dissent (e.g., Gerard, 1953; Asch, 1960; Milgram, 1965; Allen and Levine, 1969; Moscovici et al., 1969), and interest groups themselves appear to take this into account by appointing a few articulate spokesmen and sanctioning expressions of disagreement in front of opposing groups (e.g., Goffman, 1959:89-94). Evidence suggests these practices are warranted, because Lows do seem to "move in on" Highs if the latter appear to be in disagreement (e.g., Goffman, 1959:201).

There is less evidence for the effects of these conditions on Highs, but what evidence there is suggests that the effects are similar. Thus, for example, in their study of supervisors in five different light manufacturing companies, Kipnis and Cosentino (1969:465) found that "as the number of men supervised increased, the use of official warnings increased," and the use of "powers that required spending long periods of time with subordinates" decreased (Goodstadt and Kipnis, 1970). Similarly, in a subsequent experiment with college students (Goodstadt and Kipnis, 1970) "supervisors" spent less time talking with a deviant stooge when the subordinate group had eight rather than three people, and threatened to fire him sooner in the former condition. Interestingly, however, supervisors were *less* likely to correct non-problem workers in the eight-man than the three-man group. Could it be that under these circumstances (i.e., one against eight) the pressure against expressing hostility is greater for Highs than Lows, and that hostility is only expressed when Lows' behaviour actually threatens Highs' control?

COMPARING THEORIES

In very general terms, the interpersonal threat theory of micro-stratification phenomena advanced here can be summarized as follows.

1. Class, status, and power divisions entail conflicts of interest which engender interpersonal threat.

2. The engendered threat is a *sufficient*, although in some cases not a necessary condition for avoidance (Detachment), using (Means-Ends), deference and conformity (Control-Purposiveness), hostility and, under certain conditions, rebellion (Feelings).

3. Threat and/or the reactions to it vary with the degree of external and internal support for oneself and/or one's interest group and the predictability of interaction.

How, then, does the interpersonal threat theory compare with other theories which have been advanced for some of the same phenomena?

Since those who have proposed alternative theories seldom deny that the processes postulated here occur,[10] the real issue appears to be the *extent* to which "coercive power" processes (French and Raven, 1959) such as those postulated by interpersonal threat theory are associated with dimensions of stratification in liberal democracies. As with macro-theories of stratification, one

might distinguish two sets of issues. One concerns the relative utility of a *Pluralist* as opposed to a *Marxist* model of stratified conflict. Specifically, whereas a Marxist model is said to give primacy to class over occupational, racial-ethnic, or sexual conflict, a Pluralist model gives most of these dimensions roughly equal weight in either or both of two ways. (1) In any given encounter, class is usually assumed to be no more important as a source of conflict than occupation, ethnicity, or other dimensions and/or (2) to the extent that class conflict is more important than others, it is assumed to be so only at the work place; in other spheres there may be equality, or working-class people may actually make up for their disadvantaged economic position, through effective political organization, for example. The second set of issues concerns the extent to which relations between people of different classes or strata are better characterized by *consensus and exchange* than *conflict and coercion*. Here, proponents of consensus and exchange theories assume that Highs and Lows have more complementary than conflicting interests and that, for example, Lows exchange deference for the superior ability of Highs to solve mutual problems. Each of these sets of issues will be discussed in turn.

Class Versus Pluralistic Conflict

The Pluralist claim that class is no more important than other dimensions of stratification is implied in most previous sociological treatments of micro-stratification phenomena, sometimes directly (e.g., Goffman, 1961:80) and sometimes indirectly through the absence of distinctions among various "external status characteristics" in terms of their relative effectiveness (e.g., Berger et al., 1972).

Actually, however, the predictions to be made from Marxist theory are by no means as clearcut as is usually implied. Thus, the claim that class takes precedence was for Marx a long-term prediction, rather than a short-term description for bourgeois society. In the meantime, the working class would be divided along occupational and racial-ethnic lines (Marx and Engels, 1968:42, 60, 104; 1961:xiv, 280-81; 1971:293-94). The time element is therefore crucial, and some Marxists (e.g., Johnson, 1972) have suggested that in North America in particular class formation is still at a relatively undeveloped stage. While it is doubtful that Marx expected the process to take this long, the relative weight to be given different stratification dimensions at this time is unclear.[11]

Matching this theoretical ambiguity are only a few pieces of largely inconclusive empirical evidence. Jackman and Jackman (1973), for example, found that whether or not respondents in a national U.S. survey owned stocks and bonds or real estate affected the status of their neighbours and friends more than race, but less than occupation, income, and education; self-employment had no effect. Earlier Strodtbeck et al. (1958) also had found that proprietorship had only a slightly greater effect upon participation rates in a mock jury experiment than did sex.

Such studies clearly question the validity of this aspect of the Marxist model, at least if it is interpreted as predicting that class should now overshadow other dimensions of stratification. Yet several facts in the general stratification literature suggest that the issue is worth pursuing further. In the first place, occupation and income are good and reliable predictors of a host of phenomena, including occupational prestige and social class identification (e.g., Blau and Duncan, 1967; Inkeles, 1960; Jackman and Jackman, 1973). Second, these two criteria are closely related logically and empirically to large-scale capital ownership (Jackman and Jack-

man, 1973; Johnson, 1972; Zeitlin, 1974). As with capital ownership and self-employment, occupation and income are not consistently better predictors of such characteristics of interaction as avoidance patterns than are racial, ethnic, or religious status (e.g., Laumann, 1973:108); nevertheless, they often are (e.g., Artz et al., 1971:988).[12]

The second pluralist claim, that class-based coercive power does not usually generalize from the formal settings where it arises, is implied by both Berger et al. (1972: 243) and Goffman (1961:32), with the latter suggesting that the inequalities of one sphere are often reversed in another.

Earlier in this paper, work organizations were purposely distinguished from other settings in order to demonstrate that class effects *do* generalize, but only a few of the studies cited (e.g., Doob and Gross, 1968) clearly indicate that stratified coercive power itself generalizes. However, a reexamination of two studies whose results Berger et al. (1972) claim argue against the generalization of coercion actually supports the Marxist model.

One of these studies is Torrance's (1965), where bomber crews, some permanent and some constructed for the experiment, worked on a number of group tasks, some clearly related to the formal authority structure (e.g., how to survive if their plane crashed), and some clearly not related (e.g., solving a horse-trading puzzle or counting dots). While Berger et al. (1972:243) imply that coercion would not and did not operate in the latter encounters, Torrance (1965:604-7) reports that the opposite was the case—gunners did not feel free to disagree with pilots and navigators and evidenced considerable tension and hostility. That gunners in temporary crews should have had 25 percent more influence on the group decision regarding at least two of the seemingly irrelevant tasks (the horse-trading and "group story" tasks) also is consistent with a coercion interpretation, since the likelihood of Highs later exacting revenge for Lows' breach of protocol presumably would have been lower in the former.

That militarily-based coercive power generalizes is, of course, hardly startling, but we also find what appears to be a generalization effect in the second study which Berger et al. cite. In this study, Hurwitz et al. (1960) experimentally constructed discussion groups using professionals in the mental health field, ensuring that each had a mixture of High- and Low-status professions (e.g., psychiatrists and high-school teachers, respectively). Although participants need not have come from the same work organizations, they were all from the same city and many presumably knew of each other. Thus the risk for Lows of later meeting Highs, or of at least gaining a "bad reputation" for "stepping out of line," presumably would have carried over to these discussions. Supporting such a coercion interpretation of the researchers' standard participation and deference results are two additional findings: (1) Lows did not like Highs better than Lows at the end of the discussions, but (2) they did tend to overestimate the extent to which Highs liked Lows, which the authors explain as a defensive "need, realistic in these discussion groups, to feel that relations with *highs* are satisfactory and pleasant...." (Hurwitz et al., 1960:304-5).

Clearly, much more research is required before these Marxist versus Pluralist issues can be resolved. It should be stressed that a *relative decrease* in class effects as one proceeds from formal work organizations to relatively informal settings is perfectly consistent with the present theory, providing that certain conditions are met. First, external support for the formal stratification structure must remain unchanged; should external pressure actually work against it, as in Rosenberg's study (1962), there may even be *equality* in the informal setting. Second, internal support for Lows (in numbers and consensus) must remain constant. In fact, in many relatively informal settings such as political parties and other voluntary organizations, workers may well be in a small and unorganized minority, such that class effects could *increase* from those in more formal settings, where workers have much more support. Third, the predictability of interaction must remain constant; to the extent that it decreases in informal settings and workers become even more threatened with embarrassment and loss of self-esteem than they would in the formal work setting, as may often be the case, class effects should again actually increase rather than decrease.

The fact that class-based conflicts of interest and coercion-induced threat generalize beyond the work setting supports a Marxist and argues against a Pluralist model, since the latter predicts that to the extent that class inequalities exist at all, they should be restricted to only a few spheres of activity. However, at the present time there is little evidence that class takes precedence over such other dimensions of stratification as occupation, race/ethnicity, or sex, and some evidence that suggests that the opposite is sometimes the case. Future research might focus upon additional conditions which could determine when one or another dimension of stratification takes precedence and upon longitudinal designs which might permit one to test Marx's prediction that class is becoming increasingly important relative to the other dimensions.

NOTES

1. Some will question using residential segregation and label it an example of the "ecological fallacy." Nevertheless, there is evidence that the residential movements of the middle class can be partially explained as attempts to move away from working-class people (e.g., Wilmott and Young, 1960:5).

2. In a recent case (Snarky Operator and Lippy Representative, 1972:15), Canadian Bell Telephone employees have actually complained that management is eating with them, but the explanation for this anomoly is clear: information operators have a very high workload (120 calls an hour!) and want to organize against it, but management's constant surveillance hinders them.

3. See, for example, Guetzkow (1965:548) and Hage et al. (1972).

4. "Threat" is defined here as a general, aversive psychological state incorporating such tension states as "fear," "anxiety," and "embarrassment." As such, it is conceptually independent of both the stratification conditions which are presumed to produce it and the behavioural strategies which are presumed to defend one against it. While in most of what follows threat has the status of a hypothetical construct, it nevertheless has been measured directly in some studies by such things as physiological arousal and verbally expressed feelings (e.g., Cohen and Davis, 1973; Cohen, 1959).

5. Under some circumstances, workers may also be capable of damaging the interests of their immediate employers by quitting. However, such circumstances—an acute shortage of labour for the employer and attractive alternatives for the employee—have been rare, especially with regard to blue-collar workers. Nevertheless, analysts as divergent as Smith and Marx have noted that generally there has been a greater scarcity of labour, particularly skilled labour, in North America than in Europe, and this may help explain the less rigid class structure of the former.

6. The inclusion of status and power in the domain of the theory thus would seem to be justified not simply by the fact that the abovementioned generalizations seem to hold for them as well as for class, but by the fact that they, too, appear to be threatening. In fact, I shall argue later that under some circumstances status-derived threat may be greater than class and/or direct, coercive power-derived threat.

7. Thus since the Broadview Riding has relatively few middle-class residents, the latter may resort to working-class advisors because there are fewer middle-class advisors from whom to choose. Also, the Berelson et al. (1954) data are from the early 1950s and the Toronto data are from the 1970s. Aside from these difficulties, respondents' descriptions of their own behaviour may have been biased. For example, if Canada's class structure is more rigid than that of the United States, there may be more pressure on upper-class Canadians than Americans to deny that it exists. The formers' claim that they engage in less discrimination by class may result more from this greater defensiveness than from true differences in actual behaviour.

8. Resentment from middle-class persons was not eradicated, however (Rosenberg, 1962: 372).

9. Gerard himself (1957:481) makes much the same interpretation of his results as I have made.

10. For example, while clearly preferring exchange theory, Homans (1974) and Blau (1964) extensively discuss "coercive power" in stratified structures and, at one point or another, both touch upon most of the reactions to threat. Similarly, while coercive power plays no part in expectation theory, its adherents nonetheless concede that it occurs (Berger et al., 1972:243).

11. The same ambiguity exists for Weber, who Pluralists often claim assigned occupational,

racial-ethnic, and religious status an importance equal to, or even greater than class. Thus, his reference to status being "favoured" (see Gerth and Mills, 1958:193-94) includes the qualification that this is the case only in times of economic and technological stability; otherwise, he implied, class takes precedence. Similarly, in the same passage he noted that during his time, class was the major determinant of status (Gerth and Mills, 1958:190).

12. It has been suggested that the "status consistency" literature is relevant here and that the apparent consensus that status characteristics combine additively rather than interactively (see Hodge and Siegel, 1979; Jackson and Curtis, 1972) refutes the Marxist claim that class has primacy. However, this appears not to be the case; (1) the phenomena studied are different from those studied here, in terms of the dependent variables (e.g., whereas avoidance is sometimes the dependent variable, it does not pertain to avoidance of those of a different occupational status) as well as the independent variables; (2) that additive effects predominate need not contradict a Marxist model, since the latter predicts only that class will have to be weighted more heavily than status factors.

REFERENCES

Adams, Ian
> 1970   *The Poverty Wall.* Toronto: McClelland and Stewart.
> 1972   *The Real Poverty Report.* Edmonton: Mel Hurtig Ltd.

Adler, Sandra
> 1970   "Residential segregation in 23 Canadian cities," Unpublished M.A. research paper, University of Western Ontario.

Allen, Vernon L, and John M. Levine
> 1969   "Consensus and conformity," *Journal of Experimental Social Psychology,* 5:389-99.

Archibald, W. Peter
> 1974   "The empirical relevance of Marx's theory of alienation." Paper presented to the Ad Hoc Group for Alienation Theory and Research, International Sociological Association Meetings, Toronto.

Artz, Reta D., et al.
> 1971   "Community rank stratification: a factor analysis," *American Sociological Review,* 36:985-1002.

Asch, Solomon E.
> 1960   "Effects of group pressure upon the modification and distortion of judgements," in *Group Dynamics,* ed. Dorwin Cartwright and Alvin Zander, pp. 189-200. New York: Harper and Row.

Balakrishnan, T. R., and George K. Jarvis
> 1968   "Socio-economic differentiation in the metropolitan areas of Canada." Paper presented at the Annual Meeting of the Canadian Sociology and Anthropology Association, Calgary.

Bales, Robert F.
1965   "The equilibrium problem in small groups," in *Small Groups: Studies in Social Interaction,* ed. A. Paul Hare, Edgar F. Borgatta, and Robert F. Bales, pp. 444-76. New York: Knopf.

Berelson, Bernard R., et al.
1954   *Voting: A Study of Opinion Formation in a Presidential Campaign.* Chicago: University of Chicago Press.

Berger, Joseph, et al.
1972   "Status characteristics and social interaction," *American Sociological Review,* 37:241-55.
1974   *Expectation States Theory: A Theoretical Research Program.* Cambridge, Mass.: Winthrop.

Berger, Joseph, and M. Hamit Fisek
1970   "Consistent and inconsistent status characteristics and the determination of power and prestige orders," *Sociometry,* 33:287-304.

Blau, Peter M.
1964   *Exchange and Power in Social Life.* New York: Wiley.

Blau, Peter M., and O. D. Duncan
1967   *The American Occupational Structure.* New York: Wiley.

Brewer, John
1971   "Flow of communications, expert qualifications and organizational authority structures," *American Sociological Review,* 36:475-84.

Cohen, Arthur R.
1958   "Upward communication in experimentally created hierarchies," *Human Relations,* 11:41-53.
1959   "Situational structure, self-esteem, and threat-oriented reactions to power," in *Studies in Social Power,* ed. Dorwin Cartwright, pp. 35-52. Ann Arbor, Mich.: Institute for Social Research.

Cohen, Jerry L., and James H. Davis
1973   "Effects of audience status, evaluation, and time of action on performance with hidden-word problems," *Journal of Personality and Social Psychology,* 27: 74-85.

Curtis, Richard F.
1963   "Differential association and the stratification of the urban community," *Social Forces,* 42:68-77.

Davis, Kingsley, and Wilbert E. Moore
1945   "Some principles of stratification," *American Sociological Review,* 10:242-49.

Dobriner, William
1963   *Class in Suburbia.* Englewood Cliffs, N.J.: Prentice-Hall.

Doob, Anthony N., and Alan E. Gross
1968   "Status of frustrator as an inhibitor of horn-honking responses," *Journal of Social Psychology,* 76:213-18.

Doyle, Kevin
    1974   "It's dirty, dangerous," *London Free Press* (January 30):p.3.

Duncan, Otis Dudley, and Beverly Duncan
    1955   "Residential distribution and occupational stratification," *American Journal of Sociology,* 60:493-503.

Ellis, Robert A., and W. Clayton Lane
    1967   "Social mobility and social isolation: a test of Sorokin's dissociative hypothesis," *American Sociological Review,* 32:237-53.

Feldman, Arnold S., and Charles Tilly
    1960   "The interaction of social and physical space," *American Sociological Review,* 25:877-84.

Form, William H., and Joan Rytina
    1969   "Ideological beliefs in the distribution of power in the United States," *American Sociological Review,* 34:19-31.

French, John R. P., and Bertram Raven
    1959   "The bases of social power," in *Studies in Social Power,* ed. Dorwin Cartwright, pp. 150-67. Ann Arbor, Mich.: Institute for Social Research.

Gerard, Harold B.
    1953   "The effect of different dimensions of disagreement on the communication process in small groups," *Human Relations,* 6:249-71.
    1957   "Some effects of status, role clarity, and group goal clarity upon the individual's relations to group process," *Journal of Personality,* 25:475-88.

Gerth, Hans, and C. Wright Mills
    1958   *From Max Weber: Essays in Sociology.* New York: Oxford University Press.

Goffman, Erving
    1959   *The Presentation of Self in Everyday Life.* Garden City, N.Y.: Doubleday-Anchor.
    1961   *Encounters.* Indianapolis: Bobbs-Merrill.
    1967   *Interaction Ritual.* Garden City, N.Y.: Doubleday-Anchor.

Goodstadt, Barry, and David Kipnis
    1970   "Situational influences on the use of power," *Journal of Applied Psychology,* 54:201-7.

Grayson, Paul
    1973   "Comparative political networks." Unpublished paper, Atkinson College, York University.

Guetzkow, Harold
    1965   "Communications in organizations," in James G. March (ed.), *Handbook of Organizations.* Chicago: Rand McNally, pp. 534-73.

Hage Jerald, et al.
    1972   "Organization structure and communications," *American Sociological Review* 36:860-71.

Hodge, Robert W. and Paul M. Siegel
  1970   "Nonvertical dimensions of social stratifications," in Edward O. Laumann, Paul M. Siegel, and Robert W. Hodge (eds.), *The Logic of Social Hierarchies.* Chicago: Markham, pp. 512-20.

Hollingshead, A. B.
  1949   *Elmtown's Youth.* New York: Wiley.

Homans, George C.
  1974   *Social Behavior: Its Elementary Forms,* revised edition. New York: Harcourt Brace Jovanovich.

Hurwitz, Jacob I., et al.
  1960   "Some effects of power on the relations among group members," in Dorwin Cartwright and Alvin Zander (eds.), *Group Dynamics: Research and Theory.* New York: Harper and Row, pp. 800-9.

Inkeles, Alex
  1960   "Industrialized man: The relation of status to experience, perception and value," *American Journal of Sociology,* 56:20-1.

Israel, Joachim
  1971   *Alienation: From Marx to Modern Sociology.* Boston: Allyn and Bacon.

Jackman, Mary R. and Robert W. Jackman
  1973   "An interpretation of the relation between objective and subjective social status," *American Sociological Review,* 38:569-82.

Jackson, Elton F. and Richard F. Curtis
  1972   "Effects of vertical mobility and status inconsistency: a body of negative evidence," *American Sociological Review,* 37:701-13.

Johnson, Leo
  1972   "The development of class in Canada in the twentieth century," in Gary Teeple, ed., *Capitalism and the National Question in Canada.* Toronto: University of Toronto Press, pp. 141-83.

Kahl, Joseph A. and James A. Davis
  1955   "A comparison of indexes of socio-economic status," *American Sociological Review,* 20:317-25.

Kaplan, Howard B.
  1971   "Social class and self-derogation: a conditional relationship," *Sociometry,* 34:41-64.

Kelley, Harold H.
  1960   "Communication in experimentally created hierarchies," in Dorwin Cartwright and Alvin Zander (eds.), *Group Dynamics.* New York: Harper and Row, pp. 781-99.

Kipnis, David and Joseph Cosentino
  1969   "Uses of leadership powers in industry," *Journal of Applied Psychology,* 53:460-6.

Knowles, Eric S.
    1973   "Boundaries around group interaction: the effect of group size and member status on boundary permeability," *Journal of Personality and Social Psychology,* 26:327-31.

Laumann, Edward O.
    1966   *Prestige and Association in an Urban Community.* Indianapolis: Bobbs-Merrill.
    1973   *Bonds of Pluralism: The Form and Substance of Urban Social Networks.* New York: Wiley.

Lorimer, James, and Myfanwy Phillips
    1971   *Working People.* Toronto: James, Lewis, and Samuel.

Mann, Michael
    1970   "The social cohesion of liberal democracy," *American Sociological Review,* 35:423-39.

Martin, J. David
    1970   "A comment on whether American women do marry up," *American Sociological Review,* 35:327-28.

Marx, Karl
    n.d.   *Capital.* Volumes I and III. Moscow: Progress Publishers.

Marx, Karl, and Friedrich Engels
    1961   *The Civil War in the United States.* New York: International Publishers.
    1968   *Selected Works.* Moscow: Progress Publishers.
    1971   *Ireland and the Irish Question.* Moscow: Progress Publishers.

Mathewson, Stanley B.
    1969   *Restriction of Output among Unorganized Workers.* Carbondale, Ill.: Southern Illinois University Press.

Milgram, Stanley
    1965   "Liberating effects of group pressure," *Journal of Personality and Social Psychology,* 1:127-34.

Mills, C. Wright
    1956   *The Power Elite.* New York: Oxford University Press.

Moscovici, S., E. Lage, and M. Naffrechoux
    1969   "Influence of a consistent minority on the responses of a majority in a color perception task," *Sociometry,* 32:365-80.

Mulder, Mauk
    1971   "Power equalization through participation?" *Administration Science Quarterly,* 16:31-38.

Mulder, Mauk, and Henk Wilke
    1970   "Participation and power equalization," *Organizational Behavior and Human Performance,* 5:430-48.

Myers, Gustavus
    1972   *A History of Canadian Wealth.* Toronto: James, Lewis, and Samuel.

Operator, Snarky, and Lippy Representative
    1972   "Working for Ma Bell," *Canadian Dimension,* 8:11-15.

Pepitone, Albert, and George Reichling
    1960   "Group cohesiveness and the expression of hostility." Reprinted in *Group Dynamics,* ed. Dorwin Cartwright and Alvin Zander, pp. 141-51. New York: Harper and Row.

Rhodes, A. Lewis
    1969   "Residential distribution and occupational stratification in Paris and Chicago," *Sociological Quarterly,* 10:106-12.

Riecken, Henry W.
    1958   "The effect of talkativeness on ability to influence group solutions to problems," *Sociometry,* 21:309-21.

Rosenberg, Larry
    1962   "Social status and participation among a group of chronic schizophrenics," *Human Relations,* 15:365-77.

Rubin, Zick
    1973   *Liking and Loving: An Invitation to Social Psychology.* New York: Holt, Rinehart, and Winston.

Sampson, Edward E.
    1963   "Status congruence and cognitive consistency," *Sociometry,* 26:146-66.

Sennett, Richard, and Jonathan Cobb
    1972   *The Hidden Injuries of Class.* New York: Knopf.

Strodtbeck, Fred L., et al.
    1958   "Social status in jury deliberations," in *Readings in Social Psychology,* ed. Eleanor E. Maccoby, Theodore M. Newcomb, and Eugene L. Hartley, pp. 379-88. New York: Holt, Rinehart, and Winston.

Thibaut, John
    1950   "An experimental study of the cohesiveness of underprivileged groups," *Human Relations,* 3:251-78.

Torrance, E. Paul
    1965   "Some consequences of power differences on decision making in permanent and temporary three-man groups," in *Small Groups: Studies in Social Interaction,* ed. A. Paul Hare, Edgar F. Borgatta, and Robert F. Bales, pp. 600-609. New York: Knopf.

Uyeki, Eugene S.
    1964   "Residential distribution and stratification," *American Journal of Sociology,* 69:491-98.

Wilmott, Peter, and Michael Young
    1960   *Family and Class in a London Suburb.* London: Routledge and Kegan Paul.

Worchel, Philip
    1957   "Catharsis and the relief of hostility," *Journal of Abnormal and Social Psychology,* 55:238-43.

Zander, Alvin, et al.
    1959   "Power and the relations among professions," in *Studies in Social Power,* ed. Dorwin Cartwright, pp. 15-34. Ann Arbor, Michigan: Institute for Social Research.

Zeitlin, Maurice
    1974   "Corporate ownership and control: the large corporation and the capitalist class," *American Journal of Sociology,* 79:1073-119.

42. Street Crime and Suite Crime

Colin H. Goff and Charles E. Reasons

A cursory look at national and local criminal statutes attests to the diversity of behaviours defined as criminal. For example, the Criminal Code of Canada includes in its definition of crime, offences against public order (e.g., treason and other offences against the Queen's authority and person, sedition, prize fights); offences against the administration of law and justice (e.g., corruption and disobedience); sexual offences, offences against public morals and disorderly conduct (e.g., seduction of a female between 16 years and 18 years old, obscene materials, crime comics); disorderly houses, gaming and betting (e.g., common bawdy-house); offences against the person and/or reputation (e.g., homicide, venereal diseases, blasphemous libel, hate propaganda); offences against rights of property (e.g., theft, robbery, extortion);

fraudulent transactions relating to contracts and trade (e.g., fraud, breach of contract); wilful and forbidden acts in respect of certain property (e.g., arson, cruelty to animals); offences relating to currency (e.g., counterfeiting, defacing or impairing); and attempts, conspiracies, or accessories in these areas.

While in theory our freedom as citizens rests on the fact that no act is a crime unless so specified in law, in practice we have an enormous amount of behaviour defined as criminal in Canada including over 700 Criminal Code sections, 20 000 federal offences, and 30 000 provincial offences which exclude municipal laws. The sheer number of statutes is staggering to the imagination.

Most students of crime, like most citizens, take the crime problem as given, with little argument regarding its nature or scope. The crime problem is assumed to be self-evident and its dimensions are hardly arguable. This common conception of the crime problem is embodied in the term "street crime." When one talks about the crime

Revised from Colin H. Goff and Charles E. Reasons, *Corporate Crime in Canada* (Scarborough: Prentice-Hall Canada, 1978), pp. 1-15. Reprinted with permission.

505

problem, a common meaning is often assumed which emphasizes offences against the person and particularly crimes of violence (e.g., robbery, assault, murder, rape). The imagery evoked by the concept "street crime" is one of dark shadows, dirty alleys, and hordes of the criminally inclined lurking on public streets. "Street crime" has long been a rallying cry for "wars on crime" by politicians, police officials, and other civic leaders. However, when one looks beyond the rhetoric of street crimes, one discovers that most murders, rapes, and assaults are not committed in the streets, but in homes, taverns, automobiles, and parks. Such a conception is even losing meaning regarding robbery.

In actuality, most crimes in the streets are committed by vagrants, prostitutes, drunks, panhandlers, petty thieves, and auto thieves. It would appear that to avoid murder, assault, rape, or robbery, it might be advisable to stay away from home, family, friends, and local drinking establishment and to spend time in the streets. Furthermore, violent crimes account for a very small proportion of the criminal behaviour in Canada. In Canada and the United States crimes of violence account for less than 10 percent of crime.

A great deal of attention is given to "street crime" and street criminals; however, relatively little attention is paid to "suite crime" and suite criminals. By "suite crime" we are referring to the illegal behaviour which occurs in the business suites of the corporate, professional, and civil elites of society. Such crimes as misrepresentation of advertising, price fixing, fraudulent financial manipulations, illegal rebates, misappropriation of public funds, splitting fees, restraint of trade, failure to maintain safety standards, and violation of human rights are examples of suite crimes. Evidence suggests that such "suite crimes" are as pervasive as "street

crimes," if not more so, and result in a great deal more financial loss, while also entailing death and injury (Quinney, 1975:131-61). However, we have almost totally ignored such offences in Canada. Data regarding street crime and street criminals are voluminous, compared to available data on suite crime and suite criminals.

IS CORPORATE CRIME "CRIME"?

Criminologist Edwin Sutherland noted some time ago that the criminality of corporations was like that of professional thieves in that corporations are persistent recidivists; their illegal behaviour is much more extensive than the prosecutions and complaints indicate; the businessmen who violate the laws designed to regulate business do not customarily lose status among their business associates; businessmen customarily feel and express contempt for law, for government, and for governmental personnel; corporate crime, like the professional thief, is highly organized (Sutherland, 1961). However, there are important distinctions between corporate criminality and that of the professional thief. The corporate criminal does not conceive of himself as a criminal and neither do most of the public because he does not fit the stereotype of the criminal. The professional thief views himself as a criminal and is viewed as such by the general public. While the professional thief has a "mouthpiece" (attorney) to argue against specific charges, corporations employ experts in law, public relations, and advertising. Such corporate "mouthpieces" provide a much wider range of services than the "mouthpieces" of the professional thief do. Their duties include influencing the enactment and administration of the law, advising clients on how to break the law with relative impunity, defending in court those few clients who have the misfortune of being specifically charged and most importantly, building up and maintaining the corporation's status and image in the public's mind.

It is particularly those factors distinguishing the corporate criminal from the professional thief which help to maintain the appearance of non-criminality. The sharply dressed, neat appearing corporate executive who pays taxes, contributes to local charities and juvenile delinquency funds, and is an elder in the church, fails to match the stereotyped image of the criminal who, with premeditation, earns his livelihood through victimizing the public. If the mass media emphasized suite crime in the same manner it did street crime in an attempt to stress their similarities, there would likely be financial repercussions.

> Nearly all the advertising revenues of the newspapers and mass magazines, as well as of radio and television stations and networks, come from these same corporations and their smaller counterparts . . . the newspapers have never despite recent sociological revelations ventured statistical summaries of the situation as they regularly do with lower-class, police-reported crimes—a marked case of class bias. (Lundberg, 1969)

Why do we tend to evaluate "street crime" so differently from "suite crime"? The direct, personal, face-to-face threat of physical violence is significant in "street crimes," i.e., murder, rape, assault, robbery. As one student of crime states:

> I realize that muggers take much less from us than do corporate, syndicate, and white-collar criminals. I have little doubt that the average executive swindles more on his taxes and expense account than the average addict steals in a typical year. Moreover, I am well aware that concentrating on street crime provides yet another opportunity for picking on the poor, a campaign I have no wish to assist. It is a scandal

that a bank embezzler gets six months while a hold-up man is hit with five years. Yet it is not entirely their disparate backgrounds that produce this discrimination.

A face-to-face threat of bodily harm or possibly violent death is so terrifying to most people that the $20 or so stolen in a typical mugging must be multiplied many times if comparisons with other offences are to be made. I have a hunch that a majority of city dwellers would accept a bargain under which if they would not be mugged this year they would be willing to allow white-collar crime to take an extra 10 percent of their incomes. Of course we are annoyed by corporate thievery that drives up prices, but the kind of dread included by thuggery has no dollar equivalent or, if it does, an extremely high one. (Hacker, 1973)

While there is obvious physical danger and harm from some "street crimes," the belief that "suite crimes" are not violent is false.

> Corporate crime kills and maims. It has been estimated for example, that each year 200 000 to 500 000 workers are needlessly exposed to toxic agents such as radioactive materials and poisonous chemicals because of corporate failure to obey safety laws. And many of the 2.5 million temporary and 250 000 permanent worker disabilities from industrial accidents each year are the result of managerial acts that represent culpable failure to adhere to established standards. (Geis, 1974)

However, when automobile accidents, airplane crashes, or industrial disasters occur, culpability is usually found among those directly involved in the accident or disaster. In discussing the nearly 100 000 United States workers who die each year as a result of exposure to job health hazards, Swartz notes:

> One of the more insidious tactics used by the corporate perpetrators of crime is to blame the victims for what happens to them. The National Safety Council, a corporation-funded institution, frequently runs "safety" campaigns. The point of these campaigns is always that the workers are careless and lazy, and do not take

the measures necessary to protect themselves (wearing safety helmets, ear plugs, etc.). Never is the corporation held the culprit. (Swartz, 1975:19)

When alleged defects in manufactured products or violation of safety standards are investigated and substantiated, they are usually interpreted as quirks or accidents with possible civil, but not criminal, liability. In Quebec, about 45 construction workers die on the job each year while approximately 13 500 are injured.

Although persons might use the threat of violence in robbery, they will seldom employ it. Likewise, the probability of injuries and deaths from suite crime may be low related to the number of offences. Nonetheless, both types of offences periodically result in injury and death, but only street crimes bear the brunt of full prosecution. For example, mercury poisoning from the Dryden Chemical plant in Northwestern Ontario is evident among native people in the area, but it will not likely result in the laying of criminal charges. Such a decision is based largely upon legal conceptions of causation, intent, and culpability, all of which mitigate corporate responsibility. Nonetheless, physical harm, injury, and often death are the results of this disease. Whether death or injury occurs at the hands of an assailant in a face-to-face encounter, or is due to poisoning and disease caused by an impersonal corporation, the end result is similar.

ARE STREET CRIMES "CRIMES"?

The large proportion of street crimes do not involve violence. They include theft, auto offences, and "victimless crimes." "Victimless crimes" present a unique example of the politics of crime. The term "victimless crime" is applied to acts involving a willing exchange of goods and services and purported harms inflicted upon oneself. What is arguable is that victimization is more remote and/or difficult to ascertain than in "normal crimes." If someone steals a car from you or holds you up with a gun, you are obviously a victim and the other is the offender. However, public drunkenness, illicit use of drugs, gambling, abortion, prostitution, pornography, and homosexuality usually involve a willing exchange of goods and services between two or more parties, but nonetheless are often criminalized in North America. For example, a prostitute exchanges sexual favours for money from the John. It is difficult to determine who is the victim and who is the criminal. While the John may believe that he has not had fair value for his money, it is unlikely he will become a complainant due to the illegal nature of the exchange. In the United States such crimes total nearly 50 percent of all crime, while in Canada such acts constitute approximately 20 percent of the crime. Therefore, since violent crimes account for less than 10 percent of all crime, "victimless crimes" are a larger proportion of the crime in North America. (Geis, 1974)

These crimes are depicted in the media as inherently evil and subsequently dangerous. Stereotypes of the gambler, dope fiend, prostitute, homosexual, and drunk present frightening pictures which evoke both pity and fear among the "morally superior." While most users of illicit drugs, prostitutes, gamblers, homosexuals, and inebriates live relatively normal, law-abiding lives apart from their appetites, crimes of violence, personal psychopathology, and sordid environments are dramatized in the mass media as typical of such "kinds of people" and their behaviour. Such representations fail to note that most of the limited violence and personal psychopathology which is evident is largely a product of restrictive laws, not of the behaviour per se. In fact, the consequences of making and maintaining such behaviours as criminal are likely more harmful than removing them from the auspices of the criminal law (Reasons, 1976).

Report after report and study upon study have indicated that such "overcriminalization" produces the following negative consequences: artificially high profits and criminal monopolies; organized crime; secondary crime such as theft among addicts to support their habit; criminal subcultures; excessive expenditures of police and criminal justice resources; corruption of agents of the criminal justice system; contempt for the law and criminal justice system by offenders; infringement upon individual rights (Morris and Hawkins, 1970).

Public policy criminalizing such behaviours is particularly subject to criticism within democratic societies.

> To some extent crimes without victims are outlawed because of a benevolent interest in protecting an individual from himself. The difficulties here are acute. For one thing, in a democracy, freedom of an individual to determine what is best for himself, as long as he does not interfere with a similar freedom of others, is a prime ingredient. For another, it is dubious that the force of the criminal law upon marijuana smokers, abortion-seeking women, homosexuals, and numbers players adds to the sum of their happiness and makes them better persons. (Geis, 1972a:16-18)

Some students of crime are becoming increasingly aware of the ramifications of the trite observation that the formal cause of crime is the criminal law.

> Our criminal law suffers from at least four defects. It fails to differentiate between real crimes and mere regulatory offences. It descends into excessive detail. It uses a style and form of language that is inappropriate. And it is wedded to

a Victorian philosophy which is now inadequate. (Law Reform Commission of Canada, 1976:35)

The moral excesses in the criminal law can no longer be afforded. Overcriminalization in such areas as obscenity and pornography, unlawful gaming, and illicit drugs has produced more problems than it has solved. For example, there have been dramatic increases in the cost and effort of law enforcement, judicial, and correctional personnel as they attempt to enforce narcotics legislation. The irrational and oppressive way we treat users of illicit drugs is hardly any better than the way witches were treated centuries ago. The "demonological" properties attributed to these drugs have little relation to their known effects, and our actions only appear to worsen the "drug problem" rather than decrease it. Clearly the answer is not to increase penalties and personnel anticipating that there will be a decrease in illicit drug use with an increase in social control agents.

The difficulty in identifying victim(s) and offender(s) is a difference often noted between suite crime and violent street crime. While a visible, dramatic theft at gunpoint entails an obvious victim and a criminal, the taking of millions of dollars from millions of people through fraud or price fixing is less direct, with a more diffuse victim and offender. For example, the theft of a worker's income tax, unemployment insurance, and pension deductions by employers does not elicit the same response as bank robberies do, although it is a much more profitable type of crime. Failure to remit payroll deductions by employers in 1975 accounted for $7.9 million, while bank robbers, extortionists, and kidnappers gained a profit of only $5.17 million in the same year. A significant factor in such varying responses is the nonhostile, non-threatening nature of the setting and the fact that the offender is usually viewed as providing needed and legitimate goods and services.

> That we are daily victimized is not usually recognized because, for example, we do not view the grocery store or department store as an accomplice, the manufacturer as a criminal, and ourselves as victims of rising costs. (Reasons, 1974:233)

Even when "suite criminals" commit "common crimes" they tend to be evaluated differently. For example, if a person breaks into another's premises and takes something, the usual definition is breaking and entering or burglary, and the offender is subject to possible imprisonment. However, when the White House "Plumbers," CIA, FBI, RCMP, or federal narcotics agents commit such behaviours, it is likely to be evaluated in terms of national defence and/or necessary in the war against crime and therefore immune from prosecution. The innumerable offences of former U.S. President Nixon were viewed by many as the legitimate exercise of authority by the head of state.

Furthermore, the public often identifies with the suite criminal who is a respectable businessman or civic official who contributes to the community and society. The Churchill Forest Industries scandal in Manitoba attests to the significance of appearance and status in suite crime. In a multi-million dollar swindle against the people of Manitoba, one Dr. Kosser and Associates put over one of the greatest cons in the annals of crime. In the end, it was estimated by an investigating commission that Dr. Kosser made about $26 million in excessive fees and paid no Canadian taxes on more than $33 million in earnings by setting up a network of companies. Left holding the bag were business and government leaders and, of course, the taxpayers of Manitoba.

Why do we have such images of the crime problem? Where do we gain such perceptions? How are such images maintained? Our attitudes toward, and reactions to, crime are greatly affected by our perception of the nature of the crime problem. Our perception of the crime problem is largely related to our personal experiences and socialization. Since most of us do not experience rape, robbery, or other crimes of violence, our perception of the nature and scope of "street crime," i.e., the crime problem, is largely a product of the diffusion of criminal conceptions and social types. Such images of crime and the criminal are provided us by our family, educational institutions, politicians, and the mass media. Newspapers, television, radio, magazines, movies, and official governmental reports continually provide us with definitions of the nature and scope of the crime problem. Such headlines as *Violent Crimes Up 10%, Rape Increases 100%, Murder Up 20%, Serious Crime on the Upsurge* convey to citizens that the crime problem (street crime) is increasing at an alarming rate. Uniform Crime Reports in both Canada and the United States emphasize "street crimes." Therefore, headlines such as *Corporate Crime Up 100%, Price Fixing Increases 50%, Corporate Crimes Death Toll Rises* are not usually found in the media.

The mass media provide most citizens with their conceptions of the crime problem. Fear of "street crime" is widespread while fear of "suite crime" is minimal. The continual barrage of crime statistics we receive plays an important role in creating and maintaining a constant fear among the public. Both Canada and the United States have Uniform Crime Reports which are issued periodically during each year as the barometer on crime. While these reporting systems have been critically assailed for their problems, they are taken by the public as valid and reliable indicators of crime. Therefore, increases in crime noted in the media may frighten the public even though there may be little basis for fear. For example, a survey team in Toronto found in 1970 that concern with crime for many citizens was partly an artificial creation and that people were more concerned about crime in the abstract rather than actually becoming a victim. It was concluded that crime, to some extent, is an imaginary problem which is manufactured in the minds of many people (Milakovitch and Weis, 1975). The definition of crime and the criminal is constantly reinforced through television dramas, newspaper headlines, police statistical reports, and political and civic speeches. The definitions of crime and the criminal provided in these sources do not accurately reflect the nature and scope of crime in Canada.

Why Study Suite Crime?

In contemporary Canadian society we are increasingly subject to ever-larger government bureaucracies and corporations. In *The Vertical Mosaic*, John Porter (1965) reveals the extent of social stratification in Canada and the influence of elites upon our daily lives. More recently, Wallace Clement in *The Canadian Corporate Elite* extensively documents the interlocking relationships between corporations and their influence upon Canadian society (Clement, 1975). Whether corporations are multinational or domestic, they are significant and influential in the operation of our society. Canada subscribes to a liberal ideology emphasizing individualism, competition, and equality of opportunity, yet it is clear that upward mobility is the exception rather than the rule, and that class lines are becoming more rigid.

The structured inequalities in Canadian society are in part a product of corporate enterprise and economic concentration.

Andrew Armitage identifies this process in *Canadian Social Welfare* by noting "the effect of the economic elites' influence on social welfare appears to lie principally in their power to restrict the extent of welfare transfer" (Armitage, 1975:95). The great power wielded by corporations suggests they are immune from effective control. The dehumanization of our increasingly complex, urban society is compounded by the appearance, if not the reality, of corporate impersonality and disregard for social justice. While citizens are told there are controls on corporations and their power and behaviour, few data exist concerning the nature of these controls and their effectiveness. Therefore, the analysis of suite crime is particularly significant as a means of making corporations publicly accountable for their behaviour. If the power and behaviour of corporations in Canada is not checked or goes unchallenged, citizens will certainly become sceptical with regard to their ability to influence public policy.

As previously discussed, suite crime costs the public more than street crime, while also entailing injuries and sometimes death. One author has pointed out the costs of monopolies in both the United States and Canada:

A U.S. study concludes that the overall cost of monopoly and shared monopoly in terms of lost production is somewhere between $48 billion and $60 billion annually. In Canada, lost output due to the same cause would be in the order of $4.5 to $6 billion dollars. The lost tax revenues alone from this wealth would go a long way towards ending poverty and pollution. The redistribution of income from monopoly profits that transfers income from consumers to shareholders is estimated at $2.3 billion annually in the U.S. and $2 to $3 billion in Canada. Monopolistic firms thus contribute to inequality, inflation and unemployment. Unemployment results since monopolies, as noted, significantly reduce output which in turn reduces the number of workers who would otherwise be producing. (Gonick, 1975:77)

Thus, in terms of corporate accountability, financial cost, dehumanization, and physical safety there is a need for studying suite crime.

We may have to reassess our understanding of crime and criminality and its social sources. If the nature and scope of crime in a society reflects the nature of that society, then perhaps we get the criminals we deserve. Therefore, we need to direct our attention to possible criminogenic values in our society. Dominant values such as success, status and power seeking, monetary and material wealth, toughness, dupery, and shrewdness contribute to both the "of-ficial criminal's" and "law-abiding citizen's" place in society.

We still have virtually no information on the scope and magnitude of corporate crime in Canada. There has been much study and public discussion of "street crime" and "street criminals," but we have yet to direct our attention to "suite crime" and "suite criminals." "Suite crime" may victimize more of the public for much more money than street crime. Furthermore, physical injury is more evident in suite crimes through accidents, diseases, and deaths than is generally recognized. Such crimes may be more destructive to the members of society, economically and physically, than all the "common crimes" and "common criminals" which we daily pursue through the criminal justice system.

REFERENCES

Armitage, Andrew
    1975   *Social Welfare in Canada.* Toronto: McClelland and Stewart.

Clement, Wallace
    1975   *The Canadian Corporate Elite.* Toronto: McClelland and Stewart.

Geis, Gilbert
    1972a   "Crimes—but no victims," *Reason,* 4(September).
    1972b   *Not the Law's Business?* Washington, D.C.: U.S. Government Printing Office.
    1974   "Deterring corporate crime," in *The Criminologist: Crime and the Criminal,* ed. Charles E. Reasons. Pacific Palisades, Calif.: Goodyear Publishing.

Gonick, C.
    1975   *Inflation or Depression.* Toronto: James Lorimer Co.

Hacker, Andrew
    1973   "Getting used to mugging," *The New York Review of Books,* 20, no. 16(April):9.

Law Reform Commission of Canada.
    1976   *Our Criminal Law.* Ottawa: Information Canada.

Lundberg, Ferdinand
    1969   *The Rich and the Super Rich.* New York: L. Stuart.

Milakovitch, Michael E., and Kurt Weis
    1975   "Politics and measures of success in the war on crime," *Crime and Delinquency,* 21(January):1-10.

Morris, Norval, and Gordon Hawkins
    1970   *The Honest Politician's Guide to Crime Control.* Chicago: University of Chicago Press.

Porter, John
    1965   *The Vertical Mosaic.* Toronto: University of Toronto Press.

Quinney, Richard
    1975   *Criminology: Analysis and Critique of Crime in America.* Boston: Little Brown and Co.

Reasons, Charles E.
    1976   "Images of crime and the criminal: The dope fiend mythology," *Journal of Research in Crime and Delinquency,* 13(July):113-44.

Reasons, Charles E., ed.
    1974   *The Criminologist: Crime and the Criminal.* Pacific Palisades: Goodyear Publishing.

Sutherland, E. H.
    1961   *White Collar Crime.* New York: Holt, Rinehart and Winston.

Swartz, Joel
    1975   "Silent killers at work," *Crime and Social Justice,* 3(Summer).

FOR FURTHER READING

Archibald, W. Peter. 1978. *Social Psychology as Political Economy.* Toronto: McGraw-Hill Ryerson. Employing a Marxist perspective, the author describes structured social inequality from the point of view of its social psychological consequences for people. The effects of inequalities across class, race, ethnicity, and gender categories are explored. This is a sweeping and imaginative review of previous studies.

Bell, David V. J., and Lorne Tepperman. 1979. *The Roots of Disunity.* Toronto: McClelland and Stewart. This socio-historical study looks at major "fault-lines" in Canadian cultures, that is, dimensions of social inequality along which there are major differences in ways of viewing political affairs. The cleavages attributable to class, English-French differences, and regions are emphasized. This book is full of hypotheses for further study.

Black, Sir David, et al., with Peter Townsend and Nick Davidson, eds. 1982. *Inequalities in Health* ("The Black Report"). Middlesex, England: Penguin Books. This volume presents an enormous amount of material on trends in the relationships of socio-economic status and mortality at different stages in the life cycle, including infant mortality, for England. It also draws comparisons between the British trends and trends in social-class mortality from various other countries. Similar comparisons are made for patterns of health care.

Forcese, Dennis. 1986. *The Canadian Class Structure* (3rd ed.). Toronto: McGraw-Hill Ryerson. In this clear introduction to various issues in social inequality, the chapter on "Class Lifestyle and Behaviour" is of special importance for our topics in this section. The chapter presents selected information on social class as it relates to patterns of health care, household expenditures, work, criminal behaviour, political participation, party preference, participation in social movements, and religious participation.

Marchak, M. Patricia. 1981. *Ideological Perspectives on Canada* (2nd ed.). Toronto: McGraw-Hill Ryerson. (3rd edition, forthcoming, 1988). An analysis of major political ideologies in Canada and their shifting currents over time. The ideologies are liberalism, socialism, conservatism, and a new "corporatism." The policy implications for social inequality of each ideology are made abundantly clear.

Reasons, Charles E., and Robert M. Rich, eds. 1978. *The Sociology of Law: A Conflict Perspective.* Toronto: Butterworths. There are 21 chapters here, each informed by the class perspective on the function of the law (as described in the Goff and Reasons piece in this section). Only some of the chapters deal with Canadian data; most are international in scope or focussed on sociological theories of the law.